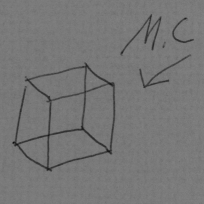

Personality Theories: *an* Introduction

Second Edition

Barbara Engler

Union County College

Houghton Mifflin Company   Boston

Dallas   Geneva, Illinois

Lawrenceville, New Jersey   Palo Alto

To my sons,
Ted and Bill

Printed in the U.S.A.
Library of Congress Catalog Card Number: 84-80709
ISBN: 0-395-34237-6

BCDEFGHIJ-H-898765

Contents

2 Carl Jung: Analytical Psychology

3 Alfred Adler: Individual Psychology

List of Explorations

Preface

Personality Theories: An Introduction examines the most important theories of personality in a way that is specially designed to facilitate learning. This Second Edition has three main objectives: to present a concise picture of the major features of each theory; to provide criteria that guide the evaluation of each theory; and to present activities, informed by the tenets of each theory, that expand a student's self-awareness.

The text's structure contributes to the first objective. Each chapter focuses on one theory or group of similar theories. A short biography of the theorist helps to shed some light on the formulation of the theory. The theory is presented succinctly (to allow adequate coverage of all of the theories) and is developed in a manner that seems most appropriate for that theory. Comparisons between theories are made when they provide a viable way to outline the distinctive characteristics and contributions of each theory. A significant amount of space is devoted to Freud's psychoanalytic theory in recognition of its influence. Because many other theories have been developed as efforts to elaborate on, modify, or refute psychoanalysis, a firm basis in Freudian theory provides the reader with a focal point from which comparisons and contrasts may be made. The text's writing style also lends itself to a clear exposition of the theories; the book has been written in easy-to-understand language and theoretical points have been illustrated by concrete examples.

The "Introduction" to the text addresses the second objective, and end-of-chapter sections labeled "Philosophy, Science, and Art" provide additional information. The subsumption of personality theories under scientific psychology is a relatively new development. Many of the theories that influence contemporary thought did not develop from strict scientific theory but reflect philosophical assumptions. In addition, the application of a theory to a real-life situation is a creative act and demonstrates that a personality theory may function as an art. Therefore, the evaluation of a personality theory is best accomplished when we break the theory down into its component parts — philosophy, science, and art — and judge whether the theory meets the criteria appropriate to each function. The "Conclusion" at the end of the text wraps up the evaluation discussion.

Finally, the third objective is accomplished through sections called "Explorations," which suggest activities that help a student experience some of the underlying principles of the theory under discussion. These "Explorations" (called "Exercises" in the previous edition) demonstrate the relevance of a theory and encourage a student's personal and academic growth. A list of "Explorations" can be found on pages xiv–xv.

The changes in the Second Edition reflect developments in the field of personality psychology as well as feedback received from instructors and students who have used the text. The work of Erik Erikson, Albert Bandura, and Julian Rotter receive more attention in this edition. Rollo May is introduced as representative of existential theorists. In addition to these content changes, some important pedagogical aids have been added. Sections called "Your Goals for This Chapter" and "Summary" frame each chapter, allowing students to read with a sense of purpose and to review important points quickly. Other pedagogical aids that were present in the previous edition ("Suggestions for Further Reading," highlighted key terms, and "Explorations") have been updated and made more effective.

Some students have told me that they sometimes touched upon unexpected feelings in the course of doing an "Exploration." If an area of resistance is probed, for example, an individual will experience anxiety. Being aware of the possibility of tapping into hidden emotions may help students deal with the experience and may ultimately help them learn more about themselves.

Once again, I would like to thank my colleagues and students at Union County College for their interest, support, and constructive comments regarding the text and its revision. I am grateful to the following reviewers for their careful consideration of the manuscript and their helpful comments:

Georgia Babladelis of California State University at Hayward
Lee Bradley of Orange Coast College
Jeffrey B. Brookings of Wittenberg University
Jonathan M. Cheek of Wellesley College
J. R. Dibble of Southwestern Oregon Community College
Juris G. Draguns of The Pennsylvania State University
Edward Grant of the College of Cape Breton, Nova Scotia

Gary Groth-Marnat of National University

P. Leslie Herold of California State College at San Bernardino

Robert L. Hiner of Texas Lutheran College

Rosina C. Chia of East Carolina University

Jean O. Love of Lebanon Valley College

Sam McFarland of Western Kentucky University

Edward R. Mosley of Passaic County College

David E. Nilsson of Primary Children's Medical Center, Salt Lake City, Utah

Tirzah Schutzengel of Bergen Community College

James R. Scroggs of Bridgewater State College

Mary Anne Sedney of Providence College

M. L. Corbin Sicoli of Cabrini College

Janet A. Simons of Des Moines Area Community College

Stephen D. Slane of Cleveland State University

Jerome Small of Youngstown State University

Auke Tellegen of the University of Minnesota

I also wish to express my appreciation to Donald Goldsmith, who offered innumerable constructive suggestions on the revision. My sons, Ted and Bill, are older now and were able to offer some useful feedback concerning portions of the text. I am grateful for their patience in the face of their mother's frequent preoccupation with the task of revising her text.

Barbara Engler

Introduction: Evaluating Personality Theories

Your Goals for This Chapter

1. Explain why the term *personality* is difficult to define.

2. Define the term *theory*.

3. Describe the three functions of personality theories.

4. Explain how to recognize *philosophical assumptions*.

5. Identify some of the basic philosophical issues on which personality theorists differ.

6. Explain how philosophical assumptions are evaluated.

7. Explain how science has its basis in philosophy.

8. Describe the five steps involved in the *scientific method*.

9. Explain the characteristics of *scientific statements*.

10. Explain how scientific statements are evaluated and describe how scientists decide between rival hypotheses.

11. Identify the three major goals of *psychotherapy* and indicate the criteria of evaluation suitable for each goal.

12. Explain why it is important to distinguish among the different functions of personality theories.

A definition for the word "personality" would be a good way to begin a book that considers various theories of personality. However, writing a definition is not that simple. A complete search for such a definition takes us back to the early history of the human race, back to the time when the first person asked, "Who am I?" thereby reflecting on his or her identity. The different answers that people have given to that question have found expression throughout history in various cultural constructs such as philosophy, religion, art, politics, and science. Each one of us begins the search anew; as children seeking identity, and later as adults reflecting upon our identity, we wonder who we are and join fellow travelers on the road in search of the self.

What Is Personality?

Although the term **personality** is frequently used, it is not easy to define. In common speech, it usually refers to one's public image. Thus people say, "Becky has a terrific personality!" or "If only Jeff had a more dynamic personality." This common usage reflects the origin of the word "personality" in the Latin *persona,* which referred to the masks that actors wore in ancient Greek plays. Such a concept of social role, however, does not include the complications that are involved in the long search to understand the self.

A psychologist, Gordon Allport, who was trying to arrive at a satisfactory definition of personality for his work, described and classified over fifty different definitions. His effort shows that there is little common agreement among personality theorists on appropriate use of the term. For Allport, personality is something *real* within an individual that leads to his or her characteristic behavior and thought. For Carl Rogers, another personality theorist, the personality or "self" is an organized, consistent pattern of perception of the "I" or "me" that lies at the heart of an individual's experiences. For B. F. Skinner, probably the most well-known psychologist in America, the word "personality" is unnecessary. Skinner does not believe that it is necessary or desirable to use a concept such as self or personality in order to understand human behavior. For Sigmund Freud, the father of contemporary personality theories, personality was largely unconscious, hidden, and unknown.

Thus, there is no definition of the word "personality" with which all personality theorists would agree. Each theorist presents us with his or her own understanding of the term. In part, this helps to explain why there are so many different personality theories. Although such a variety of definitions and theories is confusing, baffling, and even disturbing, it does not mean that the theories are not useful. Each offers insight into the question of the self and each can be helpful to us as we develop our own answers.

What Is a Theory?

Since we are referring to theories of personality, the next logical question to raise is "What is a theory?" Here you may be pleased to see that I can give a more definitive answer. The term "theory" comes from the Greek word *theōria*, which refers to the act of viewing, contemplating, or thinking about something. A **theory** is a set of abstract concepts that we make about a group of facts or events in order to explain them. A theory of personality, therefore, is an organized system of beliefs that helps us to understand human nature.

Describing a theory as a system of beliefs underscores the fact that a theory is something that we create in the process of viewing and thinking about our world. Theories are not given or necessitated by nature; rather, they are constructed by people in their efforts to understand the world. The same data or experiences can be accounted for in many different ways. As we shall see, there are many theories of personality.

How Do We Evaluate Personality Theories?

The theory of personality became a formal and systematic area of scientific specialization in American psychology during the 1930s. A personality theory is not simply an expression of science, but also involves philosophy and art. In order to understand how we evaluate personality theories, we first need to recognize how they function as philosophy, science, and art.

As I pointed out earlier, the question "What is personality?" takes us back to early human history. Awareness about the self and the world existed *before* deliberate reflection, philosophy, and science. In time, as thinkers began to reflect on their ideas, philosophy developed as a mode of understanding and expression. Later, science emerged as a way of acquiring information. Before the study of personality became a specialization of academic scientific psychology, questions of personality were generally included under the broader umbrella of philosophy. The methods of science and philosophy are distinguishable but not unrelated. Science is an offspring of philosophy and its methods are the fruit of philosophy's labors. The specific mode of study and investigation characteristic of a modern scientist arises out of an earlier philosophical encounter with the world.

If scientific theories of personality have their origin in philosophy, they also lead to some form of art, or practical application. The art of personality theory is much older than the science or even the philosophy of it; from earliest times, much has been spoken and written about how to live a good life. As science has developed, however, it has provided us with new knowledge, tools, and methods of self-understanding and improvement. Theories of personality are not just armchair speculations, but belief systems that find expression in ways that are designed to help us understand and improve ourselves and the world.

Philosophy, science, and art may be seen as three complementary activities that personality theorists engage in. As scientists, personality theorists hope to develop a workable set of hypotheses that will help us understand human behavior; as philosophers, they seek to explore what it means to be a person; as artists, they seek to apply what is known about people and behavior to make a better life. Each activity is conducted according to certain rules with its own criteria for success. Just as a potential athlete needs to become familiar with the rules, equipment, and scoring of whatever sport he or she wishes to engage in, the student of personality needs to become familiar with the different rules governing the activities of personality theorists. You will have difficulty understanding a personality theory unless you can identify the particular activity that the theorist is engaged in at a particular time and know how to evaluate it. By briefly exploring the activities of philosophy, science, and art, a foundation for understanding personality theories and evaluating them may be created.

Philosophical Assumptions

No psychologist or personality theorist can avoid being a philosopher of sorts. As we have seen, the science of personality theorizing has its origins in philosophy. The very act of theorizing, or thinking about what we see, entails making certain assumptions about the world and human nature. Every thinking person, not to speak just of personality theorists, holds basic **philosophical assumptions** as he or she reflects on the world and his or her existence. These basic philosophical assumptions profoundly influence the way in which we perceive the world and theorize about it.

The term **philosophy** comes from the Greek *philein*, "to love," and *sophia*, "wisdom"; it means the love or pursuit of wisdom. Each one of us is a philosopher insofar as we think and reflect about the world and ourselves. The search after wisdom, however, involves more than a desire for information to counter our ignorance. Wisdom denotes not merely knowing about something but knowing what ought to be done and how to do it. Wisdom touches our heart as well as our head and enables us to act out of its judgment, realizing itself in appropriate action. We are all familiar with the fool who may have a great deal of information but who lacks insight. As philosophers, we make assumptions and judgments about the good life and how to live it.

Traditionally, philosophy has encompassed five types of language and study: logic, aesthetics, ethics, politics, and metaphysics. Logic is the study of correct or normative reasoning; it describes the ideal method of making inferences and drawing conclusions. Aesthetics is the study of ideal forms and beauty; it deals with the nature of the beautiful and with judgments about beauty. Ethics is the study of ideal conduct; it deals with the knowledge of good and evil. Politics is the study of ideal social organization; it describes those forms of social and political structures that are most appropriate for human beings. Metaphysics is the study of ultimate reality; it attempts to coordinate what is real in the light of what is ideal.

Obviously, very few of us have complete and articulate stances on each of these issues. Yet, insofar as our thoughts, statements, and theorizing reflect one or more of these concerns, we can be sure that they are informed by certain basic philosophical assumptions. In the same sense, very few, if any, of the personality theorists whom we will consider aim at developing complete philosophical pictures of ourselves and the world. They consider themselves psychologists rather than philosophers. Nevertheless, in their psychologizing they raise philosophical issues and, in doing so, reflect philosophical assumptions.

Recognizing Philosophical Assumptions

It is not my purpose here to introduce you to the nature and character of philosophical assumptions. Such a topic would take us far afield and belongs more properly in philosophy textbooks. However, it is important to recognize that personality theories do entail philosophical assumptions and to identify them when they occur. I will list a few criteria that will enable you to recognize philosophical assumptions when they arise and enable you to evaluate them accordingly.

The discourses of philosophy frequently posit a distinction between what is and what ought to be. People do not always think logically, nor do they behave in ideal ways. Philosophical statements suggest that things are not necessarily what they appear to be. *What is* is not necessarily *what should be* or *what is ultimately true*. The fact that many people are aggressive does not necessarily mean that aggression is right or that aggression represents what it means to be human.

Since philosophical assumptions do not necessarily represent what happens in the everyday world, the "seeing" of philosophy cannot be the ordinary seeing of our sense organs. Rather, the "seeing" that informs our philosophical assumptions is a special act of knowing, an *extra*-ordinary intuition and visionary mode of apprehension that transcends everyday experience. Philosophical knowledge is ultimately in the form of an **epiphany** (from the Greek *epiphaneia*, which means "appearance" or "manifestation"), or a sudden perception of essential meaning.

Philosophical assumptions, therefore, differ from **empirical** statements, which are based on ordinary observation. Consider the following statements: "All blonds have blue eyes" and "All people seek what is good." On the surface, both statements look alike. But to test the first, you would look around to see if there were any non-blue-eyed blonds, whereas this kind of test would not be suitable for the second statement. The statement "All people seek what is good" does not refer to something that can be seen in everyday observation, nor does the statement rely on empirical observation. This statement refers to some kind of ultimate reality that is perceived in a different way. The first characteristic of philosophical assumptions, therefore, is that they often refer to a reality beyond appearances. They suggest that appearance and reality are not necessarily the same.

We want to be careful here because scientific statements also often refer to things that we cannot see in ordinary observation. Many important constructs in science involve imaginary concepts that cannot be seen. The difference lies in the nature of the observation that gives rise to the construct and the way in which it is tested. Statements in science are ultimately, even if indirectly, based on ordinary observation, and their means of test or validation are different from those of philosophy.

A second characteristic of philosophical assumptions is their tendency to be global. Philosophical assumptions universally embrace the world and all things. A key word to look for is "all" or some equivalent. "Everything that is real is of the nature of mind." "All people seek what is good." These statements transcend the individual and refer to the entire class of which they are speaking. Most important, they allow for no exceptions. This represents a primary distinction between scientific generalizations, which may also be global, and philosophical assumptions.

As we shall see, in science all statements must be open to falsification. In fact, science is required to indicate the conditions under which its statements might be proven incorrect. If an exception is found to a scientific generalization, that generalization must be qualified. When we philosophize, we treat exceptions in an entirely different manner. Suppose a person were to hold the philosophical assumption "All people seek what is good." A critic might counter with an exception: "How can you possibly describe the activities of Adolf Hitler as seeking what is good?" As a philosopher, a person might reply, "I agree with you, it would appear that Hitler is a man who did evil, but his evil is only in the world of appearances. In his efforts to do good, Adolf Hitler became sidetracked and his actions miscarried. In the process of trying to do what was good, he did something that appears to be evil." The exception is treated in terms of the philosophical assumption itself and explained in light of that view. Philosophical assumptions are not tentative hypotheses to be discarded when evidence contradicts them. There is no way to construct an empirical test that would let us falsify philosophical assumptions. If my philosophy is such that it involves the assumption "All people seek what is good," I will not permit any ordinary observations to convince me otherwise. On the contrary, I can account for all exceptions and seeming contradictions in terms of my philosophical assumption itself.

A third characteristic of philosophical assumptions is that they often are implicit rather than explicit. An *explicit statement* is one that is clearly stated. Its postulates are well delineated, related to one another, and organized into a unified whole. An *implicit statement* is one that is not always clearly stated. Its postulates are not always fully thought through and frequently they are not even recognized by the person who holds them. A person may be unaware that his or her theory is based on certain assumptions about the world. It is often difficult to identify a person's assumptions when they are not stated clearly. Nevertheless, almost everyone takes a stance on certain fundamental philosophical assumptions, be they explicit or implicit, which deeply influence a person's way of perceiving and understanding the world.

Some Basic Philosophical Assumptions

Many of the differences among personality theories can be attributed to fundamental differences in philosophical assumptions. Some of the issues on which personality theorists commonly disagree are described below. Each issue is presented here as a bipolar dimension. Some theorists may be seen as agreeing with one or the other extreme. Others are neutral toward the issue or seek a synthesis.

The first issue is that of *freedom versus determinism*. Theorists vary as to whether they believe that people basically have control over their behaviors and understand the motives behind them or whether they believe that the behavior of people is basically determined by internal or external forces over which they have little, if any, control. Most of us experience a subjective sense of freedom when we make a decision, but some theorists, such as B. F. Skinner, would suggest that our experience of freedom is delusive. Theorists also differ in the extent to which they would like their theories to be used to cultivate freedom in human nature or to exercise greater control over it. Carl Rogers seeks to increase a client's sense of freedom and responsibility, whereas B. F. Skinner aims to develop a technology to control human behavior.

A second dimension is that of *constitutional versus situational* factors in personality. Theorists differ over whether inherited and inborn characteristics or factors in the environment have the more important influence on a person's behavior. Some theorists, such as Raymond Cattell, stress the role of long-term personality traits in predicting behavior; others, such as Albert Bandura, emphasize situational variables. Laypersons frequently attribute the behavior of others to persistent inner dispositions, such as traits of laziness or aggression. Are such attributions valid?

A third major issue is that of *uniqueness versus universality*. Some theorists believe that each individual is unique and cannot be compared with others. Others contend that people are basically very similar in nature. Gordon Allport developed some research techniques precisely to explore the uniqueness of individuals. Eastern theories, on the other hand, tend to point toward the universality of human nature.

Proactive versus reactive is a fourth dimension that influences personality theories. Proactive theories view the human being as acting on his or her initiative rather than simply reacting. The sources of behavior are perceived as lying within the individual, who does more than just react to stimuli from the outside world. Humanist theories suggest that the human being is motivated toward growth and self-actualization. Other theorists, such as Dollard and Miller, suggest that human nature seeks primarily to maintain an internal state of equilibrium and balance through drive reduction. Such a state of balance is known as **homeostasis** as compared with **heterostasis**.

Finally, personality theorists can be compared as to whether they are *optimistic or pessimistic* about the possibility of change. Do significant changes in personality and behavior occur throughout the course of a lifetime? If an individual is motivated can he or she effect genuine changes in his or her personality? Can we help others to change by restructuring their environment? Some personality theories are decidedly more optimistic and hopeful than others concerning these possibilities. Freud, for example, is generally seen as a pessimist because he believed that early childhood experiences firmly shape an individual's personality. Behavior and learning theorists, on the other hand, are usually very optimistic concerning the possibility of change.

Exploration ////////

Examining Philosophical Assumptions

By looking at your own philosophical assumptions, you can better prepare yourself to recognize them in the theories of others. Each basic issue is presented here as a bipolar dimension along which a person's view can be placed according to the degree to which he or she agrees with one or the other extreme. You can rate your own views on a scale from 1 to 5. On each issue, if you completely agree with the first statement, rate the issue with a number 1. If you completely agree with the second statement, rate the issue with a number 5. If you only moderately agree with either statement, a number 2 or 4 would best reflect your view. If you are neutral toward the issue or believe that the best position is a synthesis of the two extremes, rate the issue with a number 3.

The first time you go through the items, rate each issue according to your

---

beliefs. The second time, consider each issue in terms of your actions, the way in which you generally behave.

1 ———————— 2 ———————— 3 ———————— 4 ———————— 5

freedom   determinism

People basically have control
over their own behavior and
understand the motives behind their behavior.

The behavior of people is
basically determined by internal or external forces over
which they have little, if any,
control.

1 ———————— 2 ———————— 3 ———————— 4 ———————— 5

constitutional   situational

Inherited and inborn characteristics have the most important influence on a person's behavior.

Factors in the environment
have the most important influence on a person's
behavior.

1 ———————— 2 ———————— 3 ———————— 4 ———————— 5

uniqueness   universality

Each individual is unique and
cannot be compared with
others.

People are basically very similar in nature.

1 ———————— 2 ———————— 3 ———————— 4 ———————— 5

proactive   reactive

Human beings primarily act
on their own initiative.

Human beings primarily react
to stimuli from the outside
world.

1 ———————— 2 ———————— 3 ———————— 4 ———————— 5

optimistic   pessimistic

Significant changes in personality and behavior can occur
throughout the course of a
lifetime.

A person's personality and
behavior are essentially stable
and unchanging.

(continued)

When you have determined where you stand on each of these major issues, a comparison of your positions can help you assess the importance of these issues to your own understanding of personality. Those assumptions that you feel very strongly about and have marked with a 1 or a 5 probably play a very important role in your personal philosophy. If you are not strongly committed to any particular issue, that issue is probably not as important in your thinking about personality.

You should note that there are no correct answers to the questions above. The different personality theorists that we shall talk about vary markedly in their position on each of these issues. Each adopts the position that appears most commendable or compelling. A comparison of your own position with that of each theorist will help you to understand why a particular theory does or does not appeal to you.

Evaluating Philosophical Assumptions

We have seen that the reality to which philosophical assumptions refer is not the world of everyday observations but a world of ultimate reality. This means that philosophical assumptions have criteria for evaluation that are different from the criteria for empirical statements or other statements based on ordinary observation. Philosophical assumptions have criteria that are suitable to the epiphanic vision that underlies them. In empirical science, as we shall see, statements are proven false by the process of perceptual observation. This method is not suitable for philosophical assumptions. In evaluating a person's assumptions, we cannot set up a crucial test or experiment that will determine whether or not his or her hypothesis is justified. Philosophical assumptions do not function as hypotheses; they have their own criteria or tests. As a matter of fact, the best way to spot whether or not a person's statements represent philosophical assumptions is to look at the way in which he or she evaluates them.

Philosophical assumptions are based on a special act of epiphanic knowing. They are evaluated by criteria that are suitable to that mode of knowing. We are going to suggest three criteria for evaluating philosophical assumptions that add up to a fourth and final criterion: compellingness.

The first criterion is that of **coherence.** Are the philosophical assumptions coherent? The verb *cohere* means "to hang together." Thus we ask, "Are the philosophical assumptions of a theory clear, logical, and consistent or are they riddled with contradictions and inconsistencies?" A philosophical system may have apparent inconsistencies, perplexing metaphors, or paradoxes and still be coherent, providing that the contradictions are ironed out within the philosophical stance itself so that the final position represents a clear, coherent whole. A person's philosophical assumptions may also be unfinished, that is, open to further growth, but to be coherent they must have a clearly recognizable, consistent thrust.

The second criterion is **relevance.** To be meaningful, a philosophical assumption must have some bearing on our view of reality. If we do not share the same view of reality, as is the case with some earlier philosophies, we will have considerable difficulty judging the assumption. We do not know what its bearing was in earlier times or how it might apply to our contemporary world. This lack of information explains why myths that posit geographical locations for heaven and hell are very difficult for us to appreciate today. Such myths were perfectly suitable in a Ptolemaic universe where the heavens revolved around the earth, since it seemed quite sensible then to think of heaven as up above and hell as down below. However, geographical location is rendered much more difficult in a Copernican universe, which is why contemporary mythic conceptualizations of heaven and hell tend to locate them within the self. Such a concept has more meaning for us today in the light of our contemporary world view. In our modern world, the criterion of relevance further implies the need to be compatible with empirical reality as best we can ascertain it; thus, philosophies are invariably reshaped by scientific discoveries.

The third criterion is **comprehensiveness.** Is the philosophical assumption "deep" enough? In part, this question refers to scope. Does it cover what it intends to cover? Further, the criterion of comprehensiveness asks whether the treatment of the subject is profound or superficial. A philosophical assumption is superficial if it leaves too many questions unanswered or if it refuses to answer them.

These three criteria add up to the final criterion, which we refer to as **compellingness.** The final and most important question to ask is "Does the assumption and its underlying philosophy convince you?" A philosophical assumption convinces you if it grabs you in such a way that you find the belief inescapable. It is as if you *have* to believe in it. Now, it is perfectly possible that a philosophical assumption may strike you as being coherent, relevant, and comprehensive, but in spite of those features it does not compel you to believe it. In such a case, the belief does not move you and you cannot "buy" it. My language here deliberately describes you as passive: "The philosophical assumption grabs you." "You are compelled." This language underscores the fact that philosophical assumptions are not merely subjective opinions that a person has about the world. Rather, philosophical assumptions emerge out of a person's encounter with the world. They entail an active meeting of the person and the world that leads to a position about reality that the person finds inescapable.

The way in which philosophers create their views of the world is similar to, although more formal than, the manner in which each one of us comes up with our own view. We may not have thought as much or written about it, but each one of us, upon reflection, can probably think of a significant incident or period in our lives when we experienced something that led us to think about ourselves and our world in a different way. Our world changed and we behaved differently as well. After an illness or accident an individual often perceives his or her life as having a new mission or purpose that was not present before. Such epiphanic experiences constitute the formative insights that shape our lives.

Inevitably, the personality theories described in this book represent philosophical points of view as well as scientific investigations. Some of the theories are explicitly philosophical. In others, the philosophical assumptions are not clearly stated, but they are nevertheless present. Carl Rogers openly acknowledges that his view of the self is philosophical and that his primary differences with other theorists, such as B. F. Skinner, are philosophical ones. Sigmund Freud initially conceived of his work as lacking any philosophy but in the end he admitted that many of his assumptions functioned philosophically. To the extent to which personality theories and our own thoughts involve philosophical assumptions, it is important that we recognize and evaluate them as such.

Scientific Statements

As scientists, personality theorists seek to develop a workable set of hypotheses, or tentative assumptions, that will help us understand human behavior. Scientists confirm their hypotheses by testing them according to generally agreed-upon methods. Thus, science, which comes from the Latin *scire,* "to know," is a group of methods of acquiring knowledge that are based on certain principles.

The Philosophical Basis of Science

Science has its origins in philosophy and, as such, it retains elements of its forebears. Thomas Kuhn, a physicist who has studied the history of science, points this out clearly when he reminds us that the ordinary observation on which scientific activity is based is not fixed once and for all by the nature of the world and our sensory apparatus but depends on a prior paradigm (1970). A **paradigm** is a model or concept of the world that is shared by the members of a community and that governs their activities. Everyday observation and perception are shaped through education and subject to change over time. Your view of the world, for example, is very different from that of a young person in ancient Greece or a member of an isolated primitive tribe. Indeed, without some sort of paradigm, we could not draw any conclusions from our observations at all.

Scientific statements, therefore, are accurately described as statements about the world based on observations arising from currently accepted paradigms. The paradigms are not derived from scientific activity but exist prior to it. The mode of knowing involved in accepting a paradigm is the same as that involved in a commitment to a philosophical assumption. This mode of knowing is quite different from that involved in adhering to the set of rules that govern scientific activity.

It may be easier for you to understand this point if you recognize that scientific activity is based on shared generalizations, beliefs in particular models, and values that cannot possibly be derived solely from the scientific activity itself. The statement that one *should* base conclusions on perceptions that can be shared by others rather than on private, intrinsically unique, perceptions is a value statement that is not mandated by our observations but chosen by the community of scientists as more useful. Likewise, the criteria for appropriate hypotheses and for choosing between rival hypotheses, which we will be outlining shortly, also function as values based on aesthetic considerations as well as empirical ones.

An Overview of the Scientific Method

There is no one method of validating hypotheses in science; rather, science consists of a variety of techniques for evaluating information. Nevertheless, one method of testing has come to be so well recognized and identified as characteristic of the scientific enterprise that it is commonly termed the **scientific method.** You should be familiar with it as an example of scientific work. This method is not unique to psychology but is shared and used by all of the sciences. Essentially, it consists of five steps.

Scientific inquiry begins with a "problem." The problem arises not in the scientific laboratory but in the everyday world. When there is an outbreak of a new virus, such as AIDS, the scientist is called upon to develop a vaccine or antidote that could alleviate it. When there is an increase in certain types of behavior, such as violence, the personality theorist might be asked to help account for that phenomenon. Thus, the *recognition of a problem* is the first step of the scientific method. The second step is to *formulate a hypothesis,* a preliminary move that directs further inquiry. A **hypothesis** is a tentative assumption that is made in order to draw out and test its empirical consequences. The hypothesis is created by the personality theorist as he or she brings creative mental powers to bear on the problem. An important point is that although the scientific method is a procedure for testing hypotheses, in and of itself it does not generate them. It presupposes them. Some scientists refer to the hypothesis as an "idea" or "hunch." Invariably the hypothesis reflects the personality theorist's underlying philosophical commitments.

The third step is to *make a prediction* from the hypothesis. This prediction refers to a state of affairs that would exist if the hypothesis were true. Predictions permit us to go beyond the situation that gave rise to the hypothesis to arrive at other consequences of it.

Testing the hypothesis is the fourth step of the scientific method. The prediction itself usually specifies the kind of test we use. Some hypotheses are tested very simply by looking somewhere. Others require an elaborate experiment in which variables are carefully manipulated and controlled. In some instances, we may not be able to find the evidence that the hypothesis requires, but as long as we can say what sort of evidence could test it, our hypothesis is considered to be legitimate.

The final step is to *draw a conclusion.* Many people like to think of a scientific hypothesis as verified, that is to say, proven true, once it has passed the test; logically, this is incorrect and is known as the **fallacy of affirming the consequent.** It is always possible that other variables could account for the test results. Therefore, the scientist never claims that the information produced by his or her methods is ultimately true, simply that it is useful.

The five steps outlined above provide an overview of scientific activity. It would be a mistake to imagine that these steps represent a clear-cut, sequential strategy. Rather, they are dissectible elements from scientific activity and do not necessarily reflect the messy, unpredictable, and exciting activity that personality theorizing really is.

Recognizing Scientific Statements

The keystone of science is empirical observation and the simplest kinds of statements in science are **empirical** statements, such as "There is a person in the room." To know whether or not an empirical statement is justified, an individual has to be shown evidence based on sensory data regarding what has been seen, heard, felt, smelled, or tasted.

Empirical statements may be based on objective data or subjective data. If someone reports, "I see a person," we can interpret the statement in two ways. The person may be saying, "I see a *person*" or "I *see* a person." In the first case, we are referring to the object of experience or **objective data.** In the second case, we are referring to an experience of seeing or **subjective data.** Both objective and subjective knowledge refer to empirical data. The difference between them lies in the position of the observer. In objective knowledge, the position is I-it: the self is looking outward on the world as

How We Behave as Scientists

The personality theorist George Kelly (1955) suggests that each one of us behaves as a scientist in our efforts to understand the world. You can gain a deeper appreciation of your own attempts to understand other people by analyzing a recent situation and your effort to understand it in terms of the scientific method that we have just outlined. Suppose one night, when you arrive home, you observe that there are tears in your roommate's eyes. You might conclude that he was upset about something. However, when you inquire what the problem is, he says, "Nothing is the matter" and points to a pile of onions that he has been chopping for tonight's stew.

Analyze this situation, or another one, in terms of the scientific method. What was the problem? What hypothesis did you develop? What prediction did you make about possible experiences you could have if the hypothesis were useful? How did you test your hypothesis and what conclusions did you draw?

object. In subjective knowledge, the position is I-me: the self is looking inward on its own experience as the object.

Reports that are concerned with the object of experience or extrospective data are relatively simple to verify. We merely indicate the conditions under which the observation may be repeated. If a second observer does not see the reported phenomenon, we suggest that the conditions were not clearly specified; for example, the observer looked for the person in the wrong room. Or we may suspect that the original observer has a distorted sense of perception or experienced a hallucination. Repeated observations of the same phenomenon under specified conditions lead to **consensual validation** or agreement among observers.

Reports that are concerned with introspective or subjective phenomena are much more difficult to validate consensually. A certain piece of art may give me much joy but fail to move someone else. This is because subjective phenomena often occur under much more complex conditions than external objects and they are more difficult to describe. Repeating such subjective observations may require the second observer to undergo extensive training or other experiences in order to duplicate all of the conditions. Undoubtedly, my joy on seeing a particular piece of art depends not simply on the art itself, but also on my mood, personal history, and so forth. Considerable effort is needed to duplicate these observations but it is not impossible (Tart, 1975).

Since reports that are concerned with subjective phenomena are much more difficult to validate, some psychologists have tended to ignore them and invest their efforts in extrospective or objective findings. In fact, John Watson (1878–1958), the father of the behaviorist movement, recommended that inasmuch as our thoughts, feelings, and wishes cannot be directly observed by another person, the psychologist should ignore them and concentrate on overt behaviors. Few psychologists today would agree with this extreme position. Most personality theorists emphasize that we need to be concerned with both subjective and objective data in order to understand behavior.

When a number of different instances of observation coincide, the scientist may make a generalization. A **scientific (or empirical) generalization** is a conclusion that something is true about many or all of the members of a certain class. Suppose I wanted to test the statement "All tough-minded people are controlling." The evidence for this statement could be a number of facts about individual members of the class. I could observe this tough-minded person, that tough-minded person, and other tough-minded persons. If all of them were also controlling, I might conclude that all tough-minded people are controlling, even though I have not examined each and every tough-minded person.

Because it is impossible for me to examine each and every tough-minded person who has existed in the past or might exist in the present or future, my empirical generalization can never be called ultimately true. Indeed, misleading stereotypes are the result of premature and unwise generalizations. As a scientist, the personality theorist must leave his or her empirical generalizations open to possible falsification.

The scientist also uses **definitions,** statements that are true because of the way in which we have agreed to use words. Some words are easy to define clearly and precisely. Other words are harder to define and subject to more disagreement. To resolve this problem, the social scientist frequently tries to develop operational definitions. An **operational definition** specifies which behaviors are included in the concept. "Stress" might be operationally defined in terms of the rate of one's heartbeat and extent of one's perspiration as measured by polygraph apparatuses, which translate such bodily changes into a printed record. It frequently is difficult to reach agreement on suitable operational definitions, and at times an operational definition distorts or even misses the concept it is trying to describe. For example, "stress" can also be defined as a subjective feeling of intense anxiety. The virtue of operational definitions lies in giving us a common ground of reference.

The most important statements in science are based on scientific constructs.

A scientist uses **scientific constructs,** which are imaginary or hypothetical and cannot be seen with the naked eye or even with sophisticated optical equipment, in order to explain what we observe. The protons and neutrons of the atom, the basic building blocks of nature, are not visible but are inferred from other observable evidence. The fact that our construct is imaginary or hypothesized does not mean that it is nonexistent or unreal. It simply means that we cannot directly observe it and have to infer it from the evidence. Hypothetical constructs such as "force" or "gravity" help to unify our world. Another familiar hypothetical construct is that of **IQ** or intelligence quotient. The concept of IQ is an imaginary construct that is used to explain certain behaviors, namely, one's likelihood for academic success. IQ is not an entity that we can see or directly observe. Indeed, it is an error to think of IQ as something substantive in the sense that if one were to cut open a person's brain, one would see the number 110 stamped on it. IQ does not represent something in the ordinary sense. It is properly used as an imaginary concept that may be more or less useful in explaining and predicting behavior. It helps to explain why John, who has a high academic record, performs in a certain way, while Mark, who studies just as hard, has difficulties pulling average grades. Many of our concepts in science, in fact almost all of the important ones, cannot be directly seen; we can only know them through their effects.

Some Basic Scientific Constructs

Constructs such as trait, reinforcement, and self have been created in efforts to understand personality scientifically. The concept of **trait** refers to a continuous dimension that an individual can be observed to possess to a certain degree. Examples of traits are emotional stability and introversion versus extroversion. Gordon Allport and Raymond Cattell make extensive use of trait constructs in their theories. The **self** is another useful construct for understanding personality that is present in many contemporary theories. In Carl Rogers's theory the self refers to those psychological processes that govern an individual's behavior. In Albert Bandura's theory the self is conceived more narrowly in terms of cognitive structures.

Indeed, some personality theories conceive of the term "personality" itself as a scientific construct. Thus Cattell defines personality as "that which permits a prediction of what a person will do in a given situation." For Cattell, personality is an imaginary construct that permits us to explain and predict behavior. The scientific constructs of a personality theory tie together the empirical findings of that theory and suggest new relationships that will hold true under certain conditions.

Evaluating Scientific Statements

As we have pointed out, there is no one method of validating scientific statements. Personality theorists use a variety of techniques, some of which are very complicated, in order to evaluate their work. We will be looking at a number of these as we discuss the specific procedures used by different personality theorists. However, we can make some general comments about the validating techniques used by scientists.

Even though scientists may build elaborate theories referring to things that they cannot observe directly, they base their theories on **everyday observation,** that is, the ordinary perceptions of our sense organs. It is true that I cannot test the statement "John has an IQ of 110" in the same way that I can test the statement "There is a person in the room." I cannot simply look. The statement must be tested indirectly, but the test is still based on ordinary empirical observation, such as looking at John's performance on an IQ measuring device. Scientific statements do not require a special act of knowing or form of intuition that goes beyond our everyday experiences. Given the identical conditions, another person could be expected to share the same perceptions and draw the same conclusions. Scientific statements, therefore, are based on *what is* and *what occurs* in our everyday world as it appears to us through our ordinary sense organs.

Second, scientific statements must be **open to falsification.** As scientist, the personality theorist is required to indicate the conditions under which his or her statements might be proven incorrect. If an exception is found to a scientific statement, that statement is considered to be false or in need of qualification. The generalization "All tough-minded people are controlling," for example, is disproven by pointing to a tough-minded person who is not controlling or qualified by indicating the conditions under which a tough-minded person will not seek to control others. This helps us to understand why a scientist never claims that the information produced by his or her methods is ultimately true. The very nature of scientific activity limits the kind of information that it can yield. This is also why the validating activity of the scientist is not as convincing or compelling as the mode of knowing that underlies philosophical assumptions. Scientific hypotheses are tentative and need to be discarded when evidence contradicts them. Although scientific methods cannot be said to yield ultimate truth, they do provide a wealth of useful information to assist us in living in the everyday world. It is to our advantage, therefore, to act as if the conclusions from our scientific methods are true. The criterion for judging scientific statements is that of **usefulness** rather than truth.

In the process of scientific investigations, the personality theorist frequently develops more than one hypothesis. Each one is checked out in turn to rule out those that do not stand up under test conditions. Occasionally, the scientist is left with rival hypotheses. Sometimes, the same phenomenon may be accounted for by two or more different hypotheses, both of which stand up under test. At other times, a sufficiently sensitive or crucial test has not been developed to eliminate all of the hypotheses but one.

Given that both are sound hypotheses, how does the scientist decide between them? In general, three criteria have been used: compatibility, predictive power, and simplicity. Each of these criteria has its advantages and limitations. **Compatibility** refers to the agreement of the hypothesis with other previously well-established information. This criterion is a sensible one since it is a lot easier for us to accept a new hypothesis if it is consistent with findings in other areas. However, it should not be too rigidly applied. Science does not necessarily grow in an orderly, straightforward manner, accumulating new facts without ever going back and changing them. There are times in science when a new idea completely shatters earlier theories, forcing us to revise and reconsider them. This is what happened with Einstein's theory of relativity. The criterion of compatibility is a good rule of thumb, but sometimes an incompatible theory proves to be more useful.

Predictive power refers to the range or scope of the statement. Scientists seek not only to explain the phenomena that we observe but also to predict and anticipate them. We have seen that, by being testable, a hypothesis is able to generate predictions about experiences that we could have if the hypothesis should turn out to be useful. The more predictions or consequences that we can infer from a hypothesis, the greater its range and usefulness in generating new ideas. On the other hand, too strict a reliance on this criterion may lead to the notion that the only value of a theory lies in the amount of research and predictions it generates. Some theories express their scope by integrating and encompassing ideas rather than by generating specific predictions and research projects.

The last criterion is that of **simplicity**, sometimes called "Occam's razor." Occam was a medieval philosopher who suggested that explanations ought to be as simple as possible. If there is too rigid an emphasis on the criterion of simplicity, the hypothesis may fail to account for all of the complexity of human behavior. However, all other things being equal, the simplest explanation is best.

The Art of Psychotherapy

If theories of personality have their origin in philosophy and seek to validate their constructs through scientific methods, they also culminate in some form of art or practical application. Personality theories have found application in many areas, such as assessment, research, and social concerns, but they are probably best known for their contribution to psychotherapy.

The art of **psychotherapy** is the effort to apply the findings of personality theory in ways that will assist individuals and meet human goals. The word **therapy** comes from the Greek *therapeia,* which means "attending" and "healing"; however, psychotherapists are not interested only in healing sick people. They are also interested in understanding "normal" people, learning how they function, and helping them to function more creatively. Although in many respects psychotherapy is the flowering of personality theory, it is also the seed of it, because the desire to help people has fostered and nourished the development of personality theories. The two go hand in hand. Many theories of personality cannot be adequately understood without understanding the theory of psychotherapy that accompanies them.

Goals of Psychotherapy

Joseph Rychlak (1968) points out that psychotherapy has three major motives or goals: the scholarly, the ethical, and the curative.

The *scholarly* motive considers therapy a means of understanding the self and human nature. Psychoanalysis, for example, was seen by Freud as a tool for discovering truths about human nature. Freud did not consider the curative effects of psychoanalysis to be its primary function or virtue. His goal was to help the individual acquire self-understanding and to develop a comprehensive theory of human nature. He developed psychoanalysis as a method of research aimed at that end.

The *ethical* motive considers therapy a means of helping the individual to change, improve, grow, and better the quality of his or her life. The effort here is not to study or understand people as much as it is to create a climate within which people can change if they wish to. Carl Rogers's work is an example of the ethical motive. His emphasis is on an attitude created by the therapist that permits change to occur within the client, rather than on cognitive understanding or the manipulation of behavior.

The *curative* motive aims directly at eliminating troublesome symptoms and substituting more suitable behavior. There is an analogy here to the work of doctors, who seek to cure people of illnesses. Most behavior therapists, for example, consider that they have been hired to do a job and seek to do it as effectively and quickly as possible. From this point of view, the therapist is responsible for creating changes, removing symptoms, and controlling behavior.

Most people enter therapy with the expectation that they will be cured or helped to improve. In this respect, the curative motive is most consistent with the popular view of psychotherapy. Because of this expectation, many people have difficulty, particularly at the beginning, in undergoing psychoanalysis or other forms of "insight" therapy. If they stay with it, however, their reasons for being in therapy change, and they begin to appreciate the value of the other motives. Obviously, the reasons for entering, continuing in, and practicing psychotherapy are many and mixed. This is why the evaluation of therapy is a difficult issue.

Evaluating Psychotherapy

How does one go about evaluating psychotherapy? What are the criteria that are appropriate to use? In 1952, a British psychologist, Hans Eysenck, stunned the therapeutic community with a report on treatment outcomes indicating that the improvement rate for patients in intensive and prolonged psychotherapy was only about 64 percent. This rate was less than that of 72 percent for patients who received treatment only from a general practitioner or were in simple custodial care. A second report (1961) did not change the general outlook. However, Eysenck's reports have subsequently been severely criticized, and it is now clear that his results are not the final word on the issue (Smith & Glass, 1977; Landman & Dawes, 1982). It appears likely that Eysenck prejudiced his results. Moreover, Eysenck's criterion for improvement was that of "symptom remission." This criterion, though perhaps appropriate for therapies governed by the curative motive, is not necessarily appropriate for those that are conducted for other purposes.

If the proportion of cures were the only criterion by which psychotherapies were to be judged, psychoanalysis and other insight therapies would have long since disappeared from the scene with the arrival of more efficient and less costly curative techniques. This, however, has not been the case. If one's criterion, on the other hand, rests on scholarly grounds, psychoanalysis emerges the clear winner. No other method of therapy has provided us with such a wealth of information about the complexity and depth of the human personality.

In brief, each method of psychotherapy must be evaluated in terms of its own goals and purposes. Behavior therapists, who aim at cure, are particularly interested in discovering the proportion of cures associated with various techniques. Ethical theorists, who aim at creating a suitable climate for therapeutic change and life improvement, have stimulated considerable research and study of those conditions that foster personality change and their effects. They have also raised ethical questions as to the desirability of certain behaviors. Freudian psychoanalysis asks to be evaluated in terms of its effectiveness as a method of research aimed at understanding human nature.

The Complexities of Evaluation

We have suggested that science, philosophy, and art are three functions that personality theories encompass. Our use of this threefold approach allows us to recognize each activity as it arises and gives us a better idea of how personality theories in general, as well as any specific personality theory, works. It is important to identify the different aspects of a personality theory because each activity has its own rules and procedures for establishing information and each has its own criteria for judging the worth of its findings.

No theory is simply one or the other: philosophy, science, or art; each theory combines elements of all three activities. Maddi (1972) points out that personality theorizing involves many different kinds of thought — rational, intuitive, and empirical. Nor are we trying to establish a model that all personality theories must follow. The fact is there is no one scientific method, philosophical approach, or psychotherapeutic strategy that would serve as an adequate model for all others.

Scientific studies of personality rely on paradigms that can only be established philosophically and generally culminate in some form of art or practical application. The desire to be scientific reflects itself in an effort to test constructs by validating evidence rather than by relying on the gut-level feeling of illumination that everyday language calls understanding something. The compelling character of a philosophical assumption is different from the scientific know-how that leads to the ability to predict. At the same time, the evidence of scientific methods can never be as strong as the compellingness of an epiphanic insight. Even though the paradigms on which scientific methods are based may be accepted as strongly as any other philosophical commitment, and this commitment may be equally resistant to change, the conclusions reached by scientific methods lack this quality of compellingness.

Some psychologists have attempted to narrow the possible activity of a personality theorist to one function or interpretation of science, such as an objective experimental methodology, and ignored the philosophical assumptions on which all scientific work is based. Others have assumed that the compelling character of philosophical assumptions is sufficient to establish their credibility as scientific findings about personality. Either position is unnecessarily limiting. It is important that we distinguish between the different kinds of functions that personality theories entail so that we can recognize them when they occur and evaluate them accordingly. Part of the current problem in personality theorizing is that the theorists are not always clear about what activity they are engaged in.

As we discuss the major personality theorists in the following chapters, we will try to clarify the function of philosophy, science, and art in each theory. This should enable you to evaluate the theories and see how they fit into the overall framework of personality theories as philosophy, science, and art.

❧ Summary

1. The term **personality** is difficult to define because there is little common agreement on how the term should be used. In everyday speech it usually

refs to one's public image. Different personality theorists present us with their own definitions of the word based on their theoretical positions.

2. A **theory** is a set of abstract concepts that we make about a group of facts or events in order to explain them.

3. Personality theories may function as philosophy, science, and art. As scientists, personality theorists develop hypotheses that help us understand human behavior. As philosophers, they explore what it means to be a person. As artists, they seek to apply what is known about human behavior to make a better life.

4. **Philosophical assumptions** suggest that things are not necessarily what they appear to be. They are based on a special **epiphanic** vision, which goes beyond the ordinary perception of our sense organs. Philosophical statements also tend to be global and do not allow for any exceptions. Finally, they often are implicit rather than explicit.

5. Some of the basic issues on which personality theorists differ are *freedom versus determinism, constitutional versus situational* factors, *uniqueness versus universality, proactive versus reactive* theories, and *optimism versus pessimism.*

6. Philosophical assumptions are evaluated by criteria appropriate to the special act of knowing that underlies them. The criteria are **coherence, relevance,** and **comprehensiveness,** all of which add up to a final criterion, **compellingness.**

7. Science has its basis in philosophy because the ordinary observation on which science relies depends upon a prior **paradigm** that is established philosophically. The values and standards of science also function as philosophical commitments.

8. The five steps that characterize the **scientific method** are *recognizing a problem, developing a hypothesis, making a prediction, testing the hypothesis,* and *drawing a conclusion.*

9. The simplest kinds of **scientific statements** are *empirical,* based directly on observation. The data on which these statements are based may be **objective** or **subjective.** When a number of different observations coincide, a scientist may make a **generalization.** Scientists also use **operational definitions,** which specify the behaviors included in a term, and **scientific constructs,** which use imaginary or hypothetical concepts to explain what we observe.

10. Scientists use a variety of techniques to evaluate their work. All of these techniques are ultimately based on **everyday observation,** the ordinary perceptions of our sense organs, although some statements can only be tested

indirectly. Scientific statements must be **open to falsification,** that is, a scientist must indicate the conditions under which a statement might be proven false. Scientists do not claim that the information produced by their methods is ultimately true. Scientific statements should be judged for their **usefulness** rather than their truth. When scientists end up with more than one hypothesis, the criteria they use to decide between rival hypotheses are **compatibility, predictive power,** and **simplicity.**

11. The three major goals of **psychotherapy** are the *scholarly, ethical,* and *curative* motives. Scholarly therapies should be evaluated on the basis of their contributions to the understanding of the self and human nature. Ethical therapies should be evaluated in terms of the suitability of the climate they create for fostering change and life improvement. Curative therapies should be evaluated on the basis of symptom remission and number of cures.

12. It is important to distinguish among the different functions of personality theories so that we can recognize each activity when it occurs and therefore evaluate each theory according to the appropriate methods.

Suggestions for Further Reading

Students who are interested in pursuing Gordon Allport's effort to define the word "personality" should see his survey in Chapter Two of *Personality: A Psychological Interpretation* (Holt, 1937). This chapter provides a compact survey of the origins of the word and the various ways in which it has been defined.

The Story of Philosophy by Will Durant (Pocket Books, 1954) is a lay introduction to philosophy that tells its story by focusing on the lives and ideas of significant philosophers. The introduction, "On the Uses of Philosophy," helps to place the work of these thinkers in perspective. J. B. Conant's *On Understanding Science* (Yale University Press, 1947) gives a concise introduction to the scientific enterprise. A comprehensive history of psychology is provided in the classic work of E. G. Boring, *A History of Experimental Psychology* (Appleton-Century-Crofts, 1929), a detailed but invaluable book for the serious student of psychology.

Books that try to place the study of psychology and personality theory within the general framework of science and philosophy are more difficult reading, but worth the effort of the interested student. The following are especially recommended: M. Turner, *Philosophy and the Science of Behavior* (Appleton-Century-Crofts, 1967); D. Bakan, *On Method: Towards a Reconstruction of Psychological Investigation* (Jossey-Bass, 1967); J. Rychlak, *A Philosophy of Science for Personality Theory* (Houghton Mifflin, 1968);

T. S. Kuhn, *The Structure of Scientific Revolutions*, 2nd ed. (University of Chicago Press, 1970); and I. Chein, *The Science of Behavior and The Image of Man* (Basic Books, 1972). These books stress the necessity of developing adequate conceptual structures of science and philosophy within which personality theorizing can flourish as efforts to understand the human being.

Part 1

The Psychoanalytic Approach

Of all the giants of intellectual history, Sigmund Freud emerges as an unquestionable leader in helping us to understand human nature. Freud's contributions are such that some people believe he did more to enhance our self-understanding than anyone else since Socrates, Plato, and Aristotle, the great philosophers of ancient Greece. Some critics, following a comment of Freud's own, have compared his activities to the Copernican revolution. Even if the comparison is not justified, Freud's achievement is highly significant. Many of the other theories that we will study were developed as efforts to elaborate on, modify, substitute for, or refute the concepts of Freud. Contemporary theories of personality cannot be studied without a prior understanding of Freud's contribution. Part 1 begins with a discussion of Freud's psychoanalytic theory.

Although he always had a group of loyal followers, it was no doubt inevitable that a dynamic figure like Freud would both attract and repel. Some of his original followers became dissatisfied with orthodox psychoanalysis, defected from the movement, and founded their own schools of thought. Carl Jung, Alfred Adler, Karen Horney, Harry Stack Sullivan, and Erich Fromm were all deeply indebted to Freud and psychoanalysis, which provided a major impetus for their work. At the same time, each reacted in varying ways against Freud's psychoanalytic theory and developed his or her own position. In many instances, certain developments in these theories have been identified as valuable elaborations or adjuncts to classical psychoanalysis. Nevertheless, each theorist presented his or her theory as one that could stand by itself. After we discuss Freud's theory, we will consider these significant theoretical departures.

1

Sigmund Freud: Psychoanalysis

Your Goals for This Chapter

1. Describe Freud's early use of the "talking method" and indicate the conclusions he drew about *unconscious processes*.

2. Describe Freud's concept of the role of emotions in human life. Explain why *wishes* are *repressed* and how they may be dealt with when brought back into consciousness.

3. Cite the instructions for *free association* and explain the premise on which the procedure is based.

4. Indicate the importance of *slips* and *dreams* and explain how they are analyzed.

5. Identify the nature of our repressed wishes and desires and explain how Freud's use of the word *libido* and his concept of *drive* lead to a new understanding of sexuality.

6. Describe the child's sexual activity and outline Freud's *psychosexual stages* of development, explaining the important events of each stage.

7. Describe how the effects of the psychosexual stages may be seen in various adult character traits and disorders.

8. Describe the characteristics and functions of the *id, ego,* and *superego*.

9. Explain how the id, ego, and superego are related in the *adjusted* and *maladjusted personalities*.

10. Explain how the id, ego, and superego are related to *conscious* and *unconscious processes*.

11. Discuss the importance of *anxiety* in the human condition and distinguish the three forms of anxiety.

12. Describe the function of *defense mechanisms* and define and give examples of common defense mechanisms.

13. Describe Freud's mature understanding of *psychoanalysis*.

14. Evaluate Freud's theory in terms of its function as philosophy, science, and art.

*T*he distinguished stature and contributions of Sigmund Freud place him at the forefront of contemporary personality theorists. For over forty years, Freud meticulously studied dimensions of human nature that were previously unknown and unexplored. Developing the technique of free association, he reached far into the depths of his own unconscious life and that of others. In the process, he created a unique method of research, psychoanalysis, for understanding the human individual. He discovered psychological processes such as repression, resistance, transference, and infantile sexuality. He developed the first comprehensive method of studying and treating neurotic problems. Not only did he revolutionize psychology, but his influence has been felt in all the social sciences, as well as in literature, art, and religion. His position in the history of intellectual thought clearly justifies an extended study of his ideas.

Biographical Background

Sigmund Freud was born in 1856 in Freiburg, Moravia (a small town in what is now Czechoslovakia), to a Jewish merchant and his young wife. Sigmund was born in a caul, that is, a small portion of the fetal sac covered his head at birth. According to folklore, this was a sign that he would be famous. Freud did not practice religion as an adult, but he remained very conscious of his Jewish origin. His mother, twenty-one at the time of her favored first son's birth, was loving and protective, and the young boy was devoted to her. Freud's father, Jacob, was a not-very-prosperous wool merchant of forty-one, almost twice as old as his wife. Jacob was stern and authoritarian, but his son respected him. Only later, through his self-analysis, did Freud realize that his feelings toward his parents were mixed: fear and hate, respect and love.

When Sigmund was eleven months old, a brother, Julius, was born, but he died eight months later. A sister, Anna, arrived when Freud was two and a half. Later, four other sisters and a brother completed the family. When Freud was very young, he had a nanny whom he described as "ugly," but he was very fond of her and impressed by her religious teachings of Catholicism. Nevertheless, shortly after Anna was born, the nanny was suddenly fired for having stolen from the family. Sigmund was also born an uncle. His father, a widower, had two grown sons by his former marriage, and Freud's elder half-brother had a child. Freud and his nephew John, who was one year older than he, were close childhood companions. Freud was to view their early relationship as very significant to his later development. Many have thought that Freud's unusual family constellation set the stage for his later discovery of the Oedipus complex.

At the age of four, Sigmund and his family moved to Vienna, where he was to live for almost eighty years. Although he was critical of Vienna, he did not

Sigmund Freud

leave the city until it was overwhelmed by Nazis in 1938, the year before he died. In his youth, Freud was a conscientious student. His parents encouraged his studies by giving him special privileges and expecting the other children to make sacrifices in behalf of their older brother. He was the only member of the family who had his own room and he studied by oil lamp while the others had to use candles. A natural student, Freud entered high school a year earlier than normal and stood at the head of the class for most of his days at the Sperl Gymnasium. He was good at languages and was an avid reader, being particularly fond of Shakespeare.

As a child, Freud had dreams of becoming a general or minister of state, but in reality professional choice was severely restricted for a Jew in Vienna. He thought of becoming a lawyer but entered medical studies at the University of Vienna in 1873 and graduated eight years later. His studies there took longer than usual since he took his time with those areas that were of particular interest to him. He never intended to practice medicine, being more interested in physiological research; practical considerations, including occupational barriers to Jewish people and the desire to marry, led him to establish a practice as a clinical neurologist in 1881. While still a student, he made substantial and noteworthy contributions to research, publishing his findings on the nervous system of fish and the testes of the eel. He developed a method of staining cells for microscopic study and explored the anesthetic properties of cocaine. Because he had no reason to believe that there were dangers connected with cocaine, he was somewhat indiscriminate in using it himself and in recommending it to others. After the addictive character of the drug was discovered, Freud said he suffered "grave reproaches." Cocaine claimed many physicians as casualties in the 1880s and 1890s.

Because the private practice on which Freud depended for a living brought him patients suffering from primarily neurotic disorders, his attention became focused on the problem and study of neurosis. **Neurosis** refers to an emotional disturbance, but one which is usually not so severe as to prevent the individual who has it from functioning in normal society. As Freud's goal was a complete theory of humanity, he hoped that his study of neurosis would eventually provide a key to the study of psychological processes in general. He studied for a year in Paris with the French psychiatrist Jean Charcot, who used hypnosis in the treatment of hysteria. He was impressed by Charcot's demonstrations but later rejected hypnosis as a therapeutic technique. On his return from Paris, Freud became influenced by a procedure developed by Joseph Breuer, a Viennese physician and friend, who encouraged his patients to talk freely about their symptoms. Breuer and Freud worked together in writing up some of their cases in *Studies in Hysteria* (1895). Freud's further investigations with Breuer's "talking cure" led to his own development of free association and later psychoanalytic techniques. Eventually they separated, as Breuer could not agree with Freud's emphasis on the role of sexuality in neurosis.

In 1900 Freud published *The Interpretation of Dreams,* a book generally considered to be the single most important work in psychology. Initially, the book was ignored by all but a few. Nevertheless, Freud's reputation grew, and he began to attract a following. He also encountered a lot of criticism; some accused his work of being pornographic. A psychoanalytic society was founded by Freud and his colleagues, and many of Freud's disciples later became noted psychoanalysts: Ernest Jones (his biographer), A. A. Brill, Sandor Ferenczi, and Karl Abraham. Originally, Carl Jung and Alfred Adler were also close associates, but later they left Freud's psychoanalytic movement to develop and stress other ideas.

In 1909, G. Stanley Hall, noted psychologist and president of Clark University in Worcester, Massachusetts, invited Freud to present a series of lectures. It was his first and only visit to the United States. These lectures contained the basic elements of Freud's theory of personality, and their delivery marked the change of psychoanalysis from a small Viennese movement to one of international scope and recognition.

Freud's work, however, was by no means over. He continued to develop and revise his psychoanalytic theory until his death. By the end of his life, psychoanalytic concepts had been applied to and were influencing almost every cultural construct of humanity. Freud's published works fill twenty-four volumes in the *Standard English Edition*. He died in London in 1939 at age eighty-three, after many years of suffering from cancer of the jaw.

The Origins of Psychoanalysis

Sigmund Freud's concepts must be appreciated historically. He did not complete a perfected system. *An Outline of Psychoanalysis,* which he began in 1938, the year before he died, had as its aim "to bring together the doctrines of psychoanalysis and to state them . . . in the most concise form." But this book was never finished; in fact much of his work has an unfinished character about it. Ideas appear and are dismissed, only to reappear in a new context. His thought moves in phases, changing and synthesizing what has gone before. The only works that Freud systematically tried to keep up to date were *The Interpretation of Dreams* (first published in 1900) and *Three Essays on Sexuality* (1905). In describing Freud's theories, therefore, it is important to recognize that psychoanalysis does not represent a finished theory, but rather an ongoing process of discovery about the self.

The Discovery of Unconscious Forces

A logical place to begin discussion of the origins of psychoanalysis is Freud's early work with Joseph Breuer. This, in fact, is how Freud began his presentation on the history of psychoanalysis to the American public in his lectures at Clark University. As we have already seen, Freud was deeply influenced by a procedure developed by Breuer, and he frequently credited Breuer with the discovery of the psychoanalytic method. Thus, psychoanalysis may be said to begin with the case history of one of Breuer's patients, who is known in the literature as Anna O. (Freud, 1910).

Anna O. was a twenty-one-year-old, highly intelligent woman. In the course of a two-year illness beginning in 1880, she had developed a number of physical and mental disturbances. Among her symptoms were a paralysis of the right arm and leg, difficulty in vision, nausea, the inability to drink any liquids, and the inability to speak or understand her mother tongue. Further, she was prone to states of **absence,** an altered state of consciousness in which there may be considerable personality change and later amnesia or forgetting of events that occurred during that period.

The medical profession of 1880 was quite puzzled by illnesses such as these and diagnosed them as cases of hysteria. **Hysteria** referred to an illness in which there were physical symptoms, such as a paralysis, but there was no organic or physiological basis for the problem. (Today such disorders are less common and are known as **conversion disorders.**) The cause of hysteria was a mystery. Because they could not understand or effectively treat the problem, many doctors tended to view patients suffering from hysteria with suspicion and to be punishing in their attitudes toward them. At times, some even went so far as to accuse their patients of feigning or faking an illness.

Breuer, however, treated his patient sympathetically. He noticed that during her states of absence, Anna frequently mumbled several words. Once he was able to determine these words, Breuer put her under hypnosis, repeated the words to her, and asked her to verbalize for him any associations that she had to the words. The patient cooperated. She began to tell him stories about herself that seemed to center on one particular event of her life: her father's illness and death.

Before he died, Anna's father had been very sick. She had taken care of him until her own illness prevented her from doing so. After she had related a number of these stories, Anna's symptoms were relieved and eventually disappeared. The patient gratefully called the cure the "talking cure," or referred to it jokingly as "chimney sweeping."

Anna at one time was unable to drink any liquids even though it was summer and she had a terrible thirst. She ate fruits, but these did not begin to quench her thirst. One day, while under hypnosis, she began to talk about her English governess, whom she had disliked. She finally told how one time she had entered her governess's room and seen the woman's little dog, whom she hated intensely, drinking water from a glass. Under the circumstances, she had kept her feelings silent, but after she had expressed her restrained anger in the session with Breuer, she asked for a glass of water and had no difficulty drinking it or drinking thereafter.

Her visual difficulties traced back in her memory to a time when she was sitting by her father's bed during his illness and was very worried about him. She was trying to hide her tears so that her father would not see them, when he asked her what time it was. Since she did not want him to see that she was crying, it was only with difficulty that she could look at her watch and make out the position of the hands on the dial through the tears that clouded her vision. Recollecting that event restored her clarity of vision.

Later she recalled another memory that also stemmed from the period when she sat by her father's bed caring for him. A black snake (common in the area in which she lived) appeared in the room and seemed to go toward her father. She tried to drive the reptile away, but it was as if she could not move her arm. She wanted to call for help, but she could not speak. Recalling these events and the emotions they included relieved her paralysis and restored her knowledge of her native tongue.

Breuer concluded that the patient's symptoms were somehow determined by traumatic or stressful events of the past and that the recollection of these events had a cathartic effect on the patient. **Catharsis** refers to emotional release. When the patient recalled the events, she did so with a great deal of emotional intensity. This evidently freed her of the symptom to which the emotion had become attached.

By mid-1882, it appeared that Anna was completely and dramatically cured. In any event, Breuer was anxious to end the treatment, because it had become obvious that his young patient was extraordinarily fond of him. Her open proclamations of love and strong demands for his services embarrassed the careful and reserved Dr. Breuer and also created domestic problems with his wife. When Breuer announced his wish to end the case, Anna offered a phantom pregnancy as a final symptom. Breuer was very shaken by this turn of events, abruptly dropped the case, and took his wife to Venice for a second honeymoon. On his return, he avoided the cathartic method in treating future patients. Fortunately, Anna eventually recovered. In time, she became well known as one of the first social workers, striving to improve the rights and status of children and women. The entire case would probably have gone unnoticed in medical history had Breuer not mentioned it to some of his coworkers, including the young doctor Sigmund Freud, who was deeply interested.

Some time later, Freud recalled the Anna O. episode and began to use the "talking method" with his own patients. He had some measure of success and, after observing his own explorations with the technique, came to the following conclusions. At the time of the original traumatic event, the patient had to hold back a strong emotion. He or she was unable, perhaps because of the circumstances that surrounded the event, to express the emotion it evoked in a normal way through thought, word, or deed. The emotion, prevented from escaping normally, had found another outlet and was expressing itself through a neurotic symptom. Further, the patient had forgotten the particulars of these past events. Until they were recalled under hypnosis, the details of the events and the emotions they involved were not a part of the patient's awareness. Thus, the patient was **unconscious,** or unaware, of these memories; but the unconscious memories were influencing present behavior.

Shortly thereafter, Freud decided to give up hypnosis. In part, it was a practical necessity, since not all of his patients could be hypnotized. He assured his patients that eventually they would be able to remember the traumatic events in a normal waking state. Abandoning hypnosis also proved to be an important step in Freud's discovery of resistances. He had found that assisting his patients to remember was a long process. This led him to think that although the patient consciously wanted to remember those events, some force within prevented the patient from becoming aware of them and kept the memories unconscious. Freud labeled this force "resistance." **Resistance** refers to the various obstacles that interfere with the analytic process and that must be overcome if the process is to be successful. Freud assumed that the same forces that originally caused the events to be forgotten were now opposing their coming into consciousness. These earlier forces he termed "repression." **Repression** is a process that shuts out undesirable thoughts or feelings from consciousness. Thus, a twofold concept emerged: repression, a force that makes ideas unconscious; and resistance, one that keeps them unconscious.

Recognizing repression and resistance leads to a dynamic understanding of **unconscious processes,** or forces of which a person is unaware. When an idea becomes unconscious, it is not simply as if it were filed in a drawer from which it can easily be recovered, as is the case with ordinary memories of which we are not always conscious. Freud called such memories, which have temporarily slipped from consciousness but are easily recovered, **pre-conscious** memories. You may not immediately be able to recall what you did on your last birthday, but with a little bit of effort you probably could remember. **Unconscious** memories are of a rather different sort. You may recall having been punished as a child but be unable, no matter how hard you try, to remember why you were punished. Such a memory has been repressed and rendered unconscious. It can only be recalled, if at all, with considerable difficulty. When one tries to regain such a memory, one discovers that the file drawer is stuck. There is a force, another aspect of the person, that prevents one from opening the drawer and recovering the memory. This force, the resistance, must be overcome in order for the memory to be recalled.

What were those ideas or thoughts that would be rendered unconscious? Freud discovered that they were **wishes.** During the traumatic event, a wish had been aroused that went against the person's ego-ideal or self-concept. Because it is hard for a person to accept the fact that he or she is not what he or she would like to be, such incompatibility causes pain. If it causes too much pain, the wish is repressed. One of Freud's patients provides an example. This patient's older sister had married a man of whom the patient was very fond. Quite soon, the sister died, and as the girl stood at her sister's bedside an idea occurred for a fleeting moment, expressing a wish. It was a wish that she could not permit to enter consciousness. "Now he is free," she thought, "and he can marry me." Shortly thereafter the girl became ill, displaying severe hysterical symptoms. Upon her recollecting that scene, the symptoms went away.

Underlying Freud's theory is the concept that events and happenings in our lives evoke strong feelings. These emotions help us to evaluate our world and surroundings in terms of being pleasurable or unpleasurable, loving or hostile, good or bad, and so forth. There may be particular cases in which the immediate expression of one's emotion may be inappropriate, ill-advised, or even disastrous. In a civilized world, we cannot express our emotions unchecked. Nevertheless, emotions must ultimately be expressed and find an outlet; they cannot be held in indefinitely. Ideally, their expression is non-destructive. One acknowledges, accepts, and then guides the emotion into constructive, or at least harmless, channels of expression. If an emotion is not expressed directly, it will seek expression indirectly. Repressed and un-recognized emotions go underground and appear in other ways, as in neurotic symptoms.

We repress emotions in order to avoid pain, because the wish the emotion represents conflicts with the self-concept. A certain amount of repression is unavoidable and necessary in order for a civilized society to exist. But the repression is not always successful or constructive. Another example, one which Freud gave during his lectures at Clark University, illustrates the problems that repressed ideas can create. Suppose, he suggested, that during the course of his lecture a young man in the back of the room decides to inter-rupt rudely by laughing, talking, and stamping his feet. Other members of the audience, disturbed by his behavior, forcibly eject the young man from the room so that the lecture may continue. Recognizing that our young man is a rowdy sort who might try to re-enter the hall, they station themselves at the door and hold it shut to make sure that he will not push it open. This unpleasant young fellow, however, refuses to be dealt with in that manner. He bangs on the outside of the door, kicks, screams, and, in short, creates a worse ruckus than he made in the first place. A new solution is required. Some compromise may be necessary. Perhaps the audience will agree to permit the young man back into the lecture hall if he will agree to behave a little bit better.

Freud admitted that his spatial metaphor was somewhat misleading, but it served to illustrate his primary concepts. We eject painful wishes, not permitting them to enter consciousness, but the repressed wishes refuse to behave agreeably. Instead, they create all sorts of problems, produce neurotic symptoms, and so forth. The need, then, is to restore the wishes to consciousness so that we can deal with them realistically.

Freud thought that there were several ways in which we could deal with the wishes once they were brought back into consciousness. First, we may recognize that we were wrong in repressing the wish in the first place. The wish that seemed so terrible at the time of the repression may be seen to represent no more than a normal desire of humanity. Therefore we can accept the wish either in whole or in part. Second, we may direct the wish into a higher goal through sublimation. **Sublimation** is a way of translating a wish, the direct expression of which is socially unacceptable, into socially acceptable behavior. Third, we may recognize that the rejection of the wish was rightly motivated but also recognize that there is a distinction between thoughts and actions. Therefore, we can control ourselves and do not act on the wish by conscious realistic thought.

Evolving a Psychoanalytic Method

Our initial discussion of the origin of psychoanalysis presented it as being simple only for the purpose of abbreviation. In fact, the process is much more complicated than the original illustrations of Breuer's and Freud's patients suggest. Essentially, several opposing forces are at work. First, there is a conscious effort on the part of the patient to remember the forgotten events. Second, there is resistance, which persists in keeping the memories unconscious. Finally, there are the expressed emotions that continue to seek expression. If a wish cannot get out on its own identity, it will seek an outlet in a disguised form. By putting on a mask, it will manage to sneak out and find expression in the person's behavior. Although the trauma cannot be immediately remembered, it may express itself in a hidden manner through the memories and thoughts that are recalled. In order to delve behind these masks and discover the repressed ideas, Freud developed two primary procedures: free association and the interpretation of dreams and slips.

Free Association   This is a technique in which the patient is told to verbalize whatever comes to mind, no matter how insignificant, trivial, or even unpleasant the idea, thought, or picture may seem. **Free association** is based on the premise that no idea that occurs to the patient is arbitrary and insignificant. Eventually, these ideas will lead back to the original problem. For example, Breuer's patient did not immediately remember the scene of her father's death, but her arm was paralyzed, her vision clouded, and she was unable to use her native tongue. Then, what she did talk about hinted at the hidden event. The instructions for free association are deceptively simple, but, in fact, they are very hard to follow. What happens when we try to verbalize everything that comes to mind? We may be flooded with thoughts and find it impossible to put them all into words. At other times, we may go blank and discover that nothing comes to mind. Also, the thoughts that do come may be very painful to discuss. These intruding ideas are like ore, however, for the analysis eventually reduces them from their crude state to a valuable metal. After free association, one reflects upon what one has said. In the process, the resistance is analyzed, understood, and weakened so that the wish is able to express itself more directly.

Exploration ///////

Free Association

A simple demonstration suggested by Theodore Reik (1956), one of Freud's followers, can convince the reader how difficult, yet potentially valuable, the task of free association is. The exercise is hardly equivalent to the genuine psychoanalytic situation, but it shares some of its elements and has the advantage of being available to anyone. Further, it shows that the value of free association goes beyond its use as a technique in psychoanalysis. It may be employed by the lay person to understand more fully experiences in his or her everyday life. By following the chain of seemingly irrelevant thoughts that we produce, we may gain new insights about ourselves.

Modern technology simplifies the demonstration. Using a tape recorder, choose a time and place where you can be alone and in relative quiet. Assume a relaxed position and then try to speak into the recorder whatever thoughts come to mind for a period of one half-hour or more. In general, we try to follow a certain direction in speaking. We try to speak logically and develop points in an orderly sequence. Free association requires that we verbalize whatever occurs to us without such order and restriction. Do not try to control your thoughts, or censor or analyze them. Moral, logical, and aesthetic considerations should be laid aside, and you should concentrate simply on recording whatever comes to mind. Many obstacles block the way. You may be surprised, ashamed, and even afraid of the thoughts that emerge. Social conventions have taught us to be silent on a great many matters. It is difficult to acknowledge hostile and aggressive tendencies, particularly toward those we love. Some of us even have difficulties expressing tender thoughts. Moreover, a petty or trivial thought is often the hardest of all to express. You will be successful if you succeed in verbalizing and recording all of your thoughts, regardless of their significance, importance, pleasantness, or logical order.

When you are finished, put the tape aside and resume your normal business. After a reasonable amount of time, perhaps the next day, play the tape back and reflect upon what you have said. You will be listening to a person who reminds you of yourself in many ways, but in other respects he or she will be unknown. You will discover that you had thoughts and impulses that you did not realize before. They may seem minor, but they will surprise you. Although such a demonstration does not even begin to approach self-analysis, it may make clear the difficulties involved, the potential for self-discovery, and the moral courage required for self-understanding.

The Interpretation of Dreams and Slips   In the process of free association, particular attention is paid to slips and dreams. **Slips** are bungled acts: a slip of the tongue, a slip of the pen, or a lapse of memory. In these cases, we consciously intend to say, write, or do one thing but something else inadvertently slips out. A word or a name may be on the tip of the tongue, but we have momentarily forgotten it. Many of us dismiss such events as trivial and meaningless, but to Freud slips like these are not without meaning. The Freudian theory assumes that in our psychic life nothing is trifling or lawless; rather, there is a motive for everything.

Here we are making an important distinction between cause and motive. *Cause* implies the action of a material, impersonal force that brings something about. *Motive* refers to personal agency and implies an emotion or desire operating on the will of a person and leading him or her to act. For Freud, all events are **overdetermined,** that is, they have more than one meaning or explanation. To illustrate: a ball is thrown into the air; after traveling a certain distance, it falls to the ground. A causal explanation of this event would use laws of gravity to account for the ball's fall. An explanation in terms of motive would emphasize that the ball was thrown by someone. This particular ball would not have fallen at this time if someone had not willingly thrown it. Both explanations are correct and they complement each other. Thus, it is not sufficient to argue that we make slips of the tongue because we are tired, although it is true that fatigue may provide the physiological conditions under which a slip may occur. Nevertheless, the slip expresses a personal motive as well. Nor, as we shall see later, is it enough to account for dreams on the basis of indigestion from last night's supper or the presence of β (beta) waves during REM sleep. The dream also expresses a personal wish that merits attention. Freudian theory is particularly concerned with the explanation in terms of motive.

Here is an example of a slip and its analysis, which Freud reports in *The Psychopathology of Everyday Life* (1904). He recalls how a friend was talking excitedly about the difficulties of his generation. The friend tried to end his comment with a well-known Latin quotation from Virgil, but he could not finish the line. Freud recognized the quotation and cited it correctly: *"Exoriare aliquis nostris ex ossibus ultor,"* which literally means "Let someone arise from my bones as an avenger." The forgotten word was *aliquis* ("someone"). Freud's friend was embarrassed but, remembering the significance that Freud attached to such slips, indicated that he was curious to learn why he had forgotten the word. Freud took up the challenge and asked his friend to tell him honestly and without any censorship whatever came to mind when he directed his attention to the word *aliquis*. The first thought that sprang to his mind was the notion of dividing the word as follows: *a* and *liquis*. Next came the words "relics," "liquify," "fluid." These associations had little meaning for him, but he continued and thought of Simon of Trent and the accusations of ritual blood sacrifices that had often been brought against the Jewish people. Next he thought of an article that he had read recently entitled "What Saint Augustine Said Concerning Women." The next thought appeared to be totally unconnected, but following the cardinal rule he repeated it anyway. He was thinking of a fine old gentleman whose name was Benedict. At this point, Freud noted that he had referred to a group of saints and church fathers: St. Simon, St. Augustine, and St. Benedict. That comment made his friend think of St. Januarius and the miracle of blood. Here, Freud observed that both St. Januarius and St. Augustine had something to do with the calendar and asked his friend to refresh his memory about the miracle of blood. The blood of St. Januarius is held in a vial in a church in Naples. On a particular holy day it miraculously liquifies. The people attach a great deal of importance to this miracle and become very upset if it is delayed. Once it was delayed and the general in command took the priest aside and made it clear to him that the miracle had better take place very soon. At this point, Freud's friend hesitated. The next thought was surely too intimate to pass on and, besides, it had little connection. He had suddenly thought of a lady from whom he might get an awkward piece of news. "Could it be," Freud guessed, "that she missed her period?"

The resolution of the slip was not that difficult. The associations had led the way. Freud's friend had mentioned the calendar, the blood that starts to flow on a certain day, the disturbance should that event fail to occur, and the feeling that the miracle must take place. The word *aliquis* and its subsequent allusions to the miracle of St. Januarius revealed a clear concern with a woman's period. That concern was what was unconsciously occupying the young friend when he made the slip. Often a slip is not so obvious and is revealed only after a long chain of associations. The meaning of the slip, you will note, is not imposed on it from outside, but comes to view only in the course of the person's associations.

A second area explored by free association is that of dreams (1900). For Freud, the dream is the *via regia,* the royal road to the unconscious. It is often easy to understand the dreams of young children, who wear their personalities on their sleeves. Because their defenses have not yet masked their motives, they dream very simply of the fulfillment of unsatisfied wishes from the day before. The child who has not received what in his or her opinion is a sufficient amount of candy during the day may dream of an abundance of it at night. Folk proverbs reinforce the concept that the dream is the fulfillment of a wish: "The pig dreams of acorns, the goose of maize." "Of what does the hen dream? Of millet."

Adult dreams also express unsatisfied wishes, but, because in the adult many of these wishes have become unacceptable to the self-concept, the dream undergoes a disguise. Therefore, Freud distinguishes between the manifest dream and the latent dream. The **manifest dream** is the dream as it is remembered the next morning. Such a dream appears frequently incoherent and nonsensical, the fantasy of a mad person. Nevertheless, it presents some kind of narrative story. The **latent dream** refers to the real meaning or motive underlying the manifest dream. Analysis seeks to discover the latent meaning that is expressed within the manifest dream. The dream wish, however, has undergone distortion, and its mask must be removed before it will reveal its true meaning.

Dreams provide a particular wealth of information because in dreams a person is more relaxed than when awake, and his or her resistance, so to speak, may be caught off guard. The wishes and desires that are forbidden access in normal conscious states have a chance to slip out. Thus, the manifest dream may be described as a disguised fulfillment of repressed wishes.

It is possible, Freud held, to gain some insight into the process that disguises the unconscious dream wishes and converts them into the manifest dream. This process is called **dream work** and it has many elements. One important element is its use of symbols. A **symbol** is a sign that stands for something else. Some symbols employed in dreams are unique to the individual dreamer and can only be understood in terms of his or her particular history and associations. Others are shared by many dreamers. In some instances, symbols have acquired universal meanings; such universal symbols find expression in our myths, legends, and fairy tales, as well as in our dreams.

The occurrence of anxiety dreams or nightmares does not contradict Freud's concept that the dream is a wish fulfillment. The meaning of a dream does not lie in its manifest context; thus, a dream that on the surface appears to provoke anxiety may serve to fulfill an unconscious wish on another level. Further, the expression of a forbidden wish, as we have seen, causes anxiety or pain to the conscious self, so an anxiety dream may indicate that the disguise was unsuccessful and permitted the forbidden wish too clear an expression.

Some examples of dreams that Freud analyzed in the course of his self-analysis and reported in *The Interpretation of Dreams* may help to illustrate the procedure of dream analysis. During the spring of 1897, Freud learned that he had been nominated for the position of professor extraordinarius (assistant professor) at the university. He was pleased even though he did not expect much to come of the nomination. In the past, such proposals had been ignored by the authorities and several other equally qualified colleagues had been waiting in vain for similar appointments. One evening a colleague visited Freud and told him of a meeting that he had with an authority, in which he asked him whether or not the fact that he was Jewish delayed the promotion. He had received an evasive and noncommittal answer, and as he stated to Freud, "Now, at least I know where I stand." The conversation reinforced Freud's notion that he would probably not get the promotion because of his own Jewish background.

The next morning, Freud recorded a dream: "My friend R. is my uncle; I have a great affection for him. His face in the dream is somewhat altered, it is elongated and has a distinct yellow beard."

An analysis of the dream (for condensation, I have omitted some of the associations) revealed that Freud had only one uncle, Joseph, who had committed a criminal offense, was arrested, found guilty, and paid the penalty. Freud's father used to say that Joseph was not a bad man, merely a simpleton, and in the dream R. appeared to be a simpleton. The composite face seen in the dream illustrates condensation in the dream work. But why would Freud wish to render his friend, for whom he had a great deal of respect, as a simpleton? At this point, Freud recalled a conversation with another colleague, N., who had also been nominated for the professorship and who had congratulated Freud on his nomination. Freud shrugged off the compliment, suggesting that the nominations were probably worthless, but N. told him not to be too certain as there was a special problem that had been delaying his. A woman had once brought criminal charges againt N. He had been acquitted, but such matters are known to show their ugly heads in considerations such as these. With these associations, the meaning of the dream was clear. Uncle Joseph represented both of Freud's colleagues: one was presented as a simpleton, the other as a criminal. If religious prejudice was really a determining factor in the delay of his friends' promotions, chances were that Freud's own promotion stood in jeopardy. If, however, in his dream he could account for their rejection by other factors, then his own chances for the appointment would be elevated.

Dreams fulfill our wishes; they do not necessarily represent reality. Freud reported that it was hard for him to analyze his dream. It was embarrassing for him to acknowledge that he had adverse thoughts about his colleagues. Of course, the analysis did not imply that Freud actually felt his colleagues were stupid or criminal; rather, it represented them in that light in order to achieve the wish fulfillment.

Another dream, which Freud traced back to his seventh or eighth year and analyzed some thirty years later, was a most vivid one in which Freud's mother, who was sleeping with a particularly calm expression on her face, was carried into the room and laid on the bed by two or three persons with birds' beaks. This dream led to an important discovery in Freud's theory and also illustrated the fact that dreams are frequently overdetermined. Dreams refer not only to the unsatisfied wishes of the day before, but also to wishes that stem back to early childhood.

Freud indicated that as a child he awoke crying from the dream, but he became calm when he saw his mother. In his subsequent analysis of the dream, the tall figures with beaks reminded Freud of illustrations in Philippson's version of the Bible. The birds appeared to be Egyptian deities such as are carved on tombs. Freud's grandfather had died shortly before the dream. Before his death, he had gone into a coma and worn a calm expression on his face identical to the expresion in the dream. At this level of interpretation, the dream appeared to express a young boy's anxiety over the possible death of his mother. Further analysis led deeper. The name "Philippson" reminded Freud of a neighborhood boy named Philip with whom he used to play as a child. Philip introduced Freud to the slang expression *völgern,* a rather vulgar German phrase for sexual intercourse. The term originates from the German word *Vogel,* which means "bird." Thus, on a deeper level, Freud had to conclude that the wish expressed in the dream was that of sexual (and therefore forbidden) desires toward his mother. This dream led Freud to the discovery of the Oedipus complex, which I will discuss shortly, and assisted him in clarifying the nature of repressed wishes and desires.

The Dynamics and Development of Personality

According to Freud, the nature of our repressed wishes and desires is erotic (from the Greek word *eros*, "love") and sexual. This reference to sexuality is an aspect of Freud's work that many people find problematic. In part, Freud's emphasis on sexuality requires understanding how Freud redefined the term "sexuality" and used it in his work. Moreover, the implications of Freud's discovery, quite frankly, offend many of us. Freud's insistence on our sexual nature tells us something about ourselves that many of us would prefer not to acknowledge.

The Importance of Sexuality

In his early work, Freud viewed sexuality as a bodily process that could be totally understood under a model of tension reduction. The goal of human behavior was simply to reduce the tension created by the accumulation of too much energy and to restore a state of balance. Sexual desires could be compared to a wish to remove an itch. However, as his work developed, Freud began to emphasize the psychological character of mental processes and sexuality. His use of the word **libido** to refer to the emotional and psychic energy derived from the biological drive of sexuality testifies to this shift in his thought.

Freud's desire to emphasize the psychological character of mental processes is also seen in the development of his concept of **drive.** The German word he used was *Trieb,* which has been variously translated as "instinct" or "drive." Since the word "instinct" generally connotes an inborn automatic pattern of activity characteristic of animals rather than humans, translation of the word as "drive," or even "impulse" (Bettelheim, 1982), seems more appropriate to Freud's intent. Freud used *Trieb* to refer to a psychological or mental representation of an inner bodily source of excitement. Drives are a form of energy, a force that cannot be reduced to either a bodily aspect or a mental one because it combines elements of both.

In his concept of drive, Freud abandoned an earlier attempt to reduce psychological processes to physiological ones and also began to resolve a problem inherited from Cartesian philosophy. In the belief that a person is more than a machine, the French philosopher René Descartes (1596–1650) had divided all reality into two separate categories: mind and matter. Matter included all material substances, inorganic and animate, including human bodies. These things, Descartes suggested, could be understood under scientific laws. Mind, which included all conscious states (thinking, willing, feeling, and so forth), was a second kind of substance that Descartes believed could not be explained by scientific laws. For the first time in history, a sharp distinction between mind and matter was made the basis of a systematic philosophy. Descartes's philosophy led people in the West to posit the center of the person in the mind rather than in the entire organism. Freud recognized that a comprehensive view of personality must see body and mind as a unity and his holistic approach began to help repair the Cartesian split.

A drive is characterized by four features: source, impetus, aim, and object. *Source* refers to the bodily stimulus or need. *Impetus* means the amount of energy or intensity of the need. *Aim* implies goal and purpose: to reduce the excitation. *Object* refers to that person or object in the environment through which the aim may be satisfied. If Freud had characterized drives simply by source and impetus, he could have continued to think of the sexual drive as just a bodily process. He chose to include also aim and object, which forced him to view sexuality differently and to emphasize its psychological and intentional character. Freud used the German verb *besetzen* (translated as **cathect**) to refer to investing libidinal energy in a mental representation of an object that will satisfy a desire; a person cathects an object that he or she wants. The importance of one's sexual life as a bodily process begins to diminish in favor of one's response to it. For this reason, Freud used the term **psychosexuality** to indicate the totality of elements included in the sexual drive.

Freud viewed human beings as predominantly hedonists or pleasure seekers. We seek to avoid painful tension and obtain pleasure. In the course of avoiding tension, psychic energy may be displaced. In other words, if the original object intended to satisfy the drive is unavailable, another object may be substituted. The substitution is known as **displacement.** Thus, the sexual drive may be satisfied in many different ways. The displacement of energy from one object to another is a very important aspect of personality development, since it helps to account for the incredible variety of human behavior.

Freud suggested that there are two basic groups of impulsive drives. **Life impulses** or drives are those forces that maintain life processes and insure reproduction of the species. The key to these forces is the sexual drive, whose energy force is "libido." **Death impulses** or drives are the source of aggressiveness and reflect the ultimate resolution of all of life's tension in death. Although Freud emphasized the importance of the death drive, his discussion of the development of personality centers around the sexual drive.

What is the purpose of sexuality? Traditionally, the answer has been reproduction. The medieval theologian Thomas Aquinas (1225–1274) gave classic expression to this position when he argued in *Summa Theologica* that according to natural law the primary purpose of sexuality was reproduction of the species. Other goals or purposes of sexual activity were seen to be secondary. The pleasure that attended sexual activity was permissible, and even encouraged by St. Thomas, but he recommended that it should be submissive to and never prevent the primary purpose of reproduction. If we think that the primary purpose of sexuality is reproduction, certain other thoughts about sexuality are logically going to follow. Fondling of the genitals that does not lead to reproduction is going to be disapproved of or regarded as perverse. It is difficult to concede that young children, prior to the age of adolescence, have a sexual life, because their immaturity inhibits reproduction.

The nineteenth-century culture in Vienna, from which Freud's theories emerged, reflected such an attitude. It is difficult for us to appreciate today the extent to which sexual impulses and desires were then forcibly repressed. The sexual act was generally viewed as beastly, unrefined, and undignified, but it was tolerated as an outlet for a natural shortcoming of men and as a necessary prelude to reproduction. Women were supposed to be above such impulses, and children were thought incapable of them. To suggest that either a woman or a child had sexual feelings was to speak evil of them. We must remember that whereas men must be orgasmic in order for reproduction to occur, the same is not true of women. Thus it was possible, and indeed required, that women hide their sexual desires. Much of the time this was done unconsciously, so that the woman was unaware of them herself.

There was considerable concern and anxiety over what were thought to be inappropriate sexual activities and perversions. Rigid taboos were put upon infants' autoeroticism (self-love and the fondling of one's own body) and limits were set on the expression of sexuality in adult life. The body's excretory functions were taken care of with embarrassment and prudery was practiced to fanatical extremes.

At the same time Vienna was undergoing a cultural renaissance in philosophy, music, and literature. The intelligentsia was seeking the realities that lay behind the facade of the decaying Austrian empire. One such reality was sex, which had been denied by the puritan climate. To a large extent, Freud did share this puritan attitude; nevertheless, he also relentlessly searched for the reality behind the mask.

Freud suggested that the primary purpose of sexual behavior is pleasure. To be specific, sexual activities aim at producing pleasure in the body. If the primary purpose of sex is pleasure, the door is open to a host of new conclusions. Activities that may not focus on the genitals are included as key expressions of sexuality to the extent to which they provide pleasure. The young child, who invariably seeks pleasure in the body, may be seen as having a rich sexual life. Activities such as sucking the thumb, previously seen as separate from sexuality, may be viewed as sexual.

Freud, in effect, turned the traditional concept upside down. This reversal permitted him to account for behaviors that were previously inexplicable, such as sexual deviations and infantile sexuality. Such activities may be more clearly understood if pleasure is seen as the primary purpose of sex, and reproduction as secondary. In effect, Freud's redefinition of sexuality is twofold. First, he divorces sex from its previous close restriction to the genitals and reproductive activity. Second, he enlarges the concept of sexuality to include activities, such as thumb sucking and sublimation, that previously were not thought of as sexual.

In Freudian terms, the child, who actively seeks pleasure from many areas of the body, is **polymorphous perverse;** that is, children differ in many respects from what is thought to be normal reproductive sexual activity. The sexual activity of children is essentially **autoerotic;** children seek pleasure from their own bodies rather than from the body of another person. They find pleasure in sucking their thumbs, exploring their genitals, and so forth. Only in the course of a long history of development do children progress toward normal, mature, heterosexual, reproductive activities.

The Psychosexual Stages of Development

Freud (1905) outlines a path that children travel as they progress from autoerotic sexual activity to normal, mature, reproductive activity. In this journey, the libido or sexual drive invests itself in various **erogenous zones** or areas of the body that provide pleasure. Indeed, observations have shown that as children grow, they do focus on different areas of the body; this attentional sequence follows the sequence outlined by Freud. He believed that by passing through a series of **psychosexual stages** in which different erogenous zones are important, children move from autoeroticism to heterosexuality and develop their adult personalities.

Oral Stage   The first stage is the **oral stage,** which lasts from birth to age one. During this time, the major source of pleasure and potential conflict is the mouth, the primary organ for young infants. From it they receive nourishment, have their closest contact with the mother (in breast-feeding), and discover information about the world. The fact that each new object infants meet is immediately placed in the mouth indicates the importance of this zone. The two main types of oral activity, ingestion and biting, are the first examples of character types and traits that may develop later on. Because the oral stage occurs at a time when infants are totally dependent on others for their needs, feelings of dependency arise. Oral activities are also a source of potential conflict because restraints may be placed on them. A mother may seek to discourage thumb sucking or stop her child from biting the breast. Thus, the focus of greatest pleasure and conflict is located for infants in the mouth.

Anal Stage   Freud's second psychosexual stage is the **anal stage,** which is experienced in the second year of life. At this time, the major source of pleasure and potential conflict is the anus. Generally, toilet training occurs during this period. Toilet training involves converting an involuntary activity,

During the oral stage, each new object an infant meets is immediately placed in the mouth.

the elimination of bodily wastes, into a voluntary one. It frequently represents the child's first experience with an attempt to regulate instinctual impulses. A clash of wills may develop. Children may obtain pain or pleasure in either retaining or expelling their waste products. These two primary modes of anal expression, retention and expulsion, are further models for possible future character traits. In their efforts to train their children, parents may forget that control over the sphincter muscles and eliminatory activity is an activity that only the child can perform. As early efforts to discipline children begin, the buttocks are frequently selected as a site on which to inflict pain. Since stimulation in that area causes both pleasure and pain, sadistic (pain-inflicting) and/or masochistic (pain-receiving) patterns of behavior may emerge. Subsequent forms of self-control and mastery have their origins in the anal stage.

Phallic Stage   The **phallic stage** of development occurs between the ages of three and six. The characteristics of this stage are pleasurable and conflicting feelings associated with the genital organs. The child's interest in the genitals is not with their reproductive function, but with their ability to give pleasure in autoerotic activity and their significance as a means of distinguishing between the sexes. At this time, children discover that not all individuals are similarly endowed. They expend considerable energy in examining their genitalia, masturbating, and expressing interest in sexual matters. They are extremely curious, even though their curiosity outstrips their ability to understand sexual matters intellectually. They spin fantasies about the sexual act itself and the birth process, which are frequently inaccurate and misleading. They may believe that a pregnant woman has eaten her baby and that a baby is expelled through the mouth or the anus. Sexual intercourse is frequently viewed as an aggressive act by the father against the mother.

Freud points out that for children a fantasy can be as powerful as a literal event in shaping personality, and so in that sense it does not matter whether or not an event really occurred. This is not to deny that some children do endure real situations of incest or sexual abuse, or that such situations can have a pervasive negative effect on a child's personality development. Recently Freud has been criticized for abandoning his early "seduction theory," which held that adult neurosis was caused by actual incidents of sexual abuse in childhood, in favor of the theory that saw childhood sexual fantasy as the primary cause of most cases of neurosis. Moreover, he has been criticized for suppressing the seduction theory for intellectually dishonest reasons (Masson, 1983). However, this criticism, as well as other recent allegations concerning Freud's personal life, seems more spurious than convincing.

The pleasures of masturbation and the fantasy life of children set the stage for the **Oedipus complex,** which Freud considered to be one of his greatest discoveries. Freud's concept of the Oedipus complex was suggested by the Greek tragedy of Sophocles in which King Oedipus unwittingly murders his father and marries his mother. The key point is that Oedipus was unaware, or unconscious, of what he was doing. He did not realize that the man whom he met on the road was his own father, nor did he know that the queen whom he married was his mother. At the same time, he played an active role in bringing about his fate. On discovering the truth, he punished himself by self-blinding. Within that Greek myth, Freud perceives a symbolic description of the unconscious psychological conflict that each one of us endures. In brief, the myth symbolizes each child's unconscious desire to possess the opposite-sexed parent and do away with the same-sexed parent.

If the Oedipus complex were to be taken literally, many people would have quickly dismissed Freud's concept as absurd and nonsensical. Incredible as it may seem, Freud suggests that children have incestuous wishes toward the opposite-sexed parent and murderous impulses toward the same-sexed parent. Do children actually desire to perform sexual intercourse and commit murder? Most preschool-age children have no clearly articulated concept of what sexual intercourse is all about. Furthermore, even if they had the will, they would lack the means to perform the act. Finally, for the preschool-age child, the permanence and reality of death are incomprehensible. As a literal depiction, Freud's concept of the Oedipus complex is clearly absurd.

Nevertheless, at this stage in development, the young boy (to tell his side of the story first) has become very fond of his mother, his primary caretaker. He loves her very much and he wants to love her as fully as possible. He senses that Mommy and Daddy have a special kind of relationship, which he wants to imitate. He becomes frustrated because he cannot imagine what the relationship is all about or perform it in a similar manner. At the same time, he wants his mother's love in return, but he views love quantitatively as a fixed amount. It is as if his mother's love constitutes an apple. Each kiss or sign of attention that his father receives indicates that a big, juicy chunk has been bitten out of that apple, so that less remains for him. He cannot conceive of love as qualitative or as able to increase to fill a void. Viewing love as a quantity, the child perceives his father as a rival who prevents him from obtaining the full love that he desires from his mother. This perception creates wishes and impulses about getting rid of the father, an activity the child is powerless to carry out.

The child's feelings are very intense, strong, and conflicting, besides being too difficult for the child to cope with directly on a conscious level. Furthermore, the feelings create guilt because the child's sentiments toward his father are not just hostile but affectionate as well. The child finds it difficult to cope with ambivalent feelings of love and hostility directed toward the same person. His rivalry culminates in **castration anxiety,** which means that he fears physical retaliation from his father, in particular that he will lose his penis.

The Oedipus complex is resolved by a twofold process. First, the son gives up his abortive attempts to possess his mother and begins to identify with his father in terms of sexual gender. In **identifying** with the same-sexed parent, he adopts the moral codes and injunctions of his father. This introjection of the parent's standards of good conduct leads to the development of a **superego** or social conscience, which assists him in dealing with his forbidden impulses. By identifying with his father, the boy can through his imagination vicariously retain his mother as his love object, because he has incorporated those characteristics of his father that his mother loves. Although he may not have his mother in fact, he can wait until he grows up and then look for "a girl, just like the girl that married dear old Dad."*

* I WANT A GIRL (JUST LIKE THE GIRL THAT MARRIED DEAR OLD DAD) written by William Dillon and Harry Von Tilzer. Copyright © 1911 Harry Von Tilzer Music Publishing Company. Copyright Renewed c/o The Welk Music Group, Santa Monica, CA 90401. International Copyright Secured. All Rights Reserved. Used By Permission.

The little girl undergoes a similar complex. Freud deliberately did not give it a separate name, because he wished to emphasize the universality of the Oedipal situation. Others have referred to the feminine version as the **Electra complex.** The primary love object for girls is also the mother. Yet girls, on discovering the genitals of the opposite sex, abandon the mother and turn to the father instead, making possible the Oedipal situation in reverse. The disappointment and shame that they feel upon viewing the "superior" penis leads to jealousy of the male, **penis envy,** a sense of inferiority, and a feeling of resentment and hatred toward the mother, who is held responsible for the effected castration. Reluctantly, the girl identifies with her mother, incorporates her values, and optimally makes the transition from her inadequate penis, the clitoris, as her chief erogenous zone, to the vagina. Because the female Oedipus complex is secondary, Freud suggests that it is resolved differently from that of the male; thus, the woman's ego-ideal (see page 60) is closer to its emotional origins and she appears to have less capacity for sublimation. Once again, to read Freud literally is to miss the point. Penis envy does not refer simply to the organ itself, but also to what it represents: the greater privileges, life choices, etc., that males have in society. The role that the girl adopts for herself is one which has been outlined for her by her society. As you might imagine, Freud's views on the development of women have been the subject of considerable criticism and debate.

Latency Period   After the phallic stage, Freud believed that there is a period of comparative sexual calm. Psychic forces develop that inhibit the sexual drive and narrow its direction. The libido is sublimated and channeled into nonsexual activities. Freud borrowed the term **sublimation** from the field of chemistry where the verb "to sublime" means to pass directly from a solid to a vapor state. Sublimation connotes passing from a lower state to a higher one. Thus, the sexual impulses, which are unacceptable in their direct expression, are channeled and elevated into more culturally accepted levels of activity, such as sports, intellectual interests, and peer relations. Freud was relatively silent about the latency period. He did not consider it a genuine psychosexual stage because nothing dramatically new emerges. Today, the latency period as such is questioned by most critics, who suggest it is more correct to observe that children learn to hide their sexuality from disapproving adults.

Genital Stage   With the onset of puberty, changes set in which transform the infantile sexual life into its adult form. Freud's final stage is termed **genital** and emerges at adolescence when the genital organs mature. There is a rebirth of sexual and aggressive desires, and the sexual drive, which was formerly **narcissistic** (aimed at obtaining gratification from one's own body), is redirected to seeking gratification from genuine interaction with others. Young adolescents prefer the company of same-sexed peers; however, in time the object of the sexual drive shifts to members of the opposite sex. The genital stage is the end point of a long journey from autoerotic sexual activity to heterosexual activity. Mature individuals seek to satisfy their sexual drives primarily through genital, reproductive activity with members of the opposite sex. The *normal* or *mature individual* is defined as one who has realized conventional genital sexuality and all its pertinent implications as defined by his or her culture. Mature people satisfy their needs in socially approved ways. They accommodate themselves to, function within, and seek to uphold the laws, taboos, and standards of their culture. These implications are clearly spelled out for both male and female. The hallmarks of maturity can be summed up in the German expression *Lieben und arbeiten,* "to love and to work." The mature person is able to love in a sexually approved way and also to work productively in his or her community and society.

Effects of the Psychosexual Stages

The lingering effects of the psychosexual stages are revealed in various adult character types or traits. Freud believed strongly that events in the past can influence the present. If the libido, the sexual drive, is prevented from obtaining optimal satisfaction during one or more of the stages, because it has been either unduly frustrated or overindulged, it may become fixated on a particular stage. **Fixation** is an arrestment of growth that creates excessive needs, characteristic of an earlier stage. Since all of us have fixated libido at some psychosexual stage or another, this dammed-up libido expresses itself in our adult life according to character types or traits that reflect the earlier level of development. Hence, an orally fixated person is likely to be dependent on and easily influenced by others. At the same time, oral personalities are optimistic and trusting to the point of being gullible. Anal personalities tend to be orderly, miserly, and obstinate. Most of us, of course, do not reflect a pure type, but these personality traits and their opposites have their origin in the various psychosexual stages.

If the development of personality is seriously inhibited or delayed, it can lead to problems later in life. We have seen how the libido, due to frustration or overindulgence, may become fixated at an earlier stage. A child who persists in thumb sucking well into the preschool years is showing evidence of an inability to satisfy oral needs in a manner suitable for his or her age. In other instances, under times of stress, the libido may regress to an earlier level of development. **Regression** refers to a temporary reverting to earlier forms of behavior. A child who was completely toilet trained may in a period of stress begin to wet the bed. Extreme instances of fixation and regression are seen in neurotic behavior and sexual perversions.

Identifying Psychosexual Character Traits

Salvadore Maddi (1972) has summarized the traits of the various character types described by Freud and his followers as bipolar dimensions. Consider each of the traits in Table 1.1; see if you recognize it as characteristic of yourself or someone you know. It would be nice if we could simply state that one polar trait indicates fixation due to frustration, and the other fixation due to overindulgence, but in reality such a view is too simple because many of us swing from one pole to its opposite. From a Freudian viewpoint, the existence of any of these traits to a marked degree presents an invitation to explore that psychosexual stage in our personal history. These basic attitudes emerge from our interactions with significant persons during these phases of development. It is important to point out that although I have described the psychosexual stages chronologically from infancy to adulthood, in psychoanalytic research the understanding of a person's history moves backwards from the present to the past. From a present attitude or trait, we can conjecture that an individual experienced certain difficulties at certain levels of his or her psychosexual development. On the other hand, we cannot suggest with any significant degree of reliability that certain present parental practices will lead to specific character traits in the future.

All of the sexual activities that we consider abnormal are at some time normal sexual activities for children. Prototypes of sadistic and masochistic forms of behavior, sexual disorders in which a person obtains pleasure by inflicting (sadism) or receiving (masochism) pain, are apparent during the toddler years. Voyeurism, obtaining pleasure from seeing sexual organs or sexual acts, is present in the curiosity of the preschool child. Homosexuality, primary attraction to the same sex, is apparent during the latency period and early adolescence when one's primary association is with same-sexed peers. Thus, sexual deviations may be accounted for in terms of arrested development.

Neurosis is also viewed as the outcome of an inadequate sexual development. In particular, it can be the result of an unsuccessfully resolved Oedipal conflict. In cases of neurosis, the individual continues to mature physically, passing from stage to subsequent stage, but with heavy residues of negative attitudes and emotions that prevent the person from functioning optimally and dealing adequately with stress and anxiety. Such people are bound to their unhappy

Table 1.1 *Psychosexual Traits*

Oral traits	
optimism	pessimism
gullibility	suspiciousness
manipulativeness	passivity
admiration	envy
cockiness	self-belittlement

Anal traits	
stinginess	overgenerosity
constrictedness	expansiveness
stubbornness	acquiescence
orderliness	messiness
rigid punctuality	tardiness
meticulousness	dirtiness
precision	vagueness

Phallic traits	
vanity	self-hatred
pride	humility
blind courage	timidity
brashness	bashfulness
gregariousness	isolation
stylishness	plainness
flirtatiousness	avoidance of heterosexuality
chastity	promiscuity
gaiety	sadness

SOURCE: Based on information in S. R. Maddi, *Personality Theories: A Comparative Analysis*, Homewood, Ill.: Dorsey Press, 1972, pp. 271–276.

past and respond in emotionally immature ways. Being unrealistic, these ways are not helpful to them in the everyday world.

Freud's presentation of the stages of human psychosexual development is clumsy, because the gradual change from one stage to another is not as distinct as the outline implies. The stages are not separate; they merge and meld into one another. Therefore, the age references should be seen not as beginning and end points, but rather as focal points, where the stage is at its height. A diagram would show each stage gradually beginning, swelling to a climax, and then waning as the following stage begins to emerge (Figure 1.1). The emergence of the genital stage does not signify the end of the earlier ones; instead it transforms them in the service of genital aims. Thus, adult behavior is shaped by a complex of earlier conflicts.

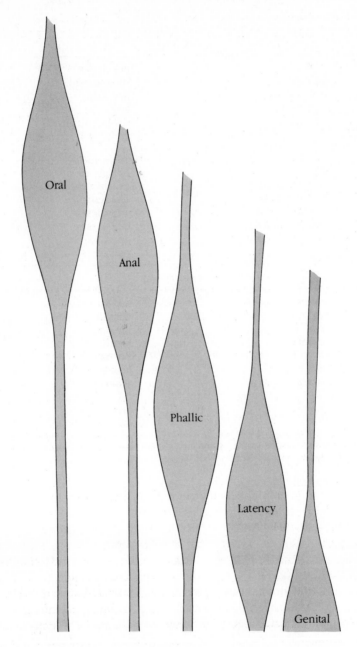

Figure 1.1 *Freud's Psychosexual Stages*
Each stage begins gradually, swells to a climax, and then wanes as the following stage begins to emerge.

Freud's discussion of the psychosexual stages of personality was set in the framework of nineteenth-century biological determinism and has been soundly criticized for its failure to appreciate deeply enough the influence of social and cultural factors. Moreover, the concept of energy that informs his theory is clearly outdated. Nevertheless, Freud's conclusion overturned almost the entire Western tradition of thought concerning humanity. In Freud's theory, human life is subsumed under a sexual model. The way in which people invest their libido determines their future. Freud used sexuality as a model for a person's style of life: character is built up by responding to one's sexuality; the way in which a person resolves the Oedipus complex is crucial to his or her adult personality; neurosis represents a fixation at an earlier stage of sexual development. The normal or mature individual is one who behaves conventionally, having attained the genital level of sexuality and all its implications. Furthermore, the development of culture and civilization is made possible by sublimated sexuality. Sexuality becomes the model for human understanding since the totality of all actual and possible human doings may be understood under its rubric.

Ever since the days of the Greek philosopher Aristotle (384–322 B.C.), people had been defined as rational animals because it was thought that reason separated the human being from other forms of life. Descartes had begun his philosophy with the assertion "I think, therefore I am." Freud did not belittle reason, which he sought to cultivate through analysis. However, he emphatically pointed out that we are essentially emotional beings, creatures of will and desire. In a sense, Freud begins his philosophy with "I love (or crave), therefore I am." In Freud's theory, our reason, which is sublimated sexuality, is no longer the master, it is a servant to the libido that brought it into being. By making sexuality, instead of reason, the prime mover or motivator of human beings, Freud radically transformed the self-consciousness of Western personality.

The Structure of Personality

Sigmund Freud did not present a completely finished model. His thought moves in phases, forever changing and synthesizing what has gone before. He did not hesitate to set forth tentative formulations. Many of his lectures and writings read as though he was thinking out loud. Ideas appear, disappear, and then reappear in a new context. Alasdair MacIntyre (1958) suggests that Freud's work is characterized by a "creative untidiness"; "he never presents us with a finished structure but with the far more exciting prospect of working through a number of possible ways of talking and thinking" (p. 79). As Freud's thought reached maturity, certain concepts about the structure of personality and the technique of psychoanalysis acquired a greater degree of sophistication and articulation. His thought moves from the physical, through the psychological, to the **metapsychological,** a term he used to refer to his effort to give the fullest possible description of psychic processes.

The familiar Freudian concept of the structure of personality as an id, ego, and superego was a rather late product of his thought. Not until 1923 with the publication of *The Ego and the Id* did Freud's final theory of a threefold structure of personality emerge. In discussing his mature understanding, we must keep in mind that the id, ego, and superego are not three separate entities with sharply defined boundaries, but rather that they represent a variety of different processes, functions, and dynamics within the person. Moreover, in his writings Freud used the German personal pronouns, *das Es, das Ich,* and *das uber-Ich.* It might have been better if they had been translated into English as "the it," "the I," and "the above-I." The usual translation into Latin pronouns has made them less personal. It is also unfortunate that the German words *Seele* (soul) and *Psyche* (psyche) are both rendered "mental apparatus" in the English versions as this further misleads us into thinking that Freud conceived of them as primarily mental (Bettelheim, 1982). Freud's description of the interactions of the id, ego, and superego tries to give us a comprehensive picture of the person as a whole.

The Id, Ego, and Superego

The **id** is the "core of our being." Freud borrowed the term *Es,* which means "it," from the title of a work, *The Book of the It,* by Georg Groddeck (1923), who suggested that we are "lived" by unknown and uncontrollable forces. Groddeck, in turn, attributed his use of the word to the German philosopher Friedrich Nietzsche (1844–1900). The id is the oldest and original function of the personality and the basis of the other two. We know little of the id, because it does not present itself to our consciousness in naked form. Therefore, we can only describe it by analogies and by comparing it with the ego. Freud referred to it as a "chaos, a cauldron full of seething excitations." The id includes all of our genetic inheritance, our reflexes and capacities to respond, and, above all, the instincts and drives that motivate us. It represents our basic drives, needs, and wishes. Further, it is the reservoir of psychic energy that provides the power for all psychological functioning.

The impersonal and uncontrollable character of the id is more readily expressed in the German language than in English. For example, the German idiom for "I am hungry" ("*Es hungert mich*") translates literally as "It hungers me," implying that I am a recipient of actions initiated *in* me, not *by* me.

The id operates according to the pleasure principle and employs primary processes. The **pleasure principle** refers to seeking immediate tension reduction. When libido (psychic energy) builds up, it reaches an uncomfortable level of tension. The id seeks to discharge the tension and return to a more comfortable level of energy. In seeking to avoid painful tension and obtain pleasure, the id takes no precautions but acts immediately in an impulsive, nonrational way. It pays no heed to the consequences of its actions and therefore frequently behaves in a manner that may be harmful to the self or others.

The id seeks to satisfy its needs through reflex action and the primary process. **Reflexes** are inborn automatic responses, like sneezing, yawning, and blinking. Such responses are spontaneous, unlearned, and operate without any conscious thought or effort. Many of our reflexes are protective in that they help us to ward off dangers in our environment. Others are adaptive and enable us to adjust to the conditions of our environment. Newborn infants have several reflexes that help to ensure their survival. They turn their heads toward the source of tactile stimulation. This "rooting reflex" assists them in locating the nipple. Sucking is also an automatic reflex enabling infants to take in nourishment.

The **primary process** is a psychological activity in which the id seeks to reduce tension by hallucinating or forming an image of the object that would satisfy its needs. Visualizing a forthcoming hamburger or sirloin steak momentarily relieves our hunger pangs; such activity is also called **wish fulfillment.** It is present in newborns, in our dreams, and in the hallucinations of psychotics. Visualizing a bottle or the breast partly pacifies the infant, but it does not satisfy his or her need. Since the primary process does not distinguish between its wish-fulfilling images and real objects in the external world that would satisfy needs, it is not very effective in reducing tension. A second structure must develop if the organism is to survive.

The **ego** ("I") emerges in order to realistically meet the wishes and demands of the id in accordance with the outside world. People who are hungry have to be effective in securing food for themselves from the environment in order to meet their needs and survive. The ego evolves out of the id and acts as an intermediary between the id and the external world. It draws on the id's energy, acquires its structures and functions from the id, and endeavors to serve the id by realistically meeting its demands. Thus, the ego is the executor of the personality, curbing the id and maintaining transactions with the external world in the interests of the fuller personality.

Whereas the id obeys the pleasure principle, the ego follows the reality principle and operates according to the secondary process and reality testing. The **reality principle** refers to satisfying the id's impulses in an appropriate manner in the external world. The ego postpones the discharge of tension until the appropriate object that will satisfy the need has been found. Although the ego does not prevent the satisfaction of the id, it may suspend or redirect the id's wishes in accordance with the demands of reality. Its task is to satisfy optimally the demands of the organism for pleasure. The id employs the fantasies and wishes of the primary process; the ego uses realistic thinking characteristic of secondary processes. **Secondary processes** are the cognitive and perceptual skills that help an individual distinguish between fact and fantasy. They include the higher intellectual functions of problem solving, which let the ego establish suitable courses of action and test them for their effectiveness. Actually, there is no natural enmity between the ego and the id. The ego is a "faithful servant" of the id and tries to fulfill its needs realistically.

Harbored within the ego as "its innermost core" is the **superego** ("above-I"). Heir to the Oedipus complex, it represents internalized values, ideals, and moral standards. The superego is the last function of the personality to develop and may be seen as an outcome of the interactions with one's parents during the long period of childhood dependency. Rewards and punishments originally placed on us from without become self-administered as we internalize the teachings of our parents and society. As a result of the activity of the superego we experience guilt when we disobey acceptable moral standards.

The superego consists of two subsystems: the conscience and the ego-ideal. The **conscience** refers to the capacity for self-evaluation, criticism, and reproach. It scolds the ego when moral codes are violated and creates feelings of guilt. The **ego-ideal** is an ideal self-image consisting of approved and rewarded behaviors. It is the source of pride and a concept of who we think we should be.

The superego strives for perfection. It seeks moralistic rather than realistic solutions. Practically speaking, the development of the superego is a necessity. The id's demands are too strong, and young children's egos are too weak to prevent them from acting on their impulses. For a period of time, strong introjected moral injunctions — "Thou shalt nots" — are required to curb behavior. But the superego may also be relentless and cruel in its insistence on perfection. Its moralistic demands may resemble those of the id in their intensity, blindness, and irrationality. In its uncompromising manner, the superego may inhibit the needs of the id, rather than permit their ultimate necessary and appropriate satisfaction.

In the mature and well-adjusted personality, the ego is the primary executor. It controls and governs both id and superego, mediating between their demands and the external world. In ideal functioning, the ego maintains a balanced, harmonious relationship among the various elements with which it has to deal. Development, though, does not always proceed optimally. If the id or superego gains control and predominates, imbalance and maladjustment follow. The ego frequently ends up harassed by two harsh masters. One demands instant satisfaction and release. The other places rigid prescriptions on that release. Drawing on an analogy of Plato's, Freud described the ego as a charioteer trying to control two strong horses, each of which is trying to run in the opposite direction from the other.

Freud's final picture of personality is that of a self divided against itself. The specific roles played by the id, ego, and superego are not always clear; they mingle at too many levels. The self is seen to consist of many diverse forces in inevitable conflict. Freud's picture of the person is not optimistic, but it is an attempt to account for the fact that as human beings we are not always able to cope with our situation. The heart of the problem is to be found in the complex inner dialogue of the self, for "the ego is not master in its own house."

Although the trifold division of personality appears to be a finished structure, essentially the person is understood as a product of development. The ego and superego have evolved historically in response to specific personal situations. In the case of the superego, that situation is also interpersonal since it involves other people. It would be wrong to freeze the id, ego, and superego into systems; instead, the personality is created by a dynamic of forces that can be divided against themselves at many levels. Thus, in his mature formulation, Freud holds in tension the biological ground of the self and its development.

Exploration /////

Recognizing the Id, Ego, and Superego

The reader can gain a more concrete picture of the various functions of the id, ego, and superego by imagining a variety of problematic situations and considering the role of the id, ego, and superego in each conflict. The id asserts our raw untempered desires and wishes; the superego places authoritarian and moralistic strictures on our behavior; and the ego seeks a realistic compromise. Thus, in the case of a young man or woman out on a date with an attractive member of the opposite sex with whom he or she might wish to engage in a sexual relationship, the id would unreservedly exclaim, "I want, I want!" while the superego might legalistically proclaim, "Thou shalt not!" Meanwhile, the ego seeks a realistic solution that fulfills the id's demands within the limitations and customs of society. In the above instance, such a solution might require waiting until one is more familiar with one's date or until certain social prerequisites have been met. Can you consider what the roles of the id, ego, and superego might be in other situations, such as that of a young child in a department store desiring a piece of sports equipment for which he or she does not have sufficient funds in his or her piggybank?

The Relationship of the Id, Ego, and Superego to Consciousness

There is no easy correlation between the words "id," "ego," and "superego" and the qualities of "conscious," "preconscious," and "unconscious." We have seen that **conscious** refers to processes of which we are aware; **preconscious** refers to psychological material that can easily become conscious when the need for it arises; and **unconscious** refers to material that has been repressed or never permitted to become conscious. At times, Freud tended to make the easy equation of ego with consciousness and id with unconsciousness; he also referred to the unconscious and conscious as systems or topographical locations. His discoveries, reflected in *The Ego and the Id,* that aspects of the ego and the superego are unconscious, as is the id, forced him to revise his theory. He could no longer use "conscious" and "unconscious" in the sense of mental provinces or systems, but simply as adjectives describing qualities that psychological processes may or may not have. Thus, in the end, "unconscious," "preconscious," and "conscious" do not imply systems. The attributes of awareness and its opposite may potentially apply to any and all of the psychic structures: id, ego, and superego. The characteristic of being conscious or unconscious is not the vital factor in their conflicts.

If one were to diagram Freud's picture of the psyche, perhaps the best image would be Freud's own: an iceberg, nine-tenths of which is submerged under water (Figure 1.2). The surface of the water represents the boundary between conscious and unconscious. Its line intersects, or potentially intersects, all three functions of id, ego, and superego. But any spatial metaphor is ultimately misleading. A topographical image does not reflect Freud's mature understanding of the person as historical. "Id," "ego," and "superego" are best understood as dynamic functions of personality, while "conscious" and "unconscious" are adjectives that describe qualities that these functions may have.

Simple correlations are inappropriate, for the dynamic forces within the self are many. The self is not simply divided against itself by id, ego, and superego but divided against itself and the world at many levels. Conflict is the keynote of Freud's final understanding of the self. The self is essentially in conflict, which is inevitable because of the very nature of things. The world, Freud once wrote, is *anake* (the Greek word for "a lack"), too poor to meet all of our needs. As the id's demands increase, tension mounts, and the ego becomes overwhelmed with excessive stimulation that it cannot control. Thus, the ego becomes flooded with anxiety.

Anxiety and the Ego

Anxiety is an inevitable aspect of the human condition, and a situation into which we all are thrust by virtue of being born. Birth represents a situation of want in which there is a realistic danger that the needs of the infant will not be met. The "birth trauma" may be seen as the model of all later anxiety,

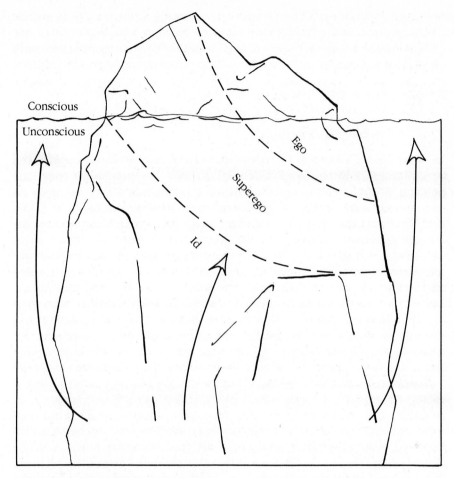

Figure 1.2 *The Psyche as an Iceberg*
Freud described the psyche as an iceberg, nine-tenths of which is submerged under water.

insofar as the infant is bombarded by unpleasurable stimuli and is unable to cope with them adequately. This means that anxiety is the key problem with which the developmental and adjustment process has to deal. An inability to cope with anxiety underlies most forms of neurosis.

Freud made a distinction among reality anxiety, neurotic anxiety, and moral anxiety. **Reality anxiety** refers to the fear of a real danger in the external world. **Neurotic anxiety** refers to the fear that one's inner impulses cannot be controlled. **Moral anxiety** is a fear of the retributions of one's own conscience. All have their basis in reality anxiety. A child who is frightened because he was almost hit by a truck is experiencing reality anxiety. However, a subsequent fear of crossing wide streets in an adult who doubts his or her own ability to cross safely is neurotic. A child who refrains from snitching cookies for fear that he or she might be beaten is experiencing reality anxiety, but most adults refrain from stealing out of moral anxiety or the fear of retribution from their own conscience.

The Defense Mechanisms

In order for an individual to cope with anxiety, the ego develops **defense mechanisms,** procedures that ward off anxiety and prevent our conscious perception of it. Defense mechanisms share two features: they occur on an unconscious level so that we are not aware of what we are doing, and they deny or distort reality so as to make it less threatening. Defense mechanisms are not necessarily maladaptive; indeed, we cannot survive without them. The stimuli that confront us as children from our outer and inner worlds are too intense to be borne in their naked reality. Without some means of warding off the intensity of our feelings, anxiety would overwhelm and paralyze us. Defense mechanisms must be created to assist the developing ego in carrying out its functions. However, should their distortion of reality become too extreme or should they be used to the exclusion of other, more effective means of dealing with reality, defense mechanisms may become maladaptive and destructive. Some of the more common defense mechanisms are as follows:

Repression involves blocking a wish or desire from expression so that it cannot be experienced consciously or expressed directly in behavior. It is an involuntary act, which prevents us from being aware of many of our own anxiety-producing conflicts or remembering certain traumatic emotional events from our past. As we have seen, the relief that repression provides is not without cost. Freud's theory emphasizes that emotions demand expression. The repressed emotion continually seeks an alternative outlet, and a continuous drain of psychic energy in the form of resistance is required to prevent its emergence into consciousness. Nevertheless, once formed, repressions are difficult to eliminate.

Projection refers to the unconscious attribution of an impulse, attitude, or behavior onto someone else or some element in the environment. An individual who is unconsciously hostile to someone may project the hostility onto the other person. Such a defense reduces anxiety by placing its source in the external world, which makes it seem easier to handle. Further, it permits us to defend ourselves aggressively against our opponent and thereby indirectly express our impulses. Freud would suggest that those who vigorously wage campaigns against pornography or other sexual practices may be projecting their own sexual impulses onto other people.

Reaction formation expresses an impulse by its opposite. Hostility, for example, may be replaced by friendship. Frequently, however, the substitution is exaggerated, thereby calling into question the genuineness of the feeling. The well-known quotation from *Hamlet,* "The lady doth protest too much, methinks," refers to a possible case of reaction formation.

Fixation refers to the settling of psychic energy at an early stage of psychosexual development, preventing the individual from moving on to the next stage. The overly dependent school-age child may be fixated, thereby prevented from becoming independent.

In **regression** the person moves backward in time to a stage that was less anxious and had fewer responsibilities. Regression frequently occurs following a traumatic experience. The child who begins bedwetting again because he is frightened by the prospect of going to school may be showing signs of regression.

Rationalization involves dealing with an emotion or impulse analytically and intellectually in order to avoid feeling it. As the term implies, it involves faulty reasoning, since the problem remains unresolved on the emotional level. Aesop's fable about the fox who could not reach the grapes and concluded that they were probably sour is a classic example of rationalization.

In **identification** we reduce anxiety by modeling our behavior on that of someone else. By assuming the characteristics of a model who appears more successful in gratifying needs, we can believe that we also possess those attributes. We may also identify with an authority figure who is resented and feared. Such identification may assist us in avoiding punishment. As we have already seen, identification with the same-sexed parent plays an important role in development of the superego and subsequent personality.

If an object that would satisfy an impulse of the id is unavailable, we may shift our impulse onto another object. Such substitution is called **displacement.** A child who has been scolded may hit a younger sibling or kick the dog. The substitute object, however, is rarely as satisfying as the original object. Thus, displacement does not bring complete satisfaction but leads to a build-up of undischarged tension.

Sublimation rechannels an unacceptable impulse into a more socially desirable outlet. It is a particular form of displacement that displaces the impulse itself rather than the object. Freud suggested that Leonardo da Vinci's interest in painting madonnas may have been a sublimation of his desire for intimacy with his own mother, from whom he had been separated at an early age. Freud also suggested that sublimation was crucial to the development of culture and civilization. However, as sublimation, like displacement, does not result in complete satisfaction, our civilization and culture are purchased at a very high price.

Defense mechanisms, in and of themselves, are not harmful. No one is free of defenses; we need them in order to survive. Defenses protect us from excessive anxiety and frequently represent creative solutions to our problems.

Different cultures and social conditions foster different patterns of defense. In Freud's day, people needed to defend themselves against their sexual and aggressive impulses. In our day, such feelings are more readily expressed, but other feelings are repressed and inhibited. Graphic portrayals of murder and violence in the media have desensitized many contemporary young people to the tragedies of social life. They react with laughter (rather than fear or empathy) at bizarre forms of horror depicted on the screen and are less able to respond to other people in a genuine emergency. The laughter may protect us from the feelings of anxiety and depersonalization generated by a high-technology society. However, if our defenses become predominant and self-perpetuating, they may block further personal and social growth. At such times, it is helpful to try to identify the defense mechanism so that we may work on it.

Exploration /////

Identifying Defense Mechanisms

Defense mechanisms are most easily recognized in preschool-age children who, to borrow Stone and Church's apt description (1984), wear their personalities on their sleeves. Because they have not yet learned to deceive other people, young children's instant translations of their impulses into actions often clearly and colorfully illustrate some of the defenses that we have described. Who has not been present when a young child who has spilled milk or broken an object immediately exclaims, "I didn't do it"? The child is trying to deny or undo the act through denial and repression. At this age, projection frequently takes the form of blaming a "crime" on a younger sibling or even the family pet.

You can familiarize yourself with the various defenses by trying to identify each of the mechanisms in Table 1.2 as you have seen them occur in someone else, and then trying to recognize instances in which you may have used them yourself. It is much easier, of course, to observe defense processes at work in someone else than to recognize them within ourselves; however, some of the following hints may help you to spot them. Have you ever "forgotten" an important event, such as an assigned test or a dentist appointment? You may also recall momentarily forgetting the name of someone you know quite well. Such activities indicate the tendency we all have to repress. Memory gaps on childhood events, in which you can recall only part of an event but not what preceded or followed, may indicate that the event involved certain traumatic elements that make it hard for you to remember it completely. Have your parents ever told you about an experience that you had as a child but cannot remember? Do you have any phobias that you know are unrealistic, such as a fear of dogs or of flying? In such instances, you may really be afraid of some of your own inner impulses and may have projected your fear onto an external object that makes it easier to handle. Have you ever found yourself laughing at an inappropriate moment? You may have compensated for an impulse you are ashamed of by reaction formation. Do you have any persistent immature habits, such as pouting and sulking when things do not go your way? Such behaviors may be signs of fixation. Have you ever provided an alibi for something you did or did not do? Could it have been an attempt to rationalize your behavior? Can you recall ever taking out your anger on someone who was helpless, such as a child or pet? Use of scapegoats is a common form of displacement. What kinds of leisure activities, sports, or creative and artistic activities do you enjoy? Through sublimation you may have been able to redirect certain antisocial impulses into socially approved and constructive behaviors. Sublimation is one of the more productive defense mechanisms available to us. In short, we all have and need defenses. Recognizing the use of a defense mechanism is not an occasion for finding fault with ourselves; rather, it is an opportunity for further exploration of our use of defense mechanisms so that they can be employed to foster instead of hinder growth.

The Synthesizing Functions of the Ego

Freud (1933) wrote, "Where id is, there shall ego be." He might also have written, "Where superego is, there shall ego be." The ego, we recall, seeks to meet realistically the needs and wishes of the organism, in contrast with the id's impulsive efforts to reduce tension and the superego's moralistic and perfectionist solutions. By strengthening the ego, an individual reduces the power of the id and superego and makes them more easily manageable. Freud believed that becoming aware of our impulses and our reasons for behaving as we do is our greatest tool for strengthening the ego and assisting its synthesizing functions. Becoming aware of one's impulses does not eliminate them or reduce their strength. However, knowledge of one's wishes and desires gives one greater opportunity for satisfying them realistically through the acceptable outlets of one's culture. All societies provide some means of expressing our sexual and aggressive impulses. Some, to be sure, are more restrictive than others and not all of the measures lead to health. However, without recognizing and understanding our impulses we cannot explore the available options. Further, an understanding of the reasons for our behavior permits us to act out of a conscience that is informed by our ego, rather than blindly obey the precepts of a moralistic and irrational superego.

Table 1.2 *Defense Mechanisms*

Repression

---

characteristics: blocking a wish or desire from conscious expression

example: being unaware of deep-seated hostilities toward one's parents

---

Projection

---

characteristics: attributing an unconscious impulse, attitude, or behavior to someone else

example: blaming somebody else for what you did or thinking that another person is out to get you

---

Reaction formation

---

characteristics: expressing an impulse by its opposite

example: treating someone whom you intensely dislike in an overly friendly manner

---

Fixation

---

characteristics: satisfying an impulse in an immature manner for one's age

example: protracted thumb sucking

Regression

---

characteristics: returning to an earlier form of expressing an impulse

example: resuming bedwetting after one has long since stopped

---

Rationalization

---

characteristics: dealing with an emotion intellectually to avoid emotional involvement

example: arguing that "Everybody else does it, so I don't have to feel guilty."

Identification

---

characteristics: modeling behavior after someone else

example: imitating one's mother or father

Displacement

---

characteristics: satisfying an impulse with a substitute object

example: scapegoating

Sublimation

---

characteristics: rechanneling an impulse into a more socially desirable outlet

example: satisfying sexual curiosity by conducting sophisticated research into sexual behaviors

---

Psychoanalysis

We have seen that for Freud neurosis basically emerges from an unsatisfactory or arrested libidinal development. An individual falls ill when the realistic satisfaction of his or her erotic needs is denied. The person turns to an illness as a surrogate satisfaction and creates a partially satisfying world of fantasy. Neurotics have no peculiar psychic content or functioning of their own that is not also found in healthy people. The conflicts of id, ego, and superego describe normal and neurotic alike. Each one of us must travel the psychosexual stages. The neurotic is simply one who falls ill from the same conflicts and complexes with which normal people struggle. There are no clearly defined boundaries between illness and health. The primary question is not "Am I normal or neurotic?" but rather "To what degree is my neurosis debilitating?" The concept of neuroses is placed under a general image of humanity.

We have briefly traced the story of the development of Freud's therapeutic method and the discovery of those techniques — free association and dream interpretation — that were to prove so fruitful to psychoanalysis. But the story of psychoanalysis was incomplete until Freud began to come to terms with the phenomenon of the transference.

Early in his work, Freud realized that the relationship between patient and physician was important in determining the outcome of the therapy. Nevertheless, it was with considerable embarrassment that he discovered one of his patients had fallen in love with him. We recall that a similar episode with his patient Anna O. had led Dr. Breuer to abandon the cathartic technique. For a man of such upright moral Victorian character as Freud, such a happening also appeared to pose a threat to his work. Only after considerable reservations and initial attempts to discourage similar occurrences did Freud begin to appreciate the dynamics of what was happening. He discovered that the feelings that were expressed toward him as a doctor were not directed at him as a person but rather were repetitions of earlier feelings of love and affection that the patient had for significant persons in his or her life. Thus, Freud was forced to recognize the value of the **transference,** a process whereby the patient transfers to the analyst emotional attitudes felt as a child toward important persons. By deliberately cultivating and analyzing the transference, Freud and his patients were able to learn a great deal.

Freud distinguished between *positive transference,* friendly, affectionate feelings toward the physician, and *negative transference,* characterized by the expression of hostile, angry feelings. By studying the transference, Freud learned that his patients were relating to him in the same unsatisfactory and inefficient ways in which they had related to other important people in their lives. The transference was simply a new segment of an old affair, repeating infantile and ineffective interpersonal relationships. However, in the security of the analytic experience, the patient could rework these earlier unsatisfactory relationships through the current relationship to a satisfactory resolution.

It is difficult to know if Freud himself ever fully recognized the implications of the transference, but its cultivation and interpretation have become crucial to the psychoanalytic technique he fathered. Transference offers the patient an opportunity to relive the emotional conflicts that led to repressions and provides the analyst with a deep understanding of the patient's characteristic ways of perceiving and reacting. The major point here is that in analysis the patient experiences his or her conflicts under a different set of circumstances. The analyst does not respond to the patient with disapproval or rejection as earlier individuals did. Rather, the analyst reacts with insight and understanding, which permits the patient to gain insight into his or her experiences and feelings and allows for change.

Freud's solution is one of insight, but the insight that psychoanalysis provides is a special kind of knowing that is not intellectual but existential. It touches the heart as well as the head. The solution does not lie in the realm of knowing but in the realm of doing: working through earlier conflicts. Discovering one's self is not only an intellectual act, but also an emotional experience. To use the Socratic expression: "To know is to do." Thus, therapy provides a more effective working through of the situation that provoked the neurosis. As the problem inevitably involves an ineffectiveness in one's psychosexual interpersonal relations, the solution must take place within the happening of a psychosexual interpersonal relationship — the transference. Freud's answer is **insight:** a deeply erotic insightful experience.

In analysis, the patient lies on a couch and the analyst sits behind, out of view. The patient is instructed to verbalize whatever comes to mind regardless of how irrelevant, absurd, or unpleasant it may seem. According to the deterministic stance, the patient's free associations are not really free at all, rather, they are determined by unconscious forces and gradually will permit these processes to be more clearly understood. During free association the patient may make a slip of the tongue or refer to a dream, both of which may be interpreted and utilized to assist the patient to acquire a deeper understanding of the problem.

In the initial phase of analysis, the patient obtains considerable relief just by being able to unburden him- or herself to a sympathetic listener. A positive transference is developed, and the patient frequently believes that the analysis has reached a successful conclusion, even though the work of analysis has barely begun. There are as yet undisclosed and conflicting feelings that the patient has not yet explored. During the next phase, the analyst gently assists the patient in exploring these emotion-laden areas by pointing out and interpreting the resistance in an effort to weaken the patient's defenses and bring his or her repressed conflicts into the open. The analyst's efforts leave the patient angry, anxious, and depressed; the analyst is now perceived as rejecting and unhelpful. Thoughts of prematurely concluding the analysis may again arise. Eventually the negative transference begins to cohere around specific areas. The patient reconstructs and re-experiences crucial episodes from childhood. The unremediated situation of the past includes not simply insufficiently resolved traumatic events but, more important, inadequately resolved interpersonal relationships and fantasies. The analyst maintains a neutral stance, interpreting the transference and encouraging the patient to re-examine those circumstances in the light of increased maturity. The analyst's stance enables the patient to work through these situations to a more satisfactory conclusion. Lastly, the analyst assists the patient in converting newly won insights into everyday existence and behavior. This emotional re-education enables the new insights to become a permanent part of the patient's personality.

In its traditional form, analysis is a protracted and expensive procedure. The patient meets with the analyst for fifty-minute sessions an average of five times a week over a period of several years. This requires a considerable commitment in terms of time, effort, and money. Contemporary analysts have refined the process further, realizing the importance of such issues as overcoming resistance, countertransference (which proceeds from the analyst to the patient), and working through issues on an emotional level. The goal of psychoanalysis is an ambitious one — a full understanding, reorganization, and basic change of the personality structure. Such goals cannot be accomplished quickly or easily. And, as Freud (1917) once wrote, "A neurotic who has been cured has really become a different person . . . he has become his best self, what he would have been under the most favorable conditions."

Therapy Excerpts /////

Psychoanalytic Therapy

In the excerpt below, Lewis Wolberg, a psychoanalytically oriented therapist, helps a relatively new patient to understand the kind of communication that occurs in psychoanalytic therapy.

PT (Patient): I just don't know what's causing these feelings. I get so frightened and upset, and I don't know why.
TH (Therapist): That's why you are coming here, to find out the reasons, so you can do something about your trouble.
PT: But why is it that I can't sleep and concentrate?
TH: That's what we'll begin to explore.
PT: But why?
TH: What comes to your mind? What do you think?
PT: I don't know.

(continued)

TH: You know, there are reasons for troubles lik yours, and one must patiently explore them. It may take a little tin   I know you'd like to get rid of this trouble right away, but the onl vay we can do this is by careful exploring.

PT: Yes.

TH: And to take your anxiety feelings, for example, you may not be aware of the reasons for them now, but as we talk about you, your ideas, your troubles, and your feelings, you should be able to find out what they are.

PT: How do I do this?

TH: When I ask you to talk about your feelings and thrash things around in your mind, you won't be able to put your finger on what bothers you immediately, but at least you will have started thinking about the sources of the problem. Right now, the only thing you're concerned with is escaping from the emotion. That's why you're just going around in a circle. While you're operating to seal off anxiety, you're doing nothing about finding out what's producing this anxiety.

PT: It sounds sort of clear when you say it. (laughs)

TH: Well, do you think you understand what I mean?

PT: What you're explaining now?

TH: Yes.

PT: Yes. (pause) The point is that I keep thinking about myself too much. It's that I feel inferior to everyone. I must win at rummy. When I play golf, I practically beat myself red if I don't get the low score. And this is silly.

TH: What happens when someone beats you at golf?

PT: I get upset and these feelings come.

TH: Now there seems to be some connection here; let's talk some more about that.*

As psychoanalytic therapy continues there are frequent long periods of silence on the analyst's part as the patient verbalizes what comes to mind. The patient is encouraged to fantasize about the analyst and these fantasies facilitate the transference. The imagined excerpt below is extremely condensed, but illustrative of what happens.

PT: You don't have anything to say about that? You should say something. (silence) You know it's very frustrating for me to come in here hour after hour and not hear you say anything. I feel as if you can't be bothered, that you don't really care.

TH: That must be very frustrating.

*L. R. Wolberg, *The Technique of Psychotherapy,* Vol. 1, New York: Grune & Stratton, 1977, p. 507. Used by permission of publisher and author.

PT: Damn right it's frustrating. There you sit with the answer to my problem, and you don't even care. You won't help me.

TH: My silence bothers you a great deal. What do you imagine that I am thinking when I'm silent?

PT: I told you — that you don't care. Either that or that you're judging me. You've decided I'm not worth it.

TH: You used the word "judge." It seems as if you feel like you're in a court room.

PT: That's right, I'm on trial and you're the judge.

TH: And the verdict is guilty.

PT: Yes, no wonder, I can't talk to you.

TH: Do your feelings seem familiar? Do I remind you of anyone?

PT: Well, hell, yes. Sure. You remind me of my father. Whenever I wanted to do anything, he'd be all over my back.

Freud's Theory: Philosophy, Science, and Art

Educated in the precise methods of nineteenth-century science, Freud established a reputation as a medical researcher before he developed the theory of psychoanalysis. In his writings he clearly defined and described the scientific enterprise. He asserted that knowledge is based on empirical observation and dogmatically maintained that his own theories were so based. His concepts, he claimed, were merely tentative constructs to be discarded if later observation failed to confirm them. He frequently revised his theories because new data had emerged that could not be accounted for by those theories.

Although Freud's research was not based on controlled laboratory experimentation, much of it was concerned with empirical data. The basic setting for his inquiry was clinical. He made careful observations of his patients in the therapeutic setting and garnered considerable information from the techniques of free association and dream analysis. He made interpretations and viewed the subsequent behavior of his patients as confirmation or disproof of his hypotheses. And he also conducted his own self-analysis, beginning in 1897 and continuing throughout his life. Data collected through self-analysis may properly be called empirical as it is based on observation. The fact that the observer is looking in ("introspection") rather than out ("extrospection") does not make the data any less empirical, although information gathered through introspection may be more difficult to test.

Nevertheless, in determining how Freud's theory functions, we have to look not only at the data on which it was initially based, but also at the method he used to test the data. Although he claimed that he was merely extending scientific knowledge by placing the psychic life of human beings under scientific observation, Freud permitted many of his concepts to function philosophically. For instance, he did not permit them to have any exceptions. We have seen that an important criterion of scientific constructs is the requirement that they be open to falsification; the desire to be scientific reflects itself in an effort to test constructs by validating evidence rather than by simply relying on the compelling character of a philosophical assumption. Freud, however, defined many of his concepts as all-controlling factors in everything we do, think, and are. For example, Freud suggested that it is impossible to conceive of any activity that does not reflect unconscious motives as well as conscious ones. The doctrine of unconscious processes is thus lifted out of an immediate empirical construct and made applicable to all possible human behavior. Even objections to the concept can be explained in terms of resistance or other unconscious processes. No one can dream a dream or make a slip that would contradict Freud's understanding of the unconscious. Anxiety dreams, seeming exceptions to the statement that all dreams fulfill wishes, can be reconciled to the theory by distinguishing between the manifest dream and the latent one; this distinction makes it clear that things are not necessarily what they appear to be. The theory of the life and death instinctual drives, which Freud lightly called "our mythology" (1933), actually does function as a mythology. Sexuality is a philosophical concept insofar as Freud asserted that all human behavior can be considered in its light.

And so we see that Freud drew conclusions from careful self-observation and the observation of his patients in a clinical setting and projected those conclusions into philosophical assumptions. Although Freud invested his theories with an aura of science, in evaluating them he made primary use of philosophical criteria, relying on their compelling power rather than validating evidence. The kind of knowing on which psychoanalysis is ultimately based is epiphanic, a form of knowing that does not rely on everyday experiences but transcends them.

Freud acknowledged that philosophy was a goal that had beckoned him all along. In later years he suggested that his dalliance with science was a detour on the road to a more ultimate quest: a comprehensive philosophy of humanity (1933). It is inaccurate to portray Freud as a scientific medical doctor. To do so distorts much of the humanism present in his writings and blunts the challenge of psychoanalysis, which is to know oneself with the constant obligation to change oneself (Bettelheim, 1982).

In evaluating Freud's work, therefore, it is most appropriate to use the criteria that apply to philosophical positions and ask if it is coherent, relevant, comprehensive, and compelling.

Although Freud changed and revised his theory, in the end it presented a clear, logical, and coherent pattern. To be sure, his theory is not a finished whole. Not only did he continually modify it, but it has been revised, modified, and updated by others working within the Freudian tradition. Freud was frequently unsympathetic to efforts to modify his theory and claimed the ultimate right to declare what should and should not be called psychoanalysis, but he was not unreceptive to changes that reflected the spirit of psychoanalysis as an evolving movement of a particular form of thought and investigation. However, he did believe that certain pillars were unassailable and must not be weakened lest the entire structure of psychoanalysis tumble. One such pillar is the concept of repression and the recognition that in large measure we are governed by forces of which we are unaware. Interpretation of transference and resistance also were seen as mainstays of psychoanalytic technique. Nevertheless, within this framework Freud often presented new points of reference for understanding personality and juxtaposed them against his earlier ones. It is only fitting that his followers do likewise. Many of Freud's arguments, informed by nineteenth-century interests, science, and philosophy, are clearly dated. For Freud's ideas to be relevant in the twentieth and twenty-first centuries, they must be reworked and reformulated in contemporary terms. Thus, Freud's theory does not constitute a finished structure; it is an open one capable of continued growth. Psychoanalytic theory not only fulfills the criterion of coherency, it also provides a consistent pattern on which one can build.

The relevance of Freud's theory is evidenced by its remarkable impact on the Western world. Freud changed, perhaps irrevocably, humanity's image of itself. Since Aristotle, the essence of humanity had been located in our ability to think. This image found ultimate expression in Descartes's phrase "I think, therefore I am." In this post-Freudian world, our self-image has changed. We no longer conceive of ourselves as primarily rational animals; rather, we are pleasure-seeking, sexual creatures driven by our emotions. Freud rephrased Descartes's statement to render it "I love, therefore I am." For many, the gospel of psychoanalysis is not "good news" because it forces us to consider aspects of ourselves that we would prefer to ignore. Still, it is virtually impossible to deny Freud his influence. The impact of Freud's accomplishments has been favorably compared with the impact of Copernicus, Darwin, and Einstein. Not only did he revolutionize psychology, but his influence has been felt in the social sciences, literature, art, philosophy, and religion. Freud's name is a household word. Errors of the pen or tongue are commonly known as "Freudian slips," and many people cannot make one without wondering what the unconscious reason is. Freud's theory, then, has relevance for our time. He grappled with ideas that were, are, and will continue to be of primary concern to us. Because of that his theories interest, allure, and excite people everywhere.

Freud's aim was to develop a comprehensive theory of humanity. He consistently maintained that his study of neurosis would eventually provide a key to the study of psychological processes in general. Freud's quest for the truth was unrelenting; no question was too small for his consideration; no probe was too trivial; no psychological process was too insignificant for his attention. To look for meaning on the surface was, for him, to settle for appearances and superficiality. Only by risking a plunge into the depths of the unconscious could one discover the truth about oneself and others. Any contradiction or opposition to his theory was to be met by analysis of the resistance, for only through such thorough analysis could true insight emerge. Freud's theory of personality, we see, is comprehensive, challenging, and profound.

Finally, Freud's theory has compelled many individuals. Some critics (see, for example, Ellenberger, 1970) have suggested that Freud founded a school comparable to the philosophical schools of ancient Greece and Rome. With the creation of psychoanalysis, Freud developed a movement characterized by its own rules, rituals, and doctrine of membership. Training in analysis entails a specific and protracted initiation into the rites of the psychoanalytic society. The didactic (or training) analysis requires sacrifices of time, money, privacy, and the self. This process serves to integrate the initiates firmly into the rituals, tenets, and wisdom of the movement. Some suggest that the development of the psychoanalytic philosophical cult will one day be seen as Freud's major contribution. As an art, Freudian psychoanalysis is a superb example of the scholarly approach to psychotherapy.

It is possible that after studying Freud, one may agree that his concepts are coherent, relevant, and comprehensive yet remain uncompelled. Freud would counter that the insight required for a full appreciation of his theory is of a particular kind, one that can be acquired only through the kind of analytic self-investigation practiced by him and his followers. Freud's theory is by no means universally accepted. Indeed, few other positions in the history of philosophical thought have been subject to as much attack, ridicule, and criticism. In modern science, only the theory of Charles Darwin has been met with equal scorn and resistance. It is not for the author to indicate to readers an appropriate judgment on psychoanalysis. Such a judgment can only arise from the reader's own encounter with Freud's theory. Nevertheless, Freud's picture of personality is one that compels many people. His picture of the personality as beset by anxieties, governed by forces of which we are largely unaware, living in a world marked by external and internal conflicts, resolving problems by solutions informed by fantasy or reality, is a concept of personality that many people find inescapable.

❧ Summary

1. The case of Anna O. may be seen as the beginning of **psychoanalysis.** Anna O. suffered from a **conversion disorder** in which her right arm and

leg were paralyzed, she had difficulty seeing, was nauseous, and was unable to drink any liquids or to speak and understand her mother tongue. She was also prone to states of **absence.** Dr. Joseph Breuer hypnotized her and asked her to verbalize associations she might have to words she mumbled during her absences. She began to tell him stories about her father's illness and death. After she had told a number of these stories, her symptoms went away.

Freud began to use the "talking method" with his own patients and he concluded that at the time of the original trauma the patient had had to hold back a strong emotion. The patient had forgotten the event and was unconscious or unaware of it. Freud's concept of **unconscious processes** is a dynamic one in which certain forces **repress** undesirable thoughts and then actively **resist** their becoming conscious.

2. An emotion, prevented from expressing itself normally, may be expressed through a neurotic symptom. **Wishes** are repressed because they go against a person's self-concept. Underlying Freud's concept is the idea that emotions which accompany events must ultimately be expressed. If they cannot find direct expression, they will find indirect ones, such as neurotic symptoms. Ideally, the expression of emotions is nondestructive.

3. Freud developed the technique of **free association** in order to help his patients recover repressed ideas. The patient is asked to verbalize whatever comes to mind no matter how insignificant, trivial, or even unpleasant the idea might be. Later he or she reflects upon those associations. Free association is based on the premise that no idea is insignificant and eventually the associations will lead back to the original problem.

4. Freud considered **slips** and **dreams** to be "the royal road" to the unconscious. They are analyzed by free associating to the slip itself or to the various elements of the dream. The analysis helps us to distinguish between the **manifest dream** and the **latent dream** that underlies it.

5. The nature of our repressed wishes and desires is sexual. Freud redefined the concept of sexuality as pleasure seeking. In doing so, he reversed many traditional concepts and was able to account for previously unexplained behaviors. As his work developed, he emphasized the psychological aspects of mental processes and sexuality, an emphasis apparent in his use of the terms **drive** and **libido.**

6. Freud outlined a set of **psychosexual stages** that children travel as they progress from **autoerotic** sexual activity to normal, mature, heterosexual, reproductive activity. The libido invests itself in various **erogenous zones.** During the **oral stage,** the major source of pleasure and pain is the mouth. The **anal stage** follows; libidinal energy is focused on the anus and the buttocks. During the **phallic stage** the genital organs become important and children experience the **Oedipus complex,** whose resolution leads to the development of a **superego** and sexual **identification.** The **latency period**

is one of rest, and the **genital stage** begins at puberty when the sexual organs mature and the individual is able to assume the sexual role outlined by his or her culture.

7. The effects of the psychosexual stages can be seen in various adult character traits and disorders. If the libido is unduly frustrated or overindulged at an early stage, it may become **fixated.** Many adult behaviors reflect early patterns that are characteristic of the different stages.

8. The **id, ego,** and **superego** represent different functions of the personality. The id is the oldest and original function. It includes our genetic inheritance, **reflexes,** and instincts and drives that motivate us. It operates according to the **pleasure principle** and uses **primary processes.** The ego develops in order to realistically meet the wishes of the id. It follows the **reality principle** and operates according to **secondary processes.** The superego consists of a **conscience** and the **ego-ideal.** It strives for perfection.

9. In the mature and well-adjusted personality, the ego is the executor controlling and governing the id and superego and mediating between their demands and the external world. In the maladjusted personality, the id or the superego gains control.

10. There is no easy correlation between the id, ego, and superego and consciousness or unconsciousness. The terms **conscious** and **unconscious** are best seen as adjectives describing qualities that the id, ego, and superego may or may not have.

11. **Anxiety** is an inevitable aspect of the human condition and the key problem with which the developmental process has to deal. Freud distinguished **reality anxiety, neurotic anxiety,** and **moral anxiety.**

12. In order to protect us against anxiety, the ego develops **defense mechanisms** which occur on an unconscious level and deny or distort reality so as to make it less threatening. Some of the more common defense mechanisms are **repression, projection, reaction formation, fixation, regression, rationalization, identification, displacement,** and **sublimation.** Freud believed that by strengthening the ego we can become more aware of our impulses and deal with them more effectively.

13. Freud's mature understanding of **psychoanalysis** emphasizes the importance of the **transference** in which the patient transfers to the analyst emotional attitudes felt as a child toward significant persons. The patient repeats with the analyst infantile and ineffective ways of relating to other people. The analysis permits the patient to re-experience and rework these relationships to a more satisfactory resolution.

14. Although Freud frequently suggested that his theory functioned as science, he permitted many of his concepts to function philosophically. He did not permit them to have any exceptions. Thus, in the final analysis, Freud's theory

needs to be evaluated in terms of a philosophy according to its coherence, relevance, comprehensiveness, and compellingness.

Suggestions for Further Reading

Freud's published works fill twenty-four volumes in *The Complete Psychological Works of Sigmund Freud: Standard Edition*, published by Hogarth Press of London, beginning in 1953. The lay reader will find the following most useful as a further introduction to the development of Freud's thought and theory. The *Five Lectures on Psychoanalysis* (1910), which were delivered at Clark University in Worcester, Massachusetts, represent a concise introduction by Freud to his own work. They are included in Vol. 11 (1957) of the complete works. More extensive presentations by Freud on his general theory are provided in *Introductory Lectures on Psychoanalysis* (1917), Vols. 15–16, 1963, and *New Introductory Lectures on Psychoanalysis* (1933), Vol. 22, 1964. Freud's classic writings on dreams, slips, and sexuality are *The Interpretation of Dreams* (1900), Vols. 4–5, 1953; *The Psychopathology of Everyday Life* (1901), Vol. 6, 1960; and *Three Essays on Sexuality* (1905), Vol. 7, 1953.

Freud's final theory of a threefold dynamic of personality was presented in *The Ego and the Id* (1923), Vol. 19, 1961. His re-evaluation of the problem of anxiety and the defense mechanisms is included in *Inhibitions, Symptoms and Anxiety* (1926), Vol. 20, 1959. The various introductory lectures provide useful information on the development of psychoanalysis as a therapeutic technique. The reader may also enjoy two later essays on the subject: "Analysis Terminable and Interminable" and "Constructions in Analysis" (both written in 1937), included in Vol. 23, 1964, in which Freud tries to assess realistically the benefits and limitations of psychoanalysis. Portions of the Standard Edition are also available in paperback editions published by Norton.

Secondary sources that provide a comprehensive picture of Freudian theory are C. Brenner, *An Elementary Textbook on Psychoanalysis* (Doubleday, 1955) and C. S. Hall, *A Primer of Freudian Psychology* (World, 1954).

The serious student of Freud will also be interested in the three-volume biography, *The Life and Work of Sigmund Freud* (Basic Books, 1953–1957), written by a close friend and follower, Ernest Jones. Briefer, more popular introductions to Freud's life and work are Irving Stone, *Passions of the Mind* (Doubleday, 1971) and P. Roazen, *Freud and His Followers* (Knopf, 1975). Bruno Bettelheim in his *Freud and Man's Soul* (Knopf, 1982) helps to clarify the essential humanism of Freud's work.

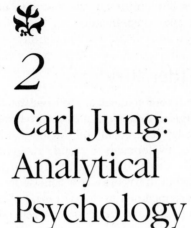

2
Carl Jung: Analytical Psychology

Your Goals for This Chapter

1. Explain how Jung uses the term *psyche*.

2. Compare and contrast Freud's and Jung's concepts of the *ego*.

3. Describe the *personal unconscious* and its *complexes*.

4. Explain how Jung's concept of the *collective unconscious* enlarges upon Freud's.

5. Discuss the following *archetypes: persona, shadow, anima* and *animus, self*. Explain the use of *active imagination*.

6. Identify two basic *attitudes* and four *functions*.

7. Explain how Jung's concept of the *libido* differs from Freud's.

8. Discuss what is involved in Jung's concept of *self-actualization*.

9. Describe some major features of Jungian psychotherapy.

10. Evaluate Jung's theory in terms of its function as philosophy, science, and art.

*C*arl Jung is recognized as one of the greatest and most controversial psychological thinkers of the twentieth century. It would be unfair to consider Jung only as a defector from the psychoanalytic movement. He was a mature scholar, with his own developing ideas, before he encountered Freud. Although he was closely associated with Freud for a period of time, he went on to develop an independent school of thought that contrasts markedly with orthodox psychoanalysis. He is indebted to Freud but is a personality theorist in his own right. His concept of the collective unconscious vastly enlarges an aspect of personality that was barely explored by Freud.

Biographical Background

Carl Gustav Jung was born in 1875 in Switzerland, where he lived all his life. He was the only surviving son of a poor country pastor and scholar of the Reformed church. Jung described his father as conventional and kind, but weak. He respected his father even though he had difficulty communicating with him, especially in matters of religion, which concerned Jung throughout his life. Skeptical of the orthodox faith in which he was reared, he searched relentlessly for adequate answers. This search is reflected in his psychology with its interest in religion, mythology, and the occult.

His mother was a powerful person. Jung felt that she was a good mother but that she suffered from emotional disturbances. He was later to describe her as possessing two personalities, one kind and loving, the other harsh and aloof. Jung's family constellation and ambivalent attitude toward his mother is echoed in his psychology, which emphasizes maternal images of woman as protector and destroyer rather than the paternal images of Freudian psychoanalysis.

Jung described his childhood as lonely and his personality as introverted. Two brothers had died in infancy before Jung was born and his sister did not arrive until he was nine. The young boy frequently played by himself, inventing games and carving a small companion out of wood to console himself. These long periods of solitude were later to find expression in his self-analysis. His psychology also reflected his predilection for being alone. Maturity for Jung is defined not in terms of interpersonal relations, as it is for Freud, but in terms of integration or balance within the self.

As a child, he not only had several close contacts and brushes with death but he was also familiar with illness. When he was a young child his mother had to be hospitalized for several months, leaving him in the care of an elderly aunt and a family maid. During his youth a series of fainting spells caused him to miss over six months of school. The boy enjoyed the consequent freedom from formal studies that his illness afforded him and the opportunity

Carl Jung

to explore other areas that interested him but were not in the traditional academic curriculum. However, shortly after he overheard his father's anguished comment to a friend, "What will become of the boy?" his health was restored and he returned to school. Later, he suggested that this experience taught him the meaning of a neurosis.

Jung originally wanted to be an archeologist, but for financial reasons he could only afford to attend the University of Basel, which did not offer courses in that area. Therefore, he chose to study medicine. He was planning to specialize in surgery when he came across a textbook by Krafft-Ebing, a German neurologist (1840–1902), that described psychiatry as invariably subjective. The description provoked Jung's interest. Here was a field that might provide the key to some of the dreams, mysteries, and obscure happenings that he had been trying to understand.

His first professional appointment was as an assistant in a mental hospital in Zurich, where he worked with Eugen Bleuler, a well-known psychiatrist. Later, he became a lecturer at the University of Zurich. He established a private practice and developed a word-association test in order to study emotional reactions.

Jung first met Sigmund Freud in 1907 after having corresponded with him about their mutual interest for a short period. The two men were highly impressed with each other and with each other's work. That meeting began an intense personal and professional relationship. For some time Freud regarded Jung as his heir apparent and he looked on him with all of the affection that a father has for his son. When the International Psychoanalytic Society was founded, Jung, with Freud's endorsement, became its first president. They traveled together to Clark University where both had been invited to lecture. Nevertheless, in 1913, Jung broke away from Freud and his school. The break was "a great loss" for Freud and shattering for Jung, who entered a period of extensive inner disorientation in which he could not read or write and which eventually led to his self-analysis. Many reasons underlay the break with Freud, the most pronounced point of disagreement being Jung's rejection of Freud's emphasis on sexuality. Whereas for Freud all higher intellectual processes and emotionally significant experiences are ultimately substitutes for sexuality and can be understood thereby, for Jung sexuality itself must be seen as symbolic. Sexuality and the reality it represents have a mysterious quality and cannot be fully analyzed or completely depicted.

Thereafter, Jung developed his own school of thought, which eventually came to be known as **analytical psychology.** He wrote extensively and his highly original theories were informed by a vast array of concerns including Eastern religions, mythology, and alchemy. Although such subjects are frequently considered to be scientifically suspect, Jung felt that they were essential to the psychologist and indispensable in understanding the mysterious forces of the unconscious. Some critics argue that Jung's theories foster racism, that Jung was psychotic, anti-Semitic, and pro-Nazi. Other critics argue that although Jung was a troubled individual, he was a sensitive historian with unique and insightful ideas, that his peculiarities were the signs of genius rather than madness. Jung died in 1961 at the age of eighty-five after a long and fruitful life.

The Nature and Structure of Personality

Whereas Freud described the structure of personality in terms of three forces that are in constant conflict — the id, the ego, and the superego — Carl Jung conceived of the structure of personality as a complex network of interacting systems that strive toward eventual harmony. The primary ones are the ego; the personal unconscious with its complexes; and the collective unconscious and its archetypes. Jung also talked about two primary attitudes and four basic functions, which together constitute separate but related aspects of the **psyche,** or total personality.

The psyche refers to all psychological processes: thoughts, feelings, sensations, wishes, and so forth. Jung used the terms "psyche" and "psychic," rather than "mind" and "mental," to avoid the implications of consciousness in the latter and to emphasize that the psyche embraces both conscious and unconscious processes.

Jung and Freud differed in their approaches to the unconscious. Freud tended to view the unconscious as essentially materials that have been repressed, whereas Jung emphasized a concept of the unconscious as the source of consciousness and the matrix of new possibilities of life.

The Ego

For Freud, the ego was ideally the executor of the personality. Although Freud initially thought that the ego was primarily conscious, he belatedly realized that a large portion of the ego was unconscious and beyond conscious control or awareness. Still, for the mature, healthy adult, the ego is the center of the personality.

Jung's concept of the ego is quite different from Freud's. For Jung, the **ego** is one's conscious perception of self. Thus, Jung suggests that the ego is responsible for our feelings of identity and continuity. It is through our conscious awareness of our feelings that we establish a sense of self. The ego, however, is not the true center of personality for Jung. This runs counter to our everyday point of view. Most of us identify ourselves or our center as that awareness or consciousness that we have of ourselves, but for Jung, as we shall shortly see, the true center of personality is located elsewhere. Jung compares the conscious aspect of the psyche to an island that rises from the sea (see Figure 2.1). We notice only the part above water, even though a much greater land mass lies below, which can be compared to the unconscious (Fordham, 1953).

The Personal Unconscious

The region immediately adjacent to the ego is termed the ***personal unconscious.*** It is a land that is not always covered by sea and thus can be reclaimed. Here those contents that have been put aside (for our consciousness can only hold a few items at a time) reside and may be easily retrieved. The personal unconscious also includes those experiences of an individual's life history that have been repressed or forgotten. This is an aspect of the unconscious that, as we have seen, Freud also emphasized. These forgotten experiences are accessible to consciousness even though becoming aware of some of them may be an arduous process.

Figure 2.1 *Jung's Concept of the Unconscious*
The Jungian notion is that each individual ego is an island, joined to others by the collective unconscious.

Experiences are grouped in the personal unconscious into clusters, which Jung calls complexes. A **complex** is an organized group of thoughts, feelings, and memories about a particular concept (1934). A complex is said to have a **constellating power,** which means that the complex has the ability to draw new ideas into it and interpret them accordingly. It can be compared to a magnet that attracts related experiences. The more drawing power a complex has, the more powerful it may become. Complexes have important implications for our interpersonal relationships, specifically influencing how we react toward others.

A complex may be organized around a particular person or object. One of Jung's examples concerns motherhood (1954). Our mother complex refers to the cluster of ideas, feelings, and memories that have arisen from our own particular experience of having been mothered. It also draws into it other experiences of mothering to which we have been exposed. Each new instance of mothering that we encounter is drawn into our mother complex and understood and interpreted by it. For example, my associations to motherhood pertained first and foremost to my own mother; later, they included other instances of mothering that I may have seen or read about. This concept of mothering deeply and individually affects my understanding of what it means to be mothered and to mother. As you can see, Jung's concept is very far removed from the everyday definition of a "mother complex" as the inability to disengage oneself from one's mother's apron strings.

A complex, however, may make it difficult for us to disengage ourselves from a situation. Jung describes a man who believed that he was suffering from a real cancer, even though he knew that his cancer was imaginary. The complex, Jung writes, is "a spontaneous growth, originating in that part of the psyche which is not identical with consciousness. It appears to be an autonomous development intruding upon consciousness" (1938). A complex may act like an independent person, behaving autonomously of our conscious self and intentions.

A complex may be conscious, partly conscious, or unconscious. Certain elements of it may extend into the collective unconscious. Some complexes appear to dominate an entire personality. Hitler is frequently described as being driven by inner forces to obtain power.

The Collective Unconscious

Whereas the personal unconscious is unique for each individual, the **collective unconscious** is shared. Jung referred to the collective unconscious as "transpersonal"; that is to say, it extends across persons. It consists of certain potentialities that we all share because we are human beings (1936). Many critics believe that Jung made a unique contribution to depth psychology in his concept of the collective unconscious. Freud's concept of unconscious forces was mostly limited to personal ones — experiences that have been repressed or forgotten. Whereas other dissenters from Freud tended to minimize the power of unconscious forces, Jung placed a greater emphasis on them and stressed the qualities that we share with other people.

All people, because they are human beings, have certain things in common. All human beings live in groups and develop some form of family life or society in which roles are assigned to various members. These roles may vary from society to society but they exist in all human groups. All human beings share certain emotions such as joy, grief, or anger. The ways of expressing these emotions may vary, but the emotions themselves are shared. All human beings develop some form of language and symbolization. The particular words may vary, but the concepts and symbols are shared. Thus, certain archetypes and symbols reappear again and again from society to society and they may be seen to have a common meaning.

Jung considers the collective unconscious an empirical concept whose existence can be demonstrated through dreams, mythology, and cross-cultural data. The workings of the unconscious are seen in experiences we have all had, such as falling in love with a "perfect other," feeling overwhelmed by a piece of art or music, or being drawn to the sea, and it expresses itself in shared symbols that have universal meaning. One such symbol is the **mandala** (1955), a concentrically arranged figure such as the circle, the wheel, or the cross, which Jung saw appearing again and again in his patients' dreams and in the artwork of all cultures. The mandala represents the self striving toward wholeness. The collective unconscious, then, consists of predispositions or possibilities of behaving in certain ways because we are human.

Archetypes   Within the collective unconscious lie the archetypes. An **archetype** is a universal thought form or predisposition to perceive the world in certain ways (1936). The word "predisposition" is crucial to Jung's concept of the collective unconscious and its archetypes. It emphasizes potentialities, for the archetypes represent different potential ways in which we may express our humanness. The archetypes can never be fully known or described. They appear to us in personified or symbolized pictorial form and may penetrate into consciousness by means of myths, dreams, art, ritual, and symptoms. Insofar as they represent the total latent potentiality of the psyche, it is helpful for us to get in touch with them. In doing so, we go beyond developing our individual potentialities and become incorporated in the eternal cosmic process.

Persona   The **persona** refers to the social role that one is assigned by society and one's understanding of it. The term comes from the Latin word *persona,* which refers to the masks that actors wore in ancient Greek dramas. Thus, one's persona is the mask that one wears in order to fulfill the demands of society. Each one of us is assigned particular roles by our society. I am assigned roles as wife, mother, and professor. The persona represents a compromise between one's true self and society. To neglect the development of a persona is to run the risk of becoming asocial. On the other hand, if one identifies too completely with one's persona, one may play the role at the expense of one's true self.

Your persona represents a compromise between your true self and the expectations of society.

The shadow The **shadow** encompasses those unsocial thoughts, feelings, and behaviors that we potentially possess. It is the opposite side of the persona, in that it refers to those desires and emotions that are incompatible with our social standards and ideal personality. It could be described as the devil within. Jung's choice of the word "shadow" is deliberate and designed to emphasize its necessity. There can be no sun that does not leave a shadow. The shadow cannot be avoided and one is incomplete without it. Jung agreed with Freud that such base and unsocial impulses may be sublimated and channeled to good ends. The shadow can also be projected onto others, with important interpersonal and social consequences such as prejudice.

To neglect or try to deny the shadow involves us in hypocrisy and deceit. Angels are not suited for existence on earth. Jung suggested a need to come to know our baser side and recognize our animalistic impulses. To do so adds dimension and credibility to personality as well as increased zest for life.

The anima and animus   Each one of us has assigned to us a sex gender, male or female, based on our overt sexual characteristics. Yet none of us is purely male or purely female. Each of us has qualities of the opposite sex in terms of biology and also in terms of psychological attitudes and feelings. Thus, the **anima** archetype is the feminine side of the male psyche and the **animus** archetype is the masculine side of the female psyche. The anima and the animus reflect collective and individual human experiences throughout the ages pertaining to the opposite sex. They assist us in relating to and understanding the opposite sex. For Jung, there was a distinct difference between the psychology of men and women. Jung believed that it was important that one express these opposite-sex characteristics in order to avoid an un-balanced or one-sided personality. If one exhibits only the traits of one's assigned sex, the other traits remain unconscious, undeveloped, and primitive. Those of us who have difficulty in understanding the opposite sex probably are not in tune with our anima and animus.

Jung has usually been considered as friendly to women because of his assertion of the need to get in touch with one's opposite-sex archetype. However, his writings have also been criticized for including naive stereotypes of women as well as overtly racist comments about other groups such as blacks and primitive people. Jung stoutly maintained that the psyche of women is different from that of men and he tended to be rigid in his discussion of those behaviors that would or would not overstep the boundaries of appropriate expression of one's assigned gender role and one's opposite-sex archetype. He warned of the dangers of pushing one's capacity to behave in the opposite-sex way too far.

Jung believed that women's consciousness was characterized by the ability to enter into relationships, whereas men's consciousness was characterized by the ability to engage in rational and analytic thought. The persona, or social mask, differs for men and women because of the various roles that society and culture have assigned to them. The anima and the animus function in ways that compensate for the outer personality and show the qualities that are missing in the outward conscious expression. In men these are traditionally feminine characteristics, in women masculine ones. The anima and the animus are determined by given biological propensities toward the opposite sex, by collective concepts of male and female that have evolved throughout history, and by the experiences that each person has in his or her own life with members of the other sex. Because psychological development involves in-tegrating one's persona and one's anima or animus, it will clearly progress differently for the male and for the female.

A woman may react to her animus in various ways. Traditionally, women have repressed their masculine qualities and striven to fulfill their feminine role. Jung thought this might lead to an imbalance in the personality and unconscious efforts on the part of the animus to intrude upon the woman's life; he pointed out that both the anima and the animus may behave as if they are laws unto themselves and have disruptive influences. Another way to react to the animus is to identify with it, but this usually makes it more difficult for a woman to fulfill her assigned role.

However, the animus in a woman need not be thought of as acting in opposition to the feminine. Indeed, one of the tasks of transcendence and self-actualization is to bring these two elements into harmony with each other. Thus, in ideal development, the animus will lead a woman to transform her femininity into a renewed form of consciousness that overcomes the traditional dualities. The same would be true of ideal development in the male. The need for such transformation is all the clearer in today's society, because the analytic, aggressive, and rational consciousness of the male has proven to be no longer a means of enlightenment. Rather, it has become a danger; we have seen that men frequently act in response to unconscious emotions that they find hard to acknowledge because they identify those emotions as feminine.

Jung's comments about the anima and the animus culminated in the now very popular concept of an androgynous ideal. **Androgyny** refers to the presence of both masculine and feminine qualities in an individual and the ability to realize both potentialities. At present, increased research is being done in the area of androgyny.

The self The central archetype in Jung's understanding is that of the self. The **self** represents the striving for unity of all parts of the personality. It is the organizing principle of the psyche that draws unto itself and harmonizes all the archetypes and their expressions in complexes and consciousness. The self directs an orderly allotment of psychic energy so that different parts of the personality are expressed appropriately. Depending upon the occasion and our personal needs, the self allows us to be socially acceptable at work (persona), outrageous at a Halloween party (shadow), emotional at a concert (shadow), and so forth. The self, rather than the ego, is the true midpoint of personality. Thus, the center of one's personality is not to be found in rational ego consciousness. Freud had already begun to discover this truth, but he wanted to rescue human beings from irrationality and so he made ego consciousness central. For Jung, the true self lay on the boundary between conscious and unconscious, reason and unreason. The development of the self is life's goal, but the self archetype cannot begin to emerge until the other personality systems have been fully developed. Thus, it usually does not become evident until one has reached middle age. Jung spoke of the realization of the self as a goal that lies in the future. It is something to be striven for but rarely achieved.

Jung described numerous other archetypes of the collective unconscious: birth, death, rebirth, power, magic, the child, the hero, God, the demon, the earth mother, and the wise old man. The point is that one cannot deny or destroy these archetypes. If one tries to (for example, if one says that God is dead), the archetype will reappear in an unlikely place because the archetypes cannot be destroyed. God will simply change into something else that will evoke human worship. Therefore, it is helpful for us to get in touch with the archetypes, as they represent our latent and inevitable personality.

Exploration /////

Active Imagination

Jung developed **active imagination** as a way of getting in touch with the archetypes, such as the anima or the animus. You are invited to imagine your anima or animus. Place yourself in a comfortable position, relax, and close your eyes. You might imagine what the fantasized archetype would say to you and enter into a dialogue with it. If a scene becomes too difficult or produces anxiety, you should discontinue it.

Because the archetypes also appear in dreams in the form of people, animals, or symbols, you may try to understand them by placing yourself in the role of one of the figures in your dreams. In dreams, the anima variously appears as a virgin, a mother, or a witch. The animus often takes on the appearance of a Prince Charming, a savior, or a sorcerer. However, they may take other forms as well. When you place yourself in the role of one of your dream figures, speak as if you were that dream individual. Describe yourself, indicate what you wanted to express in the dream, and relate to other figures in the dream.

Getting in touch with the anima or animus may permit us to feel and experience opposite-sex characteristics. Historically, the male has been associated with aggressiveness, analytic and instrumental thought, emotional control, and self-concern, while the female has been identified with passivity, intuitive and expressive thought, emotionality, and concern for others. In active imagination, a male might permit himself to feel vulnerable and hurt, and to cry. A woman might be able to express her aggression. According to Jung, each of us shares the components of our sexual opposite. If we do not get in touch with the other side of our personality, we run the risk of being lopsided and missing a valuable dimension of our experience.

The Attitudes Jung referred to two basic **attitudes** or psychotypes (1933a). **Introversion** is an attitude in which the psyche is oriented inward to the subjective world. **Extroversion** is an attitude in which the psyche is oriented outward to the objective world. These words have become so commonplace in today's vocabulary that most of us readily identify ourselves as *introverted* or *extroverted*. Jung labeled himself an introvert and Freud an extrovert. Yet this labeling refers simply to the dominant or more developed attitude. The conscious extrovert is an introvert in his or her unconscious and vice versa. The significance of the attitudes and of the functions, which are described next, is that they deeply affect how we relate to the world and to other people.

The Functions **Functions** are ways of perceiving the environment and orienting experiences (1933b). The function of **sensation** refers to sense perception of the world. **Thinking** gives meaning and understanding to the world. The function of **feeling** involves valuing and judging the world. Lastly, **intuition,** perception via the unconscious, informs us of the atmosphere surrounding experience and future possibilities. These functions group themselves into opposite pairs: thinking and feeling, sensation and intuition. Thinking and feeling are said to be rational functions because they both require acts of judgment. Sensation and intuition involve immediate experiences. Jung suggested that one of these functions tends to be dominant in each individual and its opposite inferior. The other two play an auxiliary role. A professor, for example, may have so cultivated his intellectual and cognitive powers that the feeling and intuitive aspects of his personality are submerged. Though primitive and undeveloped, they may nevertheless invade his life in the form of strange moods, symptoms, or projections. A synthesis of the four functions is required for an actualized self.

At the deepest levels, Jung believed that our unconscious remains archaic, despite our scientific technology and the development of our rational powers. Freud disclaimed Jung's plea for originality, stating that he had known all along that the unconscious is collective. And, of course, there are certain archetypal patterns in Freud's understanding of the unconscious. The psychosexual stages involve predispositions toward acting out the human drama in certain ways. The Oedipal situation that we all experience is a collective archetypal myth. Symbols in dreams may be unique to the individual, but also shared. Thus, a concept of collected unconscious forces is implied in Freud's theory although certainly not clearly articulated. And whereas Freud emphasized the unique unfolding of unconscious forces in the individual's life history and personal unconscious (it is not enough to know that one has gone through the Oedipal situation, one must fully experience its particular unfolding within one's distinct family constellation), Jung emphasized the shared and collective aspects. As you might imagine, Jung's concept is an important and controversial one in personality theorizing.

Psychic Energy

For Freud, the motive force of personality consists of libido, the sexual drive. Jung also uses "libido" to refer to psychic energy, but his use should not be confused with Freud's definition. Jung uses the term in a more generalized fashion as an undifferentiated life energy (1948b). **Libido** is an appetite that may refer to sexuality and to other hungers as well. It reflects itself as striving, desiring, and willing. Psychic energy operates according to the principles of equivalence and entropy; it seeks a balance and moves the person forward in a process of self-actualization.

Although Jung does not reject an instinctual basis of personality, he criticizes Freud's emphasis on sexuality, suggesting that it is ultimately reductive or simplistic, as it reduces any and all activities to sexual ones. Jung's point is that sexuality itself must be seen as symbolic, having a mysterious quality of otherness that cannot be fully described.

Self-Actualization

Jung suggests that the self is in the process of **self-actualization.** He did not outline stages in the development of personality nor did he consider the early childhood years to be the most important ones, as Freud did. The "psychic birth" of an individual does not really occur until adolescence, when the psyche starts to show a definite form and content. Personality development continues throughout life and the middle years (35 to 40) mark the beginning of major changes.

Although the concept of self-actualization was fully described by Jung, it cannot be said to be new with his thought. The origin of the principle takes us back to the Greek philosopher Aristotle (384–322 B.C.). Aristotle held that everything has a *telos,* a purpose or goal, that constitutes its essence and indicates its potentiality. Thus, every acorn has the essence of treeness and the potential to become a mighty oak. In the same way, each one of us has the potential to develop into a self, that is, to actualize, fulfill, and enhance our maximum human potentialities. This viewpoint is essentially *teleological,* or purposeful. It explains the present in terms of the future with reference to a goal that guides and directs our destiny. Whereas Freud's view was primarily a causal one, comprehending personality in terms of antecedent conditions of the past, Jung maintained that both causality and teleology are necessary for a full understanding of personality.

While development is largely forward moving, regression may occur under conditions of frustration. Such regression is not viewed negatively by Jung. Rather, it may, in the end, facilitate the forward movement of progression. By exploring the unconscious, both personal and collective, the ego may learn from past experiences and resolve the problem that led to the regression.

Whereas for Freud a neurosis represents the return of the repressed, for Jung it is the insistence of the undeveloped part of the personality on being heard and realized.

Self-actualization involves individuation and transcendence (1916, 1939). In **individuation,** the systems of the individual psyche achieve their fullest degree of differentiation, expression, and development. **Transcendence** refers to integration of the diverse systems of the self toward the goal of wholeness and identity with all of humanity. Jung's concepts of individuation and transcendence are difficult for the average Westerner to understand. In Western psychology, we generally think of personality in terms of an individual's uniqueness. We suggest that personality is what makes one individual different from all other people. People who do not appear to be unique are often said to "lack personality." Jung suggests that this aspect, individuation, is a lower level of total personality development. He believes that, following individuation, we need to experience transcendence. In the process of transcendence, a deeper self or essence emerges that unites a person with all of humanity and the universe at large.

The first half of life, then, is concerned with individuation, the cultivation of consciousness and gender-specific behavior. The second half of life presents us with a different task, transcendence, which permits us to come into closer contact with and express our collective unconscious and our oneness with humanity as a whole. Thus, as the self actualizes, a stormy process that is never fully completed, it perpetually rises to a greater enhancement and realization of itself and humanity. If we view the psyche as a wheel, the hub of which is the archetype of the self, we can suggest that the true self emerges when the opposites coincide (Figure 2.2). The true person does not consist of the conscious or the unconscious, mind or body, persona or shadow, overt sexual characteristics or complements, but of all of these. Neurosis results from a one-sided personality development. The coincidence of opposites is the ultimate goal of personality development in the Jungian view. Although both Freud and Jung emphasize the dynamic opposition of portions of the personality, they differ in the implications of this conflict. For Freud, the person is inescapably in conflict; for Jung, the person ultimately seeks harmony.

Jungian Psychotherapy

Jung views neurosis as a person's attempt to reconcile the contradictory aspects of his or her personality. One side of the psyche, such as the conscious, adaptive, social self, may be exaggerated at the expense of the darker, unconscious aspects. It is difficult to describe Jung's method of psychotherapy specifically because he did not clearly outline his procedures as Freud did. Further, Jung maintained that no one approach is suitable for everyone. The

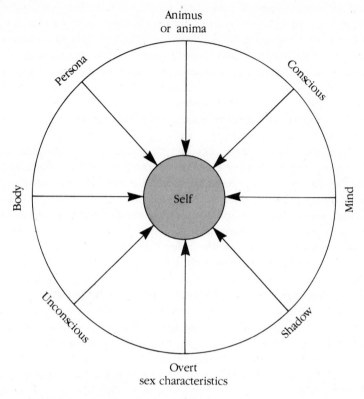

Figure 2.2 *The Coincidence of Opposites*
If we were to view the psyche as a wheel, the hub of which is the archetype of the self, the true self emerges when the opposites coincide. The resulting image is, of course, a mandala.

individual who has had difficulty in accepting the sexual and aggressive aspects of his or her life may well require a Freudian interpretation. But for others, or at different stages in development, the Freudian understanding may be insufficiently comprehensive.

In classical Freudian psychoanalysis, the analyst remains detached and reveals little of his or her personal feelings and reactions in order to facilitate the transference, whereas the Jungian analyst enters into a personal relationship with the patient and is ready to throw his or her entire personality into the work. Therapy is a "dialectical procedure," a dialogue between doctor and patient, conscious and unconscious. Although the couch may be used to facilitate procedures such as active imagination, for the most part analyst and patient sit facing each other. The Jungian also sees patients far less frequently than the Freudian analyst. The frequency of visits depends on the stage that the patient has reached.

During the early stages of treatment, there is a need for *confession*. Such confession is generally accompanied by emotional release and is viewed by Jung as the aim of the cathartic method originated by Breuer and Freud. But Jung points out that emotional release, in itself, is not therapeutic any more than temper tantrums or other emotional outbursts are curative in and of themselves. For Freud, conscious intellectual understanding and insight renders the catharsis effective. Jung emphasizes that the presence of the other, the therapist, who supports the patient morally and spiritually as well as intellectually, makes the confession curative.

Projection and transference play an important role in Jungian analysis, though Jung added to Freud's concept of transference the recognition that not only significant persons from the patient's past are projected onto the analyst but so are archetypal figures. Jung also viewed the sexual components of the transference as symbolic efforts on the patient's part to reach a higher integration of personality. In contrast to Freud, Jung did not think that transference was a necessary precondition for therapy.

Jung's attitude toward dreams differs from that of Freud. Whereas Freud treated dreams as the expression of unconscious wishes, Jung gives them a prospective function as well as a retrospective one. By prospective function Jung means that the dream represents an effort by the person to prepare for future events. Dreams also have a **compensatory** function; they are efforts to complement the patient's conscious side and speak for the unconscious. Thus, dreams speak to us of the future, revealing those aspects of our personality that we have tended to ignore and need to stress further in our movement toward wholeness.

In interpreting dreams, Jung used the **method of amplification** (1951) rather than the method of free association. In free association, each dream element is the starting place for a chain of association that may lead far afield from the original element. In amplification, one focuses repeatedly on the element and gives multiple associations to it. The dream is taken exactly as it is with no precise effort to distinguish between manifest and latent contents. The therapist joins the patient in efforts to interpret the dream, adding personal associations and frequently referring to mythology, fairy tales, and the like in order to extend the dream's meaning. Whereas Freud tended to deal with dreams singly, Jung used a series of dreams that the patient might report. Analysis of a series of dreams unfolds the inner life of the patient, which is taken as a guide to true-life meanings for the patient.

As a therapist, Jung also valued the use of active imagination as a means of facilitating self-understanding and the use of artistic production by the patient. He encouraged his patients to draw, sculpt, paint, or develop some other art form as a means of listening to their inner depths. In all of this, he emphasizes obedience to the unfolding inner life as the appropriate, ethical fulfillment of one's humanity.

The Mandalas in Your Life

The mandala is one of the oldest religious symbols and is found throughout the world. A mandala is usually circular in appearance, but at times it takes the form of a square or a squared circle and contains other geometric forms. The earliest known form of mandala was the sun wheel. Throughout the East, the mandala is a common symbol that stands for wholeness and unity and is used as an aid in meditation. In the West, mandalas appear in the four-sided cross, in symbols of the Trinity, and in stained-glass patterns of Gothic cathedral rose windows. Nature itself has provided us with many mandalas, such as the atom and the snowflake (see Figure 2.3).

Jung found the mandala symbol occurring spontaneously in the dreams and images of his patients. He believed that the mandala is an archetypal symbol of wholeness that can aid us in integrating our personality. Practically all of us doodle. Take a few minutes to look at your doodles to see if you can identify any mandalas in them. If you can, you have confirmed Jung's position that the mandala is a spontaneous symbol of expression shared by all humankind. Jung also believed that it is useful for a person to try to create his or her own mandalas. Simply draw a circle, a square, or a combined figure, and complete it in a manner that expresses your feelings and interests at the moment. Studying the mandalas that we draw and noticing subsequent changes that we make over a period of time can give us insight into our personality.

Jung believed that our art forms are important ways by which we synthesize conscious and unconscious forces. Our drawings, paintings, and other creative activities reflect aspects of our unconscious selves. Such art forms are not to be judged in terms of aesthetics, but understood as attempts at self-expression. If you are interested in exploring yourself through the medium of art, first draw, paint, or make some other effort at creative expression. Then try to explain what your creation means to you intellectually and emotionally. Take note of your self-discoveries. Develop a series of creative works and reflect on them in order to notice the changes that occur.

Jung's Theory: Philosophy, Science, and Art

Many of Jung's discoveries, like Freud's, took place in the clinical setting, based on empirical observations of his patients made during the course of treatment and research. He also obtained information from sources outside the treatment room. Observations of other cultures and studies of comparative religion and mythology, symbolism, alchemy, and the occult afforded him a

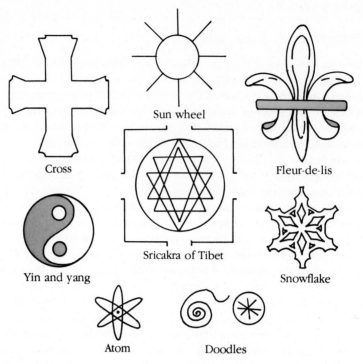

Figure 2.3 Mandalas
Mandalas appear in the symbolism of both East and West, in nature, and in our doodles.

wealth of information. Jung considered these sources secondary but legitimate ones to psychologists seeking to uncover the mysteries of the human psyche. He believed that a comparative method of study, often used in history and anthropology, was a valuable approach in science as well.

Jung did not believe that psychologists should be bound to an experimental, scientific approach. He did believe, however, that conclusions should be based on empirical data. For example, the archetypes have demonstrably clear effects on us; thus, they are psychic facts and useful psychological concepts.

Jung criticized the contemporary scientific atmosphere for limiting its concepts to those of causality and introduced the concept of teleology. After all, he pointed out, the concepts of *cause* and *goal* are not themselves found in nature but are imaginary constructs imposed by scientists. Jung urged scientists to work within a broader scope and conceptual design.

Jung's concepts are particularly difficult to study in the laboratory. As with Freud, it is virtually impossible to define many of his terms operationally or to develop a test that would disprove them. Further, Jung's interest in the occult has led many critics to dismiss him as a mystic. Consequently, scientific psychology has until recently largely ignored Jung's analytical psychology. Nevertheless, Jung has influenced developments in psychology and other disciplines. The concept of self-actualization, which is clearly teleological, reappears in the theories of Carl Rogers, Gordon Allport, and Abraham Maslow.

Jung indicated that he was more interested in discovering facts than in developing a philosophy. Because his concepts were based on empirical data, in the broadest sense of the word he operated as a "scientist." However, his theory falls short of rigorous standards of compatibility, predictive power, and simplicity. Fundamentally, the Jungian quest may be viewed as a philosophical or religious one. Jung explicitly raised philosophical questions and suggested philosophical answers. For example, asserting that questions about human nature should be answered empirically is in itself a philosophical position. For Jung, the power of self-understanding stems from an appropriate philosophy of life. It should not be surprising that although Jung has been largely ignored by experimentally-oriented psychologists, theologians have found his work very fruitful. His concept of God's revealing himself through the collective unconscious is particularly attractive to theologians who seek a more relevant articulation of traditional theistic concepts. Although it is complex, his theory is coherent; its relevance is attested to by the resurgence of interest in it today; and the comprehensive features of his theory are remarkable for their profundity.

As an art, Jungian therapy emphasizes a scholarly goal. With the resurgence of interest in Jung, training in Jungian analysis has become available in major American cities, and several new and controversial books about Jung's ideas have appeared in the past decade.

Jung's emphasis on inborn qualities, the duality of human nature, symbolism, androgyny, and the importance of inner experiences — factors that at one time led psychologists to neglect his work — are now seen as important, if not indispensable, for understanding personality. In particular, Jung's interest in the developmental process with his attention to the second half of the human life span has proved valuable to social scientists who are concerned about the needs and growth of our older population.

Jung's thinking complements the recent increase of interest in the East. His ideas appeal to those who are discontented with Western society and who seek self-understanding through Eastern thought with its emphasis on introspection and experience. The potential application of his theory is just beginning to be felt.

❦ Summary

1. Jung uses the term **psyche** to refer to all psychological processes, emphasizing that it embraces both conscious and unconscious processes.

2. Whereas for Freud the **ego** is the executor of the personality, for Jung it is one's conscious perception of self.

3. The **personal unconscious** includes experiences of an individual's history that have been repressed or forgotten. These are organized into **complexes.**

4. Freud's concept of unconscious forces is mostly limited to a personal unconscious; Jung's **collective unconscious** consists of potential ways of being that all humans share.

5. **Archetypes** are universal thought forms of the collective unconscious and predispositions to perceive the world in certain ways. Some widely recognized archetypes are the **persona,** the **shadow,** the **anima,** and the **animus.** The **self** is the central archetype and true midpoint of the personality. **Active imagination** is a method of getting in touch with the archetypes.

6. Jung described two basic **attitudes** (**introversion** and **extroversion**) and four **functions** (**sensation, thinking, feeling,** and **intuition**). In each person, one of the attitudes and functions is dominant and its opposite is weaker. A synthesis of the four functions is to be sought.

7. For Freud the **libido** consists of the sexual drive, whereas Jung uses the term in a more generalized fashion as an undifferentiated energy which moves the person forward.

8. **Self-actualization** is a teleological process of development that involves **individuation** and **transcendence.** In the process, the systems of the psyche achieve their fullest degree of differentiation and are then integrated in identity with all of humanity.

9. In his psychotherapy, Jung seeks to reconcile unbalanced aspects of the personality. It is a dialectical procedure and initially entails confession. Jung considers dreams to have a prospective function as well as a **compensatory** one; in interpreting them he uses the **method of amplification.**

10. Although Jung's concepts were based on empirical data, he raised philosophical questions and suggested philosophical answers. His theory may therefore be seen as largely philosophical.

Suggestions for Further Reading

Carl Jung was a voluminous writer. His *Collected Works* have been published in this country by Princeton University Press, beginning in 1953. Statements about his theory are scattered throughout these works, but Volumes 7, 8, and 9 present the major features. Because Jung is a difficult writer to follow, the lay person would be best advised to begin his or her study with books that are more directed to the general public. *Man and His Symbols* (Doubleday, 1964) is probably the best introduction to Jungian psychology. It was written by Jung and several of his disciples. Jung's autobiography, describing the spiritual journey that led to his position, is *Memories, Dreams, and Reflections* (Random House, 1961). A statement of the major principles of analytic psychology as well as the theory of types and functions is included in *Psychological Types* (Harcourt, Brace, 1933a). Several of Jung's lectures were also collected in a basic introduction entitled *Modern Man in Search of a Soul* (Harcourt, Brace, 1933b).

Also recommended are the *Freud/Jung Letters* (Princeton University Press, 1974). The best secondary sources introducing Jung's ideas are F. Fordham, *An Introduction to Jung's Psychology* (Penguin, 1953), and C. S. Hall and V. J. Nordby, *A Primer of Jungian Psychology* (Mentor, 1973). A more recent re-evaluation of Jung's work is V. Brome, *Jung: Man and Myth* (Atheneum, 1978).

3

Alfred Adler: Individual Psychology

Your Goals for This Chapter

1. Explain the difference between an *intrapsychic* and an *interpsychic* emphasis in personality theorizing.

2. Define what is meant by *social interest* and explain why it must be cultivated.

3. Explain what Adler meant by *finalism* and describe some *fictional finalisms*.

4. Identify the ultimate goal of the psyche.

5. Describe how *inferiority feelings* shape one's personality.

6. Tell what is meant by an individual's *style of life* and describe how *family constellation* and *family atmosphere* may shape it.

7. Discuss Adler's concept of the *creative self* and show how it restores consciousness to the center of personality.

8. Describe some of the major features of Adlerian psychotherapy.

9. Evaluate Adler's theory in terms of its function as philosophy, science, and art.

*A*lfred Adler chose the term **individual psychology** for his conception of personality because he was interested in investigating the uniqueness of personality. Nevertheless, he realized that the individual could not be considered in isolation. His emphasis shifted from a stress on **intrapsychic** ("within the psyche") phenomena such as Freud dealt with to an appreciation of **interpsychic** ("interpersonal") relations. Adler's theory holds that understanding a particular individual entails comprehending his or her attitude in relation to the world. Thus, for Adler, the human person emerged as a social creature rather than a sexual creature. According to Adler, we are motivated by social interests and our primary life problems are social ones.

Biographical Background

Alfred Adler, second of six children born to a successful merchant, was born in 1870 and raised in a suburb of Vienna. He described his childhood as difficult and unhappy. He suffered from rickets, a deficiency disease of childhood that affects the bones and made him clumsy and awkward. Initially, his parents pampered him, but when his younger brother was born he sensed that his mother transferred her attention to him. He felt dethroned and turned to his father, who favored him and expected great things from him.

When he was three, he saw his younger brother die in the next bed. Twice during his early childhood Adler was run over in the streets. His fear of death was further increased by a bout of pneumonia at the age of four. Later, he traced his interest in becoming a doctor to that near-fatal illness.

At school he was only an average student. Indeed, at one point his teacher suggested that his father take him out of school and apprentice him to a shoemaker. Nevertheless, he rose to a superior position in school, especially in mathematics, which he originally had had the greatest difficulty in mastering. In spite of his physical handicaps, he developed courage, social interest, and a feeling of being accepted in his play with other children. His interest and joy in the company of others remained throughout his life.

His weak physique and feelings of inferiority during childhood were later to find expression in his concepts of organic inferiority and the striving for superiority. His sensitivity about being the second son was reflected in his interest in the family constellation and ordinal position of birth. His efforts to get along with others found expression in his later conviction that the human being is a social animal and in the Adlerian concept of social interest.

Adler studied medicine at the University of Vienna, where Freud had received his medical training. Although he trained as an eye specialist, he became a general practitioner and later established himself as a practicing neurologist and psychiatrist. In 1902 he was invited by Freud to join a group for weekly

Alfred Adler

discussions on psychoanalysis. This group eventually grew into the Vienna Psychoanalytic Society, of which Adler was the first president, and later became the International Psychoanalytic Association.

There are many stories concerning Adler's association with Freud and their subsequent split. Adler was never a student of Freud's nor was he ever psychoanalyzed. He joined the discussions because he was interested in psychoanalysis but from the beginning he discovered points of disagreement. By 1911 these differences appeared crucial. Adler was invited to state his position to the society, which he did, but his views were denounced, he resigned, and about one-third of the members left with him.

Adler founded his own group and attracted many followers. He served in the Austrian army during World War I. Afterwards he assisted the government in establishing child guidance clinics in Vienna. Although he and Freud both practiced in Vienna during the 1920s and early 1930s, they did not associate with each other.

Adler visited the United States frequently and came here to live in 1935 to escape the Nazi regime. He continued his private practice, accepted a position as professor of medical psychology at the Long Island College of Medicine, and lectured widely. He died suddenly in 1937 of a heart attack while on a lecture tour in Scotland; he was sixty-seven.

Social Interest

A leading concept of Adler's individual psychology is his emphasis on the importance of human society. Human society is crucial not simply for the development of an individual personality, but also for the orientation of each and every behavior and emotion in a person's life.

Human beings, like all living creatures, are driven by certain innate instincts, drives, or needs. All living organisms feel an impulse to maintain life, which causes them to seek nourishment. They have a compulsion to reproduce the species, which finds its expression in sex. Although much of the behavior of lower animals appears to be regulated by instincts, this is not true of human behavior. Human beings have tamed their instincts and subordinated them to their attitudes toward the environment. At times, human beings deny or disobey their natural instincts because of their social relations. A prisoner may die rather than betray his country. A young child may refuse food if she believes that such a tactic puts her at the best advantage in a power struggle with her parents. A young woman may renounce her sexual desires if she believes it is in her best social interest to do so.

This shaping of instinctual expression in terms of one's attitude toward the environment suggests that underlying all other instincts and needs is the innate characteristic of social interest (1939). **Social interest** refers to that urge in human nature to adapt oneself to the conditions of the environment. Social interest expresses itself subjectively in one's consciousness of having something in common with other people and of being one of them. It expresses itself objectively in cooperation with others toward the betterment of human society. This innate social characteristic, while common to all, is not automatic nor does it invariably find constructive expression. It must be nurtured and cultivated if the individual is to achieve adequate fulfillment of the complex demands of his or her society and work toward its perfection.

Finalism

The personality and characteristics of an individual are developed by the attitudes that he or she adopts toward his or her social environment in early childhood. This occurs through the goal-oriented activity of the human psyche. Adler stresses the fact that the movement of all living things is governed by goals. We cannot think, feel, will, or act, except with the perception of some goal (1927). To try to understand human behavior in terms of external causes is to fail to understand psychic phenomena. If I know a person's goal, I begin to understand in a general way what is happening. It is this focus on ultimate goals that permits us to understand and recognize the unity of the human personality. Once a person's goal has been recognized, it is possible to see how the movements and behavior of that individual fall into line with both the goal and the plans that he or she has evolved for achieving the goal.

When an individual behaves in a certain way we naturally ask why. Past efforts to answer that question had emphasized material and mechanical explanations. Sigmund Freud showed us that it is not enough to look for physiological causes, that we must also try to understand the psychological motives underlying behavioral events. However, Freud was misled by the principle of causality into regarding these motives as past and looking to the past for the explanation of all human behavior. Adler emphasized the purposefulness of human behavior by recognizing that the motivational force of every human action is the goal or future orientation of that action. This means that for Adler the human psyche is teleologically oriented. We will recall from our discussion of Jung that the term "telos" means a purpose or goal. Adler agreed with Jung that teleology is necessary for a full understanding of personality. For Adler, the goal that the individual pursues was the decisive factor and he called this concept of goal orientation the principle of **finalism** (1930).

Adler suggests that many of our guiding goals are fictions. His use of the term "fiction" is puzzling, because the point is not that a fiction is false. Adler indicates that we cannot know whether or not our goals are true or false because there is no way in which we can scientifically test them. "Fiction" comes from the Latin root *fictio,* which means "to invent," "fashion," or "construct." We are unable to have a complete understanding of things as they really are, so we structure our own idea of reality. "Fictions" are an individual's or group's interpretations of the events of the world. They are philosophical assumptions. We assume that it is best to tell the truth, that all people are basically good, or that hard work will eventually pay off. In Adlerian vocabulary, such basic concepts are **fictional finalisms.** Adler was indebted to an earlier philosopher, Hans Vaihinger, for his concept of fictional finalisms. Vaihinger wrote a book, *The Philosophy of "As-if,"* in which he suggested that people create ideas that guide their behavior. Fictional finalisms cannot be tested against reality, because they are not scientific hypotheses that can be put to a crucial experiment. They are constructs or inventions of the human psyche that arise out of its encounter with the world. Under the influence of a fiction, people behave "as if" their goals were true. If people believe that it is to their best advantage to be honest, they will strive to be so, even though there is no way in which they can ultimately test that belief as a hypothesis. It is important to note that psychologists also often pose fictional finalisms in their discussion of the good life. Concepts such as the "healthy personality" and "self-actualization" function as fictional finalisms and cannot be empirically tested.

A fiction may be healthy or unhealthy. Adler's point here is that it is inappropriate to judge a fiction as true or false, right or wrong; rather, the goal should be judged according to its usefulness. Adler's concept of the **usefulness** of fictional finalisms should not be confused with the concept of usefulness in reference to scientific hypotheses, which was discussed in the introductory chapter. For Adler, a goal is useful if it fosters productive living and enhances our lives. The scientific hypothesis is useful if it can generate predictions about experiences that we might observe. Adler's point is that although fictions do not have any counterpart in reality, they do vary in terms of their usefulness: some goals foster productive living while others are harmful and hinder adjustment. Belief in a deity and the desire to serve him have proved to be a valuable fiction for many individuals. For others, however, belief in God and the desire to please him have had deleterious effects. Whether or not God really exists is beside the point; the point is that belief in God has a demonstrable effect, positive or negative, on the behavior and life of an individual. Healthy individuals (and psychologists, we might add) continually examine the effectiveness of their fictions and alter their goals when they are no longer useful. They maintain their fictions in a state of flux in order to meet the demands of reality.

Striving for Superiority

Adler suggests that the psyche has as its primary objective the **goal of superiority.** This is the ultimate fictional finalism for which all human beings strive and that gives unity and coherence to the personality. Initially, Adler conceived of the primary motivating force as aggression. Later, he identified the primary drive as a "will to power." Finally, he refined the concept of a drive toward power and suggested that the essential dynamic of human nature lies in its striving for superiority (1930).

Adler's concept of the striving for superiority does not entail the everyday meaning of the word "superiority." He did not mean that each of us innately seeks to surpass one another in rank or position, nor did he mean that we seek to maintain an attitude of exaggerated importance over our peers. Rather, the drive for superiority involves the desire to be competent and effective in whatever one is striving to do. The concept is similar to Jung's idea of self-actualization. Each one of us seeks to actualize, fulfill, and enhance our human potentialities. We strive for completion and unity — to be our best possible self. Thus, we seek to be superior within our own selves, not necessarily in competition with others. Adler frequently used the term *perfection* as a synonym for the word "superiority." This term can also be misleading unless we recognize its origin in the Latin *perfectus,* which means "completed" or "made whole."

The striving for superiority may take on the form of an exaggerated lust for power. An individual may seek to exercise control over objects and people and to play god. The goal may introduce a hostile tendency into our lives, in which we play games of "dog eat dog." But such expressions of the goal for superiority are abortive and do not reflect its constructive nature.

The striving for superiority is innate and part of the struggle for survival that human beings share with other species in the process of evolution. Life is not motivated by the need to reduce tension or restore equilibrium, as Freud tended to think; instead, life is encouraged by the desire to move from below to above, from minus to plus, from inferior to superior. This movement entails adapting oneself to and mastering the environment. The particular ways in which individuals undertake this quest are determined by their own unique history and style of life.

Inferiority Feelings

To be human, Adler suggests, is to feel inferior. The sense of inferiority is a part of the human condition that all persons share. **Inferiority feelings** have their origin in our encounter as infants with the environment. Throughout the whole period of childhood we feel inferior in our relations with parents and the world. As human infants, unlike other animals, we are born immature, incomplete, and incompetent to satisfy even our basic needs. There is a protracted period during which we are almost totally dependent on other people for our survival. Feelings of inferiority thus reflect a fact of existence. Children, in comparison to adults, are weak and inferior. Such feelings are inescapable, but also invaluable, as they provide the major motivating force that leads to growth. From our inferior position as children, we develop our goals of superiority. Our efforts and success at growth and development may be seen as attempts to compensate for and overcome our imagined or real inferiorities and weaknesses. Thus, feelings of inferiority are not deviant but are the basis for all forms of human accomplishment and improvement in life (1927).

The concept of human nature as driven by feelings of inferiority first came to Adler during his practice of general medicine. He observed that many of his patients localized their complaints in specific body organs. He hypothesized that in many cases an individual is born with a potentially weak organ that may not respond adequately to external demands (1917). This "organ inferiority" can have profound effects on both the body and the psyche. It may have a harmful effect and lead to neurotic disorders, but it can also be compensated for and lead to optimal achievements. A classic historical example of compensation is found in the story of the ancient Greek, Demosthenes, who suffered as a child from a speech impediment. He learned to overcome his stuttering and became a great orator by forcing himself to shout in front of

Our efforts to grow and develop may be seen as attempts to compensate for and overcome our inferiority feelings.

the ocean with pebbles in his mouth. Later, Adler broadened the concept of organ inferiority to include any feelings of inferiority, whether actual or imagined.

In his early writings, Adler termed the compensation for one's inferiorities the **masculine protest.** At the time, he associated inferiority with femininity. This concept finds common expression in our references to "the weaker" or "the stronger" sex. Adler himself was soon to become dissatisfied with this shortsighted view. Women may well be biologically different from men, but they are not on that account inferior. Later, he was to emphasize that inferiority has nothing to do with femininity; rather, it is a condition of existence that affects males and females alike. In that sense, Adler became an early proponent of women's liberation. He felt that none of the biological differences favored the male or justified a theory of inferiority of women. Basically, he recognized that the alleged inferiority of women was a social assignment rather than a biological one.

Adler's views were no doubt fostered by his marriage to Raissa Epstein, a member of the intelligentsia, who expected equality between them and helped him to overcome his earlier concepts of male dominance. Adler came to appreciate fully the role that society has played in perpetuating male dominance and privilege. Indeed, he went so far as to suggest that psychological differences between men and women are entirely the result of cultural attitudes. Adler pointed out the devastating effect of these attitudes on the lives of children and the development of their self-confidence. He described how such biases disturb the psychological development of women and have led them to a pervasive dissatisfaction with their role. The "excessive pre-eminence of man-liness" in our culture leads women into unhealthy forms of compensation or resignation and encourages men unwisely to depreciate and flee from women (Ansbacher and Ansbacher, 1956). Adler felt that exaggerated masculinity has a negative impact on men and women alike. He recommended the cultivation of comradeship and education for cooperation between the sexes. His ideas are confirmed today by research on sex roles and the influence of education.

Style of Life

Each individual seeks to cope with his or her environment and develop superiority in a unique way. This principle is embodied in Adler's concept of the **style of life,** which was a primary theme in his later writings (1929a, 1931). Each of us shares the common goal of striving for superiority, even though there are many different ways by which we may achieve this goal. One individual may try to develop competence and superiority through in-tellectual skills. Another may seek self-perfection by capitalizing on physical strengths. These different lifestyles develop early in childhood. Adler suggests that the lifestyle is pretty clearly established by the time a child is five years old. Thereafter it remains relatively constant. It can be changed, but only through hard work and self-examination.

The style of life results from a combination of two factors: the inner goal orientation of the individual with its particular fictional finalisms and the forces of the environment that assist, impede, or alter the direction of the individual. Each individual's style of life is unique because of the different influences of our inner self and its constructs. Adler imagines that no two individuals ever had or could have the very same style of life. Even identical twins respond to their environment in different ways.

Birth Order

Among the factors that lead to different lifestyles are the ordinal position of birth and different experiences in childhood. Adler does not postulate any stages of development but he emphasizes the importance of the atmosphere of the family and the family constellation. **Family constellation** refers to one's position within the family in terms of birth order among siblings and the presence or absence of parents and other caretakers. Adler hypothesizes that the personalities of oldest, middle, and youngest children in a family are apt to be quite dissimilar simply by virtue of the different experiences that each child has as that particular member of the family group.

Older children tend to be more intelligent, achievement-oriented, conforming, and affiliative. They often try to regain the glory that was theirs before they were dethroned by younger siblings. Thus, they are frequently oriented toward the past and show a high degree of concern with power, which may express itself as a desire to exercise authority or to protect and help others. Adler described Freud as a "typical eldest son."

The second child may feel the need to accelerate and catch up with the first child. While oldest children often dream of falling from places (dethronement), second children often dream of running to catch things. Second children are apt to be competitive and ambitious and often surpass the first-born in achievement and motivation. However, they are not as concerned with power. Adler was a second child.

Last-born children are more sociable and dependent, having been the "baby" of the family. At the same time they may also strive for excellence and superiority in an effort to surpass their many older siblings. Adler pointed out that many fairy tales, myths, and legends (for example, the biblical story of Joseph) describe the youngest child as surpassing his or her older rivals.

Only children tend to be more like older children in that they enjoy being the center of attention. Middle children show a combination of the characteristics of oldest and youngest. If children are spaced several years apart, they have more of the characteristics of only children. The family constellation becomes further complicated when one considers all the additional possibilities such as the only brother among sisters, twins, and so forth. In recent years a considerable amount of research has been done in the area of birth order and family constellation. One of the interesting findings suggests that longer marriages may occur among partners whose birth orders are complementary. Thus, an oldest brother of sisters will probably be happier with a younger sister to a brother than with an only child, because each of them is used to that familial pattern and mode of relating.

Exploration ///////

Birth Order and Personality

Read through the following lists and check those items that apply to you in comparison with your brothers and sisters. If you are an only child, check those items that apply to you in comparison with your peers.

List A
You tend to

1. be more conforming
2. be less hostile
3. have more motivation
4. be a better student
5. achieve more recognition
6. assume more leadership roles
7. be closer to your parents
8. like nurturing professions
9. consult others when making a decision
10. be less aggressive
11. associate more with others
12. receive high expectations from your parents
13. have similar values to your parents
14. seek help or nurturance from others
15. be more anxious
16. have more worries

Total ___9___

List B
You tend to

1. be more aggressive
2. be more democratic
3. be more independent
4. be more popular
5. value your parents' opinions less
6. like solitary professions
7. fight and "get into trouble" more
8. be a better mixer
9. like more dangerous activities
10. be less verbal
11. be less likely to seek help from others
12. be less conforming
13. "slide by" more
14. have been brought up less strictly by your parents
15. be more of a "loner"
16. have been given less attention by your parents

Total ___3___

Add up your totals in each list. If you are an only or a first-born child, the research indicates that more of the items on List A will apply to you. If you are a later-born (but not the youngest) more of the items on List B will apply. If you are the youngest child in a large family, your pattern will be closer to that of a first-born. If you are a middle child, you will show a combination of the characteristics of both lists. How do your findings compare with the research predictions?

Family Atmosphere

The quality of emotional relationships among members of the family reflects the **family atmosphere,** which assists in determining whether or not the child will react actively or passively, constructively or destructively, in the quest toward superiority. Children who are spoiled or neglected were thought by Adler to be particularly predisposed to a faulty style of life. The spoiled child is one who is excessively pampered and protected from life's inevitable frustrations. Such a child is actually being deprived of the right to become independent and learn the requirements of living within a social order. Parents who spoil a child make it difficult for the child to develop social feelings and become a useful member of society. The child grows to dislike order and develops a hostile attitude toward it. The neglected child is one who is unwanted and rejected. Such a child is virtually denied the right to a place in the social order. Rejection arouses resistance in the child, feelings of inferiority, and a tendency to withdraw from the implications of social life. Adler points out that child-rearing practices frequently consist of a continuing alternation between indulgence and rejection. The spoiled child demands undue attention and regard, which eventually leads to parental anger and punishment that are often interpreted by the child as rejection. Though few parents actually reject their children, many children feel humiliated and defeated.

Although parental "rejection" is overcome when parents learn better ways to handle their children, Adler stresses that the individual is fully responsible for the meaning attached to parental behavior and action. Many of us harbor deep feelings of having been rejected by our parents when in actuality they gave us their best efforts. Thus, in the end, only the person can assume responsibility for the style of life that he or she has adopted.

The Creative Self

A concept that Adler considered to be the climax of his theory is that of the **creative self** (1964). In a sense, I have been referring to the creative self all along. It is the self in its creative aspects that interprets and makes meaningful the experiences of the organism and that searches for experiences to fulfill the person's unique style of life. In other words, the creative self establishes, maintains, and pursues the goals of the individual. Adler's concept of the creative self underscored his belief that human nature is essentially active, creative, and purposeful in shaping its response to the environment.

The concept of the creative self also reinforces Adler's affirmation that individuals make their own personalities from the raw materials of their heredity and environment. In his concept of the creative self, Adler restored consciousness to the center of personality. Adler believed that we are aware of everything we do and that, through self-examination, we can understand why we behaved in a certain way. The forces of which we are unaware are simply unnoticed; they are not buried in a sea of repression.

Adler's position here was in such direct contrast to that of Freud that it is no wonder the two could not work together. Adler was not unaware of unconscious forces, but he minimized them by reducing unconsciousness to simple temporary unawareness. He opposed Freud's determinism by emphasizing the vast extent to which a person can achieve conscious control over his or her behavior. People, Adler argued, may become largely aware of their deepest impulses and fictional finalisms, and with conscious intent create their own personalities and lifestyles that will achieve their highest goals. In the end, Adler's position was almost the complete opposite of Freud's, which emphasized that our behavior is largely determined by forces of which we are unaware. Freud offered his followers the hope of being able to endure and live without crippling fear of one's unconscious conflicts, but he never offered freedom from them. By restoring consciousness to the center of personality, by again crowning the king Freud had struggled so valiantly to dethrone, Adler aroused Freud's anger. To Freud, Adler was encouraging the very illusion that Freud had sought to destroy.

For many people, Adler's optimistic view provides a welcome contrast to the pessimistic and conflict-ridden picture of human nature shown in Freudian psychoanalysis. It is comforting to believe that we make and create our personalities. Once again, we can be masters of our fate. In his optimism, Adler foreshadowed the humanistic school of personality, which I shall discuss later in Chapters 12 and 13.

Adlerian Psychotherapy

Neuroses, according to Adler (1929b), entail unrealistic life goals or fictional finalisms. Goals are not realistic unless they take into account our capacities, limitations, and social environment. A person who felt extremely inferior or rejected as a child may set goals that are too high and unattainable. A person of average intelligence cannot expect to perform at a consistently outstanding level in academic work. Some individuals adopt goals that are unrealistically low. Having felt defeated and unable to cope with certain situations, such as marriage, people may seek to avoid situations in which they could develop and perfect those skills that would enable them to perform effectively.

Neurotics also choose inappropriate lifestyles as a means of attaining their goals. In their efforts to compensate for feelings of weakness, neurotics tend to overcompensate. **Compensation** entails making up for or overcoming a weakness. **Overcompensation** refers to an exaggerated effort to cover up a weakness that entails a denial rather than an acceptance of the real situation (1954). The bully who persists in attempting to force others to play his way may be overcompensating for a difficulty in working cooperatively with others.

Adler's terms "inferiority complex" and "superiority complex," phrases that have become commonplace in our vocabulary, also describe neurotic patterns. If an individual feels highly inadequate, we suggest that he or she is suffering from an **inferiority complex.** In Adlerian terms, there is a gulf between the real person and his or her excessively high life goals. If an individual exaggerates his or her importance, we use the label **superiority complex.** In Adlerian terms, such an individual has overcompensated for feelings of weakness. Both complexes have their origin in a person's responses to real or imagined feelings of inferiority.

Adler suggests that neurotics actually live a **life lie.** Their style of life belies their actual capacities and strengths. They act "as if" they were weak, "as if" they were doomed to be losers, when in fact they could create a constructive existence for themselves. They capitalize on imagined or real weaknesses and use them as an excuse rather than a challenge to deal constructively with life. They employ **safeguarding tendencies,** compensatory devices that ward off feelings of inferiority in a maladaptive rather than adaptive fashion. To be sure, we all use such protective defense mechanisms at times, but neurotics employ them in an exaggerated manner and degree.

Adlerian therapy aims at restoring the patient's sense of reality, examining and disclosing the errors in his or her goals and lifestyle, and cultivating social interest. Adler did not establish strict rules or methods for treatment; he believed that the patient's lifestyle should determine the procedure. On the whole, Adler's approach was more informal than Freud's. He abandoned the use of the couch, suggested that the patient sit facing the therapist, and reduced the frequency of contact between patient and doctor.

The first goal of the Adlerian therapist is to establish contact with the patient and win his or her confidence (1929b). Such confidence is won by approaching the patient as a comrade, rather than an authority, and thereby eliciting cooperation. Whereas Freud viewed the transference, in which a patient works through earlier unsatisfactory relations by projecting them onto the doctor, as essential to the effectiveness of treatment, Adler suggested that therapy is effective because healthy features of the physician-patient relationship are transferred, or carried over, into the patient's life. Such transference need not have regressive features and is really another name for the cultivation of social feeling.

Second, the therapist seeks to disclose the errors in the patient's lifestyle and provide insight into his or her present condition. The patient is led gently and gradually to recognize the errors in his or her goals, lifestyle, and attitude toward life. Early memories of childhood and dreams were seen by Adler to be excellent sources of information about a person. Together, they enable us to trace an individual's "life line" or lifestyle. Early memories frequently summarize the essential characteristics of our stance toward life, because the lifestyle is generally chosen by the time we are four or five and our selective memory thereafter tends to reflect experiences that are in line with our basic attitudes. For example, Adler observed that the first memories of doctors often entail the recollection of an illness or death. Dreams, rather than reflecting the past, are goal oriented. They reveal the mood that we want to feel and suggest how we intend to deal with a problem or task of the immediate future. Taking note of the options that we choose to follow in our dream life gives us further insight into our style of life.

Adlerian therapy seeks to encourage the patient to face present problems and to develop constructive means of dealing with them. The therapist hopes to instill (or promote) the courage to act "as if" the old limiting fictions and life lies weren't true. Although the therapist does not make decisions or assume responsibilities for the patient, he or she may structure or suggest situations that will assist in cultivating the patient's own skills. Such deliberate attempts at encouragement enable the patient to become more courageous and to accept new tasks and responsibilities. In this sense, the therapist plays the role of an educator who re-educates the neurotic in the art of constructive living. Additionally, Adler sought to minimize latent feelings of rejection and resentment and to cultivate feelings of social interest and good will. Adler believed that only by subordinating our private gain to public welfare can we attain true superiority. The true and inevitable compensation for all the natural weaknesses of individual human beings is that of social justice for all.

Albert Ellis's system of rational-emotive therapy (1973), which holds that behaviors are a function of beliefs, draws on Adler's individual psychology. Many of Adler's concepts have been used to develop more effective methods of child-rearing and education (Dreikurs, 1952–1953). Adler emphasized again and again the value of education. As creative selves, we construct the primary forces that shape our existence: our goals and lifestyles. We can change these, should they become maladaptive, through insight into our errors. Thus, education and training are of the utmost importance. Through education, Adler believed, our innate and shared concept of social interest and justice could be made to flower and to provide the final and most appropriate form of compensation for our individual weaknesses. Adler was active in child guidance clinics and involved in penal reform. He was attracted to the political movement of socialism and many hours of his later years were devoted to specifying ways of educating for social justice.

Adler's Theory: Philosophy, Science, and Art

Adler's commitment to a philosophical viewpoint is clearly seen in his discussion of fictional finalisms. Human beings, he asserted, are goal-oriented organisms, and all human behavior may be understood in terms of its contribution and adherence to a goal. Difficulties in living result from an inappropriate philosophy

Exploration

First Memories

Your early memories probably refer to experiences that are in line with your basic goals, and they may be used by you to justify your present stance. It is unimportant whether or not the remembered events really happened. Even imagined memories may be revealing. Jot down your earliest memories. When you have finished, pretend that you are an observer studying someone else's actions and behavior. Ask yourself, "What goal might a person be trying to accomplish by acting in this manner?" Then, on the basis of your memories, complete these sentences: "I am _____. Others are _____. Life is _____. Therefore, I must _____." Compare the goals expressed in your early memories with those that are currently present in your dreams. In our dreams, we are not bound by realistic or common-sense solutions to our problems. Our dreams reveal how we would like to cope with issues in our lives. Running away from a dream monster may be indicative of the desire to run away from a current problem. Being paralyzed in a dream may suggest a style of playing helpless in the face of pressing demands. Look for consistencies and similar postures in your early memories and current dreams. If the goals therein appear unattainable, or the lifestyle ineffective, you may wish to examine further their usefulness. In the course of successful therapy, Adler also discovered that patients frequently recall new, previously overlooked memories that are more consistent with their newly won lifestyles.

and the inappropriate style of life that accompanies it. By recognizing and cultivating the need for social justice, a person fulfills his or her ultimate potential.

Adler added *usefulness* to the criteria for judging philosophical assumptions: a philosophy is useful if it fosters productive living and enhances our lives. In doing so, he followed the pragmatic philosophy of William James (1842–1910), who argued that the meaning of a statement lies in the particular enriching consequences it has for our future experiences and the quality of our lives. Adler's emphasis on the importance of the usefulness of our goals has been very popular among psychologists and personality theorists.

Adler added *usefulness* to the criteria for judging philosophical assumptions: a philosophy is useful if it fosters productive living and enhances our lives. In doing so, he followed the pragmatic philosophy of William James order theory (Vockell, Felker, and Miley, 1973; Howarth, 1983) and his belief that early memories reflect personality traits (Reichlin and Niederehe, 1980). Not all of the research supports Adler's findings, but it is easy to see that his theory has been valuable in stimulating further thinking and research.

Adler emphasized the factors in society that shape personality. On the other hand, he did not adopt a radical environmentalist position and suggest that personality is entirely shaped by society. There are forces within the self, such as the drive for superiority and the creative self, that assist in shaping personality.

Adler was more optimistic than Freud about human and societal potentialities. He saw human nature as flexible and changeable. The forward-moving tendency within the self, the drive for superiority, implies that obstacles to growth are imposed by society rather than by human nature itself. At the same time, through the creative self, human beings largely create their own personalities. Ultimately, Adler envisioned the possibility of creating a better society through the cultivation of our social interest. He stressed the application of personality theory through the art of psychotherapy, believing that through self-understanding and education we can construct a better world.

Adler's emphasis on the social forces that shape personality influenced subsequent social psychoanalytic theorists like Karen Horney, Harry Stack Sullivan, and Erich Fromm. Adler's optimistic constructs also influenced the humanistic school of thought in psychology. Thus, Adler's ideas and their application have become widespread even though they are sometimes not recognized as Adlerian.

❧ Summary

1. Adler's **individual psychology** marks a shift from an emphasis on **intra-psychic** ("within the psyche") phenomena to an emphasis on **interpsychic** ("interpersonal") phenomena.

2. Adler believed that human beings have an innate urge to adapt themselves to the conditions of the environment. He named this urge **social interest** but stressed that it is not automatic and must be cultivated.

3. The principle of **finalism** means that individuals are oriented toward goals that guide their behavior. However, these individual interpretations of the world cannot be proven and are therefore called **fictional finalisms.** Adler suggests that they be judged by their **usefulness.**

4. The primary objective of the psyche is the **goal of superiority,** the desire to be competent and effective in what one does. This striving may take on the form of an exaggerated lust for power.

5. As young children, we feel inferior and these **inferiority feelings** lead us to seek ways in which we can compensate for our weaknesses.

6. Each individual develops a unique way of striving for superiority that is called his or her **style of life.** The style of life is influenced by factors such as **family constellation** and **family atmosphere.**

7. Adler considered the concept of the **creative self** to be the climax of his theory. The creative self interprets the experiences of the organism and establishes a person's lifestyle. Adler's position is that the creative self is essentially conscious and he restores consciousness to the center of personality (in direct opposition to Freud's view).

8. Adlerian therapy aims at restoring the patient's sense of reality, examining and disclosing the errors in his or her goals and lifestyle, and cultivating social interest. He believed early memories and dreams are excellent sources of information about a person.

9. Adler's theory emphasizes a philosophical point of view rather than an effort to study personality empirically. He also made substantial contributions to psychotherapy, education, and child-rearing.

Suggestions for Further Reading

Alfred Adler wrote a number of books and articles. Since his writings were often intended for a lay audience, they are relatively easy to understand. The classic introduction to Adlerian thought is *The Practice and Theory of Individual Psychology* (Harcourt, Brace, 1927). A shorter summary, "Individual Psychology," appears in C. Murchison (Ed.), *Psychologies of 1930* (Clark University Press, 1930). Selections of Adler's writings have also been edited and presented by H. L. and Rowena R. Ansbacher (Basic Books, 1956, 1964).

For biographical data and an assessment of Adler's contemporary influence, the reader is referred to H. Orgler, *Alfred Adler: The Man and His Work* (New American Library, 1972); H. Musak (Ed.), *Alfred Adler: His Influence on Psychology Today* (Noyes, 1973); M. Sperber, *Masks of Loneliness: Alfred Adler in Perspective* (Macmillan, 1974); and H. L. Ansbacher, *Alfred Adler Revisited* (Praeger, 1984).

4

Karen Horney: Psychosocial Analysis

Your Goals for This Chapter

1. Describe Horney's concept of *basic anxiety* and explain how it differs from Freud's concept of anxiety.

2. Explain how ten *neurotic trends* can be summarized in terms of three ways of relating to others and three *basic orientations* toward life.

3. Distinguish between the *real self* and the *idealized self.*

4. Explain the relationship of the real self and the idealized self in normal, neurotic, and alienated individuals.

5. Compare and contrast Freud's and Horney's views of women.

6. Describe the process of *self-analysis.*

7. Evaluate Horney's theory in terms of its function as philosophy, science, and art.

Karen Horney did not try to develop a full-scale personality theory. Rather, she concentrated on the neurotic aspects of behavior in order to help us understand why we behave as we do. Horney subscribed to much of Freud's work but sought to overcome what she perceived as his limitations by emphasizing social and cultural factors and minimizing biological ones. Her work provides us with a number of fascinating insights and provocative concepts that have received a lot of attention.

Biographical Background

Karen Danielson Horney was born in 1885 near Hamburg, Germany, into an upper-middle class family that was economically and socially secure. Her father was of Norwegian descent and her mother was Dutch. As a child, Horney sometimes traveled with her father, a sea captain. Although Horney admired her father, he was frequently stern and sullen. His intense gazes frightened her and he was often critical of her intelligence, interests, and appearance. Because of her father's long absences from home, Horney spent considerably more time with her mother, a dynamic, attractive, freethinking woman who greatly influenced her daughter. Karen was devoted to her mother even though at times she felt that she favored her older brother. Mrs. Danielson encouraged her daughter to become a physician at a time when it was unusual for women to enter that profession and in spite of rigid opposition from her husband. It was not the first time that the differences of temperament in Horney's parents led to discord. Eventually they separated and Horney's mother moved near Freiburg, where her daughter was pursuing her studies at the university. Later, Horney emphasized in her writings the role that a stressful environment plays in nurturing basic anxiety. Lack of love and encouragement, quarrelsome parents, and other stressful environmental factors lead to feelings of rejection, worthlessness, and hostility. She acknowledged these feelings in herself and worked hard to overcome them.

Horney received her degree in medicine from the University of Berlin. Thereafter she was associated with the Berlin Psychoanalytic Institute. She was analyzed by Karl Abraham and Hans Sachs, loyal disciples of Freud, who were two of the foremost training analysts of the day.

In 1909 she married Oscar Horney, a Berlin lawyer. They had three daughters. As a result of their different interests and her increased involvement in the psychoanalytic movement, they were divorced in 1937. The challenges of being a career woman, a mother, and of dissolving a marriage that was no longer viable gave her considerable insight into the problems of women. We will see that she was one of the first to speak directly to the issue of feminine psychology.

Karen Horney

Horney spent most of her life in Berlin, but in 1932 she was invited to come to the United States and assume the position of associate director of the Chicago Psychoanalytic Institute. Two years later, she moved to New York City, opened a private practice, and taught at the New York Psychoanalytic Institute.

Coming to America during the Great Depression, she began to appreciate more and more the role of environmental factors in neurosis. Her patients were not troubled primarily by sexual problems but with keeping a job and paying bills. Economic, educational, occupational, and social pressures seemed to be foremost in inducing neurotic behavior. Although earlier she had had disagreements with the Freudian point of view, orthodox psychoanalysis with its stress on genetic and instinctual causes of behavior appeared increasingly one-sided. Eventually her dissatisfaction led her to leave the orthodox movement and found the Association for the Advancement of Psychoanalysis and the American Institute of Psychoanalysis. She was dean of the Institute until her death, of cancer, in 1952.

Basic Anxiety

Karen Horney suggests that anxiety is the basic human condition with which we have to deal. This idea is reminiscent of Freud's belief that anxiety is the basic human condition into which we are thrust. But, unlike Freud, Horney does not see anxiety as an inevitable part of the human condition. She suggests that anxiety is created by social forces rather than by the human predicament itself.

As human beings, our essential challenge is to be able to relate effectively to other people. **Basic anxiety** (1945) results from feelings of insecurity in these relations. According to Horney's concept of basic anxiety, the environment as a whole is dreaded because it is seen as unrealistic, dangerous, unappreciative, and unfair. Children are not simply afraid of their own inner impulses or of punishment because of their impulses, as Freud postulated in his concepts of neurotic and moral anxiety; they also feel at times that the environment itself is a threat to their development and innermost wishes. A variety of negative conditions in the environment can produce the lack of security entailed in basic anxiety: domination, isolation, overprotection, hostility, indifference, inconsistent behavior, disparagement, parental discord, lack of respect and guidance, or the lack of encouragement and warmth. Children's fears are not unrealistic, but real. In a hostile environment, the ability of children to use their energies and develop self-esteem and reliance is, in fact, thwarted. Children may be rendered powerless in the face of these encroachments on their environment. Their biological dependency and the lack of parental fostering of adaptive self-assertive behavior may leave them helpless. Although children may endure a certain amount of frustration and trauma, it is essential that they feel safe and secure.

Neurotic Trends

In the face of adverse circumstances, people develop certain defense attitudes or strategies that permit them to cope with the world and afford a certain measure of gratification (1937). Specifically, we use these strategies to deal with or minimize feelings of anxiety and to assist us in effectively relating to others. Where they become exaggerated or inappropriate these strivings may be referred to as **neurotic trends.** The trends are not instinctual in nature but highly dependent on the situation in which a person lives. Horney

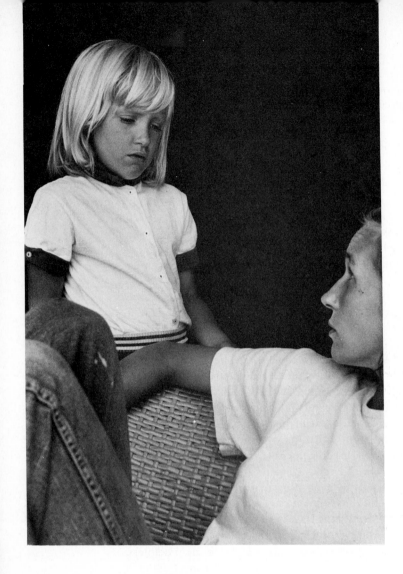

When children are threatened by a hostile environment, it is important that they be made to feel safe and secure.

criticizes Freud for his image of neurotic needs as instinctual or derivative of the instincts. She places environmental factors at the center of personality development.

Horney outlines ten different neurotic trends (see Table 4.1). These trends lead to three types of behavior toward other people: **moving toward** (compliance), **moving against** (hostility), and **moving away** (detachment). These types of behavior lead, in turn, to three **basic orientations** toward life: the **self-effacing solution,** or an appeal to be loved; the **self-expansive solution,** or a striving for mastery; and the **resignation solution,** or a desire to be free of others (1950). Normal or mature individuals resolve their conflicts by integrating and balancing the three orientations, which are present in all

Table 4.1 *Horney's Ten Neurotic Trends Reflect Three Primary Modes of Relating to Others and Three Basic Orientations Toward Life Itself.*

Neurotic trends	Primary modes of relating to others	Basic orientations toward life
Exaggerated need for affection and approval Need for a dominant partner	Moving toward: accepting one's helplessness and becoming compliant	Self-effacing solution: an appeal to be loved
Exaggerated need for power Need to exploit others Exaggerated need for social recognition or prestige Exaggerated need for personal admiration Exaggerated ambition for personal achievement	Moving against: rebelling and resisting others to protect one's self from a threatening environment	Self-expansive solution: a striving for mastery
Need to restrict one's life within narrow boundaries Exaggerated need for self-sufficiency and independence Need for perfection and unassailability	Moving away: isolating one's self to avoid involvement with others	Resignation solution: the desire to be free of others

SOURCE: Based on information in K. Horney, *Self-Analysis,* New York: Norton, 1942; K. Horney, *Our Inner Conflicts,* New York: Norton, 1945; and K. Horney, *Neurosis and Human Growth,* New York: Norton, 1950. Used by permission of W. W. Norton & Co. and Routledge & Kegan Paul.

human relations. They are able to express each mode at the appropriate time. Neurotics express one mode at the expense of the other aspects of their personality. They actively, although unconsciously, repress tendencies to react according to the other orientations. This repression, of course, is not successful; the repressed tendencies continue to seek expression and increase the neurotics' anxiety. Thus neurotics transform normal strivings into pathological ones. Table 4.1 summarizes the ten neurotic trends, three modes of relating to others, and three basic orientations toward life.

The Idealized Self

Karen Horney (1950) also distinguishes between the real self and the idealized self. The **real self** represents that which a person actually is. The **idealized**

self represents that which a person thinks he or she should be and is used as a model to assist us in developing our potential and achieve self-actualization. The dynamic of creating an idealized self in order to facilitate self-realization is universal and characteristic of each of us. In my attempt to be a competent teacher I posit an ideal of what an effective teacher is like. In the normal individual, the idealized self and the real self largely coincide because the idealized self is based on a realistic assessment of one's abilities and potentials. But in the neurotic, the real self and the idealized self are distinct or separated. This situation can be represented diagrammatically by circles as is shown in Figure 4.1.

A person is only able to recognize and develop those aspects of the real self that coincide with the idealized self. Thus, as neurosis becomes more severe, an increasing amount of the powers and potentialities of the real self may be rendered unavailable for cultivation. In an extreme neurosis, the individual may completely abandon the real self for the sake of the idealized self (see Figure 4.2). Horney refers to this situation as one of **alienation** (or *the devil's pact*). In a state of alienation, a person identifies with the ideal self in a form of neurotic entitlement and thereby loses his or her true source of strength, since our only source of strength comes from who we really are.

For example, should an individual have the concept that in order to be a good person, he must never feel jealous, he might posit an idealized self that does not permit feelings of jealousy. Because his idealized self does not include jealous feelings, he may be unable to acknowledge feelings of jealousy that arise. Therefore, the part of his real self that does experience feelings of jealousy is denied. The individual becomes estranged from a part of himself.

A classic illustration clarifies Horney's point: normal individuals, by and large, are happy with and function within the everyday world. Neurotics are unhappy with the everyday world. Therefore, they build castles in the sky. They function in the everyday world, but to the extent that they are dreaming about their castles, they do not function as effectively as they might. Extreme neurotics abandon the everyday world and attempt to go and live in their castles in the air. Such total identification with the idealized self renders these individuals virtually unable to cope.

Horney's concept of the idealized self may be seen as a constructive revision or correction of Freud's concept of the ego-ideal. We recall that Freud's concept of the superego included two aspects: an introjected social conscience and an ego-ideal that was an idealized image consisting of approved and rewarded behaviors. The ego-ideal was the source of pride and provided a concept of who we think we should be. Horney's concept of the idealized self is an elaboration of the Freudian concept of the ego-ideal. In her elaboration, Horney rejects the instinctual basis of Freud's concept of the superego that was derived from the self-destructive instinct. Instead, Horney emphasizes

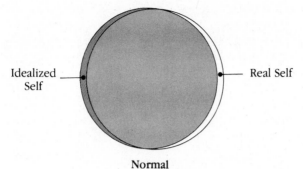

Normal
In the normal individual, the circles largely coincide.

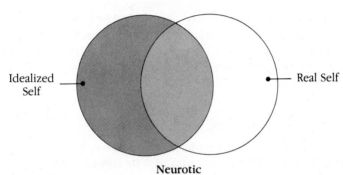

Neurotic
In the neurotic individual, the circles are increasingly distinct.

Figure 4.1 *The Normal and Neurotic Self*
Circles can be used to represent the real and idealized self in Horney's theory of personality.

social factors that influence the development of an idealized self. Furthermore, Horney does not view the idealized self as a special agency within the ego but as a special need of the individual to keep up appearances of perfection. She also points out that the need to maintain an unrealistic idealized self does not entail simply repression of "bad" feelings and forces within the self. It also entails repression of valuable and legitimate feelings that are repressed because they might endanger the mask. The repression of sexual and aggressive feelings and emotions that are thought to be socially undesirable frequently carries with it repression of spontaneous feelings, wishes, and judgments that

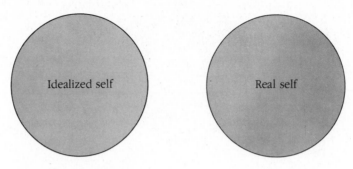

Figure 4.2 *The State of Alienation*

are legitimate and constructive to individual growth. A woman, for example, may through the repression of her sexual desires attain an appearance of being socially and morally uncorrupt, but this mask is achieved at the expense of her not fulfilling her sexual desires and it may lead to her losing touch with other important messages from her body.

Feminine Psychology

Karen Horney's interest in feminine psychology was stimulated by the fact that certain clinical observations appeared to contradict Freud's theory of the libido. In his concept of libidinal development, sexual activities and attitudes appeared to be instinctual and inevitable processes that were unaffected by culture or society.

Freud had suggested that penis envy was largely responsible for a woman's development, that women view themselves as castrated males. Horney points out that both men and women develop fantasies in their efforts to cope with the Oedipal situation. She also reminds us that many men and boys express jealousy over the woman's ability to bear and nurse children, a phenomenon that has since been clearly seen in primitive puberty rites as well as in clinical settings.

Horney termed this phenomenon **womb envy.** Her work suggests that womb envy and penis envy are complements (1967). The appearance of these attitudes does not necessarily reflect unsatisfactory development or harmful emotions but rather shows the mutual attraction and envy that the sexes have for each other.

Horney believed that the essence of sexual life lies in its biological creative powers. It follows that a greater role in sexual life belongs to the female because she is the one who is able to bear and nurse children. The woman's capacity for motherhood demonstrates her "indisputable superiority." This superiority is recognized by the male and is the source of intense envy.

Womb envy, rather than being openly acknowledged by the male, has often taken subtle and indirect forms, such as the need to disparage women, belittle their achievements, and deny them equal rights. Similar attempts to deal with these feelings have led men to equate the term "feminine" with passiveness and to conceive of activity as the prerogative of the male.

Both men and women have an impulse to be creative and productive. Women can satisfy this need naturally through procreation. Men can satisfy their need only indirectly, through accomplishments in the external world. Thus, Horney suggests that the impressive achievements of men in work or other creative fields may be seen as compensations for their inability to bear children.

The woman's sense of inferiority is not constitutional but acquired. In a patriarchal society, the attitude of the male has predominated and succeeded in convincing women of their supposed inadequacies. But these are cultural and social factors that shape development, not biological ones. If a "flight from womanhood" can be observed in our society, it is due not to instinctual developments but to the experience of real social and cultural disadvantages that women have suffered under. Sexual unresponsiveness, Horney points out, is not the normal attitude of women. It is the result of cultural factors. Our society, as has been well acknowledged, is a male society, and therefore for the most part it is not amenable to the unfolding of a woman's individuality.

Although Horney's psychology of women, which is almost a direct inversion of Freud's theory, has met with criticism from those who do not agree that the essence of being a woman lies in motherhood, her contributions to feminine psychology have been very valuable. In her own life she struggled valiantly to resolve some of the problems that face women in contemporary culture, successfully combining motherhood with an active career.

Self-Analysis

Psychoanalysis was first developed as a medical method of treatment for neurotic disorders. Karen Horney (1942) suggests and demonstrates that it can also be an assistance to normal personality development. Through the process of **self-analysis,** significant gains may be made in self-understanding and in freeing human beings from inner bondages that hinder them in developing their best potentialities.

Although Horney acknowledged that self-analysis is difficult and painful, she believed that it is possible. The world in which each one of us lives is familiar to us because it is our world. Because it is ours, in certain respects we can understand it better than any outside observer can. While it is true that many of us have become estranged from parts of our world and desire not to see them, the fact remains that knowledge about our world is available to us. By observing and then examining our observations, we can gain access to those aspects of our world that we have neglected.

To those critics who were concerned that self-analysis might be dangerous, Horney pointed out that the advantages that might accrue from self-analysis outweigh any possible dangers. The likelihood of danger is minimized in self-analysis because an individual who is attempting to analyze him- or herself will simply fail to make observations that might be intolerable and lead to further personality disorientation. While self-analysis can never be considered an adequate substitute for professional analysis of neurosis, its possible benefits for enhancing individual development merit its use.

Each one of us engages in self-analysis when we try to account for the motives behind our behaviors. A student who fails a test that she thought was unfair might ask whether she had properly prepared for it. An individual who yields to another in a disagreement might ask if he gave in because he was convinced that the other's point of view was superior or because he was afraid of a possible argument. Such analyses are a common phenomenon in normal living.

Systematic self-analysis differs from occasional self-analysis in degree rather than kind, entailing a serious and protracted effort for self-understanding undertaken on a regular basis. Systematic self-analysis employs the tool of free association, followed by reflection on what one has thought and an analysis of the resistance that aims to maintain the status quo. Obtaining insight into one's personality frees energies that were previously engaged in perpetuating neurotic trends for use in making constructive changes.

Horney's Theory: Philosophy, Science, and Art

Horney was an astute observer and talented clinician. She frequently tested, revised, and discarded her theories in the light of new observations. She asserted that certain therapeutic approaches bring forth desired and predictable changes in behavior, changes that can be observed during the course of therapy if not in a rigorous laboratory experiment. She was clearly engaged in scientific activity and believed that her method and therapy must be open to scientific investigation and research. Because her ideas do not lend themselves easily to objective test, however, her theory has not generated much specific laboratory experimentation.

Horney was not greatly interested in abstract thinking, but her theory does reflect deep philosophical commitments, such as a belief in the process of growth and forward movement (akin to Jung's concept of self-actualization)

Exploration /////

Self-Analysis

While there is no prescribed recipe, Karen Horney's general suggestions may be used by the reader who is interested in pursuing self-analysis. Horney considered the pursuit of self-knowledge a privilege and a responsibility that all of us can use to advantage.

In developing your own self-analysis, begin by investigating one problem area that you can clearly identify. Each analysis produces its own sequence or order of events. Half-hidden problems need not be tackled immediately. They will emerge in the course of analysis if they are genuine problems. Nor is it necessary to feel that you should explore every aspect of your inner life. It is enough to begin with problems that are obvious to you.

Suppose you are concerned about your relationship with your parents. Following the steps outlined by Horney, you would begin your analysis by making free associations about your parents. When thoughts stop flowing or a particular item provokes your curiosity, you might stop and begin tentatively to interpret your findings. This in essence is the heart of the analytic process: free association followed by reflection on one's thoughts. In the process, you may discover certain resistances that impede your analytic work. Further free association is helpful in dealing with such resistances.

In working through a problem, sometimes it helps to raise specific questions. You might ask, "Is my relationship a realistic matter of concern?" "Are the interpersonal standards that I have set commensurate with my abilities and willingness to change things?" "Can I identify specific problem areas?" "In my own opinion, what am I doing that might account for a poorer relationship than I desire?" "What is the simplest thing that I might do about it?" These questions can be rephrased to take account of other problems. Raising questions like these and attempting to answer them can set tendencies toward growth in motion.

and an optimistic view of human nature. Toward the end of her life she became interested in Zen Buddhist writings and practices. The underlying philosophical assumptions that support her work are both profound and compelling.

Horney's contributions to the art of psychotherapy have been particularly valuable. Her theory and therapeutic techniques have been adopted by many clinicians. Several aspects of her technique are discussed in current Freudian literature as useful additions to psychoanalysis.

Horney has been criticized for simply elaborating on concepts that were implied but not clearly expressed in Freud's writings; however, these elaborations contain valuable, original contributions. Horney clarified the ego-ideal; her concept of neurotic trends clarified Freudian defense mechanisms; and she provided more insight into the psychology of women. These substantial contributions to psychoanalysis should not be minimized.

✿ Summary

1. Horney describes **basic anxiety** as anxiety that results from feelings of insecurity in interpersonal relations. Unlike Freud, she did not believe that anxiety is an inevitable part of the human condition.

2. Basic anxiety is reflected in ten **neurotic trends,** which lead to three ways of relating to others (**moving toward, moving against,** and **moving away**) and to three **basic orientations** toward life: the **self-effacing solution,** the **self-expansive solution,** and the **resignation solution.**

3. The **real self** represents that which a person actually is; the **idealized self** represents that which a person thinks he or she should be.

4. In a normal individual the real self and the idealized self closely coincide, but in a neurotic individual they are more separate. In extreme cases of **alienation,** a person may completely abandon the real self for the sake of the idealized self.

5. Horney's view of women is almost a direct inversion of Freud's. Whereas Freud suggests the phenomenon of penis envy in women, Horney points out the phenomenon of **womb envy** in men. She emphasizes the superiority of women as reflected in their capacity for motherhood and stresses that a woman's sense of inferiority is not constitutional but acquired.

6. **Self-analysis** is difficult but not impossible. It entails a serious and protracted effort for self-understanding undertaken on a regular basis.

7. Horney's greatest contribution has been to the art of psychotherapy.

Suggestions for Further Reading

Karen Horney's writings, clear and easy to read, have attracted a large lay audience. *New Ways in Psychoanalysis* (Norton, 1939) describes Horney's disagreement with Freudian theory: her belief that its stress on instinctual determinants is one-sided and needs to be rounded out by the consideration of cultural and social elements. *The Neurotic Personality of Our Time* (Norton, 1937), *Our Inner Conflicts* (Norton, 1945), and *Neurosis and Human Growth*

(Norton, 1950) outline Horney's theory of neurosis. Identifying ten neurotic needs in the earliest book, Horney's thought develops through the concept of three modes of relating to others and, later, three basic orientations to life. In the last book, Horney introduces the concept of the idealized self. Her writings on the psychology of women have been brought together in *Feminine Psychology* (Norton, 1967). *Self-Analysis* (Norton, 1942) familiarizes the lay person with the methods and techniques of psychoanalysis. It is an invaluable work for any individual who is interested in pursuing his or her own self-understanding through analysis.

5

Harry Stack Sullivan: Interpersonal Psychiatry

Your Goals for This Chapter

1. Identify the primary emphasis in Sullivan's theory of personality.

2. Explain how Sullivan defines *personality* and explain why he conceives of it as a hypothesis.

3. Compare Sullivan's concept of *anxiety* with those of other theorists.

4. Describe Sullivan's view of unconscious forces.

5. Compare Sullivan's notion of *security operations* and Freud's concept of defense mechanisms.

6. Define and give examples of *dynamisms*.

7. Define and give examples of *personifications*.

8. Identify the stages of personality development outlined by Sullivan.

9. Describe three *cognitive processes* by which we experience the world.

10. Explain how the concept of *participant observation* defines the nature of Sullivan's method of treatment and describe four stages of the psychiatric *interview*.

11. Evaluate Sullivan's theory in terms of its function as philosophy, science, and art.

*H*arry Stack Sullivan emphasizes the interpersonal nature of personality, providing us with unusual insight into the ways in which we interact with others. He believed that the personality of an individual can never be studied in isolation, since we do not exist separately and independently from other persons. Hence he explored the dynamics of interpersonal relationships and their influence on personality development. No stranger to emotional problems himself, Sullivan had difficulties throughout his life in maintaining relationships with other people. These problems and his frequent isolation creatively informed his theory, however, and contributed to his sensitivity in understanding and working with other people.

Biographical Background

Harry Stack Sullivan was born in 1892 in Norwich, New York. He was the only surviving child of Irish Catholic farmers, who had to struggle to provide the basic necessities for their son. A shy, awkward boy, he had difficulty getting along with the other children in the predominantly Protestant Yankee community in which he lived.

Although Sullivan suggested that ethnic and religious differences were the primary contributors to his feelings of isolation as a child, personality difficulties created by his home life and own character were probably equally important. Sullivan did not have a close relationship with his father, whom he described as "remarkably taciturn." His mother, a complaining semi-invalid, was the more important figure in his life. Mrs. Sullivan resented the fact that through marriage she, a Stack, from a professional middle-class family, had sunk in social, educational, and economic status. Her son bore the brunt of her laments, tales of earlier family prominence, and unrealistic dreams.

When Sullivan was eight and a half, he developed a close friendship with a thirteen-year-old sexually mature adolescent boy. It appears that this relationship had overt and expressed homosexual characteristics (Chapman, 1976). Sullivan later wrote (1972) that close relationships between a young child and an early-blossoming adolescent of the same sex invariably lead to homosexuality. As an adult, he admitted with regret that he never achieved a heterosexual genital relationship.

Sullivan was valedictorian of his high school class and won a state scholarship to Cornell. Encouraged by one of his teachers, he decided to become a physicist in order to rise above his poverty. At Cornell, however, his grades fell and in his second year he was suspended for academic failure. During the next six years, Sullivan earned enough money to enter the Chicago College of Medicine and Surgery, an inferior school that he later described as a "diploma mill," suggesting that it granted degrees for payment of tuition rather

Harry Stack Sullivan

than academic performance. The school closed in 1917, the same year in which Sullivan received his degree.

The shabby education that Sullivan received had detrimental effects in his later life. He never learned to write well and he did not have a solid formal training in scientific methodology and research. Nor did Sullivan receive any formal training in psychiatry. Thus, there were gaps in his medical knowledge. He was also relatively ignorant of many cultural subjects. Nevertheless, Sullivan worked hard at self-instruction, and his lack of formal education may have freed him from some of the set attitudes and prejudices that a standard education can foster.

Sullivan entered psychiatry at the age of thirty when he was appointed to the staff of Saint Elizabeth's Hospital in Washington, D.C. Here Sullivan developed a working knowledge of psychiatry through his work with disturbed veterans and his attendance at lectures, seminars, and case history presentations. He later suggested that his patients were his primary teachers. In 1923 Sullivan moved to the Sheppard and Enoch Pratt Hospital in Baltimore. His energy and devotion to work and his descriptions of therapeutic techniques brought him to the forefront of American psychiatry. In 1924 he added to his duties at the hospital the responsibility of being an adjunct faculty member at the University of Maryland Medical School.

In 1930 Sullivan moved to New York and established a private practice. While in New York he had some three hundred hours of personal psychoanalysis. In 1933 Sullivan assisted in founding the William Alanson White Psychiatric Foundation, named after a neuropsychiatrist who had greatly influenced Sullivan's work. He started the journal *Psychiatry* to publicize his own views.

In his later years Sullivan served as a consultant to the Selective Service Board and to UNESCO. To the end of his life, Sullivan involved himself in the political struggles and social conflicts of the United States. He was one of the first psychoanalysts to pay serious attention to the problems of blacks in both the South and the North. After Hiroshima, he was quick to recognize the implication: either world wars or human life must end. He died suddenly in Paris in 1949 while returning from an executive board meeting of the World Federation for Mental Health at which he had been trying to enlist the support of psychiatrists from all over the continent to oppose any further use of nuclear weapons.

Personality: Its Interpersonal Basis

Sullivan (1953) defines **personality** as the characteristic ways in which an individual deals with other people. He believed that it was meaningless to think of an individual as an object of psychological study, since an individual develops and exists only in the context of relations with other people. Interpersonal relations constitute the basis of personality.

Indeed, the very term "personality" is only a hypothesis for Sullivan (1964). It is merely an imaginary construct that is used to explain and predict certain behaviors. It would be a mistake, Sullivan suggests, to consider personality as a separate entity apart from the interpersonal situations in which it emerges. Thus Sullivan's definition of personality stresses the empirical components that we can directly observe rather than intrapsychic structures. We can see, hear, and feel that an individual is relating to other people in certain ways, such as in a passive or dominant fashion.

Anxiety, Unawareness, and Security Operations

Anxiety is a central concept in Sullivan's theory, as it was for Freud and Horney. Sullivan conceives of **anxiety** as any painful feeling or emotion that may arise from organic needs or social insecurity. Like Horney, he emphasizes the anxiety that arises from social insecurity and thinks of anxiety as interpersonal in origin.

Sullivan also emphasizes the empirical character of anxiety, pointing out that it can be described and observed. The anxious person can give a subjective description of how he or she feels; objectively, anxiety can be observed by noting an individual's physical appearance and reactions or even by measuring physiological changes that are indicative of anxiety, such as heart rate.

Anxiety is interpersonal in origin. The first feelings of anxiety are transmitted by the mother whose concern for the adequate care and welfare of her child appears in worries about illness and accidents. These anxious feelings are empathetically perceived by the child. In mild or moderate amounts, anxiety serves as a warning system and motivates an individual to seek effective measures of tension reduction. In large amounts, however, it confuses and leaves one incapable of effective solutions, by limiting the ability to observe what is happening and thereby avoid repeating mistakes.

In our relationships with others, we are to some extent aware of what we are doing and why we are doing it and to some extent unaware of these things. Sullivan appreciates that an individual may be unconscious or unaware of certain of his or her motives and behaviors. This awareness or lack of it can be objectively demonstrated by talking with someone and observing his or her actions. The ease with which a person can become aware of his or her interpersonal relationships varies from individual to individual and with the person as well. Some facets of our behavior are much more easily brought to our attention than others. Thus the concepts of awareness and unawareness are empirically based.

If we are unaware of our interpersonal relationships, we cannot learn anything from them. It is as if certain events had not occurred because we do not experience them. An individual who believes that he or she is inept may only be aware of the way in which he or she bungles things. Thus, we cannot profit from our experiences and learn new patterns of relating to others. On the other hand, when we are aware of the pattern of our interpersonal relationships, we can modify and change them.

In order to reduce anxiety and enhance security, we employ security operations of which we are usually unaware (1963). A **security operation** is an interpersonal device that a person uses to minimize anxiety. These security operations may have positive or negative effects: they are healthy if they increase our security without jeopardizing our competence in interpersonal relations; they are unhealthy if they provide security at the expense of developing more effective interpersonal skills. Unhealthy security operations merely blunt our anxiety; further, they may lead to other painful emotions and psychiatric illness.

There are many parallels between Sullivan's notion of security operations and Freud's concept of defense mechanisms. Both are processes of which we are unaware and means by which we reduce anxiety. The primary difference lies in Sullivan's stress on what is observable and interpersonal. Sullivan's emphasis is not on an intrapsychic activity, such as repression, but on the way in which a person may become disassociated from certain aspects of his or her experience of the world. Sullivan points out that security operations are not unobservable processes going on inside an individual but processes that we can observe as they arise in the matrix of interpersonal relationships. In simple situations, security operations can be clearly perceived; in complex situations, we may conjecture or imagine them.

Some of the security operations that Sullivan describes are sublimation, selective inattention, and "as if" behavior. *Sublimation* is the expression and discharge of uncomfortable feelings in ways that are interpersonally acceptable. A child demonstrates sublimation by releasing anger verbally rather than by hitting or kicking the object of his or her anger. We recall that sublimation is also one of Freud's defense mechanisms, but we should note that Sullivan reconceives it to include an emphasis on learning how to behave in interpersonal situations. *Selective inattention* is the failure to observe some factor in an interpersonal relationship that might cause anxiety. A husband may not notice his wife's flirtations with other men because those activities threaten his own self-esteem. Sullivan considers selective inattention a very powerful and potentially dangerous security operation. Extensive selective inattention may blind us to what is going on in our world and make it difficult for us to cope with events effectively. "*As if*" behavior means that we act out a false but practical role. One may act "as if" he or she were stupid, to fulfill the expectations of others, when in actuality he or she is not. For the mentally disturbed person "as if" may mean acting as normally as possible. Again, we can see both the positive and negative consequences of a security operation: through the mechanism of "as if," we may discover that our capacities are greater than we thought, or we may convince ourselves that we are competent by behaving consistently in a competent fashion.

The Development of Personality

Sullivan stresses that personality arises developmentally as the result of a person's interactions with the environment. Out of innumerable social situations, we become aware of ourselves and how we relate to other people. We can observe certain processes in an individual's interpersonal relationships and these processes can be used to describe the development of his or her personality. Two such processes are dynamisms and personifications.

Dynamisms

A **dynamism** is a pattern of energy transformation that characterizes an individual's interpersonal relations (1953). Dynamisms result from experiences with other people. Many, but not all, of the dynamisms that Sullivan describes use a particular body zone by which to relate to the environment. Here his work reminds us of Freud's emphasis on the importance of bodily zones.

Sullivan's work differs from Freud's in that it rejects a Newtonian mechanical concept of the universe in terms of material objects and forces, and replaces it with a twentieth-century physicists' view of the universe in terms of the flow and transformation of energy. In Freud's theory, forces come out of the id, ego, and superego. When they collide, they create emotional conflict. Although Sullivan's concept of energy transformation is harder to describe because energy is less tangible than easily visualized structures such as the id, ego, and superego, Sullivan feels that this is a better way to view interpersonal relations. People are continually changing energy in their relationships with other people.

The description of a dynamism that occurs in infancy may help to clarify Sullivan's concept. Bodily processes within the infant cause it to feel hungry. These physiological processes provide the source for a dynamism's energy. The infant cries and by doing so summons his or her mother. Thus, the flow of energy begins an interpersonal contact between mother and child. The mother nurses the child and her activities lead the infant to respond in certain ways, such as feeling satisfied and behaving contentedly. A dynamism or pattern of energy characteristic of an individual's interpersonal relationship has begun.

In later childhood and adolescence the dynamisms become much more complex. A person who characteristically relates to others in a hostile manner is expressing a *dynamism of malevolence*. The child who is afraid of strangers illustrates the *dynamism of fear*. The young male who during adolescence seeks sexual relations with young women is expressing the *dynamism of lust*.

One of the more significant dynamisms is that of the self or **self-system**, which develops as a result of anxiety. The self-system is made up of all of the security operations by which an individual defends him- or herself against anxiety and ensures **self-esteem.** Basically, it is an individual's self-image, which has been constructed on the basis of his or her interpersonal experiences. Sullivan suggests that the concept of self is no more than a response to the interpersonal relationships in which one has been involved. The development of the self dynamism arises out of the child's recognition of situations of potential anxiety, that is, parental disapproval and rejection, and his or her attempts to avoid them.

Out of the child's experiences with rewards and anxiety, three phases of what will eventually be "me" emerge. The **good-me self** refers to the content of awareness when one is thoroughly satisfied with oneself. It is built up out of an organization of experiences that were rewarding and characterized by a lack of anxiety. The **bad-me self** is based on anxiety and refers to the content of awareness that is organized around experiences that one tries to avoid because they are anxiety producing. The **not-me self** is a gradually evolving image of aspects of the self that are regarded as dreadful and that cannot be permitted conscious awareness and acknowledgment. These dy-

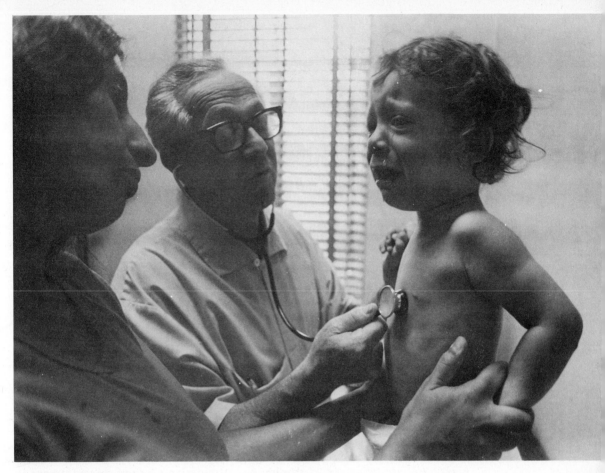

A child who is afraid of doctors is expressing a dynamism of fear.

namisms are processes rather than structures, behavior patterns that have come to characterize one's interpersonal relationships. But they can result in a dissociation of the self in which certain experiences literally become cut off from identification with the self.

Personifications

A **personification** is a group of feelings, attitudes, and thoughts that have arisen out of one's interpersonal experiences (1953). Personifications can relate to the self or to other persons. The child, for example, develops the personifications of the *good-mother* and the *bad-mother* out of either satisfying or anxiety-producing experiences with his or her own mother. In fairy tales, these personifications find expression as the good fairy and wicked stepmother or witch.

Good-Me, Bad-Me, Not-Me

You can begin to appreciate Sullivan's distinction of three phases of the self in regard to your own personality by trying to recognize certain experiences that might fit into each phase of your own self-system. Take a sheet of paper and divide it into three columns. Label them "good-me," "bad-me," and "not-me." In the column headed "good-me" make a list of those experiences that make you feel thoroughly content with yourself. For example, someone compliments you for a job you agree was well done, a significant event enhances the relationship of yourself and a friend, or you are relaxed and simply enjoying the pleasure of being you. In the column headed "bad-me" make a list of those experiences that leave you anxious and dissatisfied with yourself. For example, you have just been taken advantage of, have been caught in telling a lie, or have done something that met with the disapproval of someone very close to you. You will have to leave the column headed "not-me" blank since those aspects of the self are not permitted conscious awareness.

An individual's personifications are seldom accurate. In extreme cases, they may lead to parataxic distortions (see page 144). Nevertheless, personifications persist and are influential in shaping our attitudes and actions toward other people.

Personifications that are shared by a majority of people in any given culture are called stereotypes. **Stereotypes** are prejudgments that we make about people on the basis of their membership in certain groups. Many stereotypes, such as "all Irish are politicians," "all blacks are lazy," or "all professors are absent-minded," are based on inadequate observations. Rather than facilitating our interpersonal relations with members of those groups, they frequently serve to hinder them.

Stages of Development

Sullivan (1953) outlines six stages in personality development prior to adulthood: infancy, childhood, the juvenile era, preadolescence, early adolescence, and late adolescence. His stages remind us of Freud's in that they frequently emphasize bodily zones. However, Sullivan thought that the stages themselves were determined socially rather than biologically and were marked by the types of interpersonal relationships that are important during them.

Infancy refers to the period from birth to the emergence of meaningful speech. During this period, there is an emphasis on the significance of oral experiences. The child's perception of the nipple and his or her mother as good or bad, perceptions that crystallize around the feeding situation, will have a major impact on his or her later view of objects and persons within the environment.

Childhood extends from the emergence of meaningful speech to the development of the need for playmates. During this period, the child's primary tasks consist of developing healthy relationships with his or her parents.

The **juvenile era** begins with a strong need for playmates and ends with a need for intimacy with peers of the same sex. The juvenile era provides a broader social environment that may be useful in fostering new and more effective patterns of interpersonal relations.

Clearly, Sullivan sees the period of adolescence, which covers three of his stages, as crucial. **Preadolescence** is marked by the need for intimacy with a same-sexed peer. This "chum" relationship, as Sullivan describes it, is important because it is the beginning of genuine human relationships. One develops an intimate reciprocal relationship with another person. In healthy preadolescence, the relationship is not scarred by overt homosexual genital activity.

Early adolescence begins with physical sexual maturation and leads to the eventual development of a stable heterosexual pattern for the satisfaction of genital sexual feelings. Sullivan believed that prior to adolescence sexual impulses play an insignificant role in personality development. During adolescence, the lust dynamism emerges and impels an individual to seek intimate relations with persons of the opposite sex. Genital sexual activity in these relationships is an implied but not necessarily realized goal.

Late adolescence begins when the individual has established a stable pattern for expressing his or her feelings of lust through heterosexual genital activities. It is a period of integration and stabilization during which the individual achieves the kinds of social, vocational, and economic adjustments that his or her society considers characteristic of the adult. Adulthood is characterized by full stabilization. However, personality is never considered by Sullivan to be fixed and rigid. Blind chance, or the unpredictable and uncontrollable interpersonal situations into which a person is thrown, continues to be important in shaping an individual's interpersonal relations and in determining his or her mental health or illness throughout adulthood. Thus interpersonal relations, rather than biology, shape the development of personality.

Cognitive Processes

Sullivan describes three **cognitive processes** or ways in which we experience the world and relate to others in the course of personality development. The three cognitive modes — prototaxic, parataxic, and syntaxic — occur sequentially and show that we experience the world differently at different levels of development. They also help us understand how psychopathology may reflect an immature cognitive process.

The lowest level is the **prototaxic experience,** which is characteristic of the infant. In this experience there is no distinction between the self and the external world. Awareness is diffused and undifferentiated. The child directly perceives certain sensations, thoughts, and feelings, but he or she does not think about them or draw any conclusions. The prototaxic mode is a necessary precondition for the other two. From the masses of undifferentiated sensations, the child gradually distinguishes three different things: material objects, people, and him- or herself. This distinction moves the child into the next level of experience.

The **parataxic experience** perceives causal relations between events that happen together. It involves making generalizations about experience on the basis of proximity. The infant whose cry has brought the mother to nurse assumes that his or her crying has produced the milk. Superstitions are examples of parataxic thinking. The person who has had a bad experience after seeing a black cat assumes that the black cat is the cause of his or her misfortune. Random movements or patterns that are reinforced at an inopportune time may be repeated or avoided because they are thought to be the cause of the satisfying or anxiety-producing situation. Parataxic thinking is characteristic of the young child whose mind is too immature to understand the causal laws of nature. Yet Sullivan suggests that much of our thinking does not advance beyond the parataxic level. **Parataxic distortion** may lead us to react to another person as if he or she were someone else. Thus, a man may assume that his boss will be domineering because his father was. When he treats his boss as if he were his father, he illustrates a parataxic distortion.

The highest level of cognitive activity is that of **syntaxic experience,** which uses symbols and relies on **consensual validation,** or agreement among persons. Syntaxic experience relies upon symbols whose meaning is shared by other people in one's culture. The use of language is a primary example of such symbols. The acquisition of language illustrates Sullivan's understanding of the developmental process. When a word has been consensually validated, that is, been given an agreed-on meaning by members of a society, it loses its personal meaning and power, but the validation enables individuals to communicate with one another and provides a common ground for understanding experiences. Syntaxic thought begins to develop in childhood and increases during development so that ideally as adults our experience is almost completely symbolic and dependent on syntaxic modes of cognition.

Psychotherapy

Sullivan views psychotherapy as an interpersonal process in which one person assists another in resolving problems of living (1954). He uses the concept of participant observation to define the nature of psychiatric inquiry and treatment (1954). **Participant observation** refers to the fact that the psychiatrist is engaged in observing one or more interpersonal relationships in which he or she is an active participant. While observing what is going on, the psychiatrist is also affecting that relationship by participating in it. By his or her attitude, posture, comments, or questions, the psychiatrist alters the other person's behavior. Sullivan suggests that it is absurd to imagine that a psychiatrist could obtain from his or her patient data and/or behaviors that are uninfluenced by the therapist's own behavior in the relationship.

Sullivan, who spent his youth doing manual labor on his father's farm, suggests that psychotherapy is the hardest work he knows. It requires continual alertness, honesty, and flexibility on the therapist's part. The therapist has to be emotionally involved in the therapeutic process. He or she may be interested, bored, frustrated, or angry. The therapist must continually try to be aware of his or her reactions, understand them, and keep them at a minimum in order to continue to be an alert observer. Not only is psychotherapy hard work, it also must not be expected to provide the usual satisfactions of ordinary interpersonal relationships. The therapist does not look for friendship, gratitude, or admiration from the patient. He or she aims simply to have the patient understand him- or herself better. The therapist's rewards come from knowing that he or she is doing a job well and is being reasonably paid for it.

The work of psychotherapy primarily involves dealing with the patient's anxiety, lack of awareness, and security operations. These processes make it difficult for the person to assimilate and understand his or her experiences and thus profit by them. Exploring these areas is painful to the patient because it increases anxiety but it is necessary in order to broaden awareness. Part of the psychiatrist's task is to keep anxiety at an optimal level for furthering the therapeutic process. A certain amount of anxiety is necessary to motivate the patient to continue to work on his or her problems. Too much anxiety, however, can overwhelm and paralyze. A therapist should not hesitate to ask directed and probing questions in order to focus attention on a problem but should also make statements designed to reduce anxiety so that the patient can talk more fully about a pain-laden area. For example, a therapist might say, "Why do you think that is so horrible?" The fact that the therapist does not express alarm over the patient's behavior is, in itself, reassuring to the patient.

A major portion of the therapy is spent in examining the two-person relationship that exists between the therapist and the patient. This is one sample of the patient's interpersonal life that is made available for direct study through therapy. During therapy, the patient frequently begins to treat the physician as if he or she were someone else. Freud labeled this phenomenon transference. In Sullivan's terms, the patient develops a parataxic distortion. A patient who had a harsh, authoritarian father may react to the therapist as if he or she were also harsh and authoritarian. Such parataxic distortion is not unique to therapy. When it occurs in everyday life, however, it simply invites puzzled or angry responses from other people and interferes with effective interpersonal relationships. In therapy, it is an invitation for further exploration and study that can be used to increase the patient's self-awareness of what is happening in his or her interpersonal relationships. Eventually the parataxic distortion must be destroyed so that the patient can work cooperatively with the therapist.

In addition to examining the patient-therapist relationship and dealing with anxiety and security operations, psychotherapy involves exploring the patient's past and current relationships with others. These can be examined to see how they reiterate the processes that have been observed in the present patient-therapist relationship. Sullivan also pays attention to immediate interpersonal crises. These provide a wealth of information, especially if they can be tied to similar crises in the past. Lastly, Sullivan discusses future interpersonal relationships by asking what the patient thinks his or her relationships with certain people will be like in the future. Sullivan refers to such an exploration of the future as **constructive reverie.** Through constructive reverie the therapeutic process can take into account and deal with the patient's expectations and apprehensions about the future.

Exploration /////

Constructive Reverie

Constructive reverie provides another opportunity for the reader to further self-understanding. You can engage in constructive reverie by asking yourself what you think your relationship will be like with your mother, your father, each sibling, peer group, lover or spouse, and others in a month, a year, five years from now, and ten years from now. When you have finished outlining your expectations, ask yourself whether or not they are realistically based. Then check to see whether or not you feel comfortable with these projections of the future. If you are uncomfortable, what are some of the things that you might do in order to change these projections?

In his discussion of therapy, Sullivan pays considerable attention to the **interview,** which was his term for the interpersonal process that occurs between the patient and therapist. Sullivan suggests that each individual interview and the course of psychotherapy itself be composed of four parts: the **inception** or beginning, during which the patient introduces the problem; the **recon-**

naissance, during which the therapist raises questions in order to develop a case history and tentative hypotheses about the patient; the **detailed inquiry,** in which the therapist tests his or her hypotheses by observing the patient's behavior and responses; and the **termination,** a structured ending during which the therapist summarizes what has been learned and prescribes some kind of action that the patient might take in regard to his or her problem.

Sullivan was critical of free association as a primary therapeutic technique. He suggested that free association and introspection need to be continually questioned and further verified in a dialogue. In his discussion of dreams, Sullivan shows that he believes there is no valid distinction between a manifest and a latent dream. The dream should be taken at face value as an indication of what we are like in our everyday conscious life. For Sullivan, the key to understanding dreams lies in recognizing their interpersonal nature.

Sullivan's Theory: Philosophy, Science, and Art

Sullivan's emphasis on personality characteristics that can be directly observed within the framework of interpersonal relationships leads to a new direction in personality theorizing. The theorists studied in earlier chapters emphasized a philosophical approach to personality; Sullivan's theory veers toward a greater stress on science and empirical validation. Sullivan stopped trying to reckon with unseen mental processes and concentrated on the interpersonal processes that can be verified by observing individuals within their social contexts. With this emphasis on behaviors that can be directly observed, Sullivan points toward the behaviorists we will discuss in Chapters 15 and 16, and illustrates a scientific approach that is consistent with current American academic psychology.

This is not to say that philosophical assumptions are absent from Sullivan's theory. They are evident in his views on issues like freedom versus determinism, constitutional versus situational factors, and optimism versus pessimism, as well as in his belief that the personality of an individual can never be studied in isolation. Still, his primary intent was not to present a philosophical view of human nature but to conduct empirical research on personality.

Thus, Sullivan was more aware of the need for validating evidence in personality theorizing than the theorists we have studied to date. He emphasized that his theory was grounded in empirical data and observation, and he tried to avoid formulating imaginary concepts that could not be tested.

In his concept of dynamism as energy transformation, Sullivan is in tune with twentieth-century physics, which since Einstein (1879–1955) and Planck (1858–1947) has viewed the universe in terms of the flow and transformation of energy. The nineteenth century understood the universe in terms of material objects and forces, according to a Newtonian mechanical analogy; Freudian psychoanalysis similarly described personality processes as forces of varying strengths that collide with one another. In comparison, Sullivan's increased use of energy constructs is more consistent with the predominant twentieth-century scientific approach to nature. Sullivan's vocabulary is also consistent with current information and communication theory, which stresses interpersonal relations.

Although his concepts have a clear empirical reference, they are frequently stated in a vague or ambiguous manner; translating them into operational definitions for definitive testing is often difficult. It is hard, for example, to distinguish between dynamisms and personifications. Research on Sullivan's theory has focused primarily on the techniques of interviewing and the therapeutic process.

Sullivan demonstrated sophistication in his grasp of scientific concepts, particularly remarkable since he had no formal training in the philosophy of science. His concept of participant observation shows that he knew a scientific method can never be purely objective because it is always influenced by the observer. He was an unusually astute and perceptive scientific theorist of personality.

Sullivan's major contribution, however, has been in the area of art. He is best known for his research on the therapeutic process and, in particular, on the techniques of interviewing. His work continues to have an impact on psychotherapy, especially in the treatment of schizophrenics.

❧ Summary

1. Sullivan's theory emphasizes the interpersonal nature of personality.

2. He defines **personality** as the characteristic ways in which an individual deals with other people and calls personality a hypothesis because it is an imaginary concept used to explain and predict certain behaviors.

3. Sullivan, like Horney, thinks of **anxiety** as interpersonal in origin. He also points out that anxiety can be observed and described.

4. An individual may be unconscious or unaware of his or her motives and behaviors because of anxiety. Awareness is essential if we want to modify our interpersonal relationships.

5. **Security operations** are interpersonal devices used to minimize anxiety. They are similar to Freud's defense mechanisms but Sullivan emphasizes that they are observable and arise in the course of interpersonal relationships.

6. **Dynamisms** are patterns of energy transformation that characterize an individual's interpersonal relations. The most significant dynamism is the **self-system.**

7. **Personifications** are groups of feelings, attitudes, and thoughts that have arisen out of one's interpersonal experience. An example is the good-mother. Personifications shared by others are called **stereotypes.**

8. Sullivan outlined six stages in personality development. Three of the stages refer to adolescence, which Sullivan saw as crucial.

9. Sullivan outlined three **cognitive processes** which occur developmentally: the **prototaxic, parataxic,** and **syntaxic experiences.**

10. Sullivan uses the concept of **participant observation** to define the nature of psychiatric inquiry and treatment. In the course of therapy a **parataxic distortion** may occur. Sullivan also outlines four stages of the **interview** process: the **inception, reconnaissance, detailed inquiry,** and **termination.**

11. In his emphasis and practice of empirical research and his recognition of participant observation, Sullivan places a greater emphasis on a scientific approach than the other psychoanalytic theorists we have studied. His greatest contribution, however, has been in the area of psychotherapy.

Suggestions for Further Reading

Sullivan did not care to write much about his ideas; he published only a few articles for technical journals. He did not express his thoughts for lay people and avoided writing for his colleagues save to inform them of certain concepts and treatment techniques that he had found useful in working with patients. Only one book, *Conceptions of Modern Psychiatry,* was published during his lifetime. It was privately printed by friends through the William Alanson White Psychiatric Foundation in 1947, against Sullivan's better judgment. After his death, however, Sullivan's followers collaborated in publishing seven volumes of his ideas. These works consist of transcripts of his lectures and seminars. They are difficult reading because of uneven quality and organization, but they provide a written expression of his ideas.

The Psychiatric Interview (Norton, 1954) is probably of most interest to the lay person. It deals with the evaluation of patients and is the clearest of Sullivan's works. *The Interpersonal Theory of Psychiatry* (Norton, 1953) contains his last full series of lectures and emphasizes his concepts of personality development. *The Fusion of Psychiatry and Social Science* (Norton, 1964) consists of seventeen articles, two of which are valuable in portraying the transitional character of his work as a bridge from psychoanalysis to behaviorism: "The Data of Psychiatry" and "The Illusion of Personal Individuality."

6

Erich Fromm: Humanistic Social Analysis

Your Goals for This Chapter

1. Explain why Fromm's approach is described as humanistic social analysis.

2. Distinguish between *existential* and *historical dichotomies* and give an example of each.

3. Describe Fromm's five basic needs and explain how they are related to the development of society.

4. Discuss the *character* orientations that Fromm identifies.

5. Describe three basic types of relationship between persons.

6. Distinguish between Fromm's concept of *self-love* and narcissism.

7. Describe Fromm's concept of the role of society in structuring personality and tell how he studies the influence of society on personality.

8. Evaluate Fromm's theory in terms of its function as philosophy, science, and art.

*T*he early 1920s were a time of vibrant excitement in the academic community. Nineteenth-century scholars such as Freud, Comte, Spencer, and Marx had opened the door to the analytical study of human behavior and social institutions. New disciplines of psychology, sociology, and anthropology were emerging and efforts were being made to build interdisciplinary foundations for understanding social institutions and human behavior. Erich Fromm was particularly impressed with the writings of Freud and Marx and he attempted a synthesis of their ideas. Fromm's approach is best described, then, as humanistic social analysis.

Biographical Background

Erich Fromm was born in Frankfurt, Germany, in 1900, the only child of a deeply orthodox Jewish family. At the age of thirteen, Fromm began to study the Talmud, beginning an interest in religious literature and an admiration of the German mystic "Meister" Eckhart (1260?–1327?) that remained throughout his life. In his later years, Fromm did not formally practice religion but he referred to himself as an "atheistic mystic," and it is clear, as it is with Freud, that Fromm's early religious experiences left a distinct mark on his personality and work. The moral and committed tone of his writings has a quality that has been described as reminiscent of the Old Testament prophets. He was deeply interested in religion and both his early and recent writings reflect this concern.

Fromm wrote little about his early childhood. In his few comments, he described his early family life as tense and acknowledged that his parents were probably neurotic. His mother was "depression-prone," and his father, an independent businessman, "moody" and "overanxious." Fromm was fourteen years old when World War I broke out. He was impressed, almost to the point of being overwhelmed, by the irrationality of human behavior as it showed itself in the brutalities of war. By 1919 he had identified his political attitude as socialist and began to pursue formal studies in sociology and psychology at the University of Heidelberg. He received the Ph.D. in 1922.

Erich Fromm was trained in analysis in Munich and at the Institute of Berlin. He was one of the early *lay analysts,* that is, he had no formal medical training. The desirability of a medical background for the practice of psychoanalysis is a matter that is still currently debated. Most psychoanalysts in America view psychoanalysis as primarily a medical method of treatment for neurotic disorders and therefore consider a medical background indispensable. Freud, however, had argued against medical training as the optimal background for an analyst and had advocated the training of lay people. He felt that analysis should be viewed as more than simply a method for the treatment of neurosis and suggested that it should also be seen as a wide cultural force

Erich Fromm

offering insight into such areas as sociology, philosophy, art, and literature. Fromm's own broad understanding of the social sciences and philosophy was to enrich his understanding of psychoanalytic theory and its applications. At the same time, these interests eventually led to his severance from orthodox psychoanalysis and his criticism of Freud for his unwillingness to acknowledge the importance of social and economic forces in shaping personality.

In 1933, during the Depression, Fromm came to the United States. He helped found the William Alanson White Institute for Psychiatry, Psychoanalysis and Psychology and was a trustee and teacher for many years. He taught at other universities, such as Yale and the New School for Social Research, and maintained an active private practice. In 1949 he was appointed professor of psychiatry at the National University in Mexico. After his retirement in 1965, he continued teaching and consulting activities. He moved in 1976 to Switzerland, where he died of a heart attack in 1980. He was almost eighty years old.

Basic Human Conditions and Needs

A major theme of Erich Fromm's writings is the concept of loneliness (1941). To be human is to be isolated and lonely, because one is distinct from nature and others. Loneliness represents a basic human condition, and it is this characteristic that radically separates human nature from animal nature. As the human race has gained more freedom by transcending nature and other animals, people have become increasingly characterized by feelings of being apart and isolated. The condition of loneliness finds its ultimate expression in the problem of death. Unlike other animals, we know that we are going to die. This knowledge leads to a feeling of despair. Most of us find death incomprehensible and unjust — the ultimate expression of our loneliness.

In response to the basic condition of loneliness, human beings can resolve their problems by working with one another in a spirit of love to create a society that will optimally fulfill their needs or they can use the freedom that they gain by being human to submit to other people or forces in a form of bondage. Such an escape mechanism will alleviate feelings of isolation but it does not creatively meet the needs of humanity or lead to optimum personality development.

Existential and Historical Dichotomies

Fromm (1947) posits a number of dichotomies that arise simply from the fact that one exists. Loneliness is one of these. A **dichotomy** is a problem that has no solution because none of the alternatives it presents is entirely satisfactory. We desire immortality, but we face death; we would like to be at one with nature, but we transcend it. In short, we desire a certain kind of world, but we find the world into which we were born unsatisfactory. Dichotomies such as these are termed **existential dichotomies** because they arise from the very fact of our existence.

Finding the given world unsuitable and unsatisfactory, we attempt to create a more satisfactory environment. In doing so, we may further create **historical dichotomies,** which are problems that arise out of our history because of the various societies and cultures that we have formed. The inequitable distribution of wealth among persons is a historical dichotomy, as is our long history of war. It is important that we not confuse or mislabel the two. Historical dichotomies are created by people and thus they are not inescapable, as existential dichotomies are. They are products of history and therefore open to change.

Together existential and historical dichotomies structure our limitations and potentialities. They are the basis for our aspirations and hopes but at the same time they generate our frustrations.

Basic Human Needs

The existential dichotomies that characterize the human condition give rise to five basic needs (1955): **relatedness,** the need to relate to other people and love productively; **transcendence,** the need to rise above the animal level of creatureliness and become active creators; **rootedness,** the need to feel that we belong; **sense of identity,** the need to become aware of ourselves as separate and unique individuals; and **frame of orientation and devotion,** the need for a stable and consistent frame of reference by which we can organize our perceptions and make sense of our environment. These needs stem from our existence and they must be met in order for us to develop fully. We create society in order to fulfill these basic needs, but the type of society that humans create structures and limits the way in which the basic needs may be fulfilled. In other words, human personalities develop in accordance with the opportunities that their particular society allows. For example, in a capitalistic society, acquiring money is a means of establishing a sense of identity. A person who is unable to acquire money in a capitalistic society may have a difficult time establishing a sense of identity unless he or she is able to identify with some major corporation or find some other means of distinction.

If we cannot fulfill our needs in a constructive way, we may do so in a destructive manner. Submission or domination may become a substitute for a loving relationship; unquestioning conformity may provide a false sense of identification. Thus, one's final personality represents a compromise between one's inner needs and the ways in which society permits them to be fulfilled.

Character Orientations

Fromm identified five **character** types that are common in Western society (1947). The traits that arise from each type have both positive and negative qualities but on the whole Fromm saw the first four types as largely unproductive. A person may exhibit a combination of types. The first three types are reminiscent of Freud's oral and anal character types, and parallels can be drawn between Freud's and Fromm's typologies. However, in his discussion of the marketing orientation, Fromm is generally thought to have gone further and developed a new character type.

The primary difference between Fromm's theory of character types and orientations and that of Freud is that Freud envisions the fixation of libido in certain body zones as the basis for future character types, whereas Fromm sets the fundamental basis of character in the different ways in which a person deals with basic dichotomies. A person's character is determined in large measure by the culture and its objectives; thus, it is possible to speak of social character, qualities that frequently are shared by the people of a particular culture.

1. The **receptive orientation.** Receptive people feel that the source of all good things is outside of themselves; therefore, they believe that the only way to obtain something they want is to receive it from an outside source. They react passively, waiting to be loved.

2. The **exploitative orientation.** Exploitative people, like receptive ones, feel that the source of all good things is outside, but they do not expect to receive anything good from others. Therefore, they take the things they want by force or cunning. They exploit others for their own ends.

3. The **hoarding orientation.** Whereas receptive and exploitative types both expect to get things from the outside world, hoarding personalities are convinced that nothing significantly new is available from others. Therefore, they seek to hoard and save what they already have. They surround themselves by a wall and are miserly in their relations to others.

4. The **marketing orientation.** The modern marketplace is the model for Fromm's fourth character orientation, in which the concept of supply and demand, which judges an article of commerce in terms of its exchange worth rather than its use, is the underlying value. Marketing personalities experience themselves as commodities on the market. They see their personality as a package that is to be sold and they develop those character traits that they believe will assist them best at any particular moment in terms of being bought at the market. They are as they believe others desire them to be. Their basic character is empty. They may be described as opportunistic chameleons, changing their colors and values as they perceive the forces of the market to change.

5. The **productive orientation.** Fromm's description of the productive orientation tries to go beyond Freud's definition of the genital character, which simply suggested that the mature individual was capable of functioning adequately sexually and socially. Fromm seeks to describe an ideal of humanistic development and moral stance that characterizes the normal, mature, healthy personality. Freud's dictum "to love and to work," taken symbolically, denotes the meaning of productiveness. But the productive orientation refers fundamentally to an underlying attitude, a mode of relatedness, that governs the productive person's relationship to the world. These individuals value themselves and others for whom they are. They find themselves as the center of their powers and they are able to realize their potentialities constructively. In using their powers productively, they relate to the world by accurate perception of it and by enriching it through their own creative powers.

A further characteristic of the productive orientation is the use of humanistic rather than authoritarian ethics (1947). Whereas **authoritarian ethics** have their source in a conscience that is rooted outside the individual, **humanistic ethics** represent true virtue in the sense of the unfolding of a person's powers in accordance with the law of his or her human nature and the assumption of full responsibility for his or her existence.

Fromm's concept of the authoritarian conscience is influenced by Freud's concept of the superego, which referred to the dictates and moral values of the parents and other significant authority figures internalized and introjected into the self. The authoritarian conscience is determined not by one's own values but by those of others. Fromm points out that the source of authority is not limited to parents or other significant persons from childhood but it may be anonymous or impersonal institutions, such as cultural traditions, the scientific and philosophical ethos of one's time, or current public opinion.

Simply because an ethic is authoritarian and external does not mean that it is arbitrary and contrary to human nature. Fromm acknowledges that many of the precepts that underlie great religions may reflect humanistic ideals. All too frequently, however, the authoritarian conscience and its ethics are not based on the nature of human beings and their genuine needs. In contrast, a humanistic ethic is grounded on the true requirements of human nature. Furthermore, its source is in the individual's true self and response to his or her total functioning as a human being rather than in external authority. Whereas a comparison could be drawn between Fromm's concept of the humanistic conscience and Freud's idea that the conscience of the mature person is primarily informed by the ego rather than the superego, Fromm does not believe, as Freud did, that an authoritarian conscience is a necessary precondition of a humanistic one.

More recently, Fromm (1964, 1973) suggested a further pair of character orientations. The **necrophilous character** is attracted to that which is dead and decaying and seeks to take that which is living and destroy it. The **biophilous character** is synonymous with the productive orientation — a passionate lover of life who seeks to further the growth of living things. Fromm acknowledges that this pair is informed by Freud's life and death instincts, but he points out that for Freud both instincts are given by biology, whereas for Fromm life is the only normal biological impulse. The desire to destroy emerges only when life forces are frustrated. Thus, necrophilia is not parallel to but an alternative to biophilia.

A classic example of the necrophilous character is Adolf Hitler, who was fascinated and obsessed with death and destruction. In Fromm's description (1973), Hitler emerges as a narcissistic and withdrawn personality who, because he could not change reality, falsified, denied it, and engaged in fantasy. Hitler's coldness, apathy, and self-indulgence led to failures early in life and humiliations that resulted in a wish to destroy. This wish could not be recognized; instead, it was denied and rationalized as defensive maneuvers and actions undertaken on behalf of the glorious emerging German nation. What is unique is not the personality of Hitler, but the sociopolitical and historical situation that permitted a Hitler to rise to a position of great power. Fromm believes that malignant forms of aggression can be substantially reduced when socioeconomic conditions that favor the fulfillment of human needs and potential are developed in a particular society.

The Art of Love

The various character orientations come into being, in part, because of the particular love relationship that a child has experienced with his or her parents. Fromm describes three basic kinds of relationships (1956).

In **symbiotic relationships,** two persons are related in such a way that one of the parties loses or never attains his or her independence. One person is swallowed by the other person, the **masochistic** form of the symbiotic relationship. One person may swallow the other person, the **sadistic** form. The **withdrawal-destructive relationship** is characterized by distance rather than closeness. The relationship is one of apathy and withdrawal or direct expressions of hostility and aggression. **Love** is the productive relationship to others and the self. It is marked by mutual respect and the fostering of independence for each party.

The receptive character originates in a masochistic response to a symbiotic relationship. The exploitative type emanates from a sadistic pattern developed by the child who reacts destructively to parental withdrawal. The marketing orientation is the behavior pattern of a child who reacts to parental destructiveness by withdrawal. The productive orientation has its roots in the relationship of love.

Productive, biophilous people comprehend the world through love, which enables them to break down the walls that separate people. Productive love, Fromm asserts, is an art. We can master its theory and practice only if we make love a matter of ultimate concern. Productive love is the true creative answer to human loneliness, whereas symbiotic relationships are immature or pseudo forms of love.

Fromm (1956) distinguishes among various types of love, such as brotherly love, motherly love, erotic love, love of God, and self-love. Of particular interest are his comments on **self-love,** which he sees as a prerequisite for loving others. It is important that we distinguish Fromm's concept of self-love and affirmation from the narcissistic self-indulgence that has become so prevalent in our day and that excludes the love of others. Today many people use "self-love" as a substitute for the more difficult task of loving others. Fromm insists that the ability to love requires the overcoming of *narcissism* (experiencing as real only that which exists within ourselves). We must strive to see other people and things objectively and to recognize those times when we are limited by our subjective feelings. We need to recognize the difference between our picture of another person, as it is narcissistically determined by our feelings about and interest in the person, and the person's reality as it exists apart from our own needs and emotions. Fromm's concept of self-love foreshadows Rogers's emphasis on congruence and Maslow's discussion of self-esteem.

Exploration ////////

Relationships

Fromm suggests that there are specific standards by which a relationship may be judged healthy or unhealthy. Consider some of the relationships that you have had or observed and evaluate them according to Fromm's characteristics.

Unhealthy relationships

symbiotic: characterized by dominance or loss of independence

withdrawal-destructive: characterized by apathy and withdrawal or hostility and aggression

Healthy relationships

productive love: characterized by care (feeling concern for the life and growth of the other); responsibility (responding to the needs of the other); respect (seeing and accepting the other as he or she is); knowledge (experiencing unity with the other, yet permitting him or her to remain a mystery)

The Analysis of Society

Fromm emphasizes the role that society plays in structuring, shaping, and limiting personality. He synthesizes the insights of Freud and Marx in his analysis of different social and cultural situations and their effects on human nature (1947, 1955).

Human beings are social animals and cannot live without developing some form of social organization. We create society in order to fulfill our needs, but the type of society that we create, in turn, structures and limits the way

We create society in order to fulfill our needs. Conversely, the type of society we create structures and limits the way in which our needs may be filled.

in which our needs may be filled. Furthermore, for a particular society to function adequately, it is absolutely necessary that the people within the society be shaped to satisfy its demands. Otherwise, that system of society cannot be maintained. In a capitalistic society, for example, individuals must produce and consume goods. If they do not, a capitalistic society cannot be sustained. Nevertheless, if a particular society makes demands on its members that are contrary to their nature, that society warps and frustrates their human potential. In fact, Fromm believes that no society has yet been developed that has been able to meet all of the basic human needs constructively. He outlines specifically how both capitalism and communism have failed in their efforts to satisfy basic human needs productively. Although a great deal of lip service is given to the ideal of love in a capitalistic society, most of its relations are governed by a principle of fairness in which we give unto others only as much as they give unto us.

An example of the way in which Fromm studies society was published in 1970 (Fromm & Maccoby). Psychologists, anthropologists, historians, and other experts joined together in an interdisciplinary field study of a Mexican village. With the advent of technology and industrialization, these villagers had been lured away from their traditional values and lifestyle. Movies and television took the place of festivals and local bands. Mass-produced utensils, furniture, and clothing took the place of hand-crafted items. Trained Mexican interviewers administered an in-depth questionnaire that was interpreted and scored for characterological and motivational factors. The Rorschach Ink Blot Test, which indicates repressed feelings, attitudes, and motives, was also given. From these data, it could be seen that the three main classes in the village also represented three social character types: the landowners, productive–hoarding; the poor workers, unproductive–receptive; and the business group, productive–exploitative. The findings about the village's history, economic and social structure, belief systems, and fantasies illustrated and appeared to confirm Fromm's theory that character is affected by social structure and change.

Although Fromm did not imply that personality is entirely shaped by society, he believed that obstacles to growth are imposed by the society rather than by human nature itself. Since human beings create the societies in which they live, Fromm (1955) could envision the creation of a utopian society that would more adequately meet human needs and fulfill human potentialities. He was optimistic about the possibility of a society in which individuals would relate to one another lovingly, transcend nature creatively, and respond productively. Each individual would experience himself or herself as the source of power and would relate realistically to the world. Taking Fromm's discussion of love seriously and attempting to implement it in our society would require rather drastic changes in our social relations.

Fromm (1976) points out that two modes of existence are competing for the spirit of humanity. The **having mode,** which relies on the possessions that a person *has,* is the source of the lust for power and leads to isolation and fear. The **being mode,** which depends solely on the fact of existence, is the source of productive love and activity and leads to solidarity and joy. A person whose being depends solely on the fact that he or she *is* responds spontaneously and productively and has the courage to let go in order to give birth to new ideas.

Three and a half centuries ago, Fromm reminds us, we developed a new science that attracted the most brilliant minds and led to a highly technical society such as had only been dreamed of before. What we need now is a new social science. The goal this time "is not control over nature but control over technique and over irrational social forces and institutions that threaten the survival of Western society, if not of the human race" (1976). In his later writing, Fromm is sobered by our failure to achieve some of our goals, but he remains optimistic, believing that as long as life exists there is hope.

Fromm's Theory: Philosophy, Science, and Art

Fromm described the psychoanalytic method of investigation as genuinely scientific, its essence being the observation of facts. Over the protracted period of an analysis, the analyst observes many facts about the patient. He or she draws inferences from these observations, forms hypotheses, considers these hypotheses in the light of additional facts that emerge, and eventually arrives at a conclusion regarding the possible validity of the hypotheses. The theoretical models of the psychoanalyst do not lend themselves to scientific falsification by means of experiment, but they are based on many hours of careful empirical observation within the clinical setting. Thus, although the method of verification is different from that of the natural sciences, Fromm believed that it is a reliable method.

Fromm rejected *scientism*, or the exclusive reliance on a narrow conception of science, deeming it inadequate for the full comprehension of human nature. He was critical of a narrow scientific approach because it tends to be reductive and it does not permit the final nuances of personality to emerge. He realized, more clearly than many, that the process of scientific activity begins with an epiphanic vision that is informed by the scientist's philosophy. Fromm's theory is a speculative and transcendental one, incorporating several vantage points that initially may appear contradictory. He drew insights from religion, philosophy, psychology, sociology, and economics, permitting them to illumine his theory.

We have seen how Freud's theory was a product of nineteenth-century thought, rooted and cast in the framework of a currently outdated biological determinism. Although Freud's concepts helped to shatter the nineteenth-century understanding of human nature, they require revision to meet the demands of the twentieth century. Fromm took advantage of the emerging disciplines of psychology, sociology, and anthropology, as well as new findings in other areas, to revise Freud's theory and develop his own point of view.

Although Fromm's methods of research are empirical, based on observation, they could not be described as rigorous or precise scientific techniques. In the final analysis, Fromm, like many other followers of Freud, is philosophical in his emphasis. He considered that proof grows out of the internal coherence of a theory and the theory's ability to shed light on the human condition. This "coherence theory of truth" is characteristic of the philosopher (Rychlak, 1973).

Fromm wrote little about his technique of therapy. Although he deviated from the orthodox psychoanalytic approach to some extent, he employed a form of free association, placed considerable value on the interpretation of dreams, and recognized the importance of analyzing the transferences that arise in therapy. He indicated that he was a more active therapist than Freud and employed the term *activating* to describe the therapist's interventions to facilitate progress. Fromm emphasized that the therapist must *feel* what the patient is talking about and recognize the common humanity that both of them share. That element of empathy permits the patient to realize that his or her inner feelings are shared by others.

There are clear ethical themes in the writings of Fromm. He tried to develop a norm or an ethic that presents the best answers to the problems we all face. He considered the behaviors that are most appropriate in unifying, harmonizing, and strengthening the individual as ethical behaviors. Fromm's theory enlarges our concept of the application of personality theory to include efforts to inform and restructure society. His goals for the art of personality theory uniquely combine the scholarly and the ethical motives.

Although some of his writings may seem somewhat dated because they refer specifically to conditions surrounding the mid-twentieth century, his central ideas remain relevant. Many of Fromm's themes have been picked up by the humanist movement in psychology. His theory is coherent and sophisticated in its depth. A commitment to Fromm's point of view represents a commitment to the way of life espoused by his theory.

❧ Summary

1. Fromm's approach is termed humanistic social analysis because he attempts a synthesis of Freud and Marx.

2. He distinguishes between **existential dichotomies** that arise from existence itself and **historical dichotomies** that are created by society.

3. Fromm posits five basic needs: **relatedness, transcendence, rootedness, sense of identity,** and **frame of orientation and devotion.** We create society in order to fulfill these needs.

4. Fromm identifies **character** types in Western society, such as the **receptive, exploitative, hoarding,** and **necrophilous orientations.** In his discussion of the **marketing orientation,** Fromm is thought to have developed a new type. The **productive orientation** depicts the mature individual, who is **biophilous,** is able to love and work in the broadest sense, and uses **humanistic** rather than **authoritarian ethics.**

5. Fromm describes three basic kinds of relationship: **symbiotic, withdrawal-destructive,** and **love.**

6. Fromm believes that **self-love** is a prerequisite for loving others. Self-love requires overcoming narcissism and self-indulgence.

7. Human beings create society in order to fulfill their needs but the society they create then structures how the needs are fulfilled. Fromm believes that no society to date has been developed that is able to meet all of the basic

human needs constructively. Radical changes are needed. Fromm recommends an interdisciplinary approach to the study of society such as in his study of a Mexican village.

8. Fromm describes the psychoanalytic method of investigation as genuinely scientific and empirical, but he recognizes that a scientific approach is informed by philosophy. In the final analysis, his approach represents a deep commitment to an underlying philosophy of life.

Suggestions for Further Reading

Erich Fromm's writings have had a vast appeal. He is one of the theorists most likely to be read by the lay person, for whom he wrote expressly. Fromm's first, and in the eyes of many most important, book is *Escape from Freedom* (Holt, Rinehart, 1941). In it he explores the problem of human freedom and our tendency to submit to tyranny or authority. *Man for Himself* (Holt, Rinehart and Winston, 1947) discusses the problem of authoritarian versus humanistic ethics and outlines his five character orientations. *The Sane Society* (Holt, Rinehart and Winston, 1955) describes the five basic human needs and considers the effects of capitalism and other social forms on character development. Fromm's most popular work is *The Art of Loving* (Harper & Row, 1956), which outlines his theory of love. The distinction between the necrophilous and biophilous orientation and Fromm's case study of Adolf Hitler are included in *The Anatomy of Human Destructiveness* (Holt, Rinehart & Winston, 1973). Fromm's last work, *To Have or to Be* (Harper & Row, 1976), offers us a choice of two primary modes, one of which offers the potential for growth.

Part
2

Current
Trends
in
Psychoanalysis

In many respects Freud's theory was a product of nineteenth-century thought, cast in the framework of a now-outdated biological determinism. Yet it was Freud who shattered the nineteenth-century image of human nature and opened the door to a new point of view. Many of his concepts moved us forward into the twentieth century, but they require revision if they are to continue to meet the demands of our time and remain abreast of modern intellectual ideas. The thought of the analysts in Part 2 moves considerably beyond Freud, yet remains consistent with basic psychoanalytic doctrine. In updating and revising Freud, they have been largely responsible for the continued relevance of his theory.

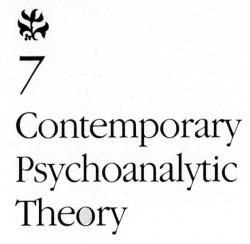

7

Contemporary Psychoanalytic Theory

Your Goals for This Chapter

1. Discuss the contributions that Anna Freud has made to psychoanalysis.

2. Explain how Heinz Hartmann has extended the functions of the ego.

3. Describe Robert White's contributions to drive theory and the understanding of the ego.

4. Discuss Margaret Mahler's concept of the *separation-individuation process.*

5. Explain how Heinz Kohut accounts for and treats *narcissistic* disorders.

6. Describe the main features of Eric Berne's *transactional analysis.*

7. Discuss efforts to test Freudian concepts experimentally.

8. Evaluate contemporary psychoanalytic theory in terms of its function as philosophy, science, and art.

A s we have seen, Freud's theory sparked a great deal of controversy and some of his original followers sought to develop separate theories. In doing so, Jung, Adler, Horney, Sullivan, and Fromm discarded a number of Freudian concepts that were considered crucial to psychoanalysis. Others, however, have worked within the mainstream of psychoanalysis to refine and update Freud's ideas.

The thought of the analysts discussed in this chapter moves considerably beyond Freud without abandoning his key concepts and principles. The focus has changed from the study of the adult to the study of the child. There has been an expansion of psychoanalysis as a therapeutic tool. Freud's concepts have been translated into terms that are easier for the lay person to understand, and there have been efforts to test Freud's concepts experimentally.

For the most part, these theorists believe that the changes they have made are consistent with basic psychoanalytic doctrine. The biological grounding of human existence remains, as does the power of sexuality. Repression and transference, keynotes of psychoanalysis, remain fast in their thought. Contemporary analysts have, however, reformed and revised psychoanalysis so that it reflects the modern world and contemporary self-understanding.

Anna Freud

Anna Freud, Sigmund's youngest daughter, was her father's intellectual heir, the only member of his family to follow in his profession. She worked closely with her father, as a highly skilled and respected colleague. After his death, she became an eminent psychoanalyst and international authority in her own right. Until her death in 1982, she was recognized as the guardian and elucidator of her father's revolutionary doctrine. She also extended the interest of psychoanalysis to the study of the child and the exploration of the ego.

In her efforts to clarify psychoanalytic theory, she presented us with some genuinely new and creative ideas. Her observations of children extended beyond normal or disturbed children growing up in average homes and included children who have met with extraordinary circumstances such as war, physical handicaps, and parentless homes. They opened the way to a new era of research in psychoanalytic child psychology, with applications to a wide area of concerns associated with child-rearing.

Some of Anna Freud's observations concerning children overturned previous notions of their reactions. For example, it had been widely assumed that children have an instinctive horror of combat, blood, and destruction and that war had a devastating effect on young children. However, her case studies of the effects of World War II bombings on British children, written in collaboration with Dorothy Burlingham, revealed that the world of the child pivots on the mother. "It is a far greater shock for a child to be suddenly

Anna Freud

separated from its mother than to have a house collapse on top of it," she wrote (1973). Her findings led her to be a strong advocate of the need to protect the natural rights and interests of the child.

Anna Freud considered infancy and childhood as prologues to greater maturity. Her therapy stressed protective, supportive, and educational attitudes. She suggested how the classic features of adult psychoanalysis could be utilized with children four years old and upward. In working with children, she recognized that child analysis could not be conducted in a manner identical to the analysis of an adult. Classical techniques such as free association, the interpretation of dreams, and analysis of the transference had to be changed to allow for the child's level of maturity. She saw the need for a long preparatory period in which the analyst is established as a trusted and indispensable figure in the child's life. She also recognized that neurotic symptoms do not necessarily have the same meaning in the life of a child as they do in the life of an adult. Her system of diagnosis, which conceives of personality as arising out of a developmental sequence, permitted her to distinguish between less serious manifestations of childhood and important threats to optimal personality growth. She produced a classification system of childhood symptoms that reflects developmental issues and a formal assessment procedure known as a **diagnostic profile** (see Table 7.1). Such profiles have since been developed for infants, children, adolescents, and adults. In each profile, different aspects of psychoanalytic theory are used to organize and integrate the data acquired during a diagnostic assessment into a complete picture of the various functionings of the patient's personality and an indication of their developmental appropriateness.

In her discussion (1965), Anna Freud uses the term **developmental line** to refer to a series of id-ego interactions in which children decrease their dependence on external controls and increase ego mastery of themselves and their world. Her six developmental lines stress the ego's ability to cope with various internal, environmental, and interpersonal situations and complement her father's discussion of psychosexual development. They are: (1) dependency to emotional self-reliance, (2) sucking to rational eating, (3) wetting and soiling to bladder and bowel control, (4) irresponsibility to responsibility in body management, (5) play to work, and (6) egocentricity to companionship.

Table 7.1   *Anna Freud's Diagnostic Profile*

Anna Freud's diagnostic profile is a careful overview of the various functionings of a patient. It provides for any stage of childhood a cross-sectional insight into the individual's overall development and mastery as well as indications for potential problems. It has nine major sections, briefly summarized as follows:

  I. Reason for referral

 II. Description of child (personal appearance, moods, manner)

III. Family background and personal history (life story and family constellation)

 IV. Possibly significant environmental influences

  V. Assessment of development in terms of:
     development and expression of the child's drives of libido and aggression
     development of the child's ego and superego sex developmental lines

 VI. Genetic assessments (signs of regression and/or fixation)

VII. Dynamic and structural assessment (signs of conflicts between the ego–id, ego–superego, or ego–reality)

VIII. Assessment of general characteristics in terms of:
     frustration tolerance
     sublimation potential
     overall attitude to anxiety
     progressive versus regressive tendencies

 IX. Diagnosis (integration and summary of above into a clinically meaningful assessment)

SOURCE: Based on information in A. Freud, *Normality and Pathology in Childhood,* Vol. 6 of *The Writings of Anna Freud,* New York: International Universities Press, 1965, pp. 138–147.

In addition, Anna Freud learned from her work with children that there are realistic limits to analysis. Certain constitutional or environmental factors may not be open to real change through analysis, though their effects may be reduced. While recognizing the greater importance of environmental factors over internal ones in childhood disturbances, she was also impressed by the efforts of children to cope with and master extremely devastating situations.

Finally, Anna Freud systematized and elaborated on Freud's discussion of the *ego's defenses.* Whereas Freud concentrated on exploring the unconscious drives of the id, his daughter realized that in order for these to emerge in an analysis, the ego must become aware of the defenses that it is using to prevent the material from re-emerging into consciousness. The ego's defenses may be inferred from observable behavior that appears to lack the normal drive components. Analysis of the defenses permits one to understand the child's life history and instinctual development. Anna Freud elaborated on the ego defenses outlined by her father and suggested some additional ones of her own (1936). She clarified the process of identification with the aggressor, in which a victim begins to react to his or her captor with gratitude and admiration. This phenomenon has since been widely recognized in prisoners of war and hostages. Her graphic case descriptions illustrating these processes have become legendary. Thus, a schoolboy's involuntary grimace caricatures the angry face of his teacher and testifies to his identification with the aggressor. Anna Freud points out that the intensity of adolescence and the extremes of acting out are not pathological but are normative and functional.

Heinz Hartmann

In Anna Freud's view, the ego remains inescapably bound to the id and necessarily regulated by the superego. Heinz Hartmann suggests that the ego is an important autonomous force (1958, 1964). Its energy is not necessarily derived from the id (as Freud thought), but both ego and id originate in inherited predispositions that follow independent courses of development. Thus, the ego's functions are not limited to the avoidance of pain and the service of instinctual gratification. Hartmann pays considerable attention to the synthesizing and integrative functions of the ego. He describes its processes of perception, attention, memory, rational thought and action and shows increased interest in accounting for normal behavior. Hartmann also suggests that certain spheres of ego activity may be "conflict free," that is to say, the ego is not perpetually in conflict with the id, external world, and superego. Through experience and adaptation, many of the ego's functions may become increasingly distinct from original instinctive and defensive maneuvers.

In Hartmann's view, memory, learning and other ego functions are *prerequisites* for the ego's interactions with the id, rather than arising out of it.

Heinz Hartmann

They emerge independently and are then brought into service. Moreover, the ego has the capacity to neutralize sexual and aggressive energy so that they function in ways other than simple drive reduction. A defense, such as regression, may be employed in the service of the ego. Thus, a college student may be able to concentrate and study better after a weekend of play. Ego functions may be autonomous of the id and practiced for their own sake.

Hartmann's emphasis on the cognitive functions of the ego is consonant with the current interest in the role of cognition in personality formation and development. He conceives of adaptation as a reciprocal relationship between the organism and the environment. The organism changes the environment in order to make it more agreeable and then changes itself in order to adapt to the changes it has created. Adaptation is never finished but is a continual process entailing ever more complex levels of mastery, molding, and synthesis. In its synthesizing function, the ego integrates and reconciles not only conflicts between itself, the id, the superego, and the external world, but also conflicts within itself.

Robert White

Robert White (1963) suggests that the ego may find intrinsic satisfaction in its own activities. He believes that there is an inherent "drive" present in living organisms to explore and manipulate things. This drive goes beyond a mere impulse to restore balance and equilibrium. White cites studies in which animals act as if they want to increase rather than decrease the amount of arousal they are experiencing. For example, monkeys will learn a new response simply in order to be given a chance to explore the laboratory. Such behaviors do not seem to occur just to reduce a biological need. Rather complex organisms are motivated by drives that reflect higher-order objectives and goals.

White suggests that an adequate theory of motivation needs to recognize an "effectance urge" that leads an organism to seek to develop *competence* in dealing with the environment. In each of Freud's psychosexual stages, White sees evidence of mastery learning that goes beyond instinctual satisfaction and id pleasures. The oral stage extends beyond the feeding situation to embrace the infant's overall capacity to cope with its environment. The anal stage involves the struggle for independence, whereas the phallic stage finds the child dealing with the world more effectively through locomotion, language, and imagination. The resolution of the Oedipal conflict involves adaptive behaviors that go beyond identification and introjection of the same-sexed parent to include an active working out of a satisfactory compromise between instinctual urges and parental demands. During the latency period, the child further develops social competencies and engages in real work tasks. The genital stage and adolescence involve the consolidation of competencies and the development of a sense of identity.*

Some personality theorists believe that a personality theory can best be judged by its ability to organize the facts in writing biographies and to present an intensive study and intimate picture of the individual. Robert White's *Lives in Progress* (originally published in 1952 with a second edition in 1966) presents some of the most complete and interesting case histories ever published in psychology.

In White's view, the ego has its own store of energy independent of the id. White observes that the ego frequently postpones gratification of an id impulse in order to secure a more satisfactory resolution. To do this, the ego must be able to anticipate future consequences. Its functions of anticipation and postponement cannot be explained as derivatives of the id but may be understood in terms of the infant learning through his or her experiences. Pathology is reinterpreted as interferences with the development of feelings of competence. Thus, in White's theory, the ego is completely free of its dependence on the id.

*White's concepts of "competence" and "effectance" are precursors of Rotter's ideas on locus of control (see Chapter 18).

Robert White

Exploration ////

Writing Your Own Case History

You can deepen your self-understanding by writing your own case history. In preparation for doing so, it is suggested that you first read some of the case histories presented in Robert White's *Lives in Progress* (2nd ed., Holt, Rinehart & Winston, 1966). You might also wish to use Anna Freud's diagnostic profile (Table 7.1) as a guide to the information that a clinician might look for. Obviously, you will not be able to supply all of the information called for in the formal profile. However, this activity should give you a better appreciation of your own history and of the complexities that are involved in a formal assessment procedure.

Margaret Mahler

Margaret Mahler (1968) explores the processes of separation and individuation by which the child emerges from a symbiotic, or intimate, fusion with the mother and assumes individual characteristics. Her findings confirm that the biological birth of an infant and the psychological birth of an individual are not the same. The former is a distinct event, whereas the latter is a gradual unfolding process.

By studying and comparing both severely disturbed and normal children, Mahler constructed a sequence of stages through which the ego passes in the process of becoming an individual. The **separation-individuation process** optimally begins about the fourth month and leads to the formation of a stable self-concept near the end of the third year. Thus, in Mahler's view the roots of identity, ego strength, and conflict resolution precede the Oedipus complex.

Prior to separation-individuation, there are two "forerunner phases," *normal autism* and *normal symbiosis,* in which the infant's ego develops from a state of absolute primary narcissism to a recognition of an external world. At this time there is no real separation of self from mother but developments may occur that promote or impede the subsequent individuation process. The separation-individuation process itself is composed of four stages: *differentiation,* the development of a body image separate from that of mother (five to nine months); *practicing,* perfecting motor abilities and developing physical independence (ten to fourteen months); *rapprochement,* increased awareness of separateness from mother, with an accompanying sensitivity to her absence that expresses a conflict between the urge to separate and the fear of loss, and a recognition that mothers have both good and bad aspects (fourteen to twenty-four months); *consolidation,* unification of the good and bad in mother with the image of her as a separate entity in the external world and the beginnings of the child's own individuality and separate personhood as seen in the development of a self-concept based on a stable sense of "me" (two to three years). Mahler's concept expresses her belief that normal, healthy infants show a "drive for and towards individuation" that is demonstrated in the separation-individuation process. Mahler's theory is receiving attention currently because it is so helpful in clarifying the separation-individuation process.

Heinz Kohut

Heinz Kohut (1971, 1977) has developed a new dimension in psychoanalysis that he calls self-theory. Extending Margaret Mahler's observations on the beginnings of individuality and the importance of the mother-child relationship,

Margaret Mahler

Kohut focuses on narcissism and narcissistic character disorders that occur when an individual fails to develop an independent sense of self.

The term **narcissism** comes from the ancient Greek myth of Narcissus, who "unwittingly" fell in love with his own reflection in a pool of water. He talked to it, made love to it, and tried to embrace it, but all in vain as it fled at his touch. The passion with which he burned was self-consuming.

Narcissistic character disorders occur when an individual fails to develop an independent sense of self. The narcissistic personality is characterized by an exaggerated sense of self-importance and self-involvement, behaviors that hide a fragile sense of self-worth.

Freud believed that narcissistic and borderline disorders could not be treated by psychoanalysis because they originated before the patient was able to talk and thus were not amenable to verbal analysis. Because the libido is withdrawn from external objects, resistance is insuperable and no object transference can be effected. However, changes in family relationships and in society have led to an increase in these types of disorder among the

Heinz Kohut

population and to more efforts to deal with them psychoanalytically. Kohut and others (such as Giovacchini, Kernberg, and Spotnitz) have expanded the psychoanalytic repertoire to include techniques designed to work through transferences and resistances that stem from pre-oedipal phases of development.

Kohut believes that disorders of the self arise from a failure in parental empathy. Children need an adequate response to their infantile needs. Most parents are able to respond appropriately to the inner needs of their children and their response helps to establish an early continuity of self. Without such response, children are likely to be left with narcissistic disorders in which they turn to others for the affirmation of self.

In the course of treatment, such patients develop idealizing or mirroring transferences to the analyst that reflect their early and troubled parent-child relationships. The analyst's task is to try and enter the patient's emotional world through empathy and be appropriately responsive in his or her words and understanding.

Eric Berne

Eric Berne, the founder of **transactional analysis** (TA), which is sometimes called "psychoanalysis for the lay person," had been associated with psychoanalysis for fifteen years when he introduced a new vocabulary (1964) that simplified the conceptualization of human relationships. TA resembles psychoanalysis in its emphasis on the importance of childhood events and unconscious forces in shaping personality but it focuses more on interactions among people and introduces more cognitive elements.

Berne suggests that in our relations with the self and others we alternate the roles of Child, Parent, or Adult. Berne's ego states parallel Freud's tripartite division of the personality in many ways: Child = id, Parent = superego, and Adult = ego. It is easier to comprehend how we frequently play the role of a Child or a Parent rather than an Adult in our interpersonal relations than it is to understand the sophisticated Freudian concepts. Berne's popular vocabulary has made it simpler for the layperson to understand him but harder for academic psychologists to take him seriously.

The **Child** consists of a recording of those feelings and experiences we had when we were children. It encompasses our hurts, angers, and affections. The Child is not childish but childlike. In our Child ego state, we tend to respond spontaneously, to strike back, or to defend ourselves, reflecting the natural, adapted, and rebellious aspects of our childhood. As we grow up, we also incorporate into our personality the admonitions, looks, gestures, and moral injunctions of significant adults. Our **Parent** is both nurturing and controlling. In our Parent ego state, we tend to scold, punish, or impose value judgments on other people. As Adults, we seek to evaluate and make realistic choices among the alternatives that confront us. Thus, in our **Adult** ego state, we seek information, weigh alternatives, and are not threatened by angry or punitive statements from others.

The point is not to eliminate the Child or the Parent, both of which have positive aspects, but to examine their data in the light of the data accumulated by the Adult. Thus, we need to ask whether or not the wisdom of the Parent is true and applicable today and whether or not the feelings of the Child are appropriate to the present (Harris, 1969).

In any given situation, an individual generally acts out of one or more of these ego states. When the other individual plays a parallel or complementary role, a reciprocal relationship exists. But if the other person does not go along, there is a crossed relationship that is mutually unsatisfying. Berne's classic example is that of a husband and wife where the husband, operating in an Adult state, asks, "Where is my watch?" A complementary Adult response might be "I haven't seen it" or "On top of your bureau." However, if the wife responds defensively as a Child, "How am I supposed to know where it is?" or judgmentally as a Parent, "You should take better care of your

Eric Berne

things," a crossed relationship exists that stops communication or causes trouble (see Figure 7.1).

In other respects, Berne's system draws heavily on the thought of Alfred Adler. Each individual develops a life script that expresses his or her attitude to him- or herself and others. These attitudes influence the *games* people play or the transactions that they have with one another. Each child begins life in the position of "I'm not OK, you're OK" because of the inferiority the infant feels. Ideally, with sufficient strokes, an individual assumes the stance of "I'm OK, you're OK" (the two other positions an individual may assume are "I'm OK, you're not OK" and "I'm not OK, you're not OK").* **Strokes** are activities that fulfill physiological and psychological needs and they are

---

*From p. 43 and after p. 80 in *I'M OK—YOU'RE OK* by Thomas A. Harris, M.D. Copyright © 1967, 1968, 1969 by Thomas A. Harris, M.D. By permission of Harper & Row, Publishers, Inc.

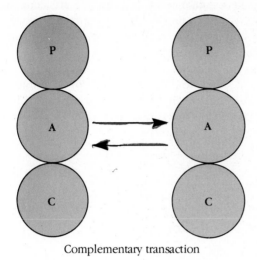

Adult stimulus:
"Where is my watch?"

Adult response:
"On top of your bureau."

Complementary transaction

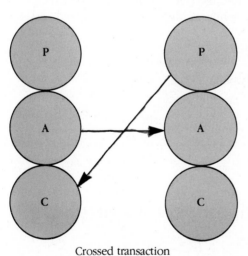

Adult stimulus:
"Where is my watch?"

Parent response:
"You should take better
care of your things."

Crossed transaction

Figure 7.1 *Berne's Relationships Represented Diagrammatically*
*In a complementary relationship, the lines indicated by the arrows are parallel
and communication can continue indefinitely. In a crossed transaction, the arrows cross over one another and make communication difficult.*

essential for human survival and self-fulfillment. Initially, we are dependent on others for our strokes; later, we learn to give them to ourselves from our nurturing Parent. Too often, however, we receive or give *cold pricklies,* negative strokes that lead to a less optimal position.

Transactional analysis seeks to help an individual understand how he or she views him- or herself and others and to analyze the kinds of interpersonal transactions or games that he or she plays. Particularly suitable for groups, TA assists people to develop a more objective view of themselves and others.

Exploration /////

Recognizing the Parent, Adult, and Child

You can become more familiar with Eric Berne's ego states by identifying them as they occur in your everyday life. The next time you have a conversation with someone or you overhear a conversation, make a transcript and reflect on it afterwards. Consider which ego state participated. For example, if you heard the following comments while waiting for a bus, you could assign these ego states.

"Buses should always be on time." (Parent)

"These buses never are!" (Child)

"I hate when the buses are late." (Child)

"There must be a problem, the bus is usually on time." (Adult)

Empirical Validation of Psychoanalytic Concepts

In recent years Freud's theory has generated a great deal of empirical research and attempts to test his concepts experimentally. A large body of literature (for example, Sears, 1943, Kline, 1972, and Fisher and Greenberg, 1977) deals with attempts to test laboratory or other setting hypotheses derived from Freud's ideas to see whether they function usefully as science.

An experimental method of test is favored by many psychologists because it permits us to infer a cause-and-effect relationship between two factors. In its simplest form, a researcher systematically varies the presence of one factor, termed the **independent variable,** in order to see whether or not these changes have any effect on a particular behavior that is being studied, the **dependent variable.** If they do, a causal relationship may be presumed. Careful precautions are taken to eliminate any alternative explanations.

Thus, for example, Lloyd Silverman (1976) designed an experiment to test the psychoanalytically informed hypothesis that depression arises from aggressive feelings that have been turned inward against the self. He tried to activate unconscious aggressive wishes to see whether or not they would result in an intensification of depressed feelings. In one session, he showed a group of subjects pictures and verbal messages that were designed to elicit unconscious aggressive wishes. The subjects were exposed to the images for only 4/1000 of a second, so that their perception was subliminal. The images included pictures such as a fierce man with a knife and the message "Cannibal eats person." In another session, Silverman showed the same group neutral images of people reading or walking. These two sets of images constituted the independent variable. Before and after the sessions, the subjects were asked to rate their feelings. Their self-ratings represented the dependent variable. As expected, the subjects reported more depressive feelings after seeing the aggressive images than after seeing the neutral ones. In subsequent studies, Silverman and his associates have demonstrated the ameliorative effects of oneness fantasies and amassed a strong body of evidence in favor of the psychoanalytic concept of the unconscious.

In yet another study, Hall and Van de Castle (1965) tested the concepts of castration anxiety and penis envy by seeing whether or not male dreamers reported more dreams expressive of castration anxiety and fewer dreams expressive of penis envy than women. They did. Of course, Hall and Van de Castle had to develop carefully a scoring manual that spelled out specific criteria for interpreting various dream themes as indicative of castration anxiety and penis envy. They also had to show that there was agreement among different scorers. As you can see, some of these efforts to test Freud's theory have demonstrated much ingenuity and sophistication.

Not all of the Freudian concepts have held up well under such scrutiny. For example, it has become untenable in light of modern research in biology and embryology to view the female as a castrated male. Other Freudian concepts, however, appear to stand up nicely under experimental conditions. The concept of repression has been operationally translated to suggest that there is a stronger tendency to forget events identified with unpleasant associations than with neutral or pleasant events (Glucksberg and King, 1967). Experimental test of this and other psychoanalytically oriented hypotheses indicates their usefulness (Shurcliff, 1968, Hammer, 1970, Silverman, 1976).

There are difficulties, however, in translating Freud's concepts into operational procedures that allow for unequivocal test. Freud's theory contains many concepts that are by their nature difficult to define operationally. There is no direct evidence that will substantiate concepts such as unconscious processes or repression. Thus, the operational translation of many of Freud's concepts may misinterpret and oversimplify his ideas. The Freudian theory of repression does not simply imply experiences associated with unpleasant thoughts; thus, laboratory studies on repression may deal with phenomena that are essentially different from the kind of phenomena that concerned Freud. If the concepts are distorted and minimized, they will not truly represent the constructs in Freud's thought. Further, a simpler rival hypothesis that has greater appeal to common sense can frequently be offered to account for the same phenomena that arise in the laboratory test. According to the rule of Occam's razor, the simpler hypothesis is preferred in science. Finally, Freud's own investigations and those of other psychoanalysts hardly allow for replication because they were carried out under conditions of privacy and confidentiality.

Although the criteria that compelled Freud are largely philosophical, the ongoing effort to validate his theories represents the need to evaluate our philosophical assumptions in light of contemporary scientific information. Moreover, some researchers are very optimistic about achieving a merger of experimental operations and clinical observations in the study of psychoanalytic phenomena. They believe it is a matter of experimenter ingenuity and creativity and that in time we will have definitive studies confirming psychoanalytic concepts.

Contemporary Psychoanalytic Theory: Philosophy, Science, and Art

Contemporary analysts have revised psychoanalysis so that it is no longer limited by nineteenth-century thought but reflects the modern world and promotes contemporary self-understanding.

Although Freud conceived of his work as science, many of his statements function philosophically; psychoanalysis has therefore been seen as primarily a philosophical point of view. Contemporary psychoanalytic theorists share many of Freud's basic philosophical concepts, emphasizing the biological grounding of human existence, the importance of sexuality, and the potency of unconscious forces. However, they recognize that Freud's ideas require revision in order to meet the demands of our time and remain intellectually viable. They also have a deepened appreciation of the need to test constructs by validating evidence. Thus, contemporary psychoanalytic theorists are more likely to develop their constructs in a way that allows the constructs to be empirically tested. They have also tested hypotheses derived from Freud's ideas to see if his constructs function usefully as science. Nevertheless, science is not the primary focus of psychoanalytic theory. The psychoanalytic understanding of human nature is first and foremost a philosophical one.

As artists, contemporary psychoanalytic theorists have made considerable contributions to the practice of psychoanalysis and psychotherapy. Anna Freud, Kohut, and Berne, in particular, have emphasized this aspect in their work, clarifying the techniques of therapy; Berne has popularized some therapeutic concepts. The expansion of psychoanalytic techniques to include the treatment of narcissistic and borderline disorders has been a very significant contribution. By enlarging upon the art of psychoanalysis, these theorists have enhanced the power, scope, and effectiveness of the psychoanalytic movement.

Contemporary psychoanalytic theorists have been criticized by traditional psychoanalysts (see Nacht, 1952; Holt, 1965; Stein, 1978), who perceive potentially destructive challenges to some of Freud's central ideas. Yet contemporary psychoanalytic theorists have brought psychoanalysis along a new path, moving closer to the stances taken by most academic, cognitive, and humanist psychologists today. In particular, their emphasis on the adaptive functions of the ego is in tune with the interest of contemporary research psychologists in the processes of cognition and their influence on personality development. The psychoanalytic approach to understanding human nature has had a wide appeal and undoubtedly will continue to compel many people.

 Summary

1. Anna Freud extended the interest of psychoanalysis to the study of the child and the exploration of the ego. She developed the **diagnostic profile** and described six **developmental lines.** She also elaborated on ego defenses.

2. Heinz Hartmann believes that the ego is an important autonomous force and has explored its synthesizing and integrative functions.

3. Robert White has posited a drive to be competent. He conceives of the ego as independent from the id and motivated by higher-order objectives.

4. Margaret Mahler has explored the processes of **separation** and **individuation** by which the child emerges from a symbiotic fusion with the mother and develops individual characteristics. She has constructed a sequence of stages through which the ego passes in the process of becoming an individual.

5. Heinz Kohut accounts for **narcissism** and narcissistic character disorders that occur when an individual fails to develop an independent sense of self. He has developed psychoanalytic techniques designed to work through transferences and resistances stemming from pre-oedipal phases of development.

6. Eric Berne's **transactional analysis** introduces a new vocabulary for simplifying our understanding of human relations. Our behavior can be analyzed in terms of roles we play: **Child, Parent,** or **Adult.**

7. Efforts to test Freud's theory experimentally have been made by Silverman

and Hall and Van de Castle, among others. The results have been mixed but illustrate the need to re-evaluate philosophical assumptions in the light of contemporary scientific information.

8. Contemporary psychoanalytic theorists recognize the necessity of validating philosophical concepts by means of scientific testing. Nevertheless, contemporary psychoanalytic theory is largely philosophical with an emphasis on practical application.

Suggestions for Further Reading

Anna Freud's significant books and papers have been collected into a seven-volume set, *The Writings of Anna Freud* (International Universities Press, 1965–1974). Her classic work, *The Ego and the Mechanisms of Defense* is found in Vol. 2. Also significant is *Normality and Pathology in Childhood: Assessment of Development* in Vol. 6. Heinz Hartmann's classic work is *Ego Psychology and the Problem of Adaption* (International Universities Press, 1958). His later papers are found in *Essays in Ego Psychology* (International Universities Press, 1964). The most comprehensive statement of Robert White's position is found in *Ego and Reality in Psychoanalytic Theory, Psychological Issues,* Monograph 11 (International Universities Press, 1963). The best introduction to Margaret Mahler's work is *The Psychological Birth of the Human Infant* (Basic Books, 1975). Heinz Kohut's position is stated in *The Restoration of the Self* (International Universities Press, 1977). Many of these works are difficult reading, but they are well worth study by the serious student.

On the other hand, most books about transactional analysis were written expressly for the lay public. Eric Berne's *Games People Play* (Grove, 1964) and Thomas Harris's *I'm OK—You're OK* (Harper & Row, 1969) are useful introductions to transactional analysis.

The classic review of empirical studies seeking to validate Freudian concepts is R. R. Sears, "Survey of Objective Studies of Psychoanalytic Concepts" (*Social Science Research Council Bulletin,* 1943). For updates on more recent efforts, see H. J. Eysenck and G. D. Wilson, *The Experimental Study of Freudian Theories* (Barnes and Noble, 1974); P. Kline, *Fact and Fantasy in Freudian Theory* (Methuen, 1972); and S. Fisher and R. P. Greenberg, *The Scientific Credibility of Freud's Theory and Therapy* (Basic Books, 1977).

The studies outlined in the text are described in L. H. Silverman, "Psychoanalytic Theory: The Reports of My Death are Greatly Exaggerated" (*American Psychologist,* 1976, *31,* 621–637) and C. Hall and R. Van de Castle, "An Empirical Investigation of the Castration Complex in Dreams" (*Journal of Personality*, 1965, *33,* 20–29).

8

Erik H. Erikson:
Psychoanalysis
and the
Life Cycle

Your Goals for This Chapter

1. Identify four ways in which Erikson extends Freudian psychoanalysis.

2. Explain how Erikson's theory enlarges our understanding of the ego.

3. Discuss the general characteristics of Erikson's *psychosocial stages* of development.

4. Discuss each one of Erikson's stages in terms of the Freudian psychosexual stage it reflects, the emotional duality that it involves, and the particular ego strength that emerges from it.

5. Describe how Erikson has explored the role of culture and history in shaping personality.

6. Discuss Erikson's findings in the area of sex differences.

7. Discuss the methods of research that Erikson uses.

8. Evaluate Erikson's theory in terms of its function as philosophy, science, and art.

E rik H. Erikson is undoubtedly the most popular and influential psychoanalytic theorist today. His phrases "identity crisis," "life cycle," and "inner space" have become commonplace. His theory incorporates cognitive elements as well as traditional psychoanalytic concepts, so that it is extremely relevant to contemporary concerns in personality research.

Erikson extends Freudian psychoanalysis in four main ways. First, he increases and extends our understanding of the ego, showing how it is a creative problem solver that emerges out of the genetic, cultural, and historical context of each individual. Second, he elaborates on Freud's stages of development, making explicit a social dimension that was implied in Freud's theory but never clearly stated. Third, he extends our concept of development to embrace the entire life span from infancy to old age. Fourth, he explores the impact of culture, society, and history on the developing personality and illustrates this in psychohistorical studies of famous people.

Biographical Background

Erik H. Erikson was born on June 15, 1902, near Frankfurt, Germany. His parents, who were Danish, separated before he was born, and his mother moved with the baby to Karlsruhe, Germany, in order to be closer to friends. There she subsequently married a local pediatrician, Theodore Homburger, who had treated young Erik for an illness when he was three years old. Dr. Homburger adopted Erik and gave him his last name. In an act that Erikson later called "loving deceit," his parents concealed from him for several years the fact of his adoption. Thus, the man who is famous for coining the term "identity crisis" did himself experience a significant identity crisis. Not only did he have to struggle with the usual quest for psychological identity but he was also unsure of his biological identity. His resolution of that problem became apparent in 1939; in the process of becoming an American citizen, he added the surname by which we know him, assuming the identity of Erik Homburger Erikson.

As a youngster, Erikson found himself rejected by his German peers because he was Jewish and rejected by his Jewish classmates because he was tall, blond, and Aryan in appearance. He was taunted as "the goy" in the synagogue. Although he lived in a comfortable house near a park and the cultural center of the city, his home was also close to the industrial area. This varied exposure helped him to recognize later how social institutions shape one's growth. In time, Erikson converted to Christianity.

Erikson was not a particularly good school student, although he excelled in art and history. He would have preferred a more general education to the classical curriculum (Latin, Greek, and German literature) in which he was

Erik H. Erikson

enrolled at the gymnasium (academic high school). The strict and formal atmosphere of the classroom turned him off. Instead of going on to the university after graduation, he wandered throughout Europe, reading, looking at the countryside, putting thoughts down in a notebook, and behaving generally as a drop-out. He studied briefly at two art schools and described himself as feeling out of place and alienated. In fact, he was involved in his own identity crisis.

In the summer of 1927, Erikson received a fateful letter from an old and like-minded friend from the gymnasium, Peter Blos. Blos had become the director of a small progressive school in Vienna that had as its clientele children and parents who were in analysis with Freud. Blos suggested that Erikson be hired to paint portraits of the children. Since Blos also wanted some time off, he further proposed that Erikson serve as his temporary replacement at the school.

In Vienna Erikson was able to find his professional identity. He and Peter Blos established a progressive, nongraded school where children were taught individually. Avoiding the excesses later present in some forms of liberal education, they provided the children with optimal freedom within an appropriate structure. After he had been at the school a short time, Erikson was asked by Anna Freud, who was turning the interests of psychoanalysts toward the study of the child, if he would be interested in beginning analysis with her and in becoming a child analyst. Thus Erikson entered the Freudian psychoanalytic circle, where he was enthusiastically accepted, and also became close to the Freud family. In those days, the conduct of analysis was different from what it is today. Analysts did not hesitate to form personal contacts with their patients. Erikson went daily to the famous building at Berggasse 19 where the Freuds lived and where father and daughter conducted analysis.

In the course of the next few years, Erikson established himself as a key figure in psychoanalysis. He published three articles on education and psychoanalysis, showing how children can become more aware of themselves through art, writing, and the understanding of historical figures. These articles and his subsequent psychoanalytic studies also reflect the precision of the Montessori philosophy. Erikson was studying simultaneously with a Montessori group and later received a diploma in that method of education. Through this happy combination of methodologies he became interested in topics such as how children arrange objects in a given space and how these arrangements reflect their inner life. The two complementary forms of training enabled Erikson to make a unique contribution to our understanding of child development.

Erikson left Vienna in 1933 when Hitler's forces threatened soon to overwhelm Europe. He settled with his wife and family in Boston, where he became the city's first child psychoanalyst. He conducted research with Henry A. Murray at Harvard University, held a position at the Harvard Medical School, and was a consultant for a number of agencies. At one point he enrolled in a graduate program in psychology at Harvard but, being unsuited to a formal program of education, he failed the first course and dropped out. Within the Harvard intellectual community, however, he was influenced by the anthropologists Margaret Mead and Ruth Benedict as well as by the gestalt psychologist Kurt Lewin.

In 1936 Erikson accepted a position in the Yale University Institute of Human Relations to teach at the medical school. Although Erikson continued to treat disturbed children, he became interested in studies that were being conducted on the growth and development of normal infants. In 1938, he learned of a unique opportunity to study child-rearing methods among the Sioux Indians in South Dakota. Here he observed at first hand how childhood events are shaped by society and its customs, a theme he was to stress again and again in his later writings.

In 1939 Erikson moved to California, where he stayed for ten years. In San Francisco he resumed his work as a child analyst and in Berkeley he pursued interests in anthropology and history. He was associated with the Institute of Child Welfare at the University of California. He also traveled north to observe a second Indian tribe, the Yurok. These observations coupled with his earlier ones of the Sioux Indians found expression in his first and perhaps most important book, *Childhood and Society* (1950), which discusses the two very different but equally valid and normal methods of child-rearing.

When the University of California began to require that its faculty sign a special loyalty oath, Erikson resigned in protest. He accepted a position at the Austin Riggs Center in Stockbridge, Massachusetts, where he worked with disturbed adolescents. In 1960 Harvard University offered him the position of professor. Erikson was considered as a sound intellectual in spite of the fact that he had never received a university or college degree. A well-liked teacher, his undergraduate course "The Human Life Cycle" was very popular. On the graduate level, he led small seminars that examined the biographies of historical figures such as Adolf Hitler, Martin Luther, and Mahatma Gandhi. Some of these psychohistorical studies were subsequently published. Erikson has been a popular speaker at colleges and universities throughout the nation. He retired in 1970 and moved to a suburb of San Francisco, where, at this writing, he continues to be active in study and research.

An Enlarged Understanding of the Ego

Freud believed that in optimal personality development the ego acted as an executor, effectively juggling the demands of the id and superego to meet their needs realistically. He emphasized the influence of the id, so that the ego only acted out of borrowed energy and was at best a harassed, if not overwhelmed, commander. In his later years, Freud conjectured that the ego might have some psychological energy of its own. As we have seen, subsequent practitioners of psychoanalysis focused on the ego and began to consider it as an independent force with a larger role.

While Erikson was training in Vienna, a lively debate was going on between Anna Freud and Heinz Hartmann. Anna Freud tended to restrict the ego's function to warding off drives, whereas Hartmann was exploring the ego's adaptive responses to its environment. Even though Anna Freud had been his training analyst, Erikson found himself attracted to Hartmann's approach. As an educator, Erikson was interested in how one might strengthen and enrich the ego of young children. He found it difficult to conceive of the ego as adaptive while limiting its role to a set of defenses used against inner drives. Erikson decided to go beyond defensiveness and emphasize adaption.

In Erikson's theory, the ego is the part of the mind that gives coherence to experiences, be they conscious or unconscious. The ego does more than simply defend itself; it also learns skills and adaptive techniques. Erikson agrees with Freud that many aspects of ego functioning are unconscious, but he believes the ego has an overall unifying purpose that leads to consistent behavior and conduct. The ego has the positive role of maintaining effective performance, rather than just a negative role of avoiding anxiety. Its defenses are adaptive as well as maladaptive (1974).

In a serious illness, the intact ego, which we usually take for granted, disintegrates. Erikson illustrates this in his description of Jean, a schizophrenic young girl whose mind, in spite of her mother's and her therapist's strenuous efforts, turned against her own body and its needs (1963). However, Erikson does *not* believe that we can best reconstruct the ego's functions from an understanding of its dysfunctions. He elaborates on its adaptive capacities, its ability to deal with stress, to resolve vital conflict, to recuperate, and to contribute to identity formation. In the final analysis, Erikson's definition of the ego is strong, vital, and positive: it is an organizing capacity of the individual that leads to "that strength which can reconcile discontinuities and ambiguities" (1975).

The ego is creative and adaptive as it comes to terms with the body, the mind, and social processes. In a vivid and awe-inspiring description, Erikson enlarges our appreciation of the ego's achievements: "The ego, in the course of its synthesizing efforts, attempts to subsume the most powerful ideal and evil prototypes (the final contestants, as it were) and with them the whole existing imagery of superior and inferior, good and bad, masculine and feminine, free and slave, potent and impotent, beautiful and ugly, fast and slow, tall and small, in a simple alternative, in order to make one battle and one strategy out of a bewildering number of skirmishes" (1968). Psychoanalysis has come a long way from its earlier view of personality development essentially as impulses and defenses against them. Erikson would measure ego strength in terms of the extremes that an individual is able to unify rather than by the extent of denial or repression.

Much of Erikson's work can be seen as a description of the social and historical forces that influence the ego's strengths and weaknesses. Whereas Freud conceived of the environment as an "outer world" with which the ego had to contend, Erikson demonstrates that the effects of one's society are not peripheral but central to the development of personality; there is an interdependence between inner and outer organization. Differences in cultural variables are significant and lead to variations in adult behavior. Different groups have different ways of rearing their children to become functioning adult members of their society. From the very beginning, the way in which an infant is handled and fed affects the development of his or her ego.

Whereas Freud tended to see society as repressive and limiting, Erikson stresses its constructive effects on development. He seeks to explore the adaptive social processes that initially protect and support the ego's development in childhood and later give strength and direction for the development of identity in adolescence. The development of the ego first depends on the nurturance of the family. Later, other social models play a significant role. It is important that social organizations permit a child's capacities and potentials to develop. The very synthesizing capacity of the ego depends on the role of social organization.

Ego development reaches a climax during adolescence when the individual is ready to establish his or her identity. Ego identity is an awareness of continuity in one's ego-synthesizing methods and one's meaning for others. It is a sense of coherent individuality that permits one to resolve conflicts. Ego identity denotes certain comprehensive gains that an individual must have derived from his or her experiences throughout childhood and adolescence in order to be ready for adulthood. It is a successful variation of one's group identity, reflecting the expectations and constructs of one's social group. Ultimately, ego identity is a psychosocial product.

The development of the ego is clearly outlined in Erikson's psychosocial stages of the life cycle. At each stage the ego develops certain strengths or basic virtues that enable it to move forward. These ego strengths further lay the basis for a set of ethical rules based on ideals that we can strive for, for Erikson also conceives of the superego and human consciousness in terms of an evolutionary process. For a fuller understanding of Erikson's position, we need to turn to the stages of development that he articulated.

The Psychosocial Stages of Development

In his discussion of the psychosexual stages of development, Freud concentrated on their biological character and thus he tended to neglect the social dimension. Nevertheless, Freud's stages reflect more than simply a psychosexual progress in which the child comes to terms with his or her sexuality. For Erikson they are definitely a psychosocial development, in which the child is trying to understand and relate to the world and others. In effect, Erikson makes explicit the social dimension implied in Freud's work.

Each of Erikson's **psychosocial stages** centers on an emotional polarity or conflict that children encounter at certain critical periods. New environmental demands introject positive and negative emotional components into the development of personality. Both emotional components are to some extent incorporated into the emerging person, but if the conflict is resolved satisfactorily, the positive component is reflected to a higher degree. If the conflict persists, or is not adequately resolved, the negative component predominates. Erikson's first four stages correspond to Freud's psychosexual stages (oral through latency). Erikson then subdivides the genital stage into four phases that represent growth and development throughout maturity.

Erikson's stages are *epigenetic* (from the Greek words *epi,* "upon," and *genesis,* "emergence"), which means that one stage develops on top of another in a sequential and hierarchical pattern. At each successive level the human personality becomes more complex. The concept of **epigenesis** also implies that it is not enough to concentrate on the early stages of development or to understand personality in terms only of its beginnings. Freud's search for origins ultimately reflects a simplistic idea of cause and effect. Without an orientation toward the future, psychoanalysis remains retrospective. Erikson stresses the prospective features of the life cycle and amends the logic of psychoanalysis so that early events are seen not only in terms of their contributions to later development, but as themselves directed by potentials that do not flower until later. Rather than speaking of cause and effect, Erikson refers to the configurational fit among different aspects of an event. This is clearly illustrated in his account of the development of ego identity and the ego's capacity for synthesis.

Erikson's psychosocial stages do not occur within a strict chronological framework. Each child has her or his own timetable. However, as in fetal development, each aspect of psychosocial development has a critical period of readiness during which, if it does not flourish, it is likely to flounder. In addition, the stages progress in a cumulative rather than a linear fashion. The behaviors of one stage do not disappear with the successive stage. Erikson suggests that we view the stages as a ground plan. "In each stage of life a given strength is added to a widening ensemble and reintegrated at each later stage in order to play its part in a full cycle" (1969).

Erikson's stages closely follow Freud's clinical observations but, instead of viewing each stage as the emergence of behavior that results from a conflict between instincts, Erikson considers the drives to be culturally modifiable. Erikson's psychosocial stages are a gradual series of decisive encounters with the environment; they are interactions between biological development, psychological capacities, and social influences.

In his theory, Erikson has modified the psychoanalytic concept of energy to be more consistent with contemporary scientific findings. Freud's original formulations were based on the imagery of energy transformation characteristic of nineteenth-century physics. Today we are guided by scientific concepts such as relativity and complementarity. Sexuality seemed to Freud to be the likely way in which quantities of excitation could arise out of body chemistry. Erikson, however, is not concerned with fixed units of energy or the channeling of energy. He sees the person as a way of being in the world. Thus the first stage, rather than a cathexis of libido onto an oral zone, is viewed as a complex of experiences centered in the mouth.

Each of the eight stages entails its own **identity crisis.** A crisis is not a catastrophe but a turning point, a crucial period in which the individual cannot avoid a decisive turn one way or the other. Each stage also provides new opportunities for particular ego strengths or basic **virtues** to develop. These psychosocial gains result from the ego's successful adaption to its environment and must be nurtured and reaffirmed continuously.

There is also a ritualization peculiar to each stage. **Ritualizations** are repetitive forms of everyday behavior, socially structured ways of doing or experiencing something, that assist us in becoming productive members of a community. Erikson also describes them as playful. Indeed, the ritualizations of some cultures may appear to the naive outsider to be symptomatic when in fact they are fruitful means of relating to that society. In any culture, the ritualizations may become distorted and turn into *ritualisms* if they are rigidly employed.

A description of each of Erikson's psychosocial stages follows.

Trust versus Mistrust

The emotional duality of **trust versus mistrust** is the key consideration of the first stage, which corresponds to Freud's oral, sensory, and kinesthetic one (1963). The basic mode of behavior at this point is an incorporative one, that of taking in. The infant takes in with all of its senses, primarily through the mouth. A complex of experiences centered on the mouth develops in relation to the mother or the primary caretaker. The basic psychosocial attitude to be learned at this stage is whether or not you can trust the world. At birth, infants are deprived of the constant attention they received in the womb and for a protracted period of time they are highly dependent on others for their care. Certain frustrations are inevitable and socially mean-ingful, but too much of either frustration or indulgence may have negative effects. Basic trust implies a perceived correlation between one's needs and one's world. The primary dilemma that infants face is whether or not the world and its people are safe, nurturing, and can be trusted to meet one's needs. If infants receive unreliable, inadequate, or rejecting care, they will perceive their world as indifferent or hostile and they will develop a high degree of mistrust. Granted, it is important that infants develop some sense of mistrust. When we enter into a situation, we need to be able to judge how much we can trust and to what degree we must be ready for danger and discomfort. The danger lies in the extremes of trust and mistrust. This crisis is not permanently resolved during the first year or two of life, but a foundation is laid that influences the subsequent course of development.

An appropriate balance of trust and mistrust leads to the development of the ego strength *hope,* a basic human virtue without which we are unable to survive. Hope represents a persistent conviction that our wishes can be satisfied in spite of disappointment and failures (1964). Once established, hope is able to maintain itself in the face of changing situations and also to change those situations. It is the basis of faith, reflected in mature religious commitments. Hope is fostered in infancy by the qualities of the ego that enable the child to pursue and take pleasure in increasingly more active and directive incorporative modes. The ritualization of this stage is the *numinous,* in which the infant recognizes the mother or primary caretaker and her affirmation of its existence by expressing devotion. The expression of devotion takes different forms in different cultures, yet the infant's attachment to a primary caretaker is easily recognized in all its societal forms. The perversion of the numinous is *idolism,* which distorts reverence for an essential source into excessive devotion to an idol or hero worship (1976).

Exploration /////

Trust Walk

You can explore your current feelings of trust by going on a trust walk with someone. Allow a partner to blindfold you and lead you around an area in which there is plenty of space and a number of objects to investigate by smelling, touching, hearing, or tasting. At one point, he or she might permit you to take a few steps by yourself. After about fifteen minutes, switch roles. When you have finished, discuss with your partner what it felt like to have to depend on someone else to take care of you. Have your feelings toward your partner been changed by the experience? What were some of the ways in which you and your partner facilitated the development of trust or made it more difficult? Your current feelings of trust are undoubtedly influenced by the foundation that was laid during the first year or two of your life.

Autonomy versus Shame and Doubt

Erikson's second psychosocial stage, **autonomy versus doubt,** arises during the second and third years of life and corresponds to the anal-muscular stage in Freud's psychosexual scheme (1963). Holding on and letting go are the basic social modalities of this phase and may have constructive or destructive effects. The primary emotional duality here is that of control over the body and bodily activities as opposed to a tendency for shame and doubt. "Just when a child has learned to trust his mother and to trust the world, he must become self-willed and must take chances with his trust in order to see what he, as a trustworthy individual, can will" (Erikson, as cited in Evans, 1967).

The struggle for autonomy is not limited to sessions on the toilet, but extends to many other areas of life as the ego begins to establish psychosocial independence. Toddlers, who are making rapid gains in neuromuscular maturation, verbalization, and social discrimination, begin to explore independently and interact with their environment. The negativism of the two-year-old whose favorite word is "no," is evidence of the child's struggling attempt at autonomy. A temper tantrum is simply a momentary loss of self-control. Cultures have different ways of cultivating or breaking the child's will, either reinforcing or rejecting the tentative explorations of the child. Doubts about their ability for self-control may give children feelings of inadequacy or shame.

Will, the virtue corresponding to this stage, is a natural outgrowth of autonomy. Clearly in the toddler years only rudiments emerge, but these will build into a mature sense of will power. Will is an unbroken determination to exercise freedom of choice and self-restraint (1964) and forms the basis for our subsequent acceptance of law. The ritualization characteristic of the second stage is the *judicious,* which makes judgments as to possible areas of self-assertion in daily life. By playfully testing his or her limits, the child learns an early sense of right and wrong that will culminate in a sense of the pragmatic. As adults we continue the ritual of the judicial in our legal procedures and courtroom trials by which we establish guilt or innocence and set rules for communal living. Rigidly applied, the judicious becomes *legalism,* in which the letter of the law triumphs over its spirit. Legalism expresses itself in vain displays of righteousness or morality and a feeling of triumph over the convicted (1976).

Initiative versus Guilt

The emotional duality that Erikson envisions for the phallic or genital-locomotor stage of psychosexuality (three to five years) is that of **initiative versus guilt** (1963). At this period, children are active in their environment, mastering new skills and tasks. Their dominant social modality is the *intrusive* mode: their bodies vigorously intrude into space and onto other people. Having gained relative independence and autonomy during the toddler years, preschoolers direct their activities toward specific goals and achievements. Their intrusion and curiosity extends not only to sexual matters but to many other concerns of life as well. If the characteristic word of toddlers is "no," the characteristic word of preschoolers is "why?" Their incessant questions are a hallmark of their curiosity. Parental responses to children's self-initiated activities determine the successful or unsuccessful outcome of this stage. If initiative is reinforced, a child's behavior will become increasingly goal oriented. Excessive punishment or discouragement of a child's general stance of initiation may lead to feelings of guilt, resignation, and the belief that it is wrong to be curious about the world and ill-advised to be active in it.

Immense new faculties develop in children at this time as they begin to imagine goals for which their locomotive and cognitive skills have prepared them. Their use of language becomes perfected. Children begin to envision themselves as growing up and to identify with people whose work and personalities they can understand and admire. Earlier fantasies are repressed or redirected and the play of preschoolers becomes more realistic and purposeful. They begin to engage in projects. Children are at no time more open to learning than during these years. They are able to work cooperatively and to profit from teachers. Their learning is vigorous, leading away from their own limitations and into later possibilities.

Erikson believes that the Oedipus complex is both more and less than Freud made of it. He would prefer to call it an early generational complex. From the point of view of evolution, it is the child's first experience with the unrelenting sequence of generations, growth, and death. The same-sexed parent becomes "naturally" involved in the child's early genital fantasies at a time when the child's initiative is ready to turn away from the present situation to new goals. At the same time, the child's strong imagination and powerful locomotive skills produce gigantic, terrifying fantasies that awaken a sense of guilt and lead to the development of conscience (Evans, 1967). Thus the oedipal stage results in a moral sense that establishes permissible limits and begins to attach childhood dreams realistically to the various possible goals of one's technology and culture.

The virtue that emerges out of the duality of initiative versus guilt is *purpose,* a view of the future giving direction and focus to our mutual efforts. Purposefulness slowly enables one to develop a sense of reality that is defined by what is attainable and is not afraid of guilt or punishment (1964).

The play activities of this age are frequently dramatic. Children engage in ambitious impersonations of victorious and evil selves. They are able to create with available objects and playmates a plot that hangs together, involves conflict, and ends in some type of resolution. Their play is often complete with costumes. The *dramatic,* then, joins the numinous and the judicial as a primary ritualization. In experimenting with self-images and images of others, children begin to develop concepts of themselves in both ideal and evil roles. However, the capacity to dramatize may be perverted into *impersonation,* a ritualism in which role-playing and the assumption of different stances prevents us from expressing who we really are and leads to the quality of inauthenticity (1976).

Industry versus Inferiority

The next stage in the child's life loosely parallels Freud's latency period. Freud gave few clues as to what was happening to personality development during this period apart from suggesting that latency involves a move from premature sexual expression to a nonactive sexual phase. Erikson agrees that during latency certain passionate and imaginative qualities of earlier years calm down so that the child is free to concentrate on learning. However, he points out that learning involves more than just suppressed or displaced sexual curiosity. Learning contains its own energy; it is a basic form of striving that takes place throughout the life cycle and undergoes a special crisis during the school years. The focus moves sharply from the id to the ego as the child applies to specific and approved goals the drives that earlier motivated dreams and play. Yet the ego can only remain strong through interaction with cultural institutions. At this time society intervenes in a more formal manner to develop the child's capacities and potentials.

During the school years (six to eleven), the primary emotional duality is that of **industry versus inferiority** (1963). The term "industriousness" might be better than "industry" as it has nothing to do with big business but rather implies being busy with something, learning to make something and to make it well. Children in all cultures receive some form of systematic instruction at this time (be it in a field, a jungle, or a classroom) to teach them skills that will be needed in their society. Indians in their native setting show little boys how to shoot an arrow. In our literate and technological society, we teach children to read, write, and operate computers. Industry, then, entails educational achievements and other skills needed to be interpersonally competent in one's social world.

New demands are placed upon children at this time. They are no longer loved simply for who they are; they are expected to master the technology of their culture in order to earn the respect of their teachers and peers. Their ability to conform and master the tasks of this level depends in large measure on how successfully they have traveled the preceding stages. A certain residue of each side of the emotional polarities is left at each stage. The question is, which predominates? If children emerge from the preceding stages with a basic sense of trust, autonomy, and initiative, they are ready for the industrious labor that "school" presupposes. But if their development has left heavy residues of mistrust, doubt, and guilt, they may have difficulty performing at an optimal level. From a psychoanalytic point of view, the child who has not adequately resolved his or her Oedipal complex may not be ready to fulfill the other demands of his or her society. If potentialities have been permitted to develop fully in the earlier stages, the child is in less danger.

The peril during this period is that feelings of inadequacy and inferiority will develop. Children begin to make comparisons between themselves and others and to perceive themselves in a more or less favorable light. The avoidance of group labels that differentiate children's performances may minimize but can in no way erase a child's consciousness of doing superior or inferior work. Children know, or think they know, where they stand.

Children at this age are ready to learn to work and need to develop a sense of *competence,* the ego strength or virtue associated with this stage. Competence entails the ability to use one's intelligence and skill to complete tasks that are of value in one's society (1964).

An element of *methodical performance* is added to the ritualizations of early years. Erikson describes this ritualization as the *formal* aspect, providing the necessary discipline and basic techniques to permit one to complete a series of tasks and put them together into a skillful, finished product. The distortions here are overformalization, perfectionism, and empty ceremonialism, leading to a ritualism of *formalism* or self-enslavement in a task (1976).

Ego Identity versus Role Confusion

For Freud, the hallmarks of the genital stage were *Lieben und Arbeiten,* "to love and to work." Erikson agrees with the importance of these accomplishments, but he further divides Freud's final stage into four substages to underscore the point that "genitality is not a goal to be pursued in isolation" (Evans, 1967). In so doing, Erikson has greatly enriched our understanding of adolescence and the adult years.

The primary duality during adolescence (twelve to eighteen) is that of **ego identity versus role confusion.** The process of forming an ego identity requires that one compare how one sees oneself with how significant others appear to expect one to be. "Ego identity, then, in its subjective aspect, is the awareness of the fact that there is a self-sameness and continuity to the ego's synthesizing methods and a continuity of one's meaning for others" (1963). Ego identity results in a sense of coherent individuality that enables one to resolve one's conflicts adaptively. Adolescents must answer the question "Who am I?" satisfactorily. If they fail to do so, they will suffer role confusion.

Erikson suggests that adolescence is a particularly crucial period. Along with rapid physical growth and changes, new psychological challenges occur. Previous continuities are called into question as young people begin to reconnect the roles and skills that they have developed into a maturer sense of identity. This integration is more than the sum total of previous accomplishments. Earlier achievements are transformed and culminate in substantial changes in the personality. Erikson often speaks of adolescence as a moratorium between childhood and adulthood. But even in the best of circumstances adolescence is a stormy period. The adolescent has to refight many battles that he or she had earlier won. "Each youth must forge for himself some cultural perspective and direction, some working unity out of the effective remnants of his childhood and the hopes of his anticipated adulthood" (1958). The period of adolescence tests the ego's accumulated capacities to integrate talents, aptitudes, and skills, to identify with like-minded people and with others' impressions of one's self, and to begin to make vocational choices.

The danger at this stage is that of role confusion, the inability to conceive of oneself as a productive member of one's society. Erikson points out that "a sound ego identity is the only safeguard against the anarchy of drives as well as the autocracy of conscience" (1958). Role confusion frequently arises out of the adolescent's difficulty in finding an occupational identity but it may also express a general inability to find a meaningful place in one's culture. The development of a positive identity depends on support from significant groups. The adolescent who cannot find a meaningful adult role runs the risk of an **identity crisis,** a transitory failure to establish a stable identity. Some young people may drop out of society for a short period, as Erikson himself did. Others may adopt a **negative identity,** one that is opposed to the dominant values of their upbringing. Where support has not been forthcoming and the climate has not been favorable to the development of inner resources, a negative identity may provide the only way of demonstrating mastery and free choice in one's culture. Negative identifications may result in unfortunate consequences — social pathology, crime, or expressions of prejudice. However, Erikson would want us to recognize that such developments are an important testimony to the adolescent's readiness for ideological involvement. The adolescent who finds him- or herself on the wave of a new technological, economic, or ideological trend is fortunate indeed. It is vitally important that a society present its young people with ideals they can share enthusiastically. These requirements are not easy to fulfill. There have been times in history, e.g., during the Nazi era, when it was impossible for large groups of youth to be anything positive. The conspicuous absence of a sense of promise in any society, due to economic conditions, population trends, high unemployment, or other problems that thwart the occupational aspirations of young people, means that those adolescents will have a difficult time establishing a clear and positive ego identity.

The virtue or ego strength developed at this time is *fidelity;* the adolescent is ready to learn to be faithful to an ideological point of view. Fidelity consists of "the ability to sustain loyalties freely pledged in spite of the inevitable contradictions of value systems" (1964). Without fidelity, the young person will either have a weak ego and suffer a "confusion of values" or search for a deviant group to be loyal to.

Although adolescents often engage in spontaneous rites, the ritualization characteristic of this age is *ideology*. Ideology indicates a readiness to assume a constructive role in the technological-political system of one's culture and to commit oneself firmly to its values. Once again, the ritualizations from earlier stages are incorporated into a coherent new whole. The young person is able to engage actively in those rites and ceremonies, be they of a religious, national, or military nature, that reflect the ideological commitments of his or her society. The corresponding ritualistic element is *totalism,* a fanatic and exclusive preoccupation with what seems to be right that excludes any other point of view.

Intimacy versus Isolation

Young adulthood (eighteen to twenty-four) is marked by the emotional duality of **intimacy versus isolation** (1963). Intimacy refers to the ability to develop a close and meaningful relationship with another person. Erikson here applies Freud's dictum "to love and to work" as the model orientation. Isolation entails self-absorption and an inability to develop deep, committed relationships. Having grown beyond the beginnings of establishing his or her own identity, the young adult is able to overcome the fear of ego loss and form a close affiliation with another individual. Although sexual exploration may have preceded genuine interpersonal intimacy, it is only now that true genitality can flower with a mature orgiastic potency and freedom from pregenital or obsessive interferences. The task of young adulthood is to couple genitality with a general work productiveness. Once again a balance is required. Clearly, genitality is an inadequate definition of health. On the other hand, an individual's dedication to work should not be such that he or she loses the capacity to love.

Thus, it is at this point that the virtue of *love* emerges as an ego strength (1964). This is not to deny the involvement of love in previous stages, but in young adulthood the individual is able to transform the love he or she received as a child and begin to care for others. Love further represents a mutual devotion that is able to overcome the natural antagonism involved in any relationship between a man and a woman. Erikson acknowledges that there are different functions of the sexes, particularly with regard to procreation; however, the capacities of the mature ego can transcend these so that male and female cooperate together.

Young adulthood adds an *affiliative* element to the list of rituals: participating and sharing with others in work, friendship, and love. Its distortion is *elitism,* the focus on an exclusive group that shuts out others (1976).

Generativity versus Stagnation

The middle years (twenty-five to fifty) are characterized by the conflict of **generativity versus stagnation** (1963). Generativity entails more than parenthood; it is the ability to be productive and creative in many areas of life, particularly those showing a concern for the welfare of ensuing generations. The adult actively participates in those elements of his or her culture that will ensure its maintenance and enhancement. Failure to do so leads to feelings of stagnation, boredom, and interpersonal impoverishment. An individual who does not have children can fulfill his or her generativity by working with other people's children or helping to create a better world for them. Thus, while the idea of generativity includes the concepts of productivity and creativity, it is much broader. A person is generative when making a contribution appropriate to his or her particular potential, be it children, products, ideas, or works of art.

Erikson suggests that because Freud stressed early inhibition of the expression of the libido or sexual drive, he underestimated the importance of the procreative desires of human beings. Erikson considers a procreative drive to be instinctual and sees generativity as a further psychosexual stage whose frustration leads to symptoms of self-absorption and indulgence.

The ego strength that emerges during the middle years is care. The adult needs to be needed. *Care* implies doing something for somebody; it entails attending to that which needs protection and avoiding destructive acts. Adults need to teach and nurture the youth of their society in order to sustain their own identities and the truth of their world. Care is also able to overcome the inevitable ambivalent feelings that are involved in the parent-child relationship. Once again, when the mature ego is able to transcend these emotions, the adult can fulfill his or her obligation to youth. Care, then, is a broad solicitude for that which has been created (1964).

The adult element in ritualization is the *generational,* which includes practices such as parenting, teaching, producing, creating, restoring: activities by which the adult guides the young. Its exaggeration is *authoritism,* a false assumption of authority in which the individual seeks to dominate rather than to care (1976).

Ego Integrity versus Despair

Maturity, the final stage of life (fifty to death), is marked by **ego integrity versus despair** (1963). Ego integrity entails the ability to reflect on one's life with satisfaction. Death is not feared but accepted as one among many facets of one's existence. Despair refers to regret over missed and unfulfilled opportunities at a time when it is too late to begin again. Ego integrity represents the fruit of the seven stages that have preceded. It witnesses the ego's culminating ability to perceive life as orderly and meaningful in a spiritual sense. Erikson indicates that the end of one's life evokes "ultimate concerns." Individuality finds its ultimate test as each person must face death alone yet owes it to the next generation to face it with strength. The virtue of this stage is *wisdom.* As we grow older, we also run the risk of a return to a second childhood. Ideally, we return to a childlikeness that is softened with wisdom. "In old age, some wisdom must mature, if only in the sense that the old person comes to appreciate and to represent something of the 'wisdom of the ages,' or plain folk 'wit' " (Erikson, as cited in Evans, 1967). Wisdom enables an

*An elderly person who shares
wisdom with younger generations helps to affirm the
meaning of the life cycle.*

individual to bring his or her life to an appropriate closure. It is the ability
to stand back and reflect on one's life in the face of impending death (1964).

In the mature years an individual has the responsibility of introducing the
integral into ritualization. The integral affirms the meaning of the life cycle.
The traditional role of the elder in society, sharing his or her wisdom, personifies
this role. However, old age also has its ritualism, *sapientism,* a pretense at
being wise (1976).

Table 8.1 summarizes Erikson's psychosocial stages, indicates their relationship
to Freud's psychosexual stages, and lists their respective ego strengths, ritualizations, and ritualisms.

Table 8.1 *The Life Cycle*

Psychosexual stage	Psychosocial stage	Ego strength or virtue	Ritualization	Ritualism
Oral sensory and kinesthetic 0-1-1½	Trust versus mistrust	Hope	Numinous	Idolism
Anal-muscular 2-3	Autonomy versus shame and doubt	Will	Judicious	Legalism
Phallic or genital-locomotor 3-6	Initiative versus guilt	Purpose	Dramatic	Impersonation
Latency period 6-pub	Industry versus inferiority	Competence	Methodical performance	Formalism
Genital (Adolescence) pub-18	Ego identity versus role confusion	Fidelity	Ideology	Totalism
(Young adulthood) 18-25	Intimacy versus isolation	Love	Affiliative	Elitism
(Adulthood) 25-50	Generativity versus stagnation	Care	Generational	Authoritism
(Maturity) 50-x	Ego integrity versus despair	Wisdom	Integral	Sapientism

SOURCE: Life Cycle Chart, based on material from CHILDHOOD AND SOCIETY by Erik H. Erikson, Copyright 1950, © 1963 by W. W. Norton & Company, Inc.; INSIGHT AND RESPONSIBILITY by Erik H. Erikson, Copyright © 1964 by Erik H. Erikson; and TOYS AND REASONS by Erik H. Erikson, Copyright © 1977 by W. W. Norton & Company, Inc. Additional rights for material from CHILDHOOD AND SOCIETY obtained from Chatto and Windus Ltd. Additional rights for material from TOYS AND REASONS obtained from Marion Boyars Ltd.

<table>
<tr><td>Exploration /////</td></tr>
</table>

The Adult Years

One of Erikson's most significant contributions has been his extension of Freud's psychosexual stages into the adult years and years of maturity. It will enrich your understanding of personality processes to talk informally with senior citizens and ask them to relate to you some of the developmental tasks that they faced during their adult years. In particular, you might wish to discuss with them the emotional dualities and ego strengths that Erikson suggests emerge during the adult period to see how they are reflected in the lives of your subjects.

Cultural and Historical Contributions to Personality

In 1938 Erikson took time off from his busy practice in New Haven to go to the Pine Ridge Reservation in South Dakota and observe the children of the Sioux Indians. It was an unusual situation. Few people would expect that a child psychoanalyst who had been in the United States for only four years would choose to investigate a group of Indians in a rural part of the country. However, Erikson was beginning to realize that the kinds of patients he had been working with did not exist everywhere. He had become increasingly interested in the work of anthropologists and enthusiastically welcomed this opportunity to observe how the events of an individual's life are shaped by societal practices. Because he traveled with an old friend of the Sioux, Erikson was able to establish a close relationship with the Indians and to observe them and speak with them freely. A few years later, he traveled to northern California to observe a very different tribe, the Yurok. Erikson's work with the Indians proved to be just a beginning. Ultimately he undertook other unique forms of investigation to study the impact of society, culture, and history on personality development.

The Study of Two Indian Tribes

The Sioux had originally been buffalo hunters. When the white settlers came, both the buffalo and the traditional way of life of the Sioux vanished amid bloody massacres. Defeated, the Sioux had become withdrawn and apathetic and appeared to resist any efforts to help them. In part the present behavior of the Sioux was undoubtedly due to their painful history, but Erikson found additional reasons in the Sioux practices of child-rearing. Unlike most American middle-class parents who impose firm structures on their children at an early age in the belief that this will help them to become productive adults, the Sioux actively encouraged their children to be free and delayed imposing restrictions on them. The Sioux mother was at ease with her tasks of mothering and liberally breast-fed her infants. Sioux toddlers were allowed extensive liberties. Generosity was encouraged, property was disregarded, and competition avoided. Boys were trained to be self-confident, boastful, spirited hunters of game and women. Girls were taught to be the wives and mothers of hunters. These child-rearing practices, probably well suited to the earlier life style of the buffalo hunter, had continued even though the historical situation of the Sioux had changed radically. The traditional practices now could not cultivate or sustain a more adaptive system of social roles. The adult Sioux, who had been given considerable freedom as a child but whose life was now severely restricted, could only cope with the dilemma by looking back to the glorious past. The future seemed "empty except for dreams of restoration."

The Yurok, on the other hand, showed "folkways of stinginess, suspicion, and anger" and an emphasis on acquiring and retaining possessions. Infants were weaned promptly at about six months and encouraged to be independent. Self-restraint was urged and the child was swiftly taught to subordinate all instinctual drives to economic considerations. The Yurok, who were fishermen along a salmon river, learned to live more easily with the white settlers because their values were similar in many ways and their present work (farming, lumbering, and fishing) was both useful and familiar to them.

In describing the behavior of these two Indian tribes, Erikson deliberately avoided talking about basic character traits even though he was aware that traditional psychoanalysts would perceive "oral" and "anal" character structures in the Sioux and the Yurok, respectively. Erikson preferred to "concentrate on the configurations with which these two tribes try to synthesize their concepts and their ideals in a coherent design for living." He points out that each society uses childhood in a number of ways: to give meaning to the child's early experiences of its body and other people, to channel the child's energies in socially constructive ways, and to provide an overall framework of meaning for the anxieties that social living provokes (1963).

Psychohistories

Erikson has also explored the contribution of culture and history to personality by examining the lives of significant historical figures. **Psychohistory** is "the study of individual and collective life with the combined methods of psychoanalysis and history" (1974). Earlier, Freud too had examined the lives of various famous people, but Erikson refined the method of psychohistory and it is his name that is typically associated with the term.

In studying historical figures, Erikson tries to understand the phenomenon of greatness. He explores how the ego strength of certain individuals is able to transform the conflicts that inhibit others so that they become leaders who make an impression on their era. Thus, in studying Martin Luther, Erikson does not focus on the pathological features of Luther's behavior as other psychiatric biographers had done. He concentrates on how Luther was able to overcome some of his limitations and become an influential leader of the Protestant Reformation.

Erikson conceives of a seizure, which Luther is said to have experienced in the choir of his monastery, as a turning point in Luther's struggle for identity. Young Luther's exclamation, "It isn't me!" expressed his need to repudiate certain roles in order to break through to what he intended to be.

Erikson suggests that when Luther entered the monastery he assumed a negative identity, for his parents wanted him to become a lawyer. Furthermore, he engaged in "foolish monkery" in his efforts to become the perfect monk. He was meticulous and scrupulous in his religious practices to the point of being absurd. It is said that his confessor once told him not to return until he had something significant, such as murder, to confess.

Luther's behavior makes sense in terms of his personal history. His parents were stern, thrifty, and superstitious Germans. They did not hesitate to employ corporal punishment in their efforts to instill the difference between right and wrong. At one point Luther relates that his father beat him so brutally that there was a subsequent period of estrangement between them. In another instance his mother beat him for stealing a single nut "until the blood came." Such child-rearing practices were probably typical of the sturdy peasant stock that gave birth to the leader of the Protestant Reformation. In light of the harshness of home and school, it is easily understandable that Luther become preoccupied with the idea of a highly judgmental and punitive God. However, Luther's ego strength enabled him to overcome this concept and rediscover a biblical meaning of the righteousness of God that stressed His mercy and care.

The focus on a key episode is also apparent in Erikson's effort to understand what led Gandhi to a position of militant nonviolence. Erikson sees Gandhi's decision to put his life on the line by fasting during a local labor dispute (which culminated in a strike in Ahmedabad in 1918) as a crisis through which Gandhi was able to transform a negative Indian identity of weakness into a positive and active political technique.

Gandhi's ideological changes occurred during his middle years when the emotional challenge of the life cycle is that of generativity. By developing *Satyagraha,* a method of nonviolent action, Gandhi assisted in the liberation of the Indian people. Erikson perceives similarities between psychoanalysis and *Satyagraha:* "Satyagraha constitutes the faith that he who can face his own propensities for hate and violence 'in truth' can count on a remnant of truth in the most vicious opponent, if he approaches him actively with the simple logic of incorruptible love" (1975). Satyagraha focuses on an external enemy whereas psychoanalysis represents a means of dealing with an inner enemy. Thus, both Freud and Gandhi developed ways in which we can cope with our instincts and learn to express them nonviolently.

Erikson's approach has been applied by other writers to the lives of significant figures, such as Robert Hogan's analysis of Malcolm X (1976). Malcolm X was a well-adjusted, superior student, yet an English teacher criticized his choice of a law career as unrealistic and suggested that he consider carpentry instead. Malcolm knew he was smarter than most of his white classmates, but society refused him the identity he wished to choose because he was black. Therefore, he turned to a negative identity, becoming a "hoodlum, thief, dope peddler, pimp," before assuming the role of the militant black leader of the 1950s and 1960s.

Sex Differences

In *Childhood and Society* (1963), Erikson reported on a unique investigation he had undertaken with a large number of children between the ages of ten and twelve in order to explore how their inner lives might be reflected in their play. He set up a table with a random selection of toys and invited each child individually to construct "an exciting scene out of an imaginary movie" and then tell the plot. The resulting constructions accurately reflected each child's inner development when compared with other sources. However, Erikson also noticed distinct sex differences in the children's configurations. Girls were apt to represent the interior of a room with a circle of furniture. Occasionally they included an intruder who was accommodated in the room. Boys, on the other hand, made towers and other high structures some of which were in a state of collapse. Erikson concluded that in order to understand a child's play construction, he had to realize that girls and boys use space differently. Girls emphasized **inner space** and qualities of openness versus closedness. Boys concentrated on **outer space** and qualities of highness and lowness. These particular tendencies reminded him of the respective structures of the female and male genitals. This discovery led him to hypothesize that "one's experience is anchored in the ground plan of the body" and that there may be a "profound difference in the sense of space in the two sexes." The development of women, for example, is influenced by their awareness of a productive inner space.

Erikson's suggestions caused a loud outcry from some who concluded that he was identifying a woman's maternal potential as the key determinant of her personality. This was not the case. Erikson was merely identifying *one* component among several. Erikson reminds us that Freud's famous dictum "Anatomy is destiny" was meant to correct Napoleon's earlier motto "History is destiny." Freud was pointing out that history is not the only component of personality development. Many factors go into one's destiny: history, anatomy, social conditions, the organization of one's ego, etc. No personality theory can ignore the fact that personality development is tied to certain conditions. There are limits to what we can be, limits of what "bodily constitution can sustain, social structures can make workable, and personality formation can integrate" (1975).

It is unfortunate that, for the most part, critics of Freud and Erikson in the area of sex differences have focused on the biological aspects of their theories and failed to consider their other statements. Freud's emphasis on overdeterminism and Erikson's extension of our understanding of the ego, as well as his elaboration of historical, social, and cultural aspects of personality, make it clear that in psychoanalytic theory many variables enter into personality development. Biological, historical, cultural, and psychological factors all interact to create a uniquely female or male experience. Only a total configurational approach can help us to understand the differences in men and women and help each individual to develop his or her unique potential as a human being.

Erikson points out that "a corollary to the attempt to raise consciousness" in the women's movement has often been "a determination to repress the awareness of unconscious motivation," particularly where this motivation is informed by the fact of sex differentiation. However, it is only by becoming aware of these motives that we can begin to exercise more control over them. "The idea of being unconsciously possessed by one's body instead of owning it by choice and using it with deliberation . . . causes much of the pervasive anger" of feminists. The solution lies not in denial, rather in undoing the repression (1975).

Unlike Freud, Erikson's clinical observations did not support the idea that a girl's awareness of her sex focused on a missing penis. Rather, in normative development, the focus is on a sense of vital inner potential. A woman's productive inner space is an inescapable factor in her development whether social, historical, and other conditions lead her to build her life around it or not. Indeed, Erikson acknowledges that the "first step of liberation is the liberty not to be what others say one must be"; then "one may be free to find a self-chosen form of being what one is." However, destiny, "for both men and women, depends on what you can make of the fact that you have a specific kind of body in a particular historical setting" (1974).

Erikson's own examples of how women differ from men are culture-bound and reflect the historical perspective of an earlier era. However, he also helps us to realize that sexual differences invariably find historical and cultural expression. Role ideologies sometimes entice us into believing we can choose roles that ignore our given limitations. Thus, Erikson points out, there is the myth of the self-made man, an unrealistic role model that individual men have emulated to their detriment. In the final analysis, both men and women need to be liberated from reciprocal roles that have exploited them both (1975).

Erikson believes that the dominant task of the adult years for both men and women is generativity. The urge to procreate is intrinsic in the sexual drive. "Genital sexuality," he maintains, "does not, in itself, assume maturity unless genitality, in turn, becomes an intrinsic part of erotic intimacy, and such intimacy, in turn, part of joint generative commitments" (1975). Neither men nor women can maintain sexual liberation without coming to terms with their profound need to be generative. The fact that social and economic conditions make it necessary to restructure the ways in which men and women express their generativity poses additional challenges and may require the redirection and sublimation of our basic human instincts. As you might imagine, Erikson's views have generated considerable controversy.

Methods of Research

Erikson's method of research is direct observation of a particular (configurational) kind followed by theoretical formulation (Coles, 1970). He has not hesitated to develop techniques of study appropriate to his subject. Thus, as a child psychoanalyst he used the media of children's play and their positioning of objects in space in order to explore their inner lives. In the clinical setting, it quickly became apparent to Erikson that "basic psychological insight cannot emerge without some involvement of the observer's impulses and defenses, and that such insights cannot be communicated without the ambivalent involvement of the participants" (1975). His anthropological field work gave him further insight into how an observer necessarily participates in the lives of his or her subjects and how his or her personality limits and structures the research. This finding was termed *participant observation* by Sullivan (1954); consistent with a twentieth-century understanding of science, it recognizes that we cannot speak of the observed without also speaking of the observer.

Erikson notes that psychoanalysis is a modern Western refinement of the technique of systematic introspection, or looking inward, previously used by Eastern mystics and Christian philosophers. Introspection is frequently belittled by extrospectively oriented psychologists who criticize it for being open to a great deal of error. It is true that in subjective reporting there is a tendency to suppress data or to supply socially acceptable data instead of the truth, but if we are aware of these tendencies to error we can take steps to avoid them. In this sense introspection is no different from any other scientific method, all of which require rigorous checks on their proceedings and honesty on the part of their participants and reporters. The subject matter of psychoanalysis, however, does not lend itself to measurement and controlled experimentation. Thus it would be neither desirable nor possible to replace the "disciplined subjectivity" that provides methodological certainty to the work of psychoanalysis with seemingly more objective methods.

There are distinct parallels between the clinical evidence obtained and used by psychoanalysts in formulating their hypotheses and that used in the study of historical events. The discipline of psychohistory permits psychoanalysts to become aware of their own historical determinants and the historian to realize that in seeking to understand history we are also making history. The analyst asks the patient to free associate and then reflect on those associations in order to perceive patterns and themes by which his or her past experiences can be reconstructed. The study of a historical figure takes into account the coherence of his or her statements, life, and time. Each event is considered in terms of its meaning for the individual at that particular stage of his or her life and also in terms of its meaning for his or her life history as a whole. This means that early events need to be compatible with the developmental stage at which they occur and that there has to be a plausible continuity in the life history as a whole, just as the pieces of the developmental puzzle of an individual's life need to fall into place.

In psychoanalysis the significance of an episode, life period, or life trend is made clear by subsequent therapeutic crises that lead to decisive advances or setbacks. In biography, the validity of any relevant theme lies in its crucial recurrence in the person's development. Psychohistory permits us to see how universal phenomena (such as the complex of emotions we term Oedipal) are re-enacted in different ways by different people in different periods of history. At the same time, the psychohistorian has to recognize that he or she influences and participates in the study out of his or her choice of subject, emotional involvement, and own intellectual tradition. Therefore, the lawfulness that is sought in psychohistory is clarification of the personal aims of an individual in terms of the goals of his or her times and the relation of both of these to the psychohistorian's values (1974).

Some critics have suggested that the difficulty we have in distinguishing between historical fact and legend jeopardizes the conclusions of a psychohistorical study. The "fit in the choir," for example, was never mentioned by Luther himself; perhaps it is merely a legend. Erikson is not distressed by such comments: "If some of it is legend, so be it; the making of legend is as much of the scholarly re-writing of history as it is a part of the original facts used in the work of scholars" (1958). Such critics are employing a correspondence theory of truth, which asks whether or not a theory corresponds to what we can observe: the empirical data. That criterion is characteristic of the scientist but it is inappropriate for the historian or psychoanalyst insofar as he or she is engaged in a retrospective activity. The reconstruction of the past in these instances can only be based on present clues, which may or may not correspond with the actual past. After all, the historical data that survive, even the most well established, survive thanks to "a previous generation's sense of the momentous" (1969).

Erikson points out that there are three aspects of reality: factuality, sense of reality, and actuality. "Only this threefold anchoring of a given world image in facts and figures cognitively perceived and logically arranged, in experiences emotionally confirmed, and in a social life cooperatively affirmed, will provide a reality that seems self evident" (1974). Thus, Erikson considers proof to be a matter of the internal coherence or consistency of a theory and its ability to illumine the human condition.

Erikson's Theory: Philosophy, Science, and Art

The "coherence theory of truth" that Erikson employs is characteristic of the philosopher (Rychlak, 1973). Unlike Freud, Erikson does not insist on a simply scientific pretense for his work; he openly acknowledges the presence of philosophical statements in his theory, believing that a sound personality theory requires a sound philosophical base.

Moreover, Erikson, like Erich Fromm, believes that important moral commitments lie within the psychoanalytic framework. To facilitate the understanding of these moral commitments, Erikson explored the evolution of the superego and distinguished among infant morality, adolescent ideology, and adult ethics. In doing so, he showed how epigenetic principles apply to the development of conscience.

The ego strengths that Erikson outlines may be seen as ethical values toward which the human race can strive. Ultimately, he aims for a universally applied ethical standard, a contemporary version of the Golden Rule, which he translates as "What is hateful to yourself, do not do to your fellow man" (1964). Erikson's philosophical statements are explicit, unlike Freud's, which are implicit.

Erikson's theory is highly comprehensive, accounting for many factors in personality development; he includes biological, cognitive, cultural, and historical variables in his discussion. It is also relevant, speaking to issues that concern us today. The fact that phrases like "identity crisis," "life span," and "inner space" are part of our everyday vocabulary testifies to its pertinence. His theory has had a heuristic value, stimulating thinking among historians, theologians, and philosophers, as well as psychoanalysts. Many people, professionals and nonprofessionals alike, find that his theory compels.

This is not to say that Erikson ignores empirical data or shuns verification of his concepts. He recognizes that one's philosophy must reflect a sophisticated understanding of contemporary scientific methods. However, he points out that a narrow scientific methodology is not able to account for his findings and is not appropriate for the study of personality. He urges a broader approach for the social scientist, including the adoption of research methods similar to those described in his own writings. His theory has not generated much laboratory research because of its lack of specificity and operational definitions; complex concepts like *identity* do not readily lend themselves to precise measurement. Some research has been conducted on the identity crisis in adolescence and for the most part the findings have been consistent with his theory. Longitudinal studies could provide us with information on the validity of his concept of the developmental process, but such studies are expensive and lengthy. Researchers have largely focused on other personality theories that are easier to translate into operational terms.

In recent years, however, there has been a renewed interest in Erikson's work because of the way his theory links cognitive and personality development. Erikson explicitly states that changes in a person's thinking skills will lead to changes in that person's social interactions and personality.

Erikson's work has had an enormous impact in the clinical area. Not only have his formulations concerning ego development enriched formal psychoanalysis, they have also found wide application in child psychology, education, psychotherapy, and vocational and marriage counseling. As the median age of our population rises, gerontologists turn to Erikson's work for insight into the needs of our senior citizens.

Erikson has been called the "closest thing to an intellectual hero" in the United States (Hall, 1983). His work is imaginative, creative, and extremely compelling. More than any other theorist, he has helped to maintain the viability and relevance of Freudian psychoanalytic theory in the contemporary world.

❦ Summary

1. Erikson extends Freudian psychoanalysis in four ways: he increases our understanding of the ego; he elaborates on Freud's stages of development; he extends the concept of development to include the entire life span; and he explores the impact of culture, society, and history on the developing personality.

2. Erikson emphasizes the adaptive qualities of the ego whereas Freud tended to emphasize defensiveness. He also describes the social and historical forces that influence the ego's strengths and weaknesses, stressing its constructive rather than its repressive effects on development. He suggests that ego development reaches a climax during adolescence.

3. Erikson's **psychosocial stages** make explicit the social dimension that was implied in Freud's work. Each of Erikson's stages is established around an emotional conflict that people encounter at certain critical periods. His stages are **epigenetic,** progressing in a cumulative fashion. The concept of energy entailed in the stages is consistent with contemporary scientific findings. Each stage provides opportunities for a basic ego strength or **virtue,** to grow and has its own **ritualization** and ritualism.

4. **Trust versus mistrust** is the emotional duality that corresponds to Freud's oral stage. It leads to the development of *hope.* **Autonomy versus doubt** marks the anal-muscular stage and culminates in *will.* The phallic stage is characterized by **initiative versus guilt.** The ego strength that emerges at this time is *purpose.* **Industry versus inferiority** is the hallmark of the latency period, whose ego strength is *competence.* Erikson subdivides the

genital stage into four stages. The primary duality during adolescence is that of **ego identity versus role confusion.** The virtue developed at this time is *fidelity.* **Intimacy versus isolation** is characteristic of young adulthood and leads to the emergence of *love.* The middle years are characterized by a conflict of **generativity versus stagnation;** the ego strength that emerges is *care.* The final stage is marked by **ego integrity versus despair** and the ego strength of *wisdom.*

5. Erikson engaged in several studies that show how culture and history shape personality. He compared the child-rearing practices of two Indian groups, the Sioux and the Yurok. He undertook a number of biographical studies on important historical figures such as Luther and Gandhi.

6. In his discussion of sex differences, Erikson has explored boys' and girls' concepts of **inner** and **outer space.** He makes it clear that many variables enter into a person's development: biological, historical, cultural, and psychological.

7. Erikson developed techniques of study appropriate to his subject. He described psychoanalysis as a modern refinement of the technique of systematic introspection. There are parallels between the evidence used by a psychoanalyst and that used in a **psychohistorical** study. Each event is considered in terms of its coherence with the individual's life.

8. The coherence method of truth that Erikson employs is characteristic of the philosopher. Erikson does not insist on a scientific pretense for his work. The philosophical statements entailed in his theory are explicit.

Suggestions for Further Reading

Erik H. Erikson's books are very readable. His first and most important book is *Childhood and Society* (Norton, 1950; 2nd ed. revised and enlarged, 1963). It describes different forms of child-rearing among the Sioux and Yurok, introduces his eight psychosocial stages of development, and discusses the growth of the ego and evolution of identity. *Insight and Responsibility* (Norton, 1964) discusses Erikson's concept of the ethical implications of psychoanalysis and introduces his idea of ego strengths. The term "identity crisis" is most associated with *Identity, Youth, and Crisis* (Norton, 1968) in which he reevaluated his theory of identity in the light of historical change. Erikson's well-known psychohistorical studies are *Young Man Luther* and *Gandhi's Truth* (Norton, 1958 and 1969), a method of research that he clarified in *Life History and the Historical Moment* (Norton, 1975). Comments on sexual differences can be found in essays throughout his writings. In particular, "The Inner Space" in *Childhood and Society* and "The Inner Space Revisited" in *Life History and the Historical Moment* are recommended.

Part
3

Dispositional Theories

The oldest and most persistent approach to personality is the dispositional. People have always described one another by talking about their differences and putting them into general categories. People have been classed as hot-tempered or placid, shy or aggressive, masculine or feminine, intelligent or dull, and so forth. Even though our specific actions may vary according to the situation we are in, we conceive of ourselves as the same person and recognize a certain regularity or pattern in our behavior. These qualities appear to be long-term dispositions or traits that can be used to characterize our personality.

One of the earliest efforts to describe personality in terms of dispositions was made by a Greek physician, Hippocrates (460?–377? B.C.), who suggested that personalities could be classified according to the predominance of certain body fluids or **humors** (see Figure 9.1). A predominance of blood led to a **sanguine** character marked by sturdiness, high color, and cheerfulness. A predominance of mucus led to the slow, solid, and apathetic **phlegmatic** personality. A predominance of black bile led to the **melancholic** or depressed personality, whereas yellow bile infused the irascible and violent **choleric** personality.

Although the humoral theory on which Hippocrates' concepts were based may strike us as quaint and outdated, his theory presages many concepts in modern psychology and continues to influence some personality theorists, such as Eysenck, whom we will consider briefly in Chapter 11. Contemporary research suggests a relationship between hormones (chemicals released into the blood stream by the endocrine glands), emotions, and behavior. Depression is thought to be attributable to a chemical reaction in the brain. Further, the ancient vocabulary has permeated our language and literature. We suggest that someone is in a "good humor" or is phlegmatic or sanguine.

Part 3 concentrates on the contributions of dispositional theorists who emphasize the importance of long-term characteristics in personality.

Choleric

Sanguine

Phlegmatic

Melancholic

Figure 9.1 *The Four Temperaments Depicted in a Fifteenth-Century Zurich Manuscript*

9
Henry A. Murray: Personology

Your Goals for This Chapter

1. Describe the study of *personology*.

2. Identify the units by which Murray suggests behavior can be studied.

3. Describe the *Thematic Apperception Test.*

4. Explain how Murray studied human *needs.*

5. Identify the twenty basic human needs.

6. Explain what Murray means by *press* and give examples.

7. Discuss Murray's elaboration of Freudian concepts.

8. Evaluate Murray's theory in terms of its function as philosophy, science, and art.

*T*he term **personology** is used by Henry A. Murray to describe his efforts to study individual persons. The theory of personality that emerges from his work is an interdisciplinary one, combining modifications of Freud's theory with a deep appreciation for biology, clinical findings, and academic research. His theory is distinguished by its explicit discussion of motivation and the careful construction of a list of needs that characterize and direct human behavior.

Biographical Background

Henry A. Murray was born in New York City on May 13, 1893. His parents were well-to-do and Murray grew up as an average privileged American boy in a time before automobiles, motorboats, or movies. Winters were spent in the city in a brownstone on what is now the site of Rockefeller Center. Summers were spent on Long Island, where he enjoyed outdoor physical activity, animals, and the woods in back of his home.

Murray does not believe that he qualifies as a typical Freudian child. It was difficult for him to recognize the presence of an oedipal complex in his life. His training analysis did not uncover any indications of hidden resentment toward his father. On the other hand, his childhood evokes several Adlerian themes. Murray recalls an incident at about four years of age when his mother suggested that the queen and her son pictured in a fairy-tale book were sad because of the prospect of death. Later he suggested that memory embodied feelings of having been abandoned (left to die) by his mother in favor of his siblings because he was difficult to care for. This led to an early development of self-reliance as well as tender feelings of pity toward his mother and others with emotional problems.

At nine years of age he came home from school one day to find the dining room transformed into an operating room and his mother offering him the choice of a general anesthetic or an aquarium as a reward for doing without it while an eminent ophthalmologist cut some of the orbital muscles that were causing a slight crossing of the eyes. Unfortunately, the eminent surgeon cut a few more muscles than were necessary. As a result, one of Murray's eyes turned out a bit and he was unable to focus on a single point with both eyes. This made him somewhat inept at sports despite his persistence and he was also a confirmed stutterer. Nevertheless, he compensated; as an adult, his analysis did not reveal any serious emotional problems.

Murray never attended public schools and received little formal training in psychology. After six years in two private schools in New York City, he went to Groton, a private preparatory school in Massachusetts. He obtained his B.A. from Harvard, where he majored in history but received only below-average grades. It appears he was more interested in going out for the crew.

Henry A. Murray

Yet he went on to medical school at Columbia University and graduated at the top of his class. Later he received an M.A. in biology from Columbia and a Ph.D. in biochemistry from Cambridge University.

He spent three weeks with Carl Jung in Zurich during an Easter vacation from Cambridge and emerged a "reborn man." He had "experienced the unconscious" and thereafter he devoted himself exclusively to psychology. He became an instructor in psychology at Harvard in 1927, where he set up the Harvard Psychological Clinic expressly to study personality. With the exception of a brief interlude during World War II, he remained at Harvard until his retirement in 1962.

Murray gathered around him a group of capable young and mature scholars, many of whom are notable psychologists in their own right. He has been awarded the Distinguished Scientific Contribution Award of the American Psychological Association and the Gold Medal Award of the American Psychological Foundation for his contributions to psychology.

The Study of Personology

Murray suggests that the concept of personality is a hypothesis, a construct that helps us account for an individual's behavior. It does not refer to any real physical substance. An individual's personality is dependent upon brain processes, and hence the anatomical center of personality is the brain. There is an intimate relationship between cerebral physiology and personality. Neurophysiological processes are the source of human behavior.

In his study of personology, Murray emphasizes the understanding of normal individuals in natural settings. He believes that psychologists should primarily concern themselves with the detailed and careful study of individual lives. In a unique interdisciplinary effort at Harvard, Murray led a staff of twenty-eight different specialists in studying fifty-two male undergraduates for a period of six months. Together they amassed a great deal of data through interviews, tests, questionnaires, and observations, using an array of clinical, psychoanalytic, experimental, physiological, and life history methods. By having several trained researchers observe the same individual, Murray believed he could cancel out personal errors in assessment. A diagnostic council permitted several observers to study the same subject and then integrate their findings into a final diagnosis. This type of interdisciplinary approach was unprecedented at the time.

In studying the individual, Murray believes that it is useful to separate the total behavior of a person into identifiable and manageable units. His basic unit is a **proceeding,** a short, significant behavior pattern that has a clear beginning and ending. Proceedings are interactions between the subject and another person or object in the environment, for example, picking up a book, writing a letter, or holding a conversation. Proceedings may be internal (imagined) or external (real). A succession of proceedings constitutes a *serial.* Thus, a friendship or a marriage consists of a serial of proceedings that needs to be studied as a whole. A planned series of proceedings is a *serial program,* which leads toward a goal such as becoming a lawyer. Serial programs may stretch into the future for months or even years. Each proceeding in the series may be seen as having a subgoal that brings the individual closer to the final goal. Serial programs are governed by a mental process known as *ordination.* This enables us, once we understand our world, to develop a strategy for coping with it. Ordination also permits us to develop *schedules* or plans for resolving conflicting proceedings. A schedule, like a family budget, tries to accommodate all of the competing needs and goals by permitting them to be expressed at different times.

More significant than the actual findings of his study at Harvard, which today would be considered unscientific, are Murray's techniques of assessing personality. The best known is the Thematic Apperception Test (TAT), which is widely used as a projective device.

The Thematic Apperception Test

Look at the picture in Figure 9.2 and describe what the picture means to you by making up a story for it. Tell what led up to the events shown in the picture, what is happening, what the characters in the picture are thinking and feeling, and how the event will turn out. When you have finished, read the material in the text on the TAT and see if you can identify the needs and press that characterized your story, as well as any thema that emerged.

The **Thematic Apperception Test (TAT)** consists of a series of thirty ambiguous pictures. The subject is asked to make up stories for the pictures, telling what led up to the event, what is happening, what the characters in the picture are thinking and feeling, and how the event will turn out. The responses to the TAT suggest how the subject thinks of him- or herself in relation to the physical and social environment. Responses are noted in terms of predominant themes and special attention is paid to those forces that emanate from the "hero" in the picture or from the environment. Through the data, the examiner can infer how the subject relates to other people and molds the environment to meet his or her needs. There are special scoring guides, but many clinicians also develop their own system of analysis.

Because the stimuli are ambiguous and the subject is free to respond in any way that he or she chooses, it is believed that any meaning the subject gives to the story must come from within. In the TAT we are dealing with imaginative projection rather than a Freudian defense mechanism of projection. Subjects unwittingly project their own attitudes and feelings onto the pictures and thereby reveal themselves.

TAT stories are interpreted in terms of *needs,* motivating forces within the individual such as the need to achieve or to be dependent, and in terms of *press,* forces from the environment that help or hinder the individual to reach his or her goals, such as rejection or physical dangers. The interaction of need and press together with the outcome of a story make up a *simple thema.* Simple themas that run through several stories become *complex themas,* which help to characterize an individual's mode of functioning. Themas are merely symbolic; they are not considered literal translations of actual subject behavior. Their inference is a hypothetical construct that guides the clinician in his or her evaluation of an individual's personality dynamics. The TAT has proven to be a most valuable assessment device.

Figure 9.2 *Thematic Apperception Test Picture*
This is a sample of the pictures in the Thematic Apperception Test. What story does the picture tell? What led up to the events in the picture? What is happening? How are things going to work out?

Human Needs

Murray's most significant contribution to the study of personality is his extensive research on human needs. He has constructed what is undoubtedly the most careful and thorough list of human needs found in psychology.

Murray (1938) defines a **need** as a construct representing a force in the brain that organizes our perception, understanding, and behavior in such a way as to change an unsatisfying situation and increase our satisfaction. A need may be aroused by an internal state, such as hunger, or by an external stimulus, such as food. It motivates us to look for or avoid certain kinds of press.

An observer can infer a need from the following signs: a typical behavior effect or pattern, the search for and avoidance of certain kinds of press, the expression of a specific emotion, and signs of satisfaction or dissatisfaction with the effects of one's behavior. In addition, a subject can usually confirm the presence of a need through his or her own subjective reports.

From his intensive study of individuals at Harvard (1938), Murray constructed a list of twenty basic needs, which are listed and briefly defined in Table 9.1. Although this list has been revised and modified since that time, it remains highly representative.

Table 9.1 *Murray's List of Needs*

Dominance	To control one's human environment
Deference	To admire and support a superior
Autonomy	To resist influence and coercion *MAKE OWN DECISIONS*
Aggression	To overcome opposition forcefully
Abasement	To submit passively to external force
Achievement	To accomplish something difficult
Sex	To form and further an erotic relationship
Sentience	To seek and enjoy sensuous impressions
Exhibition	To make an impression
Play	To relax, amuse oneself, seek diversion
Affiliation	To form friendships and associations
Rejection	To separate oneself from an object
Succorance	To seek aid, protection, or sympathy
Nurturance	To nourish, aid, or protect
Infavoidance	To avoid humiliation
Defendance	To defend oneself
Counteraction	To master or make up for a failure
Harmavoidance	To avoid pain and physical injury
Order	To put things in order
Understand	To ask or to answer questions

SOURCE: From *Explorations in Personality,* edited by Henry A. Murray. Copyright 1938 by Oxford University Press, Inc. Renewed 1966 by Henry A. Murray. Reprinted by permission of the publisher.

Sometimes multiple needs — play, sentience, and nurturance, for example — can be satisfied by a single activity.

Exploration /////

Evaluating Your Needs

Look over Murray's list of twenty needs and study their definitions. Think of instances in which the needs have applied to your life and make a list of the needs that seem to be important to you. When you have finished your list, select the five most important needs and rank them, with 1 indicating the strongest need and 5 indicating the weakest. In evaluating your own hierarchy of needs, it will be helpful if you consider specific events in your life when the needs were apparent.

Not all of the needs are present in everyone and the needs vary in their strength and intensity. Murray believes that there is a hierarchy of needs, with some being stronger than others. Where two or more needs conflict, the most insistent need will be met first. Some needs are *prepotent,* which means they become very urgent if they are not satisfied, such as the need for food or to eliminate waste. Other needs may be met together. An actor may be able to meet achievement and exhibition needs in one and the same performance.

To characterize an individual's behavior simply on the basis of needs is to give a one-sided portrait. We also need to consider the concept of **press,** forces from objects or persons within the environment that help or hinder an individual in reaching his or her goals. Examples of press are cultural discord, family discord, poverty, accident, loss of possessions, presence of siblings, maltreatment by contemporaries, religious training, encouragement, friendship, sexual abuse, and illness. It is important to distinguish between *alpha press,* actual properties or attributes of the environment, and *beta press,* the individual's subjective perception of his or her environment. The beta presses are the determinants of behavior.

Elaboration of Freudian Concepts

Other aspects of Murray's theory of personology are drawn from Freud's theory. However, Murray did not hesitate to redefine terms or to elaborate and enrich Freud's concepts. Thus, he uses the terms id, ego, and superego in describing the basic divisions of personality but adds his own meaning.

Murray agrees with Freud that the id is the source of basic drives and needs, but he emphasizes that the id contains positive impulses as well as negative ones. The superego is an internalized representation of the social environment, indicating when, where, how, and what needs can be expressed. The ego is the "organized, discriminating, time-binding, reasoning, resolving, and more self-conscious part of the personality" (1938). Its role is to facilitate the id in meeting its impulses; its effectiveness in doing so affects an individual's adjustment. Murray assumes a more active role for the ego, in line with the ego psychoanalysts discussed in Chapter 7.

Murray divides childhood into five stages, each of which is characterized by a pleasant condition that must come to an end and that leaves its mark on the personality in the form of a complex.

The first pleasurable condition is that of a secure existence within the womb, which leads to a **claustral complex,** a wish to reinstate those conditions prevailing before birth. The next two stages and complexes are very similar to those of Freud. The sensuous enjoyment of sucking nourishment while being held at the mother's breast leads to **oral complexes;** these may be expressed passively, aggressively, or through rejection. The enjoyment of sensations associated with defecation leads to **anal complexes,** which express themselves in forms of ejection or retention. The fourth complex, the **urethral complex,** originates in pleasurable sensations associated with urination. It is also called the *Icarus complex* after the figure in Greek mythology who flew too close to the sun and melted his homemade wings. An individual with an

Icarus complex aims too high and meets failure. The last stage described by Murray entails pleasurable excitations arising from genital sensations and leads to the **castration complex** defined literally by Murray as "anxiety evoked by the fantasy that the penis might be cut off" (1938). Thus, childhood events are important determinants of adult personality.

Murray's Theory: Philosophy, Science, and Art

Murray's pioneering studies helped to shape the growth of personality theory in this country. He was largely responsible for bringing Freud to the attention of academic psychologists and stimulating a great deal of scientific research on Freudian concepts. Although Murray tried to provide operational definitions and specific data, he recognized that he did not have sufficient data to justify calling his theory a scientific construct. The proceedings of his diagnostic council also fall short of today's standards in scientific research. Nevertheless, Murray was a forerunner in fostering scientific research in personality theorizing. Not only was his own work influential, several of his students at Harvard have made substantial contributions to the field of psychology.

Murray advocated an interdisciplinary approach to the study of personality, which was unprecedented. He was equally at home studying the literature of Herman Melville, the writings of Freud, and the latest empirical data as possible sources of knowledge about human nature. At the Harvard Psychological Clinic, he generated an atmosphere in which lively and creative minds could work together, exchanging ideas and developing syntheses. He spoke of the virtues of bringing different approaches and specialities together to shed light on human nature, and of the need to expand our scope beyond that of a narrow, limited model.

As a result, Murray was uniquely successful in avoiding a one-sided picture of personality. He tried to strike a careful balance between constitutional elements and environmental factors. He recognized the importance of both past and future events. His theory embraces both behavioral and experiential aspects. Although he is not explicit about his philosophical position, his efforts are clearly rooted in a humanistic philosophy that encourages a comprehensive and holistic view of human nature.

His classification of needs is considered to be more useful than any other classification of its type. His emphasis on the brain's physiological processes foreshadows contemporary appreciation of the importance of biological and chemical forces in the human organism. Finally, Murray's Thematic Apperception Test, widely used as a diagnostic tool, represents his major contribution to the art of personality theory.

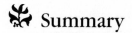 # Summary

1. Murray's term **personology** refers to his unique interdisciplinary study of the individual, which employs a wide array of clinical, psychoanalytic, and experimental methods.

2. Murray separates a person's behavior into identifiable units. The basic unit is a **proceeding,** a succession of proceedings is a *serial,* a planned series is a *serial program,* and a plan for resolving conflicting proceedings is a *schedule.*

3. The **Thematic Apperception Test (TAT)** is a projective device in which a subject makes up a story for ambiguous pictures. These stories may be interpreted in terms of needs, press, and thema.

4. A **need** is a construct representing a force in the brain that organizes our perception, understanding, and behavior in such a way as to lead us to change an unsatisfying situation. Needs can be inferred from behavioral signs and confirmed through subjective reports.

5. The twenty basic needs that Murray identifies are: dominance, deference, autonomy, aggression, abasement, achievement, sex, sentience, exhibition, play, affiliation, rejection, succorance, nurturance, infavoidance, defendance, counteraction, harmavoidance, order, and understanding.

6. A **press** is a force from the environment that helps or hinders an individual in reaching his or her goals. Murray distinguishes between *alpha press* and *beta press.* Examples of press are poverty, illness, and encouragement.

7. Murray elaborates on several of Freud's concepts, reinterpreting them in ways consistent with his own theory. He emphasizes positive impulses in the id and assumes a more active role for the ego. He divides childhood into five stages, each of which leaves its mark on the personality in the form of a complex.

8. Murray's interdisciplinary approach was unprecedented. Although it falls short of an ideal scientific model, it helps to underscore the values of an interdisciplinary approach to understanding personality and the limitations of a narrow model.

Suggestions for Further Reading

Considering the extensive amount of research that Murray has done, he has written very little. He studied Melville intensively for twenty-five years and is widely respected as a Melville scholar through his valuable articles on that author. Unfortunately, his writing tends to be stiff and formal and he has a penchant for coining new words that makes him difficult to read. The student who is interested in his work is encouraged to read *Explorations in Personality* (Oxford University Press, 1938), his major work, written in collaboration with colleagues at the Harvard Psychological Clinic, which describes the findings of his monumental study undertaken there. Also useful is "Outline of a Conception of Personality," written with C. Kluckholn and included in C. Kluckholn, H. A. Murray, and D. M. Schneider (Eds.), *Personality in Nature, Society, and Culture* (Knopf, 1953). A most delightful read is his autobiography, in E. G. Boring and G. Lindzey, *A History of Psychology in Autobiography,* Vol. 5 (Appleton-Century-Crofts, 1967).

10

Gordon Allport: A Humanistic Trait Theory

Your Goals for This Chapter

1. Discuss Allport's final definition of *personality*.

2. Distinguish between *open and closed systems* in personality theory.

3. Explain how *common traits* differ from *personal dispositions* and tell how each is established.

4. Distinguish among three levels of personal dispositions.

5. Explain why Allport coined the term *proprium* and identify his seven *propriate functions*.

6. Discuss the concept of *functional autonomy*.

7. Describe Allport's concept of maturity.

8. Distinguish between *dimensional* and *morphogenic* approaches to the study of personality and give examples of each.

9. Evaluate Allport's theory in terms of its function as philosophy, science, and art. Hi Lisa, I Love you!

When a group of clinicians were asked which personality theorist was most influential for them in their everyday work, the name of Gordon Allport ranked second only to that of Freud. Allport is a theorist of monumental influence. With the possible exception of Cattell, he has explored the concept of "trait" more fully than any other personality theorist. At the same time, his concern to do justice to the complexity of personality paved the way for the humanistic approach that we will consider in Part 4. Allport describes his theory as **eclectic:** it selects the best from a variety of different concepts and methods. He is critical of narrow conceptions of personality and research, believing new methods of study are required to capture the richness and fullness of an individual's personality. He emphasizes the uniqueness of the individual, the contemporaneity of motives, and a holistic view of the person.

Biographical Background

Gordon Allport was born in 1897 in Indiana and grew up near Cleveland, Ohio. He was the son of a country doctor and he described his practical but humanitarian home life as one characterized by "plain Protestant piety and hard work." Allport has written little about his childhood; he has indicated that he spent much of it alone. He was adept at language, but poor at sports and games.

After he graduated from high school, his brother Floyd, who also became a distinguished psychologist, encouraged him to apply to Harvard, where he had gone. As an undergraduate, Allport concentrated on both psychology and social ethics and in his spare time engaged in social service activities. He ran a boys' club in Boston's West End, served as a volunteer probation officer for the Family Society, and assisted other groups.

Upon graduation, he accepted an opportunity to teach English and sociology at Robert College in Istanbul, Turkey, in a venture that can be seen as an early forerunner of the Peace Corps. Enjoying teaching, he then accepted a fellowship from Harvard for graduate study in psychology. He received his Ph.D. only two years later, in 1922. His dissertation, "An Experimental Study of the Traits of Personality," showed an interest in the area of traits that was to endure. It was also the first American study on personality traits.

Another fellowship for travel abroad followed and gave an opportunity for Allport to meet Freud. Allport described their meeting as follows. When he arrived, Freud sat silent, apparently waiting for Allport to state the reason for his visit. Allport was simply curious. Then, an incident came to mind that he thought might interest Freud, because it concerned a phobia that appeared to be set very early in life. He told him about an event that had happened on the streetcar on the way to Freud's office. A small boy who was obviously

Gordon Allport

afraid of dirt kept saying to his mother that he didn't want to sit on a dirty seat or next to a dirty man. When Allport finished, Freud looked at him and said, "And was that little boy you?" Allport was surprised, but he regained his composure and changed the subject. Still, he was shaken and he never forgot the incident. He began to feel that Freud's ascription of most behaviors to unconscious motives was incorrect and that an alternative theory of motivation was necessary. In his own theory, Allport did not probe into the dark side of personality; he did not concur with Freud's emphasis on sexuality and unconscious motivations.

On his return from Europe, Allport became an instructor in social ethics at Harvard, where he developed and taught what was probably the first course offered in personality in this country. In 1926 he left to take up an assistant professorship in psychology at Dartmouth but in 1930 he returned to Harvard, this time to stay. His contributions to Harvard were many. Most notably, he was an early advocate of interdisciplinary studies and a leader in the creation of the department of social relations, which combined degree programs in psychology, sociology, and anthropology. His professional honors were manifold and he was a popular and respected teacher. He died in 1967, one month before his seventieth birthday.

The Nature of Personality

Allport described and classified over fifty definitions of **personality** before he developed his own in 1937. After working with this definition for many years, he revised it in 1961. His final definition is: "Personality is the dynamic organization within the individual of those psychophysical systems that determine his characteristic behavior and thought." Each word in this definition is carefully chosen. Personality is *dynamic* (moving and changing), *organized* (structured), *psychophysical* (involving both the mind and the body), *determined* (structured by the past and predisposing of the future), and *characteristic* (unique for each individual).

Allport's definition makes it clear that to him personality is not a mere fiction or imaginary concept but a real entity. He wants to suggest that one's personality is somehow really there. He refers to the concept of personality as a hypothetical construct, which is currently unobservable because it cannot be measured empirically. However, Allport suggests it is an inescapable inference that may someday be demonstrated directly as a real existence within the person, involving neural or physiological components. Allport reminds us that at one time the planet Pluto was a hypothetical construct, postulated long before any telescope could observe it. In time, science was able to point directly to it. In time, Allport also hopes that neurophysiological and psychological research will show us the way to locate directly our present hypothetical construct of personality.

Allport distinguishes between open and closed systems in personality theory and argues for an open system (1960). A **closed system** is a concept of personality that admits little or nothing new from outside of the organism to influence or change it in any significant way. In a closed system, one's personality is seen as complete within itself or as simply responding automatically to stimuli within the environment. An **open system** is one that conceives of personality as having a dynamic potential for growth, reconstitution, and change through extensive transactions within itself and also with its environment.

Allport suggests that Freud's theory of psychoanalysis tends to be closed, because it does not fully envision personality as a dynamic growth system that has significant interactions with its environment. Psychoanalysis describes the ego as seeking to maintain a balance among the id, superego, and the outside world. This emphasis on **homeostasis** (balance and equilibrium) leads to a stress on stability and permanence rather than on growth and change in the concept of personality.

Allport describes a fully open theory as one that allows for a dynamic growth process within the organism and extensive interactions with the environment. Completely open theories of personality suggest that as the organism develops, it increases in complexity and becomes something more than it was. Such systems also conceive of personality as the patterning of different experiences that characterize the interaction of the individual with his or her environment. The individual is seen as participating in extensive transactions with various elements and situations that call on him or her to assume different roles.

Another way to state the distinction between open and closed systems of personality is to refer to continuity theories versus discontinuity theories. A **continuity theory** is one that suggests that the development of personality is essentially the accumulation of skills, habits, and discriminations, without anything really new appearing in the person's make-up. Changes are merely quantitative relative to the amount of inputs.

A **discontinuity theory** suggests that in the course of development, an organism experiences genuine transformations or changes so that it reaches successively higher levels of organization. Here growth is conceived as qualitatively different. Walking is considered very different from crawling, talking is viewed as discontinuous with babbling, and so forth, even though these behaviors emerge out of the earlier ones. If we picture personality as an organism into which inputs are given, a continuity theory merely sees the inputs accumulating, whereas a discontinuity theory suggests that at times during its development, the organism reorganizes, regroups, and reshapes these inputs so that the structure of personality changes radically. Such theories view the person as active in consolidating and integrating his or her experience. Change is qualitative rather than merely quantitative. Theories that posit stages of development of personality have the potential to imply discontinuity, because each stage entails a different organization of personality from the stage before it. Freud's psychoanalytic theory, though outlining stages of development, did not fully realize this potential because of its primary emphasis on the individual and intrapsychic factors. Elements within Freud's theory point toward discontinuity, but it remains semiclosed.

Traits

According to Allport, an individual's traits are really there. In order to emphasize his belief in the reality of traits, Allport proposed a biophysical conception of them as neuropsychic structures (1937). This is to say that traits are bona fide structures within a person that influence behavior. They are not simply labels that we use to describe or classify behaviors.

Allport defines a **trait** as a determining tendency or predisposition to respond and he suggests that traits may be considered the ultimate reality of psychological organization. The trait, like personality, is not in principle unobservable. In time, trait theorists may be able to measure traits empirically.

Allport distinguished between individual traits and common traits (1937). In his later writings, to clarify his position, he used the terms *common traits* and *personal dispositions.* The difference between them is that personal dispositions are unique and peculiar to each individual. Because no two people are exactly alike, no two persons can be said to possess identical personal dispositions. On the other hand, there are times when we wish to make comparisons among individuals. To do so, it is necessary to posit the imaginary construct of common traits that are shared. In a sense, common traits are more nominal (existing primarily in name as convenient fictions for making comparisons) than veridical (really there). Nevertheless, Allport would not wish to concede that they are nonexistent.

The primary importance of the distinction between common traits and personal dispositions is the way in which each is studied. The concept of common traits lends itself to traditional psychometric research, whereas the concept of personal dispositions requires new methodologies that permit the unique individuality of the person to emerge.

Common Traits

A **common trait** is a hypothetical construct that permits us to compare individuals within a given culture. Although no two people can be said to possess identical traits, we can discover roughly comparable traits that allow us to compare the predispositions that are held in common with other persons. Normal people in any given culture tend to develop along similar modes or lines of adjustment. In a competitive society, most individuals develop a level of assertiveness or ascendance that can be compared with the level of assertiveness in others. There are several aspects of personality in respect of which all people in a given culture may be compared.

In order to establish common traits, Allport employs traditional scientific methodology and psychometric tests that measure psychological characteristics through carefully designed questionnaires and statistical techniques. In order to determine whether or not a person is aggressive, we establish the frequency, range, and intensity of his or her aggressive behaviors. We ask how often the aggressive behavior occurs, how broadly it is applied in different situations, and how strong the reaction of aggression is. These criteria of frequency, range, and intensity are quantifiable; that is to say, they can be measured through the use of an appropriate test.

The statistical proof for the existence of a trait is found in different measures of **reliability.** For example, *observer reliability* is determined by noting whether or not judgments about an individual's behavior are confirmed by several different observers. *Repeat reliability* is established by readministering the same test or an alternate version to a subject and noting whether or not approximately the same score on a trait reappears. *Internal reliability* refers to the fact that if an individual behaves in a certain way in one situation, he or she will also behave in other situations in a manner that is similar to others who share the same trait. Internal reliability is established by finding out whether or not test items correlate with one another and with the total score for a large population of people. If, for all the people who take the test, high scorers on one item have a clear tendency to be high scorers on other specified items, the test is thought to have internal reliability and to be a consistent measurement of a common trait.

In brief, the hypothesizing of common traits suggests that if one kind of behavior is usually associated statistically with other kinds of behavior, there is evidence that a trait underlies the behaviors. If that evidence is derived from a large population of people, it may be assumed to be a common trait. Many common traits — preferred patterns shared by many individuals — have been established in this manner: ascendance-submission, neuroticism, extroversion-introversion, authoritarianism, manifest anxiety, the need for achievement, masculinity-femininity, and conformity.

A characteristic of common traits is their normal distribution among the population. The bulk of people have average scores and the rest gradually taper toward the high and low extreme scores. If these scores were plotted, they would form a bell-shaped curve, which is called the **normal curve of distribution.** Such a curve is shown in Figure 10.1. Most scores cluster around

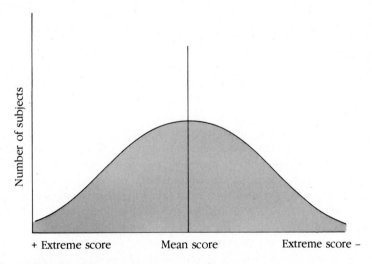

Figure 10.1 *The Normal Curve*
Allport suggests that most common traits show a normal distribution among the population.

the *mean* or average. The normal curve permits us to compare individuals with respect to a common trait. High or low scores can be considered as deviations from the group norm.

Personal Dispositions

Comparisons may be made among individuals but in the last analysis no two individuals are exactly alike. A **personal disposition** is, like a trait, a general determining characteristic but it is unique to the individual who has it. Although comparisons cannot be made among personal dispositions, personal dispositions are necessary if one is to reflect accurately the personality structure of a particular individual. Whereas common traits place individuals into comparable categories, personal dispositions, if correctly diagnosed, more accurately describe the individual in his or her uniqueness.

Each one of us has personal dispositions that are of greater and lesser importance. If a personal disposition is so pervasive that almost every behavior of the individual appears to be influenced by it, it is called a **cardinal disposition.** An example would be an extreme lust for power, so intensive that virtually every act of the individual can be seen to be governed by that desire. Allport believes that cardinal dispositions are quite rare. Nevertheless, some historical figures, such as Napoleon, have been described as possessed of a cardinal disposition like the lust for power.

Central dispositions refer to highly characteristic tendencies of an individual. They provide the adjectives or phrases a person might use in describing the essential characteristics of another individual in a letter of recommendation. Allport suggests that the number of central dispositions necessary to describe the essential characteristics of an individual normally varies between five and ten. **Secondary dispositions** are more specific, focused tendencies that are often situational in character and less crucial to the personality structure. A person may have a large number of these. A man might be domineering and aggressive at home in his role as father but behave submissively when confronted by a police officer who is giving him a ticket.

Rating scales or testing instruments are useful for determining common traits, but they are less useful in determining personal dispositions. Still, they can be helpful, as significantly high or low scores on common traits may suggest areas where personal dispositions may be found. Analysis of an individual's behaviors may also be a method of locating personal dispositions. If the investigator has data on a large number of behaviors of an individual available, he or she can look for recurring patterns. This method was used in a classic study known as *Letters from Jenny.* Over three hundred letters written by a woman throughout middle and old age were analyzed and they revealed a number of unmistakable central dispositions. We can also test hypothesized personal dispositions. Having hypothesized that an individual possesses a certain central disposition, we can make a prediction about his or her subsequent behaviors. We could then count his or her behaviors to see how many of them manifested the characteristic. Finally, studies of individuals in the clinical setting afford an excellent opportunity for investigating personal dispositions.

Exploration /////

Central Dispositions

Think of a close friend or someone whom you know well. On a blank sheet of paper, try to describe his or her personality by jotting down those words or phrases that express his or her essential characteristics. Include those qualities that you consider of major importance in an accurate description. Then do the same thing for yourself. Count the number of words or phrases necessary to describe your friend or yourself. Chances are the number falls between five and ten. Allport suggests that the number of highly characteristic central dispositions along which a personality is organized generally falls within that range. In his own research the average was seven. Does your evidence support this hypothesis?

The Proprium

Allport's humanistic orientation can most clearly be seen in his concept of the proprium. Allport coined the term "proprium" in order to avoid the terms "ego" or "self," which he believes are often used as catchall phrases for those elements of personality that cannot be accounted for in any other way. Allport's **proprium** refers to the central experiences of self-awareness that a person has as he or she grows and moves forward.

The prefix *pro-* is important. Allport conducted a study to see how frequently words containing the prefixes *re-* and *pro-* appeared in psychological literature and language (1960). The prefix *re-* means "back" and connotes backward movement, whereas the prefix *pro-* means "forth" and connotes forward movement. Allport discovered that words with the prefix *re-* outnumbered words with the prefix *pro-* nearly five to one. From psychoanalysis, we have terms like "repression" and "regression." Stimulus-response theory abounds with terms like "reflex," "reaction," "response." All these terms suggest a backward direction and preoccupation with the past rather than the future. They suggest that personality can be accounted for in terms of past events.

The proprium is defined in terms of its functions or the things that it does.

Between the ages of six and twelve, the propriate function of self as rational coper develops as children discover that they can use their intellectual capacities to solve problems.

Allport refers to these as **propriate functions.** None of them are innate; rather, they develop gradually over time as an individual grows from infancy to adulthood. Allport describes seven propriate functions (1961): sense of bodily self, self-identity, self-esteem, extension of self, self-image, self as rational coper, and propriate striving. Together, these activities of the proprium constitute an evolving sense of self as known and felt.

The first propriate function to emerge is the sense of **bodily self.** It consists of sensations in the body and entails coming to know one's body limits. Certain parts of the body are emphasized as more important than others. Thus, young children, when instructed to wash the face and hands, wash the palms and front of the face but invariably overlook the back of their hands and behind their ears. Most of us, even as adults, tend to locate the self in the head region. This bodily sense, which is learned, remains the foundation of our self-awareness.

The second propriate function, the sense of **self-identity,** refers to the awareness of inner sameness and continuity. Infants are not aware of themselves as individuals and cannot separate themselves and other objects. Gradually, out of an undifferentiated whole, the infant comes to distinguish between inner and outer. The external world is developed first; later, the child discovers a sense of "I." These first two propriate functions begin to emerge from eighteen months onward.

Between the ages of two and three the third propriate function, **self-esteem,** develops. Self-esteem refers to the feelings of pride as the child develops his or her ability to do things. It is comparable to Erikson's stage of autonomy, which reflects the child's need to feel that he or she can control him- or herself and other objects. Two-year-olds are eager to do things for themselves and do not want others to help them. One mark of the child's emerging sense of self-esteem is negativism. The child employs the word "no" to assert his or her freedom from adult control. A certain amount of negativism is necessary for the development of self-esteem.

Between the ages of four and six, two other propriate functions emerge: self-extension and self-image. **Self-extension** refers to a sense of possession. Children recognize that certain toys and certain people belong to them and identify them as "my ball," "my daddy." Self-extension leads into a valuing of others because of their relationship to oneself. In the adult years one's children are perceived as extensions of the self. **Self-image** refers to a sense of the expectation of others and its comparison with one's own behavior. The child comes to understand parental expectations and to see him- or herself as fulfilling or not fulfilling those desired roles. This early self-image lays the foundation for development of conscience and, later, intentions and goals.

Between the ages of six and twelve, the propriate function of **self as rational coper** develops. Children discover that they can use their own rational capacities to solve problems. They begin to perceive of themselves as active, problem-solving agents, who can develop a sense of competence in what they do. Allport compares the self as coper with Freud's concept of the ego as the executor of the personality.

Lastly, during adolescence, the function of propriate striving emerges. **Propriate striving** refers to the projection of long-term purposes and goals and the development of a plan to attain them. Such efforts are essential for the development of self-identity, which Erikson had pinpointed as the primary feature of adolescence.

Allport believes that there is a marked difference between the infant and the adult. The infant is a dependent, impatient, pleasure-seeking, "unsocialized horror," largely governed by unlearned biological drives, who can tolerate little delay in the fulfillment of those drives and reflexes. The infant has the potentialities for personality, but "can scarcely be said to have personality"

(1961). Given the appropriate security and affection, the child will grow in the direction of developing a proprium. The child will be transformed from a biologically dominated organism to a psychologically mature adult. The adult person is discontinuous from the child. The adult emerges from the child but is no longer governed by the child's needs.

Not only is there a radical discontinuity between the child and the mature adult, but Allport also suggests that there is a radical discontinuity between healthy adults and neurotics. The life of neurotics is marked by cognitive crippling. In their efforts to find security, neurotics react in rigid, inflexible ways. Such individuals continue to behave as children, dominated by infantile drives and conflicts. Their propriums are undeveloped and their motives remain tied to original needs.

Functional Autonomy

Closely related to Allport's concept of the proprium is his concept of **functional autonomy,** which implies that adult motivation is not necessarily tied to the past. A given behavior may become a goal in itself regardless of its original intention. Thus, adult motives are not necessarily related to the earlier experiences in which the motive or activity initially appeared.

For example, let us imagine that young Johnny's father was a baseball fan. During his spare time and on Saturdays he played baseball with his son. Originally, Johnny played baseball with his Dad to gain his attention and to please him. During his school years, Johnny also played baseball with the other children in his neighborhood and was an active member of Little League. He discovered that he was competent in the game and, what is more, he enjoyed it. In high school and college, he played in the intramural sports program. Later, he was recruited to play with a major league. Today, as he is standing at bat for the Yankees or Dodgers, does it make sense to insist that his motive for playing baseball continues to be that of pleasing his father? Does it not seem more reasonable to suggest that he plays because he enjoys the game and the financial rewards that it brings? His present motives are entirely different and free from his original motives. There may be a historical tie, but there is no functional tie. His motive is functionally autonomous.

Allport refers to two levels of functional autonomy: perseverative functional autonomy and propriate functional autonomy.

Perseverative functional autonomy refers to acts or behaviors that are repeated even though they may have lost their original function; they are not controlled by the proprium and have no genuine connection with it. A teen-age girl may, in a spirit of rebellion against her parents, begin to smoke cigarettes, which she knows will annoy them. As an adult, she may continue to smoke cigarettes, long after her period of teen-age rebellion. Perseverative functional autonomy refers to repetitive activities such as compulsions, addictions to drugs or alcohol, ritualistic or routine behaviors. Such actions are free of the original motives that spurred them into being but they cannot be said to be governed by the proprium.

Propriate functional autonomy refers to those acquired interests, values, attitudes, intentions, and lifestyle that are directed from the proprium and are genuinely free of earlier motivations. Abilities frequently convert into interests. The person selects those values that are important. He or she then organizes these motives in a fashion that is consistent with his or her self-image and lifestyle. In short, there is a radical discontinuity between the motivation of the infant and that of the healthy adult.

Allport acknowledges that not all behaviors are functionally autonomous. Among the processes that are not are: drives, reflexes, constitutionally determined capacities such as physique and intellect, habits, primary reinforcements, infantilisms and fixations, some neuroses, and sublimations. At times it is difficult to determine whether or not a motive is functionally autonomous. Further, certain motives may be autonomous only to a certain degree. Nevertheless, Allport believes that many of the motives of the healthy, mature adult may be considered to be governed by propriate functional autonomy. Allport's rationale for developing the concept of propriate functional autonomy is the desire to underscore the concept that we live in the present, not in the past. Allport does not say that there is no continuity between the present and the past but rather that the healthy adult individual is not bound to the past. He or she is free to live in the present and the future unencumbered by the past.

Allport's concept of functional autonomy has been the subject of a great deal of controversy and criticism. In presenting his theories to the public, Allport's concern has been to teach and provoke interest rather than to make statements that are above reproach. Thus, it is often very difficult to differentiate between what he assumes and what he has established through empirical procedures. The concept of functional autonomy is not a construct that lends itself to operational definition, predictions, or empirical tests. The phenomena that Allport explains as functionally autonomous can also be explained by rival constructs. Further, Allport does not clearly describe the developmental processes that underlie functional autonomy. He fails to explain how or why it occurs (Hall and Lindzey, 1978).

Still, Allport's concepts are highly congruent with recent developments in personality theory. His emphasis on discontinuity is picked up by humanist and cognitive theorists. His concepts of functional autonomy and propriate functions harmonize with recent expansions in psychoanalysis. The goal of psychoanalysis is to strengthen the functioning of the ego. The intent of the reconstruction of the past in psychoanalysis is to permit the patient to work through the past so that it loses its grip on the individual. By becoming aware of one's unconscious motivations, one is free to behave differently in the future if one so wishes. Thus, the intent of psychoanalysis is congruent, if not synonymous, with the development of propriate functional autonomy.

Allport is one of the earliest modern personality theorists to devote his attention to the mature, healthy personality rather than to the immature, neurotic one. As we have seen, Allport believes that there is a radical discontinuity between the neurotic and the healthy personality. He concurs with Jung that too many personality theorists center their discussion of personality on the characteristics of the neurotic and view health simply as the absence of neurotic symptoms. He suggests that we need a positive definition of health that will enable us to point to an ideal in adult life. In his discussion (1961), Allport posits *six criteria of maturity*: extension of the sense of self; warm relating of self to others; emotional security; realistic perception; insight and humor; a unifying philosophy of life. In essence, maturity means freedom from one's past and the expression of propriate functions. Allport's concept of maturity reflects elements of Jung's concept of self-actualization and Adler's concept of the creative self.

Methods of Research

Allport has written extensively on methods of inquiry and investigation that are useful for the study of personality, and some of his own research in the area is considered classic. Allport points out that personality is so complex that every legitimate method of study should be included in its pursuit. He is critical of those who limit their research and do not encourage or permit the study of personality concepts that are not easily submitted to empirical test. At the same time, he is also critical of applying methods appropriate to the study of neurotic individuals to the normal individual.

Allport's view of personality as open and discontinuous does not lend itself very well to study by the methods traditionally practiced in academic psychology, which seek to discover general laws that apply to all individual cases. The emphasis, particularly in American psychology, has been on the **dimensional (or nomothetic)** approach, studying large groups of individuals to determine the frequency with which certain events occur and from this to infer general variables or universal principles. Normalcy is often conceived as that behavior that occurs most regularly. Thus, the behavior that is considered normal for a two-year-old is the behavior that is shared in common by most two-year-olds. Psychologists look for common traits that are shared by a large number of the population. The individual is studied to see if and where he or she deviates from the norm. Allport encourages a **morphogenic (or idiographic)** approach that centers on the individual, employing techniques and variables that are appropriate to understanding the uniqueness of each person. Morphogenic approaches aim at discovering laws that govern the particular individual. Although such methods are difficult, time consuming, and often expensive to evolve, their aim is to account for the unique event that is theoretically just as open to lawful explanation as the frequent event. An example of a morphogenic approach that we are already familiar with is psychoanalysis, which is an extensive investigation into the historical development and psychic structure of one individual.

Most of Allport's own research was of the dimensional type but he urged the development and greater use of morphogenic approaches as an ultimately better technique for understanding and predicting behavior. This is consistent with his emphasis on the uniqueness of each individual. Allport was also a pioneer in developing morphogenic approaches to the study of personality.

With Philip Vernon and Gardner Lindzey, Allport developed a Study of Values Scale, which is a dimensional measurement designed to examine individuality. The scale measures six common traits originally delineated by Spranger (1928): the theoretical, aesthetic, social, political, religious, and economic. Because the test reflects the relative strengths of these six values within one's own personality, one individual's score cannot be compared with anyone else's. The final profile that emerges on the test is individual, personal, and relevant only to the person who has taken the test. The test has been widely used in counseling and vocational guidance and has proved to be a significant research tool in studies of selective perception.

In the 1940s, over three hundred letters written by a woman (Jenny Masterson) between her fifty-ninth and seventieth year to a young married couple came to Allport's attention. He and his students analyzed these letters to determine Jenny's central dispositions. In studying these documents, Allport tried to note the frequency with which certain themes or ideas appeared. He asked other people to read the letters and assess Jenny in terms of her traits. He also discussed Jenny's personality in terms of different personality theories. Allport believed that the study of personal documents, such as diaries, autobiographies, and letters, could be a potentially valuable morphogenic approach. Such study cannot be sloppy or loose but must be conducted under clear scientific guidelines, some of which need further refinement.

Allport and Philip Vernon initiated research into expressive behavior during the early 1930s. **Expressive behavior** refers to the study of an individual's manner of performing. Every behavior has a coping and an expressive aspect. The *coping aspect* refers to what the act does to deal with or adapt to the task at hand. The *expressive aspect* refers to how the act is done. When you listen to a lecture you concentrate on what the lecturer is saying (the coping aspect of his or her behavior) but you also take note of how he or she is delivering the lecture. The lecturer may be nervous or relaxed; he or she may talk in a loud or soft voice. These expressive aspects of behavior prompt you to make certain inferences about the lecturer as a person.

Ordinarily we pay more attention to coping behavior than to expressive behavior. But expressive behavior, because it is more spontaneous, can be highly revelatory of basic personality aspects. Allport and others conducted considerable research on several expressive features of personality: the face, voice, posture, gesture, gait, and handwriting. They discovered that there is a marked consistency in a person's expressive behavior. In some instances, Allport was able to deduce certain traits and make accurate judgments about an individual's personality. Allport acknowledges that research is not yet at the point where the study of expressive behaviors can provide a full guide to psychodiagnosis. Nevertheless, he suggests that further research in this area is highly desirable because a person's expressive manner and style may be the most important factor in understanding the personality.

Allport's Theory: Philosophy, Science, and Art

Allport's personality theory is a highly creative one. Although many of his ideas are reminiscent of other theories, he combines others' insights with his own to develop a truly unique approach. His original concepts, like personal dispositions, the proprium, and functional autonomy, are highly controversial and extremely stimulating. In his emphasis on the uniqueness of the individual, the contemporaneity of motives, and a holistic view of the person, Allport foreshadows theories that we will consider in Part 4. Indeed, the emphasis in his theory is not on the past but on forward movement.

Allport insisted that because personality is so complex, every legitimate method of study should be included in our efforts to comprehend it. He used rigorous scientific methods in the establishment of common traits. At the same time, he pointed out that the statistical methods of animal experimentation used in the psychological laboratory do not necessarily lead to a full understanding of human nature. Alternative methods that help us understand the uniqueness of each individual need to be developed. In his own research, Allport recognized the value of other methodologies and used information drawn from literature, philosophy, art, and religion, as well as from science. His most creative contributions to personality theorizing, concepts like the proprium and functional autonomy, do not lend themselves readily to operational definitions. Allport believed that an open system of personality encourages the invention of new methods of research; these methods aim at rigor but do not forfeit the study of certain aspects of personality because present scientific methodologies cannot embrace such study.

Allport realized that to understand the whole human being, it is necessary to comprehend the individual philosophically as well as scientifically. "The philosophy of the person is inseparable from the psychology of the person"

(1961). Indeed, any psychological stance, Allport pointed out, is implicitly linked to basic philosophical assumptions.

Allport was not a practicing psychotherapist and did not develop a specific therapeutic technique. Nevertheless, many of his ideas, like functional autonomy, propriate functions, and the radical discontinuity between normal and neurotic adults, have been useful to clinicians.

Allport has not developed a school of followers, but his theory has had considerable impact, as attested to by the frequent references to Allport in psychological literature. His work offers a bridge between traditional academic psychology, which emphasizes psychometrics and dimensional studies, and clinical psychology, which concentrates on a more morphogenic approach to the understanding of personality.

Summary

1. Allport described and classified over fifty definitions of **personality** before finalizing his own definition: "Personality is the dynamic organization within the individual of those psychophysical systems that determine his characteristic behavior and thought."

2. Allport distinguishes between **closed systems** of personality that are **continuous** and admit little change and **open systems** that are **discontinuous** and provide for extensive growth.

3. Allport distinguishes between **common traits,** hypothetical constructs that permit us to make comparisons between individuals, and **personal dispositions,** which are unique to each person. Common traits and personal dispositions are studied by different research methods.

4. There are three levels of personal dispositions: **cardinal, central,** and **secondary.**

5. Allport coined the term **proprium** to refer to the central experience of self-awareness that a person has as he or she grows and moves forward. He describes seven **propriate functions:** sense of **bodily self, self-identity, self-esteem, self-extension, self-image, self as rational coper,** and **propriate striving.**

6. The concept of **functional autonomy** implies that adult motivation is not necessarily tied to the past. There are two levels of functional autonomy: **perseverative** and **propriate.**

7. Allport was one of the first theorists to discuss the healthy personality. He posited six criteria of maturity.

8. The **dimensional** approach to the study of personality studies large groups

of individuals in order to infer general variables or universal principles. The **morphogenic** approach centers on the individual, using techniques that are appropriate to understanding the uniqueness of each person.

9. Allport respected and used the methods of rigorous science in establishing common traits, but he also recognized the value of other methods and the need to understand the individual philosophically as well as scientifically.

Suggestions for Further Reading

Allport was a prolific author whose many writings have a clear teaching intent. He sought to describe and illustrate his concepts vividly. His writings are enjoyable to read and of great interest to the student of personality.

Allport's pioneer effort in the field of personality theory was *Personality: A Psychological Interpretation* (Holt, 1937). This work constitutes the initial presentation of his theory: distinguishing between common and individual traits and introducing the concept of functional autonomy. A revised and updated statement of his position is given in *Pattern and Growth in Personality* (Holt, Rinehart, and Winston, 1961). In this work, Allport introduces the concept of personal disposition and emphasizes the uniqueness of each individual. The book is highly readable and strongly recommended as an introduction to Allport's thought. *Becoming: Basic Considerations for a Psychology of Personality* (Yale University Press, 1955) underscores Allport's humanistic and futuristic approach. In it he discusses the criteria for maturity. Also recommended are *The Person in Psychology: Selected Essays* (Beacon Press, 1968), which contains a group of Allport's important articles; and *The Individual and His Religion* (Macmillan, 1960), which offers a psychological interpretation of religion as a normal phenomenon of human behavior.

11
Raymond Cattell: Psychometric Trait Theory

Your Goals for This Chapter

1. Describe Kretschmer's typology and distinguish between *typologies* and *traits*.

2. State what is expressed in a *correlation*.

3. Describe Sheldon's classic study.

4. Cite Cattell's definition of *personality* and compare his interest in personality theorizing with that of other theorists.

5. Distinguish between *source* and *surface traits* and give examples of different kinds of source and surface traits.

6. Distinguish among *ergs, sentiments,* and *attitudes* and show how they may be thought of as related to one another in a *dynamic lattice*.

7. Explain how Cattell identifies traits through *factor analysis*.

8. Describe the salient features of the theories of Eysenck and Buss and Plomin.

9. Discuss how trait theories raise controversial issues with regard to the role of heredity and environment in personality.

10. Evaluate Cattell's theory in terms of its function as philosophy, science, and art.

A central issue in personality theorizing has been the importance of inherited genetic factors as opposed to environmental factors in shaping personality. In the lay person's mind, differences in behavior have often been thought to be due to general physical characteristics that are inherited. Thus we have common stereotypes such as "Fat people are jolly" or "Redheads are hot-tempered." In other instances, it has been thought that an individual's potential is clearly limited by inherited factors. Thus, although a better diet may help us grow taller or act more intelligently, there are believed to be limitations that have been imposed by our genetic make-up. Recent developments in areas such as behavioral genetics, psychophysiology, and psychopharmacology emphasize the importance of biological and chemical factors in personality and behavior. Many of these factors are inherited. This chapter discusses a number of theorists who have wrestled with these issues, focusing on Raymond Cattell.

Biographical Background

Raymond Cattell was born in Staffordshire, England, in 1905. His childhood was a happy one. His parents set high standards of behavior but gave their children considerable freedom in choosing their activities. Much outdoor activity and competition with his brothers characterized his youth. England became involved in World War I when Cattell was nine. He later acknowledged that the war had a significant impact on him. He saw trainloads of injured men being transported to a converted hospital near his home. The sight impressed upon him the "brevity of life." He became more serious and inclined to work.

Raymond Cattell received his B.S.C. from the University of London in 1924 at the age of nineteen. He majored in chemistry and physics, but his interest in social concerns led him to pursue psychology, in which he earned a Ph.D. in 1929. His graduate work was also undertaken at the University of London where he studied under Spearman, a distinguished psychologist who developed the procedure of factor analysis that Cattell would later employ.

The following years were difficult. Employment was hard to come by for a psychologist, so Cattell worked at several part-time jobs. He was a lecturer at Exeter University and he established a clinic in Leicester. Meanwhile, he continued his own research. The depressed economy and his own poor health led to several lean years, during which he was haunted by poverty and his marriage broke up. Nevertheless, he remained steadfast in his dedication to his work. He was anxious to apply Spearman's technique of factor analysis to the study of personality.

In 1937, the University of London awarded Cattell an honorary doctorate of science for his contributions to research in personality. That same year

Raymond Cattell

he received an invitation to serve as a research associate to E. L. Thorndike at Columbia University in New York. Subsequently, he became a professor of psychology at Clark University and later at Harvard. In 1945, he was offered a research professorship at the University of Illinois, which enabled him to devote his full time and energy to his research. Cattell is presently a resident professor at the University of Hawaii at Manoa.

Cattell has received several honors and made significant contributions to the study of personality. He has published a phenomenal number of books and articles on a number of different topics. Although his primary emphasis has been on the study of personality through the techniques of factor analysis, he does not lack interest in or concern with other areas of psychology. His interest in clinical psychology led him to attempt to develop a more scientific foundation for analyzing personality structure. More recently, in 1973, he established a nonprofit Institute for Research on Morality and Self-Realization in Boulder, Colorado. Here he hopes to bring together his scientific concerns and his social and religious ones.

Before discussing Cattell's theory, it will be useful to look briefly at two theories that preceded his, those of Ernest Kretschmer and William Sheldon.

Historical Background: Kretschmer and Sheldon

Ernest Kretschmer, a German psychiatrist (1888–1964), developed an early modern typology, suggesting that people could be classified on the basis of their **morphology,** or body measurements. Different clusters of personality traits were linked to different body types because hormonal secretions created both the shape of the body and personality characteristics. *Asthenics* were thin, long-limbed, and narrow-chested; they tended to be aloof, withdrawn, shy, and sensitive. *Pyknics* were short, fat, and barrel-chested; they were inclined to fluctuations in mood — being either jovial, lively, and outgoing or deeply depressed. *Athletics* were balanced in physique and muscular development and they tended to be energetic, aggressive, and sanguine. Kretschmer's theory had the advantage of further suggesting that there is a typical body structure for each of the two main forms of mental illness: schizophrenia and manic-depressive. The asthenic type was associated with schizophrenia and the pyknic type with manic-depression.

Kretschmer's work was extremely influential, but it was criticized because it was difficult to fit everyone into a proper category and many people did not behave according to their assigned body type. The difficulty was that Kretschmer could not envision mixtures; he believed that everyone was a pure type.

To avoid the problems that Kretschmer's theory encountered, William Sheldon (1899–1977) described individuals in terms of traits. Whereas **typologies** imply distinct, discrete, and separate categories into which an individual can be placed, **traits** refer to continuous dimensions that individuals possess to varying degrees. Modern **trait theories** recognize that individuals vary considerably with regard to the same characteristic. We can speak of two types of stature — tall or short. Within any given population, however, we find a continuous gradation of statures from tall to short. Most of the population, moreover, tends to fall in the middle, being neither extremely tall nor extremely short. Height is an example of a continuous dimension that varies among individuals. Traits, like typologies, are hypothetical constructs that are used to explain behavior. Sheldon's theory is important because it marks the transition from earlier typologies to a much more sophisticated approach to understanding personality in terms of traits and it foreshadows many of the concerns that occupy dispositional theorists today.

In a classic study (1940), Sheldon identifies three primary aspects of bodily constitution and demonstrates a significant positive correlation with three basic temperaments. His research is a good example of a correlational study that tries to tell us whether or not two variables are related. Whereas in an experiment one variable (or more) is systematically varied in order to see whether or not it has an effect on other variables, in a correlational study there is no effort to manipulate any of the variables. Instead, they are carefully and systematically observed as they naturally occur. A **correlation** does not imply a cause-and-effect relationship among variables, it simply tells us whether they covary directly or inversely.

The three primary aspects of bodily constitution were identified by carefully examining photographs of four thousand college-age men and noticing three extreme variations that departed most widely from the "average" male physique. Sheldon labeled the three components **endomorphy, mesomorphy,** and **ectomorphy.** *Endomorphs* have a predominance of soft roundness throughout the body. Their digestive tract appears to dominate their bodily appearance. *Mesomorphs* have a predominance of muscle, bone, and connective tissue. Their physique is generally hard, heavy, and rectangular. *Ectomorphs* have a predominance of linearity and fragility. Relative to their mass, they have the greatest surface area and sensory exposure to the outside world. Their brain and central nervous system are also more predominant. A lay person might wish to define the three basic types as a tendency to be fat, muscular, or thin, but as we shall see, this is somewhat misleading.

In order to express a given individual's body type, Sheldon used a **somatotype.** Each individual was ranked, on a scale of 1 to 7, according to the degree to which he or she exhibited a particular component. The number 1 was assigned when the component was exhibited to the least degree. The number 7 indicated the maximum manifestation of the component. Thus, three separate numbers make up an individual's somatotype. The somatotype 7–1–1 indicates that an individual's physique is extreme in endomorphy and expresses a minimum of the other two components. The somatotype 4–4–4 characterizes the individual who is at the midpoint of all three components.

The somatotype was seen as an enduring physical component that is not subject to change by weight gain or loss or nutritional factors. This is why the definition of fat, muscular, or thin ultimately misleads. A better comparison is to the concept of bone structure. Each one of us can be described as having a light, medium, or heavy bone structure that does not vary as we grow taller or gain weight. Starve an endomorph and you do not end up with an ectomorph; you simply end up with an emaciated endomorph.

Next, Sheldon made up a list of fifty personality traits and rated a group of men whom he had carefully observed over a long period of time on each of the traits. Three main clusters of traits appeared: **viscerotonia:** a general love of comfort, relaxation, sociability, people, food, and affection; **somatotonia:** a predominance of muscular activity and vigorous bodily assertiveness, and thus a tendency to seek action and power; and **cerebrotonia:** a predominance of restraint, inhibition, and the desire for concealment.

Finally, Sheldon conducted a correlational analysis to see whether or not any of the physiques and temperaments were related. The specific positive correlations he found (1944) were:

endomorphy and viscerotonia $+.79$

mesomorphy and somatotonia $+.82$

ectomorphy and cerebrotonia $+.83$

Such correlations suggest the hypothesis that physical constitution plays a large role in motivation and temperament (see Table 11.1). Sheldon himself believed that both body build and temperament are primarily the result of heredity.

Sheldon did not deny the influence of environmental forces on personality. He took an interactionist view. However, he felt that biological and constitutional factors play a role that had been largely ignored in American psychology and he sought to clarify that role. He recommended that parents, teachers, and others who are interested in the developmental process seriously consider the child's somatotype. They could then assist the child in developing aspirations and expectations that were consistent with his or her physique and temperament and avoiding those that were incompatible. They can also develop disciplinary measures that are consistent with the individual's basic nature so as to bring out rather than thwart his or her potential (1940).

Sheldon laid the groundwork for and helped to create a significant movement in contemporary personality theory — **psychometric trait theory.** Sheldon's research is firmly grounded in empirical studies and validating evidence. His introduction of continuous variables rather than discrete categories represents a distinct advance over the earlier typologies. His conscientious research provides an excellent example of the use of psychometrics in personality theory. Nevertheless, even if we agree that there is a correlation between physique and temperament, we have no proof of a causal relationship between the two. A correlation is a measure of covariance; it does not inform us about causes and effects. Further, although Sheldon looked toward constitutional

Table 11.1 *Sheldon's Relationships among Components of Physique and Temperament*

Physique		Temperament	
Component	Description	Component	Description
Endomorphy	Predominance of soft roundness	Visceratonia	General love of comfort, relaxation, sociability, people, and food
Mesomorphy	Predominance of muscle, bone, and connective tissue	Somatotonia	Tendency to seek action and power through bodily assertiveness
Ectomorphy	Predominance of linearity and fragility	Cerebrotonia	Predominance of restraint, inhibition, and concealment

factors to account for human behavior, he did not explain how body type influences temperament and disposition. This is one reason why his theory has not been widely adopted. His primary contribution was to provide us with a model of measuring and describing physique and temperament. Psychologists have used his work as a springboard for the development of even more sophisticated psychometric techniques.

Exploration ////

Estimating Your Somatotype

You can estimate your own somatotype by the following crude measurement of temperament.* Read the three scales. Study each statement and ask yourself whether that item is generally characteristic of you. Place an X next to those sentences that are characteristic of you. Do not worry about items that appear contradictory. If you are uncertain about an item, do not mark it.

Scale A

_____ 1. I am relaxed in posture and movement.
_____ 2. I love physical comfort.
_____ 3. I am slow to react.
_____ 4. I love to eat.
_____ 5. I dislike eating alone.
_____ 6. I feel pleasant after a meal.
_____ 7. I like ceremony and ritual.
_____ 8. I love people.
_____ 9. I am friendly to everyone.
_____ 10. I am miserable if someone doesn't like me.
_____ 11. I am oriented to people rather than to things.
_____ 12. I am easygoing.
_____ 13. I am tolerant.
_____ 14. I am complacent.
_____ 15. I am a deep sleeper.
_____ 16. I am malleable, finding good points to both sides of an argument.
_____ 17. I enjoy talking about my feelings.
_____ 18. I am relaxed, happy, and talkative under alcohol.
_____ 19. I need people when I am troubled.

*Adapted from the short scales of temperament in W. H. Sheldon, *The Varieties of Temperament*, New York: Harper, 1942, p. 26. Used by permission of the author.

(continued)

_____ 20. I am oriented toward childhood and family relations.

Total _____

Scale B

_____ 1. I am assertive in posture and movement.
_____ 2. I love physical adventure.
_____ 3. I am energetic.
_____ 4. I need and enjoy exercise.
_____ 5. I like to dominate and have power.
_____ 6. I love risks and chances.
_____ 7. I am bold and direct in manner.
_____ 8. I have physical courage in combat.
_____ 9. I am competitively aggressive.
_____ 10. I am unsentimental.
_____ 11. I dislike small closed-in places.
_____ 12. I am ruthless and unsqueamish.
_____ 13. I have an unrestrained voice.
_____ 14. I have a high tolerance for pain.
_____ 15. I am generally noisy.
_____ 16. I was an early maturer.
_____ 17. I am quick to make decisions.
_____ 18. I am assertive and aggressive under alcohol.
_____ 19. I need to act when I am troubled.
_____ 20. I am oriented toward goals and activities of youth.

Total _____

Scale C

_____ 1. I am restrained in posture and movement.
_____ 2. I am overly quick to respond physically to an event such as a possible accident.
_____ 3. My reactions are immediate and precise.
_____ 4. I love privacy.
_____ 5. I am hyperattentive and mentally alert.
_____ 6. I am emotionally restrained and keep my feelings secret.
_____ 7. I avoid looking directly at others.
_____ 8. I prefer small intimate groups rather than large ones.
_____ 9. I avoid talking to other people.
_____ 10. I resist habits and routines.

_____ 11. I dislike wide-open places.

_____ 12. My attitudes are hard for others to predict.

_____ 13. I am generally quiet.

_____ 14. I am hypersensitive to pain.

_____ 15. I have poor sleep habits and am often tired.

_____ 16. I look younger than my age.

_____ 17. I am introverted and a deep thinker.

_____ 18. I abstain or avoid getting intoxicated with alcohol.

_____ 19. I need to be alone when I am troubled.

_____ 20. I am oriented toward things that older people enjoy.

Total _____

When you have marked the sentences that describe you, add the number of items that you checked on each scale and divide each total by three, rounding off to the nearest whole number. The resulting three-digit number will provide you with a rough somatotype, showing the degree to which you possess each of the core components. A yields a rough measurement of endomorph-viscerotonia; B describes mesomorph-somatotonia; C depicts the ectomorph-cerebrotonia. You probably checked some items on each scale but showed a predominance in one.

It is only fair to caution you, however, that this exercise is not presented as a valid measuring device nor does it even come close to approximating the careful scrutiny Sheldon gave his subjects. But it does permit you to begin to assess the value of Sheldon's work as a means of self-exploration.

Since Sheldon asserted that his temperament characteristics hold true over time, you might wish to assess further the accuracy of your somatotype by asking your parents or a friend who has known you for a long time to rate you both as you were several years ago and as you are now. These findings can be compared with your self-rating and own historical recollection.

Cattell's Definition of Personality

Cattell begins with a tentative definition of **personality.** "Personality is that which permits a prediction of what a person will do in a given situation" (1950). He believes that a full definition of personality must await further investigation into the types of concepts that are included in the study of behavior. His general statement may be expressed in the formula $R = f(P, S)$, which reads: A response (R) is a function (f) of the person (P) and the stimuli (S). Cattell observes that the response and the stimuli can be precisely determined in an experiment in which the experimenter carefully structures the situation. However, the person is a less well-known factor that needs further exploration. Cattell believes that the investigation of traits will assist us in understanding the structure and function of the person.

Cattell's definition of personality provides a striking and important comparison between his interest and method of personality research and that of other theorists, such as the Freudians. Freud developed psychoanalysis as a means of understanding one's self and developing a comprehensive theory of human nature. He was particularly concerned not with the efficacy of psychoanalysis as a predictive tool but with the compelling character of the vision of one's self or humanity that it provided. Cattell, on the other hand, is concerned with the **heuristic value** of constructs about personality, the power of a construct to predict future events. His stance is that of the empirical scientist who derives from his or her theory propositions that are subject to empirical test. In a sense, prediction is more difficult than explanation, as it is easier to account for events that have happened than it is to predict them. Prediction is also useful in that it enables us to anticipate what will happen in certain situations. On the other hand, a theory may have considerable predictive power and garner an impressive array of validating evidence, but still fail to provide a comprehensive or compelling explanation. In his theorizing, Cattell provides an exemplary instance of a scientist who is concerned with validating evidence.

Cattell believes that the exploration of traits will assist us in understanding the structure and function of personality. Knowledge of underlying traits will allow us to make predictions about our own behavior and that of others. Cattell defines **traits** as mental or imaginary constructs; they are inferences from overt behavior that we make in order to account for its regularity and consistency. Traits are hypothetical constructs that permit us to generate conclusions about subsequent behavioral events. Although Cattell is interested in the physical and neurological components that influence behavior, unlike Allport, he does not maintain that the traits he is exploring necessarily have any real physical or neural status.

Surface Traits versus Source Traits

Cattell reminds us that if a trait theory is to be useful, the traits postulated need to go beyond the overt behaviors that an individual shows. Just as any successful hypothesis in science refers to future experiences that we might have if the hypothesis turns out to be useful, a successful trait construct goes beyond simply asserting that a particular behavior pattern exists. To argue that John is lazy because he has a lazy disposition is to argue in a circle and not provide genuinely useful information. To argue that John is honest, thoughtful, and disciplined because of an underlying source variable or trait of ego strength is a much more useful way to proceed. The underlying trait of ego strength accounts for the surface manifestation and also permits us to speculate about other related characteristics, such as assertiveness or confidence, that John will display.

Thus, Cattell distinguishes between surface traits and source traits (1950). **Surface traits** are clusters of overt behavior responses that appear to go together, such as integrity, honesty, self-discipline, and thoughtfulness. **Source traits** refer to the underlying variables that seem to determine the surface manifestation, in this case, perhaps, ego strength.

The study of source traits is valuable for several reasons. Because they are probably few in number, source traits permit economy in describing an individual. Second, source traits presumably have a genuine structural influence on personality and thus determine the way we behave. Thus, knowledge of a particular source trait may permit us to go beyond mere description and make predictions about additional behaviors that we might observe further.

Source traits may be divided in terms of their origin into constitutional traits and environmental-mold traits. **Constitutional traits** have their origin in the heredity or the physiological condition of the organism, whereas **environmental-mold traits** originate from influences of our physical and social surroundings.

Both source and surface traits may also be labeled according to the way in which they express themselves. **Dynamic traits** motivate an individual toward some goal. **Temperament traits** describe how a person behaves in order to obtain his or her goal. **Ability traits** determine how effectively a person is able to achieve his or her goal.

From extensive research, utilizing factor analysis techniques, Cattell has identified sixteen basic temperament and ability source traits that he suggests represent the "building blocks" of personality (1966). At first, Cattell did not name the traits but identified them alphabetically. Later, he gave them technical names. However, they may best be understood by the lay person by their popular labels. These labels are presented as bipolar, or opposite, dimensions, which means that a high score on one end of the dimension indicates a low score on the other and vice versa.

Sixteen basic source traits

outgoing	—	reserved
more intelligent	—	less intelligent
emotionally stable	—	emotionally unstable
assertive	—	humble
happy-go-lucky	—	sober
strong conscience	—	lack of internal standards
adventuresome	—	shy
tough-minded	—	tender-minded

trusting	—	suspicious
imaginative	—	practical
shrewd	—	forthright
apprehensive	—	self-assured
experimental	—	conservative
group-dependent	—	self-sufficient
casual	—	controlled
relaxed	—	tense

Exploration /////

Measuring a Source Trait

You can roughly measure yourself on one of Cattell's sixteen basic source traits by taking the following self-report questionnaire.* For each of the items below select the answer (a or b) that best applies to you.

1. I would rather be
   a. an engineer.
   b. a social science teacher.

2. I could stand being a hermit.
   a. true
   b. false

3. I am careful to turn up when someone expects me.
   a. true
   b. false

4. I would prefer to marry someone who is
   a. a thoughtful companion.
   b. effective in a social group.

5. I would prefer to read a book on
   a. national social service.
   b. new scientific weapons.

6. I trust strangers
   a. sometimes.
   b. practically always.

The following answers are indicative of an outgoing temperament: 1. b, 2. b, 3. a, 4. b, 5. a, 6. b. If you answered all the questions this way, you probably have a very outgoing personality. If you answered most of them the other way, you probably are reserved. Most people fall somewhere in the middle.

*Questionnaire is based on information from R. B. Cattell, *The Scientific Analysis of Personality*, Hawthorne, N.Y.: Aldine, 1965, Table A, p. 70. Used by permission of the author.

Although a person's occupation may change, the underlying ergs that influence job performance, like gregariousness, remain constant.

Cattell describes two kinds of dynamic source traits that underlie surface dynamic traits, or **attitudes.** The **erg** is a constitutional dynamic trait. Cattell prefers the neutral term "erg" over words like "instinct" or "drive" because it avoids loose connotations or associations. Ergs refer to innate motivational factors. Seven ergs have been identified through factor analysis (Cattell and Adelson, 1958):

Ergs
sex
gregariousness
parental protectiveness
curiosity
escape (fear)
self-assertion
self-indulgence

A **sentiment** is an environmental-mold dynamic source trait that arises from the interaction of the ergs and the environment. A sentiment is acquired or learned through our associations with the physical or social environment.

It is a deep, early-established feeling toward important cultural objects, such as persons or social institutions. An erg is permanent, because it is constitutional. Its intensity may increase or decrease, but the erg itself will not disappear. A sentiment, on the other hand, is less permanent because it is learned through our associations with our environment. Thus, a sentiment may be unlearned and disappear. Some of the sentiments that Cattell has identified are:

Sentiments

career or profession
sports and games
mechanical interests
religion
parents
spouse or sweetheart
self

The dynamic traits may be thought of as related to each other in a **dynamic lattice** or network (1950). The lattice shows that the traits are related according to the principle of subsidiation. **Subsidiation** means that certain traits are secondary to other traits. In general, attitudes are secondary to sentiments, which in turn are secondary to ergs. In other words, ergs are the basic motivating forces. A man's sentiment about his wife may be related to the ergs of sex, gregariousness, protection, and self-assertion. His surface attitude and behavior, that is, his attitude toward his wife's hairstyle, is influenced by that sentiment as well as other sentiments. Surface attitudes reflect sentiments, which in turn express ergs.

In Figure 11.1 the ergs are represented by the rectangles at the right. The large circles in the middle represent sentiments. Each sentiment is subsidiary to one or more ergs. The small circles at the left reflect attitudes toward particular behaviors. Each attitude is secondary to one or more sentiments, so that it expresses those sentiments and also the ergs that inform the sentiments.

A particularly important sentiment is that of the self. The **self-sentiment** refers to a person's self-image. It is reflected in almost all of the attitudes that a person holds. Cattell suggests that the self-sentiment plays a crucial role in integrating the expressions of all the various ergs and other sentiments. Although it is one of the latest sentiments to develop, it plays a major role in controlling the structure of personality.

Cattell acknowledges the importance of learning in personality development and has described stages in personality growth. Although these are not major emphases in his theory, they serve to correlate his theory with other theoretical positions, such as learning theory and developmental psychology, and indicate the connection among learning, development, and personality traits. Many of Cattell's studies have tried to analyze the changes that may occur in different

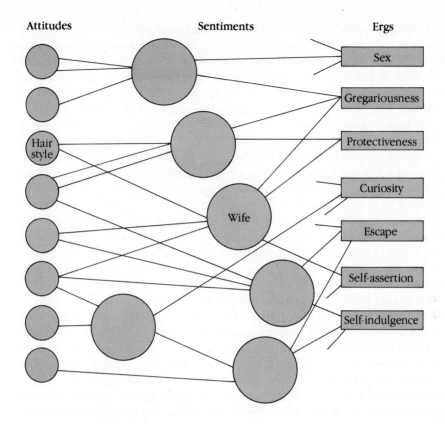

Figure 11.1 *The Dynamic Lattice*
Cattell suggests that the dynamic traits may be thought of as related to one another in a dynamic lattice.

personality traits during different age ranges. For example, in adolescence there appears to be an increase in adventurousness and ego stability and a decrease in apprehensiveness and suspiciousness. Cattell believes that further studies offer the promise of someday developing a full outline of developmental trends in personality traits.

Methods of Research

Cattell's personality theory made its major impact through his methods and techniques of researching and identifying traits. Cattell's primary tool has been factor analysis, which will be described shortly. However, before he could apply this tool, it was necessary for him to gather large masses of data from a great many individuals in a variety of different ways.

Cattell garnered his data from three main sources (1965). The first is life records and is called **L-data.** L-data refer to observations of a person's behavior in society or everyday life. Examples would be an individual's school record, number of automobile accidents, job performance reports, and so forth. L-data, therefore, involve ratings made by other people on the individual concerned. The second source involves questionnaires or self-reports and is known as **Q-data.** You were engaged in self-reports when you answered the inventories on your somatotype and tendency to be outgoing or reserved. Questionnaires permit self-ratings by the person involved. Thus, they may or may not be truthful. Cattell uses a variety of questionnaires or scales. Although he acknowledges that there are difficulties in assessing the accuracy of self-reports, he believes that they are an important mode of gathering data. Finally, Cattell uses objective tests or **T-data.** Cattell employs the term **objective test** in an unusual way, to mean that a test is constructed in such a way that the subject taking it cannot know what a particular test or test item is designed to measure. Thus, it is difficult for a subject to fake the test or distort his or her responses. An example of T-data might be Murray's Thematic Apperception Test. Cattell's definition of **objectivity** differs considerably from the definition of most other psychologists. Cattell distinguishes different media of observation because there is always measurement error associated with our observations and we must therefore replicate findings across different media in order to show that we are discovering source traits rather than measurement artifacts.

All of the data garnered from these sources are subjected to the complex, sophisticated statistical technique of **factor analysis.** Factor analysis is essentially a correlational procedure, but it involves more than just one or two correlations. It is a procedure that interrelates many correlations at one time. Hundreds, or even thousands, of variables may be considered in a single study. Factor analysis is based on the assumption that if several variables correlate highly with one another, it is possible that a common dimension underlies them.

Basically, factor analysis aims at describing larger amounts of data by smaller, more manageable units. Using complex mathematical formulas, it reduces the data to the smallest number of relatively similar dimensions or clusters, called *factors,* that can be used to account for the wider variety.

The first step in factor analysis is to make up a correlational matrix, by computing a correlational coefficient for each variable to show how it relates to every other one. This tells us the degree to which each variable covaries with the others. The second step is to scan the correlational matrix and look for any patterns that emerge. Computers are used to assist in the process. The computer looks for a set of scores that all seem to go together, that is, are similarly high or low. When it finds such a cluster, it indicates that an underlying factor could account for the many relationships in the original matrix. A factor is a subset of highly intercorrelated measures.

The next step is to compute a correlation between each of the identified factors and each of the original variables. These correlations reflect the loading

Table 11.2 *Factor Analysis*

Hypothetical correlational matrix

Variable (measure)	a	b	c	d	e	f
a (reading)	+ 1.00	+ .60	+ .50	+ .15	+ .20	+ .10
b (vocabulary)		+ 1.00	+ .50	+ .15	+ .10	+ .10
c (spelling)			+ 1.00	+ .10	+ .20	+ .15
d (addition)				+ 1.00	+ .60	+ .60
e (subtraction)					+ 1.00	+ .60
f (multiplication)						+ 1.00

A visual scan of this matrix tells us that there are clusters of variables (measures) that may belong together.

Factor matrix

Variable (measure)	Factor 1	Factor 2
a (reading)	+ .70	+ .15
b (vocabulary)	+ .60	+ .15
c (spelling)	+ .60	+ .10
d (addition)	+ .10	+ .70
e (subtraction)	+ .10	+ .65
f (multiplication)	+ .05	+ .60

The factor matrix tells us that reading, vocabulary, and spelling all have high loadings on Factor 1, whereas addition, subtraction, and multiplication have high loadings on Factor 2.

of the variables on the factors and tell us to what degree each measure is related to each factor. A high positive correlation indicates that the measure is strongly related to the factor. A high negative correlation suggests that the measure is related but in an inverse way. The final step is to name the factors. Whereas the procedures for extracting factors are established mathematically, subjective judgment enters into the process of labeling and interpreting them.

The procedure of factor analysis enables researchers to draw conclusions such as: similar scores in reading, vocabulary, and spelling tests are due to a common underlying factor of verbal ability, whereas performance in addition, subtraction, and multiplication depend on mathematical ability (see Table 11.2). Many of the studies undertaken involve a great deal of mathematical computation. Only the advent of the modern computer has made factor analysis a feasible technique for personality description.

Thus, beginning with hundreds of surface personality traits, Cattell has discovered through factor analysis which of the traits cluster and occur together with the greatest frequency. These traits are then placed together under a common source trait, thereby reducing the number of traits to be dealt with and making them easier to handle.

In the end Cattell hopes that he can use the information garnered to facilitate the prediction of behavior. Given the ability to describe an individual in terms of various traits and the understanding of how these traits enter into certain behavior response patterns, we would be able to apply this information to a particular instance. Eventually, we will be able to predict how a particular individual might respond in a given situation. Cattell (1965) suggests that this may someday be done by means of a **specification equation:**

$$R = s_1T_1 + s_2T_2 + s_3T_3 + \ldots + s_nT_n$$

This forbidding equation simply means the following: The response (R) equals the sum of the characteristics of the person ($T_1, T_2, T_3 \ldots T_n$). Each trait is weighted according to its relevance to the particular situation. That rating constitutes the situational index ($s_1, s_2, s_3 \ldots$). If a particular trait is highly relevant to the response, its corresponding situational index would be high. If a particular trait is irrelevant to a response, the situational index would be zero. If the trait inhibits or detracts from the response, the situational index would be negative. The model is basically a very simple one.

For example, suppose R were to stand for the classroom performance of a professor. The factor of intelligence would be very important because an instructor needs to understand the subject and know how to communicate it to others. Thus, the characteristic of intelligence would be assigned a high situational index. The characteristic of assertiveness might also be important, but less so than intelligence. Therefore, it would be assigned a lower number. Each trait that is relevant to classroom performance would be included until all the elements in the equation were filled in. We would then be able to predict how a candidate might behave in the classroom. Cattell has applied some of his methods to the area of personnel selection, where he has had considerable success in predicting job satisfaction and worker effectiveness.

Cattell's formula is based on addition and thus it has been criticized for not providing for possible interrelations or interactions among traits. Cattell acknowledges that we may eventually need more sophisticated formulas, but suggests that his specification equation is a useful starting point.

Current Trends in Dispositional Personality Theory

Contemporary research into the biological bases of personality has led to a renewed interest in the relationship between personality and physical characteristics. This is illustrated in the work of Hans Eysenck and Arnold H. Buss and Robert Plomin, who have combined biological, learning, and trait concepts into their theories of personality.

Hans J. Eysenck

Hans J. Eysenck has marshalled all of the forces of biology, historical typologies, learning theory, and factor analysis in order to understand personality. Eysenck uses factor analysis in his work but his use of it is more deductive than that of Cattell. In Cattell's research, conclusions were drawn from the clusters that appeared in the process of factoring. Eysenck begins with a clear hypothesis about possible underlying variables and then uses statistical analysis to test his hypothesis. Moreover, Eysenck considers factor analysis at best a preliminary tool that paves the way for subsequent laboratory and experimental research to gain a causal understanding of the factors that have been posited. Eysenck is extraordinarily rigorous in his adherence to the scientific method.

Eysenck views personality as organized in a hierarchy. At the bottom of the hierarchy are the behaviors that we can actually observe: *specific responses*. The next level is that of *habitual responses*. Above this are more generalized traits, such as the source traits that Cattell has identified. At the top of the hierarchy are broad general dimensions or basic types. Most of Eysenck's empirical research has been an effort to understand two fundamental dimensions: emotional stability versus neuroticism and introversion versus extroversion. The *emotional stability versus neuroticism dimension* refers to an individual's basic adjustment to his or her environment and the stability of behavior over time. The *introversion versus extroversion dimension* reflects the degree to which a person is usually outgoing and participative in his or her relations with other individuals.

Eysenck has been influenced by Jung's typology of introversion and extroversion as well as by the constitutional psychology of Sheldon. Indeed, he even includes the earlier classification of Hippocrates in his discussion of personality traits, suggesting that the basic dimensions and traits of personality may be summarized as shown in Figure 11.2. The inner circle shows Hippocrates' four temperaments. The outer ring shows the results of factor analysis studies of the intercorrelations among traits. The traits, which are on a continuum, clearly reflect the two fundamental dimensions of emotional stability versus neuroticism and introversion versus extroversion.

More recently, Eysenck has conducted investigations into the dimension of psychoticism versus nonpsychoticism. A **psychosis** is an abnormal personality disturbance, commonly known as insanity. It is usually characterized by loss or distortion of reality testing and inability to distinguish between reality and fantasy. Disturbances are found in thought, emotion, and motor behavior, and the person may have hallucinations or delusions. Eysenck's studies have suggested that psychotic disorders are very different from neurotic disorders. Thus, a

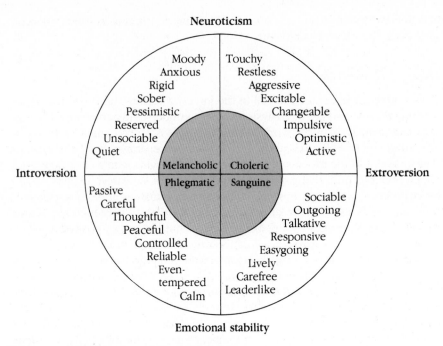

Figure 11.2 *The Intercorrelation of Traits*
The inner circle shows Hippocrates' four temperaments. The outer ring shows the results of factor analysis studies of the intercorrelations between traits done by Eysenck and others.

person may become more and more neurotic without being at all psychotic and vice versa.

Eysenck believes that there is a clear biological basis to personality. Certain constitutional structures render individuals more or less susceptible to certain personality dimensions and characteristics. In his early descriptive research, Eysenck (1957) points out that individuals differ in the speed with which they become excited and respond to stimuli. These differences are seen to correlate with the dimensions of emotional stability–neuroticism and introversion–extroversion. More recently, Eysenck (1967) has tied his theory of excitation–inhibition to specific biological functions in which introversion–extroversion is related to arousal thresholds in the reticular activating system (RAS) of the brain and emotional stability–neuroticism is related to differences in visceral brain (VB) activation.

The reticular activating system is a network of fibers that begins in the hindbrain, extends through the midbrain, and goes into the forebrain. Its primary function is to regulate levels of arousal ranging from sleep to states of high alertness. Destruction of these tissues causes an animal to sleep almost continuously whereas stimulation will cause it to become more aroused. Thus, the RAS controls the brain's level of excitability and its responsiveness to stimuli. Introverts are believed to have higher levels of RAS arousal than extroverts.

Emotional stability versus neuroticism is believed to be due to differences in visceral brain activity. The visceral brain includes the limbic system and the hypothalamus, which are both involved in motivation and emotional behavior. They exert their influence through the autonomic or involuntary nervous system. Individuals who have a low threshold of visceral brain activation are very emotional in their behavior and more susceptible to neurotic disorders.

One of the strengths of Eysenck's theory is that it allows for specific prediction and test. For example, if introverts have stronger excitatory brain processes and relatively weak inhibitory effects, they should (and do) condition more quickly in certain structured laboratory situations such as eye-blink conditioning. Electrocardiogram studies and other electrophysiological studies also support Eysenck's theory. Incredible as it may seem, it has been possible to indicate introversion or extroversion by comparing the amount of salivation produced when lemon juice is applied to the tongue of an individual with the amount created without lemon juice. Introverts produce considerably more salivation than extroverts (Corcoran, 1964). This suggests that the same physiological functions control both salivation characteristics and introversion–extroversion characteristics.

Exploration /////

The Lemon Test

You can get a rough idea of your measurement on the Lemon Test of Introversion–Extroversion by trying this simplified version. Tie a length of thread to the center of a double-tipped cotton swab so that when you hold it by the string the swab hangs perfectly horizontally.

Swallow three times and immediately put one end of the cotton swab onto your tongue. Hold it in your mouth for thirty seconds. Remove the swab and put four drops of lemon juice on your tongue. Swallow and immediately place the other end of the swab on the same spot in your mouth. Hold it there for thirty seconds and then let the swab hang.

If you are an extrovert, the swab will remain close to horizontal. If you are an introvert, one end will hang down noticeably, indicating that you produced a large amount of saliva in response to the lemon juice.

Because introverts have sensitive nervous systems, they are more easily socialized. The ease with which they become conditioned also makes them more liable to anxiety-based neuroses, which are conditioned emotional responses. Extroverts, on the other hand, have less sensitive and more inhibitive cortical processes; they seek additional stimulation and are slow to develop conditioned responses. Since socialized behavior largely depends on a well-conditioned conscience developed in childhood, extroverts are more likely to develop psychopathic disorders. Thus neurotics become so because their cortical and emotional states interfere with the learning of appropriate responses or facilitate the learning of maladaptive ones.

In short, Eysenck suggests that there is a causal connection between biological functions of the brain and the basic personality dimensions of emotional stability–neuroticism and introversion–extroversion. Neuroticism is due to excessive stimulation discharged by the visceral brain leading to a high degree of emotionality that may combine with an extremely high or low cortical arousal of the reticular activating system to form a particular neurosis. The biological basis of personality is summarized in Table 11.3.

Even though people differ in the extent to which they are genetically predisposed to neurosis, Eysenck believes that neurotic behaviors themselves are learned. In this respect, he shares similar views with the behavior and learning theorists (whose ideas are discussed in Part 5) on the origin and

Table 11.3 *The Biological Basis of Personality*

| | Visceral Brain Activation | |
	High	Low
Reticular activating system arousal — High	neurotic introvert (anxiety types)	emotionally stable introvert
Reticular activating system arousal — Low	neurotic extrovert (psychopathic types)	emotionally stable extrovert

SOURCE: Based on information in H. J. Eysenck, *The Biological Basis of Personality,* Springfield, Ill.: Charles C Thomas, 1967.

treatment of neurotic disorders. However, his recognition of the biological basis of personality suggests the possibility of altering an individual's behavior through the use of chemicals and drugs that can correct abnormalities in brain or body functions.

Eysenck has found fault with what he considers to be less empirical, factual, or scientific approaches to personality. In particular, he has been critical of Freudian psychoanalysis (Eysenck and Wilson, 1973). His concept of scientific activity, however, is extremely narrow. There are alternative ways of gathering empirical data and operationally defining terms. Moreover, Eysenck's own procedures are not as objective or purely scientific as he sometimes supposes. For example, the data of factor analysis may be analyzed in different ways and there are various methods of determining how many factors are involved as well as their level of influence. Eysenck fails to appreciate the ways in which subjectivity invariably enters into the most rigorous of scientific methodologies.

Buss and Plomin

Arnold H. Buss and Robert Plomin (1975) have developed an interaction-temperament model of personality that also combines biological, learning, and trait concepts. They suggest that there are a number of inborn or inherited dispositions (a range of response potentials) whose development is influenced by interactions with the environment. The interaction between temperament and environment in structuring personality is particularly important in early childhood and there are limits to how much the environment can modify basic dispositions.

Through factor analysis Buss and Plomin have identified four inherited temperamental dimensions:

active versus lethargic: The active person is usually busy and in a hurry compared with the slower-paced lethargic individual.

emotional versus impassive: The emotional person is easily aroused and responds more intensely than the impassive person.

gregarious versus detached: The gregarious person is affiliative, seeking others out and responding to them. The detached person tends to want the company of others less.

impulsive versus deliberate: Impulsive people respond quickly, whereas deliberate people inhibit their responses and plan them.

Research in behavior genetics involving twin studies, studies of parents and children, and the rating of an infant's behavior immediately after birth has provided evidence for a genetic factor, particularly in the first three dimensions. The evidence for a genetic component in impulsivity is uncertain because of problems of definition and measurement. Theories such as those of Eysenck and of Buss and Plomin are helping to compensate for the neglect of genetic factors that characterized American psychology for many years.

Cattell's Theory: Philosophy, Science, and Art

Cattell's theory of personality is based on highly objective and precise scientific techniques. He has generated an enormous amount of research data although his findings have not always been replicated. A perusal of the material on personality published in the *Annual Review of Psychology* over the last two decades attests to the significant research that Cattell's theory has generated.

Cattell's theory reflects a current emphasis on quantitative methods and empirical data. Few other theorists have been as precise or as operational in their definitions. Furthermore, few theorists have been as rigorous in subjecting their concepts of underlying personality variables to empirical test. In its adherence to a strict methodology and its generation of a vast quantity of research, Cattell's theory is a meritorious example of a scientific approach to personality.

Critics have pointed out that Cattell's method is not as objective as it initially appears to be (Hall and Lindzey, 1978). Although subjectivity may enter into several of the steps in factor analysis, it is impossible for any scientific methodology to be completely objective. Cattell's method of predicting behavior is an outstanding example of the use of validating evidence.

To identify Cattell as a scientist is not to ignore the fact that his theory arises out of his philosophical commitment to an empirical approach. His theory suggests that he views the world as lawful, consistent, and controllable. Moreover, Cattell suggests that a system of ethical values, which he calls *beyondism,* may be developed on the foundation of science. Beyondism is based on the view that humanity is in the process of a physical and biological advance. Moral laws that will foster and insure this evolutionary process need to be developed. Such ethics will enable us to adapt to a wider range of circumstances and will give us a better chance of survival. Strictly speaking, Cattell's new morality cannot be said to arise from science. Scientists may have discovered the process of evolution, but the judgment that such evolution is good and should be fostered is a value judgment that takes us outside the realm of validating evidence and into the realm of philosophy. The moral issues that Cattell raises, like the advisability of selective breeding as a means of cultivating desired traits, deserve serious consideration by all who are interested in the future of the human race. Herein lies the value of science for Cattell and others who cherish the importance of validating evidence: our intuition is subsequently checked by explicit logic and experimentation.

Cattell's theory is unfortunately not as popular as other theories among psychologists and it is almost totally unknown among the general public. In part this lack of popularity is due to its complexity, but it is also due to a feeling that factor analysis creates an artifact or a para-person that has no real relationship to a real person. As we have seen, it is difficult for the conclusions of a scientific method to command the same degree of compellingness as a philosophical vision.

Cattell's theory is carefully constructed and well rooted in empirical data. It has enormous potential for teaching us about human personality and for predicting behavior. In fact, Cattell believes that by applying appropriate rules of reference, psychologists will be able to predict human behavior as accurately as astronomers predict the movements of stars and planets. Cattell's rigorous methodology and approach are characteristic of the scientific enterprise at its best.

Dispositional theories, in general, are highly controversial because they imply that many personality differences are genetically based. Eysenck has said that people "are created equal in the sight of God and as regards the judicial system, but they are not created equal as far as beauty is concerned, or strength, or intelligence or a great many other things" (as quoted in Evans, 1976). This finding runs counter to this country's strong belief in equality among people and its commitment to social programs. This is not to say, however, that heredity is the sole determinant of personality. Heredity may place limits on an individual's potential, but environment probably determines where within that range his or her actual behavior will fall.

The applications of dispositional and trait theories are potentially dangerous; they may be used to foster discrimination and prejudice rather than equality and justice. The average individual has undoubtedly been more directly influenced by the trait approach to personality than by any other approach. Most people have been assessed by some device based on the trait approach, for instance, an intelligence test, an achievement test, or an aptitude test. Such psychometric measuring devices and techniques have not been used without criticism. Most of the constructs supposedly indicated by these tests cannot be measured directly. Often the validity of the tests is assumed rather than demonstrated.

On the other hand, the wise and judicious use of appropriate assessment techniques can be invaluable in developing individual and group potential. As early as the fourth century B.C., the Greek philosopher Plato advocated careful use of assessment techniques in the shaping of his ideal society, the Republic. He urged teachers to note the dominant traits of their students in order to select and prepare them for the appropriate class in society: workers, guardians, or philosopher-kings. An accurate understanding of one's limitations and abilities is important for developing one's potential.

The recognition of innate differences among people does not preclude a social philosophy that insures equal opportunity under the law. Such a recognition raises social and ethical questions and thus underscores the desirability of a reciprocal relationship between the philosophy, science, and art of a personality theory. Scientists should be aware of the ways in which philosophical assumptions inform their work and, in turn, of the ways in which their findings influence ethical and social decisions.

❧ Summary

1. Kretschmer classed individuals as asthenics, pyknics, and athletics on the basis of **morphology. Typologies** tend to separate people into distinct categories whereas **trait theories** conceive of dimensions that individuals possess to varying degrees.

2. A **correlation** tells us whether or not two variables are related directly or indirectly. In itself a correlation does not imply a cause-and-effect relationship.

3. Sheldon identified three primary components of physique and three basic temperaments. The body type can be expressed in a **somatotype.** Using a correlational study, he showed that a positive correlation exists between **endomorphy** and **viscerotonia, mesomorphy** and **somatotonia,** and **ectomorphy** and **cerebrotonia.**

4. Cattell defines **personality** as that which will permit prediction of what a person will do in a given situation. His interest in personality theorizing is clearly **heuristic.**

5. **Surface traits** are clusters of overt behavior responses that appear to go together. **Source traits** are the underlying variables, which may have their origin in heredity or in influences of the environment. Cattell has identified sixteen basic **temperament** and **ability traits.**

6. **Ergs** and **sentiments** underlie surface **dynamic traits** or **attitudes.** The dynamic traits are related to each other in a **dynamic lattice** according to the principle of **subsidiation.**

7. Cattell uses **factor analysis** to identify traits. Factor analysis is a correlational procedure that interrelates many correlations at one time and identifies common dimensions that underlie them. Cattell hopes he can use his findings to facilitate the prediction of behavior by means of a **specification equation.**

8. Eysenck identifies two fundamental dimensions of personality: emotional stability–neuroticism and introversion–extroversion. He believes that there is a biological basis to personality. Buss and Plomin have developed an interaction-temperament model of personality that also combines biological, learning, and trait concepts.

9. Trait theories are very controversial because they imply that personality disorders and human differences are genetic and due to heredity as well as

environment. These findings raise ethical questions underscoring the reciprocal relationship between science and philosophy.

10. Cattell's theory is an excellent example of an effort to comprehend personality through scientific methodology.

Suggestions for Further Reading

Cattell has been a prolific writer, authoring over thirty books and three hundred articles. His work is technical and difficult to digest. However, an introductory primer to his theory is provided in *The Scientific Analysis of Personality* (Aldine, 1965), which is not too technical and is aimed at a lay public. Also readable and exciting because of the ethical issues that it raises is *A New Morality from Science: Beyondism* (Pergamon, 1972). Beyond that the interested reader has a vast array of primary sources to choose from. Cattell's most recent findings are included in the recently published *Personality and Learning Theory*, Vols. 1 and 2 (Springer Publishing Company, 1979, 1980).

A broad critical review of Cattell's work is found in an article by S. B. Sells, "Structured measurement of personality and motivation: A review of contributions of Raymond B. Cattell," *Journal of Clinical Psychology,* 1959, *15,* 3–21. For summaries of research that Cattell's work has generated, the reader is advised to consult the selections on personality in recent issues of the *Annual Review of Psychology.*

Eysenck has written over twenty books and three hundred articles. The level of readability varies widely. A work that is relatively easy for the lay person to understand is *Psychology Is about People* (Open Court, 1972). The definitive statement of his cortical hypothesis of arousal is found in *The Biological Basis of Personality* (Charles C Thomas, 1967). A three-volume collection of research essays related to his theory has been published under the title of *Readings in Extroversion–Introversion* (Staples, 1970–1971).

Part
4

Humanist and Cognitive Theories

The humanist theories of Carl Rogers and Abraham Maslow emerged in the 1950s in an effort to correct the limited concepts of human nature of both classical psychoanalysis and radical behaviorism. Rogers and Maslow disagreed with the dark, pessimistic, and largely negative picture of personality presented by Freudian psychoanalysis. They also disagreed with the picture of the person as a machine or robot that characterized the early behavior and learning approach. The humanists suggest that the study of neurotics or infrahuman species is not particularly enlightening for the study of personality: health is more than the absence of neurotic symptoms, and there is a radical difference between a rat in a Skinner box and a human being in the everyday world.

Rogers and Maslow emphasize a view of the person as an active, creative, experiencing human being who lives in the present and subjectively responds to current perceptions, relationships, and encounters. The humanist view of personality is a positive, optimistic one that stresses the tendency of the human personality toward growth and self-actualization.

Cognitive theories of personality, exemplified here by George Kelly, emphasize the processes by which an individual becomes aware of the world and makes judgments about it. Cognitive theories stress that an individual's behavior is determined not simply by the environment but also, and primarily, by his or her attitudes, expectations, and beliefs.

Other theories have recognized the importance of cognition, but they did not make it the mainstay of their theory. Freud emphasized emotional processes of the heart rather than intellectual processes of the head. The behavior and learning tradition, until recently, was concerned with the analysis of environmental stimuli and the individual's final overt response to the environment rather than with the intermediate subjective processes that led to the behavior. Cognitive theories, on the other hand, view cognition as the primary factor governing personality and behavior.

12

Carl Rogers: A Person-Centered Theory

Your Goals for This Chapter

1. Explain how Rogers has reasserted the self as a useful construct for understanding personality.

2. Describe the philosophical movement of *phenomenology* and indicate its implications for psychology.

3. Explain the following concepts in Rogers's theory: *phenomenal field, self-actualization, organism, self.* Explain how emotions affect the process of self-actualization.

4. Explain what Rogers means by *congruence* and *incongruence* and identify denial and distortion as two processes that may lead to incongruence.

5. Discuss what is meant by *unconditional* and *conditional positive regard* and recognize their roles in influencing personality development.

6. Describe three therapist attitudes that lead to change.

7. Distinguish among five different *responses* to emotional communications.

8. Discuss *client-centered psychotherapy,* describing its supportive character, changes in Rogers's conception of it, and efforts at empirical validation.

9. Describe Rogers's concept of a *fully functioning person.*

10. Evaluate Rogers's theory in terms of its function as philosophy, science, and art.

*F*or Carl Rogers, a person's behavior is completely dependent on how he or she perceives the world and its events. Rogers's theory of personality describes the **self** as an important element of experience; it is largely due to Rogers's efforts that the self has re-emerged as a useful construct for understanding personality. In contemporary behaviorist thought the concept of the self had been ignored as a remnant of earlier religious or philosophical views that no longer appeal. Rogers presents the self as a scientific construct that helps to account for what we observe. The self is Rogers's term for those psychological processes that govern our behavior. At the same time, his theory emphasizes the organism or the total person.

Biographical Background

Carl Rogers was born in 1902 in Oak Park, Illinois, a suburb of Chicago. He was the fourth born of six children, five boys and one girl. Rogers's parents, educated and conservative middle-class Protestants, instilled in their children high ethical standards of behavior and emphasized the importance of hard work.

Rogers recalls that he had little social life outside of his large family, but this did not bother him. He was an avid reader and early in life developed a certain level of independence. When he was twelve, the family moved to a farm. Farm life spurred his interest in science and increased his ability to work independently. He was fascinated with the literature on scientific agriculture that his father brought home. Rogers worked hard at his chores on the farm; he reared lambs, pigs, and calves. He also collected, studied, and bred moths. A superior student, Rogers entered the University of Wisconsin, a family alma mater, with the full intent of studying agriculture. However, in his second year, he decided to prepare for the ministry. After his graduation in 1924, he married Helen Elliot and drove to New York City in a secondhand Model T coupe to begin preparation for the ministry at Union Theological Seminary.

Rogers's fate, however, was not to become a minister. During his final years at college, Rogers found himself departing from his parents' fundamentalist ways of thinking. The liberal philosophical approach toward religion fostered at Union Theological Seminary and insights gained from participation in several YMCA conferences led him to feel that he could not work in a field that would require him to profess a specific set of beliefs. This was a difficult period for both Rogers and his parents but it nurtured Rogers's growing conviction that the individual must ultimately rely on his or her own experiences. His interests were turning toward psychology; therefore, he transferred to

Carl Rogers

Columbia University Teachers College, where he was introduced to the philosophy of John Dewey and began his training in clinical psychology.

In 1931, Rogers received the Ph.D. and joined the staff of the Rochester Guidance Center, where he helped develop a highly successful child study department. Here, Rogers first met what was to be many years of opposition from members of the psychiatric profession who felt that psychologists should not be permitted to practice or have any administrative responsibility over psychotherapy. In 1939, when Rogers was made the director of the center, a vigorous campaign was waged to unseat him. No one criticized his work, but the general opinion was that a psychologist simply could not do this kind of work. Fortunately, the board of trustees decided in Rogers's favor.

In 1940, Rogers accepted an appointment as professor of psychology at Ohio State University. He worked with intellectually adept graduate students and began to articulate clearly his views on psychotherapy. In 1945, he moved to the University of Chicago where, as professor of psychology and executive secretary of the counseling center, he again championed his view that psychologists could effectively conduct therapy. It was largely due to his efforts that clinical psychology became a respectable field and that psychiatry and psychology have become somewhat reconciled, seeing themselves as two professions in search of a common goal. This reconciliation and challenge were reflected in his appointment as professor of psychology and psychiatry at the University of Wisconsin in 1957. Since 1963, Rogers has been a fellow at the Center for Studies of the Person in La Jolla, California.

Theory of Personality

Rogers's theory of personality developed gradually over time out of his clinical experience in working with patients.

The Phenomenal Field

Rogers (1959) maintains that each individual exists in a phenomenological field of which he or she is the center. Here we see the influence of a philosophical movement called **phenomenology.** The term phenomenon comes from the Greek *phainomenon,* which means "that which appears or shows itself." In philosophy, phenomenology seeks to describe the data, or the "given," of immediate experience. In psychology, phenomenology has come to mean the study of human awareness and perception. Phenomenologists stress that what is important is not the object or the event in itself but how it is perceived and understood by the individual. The **phenomenal field** refers to the total sum of experiences. It consists of everything that is potentially available to consciousness at any given moment. As you read you may not be aware of the pressure of the chair on your buttocks, but when attention is drawn to this fact you become conscious of it.

The organism responds to the field as it perceives it. Rogers's emphasis here is on the individual's perception of reality. For social purposes, we agree that the perceptions commonly shared by others in our culture are the correct perceptions. However, reality is essentially a very private matter. Two individuals walking along at night may see an object by the road and respond very differently. One, thinking that it is a large bear, may be afraid; the other, perceiving a tree stump, may be indifferent. The individual's perception rather than the reality in itself is what is most important. Suppose a young boy were to come to Rogers with the complaint that his father was dogmatic, authoritarian, and dictatorial. In fact, an impartial observer might conclude that the father was open and democratic. Rogers (1951) would point out that what the father is really like is not important; what is important is how the boy perceives his father.

It follows that the best vantage point for understanding an individual is that of the individual him- or herself. Rogers points out that the individual is the only one who can fully know his or her field of experience. Meaningful understanding of another person's behavior is not imposed by an outside observer interpreting behavior from an external frame of reference but is acquired by understanding the individual's behavior as he or she perceives it. Rogers acknowledges that it is not always easy to understand behavior from the internal frame of reference. We are limited to the individual's conscious perception of his or her experiences. Also, our knowledge depends on communication that is often faulty. Nevertheless, such an empathetic understanding of the experiences of another is probably much more accurate in reflecting the basic laws of personality process and behavior.

Self-Actualization

The primary tendency of the organism is to maintain, actualize, and enhance itself. This self-actualizing tendency follows lines laid down by genetics. The particular type of seed that is planted determines whether or not the flower will be a chrysanthemum or a snapdragon, but the environment can greatly influence the resulting bloom. An optimal environment that provides adequate nourishment, sun, and water leads to a healthy bloom. Conditions of drought or excessive heat may stifle the plant. The process of actualization is neither automatic nor effortless; it involves struggle and even pain. The young child does not take a first step without a struggle. The child falls and may be hurt. Yet the desire to grow moves the child forward.

Behavior is the "goal-directed attempt" of the organism to meet its needs as it perceives them (1951). Rogers's definition is very different from that of the learning theorists, who see behavior largely as a response to stimuli, or that of the psychoanalysts, who stress unconscious determinants of behavior. Behavior is a response to one's perception of his or her needs. Rogers's definition emphasizes subjective perception, values, and goal-directed activity.

The forward movement of **self-actualization** can occur only when the choices that are open are clearly perceived and adequately symbolized by the organism. When choices are unclear, the individual is unable to differentiate between progressive and regressive behavior. Given a clear choice, however, Rogers suggests that we will choose to grow rather than move backward.

Emotions accompany and usually facilitate the process of self-actualization. Pleasant emotions accompany the attainment of a goal. Even emotions that we generally think of as unpleasant, such as fear or jealousy, have a positive effect of integrating and concentrating our behavior on a goal. The intensity of the emotion varies according to the perceived significance of the behavior toward achieving the goal. Jumping out of the path of an oncoming truck is accompanied by very strong emotions, particularly if this behavior is seen as crucial to life or death. Unless they are excessive or inappropriate, emotions facilitate goal-oriented behavior.

Rogers's view of the emotions is a very positive one. Fully experiencing one's emotions facilitates growth, whereas the denial or distortion of emotions may permit them to raise havoc in our lives. In the psychoanalytic point of view the impulses of the id are savage, ignoble, and in need of civilization. Rogers has a more optimistic view of our basic motivational strivings and urges. He suggests that self-actualization occurs most freely when the person is open and aware of all of his or her experiences, be they sensory, visceral, or emotional, and the emotions that accompany them. Repression is not necessary in Rogers's view. The person who uses his or her senses and emotions, trusting them fully, is the person who is permitting the process of self-actualization to develop.

The Self

Out of the interaction of the organism and the environment, there emerges the self, or a concept of "who I am" (1951). The **self-concept** is a portion of the phenomenal field that has gradually become differentiated. Composed of those conscious perceptions and values of "me" or "I," the self-concept may or may not include all of the organism's experiences. The self, then, is an object of perception as well as a process. It is the person as he or she perceives him- or herself to be. Thus, we have a distinction between the **organism,** or real self as process, and the **self** as perceived, or object.

As young children interact with their environment, they gradually acquire ideas about themselves, their world, and their relationship to that world. They experience things that they like or dislike and things that they can or cannot control. Those experiences that appear to enhance one's self are valued and incorporated into one's self-image; those experiences that appear to threaten the self are denied and rendered foreign to the self.

The self-concept frequently includes values that are taken over from other people rather than from the actual experiences of the organism. A young boy quickly learns that his parents withdraw their affection when he hits his baby brother. Even though hitting his brother is a satisfying act, the boy forfeits his acknowledgment of its satisfaction in order to conceive of himself as lovable to his parents. Through introjection, values may become divorced from the organism's actual experiences.

When children deny or distort the symbolization of their experiences, they are no longer aware of them. They begin to experience the attitudes of others, such as their parents, as if these were the direct experiences of their organism. The "self" that one forms, therefore, may be at variance with the real experience of one's organism. An individual may come to experience any expression of anger as bad, through such distortion. He or she can no longer accurately perceive that at times its expression is satisfying. In such cases, the experiences of the self and that of the organism do not coincide.

Rogers does not believe that the self-structure must be formed on the basis of denial and distortion. The child values the experiences of his or her organism as positive or negative. If a parent is able to accept the child and his or her feeling of satisfaction and also accept his or her own feelings that certain actions are inappropriate, the parent can help the child curb actions without threatening the integrity of the child's self-concept. The parent can make it clear that the action of hitting the baby is wrong. Nevertheless, the feelings of satisfaction from the aggression and the child's desire are recognized and accepted. Such recognition provides the child with an accurate symbolization of his or her own experience. The child can weigh the satisfaction obtained from hitting the baby with the satisfaction he or she gained from pleasing the parent and then act accordingly. The child would not need to deny his or her own satisfaction nor to identify his or her own reaction with that of the parent.

The experiences that occur in one's life are either symbolized, ignored, denied, or distorted. If an experience is symbolized, it is perceived and organized into a relationship with the self. Generally, such experiences are related to the needs of the self. Experiences are ignored if one cannot perceive any relationship between the experience and the self-structure. One simply fails to pay attention to irrelevant experiences. Experiences are denied or distorted if they appear to be inconsistent with the self-structure. Young women who are brought up to believe that aggression is unfeminine may deny or distort their natural feelings of anger and find it difficult to be assertive because they seek to behave in ways that are feminine. In short, the individual's awareness is highly dependent on his or her self-concept. It is very difficult for an individual to permit the intrusion of a perception that is at variance with the self-concept. One tends to regard such perceptions as alien. The experiences occur in reality and the organism reacts to them but they are not symbolized or recognized by the conscious self.

Congruence and Incongruence

There is a need for the self as perceived and the real self, the organism, to be congruent. A state of **congruence** exists when a person's symbolized experiences reflect the actual experiences of his or her organism. When one's symbolized experiences do not represent the actual experiences, or if they distort them, there is a lack of correspondence between the self as perceived and the real self. In such a situation, there is **incongruence** and possible maladjustment. Diagrammatically, we can show this with overlapping circles, much as we depicted Horney's distinction between the real self and the ideal self (Figure 12.1).

When an individual denies or distorts significant sensory and visceral experiences, certain basic tensions arise. The self as perceived, which primarily governs behavior, is not an adequate representative of the true experiences of the organism. It becomes increasingly difficult for the self to satisfy the organism's needs. Tension develops and is felt as anxiety or uncertainty.

Rogers (1951) offers the following example. A young mother conceives of herself as a "good and loving mother." She cannot recognize her negative, rejecting attitudes toward her child because they do not coincide with her self-image. Nevertheless, these negative attitudes exist, and her organism seeks aggressive acts that would express these attitudes. She is limited to expressing herself only through channels that are consistent with her self-image of being

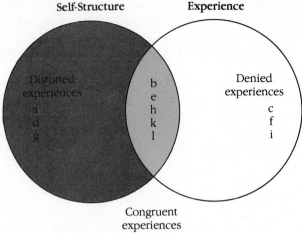

A personality in a state of psychic tension

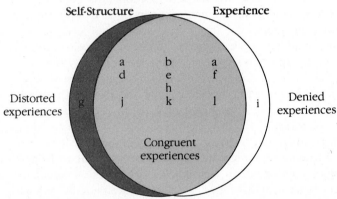

A personality in a state of relative congruence wherein more
elements of experience have been integrated into the self

Figure 12.1 *The Total Personality*

a good mother. Since it is appropriate for a good mother to behave aggressively toward her child when the child is bad, she perceives a great deal of the child's behavior as bad and punishes the child accordingly. In this manner, she can express her negative attitudes but retain her self-image of being a good mother.

When the self-concept is congruent with the experiences of the organism, the person is free from inner tension and psychological adjustment exists. Rogers makes it clear that he does not advocate the free and unrestrained expression of all our impulses and emotions. Part of the reality of the organism's experience is that certain social and cultural values require suppression of certain activities. Nevertheless, one's self-concept can include both the desire to behave one way and the desire to behave in other, more socially accepted ways. If parents can accept their feelings of rejection for their children as well as their feelings of affection, they can relate to their children more honestly.

When people become aware of and accept their impulses and perceptions, they increase the possibility of conscious control over their expression. The driver who is adept on icy roads knows the importance of going "with the skid" in order to gain control over the car. In the same manner, when a person accepts all of his or her experiences, he or she acquires better self-control.

Development of Personality

Rogers does not posit any specific stages of personality development from infancy to adulthood. He concentrates on the way in which the evaluations of others impede or facilitate self-actualization. Although the tendency to actualize follows genetic determinants, Rogers notes that it is subject to strong environmental influences.

The young child has two basic needs: the need for positive regard by others and the need for positive self-regard. **Positive regard** refers to being loved and accepted for who one is. Young children behave in such a way as to show their strong need for the acceptance and love of those who care for them. They will undergo significant changes in their behavior in order to attain positive regard.

In an ideal situation, positive regard is unconditional. It is given freely to children for who they are regardless of what they do. **Unconditional positive regard** is not contingent on any specific behaviors. A parent can limit or curb certain behaviors that he or she finds undesirable by objecting only to the behaviors and not disapproving of the child and his or her feelings. A parent who sees a child scribble on the wall may say, "Writing on the wall destroys it. Use this blackboard instead." Here, the parent limits his or her remarks to the behavior itself. But if the parent says, "You are a bad boy (girl) for writing on the wall," he or she has shifted from disapproval of the behavior to disapproval of the child. Such regard is no longer unconditional.

Conditional positive regard is given only under certain circumstances. Children are led to understand that their parents will not love them unless they think, feel, and act as their parents want them to. Such conditional positive regard tells the child that he or she is acceptable only if he or she behaves in certain ways. The parent who says, "You are a bad boy (or girl) for writing on the wall," is, in effect, saying to the child, "I will not love you if you write on the wall." In such cases, the parent is imposing **conditions of worth,** specifying the provisions under which the child will be accepted.

The young child has two basic needs: the need for positive regard by others and the need for positive self-regard.

Such conditions of worth may lead the child to introject values of others rather than of the self and lead to a discrepancy between the self-concept and the experiences of the organism.

Positive self-regard follows automatically if one has received unconditional positive regard. Children who are accepted for who they are come to view themselves favorably and with acceptance. It is very difficult, however, to view oneself positively if one is continually the target of criticism and belittlement. An individual who is merely given conditional positive regard may find it very difficult to acquire self-respect. It is clear that, for Rogers, how an individual regards him- or herself depends in large measure on the kinds of regard he or she has been given by others. Inadequate self-concepts, feelings of inferiority or stupidity, frequently arise because a person has not received adequate positive regard from others.

Rogers's point is that the valuation of others plays a significant role in development of the self-structure. If conditions of worth are posited, the self-concept may be distorted. Suppose a young boy who is jealous of his baby sister begins to hit her with a toy truck. Mother can stop the behavior: she can remove the truck. She can also remind Johnny that it is harmful to hit his sister. But if she also conveys the message that he is a bad boy and she will not love him if he feels jealous of his sister, she posits a condition of worth. Johnny's options are now limited: he can concur that he is a bad boy; he may acknowledge that his mother does not like him; or he can decide that he is not jealous of his sister and does not want to hit her with a truck. Each of these options denies certain aspects of the truth. In order to meet his mother's conditions of worth, he must deny some aspects of the experiences of his organism. In effect, the child has to put on blinders. Suppose he decides that he is not jealous of his sister. His organism remains jealous but he is unable to perceive that jealousy, because to perceive it would make him anxious lest he lose his mother's love. Introjected values take the place of his own, and he becomes divided against himself.

In the course of development, any experience that is at variance with the emerging self-concept is denied entrance into the self because it is threatening and evokes anxiety. If children are taught that it is wrong to feel angry, they may begin to perceive the emotion of anger itself rather than certain expressions of anger as dangerous or incorrect. In order to fulfill the conditions of worth, a child may become unable to perceive the very feelings of anger when they develop. Rogers would point out that there are people who literally cannot perceive when they are angry because they have been taught that the feelings of anger themselves, rather than certain actions that may emanate from those feelings, are wrong and inappropriate.

The primary distinction here is between feelings and actions. Feelings simply are. They have an important value in that they help us to understand our experience. Actions may or may not be appropriate. Some of them have to be curbed or prevented if we are going to live together in society.

When an experience is denied entrance into the self, it is not simply ignored; rather, it is falsified by the pretense that it does not exist or by distortion. In psychoanalytic terms, the experience is repressed. As Rogers (1951) explains it, an object or event may be **subceived** or unconsciously perceived as a threat. Although it produces visceral reactions in the organism, it is not consciously identified; instead, the mechanisms of denial or distortion prevent the threatening experience from becoming conscious. Rogers points out that some people will adamantly insist on a self-concept that is clearly at odds with reality. A young woman who believes that she is inferior and receives a raise may believe that the boss felt sorry for her, rather than taking credit where credit is due. The person who has achieved a significant goal may enter into a deep depression. One's self-concept may be so poor that one cannot realistically permit oneself to enjoy what has happened.

It is clear that for Rogers psychological adjustment is a function of the congruence of the self with reality. The individual who has an accurate perception of his or her self and environment is free to be open to new experiences and to fulfill his or her potential.

Exploration /////

Q-Sort Test

One method that Rogers has used for studying a person's self-concept is known as the **Q-sort technique.** The Q-sort test uses a packet of one hundred cards containing descriptive statements or words that can be used to describe the self. The person is given the cards and asked to sort them into a prearranged distribution, which resembles the normal curve, according to his or her self-perception.

The reader may explore this technique by making and sorting his or her own set of cards. Make a list of different ways in which you might perceive yourself or copy the list of twenty-five items in Table 12.1 onto individual index cards. First, sort the cards into seven different piles, ranging from "least like me" to "most like me." In order to have your distribution follow the normal curve, you will need to place most of the cards in the middle piles, indicating that the characteristic is somewhat like you but not the most or least like you. Your final distribution should be like this:

	(*least like me*)						(*most like me*)
pile #	1	2	3	4	5	6	7
no. of cards	1	2	5	9	5	2	1

After you have sorted the cards to describe your self-concept as you perceive it, you may wish to re-sort the cards to describe your ideal self — the person that you would most like to be. A comparison of these two sortings will give you a rough idea of the discrepancy between your self-concept and your self-ideal. You might also wish to ask some friends to sort the cards as they perceive you, to gain an idea of the image you project to others in comparison with your own self-perception.

Table 12.1 *Suggested Ways of Perceiving the Self*

I make strong demands on myself.
I often feel humiliated.
I often kick myself for the things I do.
I doubt my sexual powers.
I have a warm emotional relationship with others.
It is difficult to control my aggression.
I am responsible for my troubles.
I tend to be on my guard with friendly people.
I am a responsible person.
I usually feel driven.
Self-control is no problem for me.
I am disorganized.
I express my emotions freely.
I feel apathetic.
I am optimistic.
I try not to think about my problems.
I am sexually attractive.
I am shy.
I am liked by most people who know me.
I am afraid of a full-fledged disagreement with a person.
I can usually make up my mind and stick to it.
I can't seem to make up my mind one way or another.
I am impulsive.
I am afraid of sex.
I am ambitious.

Psychotherapy

Carl Rogers is best known for the method of psychotherapy that he developed: **nondirective** or **client-centered therapy.** Rogers not only originated this type of therapy but has also carefully studied it to determine what makes it work. As a scientist, he has tried to define operationally the conditions that underlie successful therapy to generate hypotheses that can be empirically tested.

Conditions for Therapeutic Change

Rogers's studies have suggested that there are three necessary and sufficient therapeutic attitudes for change. By *necessary,* Rogers means that these three therapist attitudes are essential and must be present. By *sufficient,* he means that if the client is uncomfortable with his or her present self and perceives these attitudes, change will occur. No other conditions are required. Not only does Rogers maintain that these three attitudes underlie his method of therapy but he also suggests that they underlie any successful therapeutic technique.

The first attitude is **empathy,** which is the ability to participate in another person's feelings as if they were one's own, but never lose sight of the "as if." Through empathy, the therapist is able to put him- or herself in the client's shoes without trying to wear those shoes or lose his or her own shoes. The therapist understands the client's internal frame of reference and communicates this understanding, largely through statements that reflect the client's feelings.

The second attitude is one of **acceptance,** in which the therapist does not posit any conditions of worth. Acceptance essentially means a nonjudgmental recognition of oneself and the other person. It permits each person to be him- or herself and to recognize who he or she is, without placing any restrictions or value judgments on either one's behavior. Through his or her acceptance the therapist lets the other person be.

The final attitude is that of **genuineness.** The effective therapist is genuine, integrated, free, and deeply aware of his or her experiences within the relationship. The therapist need not be a model of perfect mental health in all aspects of his or her own life. He or she may have shortcomings and difficulties in other situations. But within the relationship of therapy, the therapist needs to be congruent.

Given these conditions, Rogers believes that positive, constructive personality changes will occur. In a climate of unconditional positive regard, the patient will be able to explore those feelings and experiences that were previously denied or distorted. In doing so, the patient's self-concept will gradually become more congruent with the actual experiences of his or her organism. Rogers suggests that all successful therapy, not just his mode of client-centered therapy, shares these conditions. The factor that essentially makes psychotherapy effective is an underlying attitude of acceptance on the part of the therapist that is perceived by the client.

Responses to Emotional Communications

Rogers does not use any special techniques, such as free association or dream analysis, in his therapy. The direction of the therapy is determined by the client. Whereas in psychoanalysis the instructions are, "Say whatever comes to mind," in Rogerian therapy, if there were any instructions, they would be, "Talk about whatever you would like to talk about." These two instructions are very different. The client determines what will be discussed, when, and to what extent. This is why Rogers's form of therapy has been labeled "client-centered." If a client does not want to talk about a particular subject, he or she is not pressed to do so. The client does not even have to talk at all if he or she does not want to. Rogers feels strongly that his clients have the ability to understand and to explore their problems and that given the appropriate therapeutic relationship, that is, an attitude of acceptance, they will work toward further self-actualization.

In Rogerian therapy, the therapist communicates the attitude of acceptance largely through statements that reflect the client's feelings. We can understand this better by distinguishing between different kinds of responses to emotional communications. Rogers developed a number of studies in which he explored how people communicate in face-to-face situations (Rogers & Roethlisberger, 1952). Consider the following hypothetical communication: "The doctor keeps telling me not to worry, but I'm frightened of this operation." There are many different ways in which one could respond to such a statement. Rogers discovered that most responses fall into one of five categories: probing, evaluative, interpretative, reassuring, and reflective. Each of these responses tends to lead toward a different consequence.

A **probing response** seeks further information. One might ask, "What is it about the operation that frightens you?" Additional information can be very helpful in assisting the listener to understand the problem. All too frequently, however, a probing response is taken by the speaker to be an infringement upon his or her privacy. He or she may inwardly react, "That's none of your business." In such a case, the speaker might clam up and the listener would lose the opportunity to explore the feelings further. Rogers would recommend that a probing response be avoided or presented in such a way that the speaker is free to drop the subject if he or she chooses. One might simply ask, "Would you like to talk about it?" in which case the speaker is free to say, "No, I'd rather not," if he or she finds the subject too painful.

An **evaluative response** places a value judgment on the person's thoughts, feelings, wishes, or behavior. One might say, "You shouldn't be afraid of the operation." Evaluative responses may have their place when the listener is specifically asked to give his or her opinion or wants to disclose his or her own values or attitudes. However, because evaluative responses are judgmental, they tend to detract from an attitude of basic acceptance of the other individual. Our natural tendency to approve, disapprove, judge, or evaluate another person's comments is a primary barrier to understanding in communication. Evaluative responses frequently close the door to further communications rather than open it. Often they lead to a defensive reaction in the speaker and to a situation in which each party simply looks at the problem from his or her own point of view. A person who is defensive is no longer open to further exploration of the anxiety that he or she is trying to defend him- or herself against.

An **interpretative response** is an effort on the listener's part to tell the speaker what his or her problem really is or how he or she really feels about the situation. One might say, "That's because you're afraid of being unconscious during the operation." Interpretation is a technique that is frequently employed in intensive therapy. In the hands of a trained and skilled technician, it can be a valuable adjunct to assist in developing insight. But in the hands of an amateur, interpretation can be a dangerous tool. In the first place, the interpretation may be wrong. Second, if an interpretation is correct, it must be properly timed. If an interpretation is ill timed, it will be rejected because the speaker was not ready for it. If an interpretation is rejected it may have the further side effect of making the speaker feel misunderstood and less likely to discuss the issue further. For these reasons any interpretation should be presented only tentatively and left open for further confirmation. Further, an interpretation should be timed so that it is not given until just before the speaker is about to make the same discovery about him- or herself. When properly used and given with skill, empathy, and integrity, interpretations can be potent catalysts for growth.

A **reassuring response** attempts to soothe the speaker's feelings. It implies that the speaker need not feel the way he or she does. One might reply, "Many others have come through the same operation well." Reassuring responses may be helpful in letting the speaker know that he or she is accepted or in encouraging a person to try out new behaviors that might help to resolve a problem. However, reassurance is frequently perceived by an individual as an attempt to minimize his or her problem. At the moment he or she does not care about other people but is concerned with his or her own dilemma. Introducing other people's problems or one's own in an effort to pacify may suggest that the listener is not taking the speaker's problem seriously or wants to dismiss it.

The **reflective response** seeks to capture the underlying feelings that are expressed in the original communication. One might say, "You're very scared." An effective reflective statement does not simply echo the original words or thoughts of the speaker, it tries to zero in on the underlying emotion that was expressed. It is most effective if the listener uses his or her own words and responds in a manner that matches the depth of the original communication.

A distinction should be made between a reflective response and mere restatement. A *restatement* repeats the *thought* of the original comment, whereas a reflective comment seeks to express the underlying *emotion*. Reflective responses are useful because they tell the speaker that the listener is interested and understands what he or she is trying to say. A reflective response is most likely to encourage the speaker to elaborate and explore his or her problem further. In addition, it assists the listener to understand the other person's internal frame of reference. For these reasons, it is probably the most fruitful response to employ, particularly for a lay person and even for a skilled therapist in the initial phases of a relationship.

Nevertheless, Rogers found that in everyday life the responses were used in the following order of frequency: (1) evaluative, (2) interpretative, (3) reassuring, (4) probing, and (5) reflective. Apparently, we could use practice in cultivating the reflective response.

Cultivating a More Reflective Response

Rogers suggests this exercise as a way of cultivating a more reflective response to other people. The next time you become deeply engrossed in a conversation or an argument, agree to obey the following rule. Each person may speak for him- or herself only after he or she has reflected the thoughts and feelings of the previous speaker accurately and to that person's satisfaction. What initially sounds simple proves difficult, but it leads to a much more constructive discussion as it focuses on understanding one another rather than simply presenting different points of view.

You might also read the following emotional communications, imagine how you might respond, and try to write responses for each one that fit into each of the five categories.*

1. Mr. Jones is such an unfair teacher. I just failed another one of his tests.

2. I got so annoyed when John stood me up last night, I wouldn't come to the phone when he called.

3. I'm so depressed, I don't know what to do! Here I am twenty-nine and still unmarried.

4. I'm really worried about Bill. His grades have fallen and I think he may be into drugs.

5. What should I do about Bob? I like dating him, but I think he wants to get too serious.

6. That new kid in class really tees me off. He's such a braggart.

7. I think I'll leave home. My parents don't understand me and they make such unfair restrictions.

8. I know I should do something about the problem, but I just can't bring myself to face it.

It is helpful to compare your responses with those that others make. Discuss where and how your responses might be improved. Finally, analyze the comments that you hear people make in group situations. Note the frequency with which each type of response occurs.

Actually, there is no written exercise or book that can improve your ability to communicate reflectively. It requires continual practice, interaction, and feedback from others. Nevertheless, in everyday communications, one can

*Communications adapted from E. H. Porter, Jr., *Therapeutic Counseling*, Boston: Houghton Mifflin, 1950, pp. 33–40.

(continued)

try to attune oneself to the kinds of responses that are offered. One can ask oneself, "Do my responses reflect what the speaker really means?" One can also ask the speaker if one is reflecting him or her accurately by prefacing or ending a comment with a phrase such as, "Do you mean ..." or "... is that it?"

Supportive versus Reconstructive Psychotherapy

Different methods of psychotherapy vary in their ambitions. Some therapies aim at strengthening adaptive behaviors and others seek to reorganize the basic personality structure. At one end of the spectrum, psychoanalysis stands as an example of **reconstructive psychotherapy.** Through analysis of the resistances and transference the analyst seeks to remove defenses so that the patient can communicate his or her true feelings and integrate his or her personality. On the other hand, many psychotherapeutic techniques are best characterized as **supportive,** since they seek to strengthen adaptive instincts and defenses without necessarily tampering with the underlying personality structure.

In both instances, maladaptive behavior can be viewed as defensive behavior that has gone awry. In order to protect him- or herself against anxiety, the individual develops defense mechanisms or denials and distortions. These defense mechanisms have both constructive and destructive features. They are positive and constructive in that they ward off anxiety that would be too painful to bear in its full impact. Yet the defenses may become destructive in that they prevent us from recognizing and acting on our innermost feelings. Supportive psychotherapy seeks to strengthen and bolster adaptive defense mechanisms to assist the person in more effectively coping with his or her anxieties. Reconstructive psychotherapy entails weakening those defenses that have become maladaptive so that the original emotions and anxieties can be re-experienced and more effectively resolved.

Both modalities of treatment have their place. Some patients require supportive psychotherapy, whereas others benefit more from an intensive reconstructive psychotherapy. Age, the nature of the problem, and the ability to withstand stress are a few of the many factors that need consideration prior to selection of a method of treatment.

For example, young people typically experience anxiety over their sexual desires. However, for some women the change toward a more permissive expression of their sexuality, as encouraged by our culture during the last fifty years, has been particularly difficult to adjust to. These women were taught to frown upon their sexual impulses and desires and consider them dirty. For some of these women, supportive therapy has been very helpful in assisting them to come to terms with the acceptability of their sexual urges. In an atmosphere free of earlier parental conditions of worth, they could express their feelings without fear of punishment. Supportive therapy helps them to draw their own conclusions from their sexual experience and reassess the wisdom of the values they were taught as children.

But in other instances, supportive therapy is not sufficient. Many women are fully aware of the fallacies of the sexual views that were inculcated in them as children. But, as children, they were taught so well to repress their sexual feelings that it is very difficult for them to know or even experience their own sexual desires and responses. Even though an individual may know and be fully convinced on an intellectual level of the possibility of optimally and constructively expressing her feelings, she may find herself inhibited. Her response may be prevented from occurring by underlying unconscious conflicts. In such a situation, reconstructive therapy may be necessary. Defenses will need to be analyzed and weakened so that the underlying unconscious conflict can emerge and be worked through.

Whereas supportive therapy takes the existing personality structure and strengthens its desirable features, reconstructive therapy seeks complete rehaul and reconstruction of the personality. One might compare the one to slip-covering a chair with a fresh fabric to give it a new lease on life, and the other to an upholstery job in which the chair is stripped to the frame and then rebuilt. Clearly, reconstructive psychotherapy is a much more intensive undertaking, which accounts for the long duration of psychoanalysis. Although he is not averse to providing insight when the occasion merits it, Rogers's approach tends to be supportive rather than reconstructive.

This is not to say that one technique is better than the other; rather, we need to recognize that for different people, in different circumstances, and perhaps even at different times in their lives, one approach may be more suitable than another. Such variation may also help to explain why Rogers's therapeutic technique has been particularly successful with college-age students, many of whom are not seriously impaired but are undergoing a difficult period of identity during which supportive therapy may be very helpful. Rogers points out that we all can benefit from therapy. Although we may not be suffering from overt problems that seriously affect our lives, we may not be functioning as well as we would like. Rogers acknowledged that at one particularly stressful period of his life he was treated by a colleague. He was thankful that he was able to develop a method of therapy and train therapists who were not only independent but also able to offer him the kind of help that he needed. Since the time that he himself received therapy, Rogers has felt that his own work with patients has been increasingly free and more spontaneous.

Changes in Rogers's View of Therapy

Rogers's earlier writings on therapeutic technique stressed the idea that the potential for better health lies in the client. The therapist's role was essentially that of making the kinds of reflective responses that would enable the client's potential to flower. Later, Rogers shifted from his emphasis on technique to the counselor's need to develop an interpersonal relationship in which experiences could come into awareness. In his later writings, Rogers stresses the need for the therapist to be present as a person in the relationship. While Rogers continues to recognize the importance of nondirection, believing that the client must remain in charge of his or her own life, he maintains that the therapist needs to be aware of his or her own feelings and free to express them without imposing them on the client. Negative as well as positive feelings may be presented, simply posed as data that the client is free to cope with as he or she chooses. The therapist may point out that a client is boring him or her. This is not a mandate for the client to change, but a factor within the interpersonal relationship that the client might wish to deal with.

In recent years, Rogers has been less interested in individual therapy and more interested in group therapy, as well as broader social concerns. He is a leader in the field of encounter groups and has sponsored some interracial and intercultural groups. He has challenged some of the concepts on which our society is based, such as that power is power over or that strength is the strength to control. Instead he suggests that influence is gained only when power is shared and that control is constructive when it is self-control. He has written about education, particularly higher education, describing a plan for radical change in teacher education and researching the effects of teachers' attitudes on students' learning. He emphasizes the importance of combining experiential with cognitive learning. He has also explored various forms of partnership unions or alternatives to marriage as well as other interpersonal relationships that are found in contemporary society.

Therapy Excerpts /////

Client-Centered Therapy

In client-centered therapy, the therapist's main objective is to reflect the client's feelings. The therapist, in this case Carl Rogers, may disclose some of his or her own feelings but does so without making value judgments. In the excerpt below, the client, a thirty-year-old divorcée, begins by expressing

(continued)

---

conflict over whether or not to tell her nine-year-old daughter Pammy that she has had sexual relationships with men since her divorce.*

CL (client): I almost want an answer from you. I want you to tell me if it would affect her wrong if I told her the truth, or what.

TH (therapist): I sure wish I could give you the answer as to what you should say to her.

CL: I was afraid you were going to say that.

TH: Because what you really want *is* an answer.

The client begins to explore her relationship with her daughter and realizes that she is not sure whether or not her daughter would accept her "shady" side, because she is not certain she accepts it herself.

CL: You're going to sit there and let me stew in it and I want more.

TH: No, I don't want to let you just stew in your feelings, but on the other hand, I also feel that this is the kind of very private thing that I couldn't possibly answer for you. But I sure as anything will try to help you work towards your own answer. I don't know whether that makes any sense to you, but I mean it.

CL: I can tell that you really do mean it.

The client focuses further on the conflict she experiences between her actions and her inner standards. Again, she presses for an answer.

TH: I guess, I am sure this will sound evasive to you, but it seems to me that perhaps the person you are not being fully honest with is you, because I was very much struck by the fact that you were saying, "If I feel all right about what I have done, whether it's going to bed with a man or what, if I really feel all right about it, then I do not have any concern about what I would tell Pam or my relationship with her."

CL: Right. All right. Now I hear what you are saying. Then all right, then I want to work on accepting me then. I want to work on feeling all right about it. That makes sense. Then that will come natural and then I won't have to worry about Pammy. I guess I wanted you to tell me what to do, because I can't quite take the risk of being the way I want to be with my children unless an authority tells me that...

TH: I guess one thing that I feel very keenly is that it's an awfully risky thing

*Reproduced by permission of the publisher, F. E. Peacock Publishers, Inc., Itasca, Illinois. Adapted from Meador, B. D. and Rogers, C. R., "Person-Centered Therapy." In R. J. Corsini, *Current Psychotherapies,* 2nd edition, 1979, pp. 176–177.

(continued)

> to *live*. You'd be taking a chance on your relationship with her and taking a chance on letting her know who you are, really.
>
> CL: I wish I could take more risks, that I could act on my own feelings of rightness without always needing encouragement from others. I know what I'd like to do is to level with Pammy and tell her the kind of a person that I really am.
>
> TH: You'd like to tell her the truth.
>
> CL: Yes, I would. Now I feel like "now that's solved" and I didn't even solve a thing; but I feel relieved. I feel like you have been saying to me — you are not giving me advice, but I do feel like you are saying, "You know what pattern you want to follow, Gloria, and go ahead and follow it." I sort of feel a backing from you.
>
> TH: I guess the way I sense it, you've been telling me that you know what you want to do, and yes, I do believe in backing up people in what they want to do.

The Empirical Validation of Psychotherapy

Rogers has been exceptionally open to the empirical test of his theories. The private, confidential character of clinical treatment has made it very difficult to study in its natural setting. With the permission of his clients, however, Rogers has introduced the tape recorder and film camera into the treatment room. He does not believe that they detract from the therapy. Within a short time, both client and therapist forget about the recording equipment and act naturally and spontaneously.

The recordings Rogers has made have provided a group of actual transcriptions of therapeutic sessions that can be observed and studied. The sessions have been analyzed in various ways. A classification system permits us to note the kinds of statements made by both the client and the therapist. Rating scales monitor the progress and change that occur during therapy from the viewpoints of both the client and the therapist. The Q-sort technique has been used to measure changes that occur throughout therapy. In short, Rogers has provided and given an impetus to developing means for ongoing empirical research on the processes of therapy and the self.

From his studies, Rogers concludes that there is a clear predictability to the therapeutic process. Given certain conditions, such as the three therapist attitudes outlined earlier, certain predictable outcomes may be expected. The client will express deep motivational attitudes. He or she will begin to explore and become more aware of his or her attitudes and reactions. The client will begin to accept him- or herself more fully and will discover and choose more satisfying goals. Finally, the client will begin to behave in a manner that indicates greater psychological growth and maturity.

Research by others with troubled individuals and in education has supported the view that when facilitating conditions are present, changes in personality and behavior will occur (see Aspy, 1972; Aspy and Roebuck, 1976; Tausch, 1978).

The Fully Functioning Person

A **fully functioning person** is an individual who is functioning at an optimal level, as a result either of his or her own development or of psychological treatment. Rogers describes five characteristics of the fully functioning person (1959).

1. *Openness to experience* Fully functioning persons are aware of all of their experiences: they are not defensive and do not need to deny or distort experiences. They can recognize a feeling even if it is inappropriate to act on it. During a lecture, a young man may experience the desire to have sexual relations with the young woman sitting next to him. He refrains from acting at the moment because he recognizes that such action would be imprudent, but the feeling does not threaten him. Fully functioning people can recognize both negative and positive emotions and permit them to enter into their self-system.

2. *Existential living* Fully functioning persons are able to live fully and richly each moment of existence. Each experience is potentially fresh and new. They do not need preconceived structures to interpret each happening. Every event can speak for itself. They can deal with new, unpredicted, and unexpected situations. They are flexible and spontaneous. They discover the structure of their experiences in the process of experiencing them.

3. *Organismic trust* Fully functioning persons trust in the feel of their own organism. They may take other people's opinions and the consensus of their society into account, but they are not bound by them. The locus of their decision making lies within themselves.

4. *Experiential freedom* Fully functioning persons operate as free choice agents. They do not feel compelled by others or by some alien aspect of themselves. They assume responsibility for their decisions and behavior. Obviously, they are subject to the laws of causality. Everyone's behavior is largely determined by genetic make-up, past experiences, and social forces. Nevertheless, fully functioning people subjectively feel free to be aware of their needs and to respond accordingly.

5. *Creativity* Fully functioning persons live constructively and effectively in their environment. The spontaneity and flexibility characteristic of fully functioning people enable them to adjust adequately to changes in their surroundings and to seek new experiences and challenges. Free from constraints, they move confidently forward in the process of self-actualization.

Rogers emphasizes that his is not a "pollyanna," or naively optimistic, point of view. Terms such as "happy," "blissful," or "contented" do not necessarily describe fully functioning people; rather, such people are challenged and find life meaningful. Their experiences are "exciting," "enriching," and "rewarding." Self-actualization requires the "courage to be" and the willingness to launch oneself into the process of life.

Rogers's Theory: Philosophy, Science, and Art

Rogers has done a great deal to bring the human being back as the primary focus of psychological study. In doing so, he has clearly reasserted the philosophical character of personality theorizing. At the same time, he has been very careful to distinguish between his philosophical assumptions and his scientific hypotheses. For instance, in Rogers's theory the self is not a philosophical concept but a name for a group of processes, which can be studied scientifically.

Still, Rogers's emphasis on subjectivity and the individual's internal frame of reference has made scientific research difficult. Researchers have traditionally stressed the role of the external observer because, as we have seen, introspective reports are much more difficult to validate than extrospective reports. Rogers has been criticized for using self-reports in his research and many scientific psychologists have rejected Rogers's notion of the self because of his methods.

Tendencies to suppress data or to supply socially acceptable data instead of the truth do exist in subjective reporting. However, if we are aware of these tendencies toward error, we can take steps to avoid them. In this sense, introspection is no different from any other scientific method. Extrospection is also open to a great deal of error; sense organs may be defective or deluded. Psychologists have known for a long time that there is hardly a perfect correspondence between the stimulus, or the evidence of the world that reaches our senses, and our perception of the world. Introspection does not involve the sense organs to the same extent as extrospection and so in some respects may be more trustworthy. Thus, Rogers's emphasis on introspection is a useful correction of the emphasis on extrospection that has characterized American psychology since John Watson.

Nevertheless, a major criticism of Rogers's position is that it is based on a simplistic concept of phenomenology and does not reflect a sophisticated understanding of the complexity of the processes underlying human awareness. It also does not take into account a child's immature cognitive structures and inability to make clear distinctions between feelings and actions. To suggest that a person is the most important source of information about him- or herself because that person is the only one fully aware of his or her experiences minimizes how frequently human beings deny or distort the truth about themselves to themselves. Many of us seem bent on self-deception rather than on self-understanding. Although Rogers acknowledges that there are experiences of which a person may be unaware through the processes of denial and distortion, he does not believe that repression is inevitable. Under the proper conditions of unconditional positive regard, he suggests, repression can be avoided. Moreover, Rogers holds that an atmosphere of acceptance is sufficient to lift repression. Critics suggest that this belief is naive and that Rogers fails to recognize the power and intensity of unconscious forces.

To permit a client to say simply whatever he or she wants to say may perpetuate the process of self-deception. If one is not required to say whatever comes to mind, one can easily avoid painful topics. The topics we do not want to explore may be the locus of our difficulty and their analysis might penetrate our defenses. To be sure, the discussion of painful subjects is threatening, but a certain amount of threat may be necessary in psychotherapy to recreate the original conditions that led to the repression and to permit the unconscious forces to enter consciousness. In this sense, Rogers's philosophical assumptions lack depth.

On the other hand, Rogers's careful empirical study of the therapeutic process has shed considerable light on the phenomenon and practice of therapy. Scientific research has helped to clarify the types of situations and relationships that are conducive to change. Rogers's discussion of the therapist's attitude of acceptance is a helpful correction of Freud's overemphasis on transference. It is the real, personal relationship between therapist and client that fosters personality change. Rogers, in encouraging empirical validation of his theories, has facilitated the development of client-centered therapeutic techniques. He is largely responsible for the growth and acceptance of psychotherapy in the 1960s and 1970s.

Rogers (1961) has vigorously criticized the social and philosophical implications of a rigid behavioral science, like that proposed by B. F. Skinner, who advocated the development of a technology to control human behavior (see Chapter 16). Rogers believes that kind of society would destroy our personhood. He acknowledges that science has brought us the power to manipulate but thinks we should manipulate on the basis of certain goals. The scientific method cannot establish the goals; it can only test hypotheses that may or may not be useful. The hypotheses reflect the scientist's value system. If we value the ability to control other people, our scientific technology can tell how to achieve this goal. On the other hand, if we value individual freedom and creativity, our scientific technology can facilitate these ends as well. In either case, the goal that directs the scientific enterprise lies outside of the scientific enterprise. The basic difference between a behavioristic approach and a humanistic approach is a philosophical choice (1980). Each choice leads to different topics of research and different methods of validation.

Rogers suggests that we need to be explicit about the goals we want our scientific endeavor to serve. Rogers, in his role as scientist, studies the predictability of the therapeutic process, not to control his client's behavior but to help his client be less predictable and more free, responsible, and spontaneous.

Rogers's theory appeals to many people who prefer the optimism of his non-manipulative view to the pessimism of psychoanalysis and the reductionism of behaviorism. Psychologists have welcomed his reintroduction of the importance of subjectivity and perception in determining behavior. His therapeutic techniques have been widely applauded and adopted in education, industry, and social programs. Moreover, Rogers's theory has prompted a great deal of further study and research, particularly concerning his concept of the self and the process of psychotherapy. His emphasis on human potentiality and freedom provides an attractive alternative to theories that emphasize the idea that we are largely controlled by external or unconscious forces. His theory has tremendous appeal for those who share his humanistic and optimistic philosophy of the human being.

❧ Summary

1. Rogers has reasserted the **self** as a useful construct for understanding personality by presenting it as a scientific construct.

2. Rogers's humanist theory is influenced by **phenomenology**, which emphasized that what is important is not an object or event in itself but how it is perceived. In psychology this means an emphasis on human awareness and the conviction that the best vantage point for understanding an individual is that of the individual him- or herself.

3. The **phenomenal field** refers to the total sum of experiences an organism has, the **organism** is the individual as a process, and the **self** is a concept of who one is. **Self-actualization** is the dynamic within the organism leading it to actualize, fulfill, and enhance its potentials. Emotions accompany and facilitate the process of self-actualization. Fully experiencing emotions facilitates growth and repression is unnecessary.

4. A state of **congruence** exists when a person's symbolized experiences reflect his or her actual experiences. When denial or distortion is present in the symbolization, there is a state of **incongruence.**

5. The young child has a strong need for **positive regard.** Ideally, positive regard is **unconditional.** If it is contingent upon specific behaviors it becomes **conditional positive regard** and posits **conditions of worth** that may lead the child to introject values of others and become incongruent.

6. Rogers is best known for his method of client-centered therapy. He believes that there are three necessary and sufficient therapeutic attitudes for change: **empathy, acceptance,** and **genuineness.**

7. Rogers distinguishes among five different **responses** to emotional communications: **probing, evaluative, interpretative, reassuring,** and **reflective.** Each of them has different effects. Rogers encouraged the cultivation of the reflective response.

8. **Client-centered therapy** tends to be **supportive** rather than **reconstructive.** In his later writings, Rogers stressed the need for the therapist to be present as a person in the relationship and showed more interest in group therapy and social change. He has encouraged the empirical test of his theories and developed methods of assessing and predicting therapeutic change.

9. According to Rogers a **fully functioning person** is characterized by openness to experience, existential living, organismic trust, experiential freedom, and creativity.

10. Rogers has been very careful to distinguish between his philosophical assumptions and his scientific hypotheses. He has criticized Skinner's view of science and his goal of controlling human nature rather than increasing human freedom, responsibility, and spontaneity. He points out that our technology may be used to foster many different goals. His own position has been criticized for its reliance on a simplistic phenomenology and praised for increasing our understanding of interpersonal relationships. Rogers's careful empirical study of the therapeutic process has shed considerable light on the phenomenon of therapy.

Suggestions for Further Reading

Carl Rogers is a lucid writer whose works are relatively easy for the lay person to understand. In *Counseling and Psychotherapy* (Houghton Mifflin, 1942), Rogers first introduced his nondirective therapy technique, gave examples, and compared it with other therapeutic methods. *Client-Centered Therapy* (Houghton Mifflin, 1942) reflects the change in name Rogers gave his technique in order to focus attention on the client as the center of the therapeutic process. This book discusses the practice and implications of client-centered therapy and also describes his theory of personality and behavior. With Rosalind Dymond, Carl Rogers edited *Psychotherapy and Personality Change* (University of Chicago Press, 1954), which presents thirteen empirical studies investigating hypotheses that arose out of the client-centered approach. In a group of significant articles organized into the book *On Becoming a Person* (Houghton Mifflin, 1961), Rogers describes his own experiences as a therapist, his view of the fully functioning person, the place of research in psychotherapy and its implications for education, family life, and group functions. Also included is Rogers's critique of B. F. Skinner. *Freedom to Learn* (Charles E. Merrill, 1969) discusses ways of making classroom learning more relevant and meaningful to students. Rogers explains how the atmosphere that makes learning effective is similar to those attitudes that are conducive to personality change in therapy. *A Way of Being* (Houghton Mifflin, 1980) describes the changes that occurred in Rogers's life and thought during the 1970s.

Summaries of Rogers's own research may be found in a book edited by him, *The Therapeutic Relationship and Its Impact* (University of Wisconsin Press, 1967) and the Rogers and Dymond book mentioned above. For a discussion of the research generated by self-theory, the reader is referred to R. Wylie's chapter on "The Present Status of Self-Theory" in E. F. Borgotta and W. W. Lambert, *Handbook of Personality and Research* (Rand McNally, 1968) and his book *The Self-Concept* (University of Nebraska Press, 1974, 1978), as well as D. N. Aspy, *Toward a Technology for Humanizing Education* (Research Press, 1972) and R. Tausch's article "Facilitative dimensions in interpersonal relations: Verifying the theoretical assumptions of Carl Rogers," *College Student Journal,* 1978, *12* (1).

13
Abraham Maslow: Theory of Self-Actualization

Your Goals for This Chapter

1. Explain why Maslow has been critical of psychoanalysis and behaviorism.

2. Distinguish among *motivation, metamotivation, D-needs,* and *B-needs* and indicate the importance of these distinctions.

3. Describe Maslow's *hierarchy of human needs.* Cite studies that show that the needs are essential for optimal human life and development.

4. Describe how Maslow identified and studied *self-actualized persons.*

5. Identify four key dimensions of self-actualized persons and describe the characteristics of each dimension.

6. Explain what is meant by a *peak experience* and give examples of it.

7. Describe some of the criticisms that have been made of Maslow's portrait of the self-actualized person.

8. Distinguish between *basic needs therapy* and *insight therapy* and indicate the criteria that Maslow believed were necessary for effective and expanded therapy.

9. Evaluate Maslow's theory in terms of its function as philosophy, science, and art.

Abraham Maslow has been described as the spiritual father of American humanism. An articulate, persuasive writer, he has described humanist psychology as a "third force" in American psychology. He criticized both psychoanalysis and behaviorism for their pessimistic, negative, and limited conceptions of human nature. The study of crippled people (neurotics), characteristic of psychoanalysis, he wrote, can only lead to a crippled psychology. The study of human nature as a machine, typical of behaviorism, cannot comprehend the whole person. Maslow offered his view as a complement rather than an alternative to these two other forces. He did not reject the contributions that psychoanalysis and behaviorism have made but he believed that the picture of human nature needs to be rounded out. In particular, Maslow sought to emphasize the positive rather than the negative side of human nature. The brighter side of humanity is emphasized in his concept of the self-actualized person.

Biographical Background

Abraham Maslow was born in 1908 in a poor Jewish district of Brooklyn, New York, the first of seven children. His parents were Russian immigrants. As his father's business as a cooper (one who makes or repairs wooden casks and tubs) improved, Maslow's family moved out of the slums and into lower-middle-class neighborhoods. As a result, the young Maslow found himself the only Jewish boy in the neighborhood and a target of anti-Semitism. Taunted, isolated, friendless, and lonely, he spent a great deal of his early years cloistered in the library in the companionship of books.

His father was an ambitious man who instilled in his children a desire to succeed. At an early age, Maslow delivered newspapers. Later he spent several summers working for the family company. Today, that company, Universal Containers, Inc., is a large, successful barrel-manufacturing corporation, run by his brothers. Maslow was not close to either of his parents. He was fond of his father but afraid of him. He described his mother as schizophrenic and later wondered how he had turned out so well in spite of his unhappy childhood. His mother's brother, however, was a kind and devoted uncle, who spent a great deal of time with him and may have been responsible for Maslow's mental stability.

Maslow attended New York City schools through the eighth grade and then the Brooklyn Borough High School, where he had an excellent record. At the age of eighteen he entered New York City College, where the tuition was free. His father wanted him to study law, a subject that he was not interested in, and his grades fell. The next two years were marked by confusion. Undecided about his studies and in love with a girl of whom his parents

Abraham Maslow

disapproved, he floundered, spending time at Cornell, returning to New York City, and trying to escape by going to the University of Wisconsin.

Within a few months of his arrival at Wisconsin, he announced his intention of marrying his sweetheart. She returned with him to Wisconsin. Later, he suggested that life didn't begin for him until he married and began studying at Wisconsin. The supportiveness of his wife encouraged his academic work. Further, he had discovered John Watson and was totally absorbed in behaviorism, which he saw as a very practical way of improving society. During his college and graduate years, Maslow received a solid grounding in empirical laboratory research. He worked as an assistant to William H. Sheldon, although he was not personally impressed by Sheldon's theory of the varieties of temperament. He also studied animal behavior, working with Harry Harlow, a well-known psychologist who conducted extensive research with rhesus monkeys. Maslow's own doctoral research concerned the sexual and dominance characteristics of monkeys.

After receiving the Ph.D. from Wisconsin in 1934, Maslow returned to New York. He worked as a research assistant to Edwin L. Thorndike and then began to teach at Brooklyn College. New York was a vibrant place for a young psychologist during the 1930s. Many European psychologists, psychiatrists, and others of the intelligentsia who had come to America to escape the Nazis were in New York. Maslow eagerly met and learned from them. He was influenced by Max Wertheimer, a founder of the gestalt school, Erich Fromm, Karen Horney, and Alfred Adler. He was also impressed by the anthropologist Ruth Benedict, who inspired him with her optimism about the potentialities of society.

Within such an eclectic climate, it was probably inevitable that Maslow's interest in behaviorism would diminish. The birth of his first daughter was the "thunderclap that settled things" once and for all. All of his experimentation with rats and primates did not prepare him for the mystery of the child. Behaviorist theory might explain what was observed in the laboratory, but it could not account for human experiences. The advent of World War II also profoundly affected Maslow. His attention turned more fully to research on the human personality in an effort to improve it, "to show that human beings are capable of something grander than war and prejudice and hatred" (Hall, 1968).

Maslow remained at Brooklyn for fourteen years. In 1951, he moved to Brandeis University where he stayed until one year before his death in 1970. These later years at Brandeis were again marked by a feeling of isolation, in spite of the fact that Maslow had become a very popular figure in the field of psychology. Perhaps it was simply Maslow's nature to be a loner. He clarified and refined his theories and shortly before his death had embarked on a fellowship that would have enabled him to undertake a large-scale study developing a philosophy of economics, politics, and ethics informed by humanistic psychology.

Human Motivation: A Hierarchical Theory

Maslow believes that human beings are interested in growing rather than simply restoring balance or avoiding frustration. He describes the human being as a "wanting animal" who is almost always desiring something. Indeed, as one human desire is satisfied, another arises to take its place. In the drive to self-actualize, the individual moves forward toward growth, happiness, and satisfaction.

Maslow (1970) distinguishes between motivation and metamotivation. **Motivation** refers to reducing tension by satisfying deficit states or lacks. It entails **D-needs** or deficiency needs, which arise out of the organism's requirements for physiological survival or safety, such as the need for food or rest, and motivate the individual to engage in activities that will reduce these drives. Motivation and the D-needs are powerful determinants of behavior.

- **Metamotivation** refers to growth tendencies. It entails **B-needs** or being needs, which arise out of the organism's drive to self-actualize and fulfill its inherent potential. B-needs do not stem from a lack or deficiency; rather, they push forward to self-fulfillment. Their goal is to enhance life by enriching it. Rather than reducing tension, they frequently increase it in their quest for ever-increasing stimuli that will bring a life lived to the fullest.

Motivation and the D-needs take precedence over metamotivation and the B-needs. The deficiency needs must be satisfied first. An individual who is wondering where his or her next mouthful of food is going to come from is hardly able to be concerned with the esteem that he or she receives from other people or with spiritual goals like truth or beauty. Thus, the needs may be conceived as arranged in a hierarchy, in that the needs at the bottom must be satisfied before those at the top can be fulfilled (Figure 13.1).

In his hierarchy, Maslow (1970) describes five basic needs. In order of their strength they are: physiological needs, safety needs, belonging and love needs, self-esteem needs, and self-actualization needs. Each lower need must be satisfied before an individual can become aware of or develop the capacity to fulfill the needs above it. As each need is satisfied, the next higher order need attains importance. Some individuals, because of their circumstances, find it very difficult to satisfy even the lowest needs. The higher one is able to go, however, the greater psychological health and self-actualization one will demonstrate.

1. *Physiological needs*   The strongest needs of all are the physiological ones that pertain to the physical survival and biological maintenance of the organism. They include the need for food, drink, sleep, oxygen, shelter, and sex. For

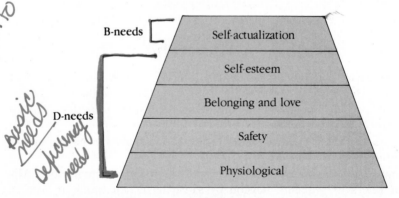

Figure 13.1 *Maslow's Hierarchy of Needs*
Maslow suggests that human needs may be conceived of as arranged in a hierarchy in which the needs that stand at the bottom must be satisfied before those at the top can be fulfilled.

many Americans, physiological needs are satisfied almost automatically. However, where biological needs are not met for a protracted period of time, an individual will not be motivated to fulfill any other needs. The person who is really starving has no other interest than obtaining food. Several experiments and tales from real life have indicated the overwhelming behavioral effects produced by a lack of food, sleep, or other life-sustaining needs. Gratification of these needs renders them less important and permits other needs to appear (1970).

2. *Safety needs* Safety needs refer to the organism's requirements for an orderly, stable, and predictable world within which to feel secure. Most normal, healthy adults have satisfied these needs but they can be seen clearly in young children and neurotics. The young child, who is helpless and dependent, prefers a certain amount of structured routine and discipline. The absence of these elements makes him or her anxious and insecure. Too much freedom is threatening because a child does not know what to do with it. The neurotic frequently behaves like the insecure child, compulsively ordering his or her world and avoiding strange or different experiences. In general, the mature adult, assured of the basic stability of his or her world, is open to the new and unexpected.

3. *Belonging and love needs* Once the physiological and safety needs are met, needs for love and belonging arise. The individual seeks affectionate and intimate relationships with other people. He or she needs to feel part of various reference groups, such as the family, neighborhood, gang, or a professional association. Maslow notes that such needs are increasingly more difficult to meet in our technological, fluid, and mobile society. Such problems may account for the rising interest in support groups and new styles of living together. Love, rather than being physiological or simply sexual, involves a healthy, mutual relationship of trust, in which each person is deeply understood and accepted.

4. *Self-esteem needs* Maslow describes two kinds of esteem needs — the need for respect from others and the need for self-respect. Self-esteem entails competence, confidence, mastery, achievement, independence, and freedom. Respect from others entails recognition, acceptance, status, and appreciation. When these needs are not met an individual feels discouraged, weak, and inferior. Healthy self-esteem is a realistic appraisal of one's capacities and has its roots in deserved respect from others. For most people, the need for regard from others diminishes with age because it has been fulfilled and the need for self-regard becomes more important.

5. *Self-actualization needs* If the foregoing needs have been met, the needs for **self-actualization** emerge. These needs are difficult to describe because they are unique and vary from person to person. In general, self-actualization refers to the desire to fulfill one's highest potential. If an individual on this

level does not fully exploit his or her talents and capacities, he or she is discontent and restless. In Maslow's words, "A musician must make music, an artist must paint, a poet must write, if he is to be at peace with himself" (1970). Each of us has different potentialities and capacities. There is no standard format for self-actualization; thus, specific forms of self-actualization differ from individual to individual.

Self-actualization is possible only if the lower needs have been sufficiently met so that they do not detract from or engross a person's basic energies. Rather than organizing their behavior toward tension reduction, individuals whose deficiency needs are satisfied may, in fact, seek states of increased optimal tension in order to enhance their opportunities for self-actualization. In short, those who are living on a B-level have a radically different motivation from those who are still striving to satisfy deficit states.

However, a number of prerequisites are necessary for a person to be motivated on the B-level. Cultural, economic, and social conditions must be such that the individual does not need to be preoccupied with physiological or safety needs. Employment settings must consider the growth needs of the employees. Emotional needs for interpersonal relationships and self-esteem must be met. This may be very difficult in periods of economic recession or in a climate that emphasizes productivity over human relations. Astute industries and organizations have taken Maslow's ideas into account and recognized that consideration must be given to workers' B-needs as well as their D-needs.

A number of clinical experiments have demonstrated that the needs that Maslow describes are essential for optimal human life and development. Studies of children in institutions where they do not receive adequate love and attention show that these children do not develop normally, although all of their physical needs are met (Spitz, 1951). Maslow's own clinical experience showed that individuals who satisfy their basic needs are happier, healthier, and more effective, whereas those whose needs are frustrated display neurotic symptoms (1970). Furthermore, other clinicians, such as Karen Horney and Carl Rogers, have pointed out that given the appropriate conditions, the individual chooses to move forward and grow. From where does such a choice or impulse come, unless it is inherent in the individual? Psychologists speak of **species-specific behavior,** that is, an inborn tendency for members of a biological subgroup to behave in a certain way. Chickens tend to scratch for their food, whereas pigs root for it. Maslow suggests that the species-specific characteristics of human beings include the hierarchical needs and a drive toward self-actualization. Of course, for an adequate test of Maslow's theory that human needs are arranged in a hierarchy in which the satisfaction of lower needs leads to the emergence of higher needs, we would have to conduct extensive longitudinal studies (Maddi and Costa, 1972). Such studies have not yet been conducted.

Motivation

You can begin to assess the level of motivation that primarily influences you by carefully analyzing the reasons for your behavior. Over the course of an entire day, take careful note of all of your activities. Ask yourself why you did what you did and try to locate your motivation on Maslow's hierarchy of needs. Do not forget to pay attention to little things that occurred while you were in the middle of another activity. You may have interrupted your study time to prepare a snack, go to the bathroom, or talk with a friend. Try to observe which needs you met in a routine fashion and which demanded your full attention. You may have found yourself motivated on all levels of Maslow's hierarchy, but chances are that you satisfied your physiological and safety needs more or less automatically and concentrated your efforts on meeting other needs that are higher in the hierarchy. In addition, it would be informative to observe the activity of young children of various ages and note the different motivations governing their behavior in order to test Maslow's hypothesis that lower-level needs become less pressing and higher-level needs assume greater dominance with age.

The Study of Self-Actualized Persons

Maslow has been described as preoccupied with healthy persons rather than with neurotics. He conducted an extensive, although informal, study of a group of persons whom he considered to be self-actualizers. His study was initially private and motivated by his own curiosity rather than by the normal demands of scientific laboratory research. Thus, it lacked the rigor and distinct methodology of strict empirical study. Nevertheless, the study generated such interest among other psychologists that Maslow felt it was wise to publish his findings (1970). He admits that his findings represent only an initial, tentative attempt to study optimum health but they may serve as a focal point for further empirical research.

Maslow defined a *self-actualizing person* as one who is fulfilling him- or herself and doing the best that he or she is capable of doing. His subjects consisted of friends and personal acquaintances, public figures living and dead, and selected college students. Some of the figures included in his study are well known, such as Abraham Lincoln, Thomas Jefferson, Eleanor Roosevelt, Albert Einstein, and Albert Schweitzer. Others are not as well known and several of them were never identified publicly. In his initial study of three thousand college students, Maslow found only one individual who could be termed self-actualizing. He hypothesized that self-actualizing tendencies probably increase with age. Thereafter, he limited his studies of the college population to the most well-adjusted 1 percent of the Brandeis College population. Not all of his subjects were deemed fully actualized. He divided them into categories: cases, partial cases, and potential or possible cases. Studying these individuals, their personalities, characteristics, habits, and abilities enabled Maslow to develop his definition of optimal mental health.

Techniques of Inquiry and Research

In his study of self-actualized individuals, Maslow used whatever techniques appeared to be most appropriate to the particular situation. In dealing with historical figures, he analyzed biographical material and written records. With living persons, he also utilized in-depth interviews and psychological tests, such as the Rorschach Ink Blot Test and the Thematic Apperception Test. He obtained global impressions from friends and acquaintances. In some cases, he found that he had to be rather careful because a number of his subjects were suspicious of the intrusions that his research constituted on their privacy.

By ordinary standards of laboratory research, what Maslow did in his study was not research. He was quick to acknowledge that his investigation was not conducted along strict scientific lines. His descriptions were not based on standardized tests nor were his conclusions obtained from controlled experimental situations. Moreover, his definition of a self-actualized person tends to be a subjective one: the self-actualized person is he or she whom Maslow deems to be self-actualized. Nevertheless, Maslow points out that the canons of rigorous scientific procedures would not have encompassed or permitted research into the problems that he was studying. Further, he presented his data as only an initial observation and effort to study health as opposed to neurosis. He hoped that future studies would yield more information as to the nature of self-actualization and confirm or disprove his own expectations.

Characteristics of Self-Actualizers

Maslow lists several characteristics of self-actualized persons that emerged out of his study (1970). For simplicity, these characteristics may be grouped under four key dimensions: awareness, honesty, freedom, and trust (1969).

Awareness   Self-actualizers are characterized by awareness. They are aware of the inner rightness of themselves, of nature, and of the peak experiences of life. This awareness emerges in an *efficient perception of reality*. Self-actualizers are accurate in their perception of the world and comfortable in it. They can see through phoniness and assess the real motives of other people. They have a clearer perception of reality and realism in areas such as politics

Bas

Intense concentration on an activity may provoke a peak experience.

and religion, which permits them to cut through extraneous issues and recognize true ones. They have a higher acuity or sharpness of perception. Colors appear brighter and more vibrant to them than to the average person. They have a more efficient sense of smell. Their hearing is more precise. Studies have suggested that mental illness may entail impaired perceptions. The neurotic does not perceive the world as accurately as the healthy person. To some schizophrenics, the world is flat, merely two-dimensional, and colors are dull. For others, colors are enhanced. The distinction between health and illness appears to be cognitive as well as emotional.

Self-actualizers display a continued *freshness of appreciation*. They can appreciate again and again the basics of life. Each sunrise and sunset refreshes them anew, and each new flower is an event that never loses its miraculous quality. Familiarization does not lessen the miracle. Self-actualizers have no preconceptions of what things ought to be. They are open to experience and let each experience speak for itself.

The self-actualized person frequently experiences what Maslow calls a peak experience. A **peak experience** is an intensification of any experience to the degree that there is a loss or transcendence of self. These kinds of experiences are often termed mystical or religious, but Maslow emphasizes that they do not necessarily entail religion. A peak experience may be provoked by a secular event as well. Events that may be mundane and ordinary to others, such as viewing a work of art or reaching a sexual climax, may be the sparks that trigger a peak experience.

During a peak experience, the individual experiences not only an expansion of self but also a sense of unity and meaningfulness in his or her existence. For that moment, the world appears to be complete and he or she is at one with it. After the experience is over, and the person has returned to the routine of everyday living, the experience lingers on. It has an illuminating quality that transforms one's understanding so that things do not seem to be quite the same afterwards. Maslow believes that all human beings are potential peakers. Some people have peak experiences but they suppress them and therefore do not recognize them when they occur. In other cases, one may inhibit a peak experience, thereby preventing its occurrence.

Self-actualizers show a high degree of *ethical awareness*. They are clear about the distinction between good and evil. Self-actualizers have definite ethical standards, although their standards are not necessarily the conventional ones; rather, they know what for them is right and do it.

Self-actualizers are able to distinguish between the end goal that they are striving for and the means by which they are accomplishing it. For the most part, they are focused on ends rather than means. At the same time, they often consider as ends activities that are simply means for other people. They can enjoy the journey and appreciate it as well as the destination.

Honesty   Self-actualizers are characterized by honesty, which permits them to know their feelings and to trust them. They can trust the wide range of feelings — love, anger, and humor — present in interpersonal relations.

Self-actualizers have a *philosophical sense of humor* rather than an ordinary one. Most humor expresses hostility, superiority, or rebellion against authority. Common jokes and wisecracks do not strike the self-actualizer as funny. His or her humor is more closely allied to philosophy. It is essentially an ability to laugh at the ridiculousness of the human situation and to poke fun at our shared human pretensions. Such humor was characteristic of Abraham Lincoln, whose jokes were not at other peoples' expense. Such humor is spontaneous rather than planned. Often it cannot be repeated or retold. Maslow suggests that he once felt this humor in a room full of "kinetic art." It seemed to him to be a "humorous parody of human life, with the noise, movement, turmoil, hurry and bustle, all of it going no place" (1970).

Peak Experiences

The following checklist of characteristics of peak experiences can be useful to you in evaluating events that have happened in your own life.* It can also serve as a focal point for discussion with other people. Think of a meaningful experience that you have had. Does it fulfill any of the criteria listed below?

1. A peak experience is fully attended to with a high degree of concentration. The person is detached, passive, and objective, able to attend to the experience without having to evaluate, compare, or judge it.

2. The universe is perceived as an integrated, united whole that is both meaningful and perfect.

3. The person is not conscious of time or space and there is a loss of ego or forgetfulness of self.

4. The person experiences wonder, humility, and reverence in the face of the experience. He or she is ready to listen and to learn. Negative emotions disappear. Some individuals experience a feeling of death and rebirth.

5. The dichotomies or conflicts of life tend to be transcended or resolved.

6. The person moves close to his or her real self, feels more like a person, and becomes more loving, accepting, spontaneous, and open.

7. The person feels responsible, an active creator who has a great deal of free will.

8. The peak experience is felt as self-validating and self-justifying.

9. After a peak experience, people characteristically feel lucky, fortunate, or graced. A common reaction is "I don't deserve this."

10. The peak experience leaves wholesome aftereffects that linger on.

*Based on information from A. Maslow, *Religions, Values, and Peak Experiences,* New York: Viking, 1964. Used by permission of Kappa Delta Pi, An Honor Society in Education, owners of the copyright, Box A, West Lafayette, Indiana 47906.

Self-actualizers experience *social interest* or a deep feeling of kinship with humanity. Maslow borrows Adler's term *Gemeinschaftsgefuhl,* which means "brotherly love," to describe the identification with humanity that is expressed. Although on occasions they may experience feelings of anger, impatience, or disgust, they have a general sense of identification, sympathy, and affection for the human race and all its members.

Self-actualizers form deep *interpersonal relations*. However, they are highly selective and therefore have a small but close circle of friends. They have no need for admirers or large groups of disciples although at times they may attract such followers, creating a situation that they try to handle with tact. Their love of others may be described as a love-being-love rather than a love-deprived-love. They are involved with the being of the other person rather than with having the love of a person who cares for them. This love stems from a fullness of being rather than a state of deprivation and need.

Their love is not indiscriminate. At times they are quick to anger; they can speak harshly to others and express righteous indignation where a situation calls for it; yet their attitude is one of pity rather than attack. They react to the behavior rather than to the person.

Self-actualizers display a *democratic character structure*. They are free of prejudice, tolerant, and acceptant of all people regardless of their background. They listen and they learn from those who are able to teach them. They react to others on the basis of character rather than on the basis of race, creed, or social status.

Freedom   Self-actualizers experience a high degree of freedom, which permits them to be detached and to withdraw from the chaos that surrounds others. They are free to be independent, creative, and spontaneous.

Self-actualizers show a high degree of *detachment* and a *need for privacy*. They enjoy solitude and like to be alone. Many of us avoid being alone and compulsively seek the company of other people. Self-actualizers relish and require times when they can be by themselves. They are not secretive but they often stand apart from other people. Maslow discovered that many of them did not particularly welcome his questions or think in terms of seeing a therapist, because they considered such activities a violation of their privacy.

This ability to be detached extends to other areas as well. It permits the self-actualizer to concentrate to a greater degree than the average person. Whereas others may become excited and involved in the storm of things around them, self-actualizers remain above the battle, calm and unruffled.

Free to be themselves, self-actualizers are also free to let other people be. They are not afraid of letting other people be who they are. As parents, this means they have the ability to refrain from meddling with a child, because they like the way he or she is growing. They do not feel that they have to interfere when it is not necessary. They do not need to make decisions for the child. They can permit the child to experience the consequences of his or her own behavior without overprotecting.

Self-actualizers are *autonomous and independent* of their physical and social environment. Motivated by growth rather than by deficiency, they do not need to depend on the world or others for their real satisfaction. Their basic needs and gratifications have been met; therefore, they are free to depend on their own development.

Autonomy also entails the ability to be a free choice agent and to govern oneself. Maslow suggests that self-actualizers have more free will than other people. Their activity stems from themselves rather than from their physical or social environment.

Maslow found that without exception all of his self-actualizers demonstrated *creativity,* originality, or inventiveness. This is not to say that they possess a special talent akin to that of a Mozart or a Picasso but that they have a drive and a capacity to be creative. They do not necessarily write books, compose music, or produce art; instead, their creativeness is projected onto and touches whatever activity they undertake. The carpenter or clerk is creative in his or her work, adding a personalized touch to whatever he or she does. Self-actualizers even perceive the world creatively, as a child does, envisioning new and different possibilities.

Self-actualizers are *spontaneous,* simple, and natural. They are free to be what they are at any given moment. Although their behavior is often conventional, they do not allow conventionality to hamper or prevent them from doing the things that they deem important. They are acutely aware of their feelings, thoughts, and impulses and do not hide them unless their expression would hurt others. Their codes of ethics are autonomous and individual, based on fundamentally accepted principles rather than on social prescriptions.

Trust Self-actualizers demonstrate a high degree of trust. They trust themselves, their mission in life, others, and nature.

Self-actualizers are generally *problem centered* rather than focused on themselves. They have a high sense of mission in life. They are task oriented and commit themselves to important tasks that must be done. They live and work within a wide frame of reference that does not permit them to get bogged down in what is petty or trivial. Problems outside themselves enlist most of their attention.

Self-actualizers demonstrate *acceptance of self, others, and nature.* They accept themselves without disappointment or regret. They recognize but are not particularly bothered by their shortcomings. This is not to say that they are smug or self-satisfied but rather that they accept their weaknesses and frailties as given. They are not embarrassed about the bodily processes that humans share with animals. The needs to eat, defecate, and express their sexuality do not distress them. They feel guilty about characteristics that they could and should improve on, but they are not overrun with neurotic guilt. Since they can respect their own limitations, their guilt arises from realistic sources. In the same way, they can accept the necessities of reality and human life. As Maslow points out, they are not disturbed because water is wet, rocks are hard, and grass is green. They can live with these things. Healthy people do not feel bad about what is per se but about differences between what is and what might realistically be.

Self-actualizers are not well adjusted in the normal sense of the term, which entails conformity with one's culture; they show *resistance to enculturation*. Essentially, they live in harmony with their culture, yet they remain somewhat detached from it. Often they are labeled "oddball," as they do not always react in the expected fashion. They generally conform in matters of dress, speech, and food, and other matters that are not of primary concern to them. But where an issue is important they are independent in their thought and behavior. This resistance to enculturation leads to their transcendence of any one particular culture. Thus their identification is with humanity as a whole rather than any one particular group.

Maslow acknowledges that the picture he draws of the self-actualized person is a composite. No one person that he studied possessed all of the above qualities. Each of them demonstrated the characteristics to varying degrees. Furthermore, Maslow emphasizes that self-actualizers are not perfect. They show many lesser human failings. They frequently have silly, wasteful, or thoughtless habits. At times they are vain and take too much pride in their achievements. They lose their tempers. Because of their concentration on their work, they often appear absent-minded, humorless, or impolite. At times their kindness toward others leads them to permit others to take undue advantage of them. At other times they may appear to be ruthless and inconsiderate in their relations with other people. Sometimes they are boring, even irritating. In short, they are not perfect; yet, Maslow's definition of self-actualization did not imply perfection: it merely suggested that an individual was basically fulfilling him- or herself and doing the best that he or she was capable of doing.

The principles and values of self-actualizers differ from those of the average person. Perceiving the world in an essentially different manner, they are not threatened by it and do not need to adopt a morality of self-protection. Maslow suggests that a great deal of that which passes for moral and ethical standards may simply be "by-products of the pervasive pathology of the average" (1970). The conflicts and anxieties that threaten the average person are simply not present. Self-actualizers can welcome differences and need not be afraid of them. Their value systems are not organized around the values of the deficiency needs. These have been satisfied, so self-actualizers can devote themselves to the values that concur with the B-needs. Thus, at one and the same time, their values are universal and reflect shared humanity but are also distinct, individual, and unique.

Maslow concluded that self-actualization entails the ability to transcend and resolve dichotomies. The usual oppositions between heart and head, reason and emotion, body and mind, work and play that fragment most of us do not exist as antagonists, because they are seen as functioning together simultaneously. For example, the distinction between being selfish and unselfish is no longer bothersome. Self-actualizers can recognize that every act is at one and the same time selfish and unselfish. That which is done for the benefit of others is frequently that which benefits the self. Maslow suggests that in the self-actualized individual the id, ego, and superego work cooperatively together. Thus, healthy individuals are both quantitatively and qualitatively different from the average.

Exploration /////

Are You Self-Actualized?

The following self-report questionnaire* may be useful in helping you determine to what extent you perceive yourself as having self-actualizing characteristics. Study each characteristic carefully and then rate yourself on a scale of 1 to 5 — 1 (always like me) to 5 (never like me) — according to how you feel that you honestly fit into each description.

1. I tend to have a more efficient perception of reality than other people and I am comfortable in the world.   1 2 3 4 5

2. I generally accept myself, others, and nature.   1 2 3 4 5

3. I am spontaneous and can do things on the spur of the moment without the need for advance planning.   1 2 3 4 5

4. I am more concerned with problems that involve society or others than with my own problems.   1 2 3 4 5

5. I enjoy and need to be alone.   1 2 3 4 5

6. Most of the time I believe that I am a free choice agent, governed by my own free will and undetermined by outside agents.   1 2 3 4 5

7. I am able to appreciate simple things, such as a sunrise, flower, or baby, again and again.   1 2 3 4 5

8. I frequently experience "peak experiences" in which there is a loss of self.   1 2 3 4 5

9. In spite of occasional anger, impatience, or disgust, I experience a deep feeling of kinship with other humans.   1 2 3 4 5

*Based on pp. 153–174 from MOTIVATION AND PERSONALITY, 2nd Ed. by Abraham H. Maslow. Copyright © 1970 by Abraham H. Maslow. Reprinted by permission of Harper & Row, Publishers, Inc.

(continued)

10. I tend to have a few close friends rather than a large number of acquaintances.   1 2 3 4 5

11. I am tolerant, free of prejudice, and relate to people equally no matter what their race, religion, or creed may be.   1 2 3 4 5

12. I have a clear and distinct sense of what is right and wrong for me.   1 2 3 4 5

13. My humor is generally nonhostile and philosophic.   1 2 3 4 5

14. I am original and perceive the world in a creative fashion.   1 2 3 4 5

15. Although I generally conform to society, it does not frighten me to be independent in my thought and behavior.   1 2 3 4 5

Compute your average total score. Do not take your results too seriously. Remember that this is not a valid test as it has not been standardized or compared with other measures of self-actualization. It is offered simply as an exploratory device. Also recall that in his initial study of three thousand college students, Maslow found only one whom he could describe as self-actualized. Nevertheless, it might interest you to note those areas where you rated yourself high and others where you felt you were low. Can you think of any reasons for these discrepancies? Also, you might wish to have a close friend or two rate you on the scale and consider the differences that emerge.

In order to develop a rating scale that would adequately measure the qualities inherent to self-actualization, the terms that are used to describe self-actualization would have to be operationally defined. We would need to specify exactly what behaviors constitute efficient perception, acceptance of self and others, spontaneity, and so forth. Maslow has not done this, although he has suggested ways in which his descriptions could be converted into hypotheses that could be empirically tested. It is important to remember that Maslow conceived of his work as merely preliminary. He recognized that considerably more scientific research needs to be done in the area of human potentialities.

Maslow's portrait of the self-actualized person is optimistic, generating much confidence in human potential. Yet some critics suggest that his picture may be simplistic, neglecting the hard work and pain that is involved in growth and development. It is important to note that Maslow's research originated in an era of growth and prosperity accompanied by a seemingly limitless view of human potential. In fact, the possibility and likelihood of self-actualization may be more remote than Maslow indicates.

Maslow suggests that in the self-actualized individual dichotomies are transcended; in Freudian terms, the id, ego, and superego work together cooperatively. But is this picture realistic? Perhaps it is naive to hope to reduce all conflict and more justified to assume that we can merely strengthen the ego, enabling it to be more effective in its executive functions. Freud, we recall, was pessimistic about reducing human conflict.

As it is, Maslow suggested that the number of people who achieve self-actualization is relatively small, less than 1 percent of the population. Concepts such as "the self-actualized person" may be elitist and apply to only a select few. Obviously, the possibility of self-actualization is limited or even closed to large numbers of the human population, whose environment and lifestyle have yet to meet the lesser needs depicted in Maslow's hierarchy, let alone the higher needs. Moreover, Maslow's concept is culture bound, reflecting his own historical period.

Critics also disagree with Maslow's choice of examples of self-actualized persons. Not everyone agrees that Eleanor Roosevelt or Abraham Maslow was self-actualized. Biographies have pointed out serious shortcomings and limitations in Maslow's historical examples. Perhaps his choice reflects his subjective preference rather than the objective application of his criteria. Others point out that as currently delineated, the concept of self-actualization would not include many genuinely creative persons such as Mozart, Tolstoy, or Wittgenstein.

More attention needs to be given to the processes within the individual and society that permit self-actualization and creativity to flower. In Maslow's words, "How good a human being does society permit?" (1970). In what instances can an individual overcome and compensate for needs that have not been met in his or her life? As it stands, Maslow's discussion of self-actualization is descriptive rather than functional. He describes the characteristics of the self-actualized individual but he does not tell how these characteristics may be concretely acquired.

For some years research on Maslow's concept of self-actualization was slow, since an adequate assessment device for measuring the variables of self-actualization was lacking. Recent years have seen the development of the Personal Orientation Inventory (**POI**) by Shostrom (1965). The POI is considered to be a reliable, valid measure of self-actualization and it has led to increased empirical research related to Maslow's constructs.

It is to Maslow's credit that he has turned the attention of the psychologist to those qualities that constitute optimal human health and functioning rather than representing human life gone awry. The example of the self-actualized individuals suggests and inspires us to improve our human condition.

Comments on Therapy

Abraham Maslow was not a practicing therapist. He did not develop any new theory or method of therapy. However, he made several comments about therapy (1970) that are worth attention. Maslow made a distinction between basic needs therapy and insight therapy. **Basic needs therapy** refers to therapeutic procedures that meet the primary needs of people: safety, belonging, love, and respect. **Insight therapy** refers to the deeper, more protracted effort of self-understanding that leads to profound motivational changes.

The first and primary criterion for both forms of therapy is a relationship between human beings. On this point Maslow concurs with Rogers. Yet Maslow goes on to point out that the kind of relationship that satisfies our basic needs is not a unique relationship but one that shares the fundamental qualities found in all good human relationships. The relationship of therapy is not at its base unique, because it shares the primary characteristics of all good human relationships.

What is needed is a more careful study of all of those relationships that foster and fulfill the satisfaction of our needs of safety, belongingness, love, respect, and, ultimately, self-actualization. A constructive marriage, close friendship, or healthy parent-child relationship permits these satisfactions to occur. Thus, every human relationship is potentially a therapeutic one. One task of psychology is to try to identify those qualities that make for good human relations as opposed to poor ones. We can then foster those relationships that enable us to grow.

Maslow criticizes Freud for limiting his discussion of the relationship that emerges in analysis to the elements of transference. By failing to recognize the underlying relationship between analyst and patient and by focusing almost entirely on the elements of transference, Freud failed to perceive the healthy character of the relationship. In effect, Freud suggested that the only feelings a patient could have toward the analyst were those of a positive or negative transference. In return, the only emotions an analyst could have toward the patient were those of countertransference. Thus, in Freud's discussion of analysis, the only feelings that emerge in the relationship are neurotic ones. Freud failed to articulate the fact that it is only because a basic healthy relationship underlies the process of analysis in the first place that elements of transference can arise, be sustained, analyzed, and worked through.

If the qualities of relationship that emerge in psychotherapy are the qualities that are found in any good, healthy relationship, we should look more closely at those everyday therapeutic happenings that occur in good marriages, good friendships, and good jobs. We ought to try to expose ourselves and others to these kinds of situations. It also follows that each human being is potentially a therapist who can function in a therapeutic way insofar as he or she can enter into these kinds of relationships that are based on love and respect.

We should approve of, encourage, and teach these fundamentals of sound human relationships and foster the development of lay psychotherapy.

However, there are times when the normal therapeutic processes of life fail and insight therapy is called for. A person who is severely ill may not be able to benefit from basic needs therapy because he or she has given up trying to satisfy those needs in favor of satisfying neurotic ones.

Insight therapy is not only invaluable for those neurotics for whom basic needs therapy is no longer helpful; it is also a valuable method by which relatively healthy persons can acquire insight and facilitate their own self-actualization. Unfortunately, psychoanalysis and psychotherapy have not become as effective or active forces of individual and cultural self-understanding as they have the potential to be. The emphasis, particularly in America, on therapy as a medical method of treatment has prevented its entrance into other fields. Interestingly, Freud did not originally conceive of analysis as simply a method for treating neurotics. That, he wrote, "is only one of its applications, the future will perhaps show that it is not the most important one" (1927). Freud also recommended that since it would be impossible to analyze each and every parent, teachers might undergo analysis in order to avoid passing on unconscious conflicts to children. Maslow picks up this suggestion, pointing out that if relatively healthy people are deeply touched by therapy, it is all the more important to invest our energies in them, particularly if they happen to be in key therapeutic positions, as teachers, social workers, and physicians. An increased proportion of time spent in didactic or training analyses, such as are presently undertaken by potential psychoanalysts, could have a profound effect on society. Additional consideration ought also to be given to furthering group therapy and personal growth groups.

Maslow's Theory: Philosophy, Science, and Art

Maslow's theory clearly points in a direction away from pure science toward the broader outlines of philosophy. Maslow acknowledged that his portrait of self-actualization is part of a larger, evolving philosophy of human nature. He reminded us that all too frequently we conceive of science as an autonomous method that exists in and of itself, governed by its own distinct rules and totally divorced from human beings or human values. We forget that human beings create science, establish its goals, and use its technology for their own purposes. Maslow believed that it is misleading to think science is value free, since its procedures are employed for human purposes. We may use science to create mechanistic robots out of human nature or we may use it to increase human freedom and potential. Maslow suggested that we conceive of science as a problem-solving activity rather than as a specific technology. Only the goals of science can dignify or validate its methods.

Maslow's study of self-actualized persons lacks the rigor and distinct methodology characteristic of strict empirical science. Nevertheless, his work underscores the fact that the canons of rigorous scientific procedures do not necessarily encompass or permit research into important human questions. It suggests the need for a broader definition of science and the development of methodologies appropriate for the human subject.

The "third force" has beome a very powerful force in psychology. A humanistic orientation has been integrated into many different approaches to therapy and has also influenced contemporary education. The impact of the third force was reflected in the creation of a new division of the American Psychological Association, called Humanistic Psychology. A separate Association for Humanistic Psychology has also been formed; it publishes the *Journal of Humanistic Psychology.* Centers for personal growth have sprung up across the United States, Canada, Mexico, and Europe. Two of the most well-known are the Esalen Institute in Big Sur, California, and the Center for the Study of the Person in La Jolla, California. These centers encourage the development of ways in which individuals can further their growth and self-actualization.

❧ Summary

1. Abraham Maslow has been called the spiritual father of American humanism. He criticizes psychoanalysis for being pessimistic and negative and behavior and learning theories for being mechanistic.

2. Maslow distinguishes between **motivation** and **metamotivation,** which entail **D-needs** and **B-needs** respectively. Motivation and the D-needs take precedence over metamotivation and the B-needs.

3. Maslow's **hierarchy of human needs** includes physiological, safety, belonging and love, self-esteem, and **self-actualization.** A number of studies have demonstrated that the needs that Maslow describes are essential for optimal human life and development.

4. A **self-actualized person** is one who is fulfilling him- or herself and doing the best that he or she is capable of doing. The subjects of Maslow's study included friends, personal acquaintances, public and historical figures, and selected college students and he used a variety of research techniques. His investigations were not conducted along strict scientific lines as he felt that those limitations would not be suitable for his research.

5. Maslow describes several characteristics of self-actualizers. These may be grouped under four key dimensions: awareness, honesty, freedom, and trust.

6. A self-actualized person often experiences a **peak experience,** which can be provoked by both religious and secular events.

7. Some critics suggest that Maslow's picture of self-actualized persons is simplistic and neglects the hard work that is involved in growth and development.

8. Maslow distinguishes between **basic needs therapy** and **insight therapy** and calls for more effective and expanded therapy.

9. Maslow's theory points in a direction away from a pure science. His work underscores the fact that rigorous scientific procedures may not encompass or permit research into important human questions.

Suggestions for Further Reading

Maslow's best-known work is *Motivation and Personality* (Harper & Row, 1970), which presents his theory of personality and describes in full his concepts of the hierarchy of needs and self-actualization. Originally published in 1954, it was completely revised shortly before his death. *Religions, Values, and Peak Experiences* (Viking, 1964) presents Maslow's argument that religion be viewed as a normal, potentially healthy phenomenon and studied scientifically. In this work he outlines his concept of peak experiences, although he does not limit them to religious experiences. Nevertheless, Maslow points out the need of human beings for spiritual expression and he suggests that science can assist us in understanding this need and its expressions. *Toward a Psychology of Being* (Van Nostrand, 1968) is a collection of papers in which Maslow discusses his theory of B-values as well as peak experiences and self-actualization; the book also makes clear Maslow's humanistic stance as opposed to those who present a mechanistic or negative picture of human nature. Maslow's last work, *The Farther Reaches of Human Nature* (Viking, 1971), is a cumulative effort to integrate his theory with the latest developments in science. It covers topics such as biology, creativity, cognition, and synergy.

Two readable secondary sources on Maslow's thought are Frank Goble, *The Third Force: The Psychology of Abraham Maslow* (Grossman, 1970) and Colin Wilson, *New Pathways in Psychology: Maslow and the Post-Freudian Revolution* (Taplinger, 1972).

→ completed cases
→ partial cases — questions inside How they feel
→ potential cases

14

George Kelly: Constructive Alternativism

Your Goals for This Chapter

1. Identify the distinguishing feature of Kelly's theory of personality.

2. Describe the philosophical position of *constructive alternativism.*

3. Explain why Kelly suggests that we view ourselves as scientists.

4. Discuss Kelly's fundamental postulate and identify eleven corollaries that support it.

5. Explain how Kelly reconceives traditional concepts in personality theorizing.

6. Describe the *Rep Test.*

7. Discuss Kelly's view of and contributions to psychotherapy.

8. Identify some of the criticisms that have been made of Kelly's theory.

9. Evaluate Kelly's theory in terms of its function as philosophy, science, and art.

R eading Kelly is like entering a new terrain, as he avoids many of the concepts traditionally present in personality theorizing. Kelly is forthright in describing the differences between his approach and that of others. "It is only fair," he wrote, "to warn the reader about what may be in store for him. In the first place, he is likely to find missing most of the familiar landmarks.... For example, the term *learning,* so honorably embedded in most psychological texts, scarcely appears at all. That is wholly intentional; we are for throwing it overboard all together. There is no *ego,* no *emotion,* no *reinforcement,* no *drive,* no *unconscious,* no *need*" (1955). It is not that these concepts are entirely omitted from Kelly's work; rather, they are given new meanings and incorporated into his philosophy of constructive alternativism.

Biographical Background

George Kelly was born on a farm in Perth, Kansas, in 1905. His father was a Presbyterian minister, but ill health prevented him from actively leading a church congregation. Kelly's parents were devout fundamentalists who practiced their faith, prescribed hard work, and rigorously shunned the evils of dancing, drinking, and card playing. As an only child, Kelly received extensive attention and love. His mother, in particular, was devoted to him.

Kelly's early education was somewhat sporadic. He attended a one-room country school and was taught by his parents at home. He was sent to Wichita, Kansas, for high school, where he attended four different schools. He studied for three years at Friends University and received the B.A. degree one year later (1926) from Park College. Kelly had majored in physics and mathematics and planned a career in mechanical engineering. However, his interests were turning to social problems. While holding a number of different jobs related to engineering and education, he pursued the M.A. degree in educational sociology at the University of Kansas.

In 1929, Kelly was awarded a fellowship for study at the University of Edinburgh in Scotland. He earned the B.Ed. degree there based on his previous academic experience and his year of residency in Scotland. Kelly wrote his dissertation on the problem of predicting teaching success and discovered that his interests were turning to psychology. On his return to the United States, he enrolled as a doctoral student in psychology at the State University of Iowa. He received the Ph.D in 1931 with a dissertation on speech and reading disabilities.

Kelly began his career as an academic psychologist in the middle of the Depression of the 1930s. Opportunities for work in physiological psychology, his speciality, were scarce, so he turned his attention to clinical psychology, a growing field. During the next twelve years, Kelly taught at Fort Hays Kansas

George Kelly

State College and developed a program of traveling psychological clinics that sought to identify and treat emotional and behavioral problems in students in the state's public school system. His experience with the clinics was crucial to his later development and theorizing. Not committed to any one theoretical approach, Kelly experimented with several different methods in his work with students referred for counseling. His position gave him a unique opportunity to try out innovative as well as traditional clinical approaches. His work with the clinics sparked several ideas that later found application in his own theory of personality and therapy.

World War II briefly interrupted Kelly's academic career. He enrolled in the navy as an aviation psychologist, headed a training program of local civilian pilots, and worked for the bureau of medicine and surgery, gaining recognition for his clinical services. After the war, a significant demand for clinical psychologists appeared as returning servicemen required help with personal problems. Clinical psychology came to be seen as an essential part of health services. Kelly played a leading role in fostering the development and integration of clinical psychology into the mainstream of American psychology. After teaching one year at the University of Maryland, he joined the faculty of Ohio State University as professor and director of clinical psychology. During the next twenty years at Ohio State, Kelly built a distinguished program of clinical psychology and refined and published his theory of personality.

In 1965, Kelly received a prestigious appointment to the Riklis Chair of Behavioral Science at Brandeis University. This appointment would have given him great freedom to pursue his research, but he died in 1967.

Kelly did not publish a great deal but he lectured extensively in the United States and abroad and he exerted a significant influence on psychology through his personal impact on his students and friends. In his later years, he spent considerable time suggesting how personal construct theory could be applied to help resolve social and international problems. He held several important positions, such as president of both the Clinical and Counseling Divisions of the American Psychological Association. He assisted the development and also served as president of the American Board of Examiners in Professional Psychology.

Constructive Alternativism

What distinguishes George Kelly's theory is his stress on **cognition** (the process of knowing) as the primary factor in personality development. Kelly pays scant attention to functions of personality that have concerned other theorists. He has little or nothing to say about drives, needs, emotions, motivation, or behavior. Nevertheless, he includes these factors by perceiving them as aspects of personality that are controlled by the higher cognitive functions. Obviously, basic biological needs must be met before a person can engage in higher cognitive functions, but Kelly believes it is more fruitful to begin personality theorizing at the point where lower needs have been satisfied and to concentrate on the higher-order functions that distinguish human nature and behavior.

Kelly's theory of personality is unashamedly based on his philosophical position of **constructive alternativism:** the assumption that any one event is open to a variety of interpretations. The world, in and of itself, does not automatically make sense to us. We have to create our own ways of understanding the events that happen. In effect, there is no reality outside our interpretations of it. Take, for example, the situation of a boy who is late for school. His father may think that it is because the boy is lazy. His mother may suggest that her son is forgetful and daydreams on the way to school. His teacher may view the pupil's tardiness as an expression of his distaste and hostility toward academic work. His best friend might see it as an accident. The boy himself could construe his lateness as an indication of his inferiority. The event itself is merely a given datum but it gives rise to many different alternative constructions that may lead to different actions. For Kelly, the objective truth of a person's interpretations are unimportant because they are unknowable. What is important is their implications for behavior and life.

In our efforts to understand the world, we develop constructs or patterns that make the world meaningful to us. We look at the world "through transparent patterns or templates" of our own creation. It is as if each person can only view the world through sunglasses of his or her own choosing. No one construct or pattern is final and a perfect reflection of the world. There is always an alternative construct that might do a better job of accounting for the facts that we perceive. Thus, our position in the world is one of constructive alternativism, as we change or revise our constructs in order to understand it more accurately.

Kelly suggests that we look at ourselves and other people as scientists, an image that he notes psychologists are quick to ascribe to themselves but perhaps not as readily to other people. In positing an analogy between the human person and the scientist, Kelly suggests that the posture we take as we attempt to predict and control the events in our world is similar to that of the scientist who develops and tests hypotheses. In our efforts to understand the world, we develop constructs that act as hypotheses that make the world meaningful to us. If these patterns appear to fit our subsequent experience, we find them useful and hold onto them. If we construe the world or certain events as hostile, we will act in certain ways to protect ourselves. If our protective behaviors appear to be useful ways to cope with the events, we will continue to hold onto the hostile interpretation. If the pattern or construct is a poor one, that is to say, if it does not lead to behaviors that help us adjust to events in our world, we will seek to alter or change the construct in order to develop a better one. Just as the scientist employs hypotheses to make predictions about certain consequences that might happen if the hypotheses were true, people employ their constructs to predict what is going to happen to them in the future. Subsequent events are then used to indicate whether the predictions and underlying constructs were correct or were misleading.

For example, at the beginning of a semester, students develop certain constructs or ideas about the subjects that they are studying. Usually, these constructs are based on a very limited sample of the actual course or the professor's behavior. One student may conclude that a particular course will be a snap, requiring a minimum of time and preparation. Another student may conclude that the same course will be a challenge, requiring considerable work and effort. As the semester progresses, each student acts on and gradually tests his or her preliminary hypothesis for its accuracy. The lectures, reading assignments, written papers, and tests are all subsequent events that serve to confirm or disprove the initial suspicions. By the middle of the semester, a student has a much clearer idea of the accuracy of his or her original construct concerning the course. Should the original hypothesis seem valid, chances are the student will continue his or her present mode of handling the course work. However, if subsequent events suggest that the original construct was incorrect, the student will re-evaluate and change the construct, developing new patterns of behavior that are more in line with the revised construct.

•

The example of a student's behavior in a college course is simply an example in miniature of what happens to us all at all times in our lives. As was pointed out earlier, the world is not a fixed given that can be immediately comprehended and understood. In order to understand the world, we have to develop constructs or ways of perceiving it. During the course of our lives, we develop many different constructs. Further, we engage in the process of continually testing, revising, and modifying them. As none of our constructs are ultimate, alternative constructs that we could choose from are always available. Thus, a person is free to change his or her constructs in an effort to make sense out of, predict, and control the world.

Fundamental Postulate and Corollaries

In order to present and explain his theory, Kelly (1955) sets forth one basic assumption, or fundamental postulate, and then elaborates on it with eleven corollaries.

The *fundamental postulate* reads:

"A person's processes are psychologically channelized by the ways in which he anticipates events."

Probably the most important word in Kelly's primary assumption is *anticipates.* Essentially, Kelly suggests that the way in which an individual predicts future happenings is crucial to his or her behavior. As scientists, people seek to forecast what is going to happen. They orient their behaviors and ideas about the world toward the goal of accurate, useful predictions. According to Kelly, the future, rather than the past, is the primary impetus of behavior.

Each of the eleven corollaries that Kelly presents to elaborate his fundamental postulate focuses on a primary word that sums up the essence of these supportive statements and his theory.

1. *Construction* The term **construe** means to place an interpretation on an event. As we have seen, the universe is not an automatically knowable given. We must create constructs or ways in which to understand it.

2. *Individuality* No two people interpret events in the same way. Each of us experiences an event from our own subjective point of view. This corollary underscores Kelly's belief that it is the subjective interpretation of an event, rather than the event itself, that is most important.

3. *Organization* Our interpretation of events in the world is neither haphazard nor arbitrary. Each one of us organizes his or her constructs in a series of ordinal relationships in which some constructs are more important and others are less important. The fact that our constructs fall into an organized pattern

The fundamental postulate maintains that the future, not the past, is the primary impetus of behavior.

means that we develop a system of constructs rather than simply a number of isolated ones.

4. *Dichotomy* In making an interpretation about an event, we not only make an assertion about it, but we also indicate that the opposite quality is not characteristic of it. A **dichotomy** is an opposite, and Kelly suggests that all of our constructs are of a bipolar form. When we construe that a person is strong, we also imply that the person is not weak. The dichotomous form of our constructs provides the basis for constructive alternativism.

5. *Choice* In developing constructs, each person tends to choose the pole that seems to be most helpful in expanding his or her anticipation of future events. The choice corollary is a very important one. It underlines Kelly's belief that a person is free and able to choose from among the various alternatives the construct that will be most useful.

6. *Range* Each construct has a certain range or focus. The construct of *tall versus short* is useful for describing people, trees, or horses, but virtually useless for understanding the weather. Some people apply their constructs broadly and others limit their constructs to a narrow focus. For instance, many political reactionaries use constructs with extremely narrow ranges. In order to understand an individual's constructs, we need to take into account both what is and what is not included in their range.

7. *Experience* People change their interpretation of events in the light of later experience. Subsequent experiences serve as a validating process by which the accuracy of anticipations can be checked out and tested. If a construct does not prove helpful in anticipating future events, it is reformulated and changed. Such reconstruction forms the basis for learning.

8. *Modulation* The extent to which changes may occur within our constructs depends on the existing framework and organization of the constructural system. Constructs are more or less *permeable,* that is, they are more or less open to change and alteration.

A concept that limits its elements to its range only is a **pre-emptive construct.** Pre-emptive constructs are very specific and difficult to penetrate, because they categorize the world in rigid ways and do not permit it to be conceived of differently. When a person insists that a spade is nothing but a spade, it is difficult to conceive of other functions for the tool. A construct that sets clear limits to the range of its elements but also permits them to belong to other realms is a **constellatory construct.** The term "constellatory," however, also implies grouping things that may not belong together. Stereotypes are examples of constellatory thinking. A construct that leaves its elements open to other constructions is a **propositional construct.** The individual who uses propositional constructs is much more open to experience and change in his or her construct system.

9. *Fragmentation* There are times when people employ constructs that appear to be incompatible with each other. Because of this, we are often surprised by other people's behavior and we cannot always infer what a person is going to do tomorrow from the way he or she behaves today. Such fragmentation is particularly apt to occur either when a person's constructs are impermeable and concrete or when they are undergoing change.

10. *Communality* When two people share similar constructs, their psychological processes may be said to be similar. This does not mean that their experiences are identical, but our ability to share and communicate with other people is based on the fact that we share similar personal constructs with them.

11. *Sociality* Our potentiality for understanding and communicating with other people depends on our ability to construe another person's constructs. We must be able to have some idea of what the other person's constructs

are. Our ability to interact socially with other people entails understanding a broad range of their constructs and behaviors.

The Reconstruction of Old Concepts

Kelly avoids many of the concepts traditionally associated with personality theorizing. Familiar landmarks and terms are given new meanings and subordinated to his theory of personal constructs.

Some of our constructs refer to self-identity or the identity of others. The **self-construct** is primarily based on what we perceive as similarities in our own behavior. We believe that we are honest, sincere, friendly, and so forth. The self-construct is developed out of our relationships with other people. When we construe other people, we also construe ourselves. When we think of another person as "hostile" or "aggressive," we are making those qualities and their opposites a dimension of our own experience. Our self-interpretation is linked to our role relationships with other people.

The **role** is a process or behavior that a person plays based on his or her understanding of the behavior and constructs of other people. We do not have to be accurate in our constructions to enter into a role. A student may play a certain role with a professor whom he or she believes to be unduly demanding and unfair when in fact the professor is not. Nor does a role have to be reciprocated by the other person. The professor may remain fair in spite of the student's misconstruction. What is needed in order to play a role is simply some construct of the other person's behavior.

Kelly's use of "role" should not be confused with its use in social psychology. In social psychology, "role" usually refers to a set of behavioral expectations or roles, such as mother, teacher, physician, ruler, and so on, set forth by a particular society and fulfilled by its members. In Kelly's theory, the role is defined by the individual in his or her efforts to understand the behavior of other people and relate to them. One's self-construct may be seen as a core or basic role structure by which one conceives of oneself as an integral individual in relation to other people.

For Kelly, the person is a process, an organism in continual activity, whose behavior is governed by a system of personal constructs. *Learning* and *motivation* are built into the very structure of the system. Conceiving of the person as a unity, Kelly believes that no special inner forces, such as drives, needs, instincts, or motives, are needed to account for human motivation. Human nature in and of itself implies motivation because it is alive and in process. Nor need behavior be accounted for in terms of external forces, such as stimuli and reinforcements. Learning is synonymous with all of the psychological processes themselves. It is simply inappropriate to conceive of an individual as motivated by internal or external forces other than him- or herself. Kelly (1958) reminds us that "There are pitchfork theories on the one hand and the carrot theories on the other. But our theory is neither of these. Since we prefer to look at the nature of the animal itself, ours is probably best called a jackass theory."

Not all constructs are verbalized; therefore, conscious and unconscious processes may be accounted for by our capacity to form constructs that are not put into words. *Emotions* are also subsumed under the general framework of personal constructs. Although some critics (Bruner and Rogers, 1956) suggest that Kelly's theory is too intellectual and mentalistic, Kelly refuses to divide the person into cognitive and emotional states. Feelings and emotions refer to inner states that need to be construed. They arise when constructs are in a transitional state.

Exploration ///////

The Rep Test*

In order to understand how a person interprets his or her world, Kelly developed the **Role Construct Repertory Test,** known more simply as the **Rep Test.** Essentially, the Rep Test permits a person to reveal his or her constructs by comparing and contrasting a number of different persons in his or her life. The following exploration will help you become acquainted with the Rep Test and also tell you about some of your own personal constructs.

Make up a list of representative persons in your life by choosing from among people you know the individual who most suits each description below. Using the form provided (Figure 14.1 on page 338), write the name of the person in the grid space above the column with the corresponding number to the description.

List of representative persons

1. Write your own name in the first blank.

2. Write your mother's first name. If you grew up with a stepmother, write her name instead.

3. Write your father's first name. If you grew up with a stepfather, write his name instead.

*Reprinted from THE PSYCHOLOGY OF PERSONAL CONSTRUCTS, Volume One, by George A. Kelly, Ph.D., by permission of W. W. Norton & Company, Inc. Copyright 1955 by George A. Kelly.

(continued)

4. Write the name of your brother who is nearest your own age. If you had no brother, write the name of a boy near your own age who was most like a brother to you during your early teens.

5. Write the name of your sister who is nearest your own age. If you had no sister, write the name of a girl near your own age who was most like a sister to you during your early teens.

From this point on do not repeat any names. If a person has already been listed, simply make a second choice.

6. Your wife (or husband) or, if you are not married, your closest present girl (boy) friend.

7. Your closest girl (boy) friend immediately preceding the person mentioned above.

8. Your closest present friend of the same sex as yourself.

9. A person of the same sex as yourself whom you once thought was a close friend but in whom you were badly disappointed later.

10. The minister, priest, or rabbi with whom you would be most willing to talk over your personal feelings about religion.

11. Your physician.

12. The present neighbor whom you know best.

13. A person with whom you have been associated who, for some unexplained reason, appeared to dislike you.

14. A person whom you would most like to help or for whom you feel sorry.

15. A person with whom you usually feel most uncomfortable.

16. A person whom you have recently met and would like to know better.

17. The teacher who influenced you most when you were in your teens.

18. The teacher whose point of view you found most objectionable.

19. An employer, supervisor, or officer under whom you served during a period of great stress.

20. The most successful person whom you know personally.

21. The happiest person whom you know personally.

22. The person known to you personally who appears to meet the highest ethical standards.

After you have written the names in the space above the columns, look at the first row. There are circles under three persons' names (20, 21, 22). Decide how two of them are alike in an important way and how they differ from the third person. Put an X in each of the two circles under the names of the persons who are alike. Then write on the line under the column headed "Construct" a word or phrase that identifies the likeness. Write the opposite of this characteristic under the heading "Contrast." Now go back and consider all the other people you listed on your grid. If any of them also share the same characteristic, put a check mark under their name. Repeat this procedure until you have completed every row on the form.

When you have completed the form, take a close look at your results. First consider the nature of the constructs you listed. How many different constructs did you list? What kind of constructs were they? Did you tend to make comparisons on the basis of appearance (skinny versus fat) or personality characteristics (thoughtful versus unthoughtful; honest versus dishonest)? Do any of the constructs overlap? You can discover this by examining the pattern of checks and X's in the various rows. If the pattern for one construct (such as honest versus dishonest) is identical to that of another construct (such as sincere versus insincere), you can suspect that these two constructs may really be one and the same for you. To how many different people did you apply each of the constructs? A construct that is applied to a large number of people may be more permeable than one that is restricted to only one person. Are the constructs divided in terms of their application to persons of the same age or sex? This may give you some idea of the limits on the range of your constructs. Now take a look at your list of contrasting constructs. Are there any constructs that you list only as a difference and never as a similarity? If so, you may be reluctant to use that construct. If you list a contrasting pole for one person only, perhaps that construct is impermeable and limited to that person. Are any names associated only with contrasting poles? If so, your relationship to those persons may be rigid and unchanging even though you get along with them. Finally, compare your own column to those of the other people on the list. Which of the other people are you most like?

This analysis will not give you definitive answers; it will simply provide a starting point for further questions. Rather than considering the results on the grid as final, you should use your findings as the basis for additional study of yourself. For example, if you discover identical patterns for two constructs, such as honest versus dishonest and sincere versus insincere, you might ask yourself, "Do I believe that all honest people are sincere?" In other words, use your findings for further questions. Numerous possibilities for self-exploration are initiated by the Rep Test.

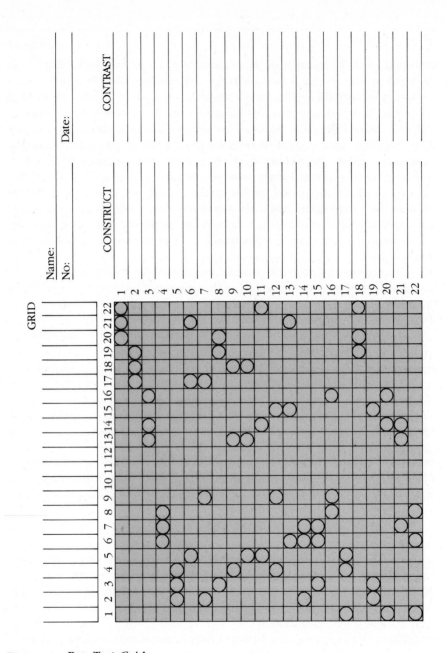

Figure 14.1 *Rep Test Grid*

Psychotherapy

According to Kelly (1955), psychological disorders arise when a person clings to and continues to use personal constructs in spite of the fact that subsequent experience fails to validate them. Such a person has difficulty anticipating and predicting events and is unable to learn from experiences. The neurotic flounders in an effort to develop new ways to interpret the world or rigidly holds onto constructs that are useless. Instead of developing more successful constructs and solving problems, the neurotic develops symptoms.

Kelly conceives of his therapeutic methods as "reconstruction" rather than psychotherapy. He seeks to help his patient reconstrue the world in a manner that will foster better predictions and control. The first step in his therapy is usually that of "elaborating the complaint." In this step, the therapist seeks to identify the problem, discover when and under what conditions it first arose, indicate what changes have occurred in the problem, discover any corrective measures that the client may have already taken, and find out under what conditions the problem is most and least noticeable. Elaboration of the complaint usually reveals many aspects of the person's construct system, but Kelly conceives of a second step as that of elaborating the construct system itself. Such elaboration gives a fuller picture of the elements encompassed in the complaint, allows more alternatives to arise, broadens the base of the relationship between therapist and client, and reveals the conceptual framework that created and sustained the symptoms.

In elaborating the construct system, Kelly uses the Rep Test previously described. He also employs the method of self-description. He might ask his client to write out a personal character sketch such as a close friend might write, identifying him- or herself in the third person. He might also ask his client to respond to questions such as "What kind of child were you?" "What kind of a person do you expect to become?" and "What do you expect from therapy?" All of these methods have proven useful in elaborating the construct system.

Many of the techniques that Kelly employed to effect psychotherapeutic change are similar to those used by other therapists. However, Kelly made a unique contribution to therapeutic methodology by developing and fostering the use of **role playing.** In the course of therapy, if a client mentioned that he or she was having difficulty with a particular interpersonal relationship, such as an overly demanding boss or unsympathetic professor, Kelly would suggest that they pretend they were in the boss's or the professor's office and re-enact the troublesome scene. Afterwards, alternative methods of handling the scene would be explored and the scene itself re-enacted and changed in the light of various alternative ways in which the client might deal with it in the future. In his use of role playing, Kelly encouraged the use of role reversal, having the client play the role of the significant figures in his or her life while he played the client. Role reversal allows the client to understand his or her own participation more fully and also to understand the framework of the other person.

Kelly also made use of fixed-role therapy, in which he had the client enact

---

Exploration /////

Role Playing

Kelly's method of role playing can be fruitfully employed as a way of understanding one's own interpersonal relationships. Ask a close friend to help as you play the role of an important figure in your life. You might wish to play the role of your mother, father, professor, boss, or boy or girl friend. Ask your friend to play yourself. Identify a problem situation or a potential problem. First consider how your parent, or whoever, would handle the situation. Then act it out, with your friend playing yourself. It is important that you try to look at the situation and behave as you believe your mother, or the other figure, would. Afterwards, discuss with your friend what happened and consider alternative ways of handling the scene. Seeing yourself through your friend's eyes may help you to a closer understanding of how you come across to other people. Playing the role of other important people in your life can help you construe their interpretation of the way in which you behave.

It is also possible for the reader to obtain some of the benefits of fixed-role therapy by employing it in a limited scope. Choose one aspect of your personality that you would like to work on. It is important that you choose only one aspect at a time and one with which you feel you can deal relatively comfortably. If you believe that you are generally too passive, you might try to become more assertive. Ask yourself, "How does an assertive person think, respond, or behave in certain situations?" Then for a period of one day, try to pretend that you are an assertive person. You might even give yourself a new name. Of course, all of your friends will call you by the same old name and assume that you are your same old passive self. However, unknown to them, the passive you is taking a day off and the new you is going to respond to them and other events as an aggressive person would. When the day is over, take time to consider how you performed in your new role. How did other people react to you? You may find yourself quite surprised by the impact that your new role has had on other people.

the role of someone else for a more protracted period of time. Beginning with the client's own character sketch, developed during the phase of elaborating the construct system, the therapist creates a fictitious role for the client to play that is different from his or her normal role and is designed to help the client explore possible ways of reconstruing his or her own experiences. The client is introduced to the fictitious role and asked to try to think, talk, and behave as if he or she were that other person for a period of a few days or weeks. Obviously, the role must be carefully contrived ahead of time. It must be realistic and not too threatening for the client. Fixed role therapy has proved to be a very creative way to reconstrue the self under professional guidance.

Kelly believed that his theory had wide implications for social and interpersonal relationships. By actively considering alternative constructions, Kelly suggests, it is possible for us individually and collectively to envision new, more creative ways of dealing with a problematic situation. Take the problem that arises when a teacher observes an inattentive student who does not listen, turns in work late, and appears to put forth very little effort. The teacher might conclude that the pupil is lazy. Kelly would ask us to pose the question: Is this the most fruitful interpretation that the teacher can make, or is it simply a cop-out? Perhaps a different construction would give the teacher more latitude in creatively dealing with the problem. At the same time, the student may have his or her own construction of the classroom situation that is hindering rather than facilitating learning. The student may, for instance, perceive that teachers are out to prove the stupidity of their pupils and may only be playing an obliging role.

Kelly also encouraged the use of group therapy to help solve individual and common problems. The technique of role playing is particularly well adapted to groups, where several people may assist an individual in acting out a scene. By the end of his life, Kelly was suggesting ways in which his theory could be applied to help solve social and international problems. Much of our difficulty as Americans in international relations has been our problem as a nation in understanding how different events are construed or interpreted variously by people in other countries.

Kelly's Theory: Philosophy, Science, and Art

Although Kelly encouraged us to think of the person as a scientist, his discussion of the way we validate personal constructs involves the compelling character of philosophical insights as well. Kelly's theory suggests that a construct is validated if the anticipations it gives rise to occur. Validation refers to the compatibility between one's predictions and one's observation of the outcome, both of which are subjectively construed. This form of everyday validation does not precisely parallel the controlled procedures of science. A scientist testing hypotheses does not look for events that will verify the hypotheses but rather sets up conditions that might falsify them. In a well-designed experiment one's anticipations are of little consequence to the outcome of the hypothesis (Rychlak, 1973). In Kelly's theory people are philosophers as well as scientists, or, at least, the scientific activities in which they engage are predicated on a philosophical stance. Kelly candidly acknowledged that his view of the person as a scientist was based on the philosophical position of constructive alternativism.

The philosophical aspect of Kelly's theory may help to account for the fact that his work has generated little research even though psychologists are paying increased attention to the role of cognitive factors in personality. Most of the empirical studies based on his work concern the Rep Test (Bannister and Mair, 1968). Other studies like Bannister and Fransella (1966) and Bannister and Salmon (1966) suggest that the Rep Test and Kelly's constructs can help us understand the disturbance of thought in schizophrenia. They conclude that the thought constructs of a schizophrenic are less interrelated and more inconsistent than other people's, particularly regarding interpersonal constructs.

Kelly has been brought to task for his overly intellectual view of the individual and therapy, his failure to deal adequately with human emotions, and his insistence on dichotomous concepts. The biggest criticism of Kelly's work has been that he has ignored the full range of the human personality in his effort to do justice to the human intellect (Bruner and Rogers, 1956).

Kelly emphasized the rationality of the human being. He believed that as the scientific world becomes increasingly sophisticated, the constructs we form are increasingly more successful approximations of reality. Nevertheless, he did not believe that the world or the person is ultimately knowable through a scientific methodology. Science is simply a construct system that helps us explain events. It is one system of constructs among many alternatives. Since we cannot posit any objective reality apart from our understanding of it, we cannot assert that science can ever comprehend the real person. It can, however, provide useful constructions that assist us in making predictions. This point of view characterized Kelly's attitude toward his own philosophizing and theorizing as well, since he readily acknowledged and expected that his own theory would ultimately be succeeded by an alternative construction (1970). "At best," he wrote, "it is an ad interim theory" (1955).

In spite of the "ad interim" character of Kelly's theory, it has attracted considerable attention and controversy. His work foreshadowed the current interest in cognitive factors of personality. And his technique of role playing has proved to be a very useful tool in psychotherapy and education.

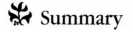 # Summary

1. Kelly's theory of personality is distinguished by its emphasis on **cognition.**

2. His theory is based on the philosophical position of **constructive alternativism,** the assumption that any one event is open to a number of interpretations.

3. Kelly suggests that we view ourselves as scientists because, in our efforts to understand the world, we develop constructs that act as hypotheses.

4. Kelly's *fundamental postulate* is "A person's processes are psychologically channelized by the ways in which he anticipates events." He elaborates on his fundamental postulate with eleven corollaries: *construction, individuality, organization, dichotomy, choice, range, experience, modulation, fragmentation, communality,* and *sociality.*

5. Kelly gives new meanings to many traditional concepts in personality theorizing, such as the *self-construct, role, learning, motivation,* and *emotion.*

6. Kelly developed the *Rep Test,* which permits a person to reveal his or her constructs by comparing and contrasting a number of different persons in his or her life.

7. In his psychotherapy Kelly sought to help his patient reconstrue the world by first elaborating the complaint and then elaborating the construct system. His unique contribution was the technique of *role playing.*

8. Kelly has been criticized for being too intellectual and for failing to deal with the whole of personality or the emotions.

9. The way in which we validate personal constructs involves philosophical insights as well as scientific methods.

Suggestions for Further Reading

George Kelly was not a prolific writer. Two books and about a dozen articles constitute the sum of his publications. His basic theory was published in a two-volume work called *The Psychology of Personal Constructs* (Norton, 1955). The first three chapters of those volumes were published separately as *A Theory of Personality: A Psychology of Personal Constructs* (Norton, 1963). Kelly's writing is rather academic and difficult reading for the lay person, who might be better advised to begin with a good secondary source such as D. Bannister and F. Fransella, *Inquiring Man: The Theory of Personal Constructs* (Penguin, 1966). Donald Bannister, an Englishman, is Kelly's most fervent disciple, and this book is a concise introduction to Kelly's theory.

Part
5

Behavior
and
Learning
Theories

One of the most puzzling questions in personality theorizing has been the dichotomy between internal and external determinants of behavior. Is behavior caused by inner predispositions or tendencies that lead a person to act in a certain way or is it caused by the situation in which one finds oneself? How much does one's "personality" really matter? A dominant trend in American psychology has been the behaviorist movement with its emphasis on learning and experience as the primary forces that shape behavior. Rather than postulating complex personality structures and dynamics within the individual, behavior and learning theories focus on those factors in the environment that determine an individual's conduct. Although internal structures are not denied, they are minimized or eliminated in favor of external forces.

Most behavior and learning theories begin in the psychological laboratory where infrahuman (lower-than-human) species, such as rats or pigeons, are studied. Theoretical speculation is avoided in favor of careful observation and experimentation. Behavior theorists have become increasingly committed to a rigorous methodology, trying to perfect the techniques of psychology and raise them to the sophistication of the natural sciences. This has permitted precision and economy in theory construction as well as clear empirical foundations for the major concepts of their theories. Part 5 presents major contributions to the behavior and learning approach to personality theory and shows their outstanding influence on psychology today.

15

John Dollard and Neal Miller: Psychoanalytic Learning Theory

Your Goals for This Chapter

1. Describe how behavior and learning theorists study personality experimentally.

2. Identify the early contributions of Pavlov, Watson, Thorndike, and Hull.

3. Define and give examples of *habits, drives,* and *reinforcers.*

4. Describe the four main conceptual parts of the learning process.

5. Discuss findings that have arisen from research into the learning process.

6. Explain how Dollard and Miller have integrated learning theory and psychoanalysis.

7. Describe Dollard and Miller's practice of psychotherapy.

8. Discuss *reciprocal inhibition* and other psychotherapeutic techniques that are based on learning principles.

9. Evaluate Dollard and Miller's theory in terms of its function as philosophy, science, and art.

J ohn Dollard and Neal Miller's orientation has been called *psychoanalytic learning theory* because it is a creative attempt to bring together the basic concepts of Freudian psychoanalytic theory with the ideas, language, methods, and results of experimental laboratory research on learning and behavior. Dollard and Miller utilize many of Freud's ideas but in doing so they integrate them with the ideas and methodology of behaviorist psychological research on learning and behavior.

Biographical Background

John Dollard and Neal Miller were both born in Wisconsin. They taught and worked together at the Institute of Human Relations at Yale University, which was founded in 1933 in an effort to explore the interdisciplinary relationships among psychology, psychiatry, sociology, and anthropology. Dollard and Miller's joint efforts resulted in a personality theory based on Hull's reinforcement theory and Freud's psychoanalytic theory. This integration resulted in a behaviorist theory that has become truly representative of the mainstream of American psychology.

John Dollard was born in 1900. He was granted the A.B. from the University of Wisconsin and the M.A. and Ph.D. from the University of Chicago. His primary interests were in sociology and anthropology and he was a strong advocate of interdisciplinary studies. Neal Miller was born in 1909. He was granted the B.S. from the University of Washington, the M.A. from Stanford, and the Ph.D. from Yale. His primary interests lay in experimental psychology. Both men undertook psychoanalytic training, each has held a number of significant positions, and each has authored several books or articles, in addition to their affiliation and collaboration at the Institute of Human Relations.

The Experimental Analysis of Behavior

Before discussing the work of Dollard and Miller, it will be useful to take a brief look at some of the origins of the experimental analysis of behavior.

Behavior and learning theories have their roots in a philosophical point of view known as **empiricism,** which suggests that all knowledge originates in experience. John Locke (1632–1704), one of the first empiricist philosophers, suggested that at birth the mind is a blank slate on which sense experience writes in a number of different ways. Locke's phrase "blank slate" (or **tabula rasa**) expressed the philosophical view of empiricism in its classic form just as Descartes's "I think, therefore I am" expressed the essence of rationalism.

Modern behavior and learning theories hold that valid knowledge arises out of experience and needs to be continually checked against it. Thus,

John Dollard and Neal Miller

behavior and learning theories are largely based on the experimental analysis of behavior. The behavior of individual organisms is carefully studied in controlled laboratory settings and the relationship between the behavior and factors in that environment is articulated. The **experimental method** seeks to investigate the effect that one phenomenon has on another. An investigator tries to determine whether a given variable or factor influences some form of behavior by systematically varying its presence or strength and then observing whether these variations have any effect on the behavior being studied.

Informed by experimental observations, theories are developed, hypotheses tested, and predictions made. Behavior and learning theories cannot predict or control human behavior in everyday life with the precision that they can obtain in the laboratory but they have been able to use these results to account for a wide range of behaviors. Principles emerging from the experimental analysis of behavior have found wide application in areas such as education, psychotherapy, industry, and corrections.

Although modern behavioral theory is singularly American, the historical background of the approach begins in Russia where Ivan Pavlov (1849–1936) demonstrated and articulated a form of learning known as **classical condi-**

tioning. In a classic laboratory situation, Pavlov took a hungry dog and presented it with food, an **unconditioned stimulus** that normally elicits salivation, an **unconditioned,** or *automatic,* **response.** Then he simultaneously paired the food with the sound of a bell, a neutral stimulus that does not normally elicit salivation. The dog salivated to the paired food and sound of the bell. After several presentations of both food and bell, Pavlov was able simply to present the sound of the bell, and the dog salivated. The sound of the bell had become a **conditioned stimulus** that elicited a **conditioned response** of salivation. In other words, Pavlov showed that by pairing an unconditioned stimulus with a conditioned stimulus, he could elicit a response that previously would have been elicited only by the original stimulus.

John Watson (1878–1958) is commonly known as the father of behaviorism. Watson expanded classical conditioning into a theory of **behaviorism** in which he recommended that psychology emphasize the study of overt rather than covert behavior. **Overt behaviors** are those that we can observe directly, such as motor movements, speaking, and crying. **Covert behaviors** are those that only the individual who actually experiences them can directly observe, such as thoughts, feelings, and wishes. Watson believed that for psychology to be an empirical science, it should base itself on phenomena that can be seen by an outside observer. Previously, psychologists had talked about a lot of phenomena that could not be directly observed by an outsider. Thoughts, feelings, and wishes can be subjectively observed by the person who is having them through the process of introspection. However, they cannot be observed directly by another individual. Because such processes cannot be objectively observed through extrospection, Watson suggested that psychology should ignore them and limit itself to discussing only the overt behaviors of an individual.

This recommendation created a curious situation. The word "psychology" refers to the study of the psyche. In everyday speech, "psychology" is often thought to refer to the study of the mind. However, Watson pointed out that it is virtually impossible to observe mental processes directly. He suggested that the psychologist should act as if the mind did not exist and simply concentrate on overt behavior. In a sense, what Watson proposed was a "psychology without the *psyche.*" Nevertheless, Watson's point of view was quickly adopted by many American psychologists. The behaviorist movement became the dominant movement in psychology in America. Even today, the distinctive methodology of American psychology reflects closely Watson's emphasis on objectivity and extrospection.

Another figure in the history of learning theory is Edwin Thorndike (1874–1949). Thorndike conducted several experiments with animals in order to gain further understanding of the learning process. He formulated many important laws of learning. The law that is particularly important for our purposes is the **law of effect,** which states that when a behavior or a performance is accompanied by satisfaction, it tends to happen again. If the performance is accompanied by frustration, it tends to decrease. We now recognize that the law of effect is not necessarily universal. Sometimes frustration leads to increased efforts to perform. Still, most psychologists believe that the law of effect is generally true.

A final figure to consider is Clark Hull (1884–1952). Hull developed a systematic theory of learning based on the concept of **drive reduction.** A **drive** is a strong stimulation that produces discomfort, such as hunger. Hull believed that learning only occurs if a response of an organism is followed by the reduction of some need or drive. The infant learns to suck a bottle of milk in order to relieve its hunger. If sucking the bottle did not result in some drive or need reduction, the infant would not learn to perform that activity.

Habits, Drives, and the Learning Process

Dollard and Miller emphasize the role of learning in personality and place less stress on personality structure. They suggest (1950) that the structure of personality can be defined very simply as habits.

Habits

Habits refer to some kind of learned association between a stimulus and response that makes them occur together frequently. Habits represent a temporary structure because they can appear and disappear: because they are learned, they may also be unlearned. This is a much simpler concept of the structure of personality than we have encountered before. The primary concern of Dollard and Miller's theory is to specify those conditions in the environment under which habits are acquired.

Drives

Dollard and Miller (1950) suggest that the primary dynamic underlying personality development is **drive reduction.** Drawing heavily upon Hull's theory, they point out that reducing a drive is reinforcing to an individual, and thus an individual will behave in ways that relieve the tension created by strong drives.

Dollard and Miller distinguish between primary and secondary **drives. Primary drives** are those associated with physiological processes that are necessary for an organism's survival. Examples would be the drives of hunger, thirst, and need for sleep. We rarely observe primary drives in a direct form because society has developed some means of reducing the drive before it becomes overwhelming. Most of us begin to feel hungry and to eat at mealtimes.

Thus, primary drives, by and large, are satisfied through secondary drives. **Secondary drives** are drives that are learned on the basis of primary ones. Dollard and Miller consider them to be elaborations of the primary drives. A person is motivated to eat at a particular time, to earn money in order to buy food, and to satisfy other drives of physical comfort in the normal mode of his culture.

Reinforcers

Dollard and Miller also distinguish between primary and secondary reinforcers. A **reinforcer** is any event that increases the likelihood of a particular response. In the case of Pavlov's dog, the food, which had originally underlaid the connection between the bell and the salivation, acted as a reinforcer. **Primary reinforcers** are those that reduce primary drives, such as food, water, or need for sleep. **Secondary reinforcers** are originally neutral but they acquire reward value on the basis of their having been associated with primary reinforcers. Money is a secondary reinforcer because you can use it to buy food. A mother's smile or a word of praise is also a secondary reinforcer, associated with a state of physical well-being.

The Learning Process

We acquire habits and develop specific behavioral responses through the process of learning. As infants each of us begins life with the basic equipment needed to reduce our primary drives: reflex responses and an innate hierarchy of response. **Reflex** responses are automatic responses to specific stimuli. All of us blink automatically to avoid an irritant to the eye or sneeze to eliminate an irritant to the nose. We pull our hand away reflexively should it touch something hot. Such reflexes are important for our survival. By **hierarchy of response,** Dollard and Miller mean that there is a tendency for certain responses to occur before others. For example, an animal runs to avoid a shock rather than cringe and bear it in pain. If a response is unsuccessful, however, an organism will try the next response on the hierarchy. If that does not work, the next will be tried, and so forth. Learning, in part, involves reinforcing and/or rearranging the response hierarchy.

Dollard and Miller (1950) suggest that *the learning process* can be broken down into four main conceptual parts:

A **drive,** as we have already seen, is a stimulus impelling a person to act, but in no way does the drive direct or specify his or her behavior. It simply impels.

A **cue** refers to a specific stimulus that tells the organism when, where, and how to respond. The sight of a bottle acts as a cue directing the infant to suck. The ringing of a bell or the time on a clock is a cue to students to enter or leave the classroom.

A **response** is one's reaction to the cue. Because these responses occur in a hierarchy, we can rank a response according to its probability of occurring. We can tell in a given situation that one response is more or less likely to occur than another response. But this innate hierarchy is not rigidly fixed or permanent; it can be changed through learning.

Reinforcement refers to the effect of the response. Effective reinforcement consists of drive reduction. If a response is not reinforced by satisfying a drive, it will undergo extinction. Extinction does not eliminate a response but merely inhibits it, enabling another response to grow stronger and supersede it in the response hierarchy. If present responses are not reinforcing, the individual is placed in a **learning dilemma.** He or she will try different responses until one is developed that satisfies the drive.

Dollard and Miller suggest that all human behavior can be comprehended in terms of the learning process. It is through the learning process that one acquires secondary drives. These drives may form a very complex system, but the underlying process by which they are developed is essentially the same: drive, cue, response, reinforcement. Even our higher mental processes can be understood in terms of the learning process. A chain of thought simply involves an internalized process of drive, cue, response, reinforcement, in which one thought serves as a cue for the next thought and so forth.

Exploration /////

The Learning Process

The four steps in the learning process as outlined by Dollard and Miller can be fruitfully used to help us understand some of our own habits and frequent responses. Choose a habit that you engage in frequently. Remember that "habit" simply means a learned association between a stimulus and a response. The habit may be positive, such as locking your car when it is parked in a questionable neighborhood, or negative, such as overeating. What are the basic underlying primary and subsequent secondary drives that your behavior seeks to fulfill? What are the specific cues that trigger your response? What are the consequences of your behavior that reinforce the habit? Such an analysis may assist you in discriminating between cues that trigger specific behaviors and reinforcements that strengthen them.

Experimental Studies of the Learning Process

Dollard and Miller have conducted extensive experimental studies on different aspects of the learning process. A number of these studies have been in the area of responses to frustration and conflict (Miller, 1944, 1951b, 1959). **Frustration** occurs when one is unable to reduce a drive because the response that would satisfy it has been blocked. If the frustration arises from a situation in which incompatible responses are occurring at the same time, the situation is described as one of **conflict.** Dollard and Miller used Kurt Lewin's (1890–1947) concept of approach and avoidance tendencies to distinguish among several different types of conflict in which an individual seeks to approach or avoid one or more goals. They developed ways of graphically presenting different types of conflict and of plotting the strengths of various forces involved in them. Thus, the child who is required to choose between two attractive objects, a toy and a bar of candy, can be diagrammed as follows:

toy *child* *candy*

with a circle representing the child and plus signs representing each desired goal. (An undesired goal would be represented by a minus sign.) The arrows indicate that there are forces moving the child in the direction of the goals (or away from them). The intensity of the force varies as the child moves closer to or further from each goal.

The value of these graphic presentations lies in the fact that if we could measure the complex forces that impel human behavior and if we could develop formulas that encompassed all of the variables involved, we could also predict a person's actions in reference to a particular goal. Human situations are so complex that such prediction is not possible at the present time. But Dollard and Miller's experiments with infrahuman species have shown that we can be quite successful in predicting the behavior of simple laboratory animals under controlled conditions.

For example, in a classic experiment, rats were placed in a harness attached to a leash so that measurements could be made as to how hard they pulled on the leash in order to arrive at or avoid a particular goal (Brown, 1948). In one case, the goal was food. Here the experimenter noted that the pull on the leash became greater the nearer the animal came to the food. This enabled him to plot a gradient of approach. In another situation, rats were placed in a similar device where they had learned to expect an electric shock at the goal. In this experiment, they were placed near the goal and permitted to run away. The experimenter noted that they pulled harder at the harness

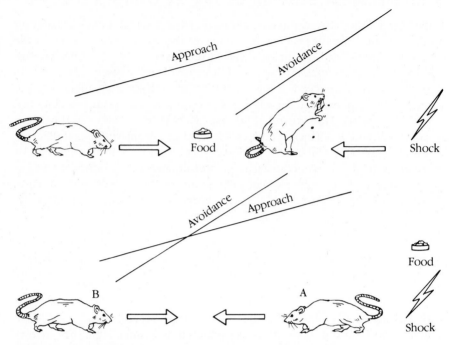

Figure 15.1 *Gradients of Avoidance and Approach*
The gradient of avoidance is steeper than the gradient of approach. Therefore, if a rat were placed in position A, it would be likely to run away from the goal, but if it were placed at position B it would go toward the goal until the gradient of avoidance became stronger.

when they were near the goal than after they had gotten some distance away from it. This enabled him to plot a gradient of avoidance. It was discovered that both the tendency to avoid and the tendency to approach reach their highest point near the goal. However, the gradient of avoidance is steeper than the gradient of approach. The rats pulled harder at the harness to avoid the shock than they did to obtain the food.

Knowing these facts and having obtained these measurements, the experimenter was able to predict what a rat would do if it were placed in any particular position within a box from which it had learned that it would receive both food and a shock at the goal, as Figure 15.1 shows. If an animal were placed in the box at position A, it would be likely to run away from the goal because the gradient of avoidance is stronger. But if it were placed in position B, it would be likely to begin to approach the goal until it reached the point where the gradient of avoidance became stronger.

The Integration of Learning Theory and Psychoanalysis

In their attempt to integrate learning theory and psychoanalysis, Dollard and Miller have adapted many Freudian concepts and reconceived them in learning theory terms. This can be seen in their discussion of unconscious processes and critical stages of development.

Dollard and Miller appreciate the importance of unconscious forces underlying human behavior but they redefine the concept of **unconscious processes** in terms of their own theory. There are two main determinants of unconscious processes. First, we are unaware of certain drives or cues because they are unlabeled. These drives and cues may have occurred before we learned to speak and therefore we were unable to label them. Other cues may be unconscious, because a society has not given them adequate labels. In our society, we have essentially one word for snow, although we might further describe it as dry or slushy. In certain Eskimo cultures, there are thirty or more different words for the various textures of snow. Such a society is certainly much more aware of the different variations in snow than we are. Distortions in labeling may also affect one's conscious perception. Through distorted labeling, an emotion such as fear may become confused with another emotion, such as guilt. Thus, an individual may react in frightening situations as if he were guilty because of a distortion in labeling. Second, unconscious processes refer to cues or responses that once were conscious but have been repressed because they were ineffective. **Repression** is essentially a process of avoiding certain thoughts that entails the loss of ability to use proper verbal labels. Thus, repressed thoughts are no longer under verbal control. Dollard and Miller point out that repression is learned like all other behaviors. When we repress, we do not think about certain thoughts or label them because they are unpleasant. Avoiding these thoughts reduces the drive by reducing the unpleasant experience.

In the same way, Dollard and Miller articulate many of the other defense mechanisms that Freud outlined: projection, identification, reaction formation, rationalization, and displacement. In each case, however, they are seen as learned responses or behaviors and they are articulated in terms of learning. For example, identification entails imitating the behavior that one has learned from another. Displacement is explained in terms of generalization and the inability to make proper discriminations.

Dollard and Miller posit four *critical training stages in child development.* These are the feeling situation in infancy, cleanliness training, early sex training, and the training for control of anger and aggression. These are **critical periods** in the child's development in which social conditions of learning imposed by the parents may have enormous consequences for future development. The parallel to Freud's stages is obvious. The conflict situation of feeding in infancy is reminiscent of Freud's oral stage, cleanliness training is reminiscent of Freud's anal stage, and early sex training as well as the effort to control anger and aggression are elements of Freud's phallic stage. Dollard and Miller agree with Freud that events in early childhood are vitally important in shaping later behavior. Further, they suggest that the logic of these events may be comprehended within the learning process as they have outlined it. Whereas Freud's stages unfold biologically, the outcomes of Dollard and Miller's stages are controlled by the learning process. Thus, the infant whose cry when hungry brings immediate relief in the sense of being fed learns that self-generated activity is effective in reducing drives. If the infant, however, is left to "cry it out," he or she may learn that there is nothing self-generated that can be done to reduce the drive and begin to develop a passive attitude toward drive reduction.

Freudian concepts like fixation and regression are also reinterpreted. Regression is understood as returning to an earlier pattern of response because a present behavior pattern has been frustrated. Fixation is described as being arrested at an earlier pattern of response because new, more appropriate behaviors have not been learned. Thus, in their incorporation of Freud's theories, Dollard and Miller reconsidered and elaborated his ideas in the light of learning theory principles.

It was easy to merge Freud's and Hull's theories because both of them are based on drive reduction and share the common feature of determinism. Dollard and Miller's work helps us to appreciate the role of learning in the development of defenses and other psychoanalytic structures. However, there are significant differences between Freud's concepts and Dollard and Miller's articulation of them, so that the translation is not exact. For example, whereas for Freud anxiety, conflict, and repression were inevitable aspects of the human condition, for Dollard and Miller they are simply learned responses. Nevertheless, by transforming Freud's concepts into the terms of learning theory and experimental psychology, Dollard and Miller rendered Freud more palatable to a large number of people. It is less threatening to believe that unconscious processes and defense mechanisms are learned and may therefore be unlearned than conceive of them as largely universal and inescapable. In Freud's view, one could merely try to recognize them in order to cope with them more effectively. In addition, Dollard and Miller's work has stimulated a great deal of scientific research and experimental testing of Freud's concepts.

Psychotherapy

We have seen that for Dollard and Miller behavior is learned in the process of seeking to reduce drives. Deviant behavior is also learned, but in the neurotic the behaviors that have been learned are frequently self-defeating and unproductive. Dollard and Miller (1950) refer to neurosis as a **stupidity-misery-syndrome.** The patient has strong, unconscious, and unlabeled emotional conflicts. Because the neurotic has not labeled the problem, he or she does not discriminate effectively, generalizing and applying old, ineffective solutions to current problems and situations. A young man whose father was a tyrant may have learned in early childhood that he had to react meekly in order to avoid his father's wrath. Unable to discriminate between his father's attitude and the attitude of other authority figures in his life, the young man may generalize his response to his father to later authority figures who in fact are not tyrants. In such situations, his meek response may not be the most appropriate one. Dollard and Miller (1950) suggest that "neurotic conflicts are taught by parents and learned by children."

Therapy involves unlearning old, ineffective, unproductive habits and substituting new, more adaptive, and productive responses. Dollard and Miller (1950) refer to two phases in therapy. In the **talking phase,** neurotic habits are studied, examined, and identified so the patient may unlearn them. Essentially, this procedure entails providing appropriate labels for the patient's responses. When we label a repression appropriately, the repression is lifted because we have erased the distortion. The reader may recall the fairy tale of Rumpelstiltskin, who loses his demonic powers once he is confronted with his name. When the repressions are correctly identified and labeled for what they are, their power to harm the individual disappears.

The second phase of therapy is the **performance phase.** During this phase, the patient acquires new, more adaptive and productive responses and habits and is encouraged to apply them. Training in **suppression** (the conscious, deliberate stopping of a thought or an action) can be helpful. The patient can be trained to suppress, rather than repress, thoughts or actions that reinforce old habits. At the same time, he or she deliberately exposes him- or herself to new cues that will evoke different responses.

Dollard and Miller's theory of therapy represents a bridge to the more directive and active therapies of other learning theories. It is pragmatic and action oriented. Whereas Freud thought it necessary to work through past problems for an analysis to be successful, Dollard and Miller believe that historical recollection is effective only if it is instrumental in creating change. If historical recollection is unnecessary for change to occur, it is only a short step to exclude that emphasis on the past and concentrate on the behaviors of the present as subsequent learning theorists do.

Dollard and Miller's theory of personality has been instrumental in stimulating the development of other psychotherapeutic techniques based on learning principles. Many of these techniques are based on the principle of reciprocal inhibition, which was formulated by Joseph Wolpe (1958). **Reciprocal inhibition**

Suppression

Suppression can be an important adaptive device that enables us to curb inappropriate responses, since it entails the conscious, deliberate stopping of a thought or action. Any learned or secondary drive can be suppressed. First, identify certain behaviors or desires that you would like to stop because they lead to unproductive results, such as a quick temper, obsession with being popular, or a tendency always to blame yourself. Recognizing these impulses and taking steps to avoid their expression can help us to achieve other goals that are more important to us. When the cues that normally trigger the unproductive response occur, try to engage in other activities that will divert your attention away from the problematic impulse. The old adage that one should count to ten before expressing one's anger is a simple device that permits suppression. If you find yourself beginning to engage in certain behaviors like self-incrimination, you might try to stop and recognize those factors in the situation that you could not realistically control before further blaming yourself. Obviously, we cannot suppress all of our desires and impulses but practice in suppression can help us acquire greater self-control.

Unlike suppression, repression and inhibition are not under conscious control. Thus, their effect is often negative rather than positive. Professional intervention is often mandated to assist in lifting repressions and inhibitions, because we are not aware of their source.

entails the introduction of a competitive response that will interfere with an original maladaptive or nonproductive response. For example, anxiety is an automatic response that an organism exhibits in the presence of painful or harmful stimuli. If anxiety becomes too intense during the process of conditioning, it may lead to neurosis, in which one becomes anxious about subsequent stimuli that are not really harmful. However, if a response that competes with anxiety can be made to occur at the same time as the anxiety-evoking stimulus is presented, it can weaken the relationship between the stimulus and the anxiety, and the anxiety may be inhibited.

Several techniques informed by learning theory will be discussed next. The particular technique employed by a behavior and learning therapist with any given patient is determined after an extensive interview process that helps to clarify what stimuli are causing the problem and what would be the best tactic to employ in eliminating the symptoms.

Systematic Desensitization

In **systematic desensitization** the patient is conditioned to stop responding with anxiety to the stimulus and to substitute a new response. Relaxation is a very successful competing response. It is difficult for a person to feel anxious in a situation in which he or she is deeply relaxed. Thus, the first step in systematic desensitization often is to train the patient in deep muscle relaxation. In the course of six or seven sessions, the patient is taught how to relax various parts of the body so that eventually he or she is able to relax practically at will.

The second step in systematic desensitization is to construct anxiety hierarchies. The therapist asks the patient to identify all of the sources of his or her anxiety. These sources are grouped into common themes. Each theme is itemized and the patient is asked to rank each item, placing the item that is most disturbing at the top of the list and the item that is least disturbing at the bottom. The following example is part of a hierarchy of fears developed by a twenty-four-year-old art student whose severe anxiety over examinations had led to several failing grades (Wolpe, 1958):

*Hierarchy of examination fears**

1. On the way to the university on the day of an examination
2. In the process of answering an examination paper
3. Standing before the unopened doors of the examination room
4. Awaiting the distribution of examination papers
5. Seeing the examination paper face down before her
6. The night before an examination
7. One day before an examination
8. Two days before an examination
9. Three days before an examination
10. Four days before an examination

Once the patient is trained in deep muscle relaxation and anxiety hierarchies have been constructed, the desensitization process itself begins. First weak and later progressively stronger anxiety-arousing stimuli are presented to the patient to imagine as he or she reclines in a deeply relaxed state. The patient is asked to imagine him- or herself four days before an examination. At the sign of any anxiety the patient is asked to inform the therapist and the scene is discontinued until the patient is able to relax again. Eventually the patient is able to imagine scenes of greater intensity and duration with less and less

*Reprinted from J. Wolpe, *The Practice of Behavior Therapy*, 1st ed., Oxford: Pergamon Press Ltd., 1969. Used by permission of the author and the publisher.

anxiety and increasing relaxation. In short, a competitive response has been established.

Assertive Training

In **assertive training** the patient is taught to express his or her feelings in various everyday situations. Training in assertion is not limited to training in aggression. The patient is taught to express friendly and affectionate feelings as well as angry and hostile ones. Many of us have been trained to inhibit expression of our feelings in social situations in order to be considered polite and socially graceful. Because of this we may let others take advantage of us without objecting to their behaviors or we may feel inhibited in expressing the positive feelings we have toward other people. Assertive training entails being taught to stand up for what one feels. If an individual butts in front of somebody in a line saying, "I'm sure you won't mind," that person should be able to say, "I'm sorry, but I do mind. Please go back to the end of the line."

Behavioral rehearsal, a form of role playing, is a useful adjunct in assertive training. The therapist will play the role of someone who is giving the patient difficulty, such as a boss who frequently asks the patient to work overtime when it is inconvenient. Through behavioral rehearsal the patient may be able to assert him- or herself and point out that it would be an imposition, rather than timidly and continually give in. Behavioral rehearsal may also help one envision a compromise in which both parties are satisfied.

Aversion Therapy

Although behavior therapists rarely consider aversion therapy the first choice of treatment, they have explored its use. The technique of **aversion therapy,** also known as *avoidance counterconditioning,* entails coupling an unpleasant stimulus of strong avoidance response, such as an electric shock, with an undesired response. This technique has been used in the treatment of alcoholism and drug addiction. Alcoholics have been given an emetic, a drug that induces vomiting, and then given an alcoholic beverage. The patient vomits violently as a result of the emetic, which is given in close proximity to the alcohol. After several such sessions the patient may begin to feel queasy or nauseous at the sight or smell of alcohol and lose the desire to drink it. Aversion therapy has been used to eliminate such undesired behaviors as drinking, gambling, nail biting, overeating, and homosexuality. Such aversive techniques will not usually be effective, however, unless the patient is also exposed to other stimuli that will reinforce the expression of the desired response. Oth-

*Assertive training can help
people stand up for what
they feel.*

erwise, when the inappropriate response is no longer negatively reinforced,
it may demonstrate spontaneous recovery. To those critics who say that
aversive therapy entails sadistic control, behavior therapists point out that it
should not be used unless the patient voluntarily agrees that this particular
treatment technique is in his or her best interest.

The successfulness of behavior therapy techniques has been demonstrated
experimentally. Nevertheless there is a widespread view among the public
that behavior therapy is inhumane and simplistic. Books and films, such as
Clockwork Orange, have misrepresented and vilified behavior therapy. Behavior
clinicians have sought to correct this misapprehension and to emphasize the
demonstrated efficacy of behavior therapy over other forms of treatment.

Behavior Modification Therapy

The following description of systematic desensitization is taken from Wolpe's account of his procedures.* The patient is the twenty-four-year-old art student whose hierarchy of examination fears was presented earlier. After having trained the patient in deep muscle relaxation and agreed on a scale for reporting anxieties, the therapist proceeds to bring about a deep state of relaxation in the patient and introduces the first desensitization session:

TH (therapist): I am now going to ask you to imagine a number of scenes. You will imagine them clearly and they will generally interfere little, if at all, with your state of relaxation. If, however, at any time you feel disturbed or worried and want to draw my attention, you can tell me so. As soon as a scene is clear in your mind, indicate it by raising your left index finger about one inch. First, I want you to imagine that you are standing at a familiar street corner on a pleasant morning watching the traffic go by. You see cars, motorcycles, trucks, bicycles, people, and traffic lights; and you hear the sounds associated with all these things.

After a few seconds the patient raises her left index finger. The therapist pauses for five seconds.

TH: Stop imagining that scene. By how much did it raise your anxiety level while you imagined it?
PT (patient): Not at all.
TH: Now give your attention once again to relaxing.

There is again a pause of twenty to thirty seconds.

TH: Now imagine that you are home studying in the evening. It is the twentieth of May, exactly a month before your examination.

After about fifteen seconds Miss C. raises her finger. Again she is left with the scene for five seconds.

TH: Stop that scene. By how much did it raise your anxiety?
PT: About fifteen units.
TH: Now imagine the same scene again — a month before your examination.

At this second presentation the rise in anxiety was five SUDs [Subjective

*J. Wolpe, *The Practice of Behavior Therapy*, 2nd ed., Oxford: Pergamon Press Ltd., 1973. Used by permission of the author and the publisher.

(*continued*)

Units of Disturbance] and at the third it was zero. ... Having disposed of the first scene of the examination hierarchy, I [the therapist] could move on to the second. ... Freedom from anxiety ... was achieved in seventeen desensitization sessions, with complete transfer to the corresponding situations in actuality.

Dollard and Miller's Theory: Philosophy, Science, and Art

Dollard and Miller have developed their theory of personality through laboratory studies and experimentation. They try to base their statements on empirical evidence and submit theoretical differences to observational tests. They recognize, perhaps more than many other theorists, that a theory is useful according to its effectiveness in leading to predictions that can be tested. As a scientific theory, therefore, Dollard and Miller's work has been very attractive to many psychologists because of its use of validating evidence.

Empirical evidence, however, has not always given as much support to Dollard and Miller's theory as the theorists imply. What an organism can learn is limited by *species specific behavior,* complex, rather than reflex, behaviors that occur in all members of a species. Some stimuli are more relevant to a particular species than others; responses also differ. Pigeons peck, chickens scratch, and pigs root. It is difficult, if not impossible, to alter these behaviors. One cannot easily generalize from a rat to a human being.

As we have seen, Dollard and Miller have taken many psychoanalytic concepts and rendered them into the imaginary constructs of a scientific theory. They have provided Freud's concepts with operational definitions and shown that they can be tested experimentally. Many consider this a substantial contribution to the viability of Freud's ideas. Whether psychoanalysis has gained or lost in the process, however, is a matter of considerable debate (Rapaport, 1953). Some would point out that in the process of translation Freudian concepts have lost considerable dynamism and have been emptied of their original intent. Others suggest that Freud's in-depth clinical study of humans illuminates the dynamics of human personality far more than Dollard and Miller's research with rats does.

Nevertheless, Dollard and Miller's views have been central to the field of personality since they first published their major work, *Personality and Psychotherapy,* in 1950. They were among the first to seek to emulate a purely scientific model in understanding personality.

Ideally, if we could measure forces that impel human behavior and develop sophisticated formulas that encompass all of the variables involved, we could predict complex human behavior; the applications of such a science would be mind-boggling indeed. Dollard and Miller's theory has been quite successful in predicting the behavior of simple laboratory animals under controlled conditions. It has not been as successful in predicting complex human behavior and this inability has limited the practical application of their theory. Nevertheless, throughout much of the twentieth century Dollard and Miller's theory has typified the mainstream of American academic psychology.

✿ Summary

1. Behavior and learning theories explore personality experimentally by studying behavior in laboratory settings. Their precise methods reflect an **empirical** point of view and the careful manipulation of variables under specified controlled conditions.

2. Early behaviorists include Pavlov, who explained the process of **classical conditioning,** Watson, whose theory recommended an emphasis on **overt behavior,** Thorndike, who formulated the **law of effect,** and Hull, who clarified the concept of **drive reduction.**

3. Dollard and Miller describe the structure of personality in terms of **habits** that may be learned and unlearned. They distinguish between **primary** and **secondary drives** and **reinforcers** as the primary motivating forces of personality.

4. Human behavior can be understood in terms of the learning process, which is broken down into four main conceptual parts: **drive, cue, response,** and **reinforcement.**

5. A number of experiments have been conducted on the learning process, especially in the area of **frustration** and **conflict.** Experiments with infrahuman species have been quite successful in predicting the behavior of simple laboratory animals under controlled conditions.

6. Dollard and Miller have adapted many Freudian concepts and integrated them into learning theory terms. **Unconscious processes** are reconceived as unlabeled drives and cues. The defense mechanisms and critical stages of development are also reconceived in terms of the learning process. The translation, though inexact, has helped to popularize Freud and stimulate experimental study of his ideas.

7. Dollard and Miller's therapy represents a bridge to the more directive and active therapies of other learning theories. Behavior therapy involves unlearning ineffective habits and substituting more adaptive responses. During a **talking**

phase, the patient learns to label responses accurately. In the **performance phase,** deliberate training in **suppression** is carried out.

8. **Reciprocal inhibition** entails developing competing responses. Behavior and learning theorists have developed other therapeutic techniques, including **systematic desensitization, assertive training,** and **aversion therapy.**

9. Dollard and Miller's theory of personality seeks to emulate a scientific model and places a great deal of emphasis on empirical research.

Suggestions for Further Reading

For students who are interested in a historical introduction to the experimental movement in psychology, E. G. Boring, *A History of Experimental Psychology* (Appleton-Century-Crofts, 1929) is an encyclopedic survey. A classic statement of John Watson's behaviorism may be found in his book *Behaviorism* (Norton, 1925).

Dollard and Miller have jointly written two books that describe their effort to develop a theory of personality. Of primary interest is *Personality and Psychotherapy: An Analysis in Terms of Learning, Thinking, and Culture* (McGraw-Hill, 1950). In this work, the authors outline how they have applied the concepts of learning theory to reconsider many of the insights and observations of Freudian psychoanalysis. They translate Freud's theory of personality, therapeutic concepts, and procedures into learning theory terms. The book is an outstanding introduction to the learning and behavior approach to personality.

Social Learning and Imitation (Yale University Press, 1941) represents an early attempt to apply Hull's principles of learning to the study of personality. It is a good introduction to an effort to use learning theory to understand personality.

Dollard and Miller have also written several articles. Some of these are cited in the References. Joseph Wolpe's therapy techniques for clinical practice are included in *The Practice of Behavior Therapy* (Pergamon, 1973).

16

B. F. Skinner: Radical Behaviorism

Your Goals for This Chapter

1. Explain why Skinner emphasizes overt behavior and avoids developing a theory of personality.

2. Describe the process of *operant conditioning,* and compare it with classical conditioning.

3. Distinguish among different *schedules* and types of *reinforcement* and indicate their effectiveness.

4. Discuss Skinner's concept of *behavior modification* and explain how it has been successfully employed.

5. Describe Skinner's concept of a utopian society.

6. Show how Skinner's position includes philosophical assumptions as well as scientific statements.

7. Distinguish between introspection and extrospection as means of acquiring empirical data and explain why learning and behavior theories have been viewed as partial or incomplete.

8. Evaluate Skinner's theory in terms of its function as philosophy, science, and art.

urrhus Frederic Skinner, who is the best-known psychologist in the United States today, espouses a point of view known as **radical behaviorism.** Skinner explicitly states that he is not concerned with positing any internal underlying motivations or structures that might be said to constitute personality. His sole concern is to study, predict, and control behavior. Thus he provides us with a rigorous application of the methods, data, and concepts that emerge out of the scientific study of learning.

Biographical Background

B. F. Skinner was born in 1904 in Susquehanna, Pennsylvania. His father, a conservative Republican, was an ambitious lawyer who eventually earned a substantial income but was unable to recognize his own success. His mother was bright, beautiful, and of high moral standards. A younger brother, of whom he was fond, died suddenly at the age of sixteen. Skinner was reared in a warm, comfortable, and stable home, permeated with the virtues and ethics of small-town, middle-class America at the turn of the century. His parents did not employ physical punishments but their admonitions succeeded in teaching their son "to fear God, the police, and what people would think." His parents and grandparents, to whom he was close, taught him to be faithful to the puritan work imperative, to try to please God, and to look for evidence of God's favor through "success."

As a child, Skinner was fascinated with machines and interested in knowing how things work. He constructed the usual childhood wagons, slingshots, and model airplanes and he also tried his hand at inventing things. He developed a mechanical device to remind himself to hang up his pajamas, a gadget that enabled him to blow smoke rings without violating his parents' prohibition against smoking, and a flotation system to separate ripe from green elderberries. For many years he tried to design a perpetual motion machine, but it did not work.

Skinner was also interested in animal behavior. He caught and brought home the small wildlife of the woodlands in western Pennsylvania, such as snakes, lizards, and chipmunks. At a county fair, he was highly impressed by a troupe of performing pigeons. Skinner later was to train pigeons and other animals to play Ping-Pong, guide a missile to its target, and perform other remarkable feats.

At school Skinner was an excellent student. He majored in English at Hamilton College, a small liberal arts school in upstate New York, and he seriously thought of becoming a writer. He sent a few short stories to the well-known poet, Robert Frost, who encouraged him in his writing aspirations. He decided to take a year or two off to write, but he quickly became discouraged and decided he could not write as he "had nothing important to say." During this interlude, he read books by Ivan Pavlov and John Watson, whose work impressed him, and he decided to begin graduate studies in psychology at Harvard. He received the Ph.D. in 1931.

He taught at the University of Minnesota for nine years and was chairman of the department of psychology at Indiana University, before he returned to Harvard in 1948, having established a reputation as a major experimental psychologist and having written his influential book *Walden II,* which describes a utopian society based on psychological principles. To this day he continues to work at Harvard, following a rigorously disciplined schedule, although his activities are, he admits, tempered by his age.

A Theory of Personality without Personality

Skinner is the leading heir of the behaviorist position, having taken the beliefs and concepts of Watson's behaviorist theory to their logical extreme. He concurs with Watson that it is unproductive and foolish to refer to structures of the personality that cannot be directly observed. Since we cannot directly observe constructs such as an id, ego, or superego, it is virtually useless for us to invoke them. We have seen that Dollard and Miller developed a psychoanalytically oriented behavioral theory in which they combined the insights of Freud's psychoanalytic position with the principles of learning theory. Skinner takes the logical step that follows from Dollard and Miller's approach. If a stimulus-response theory of psychology can account for all of the overt behaviors that psychologists seek to explain, why not omit the psychoanalytic underpinnings and simply rely on behaviorist principles (Rychlak, 1973)? Skinner, therefore, has developed a psychology that concentrates not on the person but solely on those variables and forces in the environment that influence a person and that may be directly observed. Thus, Skinner presents behaviorism and learning theory in its purest and most extreme form.

In many ways, Skinner appears to be out of place in a book that concentrates on theories of personality. Indeed, for Skinner the term "personality" is ultimately superfluous, as overt behavior can be completely comprehended in terms of responses to factors in the environment. The effort to understand or explain behavior in terms of internal structures such as a personality or an ego is to speak in terms of "fictions," because the terms are not very helpful. First, they are presented in such a way that they cannot be directly observed; second, it is very difficult to deduce operational definitions from them; and, lastly, it is virtually impossible to develop systematic and empirical means of testing them (1953). Instead, Skinner suggests that we concentrate on the environmental consequences that determine and maintain an individual's behavior. One can consider the person as if he or she were empty and observe how changes in the environment affect his or her behavior.

B. F. Skinner

It is also unnecessary to posit internal forces or motivational states within a person as causal factors of behavior. Skinner does not deny that such states occur: they are important by-products of behavior. He simply sees no point in using them as causal variables because they cannot be operationally defined and their intensity cannot be measured.

Rather than try to determine how hungry an organism is, Skinner tries to determine what variables or forces in the environment affect the individual's eating behavior. What is the effect of the time period that has elapsed since the last meal was eaten? What are the consequences of the amount of food consumed? Such factors in the environment can be specifically defined, measured, and dealt with empirically.

Some of his critics suggest that Skinner begins with the doctrine of the **"empty organism"** or the "unopened box" (e.g., Boring, 1946). These terms were not coined by Skinner, and he objects to them as well as to the label "stimulus-response theorist." Skinner fully acknowledges that at birth the infant is not a tabula rasa or blank slate. The newborn is an organism with a certain genetic inheritance, reflex capacities, and other abilities to respond, as well as certain drives and motivational states that set it in motion. These factors are given and cannot be changed. Their study is of little value. It is more important and useful to show how behavior can be modified or changed by the environment than to show how it occurs from internal structures or forces.

Skinner's work also differs from other researchers in that he emphasizes individual subjects. Typically, he studies each animal separately and reports his results in the form of individual records. Whereas other experimenters draw their conclusions on the basis of the performance of comparison groups as a whole, Skinner believes that the laws of behavior must apply to each and every individual subject when it is observed under the appropriate conditions.

The Development of Behavior through Learning

At birth, the human infant is simply a bundle of innate capacities but his or her consequent behaviors can be comprehended in terms of learning. Thorndike's law of effect stated that when a behavior or performance is accompanied by satisfaction it tends to be stamped in or increased. If the performance is accompanied by frustration, it tends to decrease. Omitting Thorndike's reference to internal states, Skinner derived a very simple definition of reinforcement. A **reinforcement** is anything that increases or decreases the likelihood of a response. It is the effect of one's behavior that determines the likelihood of its occurring again. If a young child cries or whines, perhaps he or she will get parental attention and be reinforced. If the behavior results in reinforcement, chances are the child will repeat that behavior pattern. If the behavior does not result in reinforcement, that is, if the child is ignored and does not receive attention, then it is likely that the behavioral response will cease and the child will behave in alternative ways to find patterns of behavior that are reinforced.

Operant Conditioning

Skinner (1938) distinguishes between two types of behavior: respondent and operant. **Respondent behavior** refers to reflexes or automatic responses that are elicited by stimuli. A beam of light causes the pupils of one's eye to contract. If the knee is tapped on the right spot, the leg jerks forward. When our fingers touch hot metal, we reflexively pull our hand away. Such behaviors are unlearned: they occur involuntarily and automatically.

Respondent behaviors may, however, be conditioned or changed through learning. Respondent behaviors were involved in Pavlov's demonstration of classical conditioning. Pavlov's dog learned to salivate to the tone of a bell. An infant learns to suck at a nipple. These are reflexes or automatic responses that have come to be performed in the presence of the previously neutral stimulus through the process of association.

Operant behaviors are responses that are emitted without a stimulus necessarily being present. They occur spontaneously. Not all of a newborn's movements are reflex responses. Some of them are operant behaviors in which the infant acts on his or her environment. An infant swings an arm or moves a leg and certain consequences follow. These consequences determine whether or not the response will be repeated. Skinner believes that the process of **operant conditioning** is of far greater significance than simple classical conditioning. Many of our behaviors cannot be accounted for in terms of classical conditioning. Rather, they are originally spontaneous behaviors whose consequences determine their subsequent frequency.

There is a clear distinction between the nature of a respondent behavior and an operant behavior. A respondent behavior is evoked or elicited by a stimulus. Operant behavior is emitted or freely made by the organism. The nature of reinforcement also differs in classical conditioning and operant conditioning. In classical conditioning, the stimulus is the reinforcement and it precedes the behavior. In operant conditioning, the effect of the behavior is the reinforcement. Thus, in operant conditioning the reinforcement follows the behavior.

Operant conditioning can be systematically described by depicting the behavior of a rat in an operant conditioning apparatus, a piece of laboratory equipment that Skinner designed in order to train animals and conduct research. Commonly known as a "Skinner box," the apparatus makes possible controlled and precise study of animal behavior.

When a food-deprived rat is first placed within the box, it may behave in a variety of random ways. The rat may first walk around the box and explore it. Later, it may scratch itself or urinate. In the course of its activity the rat may at some point press a bar on the wall of the box. The bar pressing causes a food pellet to drop into a trough under the bar. The rat's behavior has had an effect on the environment. The food acts as a reinforcement, increasing the likelihood of that behavior occurring again. When it occurs again it is reinforced. Eventually, the rat begins to press the bar in rapid succession, pausing only long enough to eat the food.

When a food-deprived rat is conditioned in a Skinner box to press a bar and is reinforced for that behavior with food, we can predict pretty accurately what the rat is going to do in subsequent sessions in the Skinner box. Furthermore, we can control the rat's behavior by changing the reinforcement. The person who is reinforcing determines the desired behavior. The organism emits a variety of behaviors. When the desired behavior occurs, it is reinforced. Appropriate reinforcement increases the likelihood of that behavior occurring again.

Shaping

Frequently the behavior that one wishes to train an organism to do is a complex, sophisticated one that the organism would not naturally be expected to do shortly after entering the box. Suppose one wished to train a pigeon to peck at a small black dot inside a white circle. If one were to wait until that behavior spontaneously occurred, one might wait a very long time. Therefore, Skinner employs a procedure termed **shaping**, in which he deliberately shapes or molds the organism's behavior in order to achieve the desired behavior. In shaping, undifferentiated behavior of the organism is gradually molded according to an ordered series of steps until it increasingly approximates the desired behavior.

Initially, the pigeon moves randomly about the box. When it moves in the direction of the circle, it is reinforced by a pellet of food in the trough below the circle. The next time it approaches the circle, it is again reinforced. Later, it is required to approach the circle more closely before it is reinforced. Later still, it is not reinforced until it pecks the white circle. Finally, the pigeon is reinforced only for pecking at the small black dot within the circle. Shaping can lead an organism to develop a behavior that it might never have emitted spontaneously.

Through shaping, Skinner has been able to induce behaviors in animals that they would not normally do. Some of these are unique and remarkable feats, as when Skinner taught pigeons how to play Ping-Pong. During World War II, he trained pigeons for use in air-to-ground missiles. He trained them to peck at objects that were projected onto a screen in such a way that they could guide a missile. His pigeons never actually were put to work guiding missiles, but Skinner showed that it was possible for them to do so. Using behavioral-shaping methods, other animal trainers have been able to produce unusual tricks and feats. A rabbit may be trained to jump into the seat of a toy fire truck and ring the bell. Animals have been taught to play musical instruments and baseball, jump through fiery hoops, dance complex steps, and perform other tricks. A monkey, Hellion, has been trained to act as the hands of her quadraplegic master. If you have a pet dog, chances are you have trained it to perform a few simple tricks and you have done so by shaping its behavior through reinforcement.

Skinner believes that most animal and human behavior is learned through operant conditioning. The process of learning to speak one's native tongue involves reinforcing and shaping of operant behavior. The young infant emits

Classical and Operant Conditioning

The reader can easily demonstrate the processes of classical and operant conditioning. Eye blinking is a normal reflex response that we commonly make when an irritant enters our eyes. We do not, however, normally blink simply because we hear certain words, such as "personality." But one can condition a subject to blink to the sound of the neutral word "personality" by means of the following simple process of classical conditioning. Standing close to your subject, focus a soda straw near one of his or her eyes and gently puff to elicit blinking. A few trials should help you determine the distance and strength of puff that is most effective. Then, in a rhythmic pattern say the word "personality" before you puff into your subject's eye. Repeat the process several times in rapid succession. Say the word "personality." Pause for less than a second. Puff into your subject's eye and wait for the blink. Eventually your subject will begin to blink just to the sound of the word "personality," before you have a chance to puff on the straw. Classical conditioning has occurred. Of course, you do not need to fear that your subject will be fated to blink at the sound of the word "personality" for the rest of his or her life. When the response is no longer reinforced by the original stimulus, it will undergo extinction.

You can easily demonstrate the process of operant conditioning by having a friend agree to behave as if he or she were reinforced by the sound of your clapping. Choose a *simple* uncomplicated behavior that you would like your subject to perform. Appropriate tasks might be to pick up a book lying on a table, to turn a light switch on or off, or to write (anything) with a piece of paper and pencil. Initially, you reinforce your subject by clapping whenever he or she moves in the direction of the vicinity in which the desired behavior is to be performed. Next, you require your subject to be very close to the area. Later, you only reinforce when he or she appears to be attending to the object of the desired behavior: the book, the light switch, or the paper and pencil. Eventually, you will reinforce your subject only for performing the desired task.

After the demonstration, you might ask your subject how he or she felt during the process of conditioning. Some subjects report that they feel quite frustrated when put in the position of a rat in a Skinner box. You might recognize the demonstration as a version of the game "Hot or Cold" that children play. This is Skinner's point. He suggests that learning has always occurred through reinforcement but that we now have the opportunity to study it scientifically and employ it systematically.

certain spontaneous sounds. These are not limited to the sounds of its native tongue but represent all possible languages. Initially, the infant is reinforced for simply babbling. Later, the child is reinforced for making sounds that approximate meaningful words in his or her native language. Eventually the child is reinforced only for meaningful speech. Thus, the process of shaping is involved in the process of learning to speak, as well as many other human behaviors.

Schedules and Types of Reinforcement

A practical necessity led Skinner to explore the effect of different *schedules of reinforcement.* In the 1930s, commercially made food pellets were not available. Skinner and his students found that it was a laborious, time-consuming process to make the eight hundred or more food pellets a day that were necessary to sustain his research. Skinner wondered what the effect would be if the animal was not reinforced every time it performed the desired behavior. This question led to the investigation of various schedules of reinforcement.

Skinner (1969) describes three schedules of reinforcement and indicates their effectiveness. In **continuous reinforcement,** the desired behavior is reinforced each time that it occurs. The pigeon or rat is given a food pellet every time that it pecks the small black dot or presses the bar. A continuous schedule of reinforcement is extremely effective in initially developing and strengthening a behavior. However, if the reinforcement is stopped, the response quickly disappears or undergoes extinction.

In **interval reinforcement,** the organism is reinforced after a certain time period has elapsed, regardless of the response rate. Interval reinforcement may be given on a fixed or a variable basis. If it is **fixed,** the same time period elapses each time (such as five minutes). If it is **variable,** the time periods may differ in length. This type of reinforcement schedule occurs frequently in the everyday world. Employees are paid at the end of each week. Students are given grades at certain intervals within the year. In each of these cases, the reinforcement is independent of the rate of the individual organism's performance. Interval reinforcement produces a level of response that is more difficult to extinguish than responses that have been continuously reinforced. However, the level of response tends to be lower than the level produced by other kinds of schedule. If the organism can anticipate the interval, the response may increase just before the anticipated reinforcement and drop significantly afterwards. Thus, students often cram before an exam but neglect to study during the rest of the term.

In **ratio reinforcement,** reinforcement is determined by the number of appropriate responses that the organism emits. A pigeon may be reinforced after it pecks the small black dot five times. A factory worker may be paid according to the number of pieces that he or she completes. Ratio schedules of reinforcement may also be fixed or variable. If they are **fixed,** the number of responses required prior to reinforcement is stable and the same each time. If they are **variable,** the number of appropriate operant behaviors that must occur prior to reinforcement changes from time to time. Whereas a continuous schedule of reinforcement is most effective for initially developing and strengthening a behavior, a variable ratio schedule is most effective thereafter in maintaining it. Responses maintained under the conditions of variable ratio reinforcement are highly resistant to extinction and less likely to disappear. Gambling casinos have learned this lesson well. Their use of the principle of variable ratio schedules keeps many an addicted gambler at the table long after money allotted for gambling has disappeared.

Where reinforcement is haphazard or accidental, the behavior that immediately preceded the reinforcement may be increased even if it is not the desired behavior. Athletes often engage in personal rituals before positioning themselves for play because of an earlier fortuitous connection between that behavior and success. Such behaviors are *superstitious,* yet many ineffective habits and common superstitions have their origin in chance reinforcement. Some of these behaviors are culturally transmitted and reinforced. Now that research has confirmed the effects of various types of reinforcement, we can systematically apply effective schedules of reinforcement to shape desired behavior.

In addition to primary and secondary reinforcers, Skinner (1953) describes the effects of **generalized conditioned reinforcers** such as praise and affection, which are learned and have the power to reinforce a great number of different behaviors. Moreover, an individual can give them to him- or herself. As we grow older, we move from primary reinforcers to more generalized types. Initially, young children will respond to food or something that meets their basic needs. Later, they respond to an allowance. At the same time, they associate these reinforcers with the praise and affection that accompany them. Eventually, children will work primarily for the reinforcement of praise, which can be self-given.

Skinner (1972) distinguishes positive reinforcement, punishment, and negative reinforcement. **Positive reinforcement** is anything that serves to increase the frequency of a behavior; **punishment** is an undesirable consequence that follows a behavior and is designed to stop it; **negative reinforcement** refers to an unpleasant stimulus that can be stopped by certain behavior. A negative reinforcer strengthens any behavior that reduces or terminates it. Taking an aspirin is negatively reinforcing because it relieves a headache. It is the elimination of the aversive stimulus that is reinforcing.

Skinner (1953) observes that punishment is the most common technique

Positive reinforcement seems to be the most effective technique for initiating and maintaining desired behaviors.

of behavioral control in our society. Children are spanked if they misbehave and lawbreakers are fined or imprisoned. Punishment may stop or block a behavior but it does not necessarily eliminate it. The organism may seek other means of acquiring the same ends. Punishment creates fear but, if the fear is diminished, the behavior will recur. It can also lead to undesired side effects: anger, hatred, or helplessness.

Skinner (1953, 1971) suggests the use of methods other than those based on aversive stimuli to eliminate behaviors that are not desired. One may ignore the behavior until it undergoes extinction or one may permit satiation to occur. **Satiation** entails permitting the person to indulge in the behavior until he or she tires of it. A child may be allowed to turn a light switch on and off until he or she becomes bored. One may also change the environment that provokes the behavior. Fragile objects may be placed out of a young child's reach. Finally, one can promote behaviors that counteract and inhibit the undesirable behaviors through positive reinforcement.

Skinner emphasizes that positive reinforcement is most effective in initiating and maintaining desired behaviors. We need to study it further. All too often we do not recognize how we inadvertently give positive reinforcement to a behavior that is not desirable. The child who is seeking attention may be positively reinforced by a parental scolding, rather than negatively, because the scolding affords the child attention. By identifying our reinforcement patterns, we can strengthen those that are most effective and develop more efficient means of controlling behavior.

Psychotherapy and Behavioral Change

Skinner explains maladaptive or neurotic behavior in terms of environmental contingencies that sustain and maintain it. The neurotic or psychotic is one who has been conditioned by his or her environment to behave in inappropriate ways. If we wish to change an individual's behavior, we can restructure his or her environment in such a way that it will no longer sustain his or her maladaptive behavior and it will reinforce desirable behavior. Thus, in describing neurosis, Skinner does not find it necessary to refer to concepts like repression or conflict. These explanatory fictions are not necessary because maladaptive behavior can simply be reduced to the variables in the environment that reinforce and sustain it.

The role of therapy is to identify the behaviors that are maladaptive, remove them, and substitute more adaptive and appropriate behaviors through the process of operant conditioning. There is no need to review the individual's past or encourage reliving it. Therapy is not dependent on self-understanding or insight. Some insight may occur, but such self-understanding is not necessary for behavioral change. Therapy consists simply of restructuring the environment in such a way that undesired behaviors are eliminated and more desired behaviors are substituted.

The contrast between Freud and Skinner emerges clearly in their attitudes toward therapy. As we have seen, Freud's intent was primarily scholarly. He sought to increase an individual's self-understanding, and psychoanalysis is relatively uninterested in specific behavioral change. Skinner's interest, on the other hand, is totally pragmatic and curative. **Behavior modification** seeks to eliminate undesired behaviors by changing the environment within which they occur.

Skinner's approach to behavior modification has been notably successful in areas where traditional insight therapy has failed or is inappropriate. One of its more spectacular successes has been with mute individuals, who for obvious reasons are not amenable to traditional therapies, which are largely based on talking. Dr. O. I. Lovaas (1967) has used a systematic program of shaping to teach autistic and mute children to speak. First, he identifies something that is reinforcing to the child. Since food is generally reinforcing for children, it is commonly employed. Initially, Lovaas reinforces the child with a small piece of food every time he or she makes a sound. Gradually he shapes these sounds until they approximate words. Eventually, he reinforces the child only when he or she communicates in full sentences, and so forth. The reinforcement of food is coupled with praise and affection so that the type of reinforcement grows from primary and secondary reinforcers to generalized conditioned reinforcers that can be self-applied. These methods are also generalized to include training in other desired behaviors.

Since sustaining the newly learned behavior depends on maintaining a supportive environment, Lovaas includes parents and other significant figures in his program of behavior modification. Parents and other influential figures such as teachers are taught to apply systematically the same reinforcers to similar situations in the home or school. In this way the circle of the environment is widened to permit greater control.

The several techniques employed by Skinnerian therapists may be considered **directive** rather than **nondirective.** In psychoanalysis, the course of the therapy is determined primarily by the patient's free associations, which bring to light materials for interpretation and understanding. In that sense, the patient rather than the analyst directs the course of the therapy. With behavior modification techniques, the therapist constructs a specific situation and confronts the patient with specific stimuli that are designed to facilitate unlearning of the undesired response and substitution of more appropriate behaviors. In doing so, the therapist firmly directs the course of the treatment. The patient is given specific directions to follow and may even be given homework assignments to carry out between sessions.

Skinner's influence has also extended into the area of therapeutic communities. His methods have been employed in schools for the mentally retarded, mental institutions, and rehabilitation centers. In many of these institutions, a **token economy** has been established. The patient is reinforced for appropriate behaviors by being given tokens of some kind that may subsequently be exchanged for special privileges or things that the patient would like to have. Making one's bed, getting dressed, talking to other patients, and other desirable behaviors are reinforced by tokens that can be exchanged for candy, cigarettes, watching TV, and other amenities that would not normally be provided.

The influence of Skinner's programs may also be seen in the area of education. With Sidney Presley, Skinner developed the *teaching machine,* an electronic device whereby students may be taught without the need for an ever-present human instructor. Skinnerian principles also underlie numerous systems of individualized and programmed instruction. In such programs, the work is broken down into small units each of which must be mastered before a student is permitted to proceed to the following unit. The student is virtually being shaped as he or she masters the material. There is immediate reinforcement in the sense of feedback to the student on correct and incorrect answers. There are many who suggest the need for a more systematic application of Skinnerian learning principles in our schools.

Lastly, Skinner's concepts and principles have been applied systematically in industrial and business settings to encourage greater productivity. One executive estimates that his company saved two million dollars over a three-year period through a performance-improvement system based on accurate feedback and positive reinforcement (Feeney, 1972).

Social Utopias

Skinner's interest in the environment that shapes the individual led quite naturally to his interest in the design of an ideal environment or a utopian society. We have seen how, through behavior modification, Skinner was able to induce behaviors in animals that had never been seen before. Some of his techniques offer the possibility of training infrahuman species, such as the pigeon, to handle routine work that is currently being done by human beings. Suppose one could train a pigeon to spot defective parts on an assembly line? Properly trained and reinforced, the pigeon would not be as inclined to be distracted from work by boredom as is often the case with human beings who are assigned routine tasks. The pigeon might even prove more accurate. Skinner suggests that human behavior could also reach new heights and potentialities in appropriate optimal environments.

In order to facilitate the rearing of his second daughter, Skinner developed an *air crib*. The air crib was enclosed in glass and provided an optimal germ-free environment for the child during her sleeping hours. Temperature and humidity were kept at an optimal level, eliminating the need for clothing and blankets. Toys and interesting playthings were close at hand. The crib afforded the child greater freedom of movement and it relieved the mother of many of the tedious chores normally connected with the routine of child rearing, enabling her to concentrate on other activities and positive ways of relating to the child. Skinner's eldest daughter was sufficiently impressed with the air crib to raise her own child in one. Although the air crib has by no means acquired mass popularity, many parents have chosen to use one.

In 1948 Skinner wrote *Walden II,* a book that described his concept of a utopia. **Walden II** was the name of a behaviorally engineered society designed by a benevolent psychologist who employs a program of positive reinforcements. Because positive reinforcers rather than aversive means were used to shape behavior, residents sought those reinforcers and willingly behaved in socially responsible and productive ways.

In 1971 Skinner wrote *Beyond Freedom and Dignity* and again argued for the creation of a behaviorally engineered society, pointing out that most major problems today — war, overpopulation, unemployment, inflation, and so forth — are caused by human behavior. What we need is a behavior technology that will enable us to cope with them. Such a technology cannot be established, however, unless we give up several cherished "fictions," such as the notion that people are responsible for their own behavior and the idea that human beings are autonomous. For Skinner, human behavior is controlled by forces in the environment and the concept of free will is a superstition. We feel free when we are abundantly reinforced and have learned effective behaviors. The clue to our behaviors and emotional states lies within the environment rather than the individual.

In his utopian speculation, Skinner shifts gears from the scientist to the social philosopher. Presenting us with a form of social Darwinism, he suggests that "Survival is the only value according to which a culture is eventually to be judged" (1971). Further, his concepts are informed by the philosophical assumption that a human being is nothing more than an organism, a bundle of behavior, shaped by his or her environment. During evolution, the environment shaped the behavior that survives in our genes. After birth, environmental conditioning shapes each one of us in this life. We need more, not less, control, Skinner argues. To his critics, he points out that human beings are already controlling and being controlled. The processes of controlling should not be denied but rather studied and understood so that we can implement them effectively in developing the society that we want. We have the power to develop a behavioral technology. To ignore this is to run the risk not of no control but rather of continued ineffective or deleterious control.

Skinner has mellowed as he has gotten older. Recently he conceded that psychologists and other people simply do not possess the means or the motivation to implement his utopian schemes (1981). In the end, the very reasoning of behaviorism explains its lack of success. If, as behaviorism maintains, people do not initiate actions on their own but simply act in ways in which they have been conditioned, they cannot change on the basis of predictions. Since the future does not exist, it cannot affect contemporary behavior. Problems such as pollution, energy depletion, nuclear contamination, and other environmental issues have not been dealt with effectively because they have not yet happened in sufficient extremes to reinforce behavioral change. By then, however, it may be too late.

Skinner's Theory: Philosophy, Science, and Art

Skinner has provided a great deal of experimental data and research to support his ideas. More than any other contemporary theorist, he has stimulated research, undertaken to validate the concepts of behaviorism. His own work has been characterized by the intensive study of individual subjects, primarily drawn from infrahuman species, the careful control of laboratory conditions through automated apparatus, and an emphasis on variables easily modified by manipulating the environment.

Skinner's concepts clearly evolve from experimental laboratory investigations and he has shown tremendous respect for well-controlled data. His constructs have been empirically tested and have held up well under the scrutiny of the scientific method. His theory is elegant in its simplicity. It is also admirable in its ability to predict and control behavior, particularly in infrahuman species. Although he set out to avoid theorizing, he presents a theory of human behavior, if not a theory of personality, and even plays the role of a social philosopher.

But Skinner does not always recognize the kinds of evidence on which his various statements are based. He frequently presents his social philosophy as if it were an empirical science with all the appropriate validating evidence. For example, Skinner makes the observation that an individual may be controlled by the manipulation of his or her environment. This is an empirical statement that holds up under test. However, one cannot jump from that empirical observation to the conclusion that human beings are *nothing but* organisms controlled by their environment and claim that the conclusion is simply based on validating evidence. The conclusion entails a philosophical commitment as well. Only recently has Skinner acknowledged the philosophical character of a behaviorist view (1972).

Moreover, the concept of science Skinner emulates is tied to a nineteenth-century positivistic "philosophy." *Positivism* was an intellectual movement whose adherents claimed that philosophy is an imperfect mode of knowledge that should be superseded by the empirical sciences. Positivists narrowed the scientist's activity to an objective experimental methodology and failed to recognize that all scientific work is based on philosophical assumptions.

Skinner argues that concepts like *the self, ego,* or *freedom* are useless fictions in a science. However, Skinner himself goes beyond the development of a scientific theory. In designing his utopia he invokes ethical commitments. He suggests, for instance, that the value of a society lies in its ability to survive, that human beings should give up the conceits of freedom and dignity. These are ethical considerations, not empirical ones. As such, they need to be evaluated in terms of their adequacy as philosophy. Because Skinner does not recognize these philosophical considerations, he has been criticized for being shallow and reductionistic.

Radical learning and behavior theory instituted a shift from introspection to extrospection as the primary methodology of the psychologist. As we have seen, *introspection* refers to looking inside; it is the examination of one's thought processes and sensory experiences. *Extrospection* refers to looking out; it is the examination of what is outside the self. Prior to John Watson, psychology emphasized introspection. Psychoanalysis, for example, examines the individual's own thoughts, feelings, and wishes. Watson's emphasis on overt behavior turned the gaze of the psychologist outward, to the observable behavior of others. It is important to note that both introspection and extrospection refer to empirical data. However, the growing popularity of behaviorism was accompanied by a tendency to view introspection as somehow less scientific, even though it, too, is empirical. In his emphasis on extrospection Skinner unduly limits the psychologist's activity to the study of overt behaviors and a narrow experimental methodology.

Some personality theorists have criticized Skinner on the grounds that he has not really developed a theory of personality at all. They say that Skinner has no place for the person in his theory, that he talks only about the environment. Skinner would agree with this critique. He is not, strictly speaking, a personality theorist. Indeed, he argues that a theory of personality is not necessary. He suggests that most theories of personality falsely reassure us, deluding us into thinking that we can understand or explain our behavior. Skinner is not interested in understanding or explaining behavior, rather, he is interested in predicting what behaviors will occur under certain conditions and in manipulating conditions so that behavior can be controlled. He has devoted his attention to spelling out laws that govern behavior rather than to developing a theory of personality.

Nevertheless, Skinner's theory has been strongly influential in American psychology. At one time he had acquired a large number of followers who wanted to introduce and apply his techniques and practices throughout the everyday world. The potential for the effective use of behavior modification in schools, mental institutions, and penal rehabilitation centers, for instance, was seen as great. In time, however, the shortcomings of radical behaviorism have become more apparent and enthusiasm has waned.

Skinner's theory, as we have noted, works well in predicting and controlling behavior, particularly the behavior of infrahuman species. It also deals effectively with human behavior when that behavior occurs under situations of positive or negative reinforcement; in everyday terms we would say that it is effective in dealing with human situations that are surrounded by reward or punishment.

Skinner's theory is less successful, however, in accounting for other areas of human behavior. For example, although there can be no question that operant conditioning, reinforcement, and shaping play a large role in the child's acquisition of language, these concepts alone do not provide for a full explanation of how the child learns to speak (Chomsky, 1959). Skinner's theory cannot account for the child's creative use of language. He does not tell us how it is possible for the child to come up with a new sentence that he or she has never heard before. Nor do Skinner's concepts account for the meaningful errors that the child makes in learning to speak. When a child says, "I branged it home," chances are he or she never heard the verb "branged." The error shows us that the child understands the use of the suffix -ed in expressing the past tense without the assistance of formal lessons in grammar.

Skinner suggests that his theories may be used by individuals to develop techniques of self-control. Although Skinner refers to this possibility, his concepts

Figure 16.1 *One Critique of Skinner*
Some critics have suggested that Skinner's estimate of human behavior can be summed up by looking at the laboratory animal with which he conducted a great deal of his early research.

do not explain the ability of individuals to create self-management programs. Nor do his theories explain the fact that at times an individual cannot apply these programs effectively, even though he or she is motivated to change. Skinner would say that in such cases an individual may be using ineffective controls or may even be inadvertently reinforcing the very behaviors that he or she wishes to eliminate. But these arguments do not fully convince us that Skinner's stimulus-response theory can accommodate the issues that are involved in a person's ability or inability to develop and use the techniques of behavior modification.

Nor can Skinner's own behavior and theory be comprehended solely in stimulus-response terms. Skinner has asserted that all behavior is determined by the environment. If that statement is true, then it must logically follow that Skinner's own statements are determined by his environment. Thus, his behavior as a theorist would be equally open to change by manipulation of the environment.

Human behavior is much more diverse and flexible than Skinner's radical learning theory suggests. His theory seems to be able to account for the learned behaviors of lower animal species and for the learned habits and simple behaviors of human beings; however, it is less able to account for complex human behaviors like decision making, errors, and perversity. The view that human behavior is like a machine whose output depends on the input provided does not account for the creativity of many human behaviors. It is not surprising that the radical nature of Skinner's theory led to the development of an alternative approach to learning and behavior, which, while emphasizing situational factors, also reintroduces covert factors like cognition. Some of these theories will be discussed in Part 6.

Of all the theorists discussed in this book, Skinner and Freud have generated the most controversy and criticism. Both theories offend us because they attack our illusion that we are in full control of our behaviors. Freud thought the individual is motivated by forces of which he or she is unaware. Skinner thinks the individual is shaped by forces within his or her environment. Freud described three blows to human self-esteem: the *cosmological* blow resulting from Copernicus's discovery that the earth is not the center of the universe; the *biological* blow dealt by Darwin when he demonstrated that humans are not different from or superior to animals; and the *psychological* blow afforded by Freud himself when he asserted that the ego alone does not control the organism. Skinner delivers yet another blow to human self-esteem: there is no ego and we are completely determined by forces in the environment.

Both Freud and Skinner suggest that we, as human beings, are not in control of ourselves. Yet their responses to the discovery of our lack of self-control differ widely because of the very different philosophical assumptions that undergird their work. Freud, a pessimist, offers us hope of gaining a small margin of control over the unconscious forces of which we have been unaware through the painful process of self-understanding. Skinner, an optimist, believes that the answer lies in recognizing our lack of control, renouncing our ambitions of inner control, and committing ourselves to being more effectively controlled by a behaviorally designed technology.

❧ Summary

1. Skinner chooses to describe variables and forces in the environment that shape overt behavior rather than to develop a theory of personality because he believes that the term "personality" and concepts of internal structure are ultimately superfluous. Behavior is best understood in terms of responses to the environment.

2. **Operant conditioning** involves reinforcing and **shaping** spontaneous **responses.** It differs from *classical conditioning* in terms of the nature of the behavior (which is freely made rather than elicited by a stimulus) and the nature of the **reinforcement** (which follows rather than precedes the behavior).

3. Skinner distinguishes three different schedules of reinforcement — **continuous, interval,** and **ratio reinforcement** — and describes their effectiveness. A continuous schedule is more effective for initially developing a behavior but a **variable ratio schedule** is more effective for maintaining it.

Skinner also describes the effects of **generalized conditioned reinforcers** and distinguishes among **positive reinforcement, negative reinforcement, and punishment.**

4. **Behavior modification** therapy consists of restructuring the environment so that undesired behaviors are eliminated and more desired ones substituted. Skinner's approach has been successful in situations where traditional insight methods are inapplicable. His methods have also been used in therapeutic communities, education, and industry.

5. Skinner has advocated the development of a social utopia, a behaviorally engineered society that employs a program of positive reinforcers to shape behavior.

6. In his utopian speculations, Skinner's statements reflect philosophical assumptions as well as scientific generalizations by not allowing for any exceptions and by invoking values and ethical commitments.

7. Radical learning and behavior theory constituted a shift from introspection to extrospection as the primary methodology of the psychologist. In their emphasis on extrospection, radical behavior and learning theories have been seen as incomplete.

8. Skinner's theory clearly evolved from experimental laboratory investigations and emulates a strict scientific approach. In recent years, however, Skinner has acknowledged the philosophical assumptions which underlie his theory.

Suggestions for Further Reading

B. F. Skinner's most influential work is *The Behavior of Organisms* (Appleton-Century-Crofts, 1938), in which he formulates a theory of behavior in terms of the principles of conditioning. However, the lay person will probably be more interested in *About Behaviorism* (Random House, 1974), in which Skinner clarifies his position in a highly readable way. Also of interest are his utopian speculations in *Walden II* (Macmillan, 1948) and *Beyond Freedom and Dignity* (Knopf, 1971). Skinner is in the habit of writing down ideas as they occur. In twenty-five years he has filled over one hundred spiral-bound notebooks. A selection of these have been published in *Notebooks* (Prentice-Hall, 1982). Those who are interested in a more technical presentation of his work should turn to *Science and Human Behavior* (Macmillan, 1953); *Contingencies of Reinforcement: A Theoretical Analysis* (Appleton-Century-Crofts, 1969); and *Cumulative Record* (Appleton-Century-Crofts, 1961), a collection of his research papers and detailed analysis of his experiments.

Part
6

Contemporary Cognitive and Social Learning Theories

In recent years, interest in a cognitive and social behavior and learning approach has grown rapidly. These theories emerged out of the behavior and learning tradition but they seek to correct some of the shortcomings of radical behaviorism. Cognitive and social behavior and learning theories reflect the careful scientific procedures and methodology that characterized the behaviorist approach. At the same time, they have broadened many original learning theory concepts and integrated them with other current movements in psychology.

From the 1920s until about fifteen years ago, exploration of the human mind was out of fashion in American psychology. Mainstream behaviorists, such as Watson and Skinner, discouraged speculation about what went on within the mind on the grounds that what happens there cannot be seen or proven and is unnecessary for understanding human behavior. Today, the attitude is very different. Cognitive and social behavior and learning theories appreciate that we cannot understand an individual's behavior or personality without also asking what is going on in his or her mind. Moreover, they realize that the mind and its processes can be investigated scientifically. Although we cannot directly observe the processes of the mind, we can explore them by means of circumstantial evidence. Just as a physicist infers the properties of invisible subatomic particles by the tracks they leave in a cloud chamber, so psychologists can deduce the workings of the mind from the traces they leave.

Cognitive and social behavior and learning theorists have also moved from very simple laboratory situations to more complex ones and have increasingly used human rather than animal subjects. Laboratory conditions have been made more similar to the everyday life of people. Some of the contingencies under investigation are very complex, but laboratory procedures have become increasingly sophisticated in order to deal with these complexities.

17

Albert Bandura: A Sociobehavioristic Approach

Your Goals for This Chapter

1. Explain what Bandura means by *reciprocal determinism* and identify the three factors that enter into it.

2. Explain what is meant by *observational learning*.

3. Identify three factors that influence modeling.

4. Describe the four processes that enter into observational learning.

5. Discuss the role of reinforcement in observational learning and compare Bandura's concept of reinforcement with that of Skinner.

6. Discuss the controversies surrounding television and aggression.

7. Discuss the steps that Bandura suggests might be taken to change the practices of the television industry.

8. Describe Bandura's contributions to behavioral modification.

9. Evaluate Bandura's theory in terms of its function as philosophy, science, and art.

Albert Bandura believes that human behavior can be explained by a reciprocal determinism that involves behavioral, cognitive, and environmental factors. His theory originated within the behavior and learning tradition and reflects its emphasis on extrospection. Nevertheless, recognizing the shortcomings of radical behaviorism, Bandura believes that it is desirable to reintroduce internal variables, such as *self-efficacy,* a person's perception of his or her effectiveness. Once again the organism is a part of the stimulus-response chain. In reintroducing internal variables, however, Bandura has not sacrificed the behaviorist's commitment to experimental research and rigorous methodology. The result is a theory that seeks to correct some of the flaws of earlier behavior and learning theory and combine its insights with newer findings in the area of cognition and social psychology.

Biographical Background

A small town in Alberta, Canada, was the childhood home of Albert Bandura, who was born on December 4, 1925, to wheat farmers of Polish descent. He has written little of his early years. We know that he attended a high school where there were only twenty students and two teachers. The students had largely to educate themselves, yet almost all of them went on to professional careers.

Bandura received his B.A. from the University of British Columbia in Vancouver in 1949 and his M.A. and Ph.D. from the University of Iowa in 1951 and 1952. There was a strong Hullian emphasis at Iowa, yet Bandura felt that the psychology department was very forward looking. He spent a year as a clinical intern at the Wichita (Kansas) Guidance Center and then accepted a position at Stanford University, where he has been ever since. He became a full professor in 1964 and in 1974 was awarded an endowed chair.

Bandura has been an active scholar and writer, publishing several important books and a great many articles. His first research was in collaboration with Richard Walters (1918–1967), his first Ph.D. student at Stanford. Together they authored many of the early books and articles that laid the foundation for his theory.

Bandura has received many awards for his contributions to psychology and has been a consultant to several organizations. He was elected president of the American Psychological Association in 1973. At the present time, he teaches two courses at Stanford, an undergraduate course on the psychology of aggression and a seminar in personality change.

Albert Bandura

The Self-System and Reciprocal Determinism

Unlike Skinner, Bandura does not believe that human behavior is primarily regulated through elements in the environment. On the other hand, he does not agree with a psychoanalytic position that conceives of behavior as largely determined by inner forces of which we are unaware. According to Bandura (1978), human behavior is due to a **reciprocal determinism** that involves behavioral, cognitive, and environmental factors.

Processes relating to the self play a major role in Bandura's theory, but he does not conceive of the self as a psychic agent controlling behavior. Instead he uses the term **self-system** to refer to "cognitive structures that provide reference mechanisms," a "set of subfunctions for the perception, evaluation, and regulation of behavior" (1978). Thus the self in social learning theory is a group of cognitive processes and structures by which people relate to their environment and which help to shape their behavior.

Bandura criticizes Skinner for being too extreme in his primary emphasis on external factors. The Skinnerian explanation is incomplete and leads to a "truncated" (cut-off) view of human nature because it does not take into account internal processes that also guide behavior. On the other hand, Bandura criticizes psychoanalytic theories for using circular reasoning in attributing behavior to underlying unconscious forces. To say that hostile behavior is due to underlying aggressive impulses or domineering behavior to unconscious power motives is to give us a description rather than an explanation. Such reasoning does not tell us anything new above and beyond the fact that the behavior exists. Bandura does not question the existence of motivated behavior; he simply feels that in a science of behavior such constructs are not very helpful. They do not permit us to predict how a person will behave in a given situation. Nor do they account for the wide variation of behavior in different circumstances (1977).

In Bandura's concept of reciprocal determinism, although environmental stimuli influence our behavior, individual personal factors such as beliefs and expectations also influence how we behave. My selection of a tuna-fish sandwich for lunch is not simply determined by the menu and other environmental stimuli but also by my attitude toward tuna fish and my expectation as to how it will taste. Further, the outcomes of our behavior serve to change the environment. A rush on any particular item will cause a restaurant or a household to run out of it and perhaps subsequently to order an extra supply. Thus, behavior, cognitive, and environmental factors affect each other. All three factors operate as "interlocking determinants" of one another. If we were to diagram the process, each factor would have arrows pointing toward it and toward the other two (Figure 17.1) to show their reciprocal interaction.

Many psychologists have agreed that behavior arises from the interactions of a person and his or her environment rather than from either factor alone. However, earlier conceptualizations have either seen the person and situation as separate agents that combine to produce behavior or considered the behavior that they produce as a by-product that does not enter into the causal process. Bandura believes that his concept is significant because it emphasizes the reciprocal nature of the interaction among all three factors.

Although actions are regulated by their consequences, external stimuli affect behavior through intervening cognitive processes. While they are behaving, people are also thinking about what they are doing. Their thoughts influence how their behavior is affected by the environment. Cognitive processes determine which stimuli we will recognize, how we will perceive them, and how we will act upon them. Cognitive processes also permit us to use symbols and to engage in the type of thinking that enables us to anticipate different

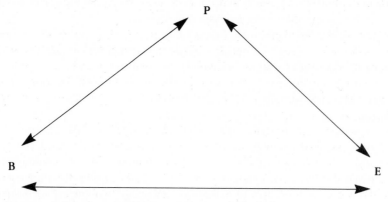

Figure 17.1 *A Diagram of Reciprocal Determinism*
In this diagram, B *signifies behavior,* P *the person, and* E *the environment.*

courses of action and their consequences. Because we act reflectively rather than automatically, we are able to change our immediate environment. In so doing, we arrange reinforcements for ourselves and influence our behavior.

Television viewing is a good example of the way in which the three factors may be interlocked.

> Personal preferences influence when and which programs, from among the available alternatives, individuals choose to watch on television. Although the potential televised environment is identical for all viewers, the actual televised environment that impinges on given individuals depends on what they select to watch. Through their viewing behavior, they partly shape the nature of the future televised environment. Because production costs and commercial requirements also determine what people are shown, the options provided in the televised environment partly shape the viewers' preferences. Here all three factors—viewer preferences, viewing behavior, and televised offerings—reciprocally affect each other. (1978)

The relative influence of the three interlocking factors varies in different individuals and in different situations. In a reciprocal interaction process, one and the same event can be a stimulus, a response, or an environmental reinforcer, depending on where in the sequence we begin our analysis. Thus, it is useless to try and search for an ultimate environmental cause of behavior. Moreover, chance encounters frequently play a role in shaping the course of a human life. In a chance encounter, each separate chain of events has its own causal determinants but their occurrence together arises fortuitously (1982). The science of psychology cannot predict the likelihood of chance encounters but it can clarify the factors that influence their impact (1982).

Learning through Observation

Bandura is best known for his emphasis on the process of learning through observation or by example. Bandura points out that most human behavior is learned by following a model rather than through the processes of classical and operant conditioning. By observing others, we develop an idea of how a certain behavior is done and that information serves as a guide for our own actions.

If learning were limited to those behaviors that are directly reinforced, it would be a very inefficient and potentially dangerous process. Most motorists do not learn to stop at red lights by being directly reinforced for their own behaviors. If direct reinforcement were required, the accident rate would be far higher than it is. Motorists learn through verbal instructions and observation of the behavior of other motorists. It would be a very dangerous world if we were unable to learn except in the presence of direct reinforcement. We have seen or heard of others who drive through red lights and we are aware of the possible consequences. These factors guide our actions as well as the direct consequences of our own behavior. Modeling reduces the time that is needed for learning and can help to eliminate the unhappy consequences of making an inappropriate response. By learning vicariously, we can avoid making costly mistakes.

Bandura suggests that most human behavior is learned through observation either intentionally or accidentally. Young children learn how to perform certain tasks by watching others do them and then repeating the task for themselves. This is how they learn to play with their toys, to perform household chores, and to develop other skills such as riding a bicycle. The young child learns to speak by hearing the speech of others and imitating it. If learning a language was totally dependent on classical or operant conditioning, it could not be accomplished so readily since the child would not be reinforced until after he or she had spontaneously uttered a sound that approximated a real word. In practice, parents repeat meaningful words over and over again to their children, who mimic those words as they learn to speak.

In many cases the behavior that is being learned must follow the same form as the modeled activity. Driving an automobile, for example, requires us to follow a prescribed method of action. However, learning through observation can also encompass new behaviors. Observers have been able to solve problems correctly even after the model has failed to solve the same problem. Thus observational learning exceeds mere imitation: the observer learns from the model's mistakes as well as from his or her successes. Learning through observation can account for innovative and creative behaviors. Bandura suggests that observers draw similar features from different responses and create rules of behavior that permit them to go beyond what they have seen

Young children learn how to perform certain tasks by watching others do them and then repeating the tasks for themselves.

or heard. Through this type of synthesis, they are able to develop new patterns of conduct that may be quite different from those they have actually observed (1974).

Experimental Analysis of the Influence of Modeling

Bandura's theory of **observational learning** is largely based on experimental analysis of the influence of modeling on behavior. In a typical modeling experiment, the subject observes another person performing a behavior or sequence of behaviors. Afterward the subject is observed to see whether or not his or her behavior imitates that of the model. The subject's behavior is compared with that of a control group who did not observe the model to see if there are any significant differences.

Bandura's most famous study involved the use of a Bobo doll, a large inflated plastic figure about four feet tall (Bandura and Walters, 1963). Young pre-school-aged children observed an adult playing with the doll in an aggressive fashion. The adult vigorously attacked the doll, hitting and kicking it while shouting things like "Sock him in the nose!" "Throw him in the air!" Other children did not see the adult playing with the doll aggressively. Later, when the experimental group was given the opportunity to play with the Bobo doll themselves, their behavior was similar to that of the model. It was twice as aggressive as that of the control group.

Through manipulating various independent variables in this kind of ex-periment, Bandura and his colleagues (1977) have demonstrated three factors that influence modeling: characteristics of the model, attributes of the observer, and reward consequences associated with the behavior.

First, the *characteristics of the model* affect imitation. We are readier to be influenced by someone who we believe is similar to ourselves than by someone who is different. Subjects are more likely to imitate a model who is similar to them in age and sex. They are also affected by the status, competence, and power of the model, and by the model's prestige. Modeling is also influenced by the type of behavior being performed by the model. Simpler behaviors are more readily imitated than complex ones and certain kinds of behavior seem more prone to imitation than others. Hostile and aggressive behaviors are readily copied, especially by young children.

A second factor that influences modeling is the *attributes of the observer*. People who are lacking in self-esteem or who are incompetent are especially prone to imitate a model. So too are highly dependent individuals and those who have been previously rewarded for conforming behavior. A highly motivated individual will also emulate a model in order to master a desired behavior. Recently, Bandura (1977) has added a developmental aspect to his theory. What a person learns and performs after observing a model changes with age. The child's attention to, understanding of, or memory of what the model did depends on his or her overall level of cognitive development.

Lastly, the *reward consequences associated with a behavior* influence the effectiveness of the modeling. Subjects are more likely to imitate a behavior if they believe that such actions will lead to positive results. The consequences do not have to be specific or immediate, although they sometimes are. Modeling behavior can be influenced by long-term rewarding and punishing effects. Bandura believes that this variable is stronger than the other ones. Thus an individual may refrain from or discontinue imitating a similar or high-status model if the reward consequences are not sufficient. Moreover, self-confident individuals will readily emulate others when the reward value is clear.

Processes of Observational Learning

Bandura believes that models influence learning primarily through their informative function. Learning through observation is not a simple matter of imitation. It is an active judgmental and constructive process. Through exposure, observers acquire symbolic representations of different ways of doing things and these ideas serve as guides for their own behavior. Observational learning is governed by four interrelated processes: attentional processes, retention processes, motor reproduction processes, and motivational processes (1977).

An individual will not learn much by observation unless he or she pays attention to the model's behavior. As any student or teacher knows, exposure alone does not guarantee learning. The subject must pay attention to the model and the perception of the modeled activity must be accurate enough to gain the information needed to reproduce it. The ability to make discriminations among observations and to process information are skills that must be present before observational learning can arise.

Every moment of every day we are bombarded by an enormous variety of sensory stimuli. We cannot attend to all of them at any given moment, so that most of them go unobserved. For example, consider your left big toe. When you focus on it you will probably become aware of a number of sensations that you were not noticing before, such as a tingling sensation in your toe itself or the pressure of your shoe upon it. Likewise, until they are drawn to your attention, you may not be aware of any other people in the vicinity or of what they are doing.

A number of variables influence *attentional processes*. Some of these have to do with the characteristics of the model, others with the nature of the activity, and still others with the subject. Some models are more noticeable than others and thus more readily copied. In a restaurant, a well-known television personality is quickly spotted. Charismatic models command considerable attention, whereas persons low in interpersonal attractiveness tend to be ignored.

Bandura points out that the people with whom one regularly associates limit and structure the kinds of behaviors that one will observe. These associations, whether by choice or circumstance, determine the types of activities that we will be exposed to over and over again. Those who live in an inner city where hostile gangs stalk the streets have more opportunity to witness aggressive behavior than those who are reared in a pacifist commune. Consequently, they are more likely to learn aggressive modes of response.

The nature of the modeled behaviors influences the amount of attention that is paid to them. Movement and rapid changes are compelling stimuli that command our attention. On the other hand, if an activity is too complex, it may overwhelm us and cause our minds to wander. Intrinsically rewarding activities, such as dancing, can hold the attention of people of all ages for long periods of time especially if they are performed by charismatic models. Bandura points out that these types of activities and models are often featured on television.

Television has greatly enlarged the range of models that are available to people today. Whereas our great-grandparents were pretty much limited to modeling sources within their own family and community, through the mass media we are exposed to a wide diversity of models that are particularly effective in capturing attention.

Finally, personal qualities, such as our own interests, needs, wants, and wishes, determine what we attend to. Our past experience and perceptual set influence our selection of observations and interpretation of them.

A second system involved in observational learning is the *retention processes.* In order to be influenced by the observation of a model, an individual must remember what the model did. When you observe someone's behavior without immediately performing the response, you have to represent it in some way in order to use it as a guide for action on later occasions. Our capacity for symbols permits us to keep feelings and experiences in long-term memory.

There are two basic forms of symbols or representational systems that facilitate observational learning: *imaginal* and *verbal.* If you are trying to remember "Big Mac" you can do it either by remembering the words *BIG MAC* or by developing a visual image of two all-beef patties, special sauce, lettuce and tomato on a sesame-seed bun. These symbols may then be present to us when the actual stimulus is not.

Visual imagery plays its largest role in observational learning during our early years when we lack verbal skills. For adults, most of the cognitive processes that govern behavior are verbal rather than visual. While watching a model, an individual might verbalize to him- or herself what the model is doing. The visual information is changed into a verbal code describing a series of events. Such codes are very useful because they can store a great deal of information in an abbreviated form. Skill in memory depends upon the ability to develop effective codes through careful verbal labeling of modeled stimuli. Precise labels and vivid images help us to retain behaviors longer, a fact that advertisers capitalize on in their campaigns.

The internal representations or symbols do not have to be exact copies of the external modeled stimuli. Subjects often draw out common features from a number of different modeling situations and then make a general higher-order code with a wider applicability than a single specified code would have. This activity underscores once again the fact that social learning theory conceives of observers as active agents. In observational learning we transform, classify, and organize modeled stimuli into memorable schemes that can be acted out creatively. Our behavior is different from that of a computer, which can only store and act upon material that has been programmed into it.

Rehearsal is another important aid to memory. Where a behavior cannot be immediately performed, it can be rehearsed mentally. Such rehearsal makes it more likely that the individual will be able to perform the activity effectively when the appropriate time comes. Rehearsal helps us retain the ability to perform an activity for a long period of time. The highest level of observational learning occurs when one first organizes and rehearses the modeled behavior symbolically and then acts it out.

The third mechanism of modeling involves *motor reproduction processes*. In order to imitate a model, an individual has to convert the symbolic representation of the behavior into the appropriate actions. The response has to be carried out in space and time in the same way that the original behavior was. Motor reproduction processes involve four substages: cognitive organization of the response, initiation of the response, monitoring of the response, and refinement of the response.

In order to perform an activity, we have to select and organize our response on the cognitive level. We decide what it is that we are going to do. Then we begin our response on the basis of an idea of how it should be carried out. Our ability to perform the response well will depend on whether or not we have the necessary skills to carry out the component behaviors involved in the activity. If we have the prerequisite skills, it is easy to learn new tasks. When these skills are missing, our reproduction of the activity will be deficient. We will have to develop the necessary skills before we can expect to perform the activity well. Highly complex tasks such as driving a car or playing a musical instrument often have to be broken down into several component parts. Each part is modeled and practiced separately and then they are all put together.

Whenever we first perform an activity, generally speaking, we are not very good at it and we make mistakes. We need to repeat the behavior and make corrections until we can accurately reproduce the model or our idea of it. Sometimes it is possible for us to act as our own critic, monitoring our own behavior and giving ourselves feedback. I know that I must improve my golf putt when the ball fails to go into the hole. If it goes past the hole, I might guess that I had swung too hard. On the other hand, it might be even more helpful if I had some feedback from others. Chances are I would improve my golf stroke more quickly if I was able to work with a pro who would demonstrate the correct positions and correct my errors.

The skills that we learn through observational learning are perfected slowly through a process of trial and error. We follow the behavior of a model and then seek to improve our approximations through adjustment and feedback.

The final system involved in observational learning is made up of *motivational processes*. Social learning theory makes a distinction between *acquisition*, what a person has learned and can do, and *performance*, what a person actually does. People do not enact everything that they learn. Most of us have the theoretical know-how to rob a store. We have seen robberies in real life or on television and we are acquainted with the behaviors that are entailed in committing that crime. However, this does not mean that we will go out and do it.

We are more likely to engage in a modeled behavior if it leads to consequences that we value and less likely to engage in it if the results are punitive. Here the traditional rules of reinforcement theory apply, although the reinforcement does not have to be direct. We also learn from observing the consequences of others' behavior. We have observed what happens to individuals who violate the law, and that prevents most of us from doing so. On the other hand, we tend to imitate those actions that seem to have been effective for others. Finally, we can engage in self-reinforcement. We generate evaluative responses toward our own behavior and this leads us to continue to engage in behaviors that we find self-satisfying and to reject those of which we disapprove or that feel uncomfortable.

No behavior occurs without sufficient incentive. Proper motivation not only brings about the actual performance of the behavior but it also influences the other processes involved in observational learning. When we are not motivated to learn something, we do not pay attention and so there is little we select to retain. Moreover, we are not willing to practice hard or to engage in the kind of trial-and-error activities necessary for the successful reproduction of a task. Thus, motivation emerges as a primary component in learning through observation.

Bandura notes that many imitative behaviors occur so rapidly that it is easy to overlook the processes underlying observational learning. However, it is important to postulate them in order to understand the phenomenon and to predict the circumstances under which learning will occur. In early development, children's modeling consists largely of instantaneous imitation. With age, children develop symbol and motor skills that enable them to follow more complex behaviors. Positing these processes helps us to specify the different variables that are involved in observational learning, develop hypotheses concerning them, and find ways of testing these hypotheses experimentally. In short, they enable us to make more accurate predictions. These constructs also help us to understand those instances in which an individual does not appear to learn from observation. Failure to reproduce a modeled behavior arises from insufficient attention, inadequate symbolization or retention, lack of physical capacities, skill, or practice, inadequate motivation, or any combination of these.

Reinforcement in Observational Learning

Whereas Skinner's studies had suggested that reinforcement is a necessary condition for the acquisition, maintenance, and changing of behavior, Bandura suggests that almost any behavior can be learned by an individual without the direct experience of reinforcement. We do not have to be reinforced to pay attention to vivid images or loud sounds: the impact of the stimulus itself commands our attention. Nor do we have to be directly rewarded in order to learn something. Driving home from work each day, I pass a gas station along the route. One day, when I am out of gas, I drive directly to the station, demonstrating that I had learned where it was even though I was not directly reinforced for doing so. Observational learning is often seen to occur where neither the model nor the observer is directly reinforced and there is a delay between the original behavior being modeled and the later response.

Bandura believes that observational learning occurs through symbolic processes *while* one is being exposed to the modeled activity and *before* any response has been made. Therefore, it does not depend on external reinforcement. Where such reinforcement plays a role in observational learning, it acts as a facilitator rather than a necessary condition. Its role precedes rather than follows a response. It serves an informative and incentive function. The individual's anticipation of a reward or punishment influences how he or she behaves.

Social learning theory considers a broad range of reinforcements including extrinsic, intrinsic, vicarious, and self-generated consequences.

Extrinsic reinforcement is external. Its relationship to the behavior is arbitrary or socially arranged rather than the natural outcome of the behavior. Being spanked for touching a hot stove is an extrinsic reinforcement. Being burnt is not. External reinforcement is clearly effective in creating behavioral change and has an important role to play in early development. Many of the activities we need to learn are difficult and tedious to perform initially. They do not become rewarding until we have become proficient in them. A young child stumbles repeatedly over letters and words while trying to read. If we did not receive positive encouragements when we were in the early stages of learning such behaviors, we would quickly become discouraged and stop learning them. Children's efforts need to be supported until they develop the competence that will make their behaviors self-rewarding.

Many studies have been conducted to determine the effects of extrinsic reinforcement on intrinsic motivation. Depending on the activities involved and the way in which rewards are used, extrinsic incentives can increase interest in activities, reduce interest, or have no effect. It is what people make of incentives rather than the incentives themselves that determines how extrinsic rewards affect motivation. Bandura recommends that incentives be used to promote competencies and hold interests. In the case of activities that are personally inconvenient or uninteresting but socially important, continuing rewards and support for doing them need to be provided.

Intrinsic reinforcement comes in three different forms. Some intrinsic reinforcement arises from without but is naturally related to the behavior by its sensory effects. Being burnt while touching a hot stove is an example of this. Other behaviors produce a natural physiological effect, for example, relaxation exercises relieve muscle fatigue. In other instances it is not the behavior itself or the feedback that is rewarding, but how we feel about it. Playing a difficult piece of music well on an instrument leads to a feeling of accomplishment. The self-satisfaction sustains the practice of the behavior.

Vicarious reinforcement occurs when we learn appropriate behavior from the successes and mistakes of others. In everyday life, we frequently watch other people in action and see what happens to them. Vicarious reinforcement can take the form of either a reward or a punishment. A child who sees a sibling being spanked for a misdemeanor quickly learns not to do the same thing.

Vicarious reinforcements alter our thoughts, feelings, and actions in different ways. First, they have an informative function, telling us what happens to others when they behave in a certain way. Second, they have a motivational function by arousing expectations in us that we will receive similar benefits or punishments for comparable actions. Third, they have an emotional learning function. The models usually express an emotional reaction while they are being punished or rewarded and these responses in turn arouse emotions in us. Fourth, vicarious reinforcements have a valuation function, affecting how we evaluate different activities and their consequences. They help us to determine whether we like or dislike various behaviors. Finally, vicarious reinforcements have an influential function. We are influenced by the way in which the models ultimately respond to the treatment they receive.

Self-reinforcement refers to the fact that people have self-reactive capacities that permit them to control their own thoughts, feelings, and actions. People do not behave like weathervanes that shift in different directions according to the external pressures that are placed upon them. Instead, people regulate their own behavior by setting standards of conduct for themselves and responding to their own actions in self-rewarding or self-punishing ways.

Bandura gives the act of writing as a common example of a behavior that is self-regulated. As I write, I do not need someone standing over me reinforcing each word and phrase. Instead, I set goals for myself and work toward them, revising my manuscript until I am satisfied with what I have written. Because of their self-reactive capacities, human beings are not completely dependent upon external supports for their behavior.

Self-reinforcement increases performance primarily through its motivational function. By creating inducements for themselves, individuals motivate themselves to live up to certain standards and goals. The amount of motivation created will vary according to the nature of the incentive and the performance standard of the individual. Individuals set different goals for themselves and react to their behaviors in different ways. One runner might be satisfied by completing a mile in five minutes; another would want to finish it in less time. The standards that govern self-reinforcing responses are established by teaching or by example. High standards are frequently emulated because they are actively cultivated through social rewards.

After individuals learn to set standards for themselves, they can influence their behaviors through self-produced consequences. They can begin to reward and punish themselves in various ways. Bandura believes that most of our behavior as adults is regulated by the continuing process of self-reinforcement.

Television and Aggression

We have seen how Bandura's investigations, which were performed under carefully controlled laboratory conditions, showed that both children and adults can develop complex patterns of behavior, emotional responses, and attitudes through the exposure to live or filmed models. Some of Bandura's experiments were specifically designed to investigate the influence of television viewing on the development of aggressive responses. In many different variations on his classic Bobo doll studies, Bandura has studied the impact of a live model as opposed to a filmed model and a cartoon model. The aggressive film model was just as effective in teaching aggressive forms of behavior as the live model. The cartoon character was somewhat less influential but nevertheless successful. In each study, children who observed an aggressive model (live, film, or cartoon) performed more aggressive responses than did children who observed a nonaggressive model or no model at all (1963).

Bandura has concluded that frequent exposure to aggression and violence on television encourages children to behave aggressively and he has been very concerned about the aggressive models that our culture provides. By the age of sixteen, the average child in the United States has spent more time in front of the television set than in school (Liebert, Neale, and Davidson, 1973). The amount of aggressive content in television shows rose continually from 1954 to 1969 and showed no reduction through 1972 (Gerbner and Gross, 1976). In the last decade the amount of violence may be decreasing (Nadar and Johnson, 1979). If that is the case, some of the credit must go to Bandura for his vigorous campaign against violence on television.

Bandura's demonstrations that the observation of live or filmed aggression leads to the development of aggressive behaviors led to a considerable amount of attention being focused on the possible relationship between violence in society and violence on television. It was suggested that several real-life instances of aggression had actually been triggered by similar episodes on television. An increase of bomb threats to airlines followed an NBC broadcast of the film *The Doomsday Flight,* in which a bomb was placed on a plane. A bizarre form of murder depicted on television was followed by a similar murder in real life. Concern over behaviors such as these led Congress to direct a number of studies throughout the 1960s and 1970s to see whether or not there is any causal relationship between televised violence and aggression in everyday life.

The results have been mixed. Most researchers believe that there is a causal relationship between observing violence on television and aggressive behavior. In laboratory studies (e.g., Liebert and Schwartzberg, 1977) children or adults have been exposed to either violent or nonviolent television programs and films and then given an opportunity to aggress against another person. Such investigations have found that the subjects exposed to violence directed stronger aggression against the victims than the subjects exposed to nonviolence. Reviews of experimental studies (e.g., Liebert, Neale, and Davidson, 1973; Berkowitz and Powers, 1979) conclude that viewing violence makes the observer more likely to be aggressive. Field research in which different groups of subjects are exposed to steady diets of violence or nonviolence in films or television and then are observed in natural settings also suggests that subjects exposed to highly aggressive films show an increase in some forms of aggression (Parke, 1977).

On the other hand, other studies suggest that exposure to aggressive behavior on television may actually reduce aggressive behavior or help to control it (Feshbach, 1959; Feshbach and Singer, 1971). A child who is stimulated to engage in aggressive fantasies may show a marked decline in aggressive behavior (Singer, 1973). Some have thought that this may be due to a *cathartic effect* in which individuals vicariously "blow off steam" while observing or fantasizing violent acts. However, the cathartic hypothesis itself has never really been investigated experimentally (Pervin, 1978).

A third group of researchers have had to conclude that the evidence is inconclusive. They have not been able to discern a distinct causal pattern between viewing different types of television programs and subsequent behavior. After one such study, Milgram and Shotland (1973) wrote, "... if television is on trial, the judgment of this investigation must be the Scottish verdict: Not proven."

In 1972, the Surgeon General's report on the behavioral effects of television was tentative, concluding that although there was some evidence linking television viewing to short-term aggression, it was unclear whether television viewing had any long-term consequences. In 1982, an update prepared by the National Institute of Mental Health was more definitive: "The consensus among most of the research community is that violence on television does lead to aggressive behavior by children and teen-agers who watch the programs."

The report described three other theories to account for the purported violence link in addition to observational learning. The theory of *arousal processes* holds that physiological arousal results from witnessing violent episodes on television. The theory of *justification processes* suggests that people who are already aggressive find justification for their actions by watching characters on television. The theory of *attitude change* suggests that people who watch a great deal of television are more suspicious and distrustful and tend to think there is more violence in the world than do others.

It is clear that a relationship exists between viewing television violence and aggressive behavior. However, scientific evidence has not yet established that the relationship is a direct causal one. The report by the National Institute of Mental Health indicates that television violence "is as strongly correlated with aggressive behavior as any other behavioral variable that has been measured." Under the appropriate conditions, violence on television has been demonstrated to have a harmful effect on viewers, but the question is a very complicated one. Other factors also play a role in fostering aggressive behaviors: influences in the home and society at large, individual dispositions, situational factors, etc. Moreover, violence as fare for children and adults is hardly unique to television and contemporary culture. Consider the long history of violence in sports and entertainment. Ancient myths and classic fairy tales are replete with aggression. Their effects are in dispute. Do they predispose their listeners to violence or might they help them deal with their aggressive impulses more effectively? (See Bettelheim, 1977.) In any event, as Bandura has pointed out, "The evidence indicates that, in general, exposure to aggression tends to increase rather than reduce aggression, but since aggression is controlled by so many different factors, predictions about the effects of modeling must include all these different determinants" (as cited in Evans, 1976).

Nevertheless, many social scientists find the extensive depiction of violent episodes on television personally repugnant and support a reduction in such programming (Pervin, 1978). Bandura (1973) has suggested four steps that might be taken to change the current practices of the television industry. First, we could appeal to governmental agencies to control the commercial marketing of violence. This is a popular route but one that is minimally effective because of political pressures and constitutional guarantees of free speech. Second, we could rely on the industry's system of self-regulation. This method is not very successful either because profits dictate content and violent shows have proven to be extremely popular among viewers and sponsors. Third, we could create a public violence-monitoring service that would periodically conduct systematic analyses of what was available on television. The service should be funded privately to avoid government and industry control. The violence ratings could be publicized through TV guides, PTA publications, and even televised reports. Bandura believes that this approach might work because sponsors who are sensitive about their public image might not want to be continually associated with fostering violent programs on television and might urge their producers to develop engrossing shows without unnecessary violence. Finally, and most constructively, we could encourage and reward desirable practices in the television industry. Programs such as "Sesame Street" demonstrate that a show can be instructive and nonviolent yet also be entertaining and attract a large audience. In short, "a viable public broadcasting system, free of commercial pressures, is perhaps the best means of improving and diversifying television offerings" (1973). Bandura recognizes that these last two steps will not eliminate the problem but they may help us begin to deal with it more constructively.

Violence and Television

It might be of interest to you to determine exactly how much violence you witness on television. For a period of one week carefully monitor your television viewing and record how many violent episodes occur in each show that you watch. For purposes of this activity, a violent episode can be defined as any form of behavior aimed at harming another living creature who wishes to avoid such treatment. Assaults on inanimate objects may be considered as emotional outbursts rather than aggressive acts unless the assault harms other people in an indirect fashion (such as destruction of another's property).

After each show, you might also wish to record your mood and desire to express yourself aggressively on a scale of 1 (not at all) to 10 (a great deal). At the end of the week's survey, you could note whether there was any correlation between your intensity of mood and the number of violent episodes watched.

Psychotherapy and Behavior Modification

Since observation is central in the learning of behaviors, it also has a useful place in modifying undesirable behaviors. Bandura has added to the techniques of behavior modification the systematic use of *modeling* as an aid in changing behaviors. Phobias (irrational fears) and other emotional reactions have been effectively altered by having the patient watch a model respond to the same situation in more appropriate ways.

Modeling has been used to reduce fears in children and adults, to teach domineering and hyperaggressive children to be more cooperative, to teach language skills to autistic children, to increase communication facility in asocial psychiatric patients, to lessen anxiety and improve performance in college students, and to facilitate many other behavior changes. In each case, a model or models illustrate or explain an appropriate way of handling a situation and the patient is encouraged to emulate the model. Thus, in order to eliminate a strong animal phobia, a subject might watch filmed and live models progressively interact with the animal in question and then be encouraged to engage in increasingly intimate interactions with the animal along with the model. Results have shown that modeling procedures are clearly instrumental in reducing and sustaining a reduction in fears and in making other behavioral changes.

Bandura (1977) points out that people who behave in abnormal ways generally have a poor sense of **self-efficacy.** They do not believe that they can successfully perform the behaviors that will enable them to cope with everyday life. Their lowered expectations lead them to avoid situations that are threatening and in which they do not believe they could perform well. Where situations cannot be avoided, they only try a little and give up quickly. As a result, they do not engage in activities that might demonstrate their abilities and serve to change their sense of self-efficacy.

Bandura's therapeutic strategies are designed to help patients improve their perception of their own effectiveness. He recommends that therapists use a variety of techniques in order to enhance their patients' self-confidence. Thus, in treating a group of *agoraphobics* (people who are afraid of public places), Bandura used a number of different procedures. Agoraphobia is a particularly disabling disorder, leading many of its victims to become virtual prisoners in their own homes. Agoraphobics cannot go to department stores or supermarkets because they are too threatened by the crowded aisles and checkout lines. They avoid theaters or restaurants or any other places where large numbers of people might congregate. They cannot travel on public forms of transportation and some of them even find it difficult to ride in a car with other people. Initially, Bandura met with the agoraphobics in small groups where he or co-therapists helped them to identify and rank those situations that aroused fear in them. He also taught them how to use relaxation techniques and how to substitute positive thoughts for self-debilitating ones. Then, through graduated field experiences, he encouraged them to engage in successful interactions with their feared objects and settings. Appropriate responses and behaviors were modeled by therapists and ex-agoraphobics. Exposure to feared situations was taken gradually, one step at a time, in order not to overwhelm or discourage the client. Through successful experiences, the subjects were able to improve their sense of self-efficacy and to increase the length of time they spent in intimidating situations. Gradually, the field therapists lessened their guided participation and support. Thus, through a variety of techniques, Bandura and his associates were able to increase self-efficacy and modify behaviors (1980).

Bandura has been particularly concerned with the effectiveness of therapeutic procedures. He reminds us that "because there is no evidence that psychotherapy kills or maims people, it is easy to adopt a casual approach of applying methods before they have been adequately assessed" (as quoted in Evans, 1976). He believes that we should base our therapeutic procedures on a sound understanding of the basic mechanisms by which change occurs and that we should not apply those procedures on a clinical level until we have clear evidence of their effects.

In those cases where behavior modification has stressed a change in the environment, Bandura points out that it usually has had only a short-term effect. As long as the person is under the control of the therapist or in a carefully monitored environment, the behavior is controlled; once that external control is gone, the behavior regresses. Reciprocal determinism assumes that behavior is controlled by both the person and the environment. It is possible, therefore, to indicate the conditions under which behavior will generalize and hold up over time and the conditions under which it will not. One condition under which change is maintained is when the new behavior has functional value for the individual. Where treatment is aimed at creating functional skills, these usually persist because they are important to the individual. A second maintenance condition arises when there are strong social and environmental supports for the behavior even though it may not have much functional value for the individual. Here, however, continued support is required for the adaptive behavior to persist. A third maintenance condition occurs when an individual's own self-evaluation becomes an important reinforcer.

Many inappropriate behavior patterns are immediately rewarding but have long-range negative effects. Examples are overeating, smoking, alcohol and substance abuse. In such cases, the task of the therapist is to help the individual acquire some capacity to control his or her own behavior. There are several different elements involved in *self-control,* but one that Bandura has explored carefully is delay of gratification. *Delay of gratification* involves the self-imposed postponement of an immediate reward in favor of a more significant reward in the future. The student who decides not to cut class may forego the fun in the coffee shop over the next hour but stands a greater chance of getting a good grade in the course. Bandura's studies have shown that modeling can influence the ability to delay gratification (Bandura and Mischel, 1965). In our achievement-oriented society, the ability to delay gratification is a desired, if not necessary, skill. Bandura believes that most individuals who are able to delay gratification were reared in homes where parents modeled the delay of reward and emphasized its importance. However, adults can also be taught to delay gratification. Bandura believes that research on self-control is our most promising approach to the management of detrimental behavior (Evans, 1976).

Exploration ///////

Developing Self-Control

Techniques informed by social learning theory can be used by the individual to develop ways of changing his or her own behavior. By carefully observing one's behavior and the factors that lead to it, one can begin to see how one can influence an undesired activity and change it. The environment can often be varied so that either the stimuli that precede the activity or the consequences

(continued)

that follow it are changed. Through a strategy of behavioral programming, a person can gradually eliminate inappropriate behaviors and substitute more desirable ones.

The student who has difficulty studying might set up a schedule of systematic rewards for him- or herself after he or she has studied for a predetermined period of time. He or she can develop positive reinforcers that may be enjoyed after passing a test with a certain grade. An overweight person may deliberately avoid purchasing foods that tempt him or her and make them unavailable in the immediate environment, then purchase a new outfit in a smaller size and work toward the day when it can be worn. An individual who wants to stop smoking can avoid lighting up a cigarette in situations that automatically seem to call for one. He or she could wait fifteen minutes after each meal before smoking. An individual could switch to a less enjoyable brand or limit the number of cigarettes that he or she carries around. Several current organizations, such as Smoke-enders and Weight-watchers, use techniques informed by learning theory to assist their members.

In developing a program of self-control, first, decide on a particular behavior pattern that you would like to modify. Carefully monitor and observe that behavior so that you can determine the conditions under which it is likely to occur. Your observation should be very specific. You need to count, chart, and evaluate each instance. It is helpful to keep a behavioral diary or chart. Next, make a list of graduated objectives that would shape you in developing a more appropriate behavior. Do not be overambitious. Select only one problem area and break it down into small, manageable steps. Consider the techniques that would help you achieve your objectives. Are there any factors in your environment that you could change in order to facilitate the development of more appropriate behaviors? A student who has difficulty studying might consider the time and place that he or she normally studies. Is it an area and time that is free from distractions and interruptions? Perhaps you would study more effectively in the library. Leaving the phone off the hook during study hours can eliminate intruding phone calls. Are there any models whose behavior you could emulate? Finally, you should develop a systematic schedule of reinforcements for appropriate behaviors that lead toward your objectives. Make sure that the reward is something that you value and are willing to work for. And then be sure that you employ it as a means of reinforcement.

Bandura has responded sharply to charges that behavior modification entails manipulation of human beings and denial of their freedom. He points out that procedures used to create a behavior pattern that is convenient to the reinforcer but of little value to the subject usually do not produce lasting results. It is unlikely that one will create permanent change in an unwilling subject. Bandura does not see this as a regrettable state of affairs because otherwise it would be too easy to develop procedures that would enslave people (Evans, 1976). A client comes to a therapist with a request for help in changing his or her behavior. The relationship is not that of a controller (however benevolent) and an unwitting subject: it is a contractual relationship between two consenting individuals. Behavior modification increases rather than limits an individual's freedoms. The individual with a strong fear is not really free but crippled by his or her behavioral responses.

Any behavioral technology can be used for constructive or destructive purposes. Bandura points out that many of our current social conditions have dehumanizing effects and separate individuals from one another. Given adequate justification, almost anyone may be willing to steal, kill, or perform an otherwise reprehensible act without having to undergo a personality transformation. It is easy in our society to provoke military and political violence because people are estranged from one another. We tend to use examples from military and political violence but similar mechanisms arise in everyday life where people are caught in activities or jobs that have dehumanizing effects. Bandura has conducted research in an effort to show that increased humanization would lead to less depersonalization, aggression, and violence. Experiments show, for example, that it is difficult to aggress against someone who is real to you as a person without evoking self-criticism for those behaviors. Thus, it might be useful if prisoners could talk with the victims of their crimes or if countries that differ would encourage intimate interchanges among their people. The implications of Bandura's findings for social planning and change are of no little importance and could have far-ranging constructive application.

Bandura's Theory: Philosophy, Science, and Art

Heir to the behavior and learning tradition in American psychology, Bandura's theory is rapidly becoming one of the most popular approaches to the study of personality. It is particularly appealing to academic psychologists because it lies within the mainstream of American psychology. It strongly emphasizes experimental research and clearly emulates a scientific model.

Bandura's reintroduction of internal variables, his emphasis on reciprocal determinism, and his investigation of human subjects allow his theory to deal with complex social responses more adequately than radical behavior and learning theories. B. F. Skinner's learning theory can account for only the learned behavior of animals and very simple learned habits and behaviors of human beings; it does not explain complex human behaviors like decision making and creativity well. Bandura's account clearly includes those kinds of complex activities, permitting a wide range of human behaviors to be subject to scientific analysis. Bandura's work has helped to overcome the earlier behaviorist view of human nature as a machine whose output depends upon the input provided. Indeed, Bandura's theory underscores the vast differences between a human being and a computer.

Bandura's theory is an excellent example of a scientific approach to personality theorizing. It is clearly grounded in empirical research and amenable to precise laboratory methods of investigation. It has stimulated research in other areas. It economically states major constructs in relatively simple terms. And it is compatible with our existing concept of the world.

Bandura's work has been criticized, however, for its emphasis on overt behaviors, in spite of his reintroduction of covert factors, and for its excessive bias against psychoanalysis, which leads him to ignore distinctly human problems such as conflict and unconscious motivation. As we have seen, learning and behavior theories tend to limit the kinds of phenomena psychologists can study and the ways in which they can investigate the phenomena. Their preoccupation with objective methodology and overt behaviors may unnecessarily constrain psychological investigation and may prevent a more holistic understanding of human nature; their scientific model may itself be unduly limited.

We have also seen that learning and behavior theorists have sometimes failed to appreciate that scientific work is based on philosophical assumptions. Skinner, for example, for many years did not acknowledge the philosophical commitments that inform his work. Although Bandura does not explicitly discuss his philosophical assumptions, with the exception of reciprocal determinism, he is more sophisticated than Skinner in his recognition that scientific efforts rest on philosophical assumptions. He also avoids elevating his empirical conclusions into philosophical ones.

In spite of their desire to limit their activities to empirical science, learning and behavior theorists invariably raise philosophical issues and ethical questions. This is particularly evident in their efforts to apply their theories toward the improvement of human behavior and society. Bandura has developed significant new forms of psychotherapy, like modeling. He has spoken candidly about the dangers of aggressive models. Other findings from observational learning theory have been taken from the laboratory and applied to problems in the everyday world, clearly demonstrating the practicality of Bandura's approach but implying an underlying philosophy as well.

Bandura has helped to revitalize the learning and behavior approach by infusing it with a cognitive dimension and by acknowledging some of its philosophical underpinnings. The scientific emphasis makes his approach an extremely popular one. His influence will undoubtedly continue to be substantial.

✿ Summary

1. According to Albert Bandura, human behavior is due to a **reciprocal determinism** that involves behavioral, cognitive, and environmental factors. Their relative influence varies in different individuals and in different situations.

2. Bandura believes that most human behavior is learned through the process of **observational learning,** by following a model.

3. Three factors influence modeling: *characteristics of the model, attributes of the observer,* and *reward consequences associated with the behavior.*

4. Bandura has described four processes that enter into observational learning: *attentional processes, retention processes, motor reproduction processes,* and *motivational processes.*

5. *Extrinsic, intrinsic,* and *vicarious reinforcement* and *self-reinforcement* all play a role in observational learning. Unlike Skinner, Bandura does not believe that direct reinforcement is necessary for learning to occur.

6. Bandura believes that frequent exposure to aggression and violence on television encourages children to behave aggressively. Research on the question has been mixed.

7. Bandura has suggested four specific steps that might be taken to change current practices of the television industry.

8. Bandura has added the systematic use of *modeling* as a therapeutic technique of behavior modification and developed strategies designed to help people improve their sense of **self-efficacy.** He has also conducted research in the area of self-control.

9. Bandura's theory clearly emulates a scientific model.

Suggestions for Further Reading

Albert Bandura's writings are quite difficult and highly technical. The most comprehensive statement of his position is *Social Learning Theory* (Prentice-Hall, 1977). His concept of personality also emerged in two articles written for the *American Psychologist:* "Behavior Theory and the Models of Man" (1974, *29,* 859–869) and "The Self System in Reciprocal Determinism" (1978, *33,* 344–358). Also significant is *Aggression: A Social Learning Analysis* (Prentice-Hall, 1973).

18

Julian Rotter: A Cognitive Social Learning Theory

Your Goals for This Chapter

1. Identify the two major trends in personality research that Rotter's theory integrates.

2. Describe the four variables that Rotter includes in his formula for predicting behavior.

3. Discuss Rotter's concepts of *need* and *minimum goal level.*

4. Describe the *I-E Scale,* discuss the construct it measures, and the findings to which it has led.

5. Discuss applications of cognitive social learning theory in the area of psychotherapy.

6. Evaluate Rotter's theory in terms of its function as philosophy, science, and art.

*J*ulian Rotter's **social learning theory** of personality represents a significant effort to integrate two major trends in personality research: learning theory and cognitive theory. In many respects, Rotter's theory is a classical learning approach based on Thorndike's law of effect, which indicated that behaviors accompanied by satisfaction tend to happen again whereas behaviors attended by frustration tend to decrease. Rotter emphasizes the importance of external reinforcement and asserts that most of our behavior is learned. However, he also stresses the fact that it is the subjective meaning and interpretation of the environment that actually regulates our lives. The effectiveness of reinforcement and the decision as to what we will learn depend on internal cognitive factors.

Biographical Background

Julian Rotter was born in Brooklyn, New York, in 1916. He has not yet written about his early life or indicated how it may have influenced his theory. He received the B.A. degree from Brooklyn College in 1937, the M.A. from the University of Iowa in 1938, and the Ph.D. in psychology from Indiana University in 1941. During his college and graduate years, he was influenced by the work of Alfred Adler and Kurt Lewin. From Adler's theory, he came to appreciate the unity of personality and the goal-directedness of behavior. From Kurt Lewin's field theory (see in Cartwright, 1948), he came to appreciate the interrelatedness of behavior and the fact that many factors are responsible for any single behavior. The influence of these figures is apparent in his writings, as well as that of learning theorists such as Thorndike and Hull.

During World War II, Rotter served as a psychologist and personnel consultant to the U.S. Army. Following the war, he took a position at Ohio State University, where George Kelly was the director of the clinical psychology program. At Ohio State, he developed his social learning theory of personality and first described it in a book entitled *Social Learning and Clinical Psychology* (1954). He also conducted a great deal of research based on his theory with the aid of graduate students. Some of these students have made significant contributions to social learning theory in their own right.

Rotter went to the University of Connecticut in 1963, where he is full professor in the department of psychology. He is also director of the Clinical Psychology Training Program and a diplomate in clinical psychology of the American Board of Examiners in Professional Psychology. In 1976–1977, he was president of the Eastern Psychological Association. Rotter's view has come to influence significantly thinking about personality in contemporary psychology.

Julian Rotter

Basic Concepts

There are four major concepts in Rotter's cognitive social learning approach: behavior potential, expectancy construct, reinforcement value, and the psychological situation (Rotter and Hochreich, 1975). These four variables can be measured and related in a specific formula that enables us to predict a person's behavior in any given situation.

Behavior Potential

The **behavior potential** refers to the likelihood that a particular behavior will occur in a given situation. Rotter uses the term **behavior** broadly to refer to a wide class of responses that include overt movements, verbal expressions, and cognitive and emotional reactions. In any given situation, an individual could react in a number of different ways. For example, faced with a competitive examination, a student might become nervous, engage in hard study, consider alternative answers, cheat, feign or actually become ill, and so on. Each of these responses may be seen to have a given potential for any individual in that type of situation. The behavior potential is specific both for the particular behavior and for the related reinforcement. Thus, we must know what goal the behavior is related to before we can tell how likely it is to occur.

Covert, as well as overt, behaviors can be observed and measured and their likelihood predicted. They can be inferred from overt behaviors. An individual who takes a longer time to answer one question than another may be considered to be evaluating alternative solutions. We can also ask an individual to report on his or her covert behaviors. Rotter believes that the principles that govern covert behaviors are the same as those that might apply to any observable behavior (Rotter et al., 1972). The objective study of internal cognitive responses is difficult but necessary for a complete understanding of behavior.

Expectancy Construct

The **expectancy construct** refers to the individual's subjective expectation about the outcome of his or her behavior. It is his or her estimation of the probability that a particular reinforcement will occur if he or she behaves in a certain way in a given situation. What does Johnny expect will be the outcome of his temper tantrum? The answer to that question will influence the likelihood of a tantrum occurring.

Expectancies are based on previous experience. An individual who has performed consistently well in mathematics will expect to do well in subsequent math courses. The expectancy is a subjective estimate; it tends to reflect the way a person feels about a subject. Therefore, it is not necessarily based on all of the pertinent objective data nor is it necessarily a true estimate.

Expectancies vary in their generalness or range. Some expectancies refer to a broad range of behaviors and therefore govern much of an individual's activities. An example of a very general expectation is the belief that one's own efforts will be effective in bringing about desired effects (called expectancy for internal control). Other expectancies are quite narrow and govern only one situation, such as the expectation that one will receive a ticket for parking too long in a metered area. Generalized expectancies are especially important when an individual faces a new situation. Here the expectancy construct can only be based on the outcomes of past similar situations.

Reinforcement Value

The **reinforcement value** refers to the importance or preference of a particular reinforcement for an individual. In a given situation, Johnny may refuse to wash Dad's car if he thinks that the only reward he will receive for the task is a verbal thank-you. On the other hand, he might be anxious to wash the car if he believes that he will receive ten dollars for the chore. The reinforcement value of a particular reward differs from individual to individual. Some children are more eager to please their parents than others. People also engage in activities for different reasons. One individual might go to a party in order to meet new friends; another might seek to get high. Some rewards are compatible and others are incompatible. A child might be asked to choose between a toy and a box of candy as a prize for winning a game. Where a choice must be made, the relative reinforcement value of each reward becomes clear.

Rotter suggests that individuals tend to be consistent in the value they place on different reinforcements. Each one of us has a characteristic set of preferences that we bring to situations. Like expectancies, the values associated with different reinforcers are based on past experiences. Out of these associations, we also form expectations for the future. Thus, there is a relationship between the expectancy construct and the reinforcement value. A chain of reinforcement sequences may also be formed based on past rewards and extending to future anticipated ones. Such chains permit future goals or expectations to influence current behavior.

Situation

The **situation** refers to the psychological context in which the individual responds. It is the situation as defined from the perspective of the person. Any given situation has different meanings for different individuals and these meanings affect the response. Rotter's concept of the psychological situation takes into account the importance of both dispositional and situational influences. It recognizes that an individual may have a strong need for aggression but may or may not behave aggressively in a particular situation depending on reinforcement expectancies. Rotter believes that the complex cues of each situation arouse in individuals expectations for behavior reinforcement outcomes and for reinforcement sequences.

These four variables can be related to a formula that will enable us to predict a person's behavior in any given situation.

$$BP\ x,s_1\ Ra\ =\ f(Ex,\ Ras_1\ +\ RVa,\ s_1)$$

The formula may be read as follows: "The potential for behavior x to occur in situation 1 in relation to reinforcement a is a function of the expectancy of the occurrence of reinforcement a following behavior x in situation 1 and the value of reinforcement a in situation 1" (Rotter and Hochreich, 1975).

If we could substitute the appropriate numbers for the above variables, we could predict the behaviors that would occur in any given situation. Of course, to date, social learning theorists have not been able to develop the precise techniques of observation and measurement that would enable them to discover the appropriate numbers. However, the formula has helped them to appreciate the complexities of the variables that must be taken into account in order to make a prediction.

Rotter has used a number of different techniques in his efforts to measure the variables that enter into his formula. Some of these rely on self-reports of the individual. Ranking methods in which individuals are asked to rank verbal descriptions of reinforcements from the most to the least reinforcing have been used to measure reinforcement value. Verbal questionnaires in which subjects are asked to predict the likelihood of success in various tasks have been used to measure expectancy. Behavior potential can be measured by asking people what they think they will do in certain situations. Behavioral observations have also been used to indicate the strength of these constructs. Individuals may be observed actually behaving in ways so as to receive one reinforcement over another. When a subject chooses one alternative over another, he or she is thought to be indicating a higher level of expectancy for the chosen alternative. Observations of an individual's behavior over a long period of time give us an indication of how frequently certain behaviors tend to occur. The development of precise measuring techniques for these constructs, however, is only at a very early stage.

The Concepts of Need and Minimum Goal Level

Other broader concepts also play an important role in Rotter's theory: the concepts of need and minimum goal level.

Rotter believes that human behavior is always directional and determined by needs that may be inferred from the ways in which an individual interacts with the environment. A **need** is "a group of behaviors which are related in the sense that they lead to the same or similar reinforcements" (Rotter and Hochreich, 1975). Rotter makes a distinction between unlearned, biologically based needs and psychological needs, which are internal cognitive conditions and are the result of experience rather than instinct. Psychological needs come into being through the association of experiences with the reinforcement of reflexes and basic needs such as hunger, thirst, freedom from pain, and sensory stimulation. As we develop, our psychological needs become less dependent on physiological needs and increasingly related to cues in the environment. Since as infants and children, we are largely dependent upon other people for the satisfaction of our needs, many of our learned goals, such as the need for love, affection, recognition, and dependency, are social in origin. Human needs also vary in terms of their generalness and predictability. Some of our motives and needs are very specific, and thus, behaviors that they include are easily predicted. Other motives are broader and more inclusive, making it difficult to predict specific behaviors that they entail.

The need for recognition and status is the need to be seen as competent in valued activities.

Through empirical research, Rotter (1975) has established six broad categories of psychological needs:

recognition-status: the need to be seen as competent in socially valued activities

dominance: the need to control the actions of others

independence: the need to make one's own decisions and rely on oneself

protection-dependency: the need to have others prevent frustration or help obtain goals *love and affection:* the need for acceptance and liking by others

physical comfort: learned needs for physical satisfactions associated with security

A need has three basic components. The first component is the **need potential,** the likelihood that a set of behaviors directed toward the same goal will be used in a given situation. The second component is **freedom of movement,** the degree of expectation a person has that a particular set of responses will lead to a desired reinforcement. Freedom of movement can be computed by adding up the individual's expectancy for each separate behavior pertaining to the goal and dividing it by the total number of behaviors. A high expectancy or freedom of movement leads to the anticipation of success in meeting one's goals. A low expectancy or lack of freedom is associated with the anticipation of failure or punishment. The third basic component of needs is the **need value,** the importance attached to the goals themselves or the extent to which an individual prefers one goal over another. It is an average of reinforcement values taken over a number of similar reinforcing circumstances. The advantage to computing these components is that they facilitate the prediction of behaviors that are likely to occur in new situations in which similar reinforcements are obtainable. Whereas the constructs of behavior potential, expectancy, and reinforcement value are useful for prediction in specific situations or in the laboratory, the constructs of need potential, freedom of movement, and need value help us to deal with broader situations and behaviors that occur in everyday life. It is clear that the prediction of behavior in the complex social situations of daily life is very difficult. It requires intense study and a great deal of information. The researcher must not only assess the need potential but also take into account the expectations and values placed on different needs, as well as how these vary from situation to situation and how they conflict with each other.

The concept of **minimum goal level** refers to the lowest level of potential reinforcement that is perceived as satisfactory in a particular situation (1954). One student might find a grade of C in a course punishing, whereas another would be happy with it. Reinforcements may be seen as existing on a continuum. Individuals vary as to their minimum goal levels or the point on the continuum that divides positively rewarding reinforcements from negative ones.

The concept of minimum goal level together with the concept of freedom of movement can be useful for predicting behavior and understanding personality adjustment. An individual who is adjusted in a particular sphere has a high freedom of movement in that area and realistic goal levels. Thus, an individual who is well adjusted in school is one who establishes academic goals for him- or herself that are commensurate with his or her abilities and engages in a wide variety of behaviors designed to meet those goals. The individual who is maladjusted sets unrealistic goals, such as the need always to obtain

A's, and engages in unproductive behaviors that reflect a low expectation of success. There are distinct parallels between Rotter's concept of the maladjusted person as one who experiences low freedom of movement yet sets unrealistic minimal goals and Adler's concept of the neurotic as one who sets unattainable fictional goals and experiences feelings of inferiority.

Internal versus External Control of Reinforcement

An important construct in Rotter's personality theory is that of *internal versus external control of reinforcement.* We have seen how an individual's expectancies concerning the effects of his or her behaviors influence his or her actions. Rotter believes that these expectancies can generalize to high freedom of movement for a larger variety of reinforcements and even to reinforcements in general. Thus, an individual may come to believe on the basis of past experiences that the reinforcements that he or she receives depend on his or her own behaviors or, conversely, may come to believe that reinforcements are controlled by outside forces (1966). Internally controlled individuals assume that their own behaviors and actions are responsible for the consequences that happen to them. Externally controlled people believe that the locus of control is out of their hands and that they are subject to the whims of fate, luck, or other people. Internal versus external control of reinforcement refers to a continuum of belief of which we have cited the two extremes. There is an entire range in between. Mary might believe that most rewards are contingent upon her own behavior but that some are controlled by external forces. John might feel that external forces control most events but his efforts can sometimes affect the results. Tom might feel that most rewards are due partly to his own efforts and partly to variables that he cannot control. Psychologists have long used concepts to describe whether or not people believe they can control their own lives. Competence, mastery, helplessness, powerlessness, or alienation are but a few of the terms that have been used. Rotter believes that his construct has an advantage over the others because it is an integral part of a formal theory from which predictions can be made.

In his early years, Rotter conducted a series of experimental studies designed to tell whether or not people learn tasks and perform differently when they see reinforcements as related or unrelated to their own behaviors. The results of these experiments led him to develop the **I-E Scale,** which measures an individual's perception of locus of control (1966). Although various measuring devices have been developed to assess locus of control as a stable personality characteristic, Rotter's scale remains one of the most widely used. The I-E scale consists of twenty-three forced-choice items and six filler items. The subject indicates which of each pair of items best describes him- or herself. The final score can range from zero to twenty-three, with higher scores indicating greater externality. Rotter does not indicate any cutoff score that separates internals from externals, but norms have been published for various groups to facilitate comparisons. On a national sample of high school students, the mean score was 8.50. The lowest mean score reported by Rotter was 5.94 among a group of Peace Corps trainees (1966).

Exploration /////

Internal-External Locus of Control

You can assess your own belief in locus of control by selecting the one statement from each pair that best describes your belief. The following are sample items taken from an earlier version of the test but not used in the final version. You can discover whether you are inclined toward internal control or external control by adding up the choices you make on each side. Items on the left indicate internality and items on the right indicate externality.

I more strongly believe that:

Promotions are earned through hard work and persistence.

In my experience I have noticed that there is usually a direct connection between how hard I study and the grades I get.

The number of divorces indicates that more and more people are not trying to make their marriages work.

When I am right I can convince others.

In our society a man's future earning power is dependent upon his ability.

If one knows how to deal with people they are really quite easily led.

Or:

Making a lot of money is largely a matter of getting the right breaks.

Many times the reactions of teachers seem haphazard to me.

Marriage is largely a gamble.

It is silly to think that one can really change another person's basic attitudes.

Getting promoted is really a matter of being a little luckier than the next guy.

I have little influence over the way other people behave.

(continued)

In my case the grades I make are the results of my own efforts; luck has little or nothing to do with it.

People like me can change the course of world affairs if we make ourselves heard.

I am the master of my fate.

Getting along with people is a skill that must be practiced.

Sometimes I feel that I have little to do with the grades I get.

It is only wishful thinking to believe that one can really influence what happens in society at large.

A great deal that happens to me is probably a matter of chance.

It is almost impossible to figure out how to please some people.

The I-E Scale has been widely used in research and has led to a number of significant findings: internality increases with age; as children grow older, their locus of control tends to become more internal; internality becomes stable in middle age and does not diminish in old age, contrary to popular views of the elderly as dependent. Certain parental practices help to foster a belief in internal control: warm, responsible, supportive conditions and the encouragement of independence (Lefcourt, 1976).

Several studies have shown that internals are more perceptive and ready to learn about their surroundings. They ask more questions and process information more efficiently than externals. They have greater mastery tendencies, better problem-solving abilities, and more likelihood of achievement. Thus, internal patients in hospital settings know more about their illnesses, are more inquisitive, and cope with their sicknesses more effectively than externals. Internal prison inmates know more about the institution and conditions affecting their parole and are more likely to be paroled (Rotter, 1966). Internals are better versed about critical political events that may influence their lives (Ryckman and Malikiosi, 1975).

Internal locus of control appears to protect one against unquestioning submission to authority. Internals are more resistant to influences from other people. They make more independent judgments and try harder to control the behavior of others (Lefcourt, 1976). They tend to assume more responsibility for their own behavior and attribute responsibility to others. As a result, they are more likely to be punitive and less sympathetic than externals.

Internals are more likely to know about the conditions that lead to good health and to take positive steps to improve their health, such as quitting smoking and engaging in regular exercise. They suffer less from hypertension and are less likely to have heart attacks. When they do become ill, they cope with the illness more adequately than externals (Strickland, 1978, 1979).

Externals tend to be more anxious and depressed, as well as more vulnerable to stress. They develop defensive strategies that invite failure in coping with a task and use defensive strategies afterward to explain their failures. They attribute their lack of success to bad luck or to the difficulties of the task (Lefcourt, 1976).

Rotter believes that extreme belief in either internal or external locus of control is unrealistic and unhealthy. He has hypothesized a curvilinear relationship between locus of control measures and assessments of maladjustment (Rotter and Hochreich, 1975). However, it is clear that many favorable characteristics have been associated with internal locus of control and it has been proposed that an internal orientation is more conducive to positive social adjustment and functioning.

Psychotherapy

Rotter's concepts have found application in the field of clinical psychology. In general, Rotter (1975) suggests that maladjusted individuals are characterized by low freedom of movement and high need value. They believe that they are unable to get the gratifications they desire through their own efforts. Instead of working toward their goals realistically, they seek to obtain them through fantasy or they behave in ways that avoid or defend against failure. Problem behaviors, such as substance abuse and delinquency, have been shown to be associated with a discrepancy between an individual's need values for recognition and his or her freedom of movement for getting it.

Low freedom of movement may result from a lack of knowledge or ability to develop the behaviors that are necessary to reach one's goals. An individual who is retarded may have low expectancies because of his or her inability to learn basic skills. Low freedom of movement may arise from the nature of the goal itself. If a goal is antisocial, behaving in ways that fulfill the goal invites punishment. An expectancy for failure can also arise from the mistaken generalization of experiences of frustration from one area to another. A child whose paralyzed leg prevents participation in sports may erroneously generalize that others will not like him. Individuals who were severely punished as children may generalize from those experiences to the present. Maladjusted individuals often apply expectations and behaviors from one situation onto another inappropriately. They tend to seek immediate rewards and deny the long-term consequences of their behaviors and they emphasize the gratification of one need to the exclusion of others.

Maladjusted individuals are frequently unaware of the self-defeating character of their own behaviors and of their actual potential for success. Rotter makes use of the defense mechanisms developed by Freud, but he reconceives them as avoidance or escape behaviors. Thus, projection entails blaming others for one's own mistakes to avoid punishment and rationalization entails making excuses in order to avoid punishment. According to social learning theory, all of the defenses and symptoms of psychopathology and mental illness may be seen as avoidance or fantasy behaviors (1975).

A social learning therapist would seek to help a maladjusted person by reducing the discrepancy between his or her need value and freedom of movement. Rotter points out that it is essential that the therapist be flexible. In time, he hopes that patients can be systematically matched to therapists since therapists vary in their effectiveness with different methods and patients. In general, cognitive learning theory emphasizes a problem-solving orientation to therapy and the development of problem-solving skills such as looking for alternative means of reaching a goal, analyzing the consequences of one's behavior, and discriminating among situations. The therapist assumes a highly active and directive role.

Rotter frequently advocates use of environmental change in order to effect personality change. He may try to alter the attitude of those who live with the patient or recommend a change in school or job. His work on the importance of an appropriate environment for change has led to a new conception of the mental hospital as a therapeutic community in itself. In other instances, Rotter employs various behavior strategies such as systematic desensitization, aversive conditioning or covert sensitization (the association of undesired behaviors with aversive stimuli in one's imagination), assertiveness training, and behavioral training in specific skills.

With its cognitive emphasis, Rotter's social learning theory also emphasizes the need to cultivate insight into one's own motives as they have developed from past experiences, insight into the motives of others, and insight into the long-term consequences of one's behavior. Rotter points out, however, that it is not enough for clients to understand the origins of their problems but they must also be taught new behaviors that will overcome them. Social learning theory conceives of psychotherapy broadly in the context of social interaction. The therapist's role is to help the patient develop a more satisfactory relationship with his or her social environment.

The cognitive approach to personality promises to be a very fruitful one. Cognitive factors may provide the link that will help us to transcend the traditional dichotomy between dispositional and situational factors in behavior. Distinctive cognitive and behavior patterns determine the unique meaning that stimuli and reinforcers have for different individuals. An individual's cognitive style influences his or her adaption to the world and interpersonal competence. Recently, there have been efforts to construct complex information-processing models that might eventually simulate a wide variety of human mental activity. In addition, there has been increased contact between cognitive psychology and neurophysiology based upon the belief that cognitive systems might be tied to underlying neural systems. Most of the research in personality today involves cognitive elements at some point. There is little doubt that the emphasis on cognition has grown and will continue as an important factor in the discussion of personality.

Rotter's Theory: Philosophy, Science, and Art

Rotter's cognitive social learning theory creatively combines traditional learning theory with an interest in cognition. Rotter's position represents a significant departure from B. F. Skinner's radical behaviorism but retains the important emphasis on a strict methodology and the classical features of the learning tradition. Thus, his theory is very appealing to experimentally-oriented researchers. It also appeals to those who are attuned to advances being made in cognitive studies. His emphasis on cognitive factors is greater than Albert Bandura's. In brief, his theory is very much in line with current trends in academic psychology.

Rotter's research is rigorous and well-controlled even though he permits introspective methods in addition to the objective observation of behavior. Indeed, he has fostered a new appreciation of introspection as a methodological technique and in doing so has made a valid correction of the rigid narrowness that characterizes radical behavior and learning theory.

As a science, Rotter's theory excels. His terms are operationally defined, measurable, and lend themselves to empirical test. His theory readily meets the criterion of verifiability. Empirical support for his theory has been strong, particularly regarding his concept of locus of control. His work has considerable heuristic value and may eventually enable us to predict behavior. Rotter's theory has stimulated research and has found wide application in the clinical setting, where the I-E Scale has proved very useful. Because his concepts are stated as simply as possible, his theory compares well to more complex rival theories.

Rotter's theory has been criticized, however, for its lack of depth (Cartwright, 1979). It takes few risks in hypothesizing and does little more than summarize existing, generally well-known knowledge. Although it provides precise, accurate, and measurable constructs, it does not evoke deep insight or new understanding. This may be the price that Rotter has paid for the precision, power, and predictability of his work. As we have seen, the validating evidence of the scientist is seldom as insightful or compelling as the epiphanic vision of a philosopher. Nevertheless, it has been Rotter's deliberate choice to restrict his assumptions and mechanisms to those that can be embraced by a precise scientific methodology.

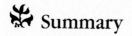 # Summary

1. Julian Rotter's theory integrates two major trends in personality research: learning theory and cognitive theory.

2. There are four main concepts in Rotter's cognitive social learning approach: **behavior potential, expectancy construct, reinforcement value,** and the psychological **situation.** These four variables can be measured and related in a specific formula that enables us to predict a person's behavior in any given situation.

3. The concepts of **need** and **minimum goal level** also help us to predict behavior and understand personality adjustment.

4. Rotter developed the **I-E Scale** to measure internal versus external control of reinforcement. The scale has been widely used in research and has led to a number of significant findings.

5. Rotter's concepts have been applied in the field of clinical psychology and therapy to account for maladjustment and develop strategies of change.

6. Rotter's theory excels as a scientific theory but has been criticized for a lack of depth.

Suggestions for Further Reading

The best introduction to Julian Rotter's theory is *Personality,* co-authored with D. J. Hochreich (Scott Foresman, 1975). Students who are interested in his point of view will also want to consult J. B. Rotter, J. E. Chance, and E. J. Phares, *Applications of a Social Learning Theory of Personality* (Holt, Rinehart & Winston, 1972) and H. M. Lefcourt, *Locus of Control: Current Trends in Theory and Research* (Erlbaum, 1976).

Part
7

Eastern and Existential Theories

During the past century we have made enormous progress in gathering together a significant amount of information about human nature and personality. However, although we have learned a great deal about ourselves, we are still far from an adequate understanding of what it means to be a human being. Our modern technology and culture have given rise to practices that may relieve many forms of human illness and suffering but they have yet to provide satisfactory answers to the most fundamental questions of human existence. Those questions about the ultimate meaning, purpose, and goal of our lives continue to haunt us and to demand answers. There has been a growing feeling that the dominant concerns of Western science and psychology have ignored the spiritual side of the person. In today's society our social security numbers and the numbers on our credit cards have become more important than our names. We feel increasingly depersonalized as automated machines perform services for us and assume vital functions once reserved for persons. We are even encouraged to think of ourselves in ways analogous to the machine, for example, as information-processing computers. In the midst of our abundant technological advance, the person appears to have been lost. Many people have turned to the East or existential philosophy in the hope of finding something that could temper or humanize the thrust of modern technology that threatens to destroy the very civilization that developed it.

As Westerners, familiar with our own brand of science and psychology, we are frequently unaware of or tend to depreciate other psychologies, such as those that emerge from the Oriental traditions. Hinduism, Buddhism, Confucianism, Taoism, and Sufism, among other Oriental traditions, have raised questions about the ultimate meaning and purpose of human life. These movements have developed psychologies insofar as they have explored the psyche or the self and all have implied personality theories insofar as they have investigated what it means to be a human being. It may come as a surprise to realize that the assumptions that constitute the consensus reality of the twentieth-century Western world are not necessarily universal and shared by other cultures. From the viewpoint of many of these movements, several of our contemporary Western ideas about personality are incredibly foreign. No wonder we have difficulty communicating, as long as we tacitly assume that our comprehension of human behavior is universally shared.

Although there are many varieties of Eastern thought, almost all of them share certain characteristics by which they may be identified and distinguished from Western thought. An examination of these shared characteristics as well as a closer look at an Eastern movement, Zen Buddhism, that is gaining popularity in the West, can give us some familiarity with the Oriental approach to personality.

Existentialism, a contemporary Western philosophy, grew directly out of the estrangement, anxiety, and conflict felt by persons in the West. It recognizes that the Western concern with conquering nature has led to the alienation of the human being from nature and from him- or herself. It undercuts the sharp antithesis between subject and object that has characterized Western thought and science since shortly after the Renaissance. Existentialism acts as a corrective to an imbalance in our thinking and emphasizes the achievement of true individuality through confronting the "givens" of one's existence.

19
Zen
Buddhism

Your Goals for This Chapter

1. Identify and discuss two general characteristics of Eastern psychology.

2. Discuss the origins of Zen by describing the story of Buddha, the teachings of Buddhism, and the main branches of thought that stemmed from early Buddhism.

3. Describe the teachings of *Zen Buddhism* and show how they represent a reaction against intellectualism.

4. Explain what is meant by *satori.*

5. Describe *zazen* and the *koan,* two key elements in the practice of Zen.

6. Describe life in a Zen monastery.

7. Compare the modes of liberation or psychotherapeutic change developed by the East and the West.

8. Evaluate Eastern theories of personality in terms of their function as philosophy, science, and art.

*T*here are many varieties of Eastern thought: Hinduism, Buddhism, Confucianism, Taoism, and Sufism, among others. Generally, we think of these movements as Oriental religions or philosophies. However, in many respects these thought systems do not resemble philosophy or religion as much as they resemble the art of psychology and psychotherapy (Watts, 1961). Their basic concern is with the human situation: the suffering and frustrations of human beings. They emphasize the importance of techniques to accomplish change. Eastern thought aims at transformations in consciousness, feelings, emotions, and one's relation to other people and the world. Each of these movements of Eastern thought may be seen to contain its own psychological categories and be understood as a quest toward self-understanding.

General Characteristics of Eastern Psychology

Although there are many differences among them, almost all Eastern movements of thought have certain characteristics in common. Jacob Needleman (1970) has singled out two features that distinguish Eastern movements from the general pattern of thought in the West: an emphasis on the self and an emphasis on the practical.

An Emphasis on the Self

For the most part, Eastern religions are centered on the self. But the self that is focused on is not the conscious ego or individual mind of Western psychology. The East conceives of the true self as a deeper, inner consciousness that identifies the individual with the universal or cosmos. Eastern thinkers point out that many of us confuse ourselves with the social role or social identity that others have assigned to us, what Jung would call the *persona* or mask. This identification is **maya,** or an illusion. Our ego is simply a social convention. When we speak of "I," "you," "him," an "individual," and so forth, we are conforming to the conventions of this world. However, the truth is that there is no "I" or "individual" in ultimate reality, and the "I" should not be confused with reality. Once we can see through the illusion of individual existence, we can recognize ourselves for who we are, both unique and universal. I am universal because my organism is inseparable from the universe at large. I am unique in that I am *I,* not whom others say or expect me to be.

Confusion of oneself with one's social role leads to feelings of isolation, alienation, and loneliness. There is a conflict between who I am and whom others say and expect me to be. Insofar as I attempt to identify myself with my social role or identity, I become further and further estranged from my true identity.

Identification with one's conscious ego or social role leads to a multitude of various contradictory wishes and desires, as well as to vigorous efforts to satisfy them. We seek to satisfy our bodily needs, to be free of pain and fear, to acquire wealth and material possessions, to be loved and love, to receive honor, recognition, and praise from our fellow human beings. At the same time, we seek to be self-sufficient, to control others, and to conquer the fear of death. The problem is that the satisfaction of one of these desires is usually at the expense of another desire, because the desires themselves contradict one another. We become caught in a many-horned dilemma, none of the solutions to which is satisfactory. We seek to satisfy our wants only to discover that in the end none of these worldly interests really satisfies our deepest needs.

In Eastern literature, these desires are frequently symbolized by animals, as if hordes of animals lived within each of us. Each animal seeks its own needs and pleasures. Carnivores feed off one another to obtain their food. If we identify with the animals, we do not relieve our suffering. As soon as we feed one animal, another appears demanding food. Often it demands for its prey the very animal that we have just cared for. When our concern is to satisfy life's secular and external conditions, we do not find happiness or release from suffering. We merely identify with the animals and increase our internal conflicts. The animals within are concerned only with their own pleasure. They are self-centered in the common meaning of the term. They are not interested in each other or in the truth. Yet it is only by recognizing the truth that their needs may be fully met.

What is required is a higher or deeper form of consciousness that can curb and care for the animals in a manner that fulfills their true needs as part of a whole. The aim of Eastern psychology is transformation of desires rather than their satisfaction. The animals cry out, "I am," "Feed me!" It is this feeling, "I am," "I must be fed," that creates the illusion of self or ego. But that ego has no correspondence with reality. True consciousness involves being whole, rising above the level of individuality and becoming one with the cosmos and universal, as in a peak experience. This is not easy, however, as the animals within try to con us into *feeling* whole rather than *being* whole (Needleman, 1970).

An Emphasis on the Practical

Eastern psychology is eminently practical. The writings of Eastern thinkers do not concentrate on telling their readers "how" to do it; they present anecdotes about a methodology that, if followed, may enable them to do it. Eastern thinkers believe the truth that we seek is not found in books. It emerges only in the course of living; to permit it to emerge, we need to undergo a process. The process is not undertaken through following a recipe but through the guidance of a **guru,** or teacher, who is seen as indispensable for such a spiritual journey.

The practice of Eastern psychology entails a systematic training of body and mind that enables one to perceive the truth that lies within his or her inner being. The follower of Eastern thought is introduced to a variety of techniques. He or she is taught to meditate and to engage in physical and psychological exercises. A disciple's life is governed by a great many rules and rituals, whose purpose is to develop a freedom beyond the rules that permits one to be oneself.

Such techniques have not been totally absent in the West. The Socratic dialectic was a particular technique in which the teacher acted as a midwife, permitting the inner life of the person to unfold. Christian monasteries and certain Jewish communities practiced and continue to practice a rich discipline and ritual in order to cultivate the spiritual side of the self. More recently, Sigmund Freud initiated his followers into a precise technique, free association, that is not unlike meditation in that it aims to alter one's normal state of consciousness and to uncover aspects of the self of which one was formerly unaware. However, for some Westerners the rituals and practices that remain or are available today in the West seem empty and meaningless. They may go to church or temple on the Sabbath and enjoy the beautiful service. They may obtain some sort of emotional release from various practices and rituals that temporarily allay their everyday discontents. But these practices do not initiate them into a process that transforms their lives: It is as if they tried to cure an illness by hearing about a new method of treatment but never went to a doctor for the treatment itself (Needleman, 1970).

Of the many forms of Eastern thought — Hinduism, Buddhism, Confucianism, Taoism, Sufism, and so forth — one in particular, Zen Buddhism, has caught the interest of the West. In order to introduce the reader to the kinds of personality theorizing characteristic of the East, it seems appropriate to focus on this movement. The study of one conceptual framework, in depth, can be more illuminating than a brief overview of several viewpoints. But we must remember that Zen Buddhism is not the only pattern of personality conception in the East. Other frameworks also illumine the human condition. Nevertheless, Zen Buddhism may be singled out as a system that, while unique, also typifies the East and has had an increasing appeal to the West.

Suzuki: Introducer of Zen to the West

The Japanese Buddhist Daisetz Teitaro Suzuki is the person who is largely responsible for introducing the concepts of Zen Buddhism to the West. Suzuki, undoubtedly the greatest authority on Buddhism and Zen in this century, dedicated his life to the study of Zen and to interpreting its concepts and philosophy for the Western reader. Suzuki was born in 1869; he was educated at Tokyo University and studied Zen Buddhism at Engakuji in Kamakura. He attained his enlightenment in 1896 under the guidance of Soyen Shaku Roshi, a well-known guru. Suzuki was a scholar who wrote and spoke with authority. He studied the original works of Zen in Sanskrit, Pali, Chinese, and Japanese, so he was very familiar with their content. Professor of Buddhist philosophy in the Otani University in Kyoto, Japan, he wrote over twenty books in English on the subject of Buddhism and at least eighteen books in Japanese, which have not yet been translated. The publication of Suzuki's *Essays in Zen Buddhism* in 1927 literally brought Zen Buddhism to the attention of the West and aroused genuine interest. In large measure the description of Zen that follows is based on the writings of Suzuki, or his followers, and his translations of Zen anecdotes and sayings.*

Suzuki was not simply a scholar, he was also a practicing Buddhist. Although he was not a priest of any Buddhist sect, he was well known, respected, and loved in Japan. Those who heard him were greatly impressed by his knowledge of spiritual things. It is true that Suzuki was sometimes described as a dilettante, popularizing Zen for the West, but those who knew him personally attested to his profound spiritual insight. It appeared clear to them that he was searching for words to describe and share his own experience of enlightenment. He spoke of a message that had transformed his life and that would transform others who permitted it to enter into their beings. He referred to a higher level of consciousness in which he dwelt. At the same time, he realized that comprehension of the secrets of Zen lies beyond the power of the intellect alone. Trying to grasp the point of Zen is like trying to hold onto a bar of wet soap. Zen eludes intellectual comprehension; it requires that it be lived. Suzuki's witness to the life of Zen continued until his death in 1966 at the age of ninety-five.

The Origins of Zen

Zen is a school of Buddhism that claims to represent the purest essence of Buddhist teachings. The origins of Zen trace back to the story of Buddha.

Siddhartha Gautama, known after his enlightenment as the Buddha or "enlightened one," was born about 560 B.C. in the city of Kapilavastu in northern India. The exact site of his birthplace is unknown. Unlike some other early religious and philosophical leaders, however, his historical existence has been

*The quotations and anecdotes in this chapter are from D. T. Suzuki, *An Introduction to Zen Buddhism.* Reprinted by permission of Grove Press, Inc., and Hutchison Publishing Group Ltd. Copyright © 1964 by D. T. Suzuki. And also from Alan W. Watts, *The Spirit of Zen.* Reprinted by permission of Grove Press, Inc., and John Murray (Publishers) Ltd. Copyright © 1958 by Alan W. Watts.

clearly established. Gautama's father was a wealthy nobleman who tried to protect his son from the harsher, seamier side of life. Gautama was brought up in luxurious surroundings and provided with every conceivable comfort. Nevertheless, he felt uneasy and tormented by the sorrows and evils that he could not avoid seeing around him. He was particularly troubled by the problems of old age, sickness, and death. He asked his father whether there was any solution to the problem of suffering, but his father, distressed by his failure to protect his son, could not answer the question.

At the age of twenty-nine, in spite of his father's judgments and attempts to prevent him, Gautama renounced everything that he had, gave up his rights to his father's throne, and left his wife and newborn son in search of something that would reduce his uneasiness. In his own words, he sought the "incomparable security of a Nirvana," or an exalted state of consciousness and bliss.

Gautama withdrew into the forest and spent the next six years as a mendicant or spiritual beggar. For a time he studied with two Hindu sages who taught him yoga and philosophy, but he continued to feel unsatisfied. Later, he joined a group of five ascetics and practiced severe deprivations. Gautama was merciless in the extremes to which he carried out his asceticism. He fasted, painfully mortified his body, and sought to renounce all human desires. These practices, however, simply brought him to a point near death from starvation. They did little to quell his uneasiness.

According to tradition, on April 8, 508 B.C., during his thirty-sixth year, Gautama, in a state of utter exhaustion, sat down under a peepul tree (an Indian fig tree), later known as the "bodhi tree" or the "tree of enlightenment." He realized that neither intellectual efforts nor ascetic extremes could provide a pathway to the truth. He resolved to wait under that tree until he attained enlightenment. He meditated throughout the night and experienced various levels of consciousness until he reached the stage after which he was known as Buddha, "the enlightened one." His enlightenment awakened him to the ultimate truth, liberating him from the cycles of cause and effect, death and rebirth as expressed in the doctrine of **karma** (the belief that a person's actions determine his or her destiny in the next life), and led to the conviction that the phenomenal world of ordinary appearances is illusory.

After a period of rest, the Buddha decided that he should share his message with others. The remainder of his life was spent teaching. He traveled from place to place and talked to whoever would listen. He led his followers in meditation and discussions. He was described as radiant, compassionate, and charismatic. He continued his work for forty-five years, until his death at the age of over eighty years in about 485 B.C.

After his enlightenment, Buddha developed his doctrine in the form of **Four Noble Truths.** The first noble truth describes our human situation as one of suffering and frustration that arise from our refusal to accept the basic impermanence and transitory character of life and all things. The second noble truth tells us that the cause of our suffering is ignorance, which arises from clinging or grasping to fixed notions about the world that are actually maya or illusions, such as the concept of a separate individual ego. These false concepts lead to the vicious cycle of karma, with its unending circle of life and death, cause and effect. The third noble truth states that we can transcend this vicious cycle and reach a state of **nirvana** or unspeakable bliss. The term *nirvana* literally means "waning out." It refers to the extinction of all desire, resentment, and selfishness that are caused by identifying with one's separate ego. Nirvana is not a place; rather, it is a condition of the mind. It entails an exalted state of consciousness in which the self is identified with Brahma, or that which is. To reach nirvana is to attain enlightenment or awakening. The fourth noble truth is Buddha's noble eightfold path that leads to enlightenment and escape from suffering. The eightfold path consists of correct seeing, knowing, speech, conduct, way of living, effort, awareness, and meditation. Essentially, the eightfold path is a method of appropriate ethical action that enjoins moderation or a middle way between extremes of behavior.

Gautama was steeped in the tradition of the *Upanishads,* an early sacred literature of India that goes back as far as 800 B.C. The term "Upanishad" is from Sanskrit and means "to sit by the side of the master and be." The Upanishads are a collection of esoteric or secret discussions between a holy man and a disciple that were designed to initiate the disciple into the inner meaning of life. Over two hundred of these little discourses are believed to have been written. Not one of them, however, is unambiguous and fully clear. They appear to us as a series of notes or aphorisms that give rise to more questions than answers. The Upanishads have also been subject to a number of different interpretations. Nevertheless, they show a general thrust that may be conceptualized as the doctrine of **Brahma,** the ground of existence, and the doctrine of **Atman,** the illusion of individuality.

According to the Upanishads, the ground of all existence is Brahma. The word "Brahma" means "that which is" and defies any further definition. Brahma is variously described as life, joy, the void, and so forth. In the Upanishads, "Brahma" encompasses all phenomena. Thus, it refers to Being, but also to non-Being. In short, Brahma has no characteristics and cannot be described as having any. Brahma is everything, yet it is nothing.

The Upanishads teach us that Brahma, that which is, expresses itself in a universe where you, Atman, find yourself. Atman denotes the inner self of an individual. In its origin the term "Atman" appears to be related to words in other languages that refer to "breath" or "the breath of life." Such a connotation also applied to Homer's "psyche." The Upanishads maintain that although it is true that Atman appears to be differentiated into individual selves (atmen) or egos, in reality there is only one Atman. The inner selves of individuals are essentially one and the same. There is only one Atman or Self.

In the final analysis, the doctrines of Brahma and Atman are one and the same. The true essence of the Self or Atman is Brahma or that which is. Therefore, Brahma is Atman and Atman is Brahma. Since there is nothing beyond what has been created, the universe and oneself are composed of Brahma.

Various analogies may be used to describe the relationship of Atman and Brahma. If you place a drop of water into the ocean, it becomes the sea. If a crystal of salt is placed in water, the water and salt mix together. Neither of these analogies, however, can capture the ultimate meaning. Since Brahma defies intellectual conceptualization, its meaning is elusive and cannot be expressed in ordinary language.

The individual "self" or separate "ego" is a misperception of what is really Atman. Thus, the experiences of the individual ego are also misperceptions. This means that the phenomenal world of appearances, as we know it, is illusory and unreal. The ordinary worldly interests and concerns that usually occupy our minds and efforts are fraudulent because they cannot begin to meet our innermost needs. The real problem is not the physical world with its karmic cycles of life and death, cause and effect, but our subjective constructs about the world that lead us to understand it in those terms. The enlightened one finds freedom in meditation on Atman and in conquering his or her individual ego through ascetic practices.

Buddha was silent on the question "What is the Self?" and the doctrines of Atman and Brahma. Most of his followers believe that he accepted the doctrines as facts beyond dispute and believed that talk about them was unimportant. He felt that it was more important to search than to know. Buddha laid speculation aside in favor of being practical and assisting others in being practical.

It is difficult to describe Buddha's original doctrine, because such a wide variety of Buddhist groups grew out of it. The two main divisions, Hinayana and Mahayana Buddhism, known as the lesser (Hina) and the greater (Maha) vessels of knowledge or wisdom, differ as much as Catholic and Protestant Christianity. These two main wings are based on the authority of certain sets of scriptures, consisting of sayings and teachings of the Buddha that his followers wrote down after his death. The southern *Theravada* or *Hinayana* school spread throughout Ceylon, Vietnam, Cambodia, Thailand, and Burma. The northern *Mahayana* school spread to Tibet, Mongolia, China, Korea, and Japan.

In general, Hinayana Buddhism is more speculative and analytical. Following a formal and rigid school of thought that sticks to the letter of Buddha's teachings as expressed in the Pali version of the scriptures, it teaches that an individual may achieve salvation and release from life's sorrows through rigorous discipline and knowledge. The Hinayana ideal is the *arhat* or monk, who seeks individual deliverance.

Mahayana Buddhism, by contrast, is more fluid. The Mahayana school continually reinterpreted the scriptures, giving rise to a wide variety of changes. Mahayana emphasizes the spiritual needs of common people. Its ideal is the *Bodhisattva,* a Buddhist saint who himself reaches enlightenment and tries to help others find salvation. Mahayana is more relaxed, emphasizing love and action rather than knowledge. Mahayana has given rise to a number of different sects. Strangely enough, in India itself today neither one of these movements is a strong force. For the most part, the Indian people who followed the Buddha incorporated his ideas into their own Hindu faith.

Both Mahayana and Hinayana Buddhism agree that the individual self or ego is an illusion. They disagree, however, over what is discovered when the person transcends the barriers of the individual ego and no longer resists the life that extends beyond it. We recall that Buddha was silent on the question "What is the Self?" The Hinayana believe that his silence meant that there is no self at all. The Mahayana, on the other hand, assume that a true Self emerges when the fallacious ego is abandoned. This true Self is identified with the whole of the universe. According to the Mahayana, to say that there is no Self at all is to be nihilistic, to deny life, and to stress only the temporary character of things. Mahayana believes that any denial must be completed by an affirmation. The individual self is denied, but the true Self is found in the totality of that which is. At the same time, Mahayana uses the term *sunyata,* or voidness, to refer to the Self, because the Self goes beyond any intellectual conceptualization of it.

Zen Buddhism stems from the Mahayana branch. It arose in China during the sixth century when an obscure and perhaps legendary patriarch called Bodhidharma brought Buddhism to China and founded the Ch'an sect. The term "Ch'an" in Chinese is the same as "Zen" in Japanese. Both words are generally translated as "meditation." This term is rather misleading, however, as Zen does not entail the speculative reflection "meditation" usually implies. On the contrary, Zen avoids all intellectual conceptualization and stresses a higher state of consciousness in which one finds union with ultimate reality. Further, Zen suggests that this higher state of consciousness is to be found in the living of everyday life rather than in solitary meditation and thought.

The Ch'an sect incorporated elements of **Taoism,** a Chinese philosophy, into their system. They identified Brahma and Atman with the *Tao,* an indefinable concept employed by Confucius and Lao-tse, Chinese philosophers who advocated a way of life that was in harmony with the course of nature. The word "Tao" has been variously translated as "the Way," "the Law," "Nature," and "Reality." The Chinese character for "Tao" consists of symbols that indicate movement. The general idea of Tao seems to be one of movement and growth. As the ultimate reality, Tao is the equivalent of the Brahma of the Upanishads. Nevertheless, the concept of Tao, like the concepts of Brahma and Atman, cannot be intellectually defined. Lao-tse told his followers that if Tao could be described in words, it would not be the true Tao. He taught that Tao was elusive and forever in motion. Trying to conceptualize Tao is like trying to catch one's shadow or swim against the current of a river. Our human suffering arises from our efforts to conceptualize and grasp the shadow or the stream that continually eludes us. We can find peace only by going along with the current and permitting it to carry us to our destination.

Tao was thought to manifest itself in two forces: **yin** and **yang.** As the classic diagram (Figure 19.1) shows, yin and yang are not static but are dynamically interrelated. One cannot move without the other. Together they compose a circle that continually rotates, and each contains within itself the seed of the other, which is represented by the small contrasting circle. Yang is frequently associated with light, creativity, masculinity, and power. Yin is often described as dark, feminine, receptive, and maternal. However, they represent different emphases rather than polar extremes. Since each is dynamically linked to the other, they express, not opposition, but the ultimate unity of all opposites.

In the twelfth century, Zen Buddhism, enriched by its contact with Chinese philosophy, was brought to Japan, where it flourished and became a major form of religion. Japanese painting, sculpture, architecture, and poetry all give witness to the wide variety of cultural expressions that Zen fostered, although Zen is no longer dominant in Japan. Within the last fifty years, Zen has been introduced to the United States where it already shows signs of giving rise to a potentially significant movement of thought.

Figure 19.1 *The Classic Diagram of Yin and Yang*

The Teachings of Zen

Zen Buddhism is a forthright, vigorous reaction against the strong intellectualism that has characterized the majority of philosophical, religious, and psychological approaches to life. Teachers of Zen suggest that the solution to life's problems cannot be found through intellectual channels, only through the paths of intuition and experience. In its essence, then, it is misleading to describe Zen as a religion or a philosophy. Zen does not set forth a doctrine of religious belief nor does it provide a method of philosophical inquiry. For that matter, it is also inaccurate to refer to Zen as a psychology, as it does not present a theory of the psyche or the self. Zen is totally devoid of all conceptual ideas. To speak of Zen is immediately to distort and misrepresent it. Ideally, one can know Zen only by experiencing its truth and bearing witness to it.

Nevertheless, as Zen spread and penetrated the Western world, it was inevitable that some of its followers would seek to articulate and describe it for the Western mind. Such descriptions are all very well, provided we realize that to talk about Zen is to conceptualize it and to miss the point at one and the same time. Although it is entirely possible to extract a philosophy or psychology of the person from Zen and its teachings, when we do so, we remain outside its secret. The following description, therefore, must immediately be identified as ultimately misleading.

Zen literature consists largely of sayings (the Zen *koan*), anecdotes, and similes. Many of them appear to be straightforward and clear, as they employ common and familiar words. However, Zen teachings are presented in such a fashion that only those disciples who have developed insight and are enlightened can comprehend their real meaning. For example, one Zen master is quoted as having said, "Empty-handed I go, and behold the spade is in my hands." Such an assertion seems simple enough, but how is it to be understood? To those who have not yet experienced Zen, such teachings appear mysterious and unintelligible, if not downright ludicrous and absurd.

There are some who suggest that teachers of Zen deliberately make their teachings unintelligible so that their profundity may not be questioned. However, followers of Zen point out that their statements are not paradoxical in an effort to hide or obscure the truth. Indeed, they claim they have nothing to hide because nothing is hidden. Their statements are enigmatic or mysterious because human language is inadequate for expressing the truths of Zen. Zen defies logical description and explanation. Its teachings must be personally experienced to be grasped. Zen neither affirms nor denies anything, it merely points the way. Zen seeks a higher affirmation beyond the antitheses of Being and non-Being, Self and not-Self, yes and no, good and evil. This is why it is misleading to identify Zen with a form of meditation. Meditation involves

Some people feel that the teachings of the East encompass truths that we have lost sight of in the West.

fixing one's thoughts on an object and extracting its vital characteristics; as such, meditation is artificial. Zen masters point out that birds and fish do not meditate — they fly and swim. Meditation is an artificial rather than a natural human activity. Zen asks us to take things as they are, to perceive things, to feel them, without any abstraction or mediation.

Suzuki reminds us that a dog behaves like a dog all of the time, yet it is not aware that it is a dog or that its nature expresses reality itself. A dog eats, sleeps, chases, and romps. It lives Zen but it does not live by Zen. Human beings, because of the unique character of their consciousness, have the potential to be conscious of living. Thus, they can live Zen and also live by Zen. Most of us are not conscious of life itself; instead, we are conscious of our individual selves and we conduct our lives according to an artificial set of subjective constructs and moralities that blind us to reality itself. As such, we are circumscribed by our self-consciousness and subjective categories and are out of touch with the innermost Self that coincides with the truth.

Zen seeks to get in touch with the innermost Self and to do it in the most direct possible way. Zen avoids anything that is external or superficial. It renounces all external authorities, stating that whatever truth there is must come from within and be experienced personally. Even human reason itself is rejected as a final authority. Our reason is seen as an intermediary that interferes with the direct perception of what is real. Zen encourages us not to be bound by rules, be they logical, moral, or spiritual; rather, we must create our own rules through the experience of life as we live it.

Truth is in the self. If one cannot find the truth in oneself, no teacher can reveal it to one. When one master was asked, "What is Enlightenment?" he replied, "Your everyday thoughts." Another answered the question "What is the Tao?" with "Usual life is the very Tao."

To search after Tao itself immediately implies a distinction between oneself and the ultimate. This distinction is the basis of egoism and lays the false foundation for an individual ego or self. It suggests that the self is somehow distinct from the rest of life. Tao is not to be sought; it is to be recognized in the commonplace events of everyday living. The individual ego disappears when the self and life move along together.

In Zen all ideas or symbols of Buddha are cast aside as misconceptions. The story is told of Tanka, a monk who burned a wooden statue of Buddha in order to keep his fire going one winter night. The keeper of the temple was outraged at his sacrilege, but Tanka merely began to search in the ashes and said that he was gathering sariras. *Sarira* refers to the holy substance that is found when a Buddha's body is burned. When the keeper inquired how he could possibly get sariras from a wooden Buddha, Tanka pointed out that if there were not sariras in his fire, then the statue was not truly a Buddha. Thereupon, he asked for the two remaining statues of Buddha for his fire. Other Zen masters teach us, "Cleanse the mouth thoroughly when you utter the word Buddha," and "If you encounter the Buddha, kill him." Such false images only serve to separate us from the truth.

Truth is life. It cannot be grasped, held, or conceptualized. All we can possess is our own subjective ideas. Zen masters say that to define is to kill. If the wind were to stop blowing so that we could catch it, it would no longer be wind. Life is elusive in the same way. We try to stop it, to preserve it, to understand it, to define it, so that we can repeat its happy moments and avoid its sad ones. But life moves on and our efforts to halt it are unsuccessful. What brings happiness one moment may bring sorrow the next. Those who try to possess life merely enslave themselves to their own illusions.

When one master was asked, "What is Tao?" he replied, "Walk on." To discuss or talk about bringing the self into harmony with life merely introduces the concept of the self and draws attention away from the process of living itself. Zen is an experience, it is not an explanation. Therefore, Zen masters do not concentrate on talk. They simply demonstrate life without making any assertions or denials about it. How can one possibly describe the sweetness of sugar? It has to be tasted. Zen masters attach no value to words, because words can only estrange us from what is real. When words are used by teachers of Zen, they are used in a different context. This is why Zen answers are short and to the point. Zen masters do not waste their time on lengthy explanations. Their statements are only to be taken as aids. Zen sayings are no more than a finger pointing to the moon. The finger remains a finger. Many of us, however, take the finger to be the moon.

When asked "Who is the Buddha?" Zen masters have given a variety of answers: "He is no Buddha." "Three pounds of flax." "See the Eastern mountains moving over the waters." In many instances, the answers appear irrelevant. At times they are contradictory. Ordinarily, they pull us away from our philosophical abstractions and draw our attention to the ordinary things of nature and life. Zen teaches that truth does not lie in our intellectual speculations but in the concrete events of daily living.

Words are words, but facts are facts. When words do not correspond to the facts, it is time to abandon words and return to facts. Most of us hang on to a logical interpretation of things. We have been taught that A is A, and it is unthinkable to suggest that A is not A. But our ordinary processes of logical reasoning do not satisfy our deeper interior and spiritual needs. Words and logic lead us to look at things, to differentiate among them, to develop an attitude toward them, and to judge them. In so doing we stand apart from them and perceive them only through our subjective constructs. Zen teaches us that A is not A. This is an apparent inconsistency. But, by becoming free of the intellect and its logic, we no longer need to be constrained by its constructs. We can stand in the rain and not be wet.

Zen aims at grasping the central fact of life. The fact of experience cannot be captured by any artificial scheme of thought or language. When we conceptualize and talk about our concepts, we make assertions or we make denials. We assert that A is A and we deny that A is B. Zen aims at a higher synthesis in which there is neither affirmation nor denial. In order to do this, it frequently proposes a series of negations that lead to a higher or more absolute affirmation. Thus we are told, "Coal is black, coal is not black." Such a statement cannot be understood philosophically. It has to be lived.

One problem is that we confuse the order of law with the order of nature. In nature, things simply happen. Our logic imposes on nature the "necessary" laws of affirmation and denial, cause and effect, and so forth. When we believe that things are necessities, life turns into a problem that must be solved. The necessities of affirmation and denial, cause and effect, and other patterns of logic are simply the necessities created by our subjective projection. They are not a problem in the natural order of things. Thus, the "problem" of life is absurd, meaningless, and need not be experienced as a problem.

The point is that we do not need to be prisoners of our thoughts and language. We can call a spade a spade if we want to and we can consider it an implement for digging. But we do not have to call a spade a spade. Nor must we confine our conception of it to that of a tool. A Zen master may hold up a spade and declare, "I hold a spade, yet I hold it not." In doing so the humble spade becomes the key to the riddle of the entire universe.

Another master may hold up a spade and say, "What do you see?" If a student answers, "I see a spade," the master knows that the student does not have Zen. But if the student replies, "I do not see anything," the master may retort, "How can you deny the fact that I am holding a spade?" To call the spade a spade is to make an assertion. To call it not a spade is to make a denial. The answer lies in perceiving the spade in a way that neither asserts nor negates. Such vision sees the spade but does not see it.

Our Western logic tells us that we cannot go beyond the dualistic antitheses of assertion and denial. Life tells us that we can and do. Most of us have been taught to conceive of life and ourselves as logical. Thus, we are encouraged to cultivate and follow our intellect. But the fact of the matter is that life has no such logic; we merely impose a logic on it. Moreover, in our everyday living, we continually behave in illogical ways. We add two and two and get five. We generally act out of our emotions and then use our logic and powers of rationalization to cover up the fact. Because we are not conscious of the illogic of our ways, we imagine that we are governed by logic and correct thought.

What answer should one give when the Zen master holds up a spade and asks his question? The question cannot be answered by logic or ordinary intellectual deduction. Actually, any answer will do, provided it comes from one's innermost being. Such an answer is always an absolute affirmation that goes beyond the logical antithesis of assertion and denial. But such an answer is very difficult to find.

Zen masters pose riddles such as the following: "If you speak I will give you thirty blows, but if you do not speak, I will give you thirty blows." "How do you interview a wise man if you neither speak nor remain silent?" "If a live charcoal is not fire, what is it?" The point of these questions is that they cannot be answered satisfactorily unless one makes the leap to an absolute affirmation that goes beyond the antithesis of the yes and no of ordinary thought. Even if the puzzle could be resolved logically, to resolve it in that way would be to miss the point. The riddles of Zen cannot be answered by our intellect but only through a consciousness of a higher order. Not to answer the question in this way is to be chained in one's own laws of thought and logic. Zen seeks to jolt us out of our intellectual ruts and conventional morality and to demonstrate a different order of things.

A monk, wanting to decide who would be his successor, brought in two of his disciples, showed them a pitcher, and said, "Do not call it a pitcher, but tell me what it is." The first replied, "It cannot be called a piece of wood." The second monk pushed the pitcher over and left the room. The monk who upset the pitcher was chosen as the new abbot.

Upsetting the pitcher appears to have qualified as an absolute affirmation. However, you would not be said to understand Zen if you were to repeat the monk's action under similar circumstances. Zen rejects any form of imitation or repetition. Each one of us must work out our own solution to the puzzle. The statement "If you find the Buddha on the road, kill him" also indicates that you must find your own salvation.

One master's assistant used to imitate his master who lifted his finger in reply to a question. When the master learned of this practice, he cut off the boy's finger. The boy could no longer imitate the master. A harsh lesson, perhaps, but a dramatic illustration that it is the spirit of Zen, not its law, that is to be followed.

The answer of absolute affirmation lies within. Each of us must find it for ourself. One's innermost self is innately perfect. Thus, each of us has the potential for perfection waiting to be actualized. The basic nature of our human consciousness is indistinguishable from the pure consciousness of the universe or the void. Our function is to arouse this deeper original consciousness that has been overlaid by intellectualization and the illusions of conventional thought. Most of us behave like someone who dies of starvation while sitting next to a bag of rice or who dies of thirst while standing in the rain. The truth lies within and can be discovered through experiencing the oneness of all things. Zen teaches us that we are ourselves the rice and the water that we need. Yet to discover this truth is more difficult than we think and may take years of work and preparation.

Enlightenment

The goal of Zen Buddhism is *satori* or "enlightenment." Suzuki wrote, "Satori is the *raison d'être* of Zen and without it there is no Zen" (1964). Satori is another concept that eludes intellectual conceptualization. Although most of us understand what the word "enlightenment" means, satori also refers to an art and a way of enlightenment. In order to communicate the message of satori, the writers of Zen again resort to similes and statements that baffle and confuse the Western mind. For example, a monk is said to have gone to a master to inquire where was the entrance to the path of truth. The master asked him, "Do you hear the murmuring of the brook?" When he replied, "Yes, I hear it," the master said, "There is the entrance."

In conceptual language, satori entails being freed of the misconception of self and becoming aware of our innermost truth. This truth enables us to recognize that we are at one with the universal. Sometimes this search for the truth is expressed in a metaphor: seeking an ox that has never gone astray. Having turned our backs on our true nature, we simply cannot see it. Satori is best conceived as intuitive perception rather than as intellectual or logical understanding. Moreover, it transforms us so that we are no longer troubled by the ordinary emotions, sorrows, and conflicts of everyday life. Satori, or enlightenment, entails an insight into the nature of the Self in which one's consciousness is freed of the illusory concept of the self as ego. In satori one breaks through the consciousness that is limited to the ego and experiences a non-ego-like-self. When the guru asks, "Do you hear the murmuring of the brook?" the reference is to something other than ordinary hearing, an experience that transcends yet is present in our everyday experience.

Satori must be personally experienced. A guru may point the way, but there are some things that a person can only do for him- or herself. If we are hungry or thirsty, another person's eating and drinking will not fill our stomach or moisten our throat. One has to eat and drink for oneself. This is why Zen masters insist that they have nothing to teach or to impart. All they can share is their own experience, but this cannot be said to be identical to anyone else's.

Satori does not yield to intellectual analysis. If it is conceptualized, it ceases to be enlightenment. A master can only indicate the way. The story is told of a master and his disciple who passed some wild laurel. "Do you smell it?" the master asked. When his disciple answered, "Yes," he remarked, "There, I have nothing to hide from you."

We are not told how enlightenment comes or what it consists of. The contents of satori cannot be encompassed in an intellectual definition or description. One disciple who acquired satori is reputed to have burned all of his commentaries on the Diamond Sutra, a Buddhist scripture, works that he had formerly cherished and kept by his side at all times. In view of his enlightenment, the wisdom contained in those writings was no more than a drop of water in a vast abyss.

Satori does not arise through concentration or meditation as they are ordinarily practiced. No effort of the will can bring it about even though many Zen Buddhists spend years preparing for it. When satori comes, it is said to come as a sudden jolt or flash. It overturns our minds and crumbles the structure of our normal patterns of thought. False pretensions and illusions disappear as our former framework of logic is torn asunder. This mental upheaval lays the foundation for a new life and a new sense of perception. Satori culminates in a new way of looking at things. It is not possible to describe the contents of satori or this new sense of perception with greater specificity. A person who has been enlightened does not doubt that he or she has been released from the ordinary perception of life. A master who has experienced the enlightenment of satori can also recognize it in his students. Beyond this, however, it belies further description. When Yakusan was asked to give a lecture on Buddhism, he did not utter a word. Another master simply stepped forward and opened out his arms.

The Practice of Zen

The practice of Zen entails a systematic training of the mind. Zen practices are designed to create in the disciples a state of mind that will permit enlightenment to occur. Zen trains the mind to see the ordinary, the everyday, as the greatest mystery of living. Zen refuses to deal with abstract concepts; it deals only with living facts of life. It points to truths in the midst of our everyday experience.

Two key elements in the practice of Zen are *zazen,* a form of meditation, and the *koan,* a paradoxical statement or question. Zen masters admit that both of these practices are actually artificial and superfluous. They are devices that are employed to open one's mind to the higher consciousness of Zen. Once the device has served its purpose, it can be discarded. The elements of zazen and the koan are used solely for their instrumental value. Nevertheless, thorough training in these techniques is provided for students of Zen. Their purpose is not the observance of rules and rituals, although the rules permit one to focus on the practice, but to obtain a freedom beyond rules and rituals that expresses the natural order of things.

Zazen (or *dhyana* in Sanskrit) refers to sitting crosslegged in quiet contemplation. The root of the word *dhyana* means to perceive or to reflect. The practice of dhyana or zazen is widespread in the East. In Zen, however, it has taken on a particular role as a means of dealing with the koan and other riddles of life.

The practice of zazen requires an appropriate posture that creates the right state of mind (see Figure 19.2). The student generally sits on a firm, round

Figure 19.2 *The Posture of Zazen*

cushion. In the full lotus position, the right foot is placed on the left thigh, and then the left foot is placed on the right thigh. This position expresses the oneness of duality. Even though we have two legs, in this posture they have become one. The head, neck, and spine are kept in a straight vertical line. The student pushes toward the sky with the back of his head as if trying to support it. The shoulders are relaxed, the chin is tucked in, and the diaphragm is pressed down toward the lower abdomen. The arms are held slightly away from the body and the hands are arranged to form a "cosmic mudra." The left hand is placed on top of the right with the middle joints of the middle fingers together. The thumbs are then held lightly together so that the hands form an oval. This posture provides a firm foundation for prolonged sitting. At first, it may be painful for the initiate since the muscles are unaccustomed to the position, but with practice the posture becomes very natural.

In Japan, students often use a variant posture for meditation. The heels are placed under the buttocks with a cushion between them and the buttocks, in order to take most of the weight off the lower legs and feet. It is also possible to meditate on a chair, a posture frequently preferred by Zen students in the West, but a cushion is placed under the buttocks so that the angle formed by the body and legs is about 95 degrees. Such an angle is mandated to keep the spine straight and erect. The perfectly vertical line of the torso and the erect spine are the hallmarks of all proper zazen postures.

When one sits correctly, the body is held in perfect balance. Everything exists in the right place and in the right way. In such a position, a person can maintain physical and mental balance and can breathe naturally and deeply. The state of consciousness that exists when one sits in the correct posture is, in itself, enlightenment, according to the teachings of Zen.

Such control over bodily reactions and processes is not unique to Zen but is shared by many other Eastern disciplines. No doubt the reader has some familiarity with the practice of yoga, a discipline cultivated by certain Hindu sects. Unfortunately, many Westerners have misinterpreted the essence of yoga, perceiving it as either a form of deception practiced by charlatans or just another set of exercises for physical fitness. In essence, however, yoga is a genuine means whereby one brings the body and mind into harmony. It consists of a series of postures gradually developed through a systematic approach by means of which one gains control over one's bodily processes. Such discipline permits the trained yogi or yogini to assume for a protracted period of time postures that for most of us would seem unbearable, such as elevating an arm or leg or standing on one's head.

There has been an increased interest in the West in transcendental meditation and biofeedback systems, practices that have grown out of essentially Asian psychologies. Studies suggest that such self-induced altered states of consciousness lead to better health and an increased ability to deal with stress and tension (Berson, Beary, and Carol, 1974). Such practices emphasize internal rather than external control as well as the unity of mind and body and they are gaining recognition for their efficacy from contemporary Western medicine.

Exploration /////

The "Corpse Posture"

One of the Hindu postures, known as the "corpse posture," is a method of inducing relaxation. Often used after strenuous exercise, it consists of lying on the back on a mat and progressively relaxing.

An effort to cultivate the Hindu "corpse posture" can be an excellent prelude to an attempt to learn to meditate. Because the posture aims at relaxation, it provides a solid foundation for all other meditational techniques. Lie down flat on your back on a mat or soft rug, your arms at your side with the palms up. You should not use a pillow. Allow yourself to relax, beginning with the toes and gradually proceeding to the rest of the body. Simply direct your attention to each part of the body as enumerated: your right big toe, each of the other toes on your right foot, the ball of the foot, arch, heel, the remainder of your foot, and your right ankle. Now direct your attention to your left foot in a similar progressive fashion. Continuing from your left ankle, attend to your leg, beginning with the lower part from the ankle to the knee, including the knee, and doing the same for the right. Attend to the upper parts of your legs and to your hips, one at a time. Then direct your attention to your pelvic area, your stomach, the sides of your body around the stomach area, and the lower part of your back. Move carefully and slowly up your spine to the upper part of your back and shoulder blades. Relax your chest, shoulders, and the upper parts of your arm. Attending to each arm separately, concentrate on the upper arm, elbow, lower arm, wrist, back and palm of the hand, and individual fingers. Pay attention to the back of your neck and its sides, your throat, jaw, and chin. Your lips, tongue, cheeks, nose, right and left ears, eyelids, eyebrows, forehead, and scalp. Gradually take three deep breaths and exhale slowly. Think about something pleasant, such as a tree, a painting, or a person. After you have relaxed for a while, gradually open your eyes, permit yourself to become mentally alert, and arise feeling refreshed.

While meditating one centers the mind on a single focus or no focus at all (emptying the mind) and seeks to control other elements. The student sits facing a blank wall in order to avoid distractions and frequently begins by concentrating on the act of breathing. When one is aware of this movement, all that exists is the rhythm of breathing. It is no longer necessary to be conscious of one's ego or self. The "I" moves along with the universal nature of breathing. Without air we cannot live and by concentrating on the experience of breathing we realize our interrelatedness with all things.

In Zen, zazen is also employed as a means for arriving at the solution to a koan. The term **koan** literally means a "public document." In the practice of Zen, it has come to refer to a paradoxical statement or question, provided by a teacher, that has no intellectual solution. The koan is an instrument for opening one's mind to the higher consciousness of Zen. Being merely a tool, appropriate use can open the mind to the inner truth of Zen. The koan itself is an intellectually unresolvable or meaningless statement or question such as "What is Mu?" "What is the sound of one hand clapping?" "How does one get a goose out of a bottle without breaking the bottle or hurting the goose?"

The koan is given to students to help them realize that what they have accepted as known facts of science or logical inferences are not necessarily so. The koan generally presents two alternatives, neither of which is intellectually possible. Its purpose is to frustrate the intellect in order to reduce its grip and allow a deeper consciousness to emerge. In their efforts to solve the puzzle of the koan, students realize that their former way of looking at things is not always correct nor is it helpful to spiritual growth. The koan cannot be resolved by the discursive intellect that reasons analytically. Our efforts at an intellectual resolution merely lead us to the edge of a mental cliff from which we have no alternative but to leap and leave the field of ordinary consciousness.

Although it might be possible to reason about the koan or intellectually try to resolve it, to do so is to miss the point. Our reasoning processes of assertion and denial obscure the truth. They stand in the way of accepting things as they are without judgments or abstractions. This is why the koan is designed to shut off the avenue of rationalization. We try to answer the koan, but our efforts are to no avail. Any answer that suggests intellectualization is abruptly dismissed by the master.

But the student's dilemma is the true starting place of Zen. Zen suggests that there are other forms of consciousness besides our ordinary consciousness of reality. Zen Buddhism distinguishes eight levels of consciousness. The first five are the ordinary senses of sight, sound, smell, taste, and touch. The sixth is thought or intellect. The seventh is mind, which entails intuition, and the eighth and highest level is universal consciousness that is at one with all of reality.

The koan arouses doubt and pushes it to its farthest limits. There is no logical way to resolve the koan through the powers of reason. It can be resolved only by a leap of consciousness in which Being is identified with non-Being, thought with non-thought, and Self with non-Self. From an intellectual viewpoint, one could say that the limits of our ordinary dualisms of logic have been transcended. But once we rise above our ordinary consciousness, we discover that in actuality there is nothing more than everyday consciousness. What appeared so mysterious was never hidden at all but was standing in front of us all the time. We realize that there was, after all, *nothing* to the koan. It was an artificial construct or dilemma, just like the other artificial constructs of our thought. When the koan is broken, we return to ordinary consciousness, yet somehow the world is perceived differently.

The koan is a miniature exaggeration of the problem of life. Just as the koan cannot be grasped and comprehended, so life itself cannot be contained and held. The koan, like life itself, cannot be understood, only accepted and lived.

In description, the process sounds deceptively simple. All one has to do is to release the grip of one's ordinary consciousness and permit a higher consciousness to emerge. But, in fact, the process is extremely hard, frustrating, and time consuming. Zen students work for years, trying to cultivate the proper state of mind that will permit enlightenment to occur. It is ironic that their strenuous efforts do not in themselves create satori. When satori comes, it comes as a flash or jolt that no amount of self-searching can produce because our efforts of will are always confined within the subjective limits of the individual ego.

Life in a Zen Monastery

The practical and disciplinary character of Zen emerges clearly in the life of a Zen monastery. The central focus of a monastery is the **zendo** or meditation hall, a rectangular building whose size varies according to the number of monks in the monastery. The zendo is the heart of a Zen monastery as it is here that the monks sleep and practice zazen. The monastery complex also includes a kitchen, dining hall, lavatories, master's quarters, guest rooms, and offices. Usually, there are gardens on the property and a farm adjacent or nearby where the monks raise fruit and vegetables for their food.

Hard work and rigid discipline characterize the life of a Zen monk. Po-chang, who founded the first Zen community, is said to have declared, "A day of no working is a day of no food" (Suzuki, 1964). Manual labor occupies a great deal of a monk's time, and no task, even the most menial, is viewed as degrading or beneath a monk's dignity. The monastery is kept immaculately clean, the gardens are beautifully cultivated, and the farm is carefully tended. There is plenty of work to be done: wood to be chopped, food to be prepared, and laundry to be washed. The hard work performed by Zen monks has gained them a reputation for being very industrious. Nevertheless, the monks

Exploration ////

Meditation

For a fuller understanding of the practice of Zen, it will be helpful if you try to meditate yourself. Carefully reread the description of meditation given in the text. Sit in a relaxed position, approximating the classic posture if you wish. Close your eyes and begin to meditate. At the beginning it will probably be most helpful if you concentrate on your breathing. This is most easily done by counting breaths up to ten and then beginning to count again. Try to concentrate solely on the experience of breathing. If anything else comes into your mind, say to yourself, "This is a passing thought," and go back to counting. In the beginning, you may find it difficult to focus your attention solely on the act of breathing but with time and practice you will be able to increase the amount of time spent in alert but relaxed concentration.

As you become more at ease with the process of meditating, it may facilitate your efforts to try to ponder one of the koans cited in this chapter or to contemplate a mantra. A **mantra** is a spiritual word or formula chanted throughout meditation in order to evoke a deeper level of consciousness. Sometimes the mantra is a syllable or word such as "*Om,*" which appears to have no intellectual meaning but which through use as a meditational tool reveals the essence of the divine. Other mantras are spiritual formulas: *Om Sivoham,* "I am a part of the cosmos," and *Aham Brahmo Smi,* "I am a unique creative center of Being." These formulas focus attention on the individual's true identity as part of the unity of the universe. A Zen master frequently assigns personal mantras to each of his students. The mantra then becomes the student's secret meditational device.

---

attend to their chores and labors in a spirit of zest and joy. Laughter and happy facial expressions accompany their efforts at tough manual work.

Economy and simplicity are the hallmarks of the life. In the monastery wants are reduced to a minimum, and the Zen monk leads the simplest of lives. There is little private property. Each monk has his *kesa* and *koromo* (priestly robes), a few books, a razor, and an *oryoki* (set of eating utensils). A monk's possessions are so few that they can be packed into a small wooden box. This box is suspended from the neck by a broad sash and carried in front of the body when the monk is traveling. In the zendo, each monk is provided with a *tatami* (a three by six foot mat) for sitting, meditating, and sleeping. In cold weather, a large quilt provides some protection and warmth.

A monk's day begins long before sunrise, as early as 4:00 A.M. The sound of a gong or bell summons the monks to rise, wash, dress, and prepare for the period of zazen that precedes the early morning meal. The gong also notes the times for the remaining activities of the day. The schedule is demanding and precise. There is no time to waste. A monk has just enough time to do what he has to do but little if any time to ponder how he feels about it. The purpose of such an exacting schedule is to remove attention from one's personal feelings or tendency to always consider how things ought to be done differently, so that a person may simply do what needs to be done. Zen teachings hold that truth does not reside elsewhere, but in the world of everyday living. By living each moment fully and concentrating simply on what one is doing, one can gain the awareness that he or she is perfect. Usually, we try to change ourselves and to be something or someone other than whom we already are. Likewise, when we are doing something, we tend to be concerned with what we think we should be doing rather than with what we are doing in the present. In the beginning, it is difficult for an initiate to get used to the rigid schedule and to cope with the utter lack of personal time. However, with practice, the schedule becomes second nature, an automatic routine, whose effect is freedom rather than restriction. The purpose of the rules in a Zen monastery is not to restrict the self but to enable a monk to express himself most freely. Such freedom arises when we no longer have to concentrate on what we should do but simply on what is being done and how we are doing it.

When it is time for meditation, the monks proceed into the zendo in single file and take their places on low platforms that face the center of the room. The head monk steps forward, prostrates himself before a shrine, and lights a stick of incense to mark the time. Other monks act as monitors and strike the meditators at various times with a *kyosaku* or wooden stick to arouse any of them from drowsiness. This procedure is also believed to stimulate psychic energy. The periods of sitting meditation generally last for about half an hour. A gong summons the monks to *kinhin,* or walking meditation. They proceed slowly around the zendo in single file, still focusing on the koan or some other practice. The combination of sitting and walking meditation provides a perfect balance of needs for both body and mind.

A gong indicates the time for a meal. The monks take their oryoki into the dining hall. The **oryoki** consists of a nest of four or five lacquered wooden bowls, chopsticks, spoon, scraping implement, napkin, and cloth for wrapping all the utensils together. Each activity entailed in eating with the oryoki is carefully prescribed. The monks unfold the cloth in a certain manner, remove and place the bowls on the table according to a set pattern, and so forth.

The food is simple but it provides the essentials for a well-balanced diet. Breakfast, eaten when it is still dark, generally consists of rice gruel and pickled vegetables. The main meal of the day is eaten at about ten in the morning and includes rice, vegetable soup, and pickles. Later in the afternoon, the monks eat what is known as a "medicinal meal." The Zen monk is not supposed to have an evening meal, but the climate of Japan made a compromise mandatory. The final meal of the day, therefore, consists of leftovers from the main meal and entails no special preparation.

Each meal begins with a special ceremony during which a short *sutra,* or sacred scripture, and the "Five Meditations on Eating" are recited:

> Firstly, let us reflect on our own work, let us see
>   whence comes this offering of food;
> Second, let us reflect how imperfect our virtue is,
>   whether we deserve this offering;
> Thirdly, what is most essential is to hold our minds
>   in control and be detached from the various faults;
> Fourthly, that this is medicinal and is taken to keep
>   our bodies in good health;
> Fifthly, in order to accomplish the task of
>   enlightenment, we accept this food.
>
> (Trans. Suzuki, as quoted in Watts, 1958)

Monks act as waiters and serve the food from large bowls. Before they eat, each monk sets aside a few grains of rice and offers them to spirits unseen. Later, these will be taken out to the garden for the birds. The meal is eaten in absolute silence. As they eat, the monks meditate on the principles of Zen Buddhism. The way in which each eating utensil is held and handled is meticulously prescribed. The monks communicate their need for more food with hand gestures. After the meal is finished, the waiters bring in hot water. Each monk fills his largest bowl and carefully washes and wipes all of his utensils according to a predetermined ritual. The bowls are then reassembled and precisely wrapped in their cloth. The monks leave the dining room, as they arrived, in silent procession.

Eating with an oryoki entails much more than simply a Zen version of etiquette. It is essentially a very simple way to eat, in which each movement is accounted for and reduced to the bare minimum. Although it takes practice and initial concentration, eventually one's attention is free to focus simply on eating. The practices and rituals of eating with an oryoki, just like the practice of zazen, are designed to remove attention from one's individual self or ego. When one eats in the prescribed manner, just as when one sits in the appropriate posture for zazen, one's movements are symbolic of the truth. Thus, in following these practices, one no longer needs to be concerned with cultivating a proper state of mind, because the practice itself provides the proper framework. The person is not restricted but is allowed to express him- or herself most freely. When we assume the right posture for zazen, the correct stance for eating, and so forth, we are already enlightened.

During periods of *sesshin,* which means "collecting or concentrating the mind," the usual manual labor of monastery life gives way to intensive spiritual training and discipline. Sesshin lasts for a week and is held about four times a year. During sesshin the monks rise even earlier than usual, stay up later, and remain in the zendo for extensive periods of meditation. Sesshin provides extensive opportunites for teisho and sanzen. *Teisho* refers to a lecture or discourse on the inner meaning of Zen that is given by the master. It is generally based on one of the sacred texts. The presentation of a teisho is accompanied by a great deal of ceremony and ritual. The sermon itself is frequently mystifying and obscure to the unenlightened. One master is reported to have said nothing at all. Instead, he called attention to the song of a bird and remarked that the sermon had been given. Such discourses are to be viewed in the same vein as a koan. They baffle the intellect and prepare the mind for a new point of view. **Sanzen** consists of individual consultations between a monk and his master. Many of the written teachings of Zen refer to such interviews. The sanzen is a formal, solemn conference during which the monk presents his view on the koan or some other questions. Before he enters the master's quarters, the monk bows three times. He enters the room with his hand held palm to palm in front of his chest and prostrates himself. Once the conference begins, however, all formalities and conventions are laid aside, and unexpected exchanges may occur. The purpose of sanzen is to make manifest the truth of Zen. Blows and other physical combat may be used to this end. It has been said that a smack on the face expresses the truth of Zen far more than do words. As long as the student gives an intellectual solution to his koan, the master will abruptly reject his answer. The student who attempts to resolve a koan with the intellect is as inept as a mosquito that tries to bite an iron rod. Once the student forgets himself, however, and abandons the pretensions of his individual ego, the flash of satori comes, and he is able to realize that there was nothing in the koan after all. Such enlightenment does not come quickly, however, but only after several years of hard work and innumerable impasses during sessions of sanzen.

This description of life in a Zen community has focused on the life of a monk, or male. Unfortunately, we know little about the role of women in Zen. There are Zen Buddhist nunneries in Japan, but few women have written about their experiences and it appears that the leadership is predominantly male. In America, however, Zen centers are integrated and women are slowly assuming a more active role.

Zen monks do not remain forever in the monastery. Many return to the everyday life of the world and some of them marry. Monastic separateness is not an ideal of Zen Buddhist life. Zen Buddhism requires that its disciples be in the world but not of the world. Returning to the world permits a further maturing of one's character. This requires one to act out of one's full being in the ordinary affairs of everyday life.

Some have suggested that Zen permits and justifies any kind of behavior inasmuch as Zen accepts all things, both good and evil, as evidences of reality. This is not the case. Zen disciples observe a rigorous discipline, both within the monastery and outside in the everyday world. It would be more correct to suggest that Zen commences where conventional morality ceases. Our ordinary morality is a tool that enables us to live in society and get along with other people. As such, it is useful but it can also become enslaving. Nevertheless, mastery of the moral law is a necessary precedent for awakening to a higher spiritual law. An analogy could be drawn to the cultivation of a garden. A garden must be carefully planned and laid out so that the plants do not choke one another and crowd each other out. But the beauty of a garden does not lie in the planning or position of each individual flower. The beauty resides in the glory of the finished garden as a whole.

In short, Zen is life. Alan Watts, a convert to Zen, describes it as follows: "to chase after Zen is like chasing one's own shadow, and all of the time one is running away from the sun. When at last it is realized that the shadow can never be caught, there is a sudden 'turning about,' a flash of satori, and in the light of the sun the dualism of self and its shadow vanishes; whereas man perceives that what he was chasing was only the unreal image of the one true Self — of That which he ever was, is and shall be. At last he has found Enlightenment" (Watts, 1958).

Eastern Thought and Psychotherapy

Alan Watts, one of the leading Western authorities on Eastern thought, compared the modes of liberation or psychotherapeutic change developed by the East and the West (1961). Both Western psychotherapy and Eastern ways of life aim at change. However, whereas Western psychotherapy has emphasized change for neurotic or disturbed individuals, Eastern disciplines are concerned with change in the consciousness of normal or healthy people. Eastern psychotherapies recognized long ago that the culture in which one lives not only defines what is normal and abnormal in that particular society but also provides the context for and fosters a more pervasive form of neurosis that is endured by all of its members.

In the West, Sigmund Freud drew our attention to the offenses that are made against the human being by social repression. In large measure, the task of the psychoanalyst is to liberate his or her patient from stressful social conditioning so that he or she can function more effectively. Eastern psychotherapy, however, goes further than classical Freudian psychoanalysis and other Western psychotherapies. It seeks not just to restore the disturbed individual to normal, healthy, social functioning but to point out that the distress of the normal person, as well as the abnormal, is caused by maya or illusion. The neurosis of all humanity lies in the fact that we take the world picture of our culture too literally and identify ourselves with our social role.

The construct of the self as "individual" is a social process created in the history of our relations with others that gives us our categories of subjective identity. The "I" of the individual ego becomes conscious of itself only in terms of the view of itself given to it by other people. Because the ego is socially constituted, it cannot be identified with anything ultimate or real. The answer lies not in destroying the illusion but in recognizing it for what it is.

In his theory of psychoanalysis, Freud emphasized the conflict that arises between the person's sexual desires and impulses and the cultural mores and standards that require him or her to repress them. Eastern thought sees more clearly that social institutions repress not only sexuality but also the deeper relationship and involvement of the person and the environment. The person does not emerge from the socially created boundaries of self and not-self, inner and outer, subject or object, but from an encounter with what is real. As long as we insist on the reality of these social constructs, we will not encounter ourselves in our full potentiality.

In Eastern ways of liberation, a guru or master points toward enlightenment by persuading disciples to act on their own delusions. Initiating a countergame, the guru provides students with new ways of acting on their premises until they convince themselves that they are false. The students are placed in a dilemma or double bind from which they cannot escape unless they abandon their former conceptions and risk the leap of simply recognizing and accepting things for what they are. To answer a koan, the ego must get rid of the ego. Once we get rid of the ego, we can return to the master and demonstrate that we see through the koan's pretext. There is an obvious parallel here between Eastern liberation and Western psychotherapy, which permits the patient to act on his or her symptoms until he or she realizes their inappropriateness and ceases to use them. Nevertheless, Watts points out that Western psychotherapy falls short of being a way of liberation because it fails to deal with the bigger problem of rectifying the breach between the individual and the world. It is content to limit itself to the individual's adjustment to his or her society. Frequently, its aim is to fortify the ego rather than to dissolve it.

Freud could not begin to resolve the problem of the individual and his or her relationship to reality, partly because he believed that there was an irreparable conflict between the ego and the world. The world, he held, was too poor to meet our needs. Zen points out that we construct our own reality through the development of culture and society. Only by recognizing our construction for the maya that it is can we envision a way to resolve the seemingly irreconcilable opposites brought forth in the Taoist symbol of yin and yang, each of which actually contains the seed of the other.

Eastern Theories: Philosophy, Science, and Art

Eastern thinkers have not developed theories of personality comparable to modern Western theories. They have merely said and written a great deal about the relationship between the self and the cosmos. Although it is possible to abstract a theory of personality from the writings of the East, to do so really violates the spirit in which they are presented. Eastern reflections on the self and the cosmos represent an art, rather than a philosophy or a science.

Nevertheless, it is possible to outline certain broad concepts about personality that are present in Eastern thought, which provide a basis for comparison with other theories. For example, in the East the emphasis is relational rather than individual. The person is not considered in isolation but in relation to the self, to others, and to the larger cosmos.

Most certainly, Eastern concepts of personality do not qualify, nor do they aspire to qualify, as science. The very need to evaluate and demonstrate a personality theory's usefulness constitutes a bias that is foreign to Eastern thought. Although some efforts have been made in the West to validate objectively the claims that certain meditational techniques lead to effective results, for Eastern thinkers the truth could never rest on such grounds. In Zen truth resides in satori, the compelling vision that accompanies enlightenment.

Eastern theories are sometimes considered a philosophy or a religion. However, they do not entail the speculation or logic that characterizes Western philosophy and religion. Thus, for our purposes it is most accurate to call them an art. Eastern theories are highly practical. They offer a variety of techniques for cultivating a deeper understanding of self. These practices move the individual away from intellectual, rational consciousness and cultivate a deeper awareness that transcends everyday consciousness. Systematically training the body and the mind, Eastern disciplines aim at enabling the individual to perceive the truth that lies within his or her inner being.

As we have seen, there has been a steady growth of interest in the ideas and practices of the East. The influence of Eastern concepts is apparent in the work of several personality theorists included in this book: Jung explicitly incorporated Eastern concepts into his theory; both Fromm and Horney turned to the East to enrich their theories and practices. Today, with increased opportunities for cooperation or combat, it is vitally important that East and West appreciate each other's attempts to understand the self. To do so can only enrich us both.

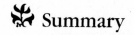 Summary

1. Eastern psychology is characterized by an emphasis on the self and an emphasis on practical techniques.

2. Siddhartha Gautama, the Buddha, renounced everything that he had and left home in search of **nirvana.** After several years of extreme asceticism, he attained enlightenment. He developed the doctrine of **Four Noble Truths** and articulated teachings about **Brahma** and **Atman.** Hinayana and Mahayana Buddhism grew out of his doctrine. **Zen Buddhism** stems from the Mahayana branch and includes elements of **Taoism.**

3. Zen Buddhism is a vigorous reaction against the intellectualism that characterizes many philosophical, religious, and psychological approaches to life. The solution to life's problems according to Zen cannot be found through intellectual channels, only through intuition and experience.

4. The goal of Zen Buddhism is **satori** or enlightenment, a concept that does not yield to intellectual analysis but must be experienced personally.

5. The practice of Zen entails a systematic training of the mind. Two key elements in the practice of Zen are **zazen,** a form of meditation, and the **koan,** a paradoxical statement or question.

6. Life in a Zen monastery is characterized by hard work and rigid discipline, economy, and simplicity. These are reflected in rituals of eating, working, and meditating.

7. Whereas Western psychotherapy has emphasized change for neurotic or disturbed individuals, Eastern disciplines are concerned with change in the consciousness of normal or healthy people, pointing out that the distress of both is caused by **maya,** or illusion.

8. Eastern theories do not entail the speculation or logic characteristic of Western theories. For our purposes, it is most accurate to characterize them as art.

Suggestions for Further Reading

The writings of D. T. Suzuki and Alan Watts, leading exponents of Zen Buddhism in America, provide an excellent introduction to the thought of Zen. Having introduced Zen to the English-speaking world in his renowned series of *Essays in Zen Buddhism* (Rider and Company, London, beginning in 1927), Suzuki wrote some twenty additional major works in English and at least eighteen in Japanese. Recognizing that the entire set of essays was somewhat lengthy and cumbersome, in 1934 Suzuki re-edited several of the major essays to constitute a shorter work, *An Introduction to Zen Buddhism* (Grove Press,

1964), that is probably the best introduction to Zen for the lay person. The companion volume, *Manual of Zen Buddhism* (Grove, 1960), is recommended for use with it.

Alan Watts wrote numerous books on Eastern thought that have attracted a wide lay audience. His best known is probably *The Spirit of Zen* (Grove Press, 1958), describing the way of life, work, and art in the Far East. Watts's *Psychotherapy East and West* (Pantheon Books, 1961) relates Eastern thought to the needs of Western culture and offers reflection on Western psychotherapy.

A good additional reference for the student who wishes to enter further into the spirit of Zen is R. H. Blyth, *Haiku* (Hokuseido, 1952). Haiku is a short Japanese poem form consisting of only three lines, with usually the first and last lines of five syllables and the second line seven syllables. Other books that are easily available and meaningful to students are Chuang Tsu, *Inner Chapters*, translated by Gia-Fu Feng and Jane English (Vintage Books, 1974); Lao-Tse, *Tao Te Ching*, translated by Gia-Fu Feng and Jane English (Vintage Books, 1972); Jane Hamilton-Merritt, *A Meditator's Diary* (Harper & Row, 1976); and Sheldon Kopp, *If You Meet the Buddha on the Road, Kill Him* (Science and Behavior Books, 1972). A more difficult but useful book is Rune E. A. Johansson's *The Psychology of Nirvana* (Doubleday Anchor, 1970).

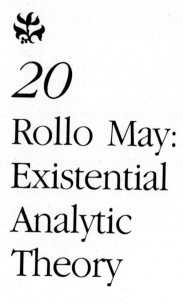

20
Rollo May: Existential Analytic Theory

Your Goals for This Chapter

1. Identify two major traditions that Rollo May combines.

2. Describe the philosophy of *existentialism.*

3. Explain the existentialist approach to scientific methodology.

4. Describe the central problem May believes we face at the end of the twentieth century.

5. Explain how May conceives of *anxiety* and tell how it is intensified in contemporary culture.

6. Discuss the source of the human dilemma according to May.

7. Identify four ontological assumptions May makes concerning human beings and explain how they can give us a structural basis for a science of personality.

8. Discuss what is involved in rediscovering selfhood.

9. Show how May confronts the paradoxes involved in each of the following goals of integration: love, intentionality, the daimonic, courage and creativity, power, freedom and destiny.

10. Describe the existentialist approach to psychotherapy.

11. Describe May's methods of research.

12. Evaluate May's theory in terms of its function as philosophy, science, and art.

*R*ollo May's work represents a unique effort to bring together the psychoanalytic tradition in psychology and the existentialist movement in philosophy. As we have seen, Freud's writings, though transcending his own era, nevertheless clearly reflect tendencies of nineteenth-century philosophy that are inappropriate today. In combining the insights of psychoanalysis and existentialism, May has not only ensured the continued impact of many of Freud's contributions but he has also developed his own original stance. In doing so, he has helped to underscore the importance of philosophy and the understanding of values for the psychologist and the theory of personality.

Biographical Background

Rollo May was born on April 21, 1909, in Ada, Ohio, and grew up in Marine City, Michigan, where a middle-American anti-intellectual attitude prevailed. His father commented several times that a psychotic breakdown experienced by Rollo's older sister was due to "too much education." May felt that the comment was "inhumane and destructive" and came to hate the disease of anti-intellectualism. However, he indicates that in other respects his father was a very sympathetic man (1983).

May enrolled in college at Michigan State, but his studies there were abruptly ended when he began to edit a radical student magazine. He transferred to Oberlin College in Ohio where he completed the A.B. in 1930. There, fresh from Michigan, he marveled at the simple yet beautiful lines of an antique Greek vase displayed on a table in one of the classrooms and resolved to go to Greece, which he did immediately after his graduation. He worked in Greece for three years, teaching at Anatolia College in Salonika and traveling during the summer. He spent two summers with a group of modern artists, painting and studying peasant art. The impact of Greek philosophy and mythology is clear in his writings. He also went to Vienna and studied briefly with Alfred Adler whose approach influenced him considerably.

Europe's tragic view of human nature prevented May from ever accepting a mechanistic concept of the person. Upon his return, American psychology seemed "naive and simplistic." So he enrolled at Union Theological Seminary in New York — not with the intent of becoming a preacher, but with the intent to ask questions. There he could raise penetrating inquiries into the meaning of despair, suicide, and anxiety, issues largely ignored by psychologists. He also hoped that in doing so he might learn about their counterparts: courage, joy, and the intensity of living (1983). At Union, he began a lifetime friendship with the eminent Protestant theologian Paul Tillich, an association that enriched the lives, work, and writings of both of them.

May's parents were divorced while he was at Union, so he interrupted his

Rollo May

studies and returned to East Lansing, Michigan, to take care of what remained of his family, his mother, a younger sister, and a brother. During that time, he served as an advisor to students at Michigan State College. He was able to return to New York and complete the B.D. in 1938. During his senior year at Union, his first book, *The Art of Counseling,* was written.

Thereafter, May served briefly as a parish minister in Montclair, New Jersey, before going back to New York to study psychoanalysis at the William Alanson White Institute for Psychiatry, Psychoanalysis, and Psychology. He enrolled at Columbia University and eventually received the first Ph.D. in clinical psychology.

May's life, however, was sharply interrupted when as a young man in his early thirties, he came down with tuberculosis. At the time there was no medication for the disease. May had to spend three years at the Saranac TB Sanatorium in upstate New York, not knowing whether he would live or die. During his illness, he read, among other works, *The Problem of Anxiety* by Freud and *The Concept of Dread* by Sören Kierkegaard, the founder of the existential movement in philosophy. He appreciated Freud's careful formulations but felt that Kierkegaard "portrayed what is immediately experienced by human beings in crisis" (1969a). May's illness helped him to appreciate the importance of an existential point of view. His own book *The Meaning of Anxiety* (1977) has been widely recognized as the first to encourage a genuine union between psychology and philosophy and to demonstrate the importance of values for psychology.

May's professional life has been busy and productive. He served as a counselor to college students at City College of New York, developed a private practice in psychoanalysis, and became a member of the White Institute. He has taught at The New School for Social Research, New York University, Harvard, Yale, and Princeton. He has numerous publications and has been honored with several awards. He married Florence deFrees and has one son and two daughters. At present, May lives in Tiburon, California.

The Existential Attitude

Existentialism is a movement in contemporary psychology and psychotherapy that sprang up spontaneously in different parts of Europe and among different schools. It has its roots in the resistance movements during World War II and in the earlier philosophies of Sören Kierkegaard (1813–1855), Martin Heidegger (1889–1976), and Jean Paul Sartre (1905–1980). The name existentialism comes from the Latin *exsistere,* which means "to stand out" or "to emerge," and the existential approach focuses upon the human being as he or she is emerging and becoming.

In the past, Western philosophy has traditionally looked for the **essence** of being, the unchangeable principles and laws that are believed to govern existence. Mathematics is the purest form of this approach. In psychology, the essentialist attitude expresses itself in the effort to understand human beings in terms of forces, drives, and conditioned reflexes. Existentialists point out that a law can be true and still not be real. "Two unicorns plus two unicorns equals four unicorns" is a logically true statement but it does not talk about anything that is real. Existentialism seeks to bridge the gap between what is abstractly true and what is existentially real (May et al., 1958).

The existential attitude is a bewildering one that defies simple definition. We can illustrate it, however, by comparing two possible postures that a person might have at a football game. The first is that of the spectator up in the stands; the second is that of the player on the field. Both spectator and player are involved in the football game, but there is a considerable difference in their involvement. The spectator may get very agitated and excited as the game proceeds. He or she may urge and cheer on a favorite team. But his or her involvement is very different from that of the player. The outcome of the game does not depend on the activity of the spectator, who remains outside the game as an observer. The outcome does depend very much on how the player behaves and performs on the field. What he or she does is not indifferent to the game. The player cannot stand back and observe the game while involved in it.

The posture of existentialism is that of the player, and the game of existentialism is the game of life. In the game of life, existentialists point out, we cannot play the role of a detached or uninvolved spectator because we are already participants in the game.

Existentialists suggest that there is no truth or reality for us as human beings except as we participate in it, are conscious of it, and have some relation to it. Knowledge is not an act of thinking but an act of doing. Existentialists do not necessarily rule out essences. May, for example, does not deny the validity of concepts such as conditioning or drives; he simply points out that we cannot adequately explain a person on that basis because when we try to, we end up talking about abstractions rather than the living person. It is all right to have concepts, but we must recognize that they are only tools and not substitutes for the living person. Thus, when we use concepts, we must make it clear that we are abstracting them from the living person and we are not talking about the real person.

Psychologists have generally tended to study those phenomena that lend themselves to control and analysis and permit one to formulate abstract laws. They are not particularly concerned with whether or not the phenomena are real or even close to everyday life. Indeed, in some laboratory experiments, the phenomenon under consideration is far removed from real life. Existentialists believe that the psychologists' preoccupation with lawfulness and predictability, as these are usually conceived, stands in the way of our understanding the real person. May points out that the behavior of a neurotic is quite predictable because it is compulsive, whereas the healthy person is "predictable" in that his or her behavior is integrated and unified, but at the same time he or she can be flexible and spontaneous. The existentialist approach has been criticized for rendering the individual unlawful and unpredictable. It is true that existentialists do not see the human being in terms of our traditional conceptual theories, looking instead at the structure of a particular person's existence and its own lawfulness.

The existentialist approach is not antiscientific. It arose out of a desire to be not *less* but *more* empirical, but it does urge a greater breadth to our scientific methodology. Contrary to the conventional approach of the scientist in which the more complex is explained by the simpler, existentialists believe that a reductionistic approach misleads and that the "simpler can be understood and explained only in terms of the more complex" (May, 1969). When a new level of complexity emerges, it becomes crucial for understanding the forms that have preceded it. What makes a horse a horse is not what it shares with the organisms it evolved from but what constitutes its distinctive "horseness"

(1983). Science, therefore, must look for the distinguishing characteristic of what it is trying to understand, namely, the human being.

The existentialist view takes the inquiry to a deeper level to look at the structure in which those concepts are rooted. It seeks to develop an empirical science that deals with the whole of our knowledge of what it means to be human. As such, it looks at the unity of the person prior to any split into subject versus object, body versus mind, nature versus nurture, or any other conceptual "either-or" dimensions. It asks what does it mean to be and to exist under these particular psychological, cultural, and historical conditions.

In studying the structure of human existence, the very nature of the subject shapes the science that investigates it. Existentialists have made clear the limits of objectivity in our understanding and the need to broaden the scope of our methodology. Objectivity is a goal that many psychologists have prized and sought to achieve. They believe that unless we are objective, our emotions and prejudices will come between us and the facts, clouding our reasoning processes. Students of psychology are encouraged to take a detached, objective stance. At times, however, objectivity prevents understanding. Some truths, such as understanding what it means to be, are discovered not by objectivity but by intense personal involvement. Although objectivity may tell us that the study of a rat's behavior in a Skinner box shows something about ourselves, we do not really understand ourselves except as we enter into personal relations with others. The existentialist attitude strongly resists the tendency to treat a person as an object.

In their insistence that human knowledge is ultimately interpersonal, May and other existentialists are indebted to the thought of Martin Buber (1878–1965), whose book *I-Thou* made a classic distinction between knowing that is transpersonal (I-Thou) and knowing that is objective or subjective (I-it). In his book, Buber describes an entirely different way in which the world, particularly the world of persons, reveals itself to us. Knowledge is not simply objective (of an external object) or subjective (of the self) but also interpersonal, arising out of the encounter of human beings with one another. Understanding through encounter is just as real as understanding through objectification. Most personality theorists have tended to reduce persons to I-it descriptions. For example, Cattell describes a person by means of sixteen numbers. May would suggest that real persons — Ted Clifford, Kathy Kapner — are not "known" by this process, merely abstracted.

Existentialism begins with personal existence. It asks, "What does it mean to be a self?" It questions the purpose and nature of existence. It views each individual as an agent with free choice who is responsible for his or her actions. Each one of us carves out our own destiny. We are literally what we do. The existentialist posture leads to an emphasis on choice and responsibility and to the view that a worthwhile life is one that is authentic, honest, and genuine.

Depersonalization

Almost everyone has experienced being processed by some large institution such as a school, a hospital, the military, or a service organization. In the course of such an experience, we often feel as if we are being treated as numbers or objects rather than as people. We experience *feelings of depersonalization.* You can better understand the factors that contribute to feelings of depersonalization by focusing on an experience in which you felt depersonalized and trying to identify as clearly as possible some of the things that caused those feelings. Were there any physical characteristics of the institution that contributed to your feelings of depersonalization (such as long corridors, identical offices or rooms, uniforms, standardized furniture or equipment)? How did the procedure itself foster depersonalization (for example, long waiting periods, routine questions, limits placed on your behavior or statements)? How did the behavior of others and your interchanges with them contribute to your feelings (for example, lack of eye contact, impersonal treatment)? What are some of the ways in which you believe feelings of depersonalization could be minimized?

Our Predicament

Existentialism and psychoanalysis grew out of the same cultural situation. Both seek to understand anxiety, despair, and the alienation that people feel today from themselves and society. During the last half of the nineteenth century, the concept of personality was fragmented into separate elements such as the will, the reason, and the emotions. There was a strong tendency to make the person over into a machine, thinking of people in terms of the industrial system for which they worked. This segmentation of culture had a psychological counterpart in extreme repression within the individual. It was Freud's genius to speak to, and help cure, the problem of repression (May et al., 1958). However, the problem went deeper than neurotic repression in the individual. Kierkegaard, Nietzsche, and other forerunners of the existentialist position foresaw that the forces of disintegration were gradually destroying the inner emotional and spiritual life of the person and leading to ultimate despair and alienation from him- or herself and from society. Thus, May points out (1967), in the second half of the twentieth century, the central problem that we face is a feeling of *powerlessness,* a "pervasive conviction that the individual can not do anything effective in the face of enormous cultural, social, and economic problems."

*Feelings of impotence may
breed violence and hostility.*

Powerlessness

The problem of powerlessness goes much deeper than the fact that this is
an age of uncertainty and social upheavals. The unwanted war in Vietnam
illustrated how we could become caught in a historical situation in which
no one person or group of persons felt capable of exercising significant power.
With our increased technology, power has become impersonal, an autonomous
force, acting on its own behalf (1967).

In the early 1950s, May observed that many of the patients who came to
see him were suffering from inner feelings of emptiness (1953). He noted that
the neurotic frequently acts out what others are temporarily unaware of. The
sexual problems that Freud saw in his patients at the turn of the century
became widespread among the population after World War I. May anticipated
that the experience of emptiness and powerlessness he was seeing in his
patients would in time become epidemic, and of course it has. The 1970s saw
considerable talk about human potentialities, yet very little confidence on

the part of the individual about his or her power to make a significant difference (1975). This feeling of paralysis has accompanied us into the 1980s.

The most striking example of the individual's sense of insignificance and powerlessness is the impotence each one of us feels concerning the threat of nuclear war. The potentiality for such a war rapidly increases along with a recognition that such a war will most likely begin through a computer malfunction or accident. The threat of nuclear war and other unsettling social conditions are but symptoms of the deeper problem. Contemporary men and women feel helpless and insignificant. Our impotence leads to anxiety and repression, leading in turn to apathy, which is a form of protection. Impotence and apathy, however, also breed violence and hostility that further alienate us from one another and only serve to increase our isolation (1972).

Anxiety

It has become commonplace to describe our age as an age of anxiety. However, prior to 1950, only two books had been written that concerned themselves specifically with presenting an objective picture of anxiety and suggesting constructive ways of dealing with it: Freud's *The Problem of Anxiety* and Kierkegaard's *The Concept of Dread.* After May wrote *The Meaning of Anxiety,* which was first published in 1950, hundreds of works followed on the same topic. May's efforts helped to spur research into this area. *The Meaning of Anxiety* was revised in 1977 and at that time May pointed out that the tremendous interest in anxiety that attended its initial publication had indicated the need for an integrated theory of anxiety. May's work is distinguished by its efforts to synthesize the insights of both psychology and philosophy. Since that time, he has applied his analytic synthesis to the dilemmas of love and will, power and innocence, creativity, and freedom and destiny.

Some psychologists prefer to use the term *stress* in place of anxiety. May believes that this tendency is unfortunate and inaccurate. The word stress has become popular, because it comes from engineering and physics; it can be defined easily and measured accurately. The problem with the concept of stress is that it does not adequately describe the apprehension we ordinarily refer to as anxiety. Moreover, it puts the emphasis on what happens *to* a person, whereas anxiety is distinctly bound up with consciousness and subjectivity (1977).

May proposes the following definition of **anxiety:** "Anxiety is the apprehension cued off by a threat to some value that the individual holds essential to his or her existence as a person" (1977). Anxiety is an ontological characteristic of being human (1983), a given. Anxiety is objectless, "because it strikes at that basis of the psychological structure on which the perception of one's self as distinct from the world of objects occurs" (1977). It threatens the security base that permits the individual to experience him- or herself as a self in relation to objects. Thus, in anxiety, the distinction between self and object breaks down.

The potential for anxiety is innate, although the particular events that may become threatening are learned. Fear is the expression of anxiety in a specific objectified form. May suggests that anxiety is intensified in our contemporary competitive culture by the interpersonal isolation and alienation that have emerged out of a particular pattern in which one's self is viewed as an object and self-validation depends upon winning over others (1977). Anxiety, therefore, is another symptom of the deeper problem.

Our current stepped-up efforts to dispel anxiety actually end up increasing it. Indeed, the ultimate self-destruction of our technology is found in our abortive efforts to use it to fill the vacuum of our own diminished consciousness. May reminds us that we cannot live in an empty condition for a sustained period of time (1953). We need something to fill the gap, be it a destructive authority, drugs, or alcohol. Earlier in this century, the emotional vacuum in Europe permitted fascist dictatorships to seize power. Currently, large numbers of young people systematically and deliberately "waste" themselves on alcohol and drugs. The problem is that human consciousness, responsibility, and intentions have not been able to keep up with all of the rapid changes in contemporary society. If we were able to recognize our historical situation and its psychological implications, we might be able to move from self-defeating activities to constructive ones.

The Loss of Values

The source of our problem lies in the loss of the center of values in our society (1967). Ever since the Renaissance, the dominant value in Western society has been competitive prestige measured in terms of work and financial success. Such values are no longer effective in the contemporary world in which we have to learn to work with other people in order to survive. Individual competition no longer brings the greatest good to one's self or to the community. Instead, it creates problems where previously it did not.

Our human dilemma arises out of our ability to stand outside of ourselves and relate to ourselves. This ability permits us to create values; it is a distinguishing mark of the human being that he or she is an animal that values (1967). For several centuries, we were able to validate ourselves by our power over nature. Then we began to supply the methods that had been so successful in controlling nature to ourselves. In so doing, we rendered ourselves impersonal objects that could be exploited. Along with the loss of the dominant value of individualism, we lost a sense of the worth and dignity of the human being. We became estranged from nature and from one another. Today, many young people are more comfortable conversing with a computer than with another human being. The loneliness and isolation that were potential in Western technology have become widely apparent in our time.

The answer to our dilemma is to discover and affirm a new set of values. There are those who would suggest that we need to reaffirm the traditional values, embodied in earlier philosophies and religion, that we have permitted to go by the wayside. Here, May's existential stance becomes apparent. Because we have no "essence," there are no given or pre-established values to which we can turn. Our values are established in the course of our existence and our destiny now includes the historical situation in which we have placed ourselves (1981). There can be no simple reaffirmation of our human "essence," because there is none; the human being is forever in the process of becoming. We have to choose our values in the process of living.

The choice is ours, and so is the responsibility. We can withdraw in anxiety, giving up our distinctive human capacity to influence our own development through our awareness, and surrender to the power of the technology that we created or we can muster together the courage that we need to preserve our sensitivity and responsibility and consciously work together in developing a new society (1975).

Rediscovering Selfhood

May (1953) believes that *consciousness of self* is the unique mark of the human person. Self-consciousness is the source of our highest qualities. It enables us to distinguish between ourselves and the world, to learn from the past and to plan for the future, to see ourselves as others do, and to have empathy with others. However, such self-consciousness comes at the price of anxiety and inward crisis. It means that we must stand on our own and develop an identity apart from that of our parents and forebears. We can even stand against them, if necessary.

Unlike the acorn that grows automatically into an oak tree, the human being, in fulfilling his or her nature, must do so in self-consciousness through choice and affirmation. Self-actualization is not automatic. Selfhood is born in a social context and grows in interpersonal relations. However, May's emphasis is not on the extent to which we are created by others, but rather on our capacity to experience and create our own selves.

Some psychologists avoid the concept of self because it separates humans from animals and complicates scientific experimentation. May, along with Rogers and Maslow, believes that in doing so psychologists miss an important feature of the human experience. Our capacity for self-relatedness is prior to, not established by, our science. It is presupposed in the fact that one can be a scientist. May would like to see us develop a science to illuminate the concept of self.

Ontological Assumptions Concerning the Person

Psychologists need to ask questions on an *ontological* level, the level of being. What is the nature of the person as a person? The problem with emphasizing the study of behaviors is that the psychologist does not clarify the assumptions that led to the choice of a particular behavior to study or indicate the way in which he or she proposes to unite them. The principle of selection and the form of union constitute the original contribution that existential analysis can make to the problem (1967).

As a clinician, May frankly admits that he makes certain ontological and philosophical assumptions about what it means to be a human being (1967). First, he assumes that all living organisms are potentially centered in themselves and seek to preserve that center. In psychotherapy, a patient is engaged in the process of such preservation. Second, human beings have the need and the possibility of going out from their centeredness to participate with other people. This entails risk and is illustrated in psychotherapy in the encounter with the therapist. Third, May suggests that sickness is a method whereby an individual seeks to preserve his or her being, a strategy for survival, even though that method may be limiting and block off potentials for knowledge and action. Finally, May asserts that human beings can participate in a level of self-consciousness that permits them to transcend the immediate situation and to consider and actualize a wider range of possibilities. These ontological assumptions can give us a structural basis for a science of personality. They precede our analytic activity and make it possible. In turn, our analytic activity can help to illumine them.

Psychological concepts need to be oriented within an ontological framework. Thus, May suggests that the concept of *unconscious experience* can be understood in terms of self-deception and experiences that an individual cannot permit him- or herself to actualize. May reinterprets the oedipal myth and conflict as describing the problems involved in a person's relation to the world and others through the emergence and development of consciousness (1967). The main question in the drama does not concern murder and incest but is "Shall Oedipus recognize what he has done?" What is at issue is seeing reality and the truth about oneself.

May believes that the theme of exile in the story is very important. Oedipus was exiled as a baby and at the end of the drama he exiles himself. Being aware that one is the conscious being responsible for one's life, a person can confront his or her life and death and choose how to live it. This is why the symbol of suicide is centrally placed in the existentialist approach. May reminds us that Sophocles wrote a sequel to *Oedipus Rex, Oedipus at Colonus,* in which the old king reflects on all that has happened to him and experiences a new unity that emerges after the tragic experience of consciousness. The "tragic experience of consciousness" involves admitting what one has done, assuming responsibility for it, and also assuming the responsibility for what one shall do in the future.

Rediscovering Feelings

In rediscovering selfhood, most people have to start back at the beginning and rediscover their feelings (1953). Many of us have only a vague idea of what we are feeling at any given time. We react to our bodies as if they were separate and distinct. While denying our own emotions, we ascribe feelings to machines, describing them as "friendly," "affectionate," and so forth. We need to recognize that we play an active role in creating our bodies and feelings. Awareness of one's body and feelings lays the groundwork for knowing what one wants. Surprisingly few people are actually clear on what it is that they want. Being aware of one's desires does not imply that one must act on them. But we cannot have any basis for judging what we will and will not do unless we first know what it is that we want to do.

Exploration /////

Getting in Touch

You can become more aware of your body by frequently asking yourself how different parts of your body feel to you at any given moment. What sensations and feelings are you receiving from your leg, your ring finger, your head, and so forth? Learn to feel what is happening as you walk or as you rest. Many of us only become aware of a part of our body when it malfunctions. Then we say, "I got sick," as if my body is something outside that happens to me. It is important that you try to experience your body as an aspect of your acting self, an expression of yourself in its unity.

Becoming a person requires not only getting in touch with one's feelings and desires but also fighting against those things that prevent us from feeling and wanting (1953). The development of a human being is a process of differentiation from an original unity with the mother toward freedom as an individual. The physical umbilical cord is cut at birth, but the infant is still dependent on its parents. Unless the psychological cord is severed in due time, the individual's growth is stunted. In order to advance and be oneself, a person has to become free of the domineering and auhoritarian powers that imprison even if that requires taking a stand against one's parents or other authorities. It is our infantile ties of dependency that keep us from being clear as to our feelings and wants. The early struggle against authority is external: as we grow, the problem becomes internal. Thus, as adults many of us continue to act as if we still have to fight the original forces that enslaved us, when in fact we are now enslaving ourselves.

Four Stages of Consciousness of Self

May (1953) suggests that there are four stages of consciousness of self. The first is the *stage of innocence* before consciousness of self is born. This stage is characteristic of the infant. The second is the *stage of rebellion* in which the individual seeks to establish some inner strength in his or her own right. The toddler and the adolescent illustrate this stage, which may involve defiance and hostility. The third stage is *ordinary consciousness of self.* This is the stage most people refer to when they speak of a healthy personality. It involves being able to learn from one's mistakes and live responsibly. May refers to the last stage as *creative consciousness of self.* It involves the ability to see something outside one's usual limited viewpoint and gain a glimpse of objective truth as it exists in reality. This level cuts through the dichotomy between subjectivity and objectivity. Not everyone achieves each level of consciousness. As we have seen, part of our predicament is the lessening of human consciousness. The fourth stage, achieved only rarely, is somewhat analogous to Maslow's peak experience. Nevertheless it is the level that gives meaning to our actions and experiences on the lesser levels.

The Goals of Integration

May conceives of the human being as conscious of self, capable of intentionality, and needing to make choices. In his existential analysis of personality, May undercuts the traditional dualism of subject and object by seeing the self as a unity and pointing toward a creative consciousness of self that goes beyond the consciousness of one's self as a subject or an object. In his discussion of the goals of integration, May further reveals an intent to discuss key issues in personality in such a way as to avoid the tendency to abstract the real person and life itself into artificial dualisms and constructs. Instead of abstract conceptualizations, we need to recognize and confront the paradoxes of our own lives (1981). In **paradox** two opposing things are posited against and seem to negate each other yet they cannot exist without each other. Thus, good and evil, life and death, beauty and ugliness appear to be at odds with each other but the very confrontation with the one breathes life and meaning into the other. "Harmony," as Heraclitus reminded us, "consists of opposing tension, like that of the bow and the lyre" (May, 1981). The goals of integration include confronting one's potentialities for love, intentionality, the daimonic, courage and creativity, power, and freedom and destiny.

Love

Love used to be seen as the answer to human problems. Now love itself has become the problem (1969). The real problem is that of being able to love. Our world is schizoid, out of touch, unable to feel or to enter into a close relationship. Affectlessness and apathy are predominant attitudes toward life, forms of protection against the tremendous overstimulation of modern society.

Our highly vaunted sexual freedom has turned out to be a new form of puritanism in which emotion is separated from reason and the body is used as a machine. Commercialization of sex destroys true feelings as badly as traditional taboos once did. We have set sex against eros, the drive to relate and create new forms of life. It is now socially sanctioned to repress eros, and we rush to the sensation of sex in order to avoid the passion and responsibility that eros commands. The sexual freedom established during the past few decades has not led to the increase in happiness that many thought would follow a freeing of sexual mores. In the midst of wide availability of information and birth control, unwanted pregnancies are on the rise. Why? The real issue is not on the level of conscious rational intentions but in the deeper realm of intentionality where a deep defiance mocks our withdrawal of feeling.

The psychological meaning of contraception is that it expands the realm of personal responsibility and commitment. No longer does God or some factor of chance physiology decide whether or not we will have children: we do. It now rests with the individual person or couple to choose the value of the sexual experience and the reasons for participating. With our increased technology, we hold within our hands the possibility of creating new forms of life. And with the possibility of artificial body parts, we may also choose how long we are going to live. Since God and philosophy are dead, we are the only ones who can decide the values that will guide us in these decisions. May suggests that only the experience and rediscovery of *care,* the opposite of apathy, will enable us to stand against the cynicism that characterizes our day. The mythos of care points to the need to develop a new morality of authenticity in human relations.

Intentionality

May believes that we must put decision and will back into the center of our picture of personality. His intent is not to rule out deterministic influences but to place the problem of determinism and freedom on a deeper level. May does this by introducing the concept of **intentionality** (1969), which underlies will and decision. It is a dimension that cuts across and includes the polarities of conscious and unconscious, determinism and freedom, cognition and conation. A distinctly human capacity, intentionality is an imaginative attention that underlies our intentions and informs our actions. It is the capacity to participate in knowing. Intentionality bridges the gap between subject and object because it is the structure of meaning that permits a subject to understand the world as object. Perception is directed by intentionality. How I perceive a piece of paper will differ depending on whether I intend to write on it or to make a paper airplane. Through intentionality, we give meaning to the world. Contrary to the popular belief that truth is perceived through a detached objective stance, May holds that we cannot know the truth until we have taken a stand on it. Both the detached type and the asocial personality are avoiding confronting their intentionality. When I face my intentionality, then I can decide whether or not to act it out in my behavior.

The Daimonic

In a world that vaunts rationality, May (1969) reintroduces the concept of the daimonic and insists that we come to terms with it. The **daimonic** is "any natural function which has the power to take over the whole person." Sex, anger, a craving for power, all of these may become evil when they take over the self without regard for the integration of the self. We can repress the daimonic but we cannot avoid its consequences. In repressing it, we become its pawns — as millions did in the optimistic era that led to the rise of Hitler.

The daimonic is potentially creative and destructive at the same time. By becoming aware of it, we can integrate it into ourselves. We can learn to cherish our internal demons and permit them to give us the salt of life. The daimonic begins as impersonal; by bringing it into my consciousness, I make my daimonic urges personal. With a more sensitive understanding of these forces in my body and my life, the daimonic pushes me toward the universal. "The more I come to terms with my daimonic tendencies, the more I find myself conceiving and living by a universal structure of reality." The movement is from impersonal to personal to a transpersonal dimension of consciousness (1969).

Courage and Creativity

Courage is the capacity to move ahead in spite of despair. In human beings, courage is necessary in order to make being and becoming possible. Courage is not a virtue but a foundation that underlies and gives reality to all other values. The paradox of courage is that we must be fully committed but we must also be aware at the same time that we might be wrong. Creative courage is the discovery of new forms, symbols, and patterns on which a new society can be built. The creative person must fight the actual order so as to bring about what is new. Thus, creativity brings upon us the wrath of the gods, the anger of the authority of the past. Psychologists frequently ignore creativity because, as an act of encounter between two poles, it is very difficult to study. Yet our contemporary crisis requires creativity if we are to deal with it effectively (1975).

Power

As we have seen, a basic factor in our contemporary crisis is the feeling of insignificance and powerlessness. Human life can be seen as a conflict between achieving a sense of the significance of one's self on the one hand and the feeling of powerlessness on the other. We tend to avoid both sides, the former because of evil connotations associated with being too powerful and the latter because our powerlessness is too painful to bear.

However, violence has its breeding ground in impotence and apathy. As we make people powerless, we encourage their violence rather than control it. Violent deeds are done by those who seek to enhance their self-esteem. Powerless people sometimes invite exploitation in order to feel significant or seek revenge in passive-aggressive ways, such as the use of drugs and alcohol.

May points out that the argument against violence on television would be stronger if it were made against the passive character of television viewing rather than the emulation of aggressive models. Televised entertainment cultivates the spectator role rather than active participation; as such, its greatest danger may lie in the cultivation of feelings of impotence that contribute to violent behavior.

May's theory (1972) cuts beneath the controversy of internal versus external determinants of aggression and tries to show how power is central to the problem. Aggression is fundamental to human life; it is naive to see it as merely culturally induced.

It is true that the exercise of power in the modern world has done enormous harm. However, by trying to rid ourselves of our tendencies toward aggression, we also discard values that are essential to humanity. We deny the positive side of self-affirmation and self-assertion, and these denials add to our feelings of powerlessness.

"The culture admittedly has powerful effects upon us. But it could not have these effects were these tendencies not already present in us, for, . . . we constitute the culture" (1983). The ontological view does not deny development but it takes the inquiry down to a deeper level by cutting below the structure of nature versus nurture and directing our attention at a structure in which both nature and nurture are rooted. Power is an ontological state of being. The potentiality to experience and to express power is present in all of us. No one can escape experiencing power in desire or in action. Our goal is to learn how to use our power in ways that are appropriate for the situation, to be assertive rather than aggressive. We must find social ways of sharing and distributing power so that every person can feel that he or she is significant.

Freedom and Destiny

The existentialist attitude is sometimes criticized for portraying the individual as absolutely free with no restraints whatsoever. May, however, reminds us that freedom can only be considered together with destiny (1981). Freedom means "openness, readiness to grow, flexibility, and changing in pursuit of greater human values" (1953). It entails our capacity to take a hand in our own development. Freedom is basic to the existentialist understanding of human nature because it underlies our ability to choose and to value. However, freedom can only be experienced in juxtaposition with human destiny.

May (1981) defines *destiny* as the vital design of the universe expressed in each one of us. In its extreme form, our destiny is death, but it also expresses itself in our individual talents, our personal and collective histories, and the culture and society into which we were born. A person's destiny is a combination of his or her own nature and external reality. Destiny sets limits for us but it also equips us to perform certain tasks. Confronting these limits yields constructive values.

Freedom is in crisis today because we have viewed it without its necessary opposite. We have become irresponsible with our laissez-faire free enterprise system and culture of narcissism. We have lost sight of the fact that we can only exist as a community. The tendency, especially in America, to believe that nothing is fixed and that we can change everything we wish is not only a misperception of life but also a desecration of it. When people cannot or will not accept their destiny, it is repressed and often projected onto others as in witchcraft or the perception of one's enemy as totally bad (1981).

On the other hand, the denial of the possibility of freedom expressed in Skinner's radical behaviorism also increases our feeling of a lack of responsibility by placing on the environment the very responsibility that is needed if we are to influence it effectively. May points out that "freedom and determinism give birth to each other. Every advance in freedom gives birth to a new determinism, and every advance in determinism gives birth to a new freedom" (1981). Freud's and Darwin's theories, deterministic as they were, opened the door to new possibilities. However, the word **determinism,** borrowed from physics, is not very adequate for the rich nuances of human experience. To the extent to which one is unaware of one's responses, the term determinism may be appropriate, yet May suggests that we reserve it for inanimate objects, such as billiard balls, and use the term *destiny* for human beings. Determinism is merely one aspect of destiny. The shift from determinism to destiny occurs when a person is self-conscious about what is happening to him or her (1981).

One of the goals of psychotherapy is to increase the patient's awareness of his or her destiny in order that he or she can experience a greater sense of freedom. We gain our personal freedom only when we come to terms with the limitations of our own lives. The past, for example, cannot be changed: it can only be acknowledged and learned from so that we can choose the future. Some things we cannot change, but we can change our attitude toward them. Survivors of prison or concentration camps frequently testify how they retained their sense of self by concentrating on those limited areas in which they were free to choose, even if it was merely an inner attitude toward their fate (1981).

Freedom is not to be confused with rebellion, although rebellion is a necessary step in the evolution of consciousness and freedom. People earn their right to be free through an inner act of rebellion. Destiny structures the shape that struggle will take and also the effect of any outward expression of it. In the Western world, we experience freedom as individual self-expression. In the East, freedom is experienced as participation in a group. These are two very different situations, yet both permit the experience of freedom. When the social order breaks down, Eastern countries are apt to use force to hold the society together. Nevertheless, in America our underestimation of the significance of community ultimately stifles freedom also. Our need is not to imitate but to develop a form of community and means of experiencing freedom in the West that is compatible with our own history and nature (1981).

Are we responsible for our destiny? May reminds us that responsibility is inseparable from freedom. Acknowledging one's destiny is to accept personal responsibility. In the terms of our psychology, freedom is the capacity to pause between a stimulus and a response. The key word here is *pause.* The significance of the pause is that it breaks the rigid chain of cause and effect. In the debate between situational and dispositional factors, May reminds us that there is a third alternative. Human beings can choose when and whether they are to be acted upon or to do the acting. In moving between being controlled and controlling, one moves on a deeper level of freedom, the freedom of being (1981).

The past and future live in the psychological present. On the deepest level, the question of which age we live in is irrelevant. Instead the question is how, in our awareness of self and the period we live in, are we able through our choices to attain inner freedom and live according to our own inner integrity (1953). One reason why we are reluctant to confront our destiny is that we are afraid it will lead us to despair. But despair may be a prelude to better things. Indeed, authentic despair is the emotion that forces us to come to terms with our destiny and permits us to let go of false hopes (1981).

Psychotherapy

The existential approach to psychotherapy maintains that the central goal of therapy is to help the patient understand him- or herself and his or her mode of being in the world. Psychological constructs for understanding human beings are, therefore, placed on an ontological basis and take their meaning from the present situation. Drives, dynamisms, or behavior patterns are understood only in the context of the structure of the existence of the particular person.

May points out that *being* in the human sense is not given once and for all. As humans we have to be aware of ourselves, be responsible for ourselves, become ourselves. "To be *and* not to be" (there is no typographical error in May's rephrasing of Hamlet) is a choice we make at every moment. An "I am" experience is a precondition for solving specific problems (1983). Otherwise, we merely trade one set of defenses for another.

Becoming aware of one's own being is not to be explained in social terms. The acceptance of the therapist may facilitate the "I am" experience but it does not automatically lead to it. "The crucial question is what the individual himself, in his own awareness of and responsibility for his existence, does with the fact that he can be accepted" (1983). Nor is the emergence of an "I am" experience identical to the development of the ego. It occurs on a more basic level, an ontological one, and is a precondition for subsequent ego development.

In order to grasp what it means to exist, one also needs to grasp the option of nonbeing. Death is an obvious form of the threat of nonbeing, but conformity is an alternative mode that May finds very prevalent in our day. People give up their own identity in order to be accepted by others and avoid being ostracized or lonely but in doing so they lose their power and uniqueness. Whereas repression and inhibition were common neurotic patterns in Freud's day, today *conformism* is a more prevalent pattern. Such denial of one's potentialities leads to the experience of guilt. Ontological guilt does not come from cultural prohibition but arises from the fact of self-awareness and the recognition that one has not fulfilled one's potentialities. Facing such guilt in the process of therapy leads to constructive effects.

Thus, the central task of the therapist is to seek to understand the patient and his or her mode of being and nonbeing in the world. It is the context that distinguishes the existential approach rather than any specific techniques. The human being is not an object to be managed or analyzed. Technique follows understanding. Various psychotherapeutic devices may be used, depending on which method will best reveal the existence of a particular patient at any given moment of his or her history.

May believes that free association is particularly useful in revealing intentionality. There is an emphasis on presence. The relationship between the therapist and patient is seen as a real one. When transference occurs, May points out that it distorts the therapeutic encounter. The therapist seeks to "analyze out" the ways of behavior that destroy presence and to help the patient experience his or her existence as real. This does not imply simply adjusting to one's culture or relieving anxiety but rather experiencing one's existence, whatever that may be.

May warns against the use of drugs in psychotherapy. For the most part, he believes they have a negative effect because, in removing the patient's anxiety, they may remove his or her motive for change and thereby deny an opportunity for learning and destroy vital resources. Occasionally, May employs techniques developed by **gestalt therapists** such as Fritz Perls. An emphasis might be placed on nonverbal behaviors to show the inconsistency between a verbal and nonverbal statement. If a patient states that she is frightened but has a smile on her face, May might point out that a frightened person does not smile and seek to explore the meaning of the smile. A patient might be asked to fantasize that a significant other was sitting in a chair opposite him or her, to have a conversation with that person, and then to reverse roles. Such techniques are designed to help the patient confront his or her self and experience his or her actual present feelings. Finally, the existential approach emphasizes commitment, believing that the patient cannot receive any insight until he or she is ready to decide and take a decisive orientation to life.

Methods of Research

May believes that in their efforts to be "scientific" many psychologists lose sight of the real person that they seek to understand. However, while May is critical of some of the so-called scientific forms of psychology, he is by no

The Empty Chair

The empty chair technique originated with gestalt therapy and is a useful way of encountering and enriching our understanding of a neglected aspect of ourselves or another person. Place two chairs opposite one another so that they are about four feet apart. Sit in one of the chairs and then begin to fantasize a significant other in your life or an aspect of yourself that you can personalize in the other chair. Try to visualize the person in the empty chair as vividly as possible. How tall is she? What is he wearing? What is his posture? What do you imagine she is feeling? Say something to the person in the empty chair about your relationship. Then reverse roles. Actually get up and go and sit in the other chair and pretend that you are the other person or the other aspect of yourself. Respond to yourself as fully and completely as you possibly can. When you have finished, return to the original chair and say a final word as yourself to the person in the empty chair. Many people find that this experience is very helpful to them in getting to see things from a different perspective.

means antiscientific. His aim is to speak out against concepts of personality that dogmatically foreclose avenues of research.

In the 1950s, May criticized psychologists for having singled out for study those aspects of human behavior that overlap with animal behavior and can ultimately be described in physiological or stimulus-response terms. In doing so, May pointed out that psychologists neglected the problem of symbols, even though the use of symbols is part of the distinct human condition (1958). Behaviorism has been superseded by cognitive psychology, which studies symbols and other events that occur in the mind, yet May does not look to cognitive psychology either for answers to the psychological problems of our time because its conceptions are also too limited (1981).

May criticizes contemporary psychological research for being impressed with data and numbers at the expense of theory. Psychologists tend to be contemptuous of imagination and speculation, yet the most important scientific discoveries (Copernicus's concept of the universe, Darwin's theory of evolution, Freud's discovery of unconscious forces, Einstein's theory of relativity) were made not by accumulating facts but by perceiving the relationship among them (1983). Human nature can only be understood within a theoretical framework.

The existential approach suggests three basic changes in psychological methods of research on personality. First, "we must cut through the tendency in the West to believe we understand things only if we know their causes, and to find out and describe instead what the thing is as a phenomenon — the experience, as it is given to us, in its 'givenness.' First, that is, we must know what we are talking about. This is not to rule out causation and genetic development, but rather to say that the question of *why* one is what one is does not have meaning until we know *what* one is" (1967). This phenomenological approach is very similar to the view maintained by Rogers.

Second, psychologists must recognize that all ways of understanding what it means to be a human being are based on philosophical presuppositions. We need to examine these presuppositions continually for it is one's philosophical concept of human being that guides one's empirical research. Here May also reminds us of Rogers's and Maslow's emphasis on science serving previously chosen goals.

Finally, we must ask the question of the nature of person as person, the ontological question of what it means to be. Understanding the being of another person occurs on a very different level from knowing specific things about her or him. This is the classical distinction between *knowing* and *knowing about.* Our culture tends to believe that something is not real unless we can reduce it to a mathematical abstraction. But according to May, this denies the reality of our own experience. May suggests that it would be more scientific to first try and see clearly what it is we are talking about and then try and find symbols to describe what we see with a minimum of distortion (1983).

At the present time, much of our research is governed by the myth of the technological man, which May describes as "a set of assumptions postulating that the human being is governed by what he can rationally understand, that his emotions will follow this understanding, and that his anxiety and dread will thus be cured" (1969). What May is trying to do is to help us develop a new form, a new myth that will be more adequate for our day. After all, he reminds us, "Anyone can do the research . . . The original contribution lies in seeing a new *form* for the problem" (1967). May believes that new forms of symbols and myths for understanding human nature are more likely to come from our art, literature, humanities, and religion than from our present psychology (1983).

May's unique approach to research may be seen in two specific research activities that he describes: the study of unmarried mothers and the study of a dream sequence. May undertook a study of unmarried mothers in order to illuminate the meaning of anxiety (1969). Because he believed that there might be damaging effects in inducing anxiety experimentally, he took what was an anxiety-creating situation at that time in our society and studied it to reveal a pattern that would be characteristic of other anxiety-creating situations as well. May believes that the more intensely we study the individual, the

Exploration ///

Three Types of Description

You can begin to develop an appreciation of one aspect of the existentialist point of view by describing someone with whom you have a close relationship in three different ways. First, give an objective description of the other person, indicating as accurately as possible his or her age, height, weight, coloring, background, occupation, and other important information. Second, give a subjective description of how you feel about the other individual. Express in considerable detail what your thoughts and emotions are when you are in the other person's presence and how you feel when you are apart. Finally, commit to writing the story of your relationship with the other person. Tell how you met, what you have said to one another at various times, and some of the things that you remember doing together. When you have finished, compare the different descriptions to see which one conveys best a real sense of that individual. Existentialists would suggest that the story of your relationship together undoubtedly provides the most adequate understanding.

more we arrive at data that lie below individual differences and are applicable to human beings in general.

In studying each woman May used personal interviews, the Rorschach Ink Blot Test, anxiety check lists, and collateral data, such as medical examinations. He tried to see each woman in light of the data on three dimensions: (1) behaviorally, the woman's present behavior; (2) structurally, in terms of underlying structure; and (3) genetically, in terms of childhood background. From these three dimensions, he sought to arrive at a picture of the constellation of each personality. The central criterion for the validity of his conceptualization of each case was internal consistency. He asked, "Do the data arrived at by the various methods exhibit inner consistency within the framework of the conceptualization of the case and with the other elements in the constellation of the personality?" (1977). His study led to some rich observations concerning the meaning of anxiety itself, the origin of neurotic anxiety in a particular parent-child relationship in which rejection is covered over with pretenses of love so that it cannot be appraised realistically, and the greater prevalence of neurotic anxiety among women of the middle class.

In his study of dreams and symbols, May undertook an analysis of Susan Berman, a patient of Leopold Caligor, simply on the basis of her narration of her dreams. The purpose was to test his belief that we can often get a more accurate and meaningful picture of the significant changes in a person's life from the symbols and myths that he or she creates in dreams than we can from what he or she says (1968).

May believes that dreams reflect an individual's way of perceiving, coping with, and giving meaning to his or her world. Our dream life reflects our intentionality and deepest concerns. It permits the person to experience rather than merely explain the symbols and myths that are important to him or her. In analyzing the dreams, May took them phenomenologically as self-revealing givens, patterns of data within themselves. He looked for consistency over a period of time and noticed that latent meanings in earlier dreams became manifest in the later dreams. The latent meaning of dreams is thus reconceived by May as a dimension of communication that the patient is unwilling or unable as yet to actualize.

Each dream has a theme and a motif. The *theme* is the unity and inner consistency that is a part of the dreamer. It is characteristic of all of his or her dreams and reflects the unity of his or her character. The *motif* is the central thread running through the various dreams and the goal one is moving toward. Susan was frequently represented in her dreams by the symbol of her hair. Hair may appear to be a rather uninspiring symbol, yet May demonstrates how it had rich historical, social, and individual connotations in this case. The purpose of interpreting a dream is not to tell the individual what it means but to expand the individual's consciousness so that what is going on can be more fully and deeply experienced. In dreams we successfully resist the temptation to intellectualize and, instead, wrestle with our real problems.

After May had painted a portrait of Susan from her dreams, he compared his picture with that which had emerged in the course of her three-year analysis with Dr. Caligor by comparing his findings with the doctor's case notes. He found a remarkable consistency between the two accounts, confirming his hypothesis that one can get an accurate and meaningful picture of a person from the symbols and myths that he or she creates in dreams.

May's Theory: Philosophy, Science, and Art

May clearly recognizes that science derives from prior philosophical forms and is fundamentally dependent upon them. He believes the reason why we don't understand the truth about ourselves is not that we haven't amassed enough data, conducted the right experiments, or read enough books, but because we "do not have enough courage." Scientific facts and technical proofs rarely help us answer the questions that really matter. We have to "venture" (1953).

In psychotherapy May is "the implacable friend," demanding that his patients "grapple with the disabling forces inside of them and fight their way back into life" (Harris, 1969). He has not been afraid to risk looking foolish because of his introduction of concepts vehemently rejected by mainstream psychologists — intentionality, the will, the daimonic. He introduced these concepts because he believes that they are vital to an understanding of what it means to be human today. There is a prophetic note to his writing, reminiscent of Erich Fromm, and his thinking frequently has a theological quality. Indeed, there are those who suggest that May has taken up where Paul Tillich, the theological giant of our century, left off (Harris, 1969). This suggestion does not bother May; he acknowledges that for him the great periods in history were not those when psychological concerns were dominant but those when philosophical and religious concerns were uppermost (1983).

May's theory is not a scientific theory of personality; he does not give us a series of hypotheses that may be tested by empirical procedures. Instead, he gives us a philosophical picture of what it means to be a person in today's world. Reasons are offered in support of his affirmations, but they do not serve as proof; they cooperate as pieces of evidence in favor of a certain picture of reality. It is important to maintain the distinction between philosophical assumptions and scientific statements. Failure to notice the difference leads to ambiguity and confusion. A philosophical view of human nature may illumine our condition, but it does not function as a scientific theory with a utilitarian goal. On the other hand, a scientific theory that neglects its philosophical assumptions is arid and fruitless, if not destructive. To reduce our understanding of personality to scientific, causative, and abstract terms means that we will lose some significant content and fail to understand the full reality of a human being. May encourages us to examine the philosophical assumptions of our scientific endeavor so that we can maintain a creative dialogue between our science and our philosophy.

May's philosophical picture of human nature is coherent, relevant, comprehensive, and compelling. He successfully avoids the Cartesian dualisms. The existential framework that informs his theory is more compatible to our world than the philosophical assumptions of nineteenth-century science that informed Freud's work. An existential philosophy provides a helpful background for discussing what Freud meant to say about the nature of psychic functioning. Although Freud was not an existentialist, existentialism provides categories that clarify Freudian thought and intent. Thus, May fruitfully reconceives many Freudian concepts.

Whereas Freud's philosophy was an extension of the assumptions inherent in the scientific community of his time, May begins as a philosopher. His image of human nature provides a welcome antidote to the technological view of the person that permeates radical behavior and learning theories as well as to the naive optimism of the humanists. May differs from traditional learning and behavior theories in his open examination of his philosophical assumptions. He differs from the humanists in his insistence that we directly confront our own evil.

For the most part, psychologists tend to ignore May's theory because they cannot treat it as a scientific hypothesis. Concepts like intentionality and the daimonic are virtually impossible to define operationally and test empirically, but the findings of an empirical test do not establish a philosophical assumption; they may not even significantly relate to it. Nevertheless, the very strength of May's theory, the fact that it has its roots in a new philosophical conception of human life, may also be its greatest liability. May runs a strong risk of being given short shrift by the psychological establishment and having little impact on personality theorizing. This is ironic because in many ways the humility and openness to change characteristic of May's theory are more in keeping with the nature of the scientific enterprise than the attitude of those who seek to limit and confine research. By ignoring May, psychologists deprive themselves of the challenge of re-examining their own philosophical assumptions and, perhaps, reconceiving the goals and methods of their science.

In any event, a response to May can take one of three forms. We can agree with him and adopt his philosophical categories as part of our scientific activity. We can object to his views on philosophical grounds and maintain that another view, like the technological or humanistic view of the person, is more compelling. Or we can maintain that none of these views is adequate. If we adopt the third position, we are then faced with the responsibility of suggesting an alternative philosophical framework that provides a more convincing model for understanding personality.

❧ Summary

1. Rollo May's work brings together the psychoanalytic tradition in psychology and the existentialist movement in philosophy.

2. **Existentialism** emphasizes *existence* rather than **essence.** It suggests that there is no truth or reality except as we participate in it. Knowledge is an act of doing.

3. Existentialists believe that the psychologist's preoccupation with lawfulness and predictability stands in the way of understanding the real person and they urge a greater breadth to our scientific methodology. They seek to study the structure of human existence and to look at the unity of the person prior to any split into subject and object.

4. The central problem we face in the second half of the twentieth century, according to May, is a feeling of *powerlessness* in the face of nuclear war.

5. May defines **anxiety** as the apprehension cued off by a threat to an essential value. It is intensified in contemporary culture by the interpersonal isolation and alienation that have come out of the way in which we view ourselves. Many of our present efforts to dispel anxiety actually end up increasing it.

6. The source of the human dilemma lies in the loss of the center of values in our society. A distinguishing mark of the human animal is that he or she creates values. The need today is to discover and affirm a new set of values.

7. May assumes (a) that all living organisms are centered on themselves and seek to preserve that center; (b) they can go out from their centeredness to participate with other people; (c) sickness is a means of preserving one's being; (d) human beings can engage in a level of self-consciousness that permits them to transcend the present and consider alternatives. These *ontological assumptions* precede our scientific activity and make it possible, but our analytic activity may in turn illumine them.

8. *Rediscovering selfhood* involves rediscovering our own feelings and desires and fighting against those things that prevent us from feeling and wanting. There are *four stages of consciousness* of self: innocence, rebellion, ordinary consciousness of self, and creative consciousness of self.

9. May discusses key issues in personality in ways that avoid abstraction and facilitate the confronting of **paradoxes.** *Love,* which used to be seen as the answer to human problems, has now become the problem. We are unable to love. We need to experience and rediscover *care.* May introduces the concept of **intentionality** to bridge the gap between subject and object and to place the problem of determinism and freedom on a deeper level. He reintroduces the concept of the **daimonic** and insists that we must come to terms with it. He emphasizes our need to be *courageous and creative.* We also need to rediscover our *power* and express it in constructive ways. May points out how our *freedom* needs to be considered in light of our *destiny.*

10. In psychotherapy the existentialist seeks to understand the patient and his or her mode of being in the world. It is the context that distinguishes the existential approach rather than any specific technique. Use has been made of the psychotherapeutic devices of both Freud and **gestalt psychotherapists.**

11. May criticizes contemporary psychological research for being impressed with data and uninterested in theory. We need continually to re-examine our presuppositions and raise ontological questions. Two specific research activities that May engaged in were a study of unmarried mothers and the study of a dream sequence.

12. May's theory is not a scientific theory of personality giving us a series of hypotheses that may be tested by an empirical procedure. Instead he suggests a philosophical picture of human nature that is coherent, relevant, comprehensive, and compelling.

Suggestions for Further Reading

Rollo May's books are extremely readable and enlightening for the lay person. His theory of personality was initially outlined in *Man's Search for Himself* (Norton, 1953) and *Psychology and the Human Dilemma* (Van Nostrand Reinhold, 1967). *The Meaning of Anxiety* (Norton, 1950; revised, 1977) is now considered a classic. In it May encouraged a genuine union between psychology and philosophy and demonstrated the importance of values for psychology. *Love and Will* (Norton, 1969) explores the experience of sex and love in contemporary society. It was hailed by the *New York Times* as the "most important book of the year." May's most recent works are *Freedom and Destiny* (Norton, 1981), which rethinks the problem of determinism and personal freedom, and *The Discovery of Being* (Norton, 1983), which describes the human search for being and nonbeing in an age of anxiety.

Conclusion: Personality Theory in Perspective

Your Goals for This Chapter

1. Compare different personality theories in terms of their emphasis on philosophy, science, and art.

2. Compare different personality theories in terms of their stand on some basic philosophical issues.

3. Discuss the history of the terms *psyche* and *psychology* from their origins in Greek thought to their present-day use.

4. Indicate how Western psychology has narrowed the definition of *empirical*. Explain how the scientific method may separate us from experience rather than illuminate it.

5. Explain why it is important to conceive of personality theories as philosophy and art as well as science.

T his final chapter seeks to place the personality theories we have studied into perspective by making some comparisons and contrasts among them and by pointing to a problem in contemporary personality theorizing, suggesting a view toward the future.

Personality Theories: Philosophy, Science, and Art

Although personality theories are a branch of academic scientific psychology, they also entail philosophy and art. As scientists, personality theorists seek to develop workable hypotheses that enable us to understand human behavior. As philosophers, personality theorists seek to give us insight into what it means to be a person. As artists, personality theorists seek to apply what is known about people and behavior to foster a better life. Some critics evaluate theories simply in terms of their efficacy as science. Yet, as we have seen, few of the theories described in this text demonstrate purely scientific concerns. Most theories reflect a great variety of concerns and need to be evaluated in terms of the criteria that suit their goals.

Some of the theories we have considered clearly reflect philosophical concerns. The psychoanalytic tradition, for instance, tends to be philosophical, rather than scientific, in its approach. Psychoanalytic theories develop out of a clinical setting. These theorists, by and large, are physicians who develop their theoretical structures within the context of therapy. Although their methods and results are frequently empirical, that is, based on observation, they could not be described as rigorous or precise scientific techniques. Psychoanalytic theorists tend to consider proof as arising from the internal consistency of a theory and the ability of the theory to illumine the human condition. Their work is ultimately evaluated in terms of its coherence, relevance, comprehensiveness, and compellingness. The theories of Sigmund Freud, Carl Jung, Alfred Adler, and Erich Fromm represent a deep commitment to an underlying philosophy of life. Harry Stack Sullivan placed a greater emphasis on empirical research than the other early psychoanalytic theorists; contemporary psychoanalytic theorists appreciate the need to validate their constructs and are thus open to scientific test. But psychoanalytic theory remains largely philosophical. This is best seen in the work of Erik Erikson, an outstanding contemporary psychoanalytic theorist, who does not insist on a scientific pretense for his work but tries to make his philosophical assumptions explicit.

Other theories make a greater effort to be successful scientific theories. Behavior and learning theories are expressly scientific in their approach. Committed to a rigorous methodology, behavior and learning theories shun theoretical speculation in favor of careful observation and experimentation. Thus, John Dollard and Neal Miller emphasize empirical research in their efforts to combine psychoanalytic theory with the best aspects of the behaviorist tradition. B. F. Skinner's theory also evolves from experimental laboratory investigations. This emphasis has continued in the work of cognitive and social learning theorists, like Albert Bandura and Julian Rotter, whose theories are superb examples of a rigorous scientific approach to personality. Their methodologies have produced precise and economical theories and have given strong empirical support to their constructs. Psychometric trait theories also demonstrate a deep commitment to scientific methodologies and validating evidence; Raymond Cattell's theory is an excellent example of an effort to comprehend personality through a scientific model.

Some theorists deliberately seek an interdisciplinary approach. Henry A. Murray was one of the first to recognize the value of an interdisciplinary methodology; the diagnostic council that he established at Harvard was unprecedented in its vision and scope. Jung, Fromm, Gordon Allport, and Abraham Maslow all drew upon several areas of research — art, literature, history, philosophy, and science — in their efforts to understand human nature. Carl Rogers very carefully distinguishes between his philosophical assumptions and his scientific hypotheses, emphasizing the need for a balanced view.

Other theories are primarily concerned with the art of personality theory, or the practical applications. We saw how Eastern thinkers do not seek to demonstrate the validity of their constructs or engage in philosophical speculation; rather, they are concerned with offering a variety of practices for cultivating a deeper understanding of the self. Freud, Karen Horney, Sullivan, Adler, and Rogers have also made substantial contributions to the understanding and practice of psychotherapy.

Although certain personality theories stand out as excellent examples of one of the three primary concerns — philosophy, science, or art — none of the personality theories that we have studied can be appropriately pegged as simply philosophy, science, or art. All of the theories reflect each of these concerns to a greater or lesser degree. For instance, although behavior and learning theories largely seek to present a scientific conception of personality, they also reflect basic philosophical assumptions that influence their scientific hypotheses and their practical applications.

Initially, behavior and learning theorists were unable to recognize the philosophical roots of their approach. In recent years, however, they have acknowledged the philosophical assumptions that undergird their work. It is now widely recognized that even the most scientific approach to understanding personality addresses philosophical questions and suggests philosophical answers. Indeed, the basic difference among personality theories appears to be one of philosophical stance rather than one of methodology.

Philosophical Issues

Personality theories, then, can be compared in terms of where they stand on each of the basic philosophical issues outlined in the Introduction.

First, theorists differ as to whether they believe people are basically free to control their own behavior or whether they believe that behavior is essentially determined by forces over which people have little, if any, control. Both Freud and Skinner saw the individual as determined but for very different reasons. For Freud, the individual is motivated by internal forces of which he or she is unaware. For Skinner, the individual is shaped by forces within his or her environment. Theorists also differ in the extent to which they would like their theories to be used to cultivate freedom in human nature or to exercise greater control over it. Skinner seeks to develop a technology to control human behavior, whereas Rogers tries to increase a client's sense of freedom and responsibility.

As we have seen, another of the most puzzling questions in personality theorizing has been the dichotomy between constitutional and situational determinants of behavior. Theorists differ over whether they believe that inborn characteristics or factors in the environment have the more important influence on a person's behavior. Dispositional theorists stress the importance of long-term personality traits in understanding behavior; behaviorists emphasize situational factors. These philosophical differences also lead to different recommendations for action. An emphasis on inborn factors sometimes leads to the support of selective breeding; an emphasis on situational factors may lead to efforts to change the environment. Thus, Cattell urges consideration of *eugenics,* the study of improving hereditary qualities by genetic control, and Bandura encourages *euthenics,* the study of advancing human life by improving living conditions.

A third major issue is that of uniqueness versus universality. Allport clearly grappled with this issue. On the one hand he recognized that common traits permit us to make generalizations and comparisons among individuals, but in the final analysis he held that each individual is particular and unique. Eastern theories point out that we need to see through the illusion of individual existence, called maya. Jung thought that the earlier part of one's life is devoted to the task of individuation, whereas the later years reflect the need for transcendence.

Proaction versus reaction is a fourth dimension that influences personality theories. Allport discovered in his study of psychological terms with the prefixes *re-* and *pro-* that most theories tend to be reactive. Concepts such as "repression" and "regression" in psychoanalysis and "reflex" and "reinforcement" in stimulus-response theory suggest an emphasis on the past and a preoccupation with homeostasis. Humanist theories, on the other hand, suggest that the human being is motivated toward heterostasis, that is, growth and self-actualization. Cognitive theories also emphasize the present and the future rather than the past, viewing the individual as purposeful and active rather than passive.

Finally, personality theories can be compared according to whether they are optimistic or pessimistic about the possibility of change. Freud is generally seen as a pessimist because he believed that adult behavior is deeply structured by early childhood. Dispositional theorists believe that constitutional factors place firm limits on personality change. Behavior and learning theorists and humanist theorists, on the other hand, are usually very optimistic concerning the possibility of change.

These basic issues are typically presented as bipolar dimensions. However, Rollo May reminds us that they are actually paradoxes of human existence that seek resolution in a creative synthesis. An either/or position is generally misleading. Personality theorists must avoid being impaled on either horn of the dilemma as they try to reflect the truth of human existence.

The Challenge of Contemporary Personality Theorizing

Although psychology is a young science, it represents the oldest of human concerns. Our Western tradition initially fostered a mystical view of the self, emphasizing the spiritual side of the person. The effort to comprehend the human personality within the framework of a scientific methodology is largely the recent product of the twentieth century.

The term *psychology* comes to us from the ancient Greek word *psyche,* first introduced by the poet Homer to express the essence of a human being, or "the self." During the early Christian era as philosophy and rhetoric replaced poetry and mythology, the term "psyche" came to be identified with *pneuma,* or "spirit." It later became identified with the more rationalistic and intellectual concept of *nous,* or "mind." By the time of the enlightenment, "psyche" had become synonymous with consciousness or mental processes. As we have seen, John Watson, the founder of behaviorism, subsequently pointed out that states of consciousness are not objectively verifiable. He deemed them unfit as data for science and encouraged psychologists simply to study behavior. Under Watson's leadership, psychology was transformed from the largely introspective study of consciousness into the study of overt or observable behaviors. Thus, in the typical American university a strange situation prevailed throughout most of the twentieth century. Students of psychology discovered that, for the most part, they were not engaged in the study of the psyche; they were engaged in the study of behavior.

Behaviorism came to be the dominant position of psychology in American universities. Psychologists sought to pursue psychology as an experimental science that emulated the natural science of physics, an aspiration that largely remains with us today. The mainstream of American psychology still emphasizes extrospective observation and a rigorous scientific methodology. This emphasis is found in the cognitive approach, which has currently superseded behaviorism as the dominant trend.

Not all of the personality theorists that we have considered agree that a rigorous scientific method is the best way to understand personality. Indeed, some (Allport, Maslow, Rogers, and May, for example) have been very critical of the narrow view of psychology as an experimental science. Their critiques have fostered trends toward a more humanistic approach and an interest in alternative means of studying the person.

Unfortunately, however, humanistic psychology has become a rather "divisive force." Its adherents frequently belittle the usefulness of science and generate little research to support their concepts. Thus, "the early promise of this approach, as emphasized by Abraham Maslow and Carl Rogers, was never realized in the mainstream of psychology." Psychologists tend to be divided as to whether they belong to a "humanistic" or a "scientific" camp (Ornstein, 1977).

The behaviorist and cognitive positions, with their emphasis on extrospective observation and experimental research, continue to represent the strongest and most predominant modes of psychological study in the American academy today. Those theorists who choose not to imitate the mainstream run the risk of being considered less respectable because of their lack of allegiance to a purely scientific approach and methodology. They are tolerated, particularly when they are willing to subject their findings to scientific scrutiny, but their theories are not fully recognized as sound.

We have seen that the keynote of science is observation. Scientific theories rest on empirical data, that which is based on experience. In Western psychology, however, the term *empirical* has been rendered practically synonymous with "relying on or derived from extrospective observation." Empirical data have been largely limited to objective findings. Other data of experience or observation, such as subjective introspection, have been discouraged or depreciated, largely because it is so difficult to test these findings experimentally.

Historical, philosophical, and mythological data, because they invariably entail subjective as well as objective elements, are often viewed as incompatible with science. According to this conception, a competent scientist does not permit subjective assumptions to interfere with his or her work. The scientist remains detached, objective, and value free. As a result, Western psychology has tended to isolate itself. It has divorced itself from other possible modes of investigation on the grounds that their findings, because they are difficult to test experimentally, are not objective and are therefore incompatible with science.

David Bakan has pointed out that the rigorous scientific methodology of the Western experimental psychologist may, at times, actually stand in the way of the empirical and divorce us from experience rather than illuminate it (1969). Any experiment, precisely because it is artificial and contrived, loses its effectiveness in illuminating the everyday world as it becomes more distant from the everyday world. In a well-developed experiment the experimenter does not deal with the everyday world; instead, he or she creates a **para-world** of quantified, logico-mathematical imaginary constructs. In this para-world, events are carefully chosen and precisely controlled in order to avoid the haphazard occurrences of the everyday world that might jeopardize the results. Further, in a well-designed experiment all the possible alternatives and outcomes are anticipated in advance. The experimenter can predict within limits what is going to happen as a result of his or her manipulation of the variables in the experiment. And so the more carefully designed an experiment is, the more separate it becomes from the world of experience that it seeks to clarify. Rather than talking about the world, the psychologist constructs a para-world. Rather than talking about the person, the psychologist constructs a para-person. The Western psychologist's reliance on a rigid experimental method may, therefore, interfere with the possibility of learning from experience.

The emphasis on extrospection and rigorous scientific methodology also constrains the scope of psychological findings and personality theorizing. Such an emphasis limits the findings of psychology to those that can be demonstrated within the experimental laboratory. It circumscribes the study of personality to merely those aspects about the person that can be comprehended in specifically scientific terms. Because of this, many questions about the ultimate meaning, purpose, and goal of human living, questions that traditionally have been and could be included in the study of personality, are ruled out of inquiry.

Few theories of personality resemble an ideal scientific theory. Their assumptions lack explicitness, making it difficult for us to derive empirical statements that would permit us to move from abstract theory to empirical observation. Many personality theories, although provocative, have failed to generate a significant amount of research, thus depriving us of the "most important evaluative comparison" that can be made among theories (Hall & Lindzey, 1978). And yet, those personality theories that successfully emulate a scientific model gain their precision, accuracy, and predictive power at the price of evoking little depth of insight or new understanding.

In part, the problem results from the fact that theories of personality explore phenomena that by their very nature elude a narrow definition of science. At the heart of the experimental method is the search for cause and effect. Theories that emphasize motivation or free will make it difficult to look for underlying causes and limit the possibility of prediction and control. Moreover, they call into question the value of experimentation as a primary means of gaining insight into the human condition.

We need to recall that American psychology struggled valiantly to become a respectable science. This struggle entailed severing its early ties with philosophy and modeling itself along the lines of the natural sciences. Sound training in experimental design and statistical methods characterize the curriculum of academic psychology. Because of the earlier struggle to gain recognition as a science, many psychologists, particularly those with a behaviorist orientation, are suspicious of recent efforts by personality theorists to defy strict scientific methodology and reassert the philosophical character of psychology.

As a result, much of the current research in personality is fragmented, limited to a specific domain that can be precisely defined, articulated, measured, and tested. A particular variable, like locus of control, need to achieve, or cognitive style, is isolated for study, leading to a multiplicity of interesting and stable empirical findings. However, as May reminds us, contemporary psychological research is preoccupied with data and numbers at the expense of theory. The most important scientific discoveries were not made by accumulating facts but by perceiving relationships among the facts (1982). Human nature can only be understood within a theoretical framework. The real contribution lies in seeing a new *form* that avoids the misconceptions of an existing mythology.

The reluctance to reassert the philosophical character of psychology to some extent reflects a realistic fear that our present disillusionment with science may foster a tendency to disregard the substantial contributions that it has made to our understanding. We developed the experimental method as a tool because we discovered that we could increase our understanding and act more efficiently if our activities were guided by information about the determined aspects of our everyday world. Although it may be true that the experimental method cannot establish truth, it has provided a very pragmatic means of testing some of our assumptions.

Still, we should recognize that a purely experimental approach is not the only option available to the personality theorist and we should be aware of the effects of a purely scientific conception of psychology. Moreover, we must not allow the popularity of the experimental approach in the American academy to close our eyes to the importance of other methods or to the reality of the phenomena that other methods draw to our attention. We should seek a higher perspective in which science and philosophy are no longer in opposition to one another but complement each other.

Many contemporary personality theorists urge us to be more, not less, empirical. They point out that our traditional scientific methods may not only fail to do justice to the data but may also camouflage it. They suggest that when we limit our analysis to those phenomena that can be comprehended in terms of current experimental methodology, we prejudice our results. By becoming "less scientistic," psychology could become "more scientific" (Bakan, 1969).

It is not wise for a field of investigation that claims to explore the human condition to refuse to deal with a wide variety of concepts and data simply because they are difficult to state in scientific terms. The crises in living that we face today mandate that we marshal whatever means are available to assist us in self-understanding. A true portrait of personality must come to terms with all of the experiences that are central to being a person. It needs to grapple with and express all of the facets of personality, even though they may be difficult to conceptualize, test, or express. To ignore or deny anything that is part of the human condition means that we lose an important aspect of what it means to be human. Lopsided theories err not simply because they present us with incomplete portraits that are often biased or stereotyped but because they fail to develop concepts that adequately represent a human being's potential. In doing so, lopsided theories deprive us of important aspects of our own consciousness.

This book has suggested that personality theorizing invariably entails more than science; it also involves philosophy and art. Every activity that we engage in rests on certain philosophical assumptions. Contemporary personality theorizing is tied to and limited by certain assumptions that characterize our view of the world. Frequently, these assumptions are implicit rather than explicit; that is, they are not clearly recognized. Nevertheless, they profoundly influence our concept of the world and its inhabitants. Only by making our assumptions explicit and continually re-examining them can we place ourselves in a better position to understand ourselves. Herein lies the value of the scientific method: it has provided us with a means of testing and consensually validating our theoretical speculations. What we need to do is twofold. We need to evaluate our philosophical assumptions in the light of contemporary scientific information and to judge our scientific findings in the light of their adequacy as philosophy. In the final analysis, however, neither the speculations of science nor the speculations of philosophy can express the ultimate meaning of personality. The ultimate expression of personality does not lie in the constructs of science or philosophy. It lies in the art of living.

❀ Summary

1. Personality theories can be compared in terms of their emphasis on philosophy, science, and art. For example, psychoanalytic theories tend to emphasize philosophy, whereas behavior and learning theories emphasize science.

2. They can also be compared in terms of where they stand on basic philosophical issues, like freedom versus determinism, constitutionalism versus situationalism, uniqueness versus universality, proactive versus reactive em-

phases, and optimism versus pessimism. For instance, humanist theories stress an individual's responsibility and free will; psychoanalytic and behaviorist theories see the individual as determined.

3. Although psychology is a young science, it represents one of the oldest human concerns. The term *psyche* is an ancient Greek term that originally referred to "the self." Later it came to mean "spirit" and, finally, "mind." Through the influence of the behaviorist movement, *psychology* came to be the study of behavior, emphasizing a rigorous scientific method based on extrospective observation.

4. In Western psychology the term *empirical* has been rendered synonymous with "relying on or derived from extrospective observation." The rigorous scientific methodology of the Western experimental psychologist may at times tend to divorce us from experience, rather than illumine it, by separating us from the everyday world.

5. Personality theories need to be seen as philosophy, science, and art in order to do justice to the full range of human existence and potentiality.

Suggestions for Further Reading

For additional information on problems in current psychological research, see David Bakan, *On Method: Toward a Reconstruction of Psychological Investigation* (Jossey-Bass, 1969). Bakan points out that our enormous expenditures on psychological research are not yielding much new information. He suggests ways in which psychology might become "more scientific" and "less scientistic."

The following three books were previously recommended in conjunction with the Introduction; they are again suggested as invaluable for the student who is interested in pursuing personality theory in greater depth: Joseph Rychlak, *A Philosophy of Science for Personality Theory* (Houghton Mifflin, 1968); T. S. Kuhn, *The Structure of Scientific Revolutions,* 2nd ed. (University of Chicago Press, 1970); and I. Chein, *The Science of Behavior and the Image of Man* (Basic Books, 1972).

Glossary

ability traits In Cattell's theory, traits that determine how effectively a person is able to achieve his or her goal.

absence An altered state of consciousness in which there may be considerable personality change and later amnesia or forgetting of the events that occurred.

acceptance A nonjudgmental recognition of oneself, others, and the world.

active imagination In Jung's psychotherapy, a method for getting in touch with the archetypes.

Adult In Berne's transactional analysis, an ego state that seeks to evaluate and make realistic choices among the alternatives that confront an individual.

alienation In Horney's theory, a state in which the real self and the idealized self are disjunct.

anal stage One of Freud's psychosexual stages, in which the major source of pleasure and conflict is the anus.

analytical psychology The school of psychology founded by Carl Jung.

androgyny The presence of both masculine and feminine qualities in an individual and the ability to realize both potentials.

anima In Jung's theory, an archetype representing the feminine side of the male personality.

animus In Jung's theory, an archetype representing the masculine side of the female personality.

anxiety An emotional state characterized by a vague fear or premonition that something undesirable may happen. a) In Freud's theory, a situation into which we are thrust at birth because of the realistic danger that our needs as helpless infants will not be met. b) In Sullivan's theory, any painful feeling or emotion. c) In May's theory, the apprehension cued off by a threat to some value that the individual holds as essential to his or her existence as a person.

archetype In Jung's theory, a universal thought form or predisposition to perceive the world in certain ways.

"as if" a) A philosophical position espoused by Vaihinger and reflected in Adler's concept of fictional finalisms. b) In Sullivan's theory, a security operation in which an individual acts as if he or she were someone else in interpersonal relations.

assertive training A behavior therapy to assist a person to express his or her feelings.

Atman In Buddhist thought, the doctrine of the illusion of individuality.

attitude A positive or negative feeling toward an object. a) In Jung's theory, a basic psychotype. b) In Cattell's theory, a surface dynamic trait.

authoritarian ethic In Fromm's theory, a value system whose source lies outside the individual.

autism A disorder characterized by absorption into fantasy.

autoeroticism Self-love. In Freud's theory, the child's sexual activity.

autonomy versus shame and doubt Erikson's psychosocial stage, corresponding to Freud's anal stage, in which the child faces the task of developing control over his or her body and bodily activities.

aversion therapy A type of treatment in which an unpleasant stimulus is countered with an undesirable response.

bad-me self In Sullivan's theory, the content of awareness organized around anxiety-producing experiences concerning the self.

basic anxiety In Horney's theory, feelings of insecurity in which the environment as a whole is dreaded because it is seen as unrealistic, dangerous, unappreciative, and unfair.

basic needs therapy Therapeutic procedures that seek to meet the primary needs of people.

basic orientations In Horney's theory, fundamental modes of interaction with the world.

behavior The activity of an organism. a) In learning theory, a response to stimuli. b) In Rogers's theory, the goal-directed attempt of the organism to meet its needs as it perceives them.

behavior modification A form of therapy that applies the principles of learning to achieve changes in behavior.

behavior potential In Rotter's theory, a variable that refers to the likelihood that a particular behavior will occur.

behavior therapy A form of therapy that aims to eliminate symptoms of illness through learning new responses.

behavioral rehearsal A form of role playing used in therapy.

behaviorism A movement in psychology founded by John Watson, who suggested that psychologists should focus their attention on the study of overt behavior.

being mode In Fromm's theory, a way of life that depends solely on the fact of existence.

biophilous character In Fromm's theory, a character orientation that is synonymous with the productive orientation.

B-needs A term used by Maslow to refer to being needs that arise from the organism's drive to self-actualize and fulfill its potential.

bodily self In Allport's theory, a propriate function that entails coming to know one's body limits.

Brahma In Buddhist thought, the ground of existence.

cardinal disposition In Allport's theory, a personal disposition so pervasive that almost every behavior of an individual appears to be influenced by it.

castration anxiety In Freud's theory, the child's fear of losing the penis.

catharsis An emotional release that occurs when an idea is brought to consciousness and allowed expression.

cathect In Freud's theory, to invest libidinal energy into an object.

causal laws Established laws of cause and effect.

central disposition In Allport's theory, a highly characteristic tendency of an individual.

cerebrotonia In Sheldon's theory, a component of temperament characterized by a predominance of restraint, inhibition, and the desire for concealment.

character a) In Fromm's theory, a system of strivings or objectives that underlies one's behavior. b) In Allport's theory, a certain moral standard or code of behavior against which a person's actions or behaviors may be evaluated or judged.

Child In Berne's transactional analysis, an ego state that records those feelings and experiences one had as a child.

choleric One of Hippocrates' temperaments, referring to an individual who tends to be irascible and violent.

classical conditioning A form of learning in which a response becomes associated with a previously neutral stimulus.

claustral complex In Murray's theory, a wish to reinstate conditions prevailing before birth.

client-centered psychotherapy A therapeutic technique developed by Rogers that focuses attention on the person seeking help.

closed system A concept of personality that admits little or nothing new from outside the organism to influence or change it in any significant way.

cognition The process of knowing.

cognitive processes In Sullivan's theory, developmental modes by which an individual experiences the world and relates to others.

cognitive theories Theories of personality that emphasize cognitive processes such as thinking and judging.

coherence One of the criteria for judging philosophical statements: the quality or state of logical consistency.

collective unconscious In Jung's theory, a shared, transpersonal unconscious consisting of potential ways of being human.

common traits In Allport's theory, hypothetical traits that permit us to compare individuals according to certain shared dimensions.

compatibility A criterion for evaluating rival hypotheses: the agreement of the hypothesis with other previously well-established information.

compellingness One of the criteria for evaluating philosophical statements: The quality of appealing to someone with a driving force.

compensation Making up for or overcoming a weakness.

compensatory mechanisms In Adler's theory, safeguarding tendencies that ward off feelings of inferiority.

complex In Jung's theory, an organized group of thoughts, feelings, and memories about a particular concept.

comprehensiveness One of the criteria for evaluating philosophical statements: the quality of having a broad scope or range and depth of coverage.

conditional positive regard In Rogers's theory, positive regard that is given only under certain circumstances.

conditioned response A response that becomes associated with a stimulus through learning.

conditioned stimulus A previously neutral stimulus that becomes associated with a response.

conditions of worth In Rogers's theory, stipulations imposed by other people indicating when an individual will be given positive regard.

conflict a) In Freud's theory, the basic incompatibility that exists among the id, ego, superego, and the external world. b) In Dollard and Miller's theory, frustration that arises from a situation in which incompatible responses occur at the same time.

congruence In Rogers's theory, the state of harmony that exists when a person's symbolized experiences reflect the actual experiences of his or her organism.

conscience In Freud's theory, a subsystem of the superego that refers to the capacity for self-evaluation, criticism, and reproach.

conscious In Freud's theory, the thoughts, feelings, and wishes that a person is aware of at any given moment.

consensual validation Agreement among observers about phenomena.

constellating power In Jung's theory, the power of a complex to admit new ideas into itself.

constellatory construct In Kelly's theory, a construct that sets clear limits to the range of its elements but also permits them to belong to other realms.

constitutional traits In Cattell's theory, traits that have their origin in heredity or the physiological condition of the organism.

constructive alternativism In Kelly's theory, the assumption that any one event is open to a variety of interpretations.

constructive reverie In Sullivan's therapy, exploration of the future.

construe To place an interpretation on events.

continuity theory A theory that suggests that the development of personality is essentially an accumulation of skills, habits, and discriminations without anything really new appearing in the make-up of the person.

continuous reinforcement A schedule of reinforcement in which the desired behavior is reinforced every time it occurs.

control group In an experiment, a group equally matched to the experimental group and used for comparison.

conversion disorder A reaction to anxiety or stress expressed through physical symptoms; the modern term for hysteria.

correlation A statistical tool for making comparisons by expressing the extent to which two events covary.

covert behavior A behavior that can be observed directly only by the individual actually experiencing it.

creative self In Adler's theory, that aspect of the person that interprets and makes meaningful the experiences of the organism and establishes the lifestyle.

criterion analysis A method of analysis employed by Eysenck that begins with a hypothesis about possible variables and conducts statistical analyses in order to test the hypothesis.

critical periods Periods during which an organism is highly responsive to certain influences that may enhance or disrupt its development.

cue In Dollard and Miller's theory, a specific stimulus that tells the organism when, where, and how to respond.

daimonic In May's theory, any natural function that has the power to take over a person.

death impulses In Freud's theory, drives or forces that are the source of aggressiveness.

defense mechanism In Freud's theory, a procedure that wards off anxiety and prevents its conscious perception.

definition A statement that is true because of the way in which we have agreed to use words.

delayed reinforcement Reinforcement that is delayed after a response.

dependent variable In an experiment, the behavior under study.

detailed inquiry In Sullivan's theory, the third phase of the interview, in which the therapist tests his or her hypotheses about the patient.

determinism The philosophical view that behavior is controlled by external or internal forces and pressures.

developmental line In A. Freud's theory, a series of id-ego interactions in which children increase ego mastery of themselves and their world.

diagnostic profile A formal assessment procedure developed by Anna Freud that reflects developmental issues.

dichotomy An opposite or bipolar construct.

dimensional (or nomothetic) In Allport's theory, an approach to studying personality that considers large groups of individuals in order to infer general variables or universal principles.

directive A term used to describe therapies whose course is primarily structured by the therapist.

discontinuity theory A theory of personality that suggests that in the course of development an organism experiences genuine transformations or changes so that it reaches successively higher levels of organization.

discrimination The learned ability to distinguish among different stimuli.

displacement In Freud's theory, a defense mechanism in which one object of an impulse is substituted for another.

D-needs A term used by Maslow to refer to deficiency needs that arise out of a lack.

dream analysis A technique used by Freud and other analysts to uncover unconscious processes.

dream work In Freud's theory, the process that disguises unconscious wishes and converts them into a manifest dream.

drive The psychological correlate of a need or stimulus that impels an organism into action. a) In Freud's theory, a psychological representation of an inner bodily source of excitement characterized by its source, impetus, aim, and object. b) In Dollard and Miller's theory, the primary motivation for behavior.

drive reduction A concept formulated by Hull that suggests that learning occurs only if an organism's response is followed by the reduction of some need or drive.

dynamic lattice In Cattell's theory, a network by which dynamic traits are related.

dynamic traits In Cattell's theory, traits that motivate an individual toward some goal.

dynamism In Sullivan's theory, a pattern of energy transformation that characterizes an individual's interpersonal relations.

early adolescence In Sullivan's stages of development, a period marked by physical sexual maturation and the development of a stable heterosexual pattern of expressing sexual feelings.

eclectic Selecting the best from a variety of different theories or concepts.

ectomorphy In Sheldon's theory, a component of physique indicating a predominance of linearity and fragility.

effectance urge In White's theory, a drive that leads an organism to develop competence in dealing with the environment.

ego The self. a) In Freud's theory, a function of the personality that follows the reality principles and operates according to secondary processes and reality testing. b) In Jung's theory, one's conscious perception of self.

ego-ideal In Freud's theory, a subsystem of the superego consisting of an ideal self-image.

ego identity versus role confusion Erikson's psychosocial stage of adolescence in which one faces the task of developing a self-image.

ego integrity versus despair Erikson's psychosocial stage of maturity that entails the task of being able to reflect on one's life with satisfaction.

ego-psychoanalytic theory Psychoanalytic theory that emphasizes the role of the ego in personality development.

Electra complex A term that some critics have used to express the feminine counterpart to the male Oedipus complex.

empathy The ability to recognize and understand another's feelings.

empirical Based on experience and observation.

empiricism The philosophical view that human knowledge arises slowly in the course of experience through observation and experiment.

empty organism A phrase used by Skinner's critics to describe his concept of the infant at birth.

endomorphy In Sheldon's theory, a component of physique indicating a predominance of soft roundness throughout the body.

environmental-mold traits In Cattell's theory, traits that originate from the influences of physical and social surroundings.

epigenesis Development in a sequential pattern implying a hierarchy.

epiphany A usually sudden manifestation of the essential nature of something.

equilibrium Balance or harmony.

erg In Cattell's theory, a constitutional dynamic trait.

erogenous zones Areas of the body that provide pleasure.

essence In philosophy, the unchangeable principles and laws that govern being.

evaluative response In Rogers's theory, a response that places a value judgment on thoughts, feelings, wishes, or behavior.

existential dichotomy In Fromm's theory, a dilemma or problem that arises simply from the fact of existence.

existentialism A philosophical movement that studies the meaning of existence.

expectancy construct In Rotter's theory, the individual's subjective expectation about the outcome of his or her behavior.

experimental method A scientific method involving a careful study of cause and effect by manipulating variables and observing their effects.

exploitative orientation In Fromm's theory, a character type in which a person exploits others and the world.

expressive behavior In Allport's theory, an individual's manner of performing.

extinction The tendency of a response to disappear when it is not reinforced.

extrinsic A quest that serves other purposes outside the original goal.

extroversion An attitude of expansion in which the psyche is oriented toward the external world.

factor analysis Employed by Cattell, a procedure that interrelates many correlations at one time.

fallacy of affirming the consequent An invalid form of reasoning in which affirming the consequence of a premise is thought to affirm the premise itself.

falsification The act of disproving.

family atmosphere In Adler's theory, the quality of emotional relationships among members of a family.

family constellation In Adler's theory, one's position within the family in terms of birth order among siblings and the presence or absence of parents and other caretakers.

feeling One of Jung's functions, involving valuing and judging the world.

fictional finalism In Adler's theory, a basic concept or philosophical assumption that cannot be tested against reality.

finalism In Adler's theory, a principle that reflects the concept of goal orientation.

fixation In Freud's theory, a defense mechanism in which there is an arrestment of growth and excessive needs characteristic of an earlier stage are created by over-indulgence or undue frustration.

fixed schedule of reinforcement A schedule of reinforcement in which the time period or number of responses before reinforcement is identical.

Four Noble Truths A doctrine developed by Buddha.

frame of orientation and devotion In Fromm's thought, the need for a stable thought system by which to organize perceptions and make sense out of the environment.

free association In Freud's psychoanalysis, a technique in which a person verbalizes whatever comes to mind.

freedom of movement In Rotter's theory, the degree of expectation a person has that a particular set of responses will lead to a desired reinforcement.

frigidity The quality of marked sexual indifference or lack of sexual response.

frustration In Dollard and Miller's theory, an emotion that occurs when one is unable to satisfy a drive because the response that would satisfy it has been blocked.

fully functioning person A term used by Rogers to indicate an individual who is functioning at an optimum level.

functional autonomy In Allport's theory, a concept that present motives are not necessarily tied to the past but may be free of earlier motivations.

functions In Jung's theory, ways of perceiving the environment and orienting experiences.

generalization A statement that may be made, when a number of different instances coincide, that something is true about many or all of the members of a certain class.

generalized conditioned reinforcers In Skinner's theory, learned reinforcers that have the power to reinforce a great number of different behaviors.

generativity versus stagnation Erikson's psychosocial stage of the middle years, in which one faces the dilemma of being productive and creative in life.

genital stage Freud's final psychosexual stage, in which an individual reaches sexual maturity.

gestalt Configuration or pattern that forms a whole.

gestalt principle The notion that the whole is more than the sum of its parts.

gestalt psychology A branch of psychology that studies how organisms perceive objects and events.

gestalt therapy A method of psychotherapy developed by Fritz Perls that emphasizes awareness and seeks to discover the how and now of behavior.

goal of superiority In Adler's theory, the ultimate fictional finalism, entailing the desire to be competent and effective in whatever one strives to do and to actualize one's potential.

good-me self In Sullivan's theory, the content of awareness that accompanies being thoroughly satisfied with oneself.

gradient The changing strength of a force, which may be plotted on a graph.

guru Teacher.

habit In Dollard and Miller's theory, the basic structure of personality: a learned association between a stimulus and response.

having mode In Fromm's theory, a way of existence that relies on possessions.

heterostasis The desire not to reduce tension, but to seek new stimuli and challenges that will further growth.

heuristic value The ability of a construct to predict future events.

hierarchy of response In Dollard and Miller's theory, a tendency for certain responses to occur before other responses.

historical dichotomy In Fromm's theory, a dilemma or problem that arises out of human history because of various societies and cultures.

hoarding orientation In Fromm's theory, a character type in which the person seeks to save or hoard and protects him- or herself from the world by a wall.

homeostasis Balance or harmony.

homosexuality Primary attraction to the same sex.

hormones Chemicals released into the blood stream by the endocrine glands.

humanist theories Theories of personality that emphasize human potential.

Humanistic Communitarian Socialism The name of Fromm's ideal society.

humanistic ethic In Fromm's theory, a value system that has its source in the individual acting in accord with the law of his or her human nature and assuming full responsibility for his or her existence.

humors In earlier psychology, bodily fluids thought to enter into the constitution of a body and determine by their proportion a person's constitution and temperament.

hypothesis A preliminary assumption that guides further inquiry.

hysteria An earlier term for an illness in which there are physical symptoms, such as paralysis, but no organic or physiological basis for the problem.

id In Freud's theory, the oldest and original function of the personality, which includes genetic inheritance, reflex capacities, instincts, and drives.

idealized self In Horney's theory, that which a person thinks he or she should be.

identification In Freud's theory, (a) a defense mechanism in which a person reduces anxiety by modeling his or her behavior after that of someone else, and (b) the process whereby the child resolves the Oedipus complex by incorporating the parents into the self.

identity crisis In Erikson's theory, transitory failure to develop a self-image or identity.

I-E Scale A questionnaire developed by Rotter to measure internal versus external locus of control.

immediate reinforcement Reinforcement that immediately follows a response.

imprinting A bond of attraction that develops among members of a species shortly after birth.

inception In Sullivan's theory, the first phase of an interview in which the patient describes the problems that have brought him or her to the session.

incongruence In Rogers's theory, the lack of harmony that results when a person's symbolized experiences do not represent the actual experiences.

independent variable In an experiment, the factor that is manipulated by the experimenter.

individual psychology The school of psychology developed by Adler.

individuation In Jung's theory of self-actualization, a process whereby the systems of the individual psyche achieve their fullest degree of differentiation, expression, and development.

industry versus inferiority Erikson's psychosocial stage, corresponding to Freud's latency period, in which children face the task of learning and mastering the technology of their culture.

infancy In Sullivan's stages of development, the period from birth to meaningful speech, in which the significance of oral experiences is emphasized.

inferiority complex In Adler's theory, a neurotic pattern in which an individual feels highly inadequate.

inferiority feelings In Adler's theory, feelings of being inadequate that arise out of childhood experiences.

infrahuman species Species lower than human organisms.

inhibition The prevention of a response from occurring because it is in conflict with other strong unconscious responses.

initiative versus guilt Erikson's psychosexual stage, corresponding to Freud's phallic stage, in which children face the task of directing their curiosity and activity toward specific goals and achievements.

inner space In Erikson's theory, tendency on the part of girls to emphasize qualities of openness versus closedness in space.

insight A form of therapeutic knowing that combines intellectual and emotional elements and culminates in profound personality change.

insight therapy Therapeutic procedures that seek to increase self-understanding and lead to deep motivational changes.

intentionality In May's theory, a dimension that undercuts conscious and unconscious, and underlies will and decision.

interpretative response In Rogers's theory, a response that seeks to capture the underlying meaning or motive.

interpsychic Between psyches or persons.

interval reinforcement A schedule of reinforcement in which the organism is reinforced after a certain time period has elapsed.

interview Sullivan's term for the interpersonal process that occurs between patient and therapist.

intimacy versus isolation Erikson's psychosocial stage of young adulthood in which one faces the task of establishing a close, deep, and meaningful genital relationship with another person.

intrapsychic Within the psyche or individual self.

introversion An attitude of withdrawal in which personality is oriented inward toward the subjective world.

intuition One of Jung's functions, entailing perception via the unconscious.

IQ Intelligence quotient: a number used to express the relative intelligence of a person.

juvenile era In Sullivan's stages of development, a period when the child has a strong need for playmates.

karma In Hindu thought, cycles of cause and effect.

koan In the practice of Zen, a paradoxical statement or question that has no intellectual solution.

late adolescence In Sullivan's stages of development, the last stage before adulthood in which an individual achieves social, vocational, and economic integration and stability.

latency period A period in Freud's psychosexual stages of development in which the sexual drive was thought to go underground.

latent dream In Freud's theory, the real meaning or motive that underlies the dream that we remember.

law of effect A law formulated by Thorndike that states that when a behavior or a performance is accompanied by satisfaction it tends to increase; if accompanied by frustration, it tends to decrease.

L-data In Cattell's theory, observations made of a person's behavior in society or everyday life.

learning dilemma In Dollard and Miller's theory, the situation an individual is placed in if present responses are not reinforced.

libido a) In Freud's theory, an emotional and psychic energy derived from the biological drive of sexuality. b) In Jung's theory, an undifferentiated life and psychic energy.

life impulses In Freud's theory, drives or forces that maintain life processes and insure propagation of the species.

life lie In Adler's theory, a style of life that belies one's actual capabilities and strengths.

love In Fromm's theory, the productive relationship to others and the self, entailing care, responsibility, respect, and knowledge.

mandala A concentrically arranged figure often found as a symbol in the East that denotes wholeness and unity. In Jung's theory, a symbol for the emerging self.

manifest dream In Freud's theory, the dream as it is remembered the next morning.

mantra In Eastern thought, a spiritual word or formula chanted throughout meditation to evoke a deeper level of consciousness.

marketing orientation In Fromm's theory, a character type in which the person experiences him- or herself as a commodity in the marketplace.

masculine protest In Adler's early theory, the compensation for one's inferiorities.

masochism A sexual disorder in which a person obtains pleasure by receiving pain.

maya In Eastern thought, a term that means illusion.

melancholic One of Hippocrates' temperaments, referring to an individual characterized by depression.

mesomorphy In Sheldon's theory, a component of physique indicating a predominance of muscle, bone, and connective tissue.

metamotivation A term used by Maslow to refer to growth tendencies within the organism.

metapsychological A term used by Freud to indicate the fullest possible description of psychic processes.

method of amplification In Jungian therapy, an analytical method whereby one focuses repeatedly on an element and gives multiple associations to it.

minimum goal level In Rotter's theory, the lowest level of potential reinforcement that is perceived as satisfactory in a particular situation.

moral anxiety In Freud's theory, fear of the retribution of one's own conscience.

morphogenic (or idiographic) In Allport's theory, an approach to studying personality that centers on understanding the uniqueness of the individual.

morphology Body measurement.

motivation Maslow's term for the reduction of tension by satisfying deficit states or lacks.

moving against One of Horney's three primary modes of relating to other people, in which one seeks to protect him- or herself by revenge or controlling others.

moving away One of Horney's three primary ways of relating to other people, in which one isolates him- or herself and keeps apart.

moving toward One of Horney's three primary modes of relating to other people, in which one accepts his or her own helplessness and becomes compliant in order to depend on others.

narcissism a) A form of self-encapsulation in which an individual experiences as real only that which exists within him- or herself. b) In Kohut's theory, a disorder that occurs when an individual fails to develop an independent sense of self.

necrophilous character In Fromm's theory, a character orientation in which an individual is attracted to that which is dead and decaying and seeks to destroy living things.

need a) In Murray's theory, a force in the brain that organizes perception, understanding, and behavior in such a way as to change an unsatisfying situation and increase satisfaction. b) In Rotter's theory, a behavior that leads to a reinforcement.

need potential In Rotter's theory, the likelihood that a set of behaviors directed toward the same goal will be used in a given situation.

need value In Rotter's theory, the importance placed on a goal.

negative identity In Erikson's theory, an identity opposed to the dominant values of one's culture.

negative reinforcement Unpleasant or aversive stimuli that can be changed or avoided by certain behavior.

neo-psychoanalytic theories Psychoanalytic theories that revise or modify Freud's original theories.

neurosis An emotional disturbance, usually not so severe as to prevent an individual from functioning in normal society.

neurotic anxiety In Freud's theory, the fear that one's inner impulses cannot be controlled.

neurotic trends In Horney's theory, exaggerated defense strategies that permit an individual to cope with the world.

nirvana In Buddhist thought, the extinction of all desire, resentment, and selfishness caused by identification with one's separate ego.

nondirective A term used by Rogers to describe therapies whose course is primarily determined by the patient.

normal curve of distribution A bell-shaped curve representing many events in nature in which most events cluster around the mean.

not-me self In Sullivan's theory, an aspect of the self-system, a gradually evolving image of the self that is regarded as dreadful and cannot be permitted conscious awareness and acknowledgment.

objective test In Cattell's theory, a test that is constructed in such a way that the subject taking it cannot know its purpose.

objective data Data acquired through extrospection, the act of looking outward on the world as object.

objectivism The philosophical view that valid knowledge arises gradually in the course of experience through observation and experimentation.

objectivity The quality of recognizing or expressing reality without distortion by personal feeling. In test construction, construction of a test in such a way that it can be given and scored in a way that avoids the scorer's subjective bias.

observational learning In Bandura's theory, learning that occurs through observation without any direct reinforcement.

Oedipus complex In Freud's theory, an unconscious psychological conflict in which the child loves the parent of the opposite sex.

open system A concept of personality that conceives of it as having a dynamic potential for growth, reconstitution, and change through extensive transactions within itself and the environment.

operant behavior In Skinner's theory, a response that acts on the environment and is emitted without a stimulus necessarily being present.

operant conditioning In Skinner's theory, the process by which an operant response becomes associated with a reinforcement through learning.

operational definition A definition that specifies those behaviors that are included in the concept.

oral stage One of Freud's psychosexual stages, in which the major source of pleasure and potential conflict is the mouth.

oryoki Utensils used for eating in a Zen monastery.

outer space In Erikson's theory, tendency on the part of boys to emphasize qualities of highness or lowness in space.

overcompensation In Adler's theory, an exaggerated effort to cover up a weakness that entails a denial rather than an acceptance of the real situation.

overdetermination In Freud's theory, the view that all events have more than one meaning or explanation.

overt behavior Behavior that can be observed by an external observer.

paradigm A pattern or model.

paradox Two opposites that seem to negate each other but cannot exist without each other.

parataxic distortion In Sullivan's theory, reacting to someone as if he or she was someone else.

parataxic experience In Sullivan's theory, a cognitive process in which one perceives causal relations but not on the basis of reality or logic.

para-world A world of quantified, logical, and mathematical imaginary constructs used by the scientist to draw conclusions about the everyday world.

Parent In Berne's transactional analysis, an ego state that incorporates the values of others.

participant observation In Sullivan's theory, a concept that refers to the fact that an observer of an interpersonal relationship is also a participant in it.

peak experience In Maslow's theory, an intensified experience in which there is a loss of self or transcendence of self.

penis envy In Freud's theory, the concept that women view themselves as castrated males and envy the penis.

performance phase In Dollard and Miller's therapy, a phase in which the patient acquires new, more adaptive responses and habits.

perseverative functional autonomy In Allport's theory, acts or behaviors that are repeated even though they may have lost their original function.

persona In Jung's theory, an archetype referring to one's social role and understanding of it.

personal dispositions In Allport's theory, traits that are unique to an individual.

personal unconscious In Jung's theory, experiences of an individual's life that have been repressed or temporarily forgotten.

personality a) In social speech, one's public image. b) In Sullivan's theory, an imaginary construct used to explain and predict certain behaviors. c) In Fromm's theory, the totality of an individual's psychic qualities. d) In Allport's theory, the dynamic organization within the individual of those psychophysical systems that determine his or her characteristic behavior and thought. e) In Cattell's theory, that which permits prediction of what a person will do in a given situation.

personification In Sullivan's theory, a group of feelings, attitudes, and thoughts that have arisen out of one's interpersonal experiences.

personology Murray's term for his study of individual persons.

phallic stage One of Freud's psychosexual stages, in which pleasurable and conflicting feelings are associated with the genital organs.

phenomenal field In Rogers's theory, the total sum of experiences an organism has.

phenomenology The study of phenomena or appearances.

philosophical assumption An underlying view of the world that influences a person's thinking.

philosophy The systematic love and pursuit of wisdom.

phlegmatic One of Hippocrates' temperaments, referring to an individual who is slow, solid, and apathetic.

pleasure principle In Freud's theory, the seeking of tension reduction followed by the id.

POI Personal Orientation Inventory: a test developed by Shostrom to measure self-actualization.

polymorphous perverse A phrase used by Freud to emphasize the point that children deviate in many ways from what is thought to be normal reproductive sexual activity.

positive regard In Rogers's theory, being loved and accepted for who one is.

positive reinforcement Anything that serves to increase the frequency of a response.

preadolescence In Sullivan's theory, a stage of development marked by the need for intimacy with a same-sexed peer.

preconscious In Freud's theory, memories of which we are unaware but which are easily accessible to consciousness.

predictive power A criterion for evaluating rival hypotheses: the range or scope of the hypothesis.

pre-emptive construct In Kelly's theory, a construct that limits its elements to one range only.

press In Murray's theory, a force coming from the environment that helps or hinders an individual in reaching goals.

primary drive A drive associated with a physiological process that is necessary for the organism's survival.

primary process In Freud's theory, a psychological activity of the id characterized by immediate wish fulfillment and disregard of realistic concerns.

primary reinforcer A reinforcer that is inherently rewarding as it satisfies a primary drive.

proactive Referring to theories of personality that view the human being as acting on his or her own initiative rather than simply reacting.

probing response In Rogers's theory, a response that seeks further information.

proceeding In Murray's theory, a short, significant behavior pattern that has a clear beginning and ending.

productive orientation In Fromm's theory, the character type that represents the ideal of humanistic development.

projection In Freud's theory, a defense mechanism that refers to the unconscious attribution of an impulse, attitude, or behavior to someone else or some element in the environment.

projective techniques Personality tests in which an ambiguous stimulus is presented to the subject who is expected to project aspects of his or her personality into the response.

propositional construct In Kelly's theory, a construct that leaves its elements open to other constructions.

propriate functional autonomy In Allport's theory, acquired interests, values, attitudes, intentions, and lifestyle that are directed from the proprium and are genuinely free of earlier motivations.

propriate functions In Allport's theory, the functions of the proprium.

propriate striving In Allport's theory, a propriate function that entails projection of long-term purposes and goals and development of a plan to attain them.

proprium In Allport's theory, a term that refers to the central experiences of self-awareness that a person has as he or she grows and moves forward.

prototaxic experience In Sullivan's theory, a cognitive process in which the infant does not distinguish between the self and the external world.

psyche From the Greek term meaning "breath" or "principle of life," often translated as "soul" or "self." a) In Freud's theory, the id, ego, and superego. b) In Jung's theory, the total personality encompassing all psychological processes: thoughts, feelings, sensations, wishes, and so on.

psychoanalysis A method of therapy developed by Freud that concentrates on cultivating a transference relationship and analyzing resistances to the therapeutic process.

psychohistory The combined use of psychoanalysis and history to study individuals and groups.

psychometrics The quantitative measurement of psychological characteristics through statistical techniques.

psychophysical Entailing components of both the mind and the body.

psychosexual stages In Freud's theory, a series of developmental stages through which all people pass as they move from infancy to adulthood.

psychosexuality In Freud's theory, a term used to express the totality of elements included in the sexual drive.

psychosis An abnormal personality disturbance characterized by loss or distortion of reality testing and the inability to distinguish between reality and fantasy.

psychosocial stages A series of developmental stages proposed by Erikson to emphasize the social dimension of personality.

psychotherapy Treatment of emotional disorders by psychological means.

punishment An undesirable consequence that follows a behavior and is designed to stop or change it.

Q-data In Cattell's theory, questionnaires and self-reports.

Q-sort technique A card-sorting technique employed by Rogers for studying the self-concept.

radical behaviorism A label that has been given to B. F. Skinner's point of view.

random assignment In an experiment, insuring that every subject has an equal chance of being assigned to any of the treatment groups.

ratio reinforcement A schedule of reinforcement in which the organism is reinforced after a number of appropriate responses.

rationalism The philosophical view that the mind can, in and of its own accord, formulate ideas and determine their truth.

rationalization In Freud's theory, a defense mechanism that entails dealing with an emotion or impulse analytically and intellectually, thereby not involving the emotions.

reaction formation In Freud's theory, a defense mechanism in which an impulse is expressed by its opposite.

reactive Referring to theories of personality that view the human being as primarily responding to external stimuli.

real self In Horney's theory, that which a person actually is.

reality anxiety In Freud's theory, the fear of a real danger in the external world.

reality principle In Freud's theory, the way in which the ego satisfies the impulses of the id in an appropriate manner in the external world.

reassuring response In Rogers's theory, a response that attempts to soothe feelings.

receptive orientation In Fromm's theory, a character type in which the individual reacts to the world passively.

reciprocal determinism In Bandura's theory, the regulation of behavior by an interplay of behavioral, cognitive, and environmental factors.

reciprocal inhibition In Wolpe's therapy, the introduction of a response that will compete with a maladaptive response.

reconnaissance In Sullivan's theory, the second phase of the interview, during which the therapist develops a case history and tentative hypotheses.

reconstructive (or intensive) psychotherapy Therapeutic methods that seek to remove defenses and reorganize the basic personality structure.

reflective response In Rogers's theory, a response that seeks to capture the underlying feeling expressed.

reflexes Inborn automatic responses.

regression In Freud's theory, a defense mechanism that entails reverting to earlier forms of behavior.

reinforcement The process of increasing or decreasing the likelihood of a particular response.

reinforcement value In Rotter's theory, a variable that indicates the importance or preference of a particular reinforcement for an individual.

reinforcer Any event that increases or decreases the likelihood of a particular response.

relatedness In Fromm's theory, the basic need to relate to and love other people.

relevance One of the criteria for evaluating philosophical statements, the quality of having some bearing or being pertinent to one's view of reality.

reliability The quality of consistently yielding the same results over time.

Rep Test Role Construct Repertory Test: a device developed by Kelly to reveal personal constructs.

repression a) In Freud's theory, the key defense mechanism, which entails blocking a wish or desire from expression so that it cannot be experienced consciously or directly expressed in behavior. b) In Dollard and Miller's theory, a learned process of avoiding certain thoughts and thereby losing verbal control.

resignation solution One of Horney's three basic orientations, representing the desire to be free of others.

resistance In Freud's theory, a force that prevents an individual from becoming aware of unconscious memories or any obstacle that interferes with the analytic process.

respondent behavior In Skinner's theory, reflexes or automatic responses elicited by a stimulus.

response A behavior that results from a stimulus. In Dollard and Miller's theory, one's reaction to a cue or stimulus.

ritualization In Erikson's theory, a form of behavior that is repeated and has an adaptive function.

role a) In social psychology, a set of behavioral expectations set forth by a particular society and fulfilled by its members. b) In Kelly's theory, a process or behavior that a person plays based on his or her understanding of the behavior and constructs of other people.

role confusion In Erikson's theory, an inability to conceive of oneself as a productive member in one's society.

role playing A therapeutic technique introduced by Kelly.

rootedness In Fromm's theory, the basic need to feel that one belongs in the world.

sadism A sexual disorder in which a person obtains pleasure by inflicting pain.

safeguarding tendencies In Adler's theory, compensatory mechanisms that ward off feelings of insecurity.

sanguine One of Hippocrates' temperaments, referring to a personality marked by sturdiness, high color, and cheerfulness.

sanzen Individual consultations between a Zen Buddhist monk and his master.

satiation Engaging in a behavior until one tires of it.

satori In Zen Buddhism, enlightenment.

science A system or method of acquiring knowledge based on specific principles of observation and reasoning.

scientific construct An imaginary or hypothetical construct used to explain what is observed in science.

scientific (or empirical) generalization An inductive conclusion based on a number of different instances of observation.

scientific method A method of inquiry that consists of five steps: recognizing a problem, developing a hypothesis, making a prediction, testing the hypothesis, and drawing a conclusion.

scientific statement A statement about the world based on observations arising from a currently held paradigm.

scientism Exclusive reliance on a narrow conception of science.

secondary dispositions In Allport's theory, more specific, focused tendencies of an individual that tend to be situational in character.

secondary drive A drive that is learned or acquired on the basis of a primary drive.

secondary processes In Freud's theory, higher intellectual functions that enable the ego to establish suitable courses of action and test them for their effectiveness.

secondary reinforcer A reinforcer that is originally neutral but that acquires reward value on the basis of association with a primary reinforcer.

security In Sullivan's theory, a state of emotional well-being, self-confidence, and optimism in which there are no painful feelings or emotions.

security operation In Sullivan's theory, an interpersonal device that a person uses to minimize anxiety and enhance security.

selective inattention In Sullivan's theory, a security operation in which one fails to notice some factor in an interpersonal relationship that might cause anxiety.

self a) In Jung's theory, a central archetype representing the striving for unity of all parts of the personality. b) In Rogers's theory, the psychological processes that govern a person's behavior.

self-actualization In the theories of Aristotle, Jung, Rogers, and Maslow, a dynamic within the organism leading it to actualize, fulfill, and enhance its inherent potentialities.

self-analysis In Horney's theory, a systematic effort at self-understanding conducted without the aid of a professional.

self-as-rational coper In Allport's theory, a propriate function that entails the perception of oneself as an active problem-solving agent.

self-concept In Rogers's theory, a portion of the phenomenal field that has become differentiated and is composed of perceptions and values of "I" or "me."

self-construct In Kelly's theory, perception of similarities in one's behavior based on role relationships with other people.

self-effacing solution One of Horney's three basic orientations toward life, which represents an appeal to be loved by others.

self-efficacy In Bandura's theory, a person's perception of his or her effectiveness.

self-esteem a) In Sullivan's theory, all the feelings of competence and personal worth that hold a person together. b) In Allport's theory, a propriate function that entails feelings of pride as one develops the ability to do things.

self-expansive solution One of Horney's three basic orientations toward life, which represents a striving for mastery.

self-extension In Allport's theory, a propriate function that entails a sense of possession.

self-identity In Allport's theory, a propriate function that entails an awareness of inner sameness and continuity.

self-image In Allport's theory, a propriate function that entails a sense of the expectations of others and its comparison with one's own behavior.

self-love In Fromm's theory, love of self that is a prerequisite for love of others.

self-sentiment In Cattell's theory, an environmental-mold dynamic source trait composing a person's self-image.

self-system a) In Sullivan's theory, a dynamism of self-understanding that emerges as a result of interpersonal experiences. b) In Bandura's theory, cognitive structures that underlie the perception, evaluation, and regulation of behavior.

sensation One of Jung's functions, referring to sense perception of the world.

sense of identity In Fromm's theory, the need to be aware of oneself as an individual.

sentiment In Cattell's theory, an environmental-mold dynamic source trait.

separation-individuation process A sequence of stages posited by Mahler through which the ego passes in the process of becoming an individual.

shadow In Jung's theory, an archetype that encompasses one's animalistic and unsocial side.

shaping In Skinner's theory, a process by which an organism's behavior is gradually molded until it approximates the desired behavior.

simplicity A criterion for evaluating rival hypotheses: the quality of being simple and avoiding complicated explanations.

situation The psychological context within which an organism responds.

slips In Freud's theory, bungled acts, such as a slip of the tongue, a slip of the pen, or a memory lapse.

social interest In Adler's theory, an urge in human nature to adapt oneself to the conditions of one's environment and society.

social learning theories Theories that attempt to explain personality in terms of learned behavior within a social context.

social psychoanalytic theories Psychoanalytic theories that emphasize the role of social forces in shaping personality.

somatotonia In Sheldon's theory, a component of temperament characterized by a predominance of muscular activity and vigorous bodily assertiveness.

somatotype Sheldon's term for the expression of body type through three numbers that indicate the degree of each physical component.

source traits In Cattell's theory, underlying variables that determine surface manifestations.

species-specific behavior Complex automatic behaviors that occur in all members of a species.

specification equation An equation by which Cattell suggests we may eventually be able to predict human behavior.

spontaneous recovery Following extinction, the return of a learned behavior.

standardization Pre-testing of a large and representative sample in order to determine test norms.

statement An utterance that makes an assertion or a denial.

statistics The application of mathematical principles to the description and analysis of measurements.

stereotype Prejudgment that we make about people on the basis of their membership in certain groups.

stimulus An agent that rouses or excites a response.

stroke In Berne's transactional analysis, an activity that fulfills a physiological or psychological need.

structuralism Early school of psychology that suggested that psychology study conscious experience.

stupidity-misery syndrome Dollard and Miller's term for a neurosis.

style of life In Adler's theory, the specific ways in which an individual seeks to attain the goal of superiority.

subception In Rogers's theory, a discriminative evaluative response of the organism that precedes conscious perception.

subjective data Data acquired through introspection, the act of looking inward on the self as subject.

subjectivism A philosophical view that constructs of knowledge are creations of the self.

sublimation In Freud's theory, a defense mechanism that refers to translating a wish, the direct expression of which is socially unacceptable, into socially acceptable behavior.

subsidiation In Cattell's theory, the principle that certain traits are secondary to other traits.

successive approximations In Dollard and Miller's therapy, the interpretations of the therapist that provide increasingly more accurate labels for the patient's responses.

superego In Freud's theory, a function of the personality that represents introjected and internalized values, ideals, and moral standards.

superiority complex In Adler's theory, a neurotic pattern in which an individual exaggerates his or her importance.

supportive psychotherapy Therapeutic measures that seek to strengthen adaptive instincts and defenses.

suppression The conscious, deliberate stopping of a thought or an action.

surface traits In Cattell's theory, clusters of overt behavior responses that appear to go together.

symbiotic relatedness In Fromm's theory, a relationship in which one or the other of two persons loses or never attains his or her independence.

symbol An element in a dream that stands for something else.

syntality In Cattell's theory, the behavior of a group as a whole or its "group personality."

syntaxic experience In Sullivan's theory, the highest level of cognitive activity, entailing the use of symbols and relying on consensual validation.

systematic desensitization A behavior therapy developed by Wolpe to condition a patient to substitute a new response for an undesired one.

tabula rasa A blank slate, a phrase associated with John Locke, suggesting that the mind is a blank tablet on which experience writes.

talking phase In Dollard and Miller's therapy, a phase in which neurotic habits are studied, examined, and identified so that the patient may unlearn them.

Taoism A Chinese philosophy that advocates a way of life in harmony with the course of nature.

TAT Thematic Apperception Test: a projective test consisting of ambiguous pictures to which a subject is asked to respond.

T-data In Cattell's theory, objective tests.

teisho A lecture or discourse on the inner meaning of Zen.

telos A purpose or goal.

temperament traits In Cattell's theory, traits that determine how a person behaves in order to obtain his or her goal.

termination In Sullivan's theory, the final phase of the interview, which represents a structured conclusion and suggestion for action.

theory A set of abstract concepts made about a group of facts or events to explain them.

therapy The practical application of psychology in ways that will assist individuals.

thinking One of Jung's functions, referring to giving meaning and understanding to the world.

token economy A community based on Skinnerian principles in which individuals are rewarded for appropriate behavior with tokens that can be exchanged for various privileges.

tracing the life line In Adlerian psychotherapy, a method of analyzing early memories and dreams to determine an individual's lifestyle.

trait Continuous dimension that an individual can be seen to possess to a certain degree. a) In Allport's theory, a determining tendency to respond that represents the ultimate reality of psychological organization. b) In Cattell's theory, an imaginary construct or inference from overt behavior that helps to explain it.

trait theories Theories that conceive of personality as being composed primarily of traits.

transactional analysis A system of therapy developed by Eric Berne that conceptualizes human relationships in terms of the roles of Parent, Child, and Adult.

transcendence a) In Jung's theory of self-actualization, a process of integrating the diverse systems of the self toward the goal of wholeness and identification with all humanity. b) In Fromm's theory, the basic human need to rise above the accidental and passive creatureliness of animal existence and become an active creator.

transference In Freudian psychoanalysis, a process in which the patient projects onto the analyst emotional attitudes felt as a child toward important persons.

transjective knowledge In Buber's philosophy, the knowledge that arises out of an encounter between persons.

trust versus mistrust Erikson's psychosocial stage, corresponding to Freud's oral stage, in which infants face the task of trusting the world.

typology Division of human beings into distinct, separate categories.

unconditional positive regard In Rogers's theory, positive regard that is not contingent on any specific behaviors.

unconditioned response A reflex or automatic response to a stimulus.

unconditioned stimulus A stimulus that normally elicits a particular reflex or automatic response.

unconscious processes a) In Freud's theory, processes of which a person is unaware because they have been repressed or never permitted to become conscious. b) In Dollard and Miller's theory, drives or cues of which we are unaware because they are unlabeled or repressed.

urethral complex In Murray's theory, a complex that originates in pleasurable associations with urination.

usefulness a) In scientific theorizing, the ability of a hypothesis to generate predictions about experiences that we might observe. b) In Adler's theory, the ability of a goal to foster productive living and enhance one's life.

validating evidence Observable consequences that follow an experiment designed to test a hypothesis and are used to support a construct or theory.

validity The quality of measuring what a construct is supposed to measure.

variable A characteristic that can be measured or controlled.

variable schedule of reinforcement A schedule of reinforcement in which the time period or number of responses prior to reinforcement varies.

virtues In Erikson's theory, ego strengths that develop out of each psychosocial stage.

viscerotonia In Sheldon's theory, a component of temperament characterized by a general love of comfort, relaxation, sociability, people, food, and affection.

voyeurism A sexual disorder in which a person obtains pleasure from seeing sexual organs or acts.

Walden II Skinner's name for his utopian community.

wish fulfillment In Freud's theory, a primary-process activity that seeks to reduce tension by forming an image of the object that would satisfy needs.

withdrawal-destructiveness In Fromm's theory, a relationship characterized by distance, apathy, or aggression.

womb envy In Horney's theory, the concept that men and boys experience jealousy over woman's ability to bear and nurse children.

yin and yang In Taoism, two forces by which Tao manifests itself.

zazen A practice of meditation widespread in the East.

Zen Buddhism A branch of Mahayana Buddhism that teaches meditation and the attainment of enlightenment.

zendo The meditation hall of a Zen monastery.

References

Adler, A. *Study of organ inferiority and its psychical compensation.* New York: Nervous and Mental Diseases Publishing Co., 1917.

Adler, A. *The practice and theory of individual psychology.* New York: Harcourt, Brace, & World, 1927.

Adler, A. *The science of living.* New York: Greenberg, 1929a.

Adler, A. *Problems of neurosis.* London: Kegan Paul, 1929b.

Adler, A. Individual psychology. In C. Murchison (Ed.), *Psychologies of* 1930. Worcester, Mass.: Clark University Press, 1930.

Adler, A. *What life should mean to you.* Boston: Little, Brown, 1931.

Adler, A. *Social interest.* New York: Putnam, 1939.

Adler, A. *Understanding human nature.* New York: Fawcett, 1954.

Adler, A. *Superiority and social interest: A collection of later writings.* H. L. & R. R. Ansbacher (Eds.). Evanston, Ill.: Northwestern University Press, 1964.

Allport, G. W. *Personality: A psychological interpretation.* New York: Holt, 1937.

Allport, G. W. *The nature of personality: Selected papers.* Cambridge, Mass.: Addison Wesley, 1950.

Allport, G. W. *Becoming: Basic considerations for a psychology of personality.* New Haven, Ct.: Yale University Press, 1955.

Allport, G. W. *The individual and his religion.* New York: Macmillan, 1960.

Allport, G. W. The open system in personality theory. *Journal of Abnormal and Social Psychology,* 1960, 60, 301–310.

Allport, G. W. *Pattern and growth in personality.* New York: Holt, Rinehart, and Winston, 1961.

Allport, G. W. *The person in psychology: Selected essays.* Boston: Beacon, 1968.

Ansbacher, H. L. *Alfred Adler revisited.* New York: Praeger, 1984.

Ansbacher, H. L., & Ansbacher, R. R. *The individual psychology of Alfred Adler.* New York: Basic Books, 1956.

Aspy, D. *Toward a technology for humanizing education.* Champaign, Ill.: Research Press, 1972.

Aspy, D., & Roebuck, F. *A lever long enough.* Washington, D.C.: National Consortium for Humanizing Education, 1976.

Bakan, D. *On method: Toward a reconstruction of psychological investigation.* San Francisco: Jossey-Bass, 1969.

Bandura, A. *Principles of behavior modification.* New York: Holt, Rinehart & Winston, 1969.

Bandura, A. *Aggression: A social learning analysis.* Englewood Cliffs, N.J.: Prentice-Hall, 1973.

Bandura, A. Behavior theory and the models of man. *American Psychologist,* 1974, *29,* 859–869.

Bandura, A. *Social learning theory.* Englewood Cliffs, N. J.: Prentice-Hall, 1977.

Bandura, A. The self system in reciprocal determinism. *American Psychologist,* 1978, *33,* 344–358.

Bandura, A., Adams, N. E., Hardy, A. B., & Howells, G. N. Tests of the generality of self-efficacy theory. *Cognitive Therapy and Research,* 1980, *4,* 39–66.

Bandura, A., & Mischel, W. Modifications of self-imposed delay of reward through exposure to live and symbolic models. *Journal of Personality and Social Psychology,* 1965, *2,* 698–705.

Bandura, A., & Walters, R. *Social learning and personality development.* New York: Holt, Rinehart, & Winston, 1963.

Bannister, D., & Fransella, F. A grid test of schizophrenic thought disorder. *British Journal of Social and Clinical Psychology,* 1966, *5,* 95–102.

Bannister, D., & Mair, J. M. M. *The evaluation of personal constructs.* New York: Academic Press, 1968.

Bannister, D., & Salmon, P. Schizophrenic thought disorder: Specific or diffuse? *British Journal of Medical Psychology,* 1966, *39,* 215–219.

Berkowitz, L., & Powers, P. Effects of timing and justification of witnessed aggression on observers' punitiveness. *Journal of Research in Personality,* 1979, *13,* 71–80.

Berne, E. *Games people play.* New York: Grove Press, 1964.

Berson, H., Beary, J., & Carol, M. The relaxation response. *Psychiatry,* 1974, *37,* 37–46.

Bettelheim, B. *The uses of enchantment.* New York: Knopf, 1977.

Bettelheim, B. *Freud and man's soul.* New York: Knopf, 1982.

Borgatta, E. F., & Lambert, W. W. (Eds.). *Handbook of personality and research.* Chicago: Rand McNally, 1968.

Boring, E. G. *A history of experimental psychology.* New York: Appleton-Century-Crofts, 1929.

Boring, E. G. Mind and mechanism. *American Journal of Psychology,* 1946, *59,* 179–192.

Boring, E. G., & Lindzey, G. (Eds.). *A history of psychology in autobiography* (5 vols.). New York: Appleton-Century-Crofts, 1930–1967.

Bottome, P. *Alfred Adler.* New York: Vanguard, 1957.

Brenner, C. *An elementary textbook on psychoanalysis.* New York: Doubleday, 1955.

Brome, V. *Jung: Man and myth.* New York: Atheneum, 1978.

Brown, J. A. C. *Freud and the post-Freudians.* Baltimore: Penguin, 1961.

Brown, J. S. Gradients of approach and avoidance responses and their relation to motivation. *Journal of Comparative and Physiological Psychology,* 1948, *41,* 450–465.

Bruner, J. S. A cognitive theory of personality. And Rogers, C. R., Intellectualizing psychotherapy. [Reviews of G. A. Kelly. *Psychology of personal constructs.*] *Contemporary Psychology,* 1965, *1,* 355–358.

Buber, M. *I and Thou.* New York: Scribner, 1937.

Cartwright, D. (Ed.). *Field theory in social science: Selected theoretical papers.* New York: Harper & Row, 1948.

Cartwright, D. S. *Theories and models of personality.* Dubuque, Iowa: W. C. Brown Co., 1979.

Cattell, R. B. *Personality: A systematic, theoretical and factual study.* New York: McGraw-Hill, 1950.

Cattell, R. B. *The scientific analysis of personality.* Chicago: Aldine, 1965.

Cattell, R. B. (Ed.). *Handbook of multivariate experimental psychology.* Chicago: Rand McNally, 1966.

Cattell, R. B. *A new morality from science: Beyondism.* New York: Pergamon, 1972.

Cattell, R. B. Personality pinned down. *Psychology Today*, July 1973, 40–46.

Cattell, R. B. *Personality and learning theory* (Vols. 1 & 2). New York: Springer, 1979–1980.

Cattell, R. B., & Adelson, M. The conformation of ergic and engram structures in attitudes objectively measured. *Australian Journal of Psychology*, 1958, *10*, 287–318.

Cattell, R. B., & Dreger, R. M. (Eds.). *Handbook of modern personality theory.* Washington, D.C.: Hemisphere Publishing Corp., 1977.

Chapman, A. N. *Harry Stack Sullivan: His life and work.* New York: Putnam, 1976.

Chein, I. *The science of behavior and the image of man.* New York: Basic Books, 1972.

Chomsky, N. Review of Skinner's *Verbal behavior. Language*, 1959, *35*, 26–58; *234*, 246–249.

Coles, R. *Erik H. Erikson: The growth of his work.* Boston: Little, Brown, 1970.

Conant, J. B. *On understanding science.* New Haven: Yale University Press, 1947.

Corcoran, D. W. J. The relation between introversion and salivation. *American Journal of Psychology*, 1964, *77*, 298–300.

Corsini, R. J. *Current personality theories.* Itasca, Ill.: F. E. Peacock, 1977.

Dana, R. H. *A human science model for personality assessment with projective techniques.* New York: Charles C Thomas, 1982.

Dollard, J., & Miller, N. *Social learning and imitation.* New Haven: Yale University Press, 1941.

Dollard, J., & Miller, N. *Personality and psychotherapy: An analysis in terms of learning, thinking, and culture.* New York: McGraw-Hill, 1950.

Dreifurs, R. Adler's contribution to medicine, psychology, education. *American Journal of Individual Psychology*, 1952–1953, *10*, 83–86.

Ellenberger, H. F. *The discovery of the unconscious.* New York: Basic Books, 1970.

Ellis, A. *Reason and emotion in psychotherapy.* New York: Lyle Stuart, 1962.

Ellis, A. *Humanistic psychotherapy.* New York: Julian Press, 1973.

Erikson, E. H. *Young man Luther.* New York: Norton, 1958.

Erikson, E. H. *Childhood and society* (2nd ed.). New York: Norton, 1963.

Erikson, E. H. *Insight and responsibility.* New York: Norton, 1964.

Erikson, E. H. *Identity, youth and crisis.* New York: Norton, 1968.

Erikson, E. H. *Gandhi's Truth.* New York: Norton, 1969.

Erikson, E. H. *Dimensions of a new identity.* New York: Norton, 1974.

Erikson, E. H. *Life history and the historical moment.* New York: Norton, 1975.

Erikson, E. H. *Toys and reasons.* New York: Norton, 1976.

Evans, R. I. *Conversations with Carl Jung and reactions from Ernest Jones.* Princeton: Van Nostrand, 1964.

Evans, R. I. *Dialogue with Erich Fromm.* New York: Harper & Row, 1966.

Evans, R. I. *Dialogue with Erik Erikson.* New York: Harper & Row, 1967.

Evans, R. I. *B. F. Skinner: The man and his ideas.* New York: Dutton, 1969.

Evans, R. I. *Gordon Allport: The man and his ideas.* New York: Dutton, 1970.

Evans, R. I. *Carl Rogers: The man and his ideas.* New York: Dutton, 1975.

Evans, R. J. *The making of psychology: Discussions with creative contributors.* New York: Knopf, 1976.

Eysenck, H. J. The effects of psychotherapy: An evaluation. *Journal of Consulting Psychology*, 1952, 16, 319—324.

Eysenck, H. J. *The dynamics of anxiety and hysteria.* London: Routledge & Kegan Paul, 1957.

Eysenck, H. J. (Ed.). *Handbook of abnormal psychology: An experimental approach.* New York: Basic Books, 1961.

Eysenck, H. J. *The biological basis of personality.* Springfield, Ill.: Thomas, 1967.

Eysenck, H. J. *Psychology is about people.* New York: Open Court, 1972.

Eysenck, H. J., & Rachman, S. *The causes and cures of neurosis.* San Diego: Knapp, 1965.

Eysenck, H. J., & Wilson, G. D. *The experimental study of Freudian theory.* London: Methuen, 1973.

Feeney, E. (Vice President, System Performance, Emery Air Freight). Statement made in *Business, behaviorism, and the bottom line* [Film]. CRM Films, Del Mar, Calif.: 1972.

Feshbach, S., & Singer, J. *Television and aggression.* San Francisco: Jossey-Bass, 1971.

Fisher, S., & Greenberg, R. P. *Scientific credibility of Freud's theory and therapy.* New York: Basic Books, 1977.

Fordham, F. *An introduction to Jung's psychology.* Baltimore: Penguin, 1953.

Freud, A. *The Writings of Anna Freud.* New York: International Universities Press, beginning in 1965.

Freud, S. *The complete psychological works: Standard edition* (24 vols.). J. Strachey (Ed.). London: Hogarth Press, 1953—   . (Hereafter referred to as *SE* with year of original publication.)

Freud, S. Studies in hysteria. *SE* (Vol. 2), 1895.

Freud, S. The interpretation of dreams. *SE* (Vols. 4 & 5), 1900.

Freud, S. The psychopathology of everyday life. *SE* (Vol. 6), 1901.

Freud, S. Three essays on sexuality. *SE* (Vol. 7), 1905.

Freud, S. Five lectures on psychoanalysis. *SE* (Vol. 11), 1910.

Freud, S. Instincts and their vicissitudes. *SE* (Vol. 14), 1915.

Freud, S. Introductory lectures on psychoanalysis. *SE* (Vols. 15 & 16), 1917.

Freud, S. Beyond the pleasure principle. *SE* (Vol. 18), 1920.

Freud, S. The ego and the id. *SE* (Vol. 19), 1923.

Freud, S. Inhibitions, symptoms and anxiety. *SE* (Vol. 20), 1926a.

Freud, S. The question of lay analysis. *SE* (Vol. 20), 1926b.

Freud, S. New introductory lectures on psychoanalysis. *SE* (Vol. 22), 1933.

Freud, S. Analysis terminable and interminable. *SE* (Vol. 23), 1937.

Freud, S. An outline of psychoanalysis. *SE* (Vol. 23), 1940.

Fromm, E. *Escape from freedom.* New York: Rinehart, 1941.

Fromm, E. *Man for himself.* New York: Rinehart, 1947.

Fromm, E. *The sane society.* New York: Rinehart, 1955.

Fromm, E. *The art of loving.* New York: Harper & Row, 1956.

Fromm, E. *The heart of man.* New York: Harper & Row, 1964.

Fromm, E. *The anatomy of human destructiveness.* New York: Rinehart, 1973.

Fromm, E. *To have or to be.* New York: Harper & Row, 1976.

Fromm, E., & Maccoby, M. *Social character in a Mexican village.* Englewood Cliffs, N.J.: Prentice-Hall, 1970.

Gerbner, G., & Gross, L. Living with television: The violence profile. *Journal of Communication*, 1976, 26, 173—199.

Giovacchini, P. L. *Psychoanalysis of character disorders.* New York: Jason Aronson, 1975.

Giovacchini, P. L. *Psychoanalysis of primitive mental states.* New York: Jason Aronson, 1977.

Glucksberg, S., & King, I. Motivated forgetting mediated by implicit verbal chaining: A laboratory analog of repression. *Science*, October 27, 1967, 517—519.

Goble, F. *The third force: The psychology of Abraham Maslow.* New York: Grossman, 1970.

Hall, C. S. *A primer of Freudian psychology.* New York: World, 1954.

Hall, C. S., & Lindzey, G. *Theories of personality* (3rd ed.). New York: Wiley, 1978.

Hall, C. S., & Nordby, V. J. *A primer of Jungian psychology.* New York: Mentor, 1973.

Hall, C. S., & Van de Castle, R. An empirical investigation of the castration complex in dreams. *Journal of Personality*, 1965, 33, 20—29.

Hall, M. A conversation with H. A. Murray. *Psychology Today*, 1968, 4, 56—63.

Hall, M. A conversation with Abraham H. Maslow. *Psychology Today*, July 1968, 34—37; 54—57.

Hall, M. A conversation with Erik Erikson. *Psychology Today*, 17(6), June 1983.

Hammer, J. Preference for gender of child as a function of sex of adult respondents. *Journal of Individual Psychology*, 1970, 33, 20—29.

Harris, T. *I'm O.K. — You're O.K.* New York: Harper & Row, 1969.

Hartmann, H. *Ego psychology and the problem of adaption.* New York: International Universities Press, 1958.

Hartmann, H. *Essays in ego psychology: Selected problems on psychoanalytic theory.* New York: International Universities Press, 1964.

Hilgard, E. R., & Bower, G. H. *Theories of learning.* Englewood Cliffs, N.J.: Prentice-Hall, 1975.

Hogan, R. J. *Personality theory: The personological tradition.* Englewood Cliffs, N.J.: Prentice-Hall, 1976.

Holt, R. R. Individuality and generalization in the psychology of personality. *Journal of Personality*, 1962, 30, 3.

Holt, R. R. Ego autonomy re-evaluated. *International Journal of Psychiatry*, 1965, 46, 151—167.

Honig, E.K. (Ed.). *Operant behavior: Areas of research and application.* New York: Appleton-Century-Crofts, 1960.

Horney, K. The neurotic personality of our time. New York: Norton, 1937.

Horney, K. *New ways in psychoanalysis.* New York: Norton, 1939.

Horney, K. *Self-analysis.* New York: Norton, 1942.

Horney, K. *Our inner conflicts.* New York: Norton, 1945.

Horney, K. *Neurosis and human growth.* New York: Norton, 1950.

Horney, K. *Feminine psychology.* New York: Norton, 1967.

Howarth, E. Birth order and personality. *Personality and Individual Differences,* 1983, *3* (2), 205–210.

Johnson, J. H., & Sarason, I. G. Life stress, depression and anxiety: Internal-external control as a moderator variable. *Psychosom. Res.,* 1978, *22,* 205–208.

Jones, E. *The life and work of Sigmund Freud* (3 vols.). New York: Basic Books, 1953–1957.

Jung, C. G. *Collected works.* H. Read, M. Fordham, & G. Adler (Eds.). Princeton: Princeton University Press, 1953–   . (Hereafter referred to as *CW* with year of original publication.)

Jung, C. G. *Psychological types.* New York: Harcourt, Brace, 1933a.

Jung, C. G. *Modern man in search of a soul.* New York: Harcourt, Brace, 1933b.

Jung, C. G. A review of complex theory. *CW* (Vol. 8), 1934.

Jung, C. G. The archetypes and the collective unconscious. *CW* (Vol. 9), 1936.

Jung, C. G. Psychology and religion. *CW* (Vol. 11), 1938.

Jung, C. G. The shadow. *CW* (Vol. 9), 1948a.

Jung, C. G. On psychic energy. *CW* (Vol. 8), 1948b.

Jung, C. G. Psychological aspects of the mother archetype. *CW* (Vol. 9), 1954.

Jung, C. G. Mandalas. *CW* (Vol. 9), 1955.

Jung, C. G. *Memories, dreams, and reflections.* New York: Random House, 1961.

Jung, C. G. *Man and his symbols.* New York: Doubleday, 1964.

Kauffman, R. A., & Rychman, R. M. Effects of locus of control. *Personality and Social Psychology Bulletin,* 1979, *5,* 340–343.

Kelly, G. A. *The psychology of personal constructs* (2 vols.). New York: Norton, 1955.

Kelly, G. A. Man's construction of his alternatives. In G. Lindzey (Ed.), *Assessment of human motives.* New York: Rinehart & Winston, 1958.

Kelly, G. A. A brief introduction to personal construct theory. In D. Bannister (Ed.), *Perspectives in personality construct theory.* New York: Academic Press, 1970.

Kline, P. *Fact and fantasy in Freudian theory.* London: Methuen, 1972.

Kluckholn, C., Murray, H. A., & Schneider, D. M. (Eds.). *Personality in nature, society, and culture.* New York: Knopf, 1953.

Koch, S. (Ed.). *Psychology: A study of a science.* New York: McGraw-Hill, 1959.

Kohut, H. *The analysis of the self.* New York: International Universities Press, 1971.

Kohut, H. *The restoration of the self.* New York: International Universities Press, 1977.

Kuhn, T. S. *The structure of scientific revolutions.* Chicago: University of Chicago Press, 1970.

Landman, J. T., & Dawes, R. M. Psychotherapy outcomes. *American Psychologist,* 1982, *37* (5), 504–516.

Lefcourt, H. *Locus of control: Current trends in theory and research.* Hillsdale, N.J.: Erlbaum, 1976.

Lewin, K. The conflict between Aristotelian and Galileian modes of thought in contemporary psychology. *Journal of General Psychology,* 1931, *5,* 141–177.

Liebert, R. M., & Baron, R. A. Some immediate effects of televised violence on children's behavior. *Developmental Psychology,* 1972, *6,* 469–475.

Liebert, R. M., Neale, J. M., & Davidson, E. S. *The early window: Effects of TV on children and youth.* New York: Pergamon, 1973.

Liebert, R. M., & Schwartzberg, N. S. Effects of mass media. *Annual Review of Psychology,* 1977, *28,* 141–173.

Lovaas, O. T., et al. Acquisition of imitative speech in schizophrenic children. *Science,* 1966, *151,* 705–707.

Lundin, R. W. *Personality: A behavioral analysis (*2nd ed.). New York: Macmillan, 1974.

MacIntyre, A. *The unconscious: A conceptual analysis.* London: Routledge & Kegan Paul, 1958.

Maddi, S. R. *Personality theories: A comparative analysis* (rev. ed.). Homewood, Ill.: Dorsey Press, 1972.

Maddi, S., & Costa, P. *Humanism in perspective: Allport, Maslow, and Murray.* Chicago: Aldine Altherton, 1972.

Mahler, M. *The psychological birth of the human infant.* New York: Basic Books, 1975.

Mahler, M. *On human symbiosis and the vicissitudes of individuation.* New York: Library of Human Behavior, 1976.

Mahoney, M. J. *Cognition and behavior modification.* Cambridge, Mass.: Ballinger, 1974.

Maslow, A. *Religions, values, and peak experiences.* New York: Viking, 1964.

Maslow, A. *The psychology of science: A reconnaissance.* Chicago: Henry Regnery, 1966.

Maslow, A. *Toward a psychology of being* (2nd ed.). New York: Van Nostrand, 1968.

Maslow, A. *Maslow and self-actualization* [Film]. Orange, Calif.: Psychological Films, 1969.

Maslow, A. *Motivation and personality* (2nd ed.). New York: Harper & Row, 1970.

Maslow, A. *The farther reaches of human nature.* New York: Viking, 1971.

Masson, J. M. *The assault on the truth: Freud's suppression of the seduction theory.* New York: Farrar, Straus, & Giroux, 1983.

May, R. *Man's search for himself.* New York: Norton, 1953.

May, R. *Existential psychology.* New York: Random House, 1961.

May, R. *Psychology and the human dilemma.* New York: Van Nostrand Reinhold, 1967.

May, R. *Love and will.* New York: Norton, 1969.

May, R. *Power and innocence.* New York: Norton, 1972.

May, R. *The courage to create.* New York: Norton, 1975.

May, R. *The meaning of anxiety.* New York: Norton, 1977.

May, R. *Freedom and destiny.* New York: Norton, 1981.

May, R. *The discovery of being.* New York: Norton, 1983.

May, R., Angel, E., & Ellenberger, H. F. (Eds.). *Existence: A new dimension in psychiatry and psychology*. New York: Basic Books, 1958.

McGuire, W. (Ed.). *The Freud-Jung letters*. Princeton: Princeton University Press, 1974.

McGuire, W., & Hull, R. F. (Eds.). *C. G. Jung speaking: Interviews and encounters*. Princeton: Princeton University Press, 1977.

Meichenbaum, D. *Cognitive behavior modification*. New York: Plenum Press, 1977.

Milgram, S., & Shotland, R. L. *Television and antisocial behavior*. New York: Academic Press, 1973.

Miller, N. E. Experimental studies of conflict. In J. McV. Hunt (Ed.). *Personality and the behavior disorders* (Vol. 1). New York: Ronald Press, 1944.

Miller, N. E. Comments on theoretical models: Illustrated by the development of a theory of conflict behavior. *Journal of Personality*, 1951, *20*, 82–100.

Miller, N. E. Liberalization of basic S-R concepts: Extensions to conflict behavior, motivation, and social learning. In S. Koch (Ed.), *Psychology: A study of a science* (Vol. 2). New York: McGraw-Hill, 1959.

Miller, N. E., & Dollard, J. *Social learning and imitation*. New Haven: Yale University Press, 1941.

Murchison, C. (Ed.). *A history of psychology in autobiography* (Vol. 3). Worcester, Mass.: Clark University Press, 1936.

Murray, H. A. *Explorations in personality*. New York: Oxford University Press, 1938.

Murray, H. A. *Thematic apperception test*. Cambridge, Mass.: Harvard University Press, 1943.

Murray, J. R. Television and violence: Implications of the surgeon general's research program. *American Psychologist*, 1973, *28*, 472–478.

Musak, H. (Ed.). *Alfred Adler: His influence on psychology today*. New York: Noyes, 1973.

Nacht, S. Discussion of "The mutual influences in the development of the ego and id." In A. Freud et al., *The Psychoanalytic Study of the Child* (Vol. 7). New York: International Universities Press, 1952.

Nadar, R., & Johnson, N. *Television violence survey*. Report of the National Citizens Committee for Broadcasting. Washington, D.C., July 1979.

Needleman, J. *The new religions*. New York: Doubleday, 1970.

Nordby, V. J., & Hall, C. S. *A guide to psychologists and their concepts*. San Francisco: W. H. Freeman, 1974.

Orgler, H. *Alfred Adler: The man and his work*. New York: New American Library, 1973.

Parke, R. D., et al. The effects of repeated exposure to movie violence on aggressive behavior in juvenile delinquents. In L. Berkowitz (Ed.), *Advances in experimental social psychology* (Vol. 8). New York: Academic Press, 1974.

Parke, R. D., et al. Some effects of violent and nonviolent movies on the behavior of juvenile delinquents. In L. Berkowitz (Ed.), *Advances in experimental social psychology* (Vol. 10). New York: Academic Press, 1977.

Perls, F., Hefferline, R. F., & Goodman, P. *Gestalt therapy*. New York: Julian Press, 1958.

Perry, H. S. *The life of Harry Stack Sullivan*. Boston: Belknap Press, 1981.

Pervin, L. A. *Current controversies and issues in personality*. New York: John Wiley, 1978.

Phares, E. J. *Locus of control in personality*. Morristown, N.J.: General Learning Press, 1976.

Pines, M. The only child. *Psychology Today*, 1981, 4.

Porter, E. H., Jr. *Therapeutic counseling*. Boston: Houghton Mifflin, 1950.

Rapaport, D. A critique of Dollard and Miller's *Personality and psychotherapy*. *American Journal of Orthopsychiatry*, 1953, 23, 204–208.

Rapaport, D. The structure of psychoanalytic theory: A systematizing attempt. *Psychological Issues*, 1960, 6.

Rees, L. Constitutional factors and abnormal behavior. In H. J. Eysenck (Ed.). *Handbook of abnormal psychology*. New York: Basic Books, 1961.

Reichlin, R. E., & Niederehe, G. Early memories: a comprehensive bibliography. *Journal of Individual Psychology*, 1980, 36 (2), 209–218.

Reik, T. *The search within*. New York: Farrar, Straus, & Cudahy, 1956.

Roazen, P. *Freud and his followers*. New York: Knopf, 1975.

Roazen, P. *Erik H. Erikson: The power and limits of his vision*. New York: Free Press, 1976.

Rogers, C. R. *Counseling and psychotherapy: Newer concepts in practice*. Boston: Houghton Mifflin, 1942.

Rogers, C. R. *Client-centered therapy: Its current practice, implications, and theory*. Boston: Houghton Mifflin, 1951.

Rogers, C. R. A theory of therapy, personality and interpersonal relationships as developed in the client-centered framework. In S. Koch (Ed.). *Psychology: A study of a science* (Vol. 3). New York: McGraw-Hill, 1959.

Rogers, C. R. *On becoming a person*. Boston: Houghton Mifflin, 1961.

Rogers, C. R. *Freedom to learn*. Columbus, Ohio: Charles E. Merrill, 1969.

Rogers, C. R. *A way of being*. Boston: Houghton Mifflin, 1980.

Rogers, C. R., & Dymond, R. F. (Eds.). *Psychotherapy and personality change: Co-ordinated studies in the client-centered approach*. Chicago: University of Chicago Press, 1954.

Rogers, C. R., & Roethlisberger, F. J. Barriers and gateways to communication. *Harvard Business Review*, July-Aug. 1952, 28–35.

Rotter, J. B. *Social learning and clinical psychology*. Englewood Cliffs, N.J.: Prentice-Hall, 1954.

Rotter, J. B. Generalized expectancies for internal versus external control of reinforcement. *Psychological Monographs*, 1966, 80 (whole no. 609).

Rotter, J. B., Chance, J. E., & Phares, E. J. *Applications of a social learning theory of personality*. New York: Holt, Rinehart & Winston, 1972.

Rotter, J. B., & Hochreich, D. J. *Personality*. Glenview, Ill.: Scott Foresman, 1975.

Rubins, J. L. *Karen Horney: Gentle rebel of psychoanalysis*. New York: Dial, 1978.

Rychlak, J. *A philosophy of science for personality theory*. Boston: Houghton Mifflin, 1968.

Rychlak, J. F. *Introduction to personality and psychotherapy*. Boston: Houghton Mifflin, 1973.

Ryckman, R. M., & Malikiosi, M. X. Relationship between locus of control and chronological age. *Psychological Reports*, 1975, *36*, 655–658.

Scarf, M. Psychoanalyst Adler: His ideas are everywhere. *New York Times Magazine*, February 28, 1971, pp 10–11, 44–47.

Schuyler, H., & Sandler, H. M. *Rival hypotheses: Alternative interpretations of data based conclusions*. New York: Harper & Row, 1979.

Sears, R. R. Survey of objective studies of psychoanalytic concepts. *Social Science Research Council Bulletin*, 1943, *51*.

Seligman, M., and Hagar, J. *Biological boundaries of learning*. Englewood Cliffs, N.J.: Prentice-Hall, 1972.

Sells, S. B. Structured measurement of personality and motivation: A review of contributions of Raymond B. Cattell. *Journal of Clinical Psychology*, 1959, *15*, 3–21.

Sheldon, W. H. (with the collaboration of S. S. Stevens & W. B. Tucker). *The varieties of human physique: An introduction to constitutional psychology*. New York: Harper, 1940.

Sheldon, W. H. (with the collaboration of S. S. Stevens). *The varieties of temperament: A psychology of constitutional differences*. New York: Harper, 1942.

Sheldon, W. H. Constitutional factors in personality. In J. McV. Hunt (Ed.). *Personality and the behavioral disorders*. New York: Ronald Press, 1944.

Shostrom, E. An inventory for the measurement of self-actualization. *Educational and Psychological Measurement*, 1965, *24*, 207–218.

Shurcliff, J. Judged humor, arousal, and the relief theory. *Journal of Personality and Social Psychology*, 1968, *8*, 360–363.

Silverman, L. H. Psychoanalytic theory: The reports of my death are greatly exaggerated. *American Psychologist*, 1976, *31*, 621–637.

Singer, J. L. *The child's world of make-believe*. New York: Academic Press, 1973.

Skinner, B. F. *The behavior of organisms*. New York: Appleton-Century-Crofts, 1938.

Skinner, B. F. *Walden II*. New York: Macmillan, 1948.

Skinner, B. F. *Science and human behavior*. New York: Macmillan, 1953.

Skinner, B. F. *Cumulative record*. New York: Appleton-Century-Crofts, 1961.

Skinner, B. F. *Contingencies of reinforcement: A theoretical analysis*. New York: Appleton-Century-Crofts, 1969.

Skinner, B. F. *Beyond freedom and dignity*. New York: Knopf, 1971.

Skinner, B. F. Will success spoil B. F. Skinner? (Interview). *Psychology Today*, Nov. 1972, *6*, 66–72, 130.

Skinner, B. F. *About behaviorism*. New York: Random House, 1974.

Skinner, B. F. Why are we not acting to save the world? Paper prepared for the annual meeting of the American Psychological Association, 1981.

Skinner, B. F. *Notebooks*. Englewood Cliffs, N.J.: Prentice-Hall, 1982.

Skinner, B. F. Origins of a behaviorist. *Psychology Today*, *17* (9), September 1983.

Smith, M., & Glass, J. Metaanalysis of psychotherapy outcome studies. *American Psychologist*, Sept. 1977, 752–760.

Sperber, M. *Masks of loneliness: Alfred Adler in perspective*. New York: Macmillan, 1974.

Spitz, R. A. The psychogenic diseases in infancy: An attempt at the etiologic classification. *Psychoanalytic Study of the Child*, 1951, *6*, 255–275.

Spotnitz, H. *Psychotherapy of preoedipal conditions*. New York: Jason Aronson, 1976.

Spranger, E. *Types of men*. New York: Stechert, 1928.

Stein, M. H. Review of Kohut's *Restoration of the Self. Journal of the American Psychoanalytic Institute*, 1978.

Stone, I. *Passions of the mind*. New York: Doubleday, 1971.

Stone, L. J., & Church, J. *Childhood and adolescence: A psychology of the growing person*. New York: Random House, 1984.

Strickland, B. R. I-E expectations and health-related behaviors. *Journal of Consulting and Clinical Psychology*. 1978, *46*, 1192–1211.

Strickland, B. R. I-E expectations and cardiovascular functioning. In L. C. Perlmuller & R. A. Monty (Eds.). *Choice and perceived control*. Hillside, N.J.: Erlbaum, 1979.

Sullivan, H. S. *The interpersonal theory of psychiatry*. New York: Norton, 1953.

Sullivan, H. S. *The psychiatric interview*. New York: Norton, 1954.

Sullivan, H. S. *The fusion of psychiatry and social science*. New York: Norton, 1964.

Sullivan, H. S. *Personal psychopathology*. New York: Norton, 1972.

Suzuki, D. T. *Essays in Zen Buddhism*. London: Rider and Company, 1927.

Suzuki, D. T. *Manual of Zen Buddhism*. New York: Grove, 1960.

Suzuki, D. T. *An introduction to Zen Buddhism*. New York: Grove, 1964.

Tart, C. T. (Ed.). *Transpersonal psychologies*. New York: Harper & Row, 1975.

Tausch, R. Facilitating dimensions in interpersonal relations: Verifying the theoretical assumptions of Carl Rogers. *College Student Journal*, 1978, *12* (1).

Vockell, E. L., Felker, D. W., & Miley, C. H. Birth order literature 1967–1971: Bibliography and index. *Journal of Individual Psychology*, 1973, *29*, 39–53.

Watson, J. *Behaviorism*. New York: Norton, 1925.

Watts, A. W. *The spirit of Zen*. New York: Grove, 1958.

Watts, A. W. *Psychotherapy east and west*. New York: Pantheon, 1961.

White, R. S. *Lives in progress*. New York: Holt, Rinehart & Winston, 1952.

White, R. S. Ego and reality and psychoanalytic theory. *Psychological Issues Monographs*, *11*, 1963.

Wilson, C. *New pathways in psychology: Maslow and the post-Freudian revolution*. New York: Taplinger, 1972.

Witkin, H. *Psychological differentiation*. New York: Halsted, 1974.

Wolpe, J. *Psychotherapy by reciprocal inhibition*. Stanford, Calif.: Stanford University Press, 1958.

Wolpe, J. *The practice of behavior therapy*. Oxford: Pergamon Press, 1973.

Wolpe, J. Behavior therapy versus psychoanalysis: Therapeutic and social implications. *American Psychologist*, 1981, *36* (2), 159–164.

Wolpe, J., & Lazarus, A. *Behavior therapy techniques*. Oxford: Pergamon Press, 1966.

Wylie, R. C. *The self concept* (2 vols.). Lincoln: University of Nebraska Press, 1974, 1978.

Index

Family constellation, 111
Feelings, 474–475; *see also* Emotions
Feminine psychology, 89–90, 110, 121, 128–129
Fictional finalisms, *see* Finalism
Finalism, 105–106, 117
First memories, 115–116, 117
Fixation, 65, 68, 356
Four Noble Truths, 436–437
Free association, 38–39, 147, 161, 168, 434, 482
Freedom, 7, 316–317, 379, 381, 479–481, 494
Freedom of movement, 419, 420, 423, 424
Freud, A., 167–170, 173, 183, 188, 189, 275
Freud, S., 2, 27, 28–79, 137, 139, 158, 165, 167, 175, 180–182, 190, 196, 201, 207, 230, 233, 256, 269, 300, 322, 323, 384, 424, 434, 457–458, 463, 464, 465, 468, 469, 470, 480, 483, 487, 492, 493, 494
   and Adler, 32, 114, 118
   and Allport, 230
   and Dollard and Miller, 355–356, 363
   and Erikson, 186, 191–192, 207–208
   and Fromm, 151, 154, 161
   and Horney, 123, 129
   and Jung, 32, 81, 83, 93, 96
   and Maslow, 322–323
   and May, 463, 487
   and Murray, 225
   and Skinner, 377, 384
   and Sullivan, 140, 142
   biographical background, 30–33
   methods of research, 33–44; *see also*
      Dreams: analysis of, Free association, Psychoanalysis
   personality theory, 45–68
   psychotherapy, 68–73
   theory as philosophy, science, and art, 73–76
Fromm, E., 27, 118, 150–163, 167, 211, 307, 459, 487, 492, 493
   and Freud, 151, 154
   biographical background, 151–153
   methods of research, 160, 161
   personality theory, 153–160
   psychotherapy, 161–162
   theory as philosophy, science, and art, 161–162
Fully functioning person, 298–299
Functional autonomy, 240
Functions, 92

Gautama, S., *see* Buddha
Generativity, 200–201, 208
Genital stage, 52–53, 198
Genuineness, 289
Gestalt therapy, 482, 483
Ghandi, M., 206–207
Goals, 110; *see also* Motivation, Motives, Teleology
Guilt, 195–196

Habits, 350
Hall, C., 181
Hall, S., 32
Harlow, H., 306
Hartmann, H., 170–171, 189
Having mode, 160
Heidegger, M., 465
Heredity and environment, 271; *see also* Constitutional factors in personality, Situational factors in personality
Heterostasis, 8, 494
Hierarchy of needs, *see* Needs: hierarchy of
Hierarchy of response, 351
Hippocrates, 215, 265
Historical dichotomies, 153
Hitler, A., 156
Homeostasis, 8, 232
Homer, 437, 495
Honesty, 314–316
Hope, 193
Horney, K., 27, 118, 120–133, 137, 167, 307, 310, 459, 493
   and Freud, 123, 129
   biographical background, 121–123
   methods of research, 131
   personality theory, 123–129
   psychotherapy, 129–131
   theory as philosophy, science, and art, 130–133
Hull, C., 350, 356, 389, 413
Humanist and cognitive theories, 275–343, 487, 488, 494, 496
Humanistic ethics, 154–155
Hypnosis, 34, 35
Hypotheses, 13–14, 330, 342
Hysteria, 34

Icarus complex, *see* Complexes
Id, 58–59, 60–62, 67, 169, 170, 171, 172, 177, 189, 319, 321
Idealized self, 125–128